Oh! 1001 Homemade Asian Recipes

(Oh! 1001 Homemade Asian Recipes - Volume 1)

Wendy Ross

Copyright: Published in the United States by Wendy Ross/ © WENDY ROSS

Published on October, 13 2020

All rights reserved. No part of this publication may be reproduced, stored in retrieval system, copied in any form or by any means, electronic, mechanical, photocopying, recording or otherwise transmitted without written permission from the publisher. Please do not participate in or encourage piracy of this material in any way. You must not circulate this book in any format. WENDY ROSS does not control or direct users' actions and is not responsible for the information or content shared, harm and/or actions of the book readers.

In accordance with the U.S. Copyright Act of 1976, the scanning, uploading and electronic sharing of any part of this book without the permission of the publisher constitute unlawful piracy and theft of the author's intellectual property. If you would like to use material from the book (other than just simply for reviewing the book), prior permission must be obtained by contacting the author at author@ontariorecipes.com

Thank you for your support of the author's rights.

Content

CHAPTER 1: THAI CUISINE RECIPES ...16

1. Adrienne's Tom Ka Gai..................16
2. Ajad (Authentic Thai Cucumber Salad).....16
3. Amazing Simple Thai Tofu 17
4. Andrew's Tom Kha Gai..............17
5. Authentic Pad Thai Noodles 18
6. Authentic Thai Cashew Chicken 18
7. Barbequed Thai Style Chicken 19
8. California Thai Flank Steak 19
9. Carrie's Pad Thai Salad 20
10. Chicken Salad With Thai Flavored Dressing 21
11. Chicken Satay................................21
12. Chicken Satay With Peanut Sauce 22
13. Classic Pad Thai 22
14. Coconut Rice Salad 23
15. Curried Coconut Chicken 23
16. Dad's Pad Thai 24
17. Duck Legs In Green Curry............24
18. Easy Red Thai Curry With Chicken And Broccoli..25
19. Easy Spicy Thai Slow Cooker Chicken......26
20. Egg And Coconut Custard Jellies 26
21. Fabienne's Leeks And Monkfish 26
22. Fresh Spring Rolls With Thai Dipping Sauce...27
23. Fried Whole Tilapia With Basil And Chilies 28
24. Gaeng Daeng Sai Fak Thong Lae Moo (Red Curry With Pork And Squash) 28
25. Goong Tod Kratiem Prik Thai (Prawns Fried With Garlic And White Pepper)................29
26. Green Curry Lamb Balls 29
27. Green Curry Thai For Kings 29
28. Green Curry Tofu 30
29. Grilled Mahi Mahi In Thai Coconut Sauce 30
30. Guay Diaw Lawd (Pork Belly, Chicken Wing, And Noodle Stew) 31
31. Hot And Sour Prawn Soup With Lemon Grass 32
32. How To Make Peanut Dipping Sauce 32
33. Jet Tila's Tom Yum Goong Soup................33
34. Kal Pot..33
35. Khao Soi Soup..............................34
36. Larb Gai Nikki Style 34
37. Mango With Sticky Coconut Rice (Kao Niaw)..35
38. Mild Thai Beef With A Tangerine Sauce...36
39. Mung Beans Cooked In Sweet Syrup 36
40. Nam Sod (Thai Pork Salad).......................37
41. Nong's Khao Man Gai 37
42. Oriental Cold Noodle Salad 38
43. Pad Krapao (Thai Stir Fry Pork With Basil) 38
44. Pad Se Eew...................................39
45. Peanut Butter Noodles................................40
46. Poached Eggs In Ginger Syrup..................40
47. Potsticker Salad 40
48. Pumpkin Coconut Curry.............................41
49. Quick Red Curry Soup 42
50. Satay Chicken Pizza 42
51. Satay Sauce 43
52. Scot's Thai Soup..........................43
53. Shrimp Fried Noodles Thai Style 44
54. Shrimp Summer Rolls With Asian Peanut Sauce...44
55. Spaghetti With Peanut Butter Sauce 45
56. Spiced Thai Iced Tea 45
57. Spicy Chicken Thai Noodle Soup..............46
58. Spicy Devil's Tom Yum Soup 46
59. Spicy Thai Basil Chicken (Pad Krapow Gai) 47
60. Spicy Thai Shrimp Pasta............................48
61. Spicy Thai Vegetable Soup 48
62. Steamed Lemon Grass Crab Legs 49
63. Sticky Rice With Coconut Milk And Mango 49
64. Stir Fried Sweet And Sour Vegetables.......50
65. Stir Fried Tofu With Cashews....................50
66. Sukhothai Pad Thai......................51
67. Sweet Rice And Mango 51
68. Sweet Sticky Rice And Mango 52
69. Sweet Sticky Rice With Mangoes................52
70. Sweet Thai Style Chicken Bowl 53
71. Tantalizing Pad Thai....................53
72. Tapioca Pudding With Tender Coconut ...54
73. Tender Taro Root Cooked In Coconut Milk 55
74. Thai Buffalo Wings.....................55

#	Recipe	Page
75.	Thai Cashew Chicken	55
76.	Thai Chicken Dip	56
77.	Thai Chicken Satay	56
78.	Thai Chicken Stock	57
79.	Thai Chicken Wings	57
80.	Thai Chicken With Basil Stir Fry	58
81.	Thai Chicken With Cashew Nuts	59
82.	Thai Coconut Chicken	59
83.	Thai Coffee	60
84.	Thai Crab Rolls	60
85.	Thai Cucumber Salad	60
86.	Thai Dipping Sauce	61
87.	Thai Fried Bananas	61
88.	Thai Fried Rice With Pineapple And Chicken	62
89.	Thai Ground Chicken Basil	62
90.	Thai Hot And Sour Soup	63
91.	Thai Monkfish Curry	63
92.	Thai Peanut Butter Sauce	64
93.	Thai Peanut Noodle Stir Fry	64
94.	Thai Pork Satay	65
95.	Thai Pork With Peanut Sauce	65
96.	Thai Pumpkin Soup	66
97.	Thai Red Curry Paste	66
98.	Thai Salmon Salad	67
99.	Thai Shrimp And Clam Curry	67
100.	Thai Shrimp, Chicken, Grapefruit, And Coconut Salad	68
101.	Thai Steamed Banana Cake	69
102.	Thai Sweet Sticky Rice With Mango (Khao Neeo Mamuang)	69
103.	Thai Tofu Soup	70
104.	Thai Dipped Beef Tri Tip	70
105.	Thai Style Chicken Wings	71
106.	Thai Style Chicken With Noodles	71
107.	Thai Style Ground Pork Skewers	72
108.	Thai Style Steamed Pumpkin Cake	73
109.	Thai Style Steamed Tapioca Cake	73
110.	The Best Thai Coconut Soup	74
111.	The Best Thai Curry Peanut Sauce	74
112.	Todd's Famous Thai Peanut Sauce	75
113.	Tom Byoo (Sour Fish Soup)	75
114.	Tom Ka Gai (Coconut Chicken Soup)	76
115.	Tom Kha Gai	76
116.	Tom Yum Koong Soup	77
117.	Vegan Pad Thai With Baked Tofu	77
118.	Vegetarian Phad Thai	78
119.	Yam Taeng (Spicy Cucumber Salad)	79
120.	Yellow Mung Bean Pudding With Coconut Cream	79

CHAPTER 2: JAPANESE CUISINE RECIPES..........80

#	Recipe	Page
121.	Agedashi Esque Tofu	80
122.	Ashley's Chicken Katsu With Tonkatsu Sauce	80
123.	Asian Crab And Cuke Salad	81
124.	Authentic Miso Soup	81
125.	Beef Bowl (Gyudon)	81
126.	Beef Short Ribs Rice Bowl (Gyu Kalbi Don)	82
127.	Black Sesame Pudding	83
128.	Broiled Mochi With Nori Seaweed	83
129.	Butter Mochi	83
130.	California Roll	84
131.	Chicken Hekka	85
132.	Chicken Yakisoba	85
133.	Chicken And Sweet Potato Rice	86
134.	Coffee Gelatin Dessert	86
135.	Coffee Jelly	87
136.	Cucumber And Avocado Sushi	87
137.	Dango (Sweet Japanese Dessert)	88
138.	Dashi Stock (Konbudashi)	88
139.	Dynamite Sauce	89
140.	Easy Japanese Okonomiyaki	89
141.	Easy Mochi	89
142.	Eel Sauce	90
143.	Famous Japanese Restaurant Style Salad Dressing	90
144.	Ginger Spiced Cucumbers	91
145.	Glo's Sausage Fried Rice	91
146.	Goya Champuru (Bitter Melon Stir Fry)	92
147.	Green Tea Kasutera (Green Tea Bread)	92
148.	Green Tea Mousse Cheesecake	93
149.	Green Tea Muffins	93
150.	Gyoza (Japanese Potstickers)	94
151.	Hiyashi Chuka Noodles	94
152.	Home Rice	95
153.	Homemade Japanese Curry	96
154.	Homemade Pickled Ginger (Gari)	97
155.	Hoshi Shiitake Dashi	97
156.	Japanese Agedashi Deep Fried Tofu	97
157.	Japanese Beef Rolls	98
158.	Japanese Beef Tongue Stir Fry	98

159. Japanese Deviled Eggs 99
160. Japanese Egg Yolk Sauce 99
161. Japanese Fruitcake 100
162. Japanese Ginger Pork 101
163. Japanese Green Tea Petits Fours 101
164. Japanese Gyudon (Beef Bowl) 102
165. Japanese Minced Beef 102
166. Japanese Miso Glazed Cod 103
167. Japanese Okonomiyaki 103
168. Japanese Onion Soup 104
169. Japanese Pan Noodles 104
170. Japanese Restaurant Cucumber Salad 105
171. Japanese Scrambled Eggs With Pacific Saury 105
172. Japanese Spinach With Sweet Sesame Seeds 105
173. Japanese Tamago Egg 106
174. Japanese Tofu Salad 106
175. Japanese Style Deep Fried Chicken ... 107
176. Japanese Style Sesame Green Beans ... 107
177. Juicy Chicken 108
178. Kasutera (Castella), The Japanese Traditional Honey Cake 108
179. Kimchi Goya Champuru 109
180. Kiyoko's Miso Sauce 109
181. Lucy's Quick Tonkatsu Sauce 110
182. Manju (Japanese Sweet Bean Paste Cookies) 110
183. Marshmallow Cake 111
184. Marvel's Japanese Fried Oysters (Kaki Fuh Rai) With Lemony Tartar Sauce 111
185. Matcha Green Tea Ice Latte 112
186. Michelle's Chicken Yakitori 112
187. Miso Salmon 113
188. Miso Salmon (Sake Misozuke) With Spinach Sauce 113
189. Miso Soup With Shiitake Mushrooms 114
190. Miso And Soy Chilean Sea Bass 114
191. Mizu Shingen Mochi With Strawberry Compote 115
192. My Fly Stir Fry 115
193. Nigiri Sushi 116
194. Nona's Tableside Homemade Soft Tofu ... 117
195. Okonomiyaki (Japanese Pancake) 117
196. Okura And Sakura Shrimp Japanese Style Spaghetti 118
197. Onigiri (Japanese Rice Balls) 118
198. Orange Ponzu 119
199. Oyako Donburi 119
200. Oyakodon (Japanese Chicken And Egg Rice Bowl) 120
201. Pan Roasted Beef Tenderloin With Ginger Shiitake Brown Butter 120
202. Pan Roasted Miso Marinated Sea Bass 121
203. Perfect Sushi Rice 121
204. Pork Gyoza 122
205. Restaurant Style Shoyu Miso Ramen 123
206. Seaweed (Nori) Soup 124
207. Semi Homemade Japanese Kare Pan (Curry Bread) 124
208. Sesame Crusted Mahi Mahi With Soy Shiso Ginger Butter Sauce 125
209. Sesame Tuna With Soy Miso Dressing 126
210. Smoked Salmon Sushi Roll 126
211. Spicy Chile Oil Squid 127
212. Spicy Japanese Crab Noodle Salad ... 127
213. Spongy Japanese Cheesecake 128
214. Steamed Clams In Butter And Sake ... 128
215. Sukiyaki 129
216. Sukiyaki Beef 129
217. Sunomono (Japanese Cucumber And Seafood Salad) 130
218. Sushi Party 130
219. Sushi Roll 131
220. Sweet Miso Soup With Baby Turnips 132
221. Tamagoyaki With Mushroom And Mozzarella Cheese 132
222. Tempura Shrimp 133
223. Teriyaki Rib Eye Steaks 134
224. Teriyaki Sauce And Marinade 134
225. The Perfect Simplified Sushi Vinegar 134
226. Thick Kabocha Soup 135
227. Tofu Chanpuru 135
228. Tofu Hiyayakko 136
229. Tonkatsu 137
230. Tonkatsu Asian Style Pork Chop 137
231. Tonkatsu Shoyu Ramen (Pork Cutlet Soy Sauce Ramen) 138
232. Traditional Beef Sukiyaki 138
233. Tuna Tartare 139
234. Vegan Edamame 139
235. Vegan Japanese Spinach Salad 140
236. Vegetarian Nori Rolls 140
237. Yakitori Chicken 141

238. Yakitori Don..................................141
239. Yakitori Marinade 142
240. Yummylicious Japanese Beef Croquettes 142

CHAPTER 3: INDIAN CUISINE RECIPES
....142

241. Alicia's Aloo Gobi...........................142
242. Aloo Gobi Masala (Cauliflower And Potato Curry)...143
243. Alu Baigan 144
244. Apple Chutney................................144
245. Authentic South Indian Biryani 145
246. Awadi Dahi Murg (Chicken In Yogurt Gravy) 145
247. Baingan Bharta (Eggplant Curry) 146
248. Banana Lassi 146
249. Best Potatoes Ever!........................147
250. Bhuna Gosht..................................147
251. Biryani With Yogurt Marinated Chicken.148
252. Chai Tea Concentrate...................149
253. Chai Tea Ice Cream 149
254. Chef John's Chicken Tikka Masala...........150
255. Chef John's Tandoori Chicken 150
256. Chicken Biryani..............................151
257. Chicken Cauliflower Korma...........152
258. Chicken Chicken Curry 153
259. Chicken Chutney Sandwiches With Curry 153
260. Chicken Makhani (Indian Butter Chicken) 154
261. Chickpea Coconut Salad 154
262. Coconut Chutney..........................155
263. Coconut Curry Chili 155
264. Cod Curry.......................................156
265. Country Captain Chicken With Rice........156
266. Culture Blend Spaghetti 157
267. Curried Celery................................158
268. Curried Chicken With Rice............158
269. Curried Corn..................................158
270. Curried Cream Of Cauliflower Soup 159
271. Curried Cumin Potatoes 160
272. Curried Scallops With Angel Hair Pasta..160
273. Dal Makhani (Indian Lentils) 161
274. Easy Baked Indian Samosas 161
275. Easy Chickpea Curry 162
276. Easy Curried Cauliflower 163
277. Easy Curry Rice..............................163
278. Easy Masoor Daal 163
279. Easy Paneer Tikka.........................164
280. Easy Veggie Samosas...................164
281. Faux Bombay Potatoes 165
282. Four Seasons Chicken Curry.....................165
283. Garam Masala Seared Salmon With Coconut Curry Butter....................................166
284. Garam Masala Spice Blend.........................167
285. Goan Pork Vindaloo 167
286. Green Chutney 168
287. Green Curry With Sweet Potato And Aubergine (Eggplant) 168
288. Grilled "Tandoori" Lamb 169
289. Grilled Chicken Thighs Tandoori 169
290. Gujarati Carrot And Peanut Salad...........170
291. Gujarati Kadhi................................170
292. Hara Masala Murgh 171
293. Indian Cabbage Patties................171
294. Indian Chai Hot Chocolate 172
295. Indian Chicken Korma In The Slow Cooker 172
296. Indian Crepes................................173
297. Indian Eggplant Bhurtha 173
298. Indian Hot Curried Mangos With Tofu..174
299. Indian Onion Dipping Sauce 175
300. Indian Salad...................................175
301. Indian Style Sheekh Kabab..........175
302. Indian Style Shrimp Fry 176
303. Indian Tomato Chicken 177
304. Indian Style Butter Chicken (Murgh Makhani)...177
305. Indian Style Chicken And Onions 178
306. Kachori With Fresh Peas 178
307. Kashmiri Lamb...............................179
308. Kashmiri Style Kidney Beans With Turnips 180
309. Keema Aloo (Ground Beef And Potatoes) 180
310. Keon's Slow Cooker Curry Chicken 181
311. Kheema Pulao 182
312. Kobbari Annam (Coconut Rice) 182
313. Lamb (Gosht) Biryani 183
314. Lamb Meatballs Over Tandoori Naan 184
315. Lamb Shank Vindaloo...................185
316. Lemon Lentil Rice 186
317. Lucy's Tomato And Peach Chutney 186
318. Makhani Chicken (Indian Butter Chicken)

319. Mangalore Mutton Curry 187
320. Mango Lassi Come Home 188
321. Minty Cucumber Raita 188
322. Mixed Grill Of Sausage, Chicken And Lamb With Tandoori Flavorings 189
323. Moong Dal 189
324. Mulligatawny Soup I 190
325. Mulligatawny Soup II 190
326. Nitya's Cauliflower 191
327. Nuvvu Podi (Sesame Seed Powder) 192
328. Paneer (Home Made) 192
329. Paneer Tikka Masala 192
330. Pork Vindaloo 193
331. Potato Cutlets 194
332. Potatoes Madras 194
333. Pressure Cooker Sambar (Indian Lentil Curry) 195
334. Punjabi Chicken In Thick Gravy 195
335. Punjabi Sukha Urad Dal 196
336. Quick Cranberry Chutney 196
337. Quick And Savory Indian Peas 197
338. Ras Malai 197
339. Red Split Lentils (Masoor Dal) 198
340. Restaurant Style Mango Lassi 199
341. Sabudana Khichdi (Tapioca With Potatoes And Peanuts) 199
342. Saffron Rice With Raisins And Cashews ... 200
343. Savory Lassi 200
344. Serena's Strawberry Lassi 200
345. Shahi Tukra (Sweet Bread Dessert) 201
346. Shahi Tukray (Indian Bread Pudding) 201
347. Shahi Tukri (Sweet Fried Bread) 202
348. South Indian Style Okra Fritters 202
349. Spiced Chickpeas (Chole) 203
350. Spiced Moong Beans 203
351. Spicy Banana Curry 204
352. Spicy Chicken In Tomato Coconut Sauce 204
353. Spicy Fried Shrimp 205
354. Spicy Indian Chicken Curry Yummy 206
355. Spicy Potato Noodles (Bataka Sev) 206
356. Spicy Tomato Chutney 207
357. Spicy Tomato Soup 208
358. Spicy Yogurt Dressing 208
359. Steve's Chicken Korma 208
360. Stuffed Okra 209
361. Sweet Lentil Soup With Asparagus Tips . 209
362. Tamarind Date Chutney 210
363. Tandoori Chicken I 210
364. Tandoori Grilled Chicken 211
365. The Maharajah's Mulligatawny 211
366. Tim Perry's Soup (Creamy Curry Cauliflower And Broccoli Soup) 212
367. Tomato Cucumber Kachumbar 212
368. Traditional Chicken Curry 213
369. Turmeric Milk 213
370. Ullipaya (Onion) Tomato Chutney 214
371. Vankaya Pulusu Pachadi (Andhra Sweet And Sour Eggplant Stew) 215
372. Veg Biryani 215
373. Vegan Sweet Potato Chickpea Curry 216
374. Vegetable Masala 216
375. Vegetarian Splendor Chickpea Curry 217
376. Vendakka Paalu 217
377. Whole Wheat Chapati 218
378. Yogurt Samosas 218
379. Yogurt Marinated Salmon Fillets (Dahi Machhali Masaledar) 219
380. Yummy Curd Rice 220

CHAPTER 4: FILIPINO CUISINE RECIPES 220

381. Abalos Style Hamburger Soup (Picadillo Filipino) 220
382. Adobo Twist 221
383. Adobong Pusit (Squid Adobo) 221
384. Atsara (Papaya Relish) 222
385. Barbecued Pork Kebabs 222
386. Barbecued Spareribs 223
387. Barquillos (Wafer Rolls) 223
388. Beef Asado 224
389. Beef Nilaga 224
390. Bringhe 225
391. Buko (Young Coconut) Chiller 225
392. Buko (Young Coconut) Pie 226
393. Caldereta (Filipino Beef Stew) 226
394. Caldereta (Filipino Beef And Chorizo Stew) 227
395. Cassava Cake 227
396. Champorado 228
397. Chicken Adobo I 228
398. Chicken Adobo II 229
399. Chicken Adobo With Noodles Filipino

Mexican Fusion 229
400. Chicken Afritada (Filipino Stew) 230
401. Chicken Arroz Caldo (Chicken Rice Porridge) 230
402. Chicken Binakol 231
403. Chicken Teriyaki 231
404. Chicken With Chicharo (Snow Peas) 232
405. Chinky's Bibingka 232
406. Chinky's Mango Bread 233
407. Chinky's Puto Bread 233
408. Chocolate Orange Rice Pudding 234
409. Coconut Sauce 234
410. Corned Beef Hash (Abalos Style) 235
411. Crab Omelet 235
412. Dinengdeng 236
413. Duck Adobo 236
414. Empanada Dough 237
415. Filipino Baked Milkfish (Baked Bangus) .237
416. Filipino Banana Blossoms Sisig 238
417. Filipino Beef Giniling (Afritada Style) 238
418. Filipino Beef Stir Fry 239
419. Filipino Chicken Binakol 239
420. Filipino Chicken Relleno 240
421. Filipino Chicken Salad 241
422. Filipino Fish Stew (Paksiw Na Bangus) ... 241
423. Filipino Fried Chicken 242
424. Filipino Leche Flan 242
425. Filipino Lechon (Roasted Pork Leg) 243
426. Filipino Lumpia 243
427. Filipino Menudo (Pork And Liver Stew) 244
428. Filipino Pancit Bihon With Canton 244
429. Filipino Pork Adobo 245
430. Filipino Pork Sinigang 245
431. Filipino Rice (Arroz Valenciana) 246
432. Filipino Spaghetti 246
433. Filipino Stew (Caldereta) 247
434. Filippino Lechon Kawali 248
435. Fish Sinigang (Tilapia) Filipino Sour Broth Dish 248
436. Fresh Lumpia 249
437. Fresh Lumpia With Ubod 249
438. Fried Rice (Sinangag) 250
439. Fried Tulingan (Mackerel) 250
440. Garlic Rice 251
441. Ginataan 251
442. Ginataang Manok (Chicken Cooked In Coconut Milk) 252
443. Grandma Nena's Lumpia And Pancit 252
444. Grilled Chicken Adobo 253
445. Guinataan Chicken Adobo 253
446. Halo Halo Especial 254
447. Ham Hocks With Lima Beans 254
448. Healthier Crema De Fruta 255
449. Karioka Sweet Rice Balls 255
450. Leyley's Spicy Chicken Adobo Wings 256
451. Lipardo's Puto Seco 256
452. Lisa's Adobo 257
453. Lolah's Chicken Adobo 257
454. Lumpia 258
455. Lumpia (Shanghai Version) 259
456. Lumpia Filipino Shrimp And Pork Egg Rolls 259
457. Lumpia Mollica 260
458. Maja Blanca (Coconut Pudding) 260
459. Maja Blanca Maiz (Corn Pudding) 261
460. Melon Chiller 261
461. Mongo Guisado (Mung Bean Soup) 262
462. Paksiw Na Pata (Pig's Feet Stew) 262
463. Pan De Sal I 263
464. Pan De Sal II 263
465. Pan De Sal Filipino Bread Rolls 264
466. Pancit 265
467. Pancit Luglug 265
468. Pandesal 266
469. Party Pancit 266
470. Philippine Longanisa De Eugenio (Sweet Sausage) 267
471. Pinoy Chicken Adobo 268
472. Plantain Egg Rolls (Turon) 268
473. Pochero 269
474. Pork Afritada 269
475. Pork Sinigang 270
476. Pork Tocino (Sweet Cured Pork) 270
477. Pork And Chicken Adobo 271
478. Prawns In Peanut Soup 271
479. Puto 272
480. Quick And Easy Pancit 272
481. Rumaki 273
482. Salmon Sarciado 273
483. Salmon Stew (Abalos Style) 274
484. Salpicao Jalisco 274
485. Sati Babi 275
486. Savory Mussels 275
487. Singkamas (Jicama) Salad 276

488. Sinigang (Pork Spare Ribs In Sour Soup) 276
489. Sinigang Na Bangus (Filipino Milkfish In Tamarind Broth) 277
490. Sinigang Na Isda Sa Miso (Fish Stew With Miso) 277
491. Siopao (Filipino Steamed Buns) 278
492. Siopao (Filipino Steamed Dumplings) 278
493. Siopao Chicken And Pork Filling 279
494. Slow Cooker Adobo Chicken With Bok Choy 280
495. Slow Cooker Chicken Afritad 280
496. Squash And Coconut Milk Stew 281
497. Stuffed Filipino Fish (Bangus Relleno) 281
498. Tokneneng (Filipino Street Food) 282
499. Traci's Adobo Seasoning 282
500. Turon (Caramelized Banana Triangles) ... 283

CHAPTER 5: KOREAN CUISINE RECIPES
.... 283

501. Awesome Korean Steak 283
502. Baechu Kuk (Napa Cabbage And Soya Bean Paste Soup) 284
503. Baek Kimchi (Korean White Non Spicy Kimchi) 285
504. Baek Kimchi (White Kimchi) 285
505. Barbecued Korean Ribs 286
506. Beef Bulgogi 286
507. Beef Bulgogi Lettuce Wraps 287
508. Best Bulgoki Korean Barbeque Beef 287
509. Best Korean Bulgogi 288
510. Bibimbap With Beef 289
511. Bill's Kimchi 289
512. Bulgogi (Korean BBQ) 290
513. Chinese Korean Cucumber Kimchi 290
514. Chompchae Deopbap (Korean Spicy Tuna And Rice) 291
515. Daeji Bulgogi (Pork Bulgogi) 291
516. Dak Bulgogi (Korean Barbeque Chicken) 292
517. Dak Dori Tang (Spicy Korean Chicken Stew) 292
518. Dak Galbi (Korean Spicy Chicken Stir Fry) 293
519. Dakdoritang (Korean Spicy Chicken Stew) 294
520. Dakdoritang (Spicy Chicken Stew) 294
521. Dol Sot Bi Bim Bap 295

522. Dubu Jeon (Korean Pan Fried Tofu) 296
523. Easy And Simple Korean BBQ Ribs 296
524. Eunah's Korean Style Seaweed Soup 297
525. Fiery Red Pepper Potatoes 297
526. Fried Kimchi 298
527. Galbitang (Korean Beef Short Rib Soup) 298
528. Gluten Free Kalbi Beef 299
529. Gochujang Barbeque Sauce 299
530. Gochujang Pulled Pork In The Slow Cooker 300
531. Gochujang Sauce 301
532. Godeungeo Jorim (Korean Braised Mackerel With Radish) 301
533. Grilled Korean Style Beef Short Ribs 302
534. Haemoolpa Jun (Pan Fried Seafood And Green Onion Pancake) 302
535. Herb Samgyupsal (Korean Grilled Pork Belly) 303
536. Hobak Namul (Zucchini Side Dish) 303
537. Hotteok 304
538. Jab Chae (Korean Noodles) 305
539. Jajangmyeon (Vegetarian Korean Black Bean Noodles) 305
540. Jang Jorim With Hard Boiled Eggs (Korean Soy Beef Strips) 306
541. Jap Chae Korean Glass Noodles 307
542. Japchae 307
543. Kalbi (Korean BBQ Short Ribs) 308
544. Kalbi (Korean Marinated Short Ribs) 308
545. Kalbi (Marinated Beef Short Ribs) 309
546. Kim Chee Squats 309
547. Kimchi (Korean Fermented Spicy Cabbage) 310
548. Kimchi Fried Rice With Bell Pepper 311
549. Kimchi Jigae (Kimchee Soup) 311
550. Kimchi Jun (Kimchi Pancake) And Dipping Sauce 312
551. Kimchi Jun (Kimchi Patty) 312
552. Kkakdugi (Korean Radish Kimchi) 313
553. Kongnamool (Korean Soybean Sprouts) 313
554. Korean BBQ Chicken Marinade 314
555. Korean BBQ Galbi 314
556. Korean BBQ Short Ribs (Gal Bi) 315
557. Korean BBQ Inspired Short Ribs 315
558. Korean Barbequed Beef 316
559. Korean Bean Curd (Miso) Soup 316

560. Korean Beef Simmered In Soy Sauce (Jangjorim) 317
561. Korean Crab Cakes 317
562. Korean Cucumber Salad 318
563. Korean Egg Roll Triangles 318
564. Korean Fried Chicken 319
565. Korean Fried Chicken Sauce 319
566. Korean Fusion Chicken Burrito 320
567. Korean Hot Wings 320
568. Korean Kalbi Jjim (Braised Beef Short Ribs) 321
569. Korean Kebabs 322
570. Korean Kimchi 322
571. Korean Marinated Flank Steak 323
572. Korean Oxtail Soup 323
573. Korean Pizza 324
574. Korean Pork Curry 324
575. Korean Rice Cake (Tteok) 325
576. Korean Rice Cakes And Lentils With Gochujang 325
577. Korean Seafood Tofu Soup (Soondubu Jjigae) 326
578. Korean Short Ribs (Kalbi Jjim) 327
579. Korean Soft Tofu Stew (Soon Du Bu Jigae) 328
580. Korean Soybean Noodles (Kong Kook Su) 328
581. Korean Spicy Chicken And Potato (Tak Toritang) 329
582. Korean Squash 329
583. Korean Style Salad Dressing 329
584. Korean Sushi 330
585. Korean Take Out Rice Noodles (Vegan) 330
586. Korean Tofu And Vegetable Soup 331
587. Korean Tteokguk (Rice Cake Soup) 332
588. Korean Style Braised (Slow Cooker) Baby Back Ribs 332
589. Korean Style Seaweed Soup 333
590. Las Vegas Galbi (Korean Style Beef Ribs) 333
591. Mae's Kimchi Stew 334
592. Maple Syrup Korean Teriyaki Chicken 334
593. Mom's Kimchi Egg 335
594. Moose's Close Enough Bulgogi 335
595. My Auntie's Real Bulgogi 336
596. Nabak Kimchi (Water Kimchi) 336
597. Oi Sobagi (Korean Cucumber Kimchi) ... 337
598. Pine Nut Rice Soup 338
599. Quick And Easy Kimchi Salad 338
600. Quick And Simple Korean Doenjang Chigae (Bean Paste/Tofu Soup) 338
601. Refreshing Korean Cucumber Salad 339
602. Russian Carrot Salad (Korean Style) 339
603. Samgyetang (Chicken Soup With Ginseng) 340
604. Simple Slow Cooked Korean Beef Soft Tacos 340
605. Soondubu Jjigae (Korean Soft Tofu Stew) 341
606. Spicy Korean Chicken 341
607. Spicy Korean Ribs 342
608. Spicy Korean Rice Cakes (Ddeokbokki Or Tteokbokki) 342
609. Spicy Mandoo (Korean Dumpling) 343
610. Stewed Korean Short Ribs (Kalbi Jim) 344
611. Sweet And Spicy Shrimps 344
612. Toasti 345
613. Tteokbokki (Korean Spicy Rice Cakes) ... 345
614. Umma's Kimchi Jigeh 345
615. Vegan Korean Kimchi Fried Rice 346
616. Vegan Korean Tofu And Leek Barbeque 347
617. Vegetarian Bibimbap 347
618. Vegetarian Kimchi 348
619. Yaki Mandu 348
620. Yummy Korean Glass Noodles (Jap Chae) 349

CHAPTER 6: CHINESE CUISINE RECIPES 349

621. 8 Treasures 349
622. Adriel's Chinese Curry Chicken 350
623. Adzuki Mooncake 351
624. Ahi Tuna Spice Rub 352
625. Anise Wine Chicken 352
626. Asian Beef With Snow Peas 353
627. Authentic Chinese Egg Rolls (from A Chinese Person) 353
628. Authentic Chinese Steamed Fish 354
629. Beefy Chinese Dumplings 354
630. Broccoli And Carrot Stir Fry 355
631. Cantonese Barbecued Pork 355
632. Cantonese Style Pork And Shrimp Dumplings 356

633. Chi Tan T'ang (Egg Drop Soup) 357
634. Chicken Broccoli Ca Unieng's Style 357
635. Chicken Vicious 358
636. Chicken And Chinese Vegetable Stir Fry 358
637. Chicken And Cold Noodles With Spicy Sauce 359
638. Chicken In Garlic And Black Bean Sauce 359
639. Chicken With Green Peppers In Black Bean Sauce 360
640. Chinese Barbeque Pork (Char Siu) 361
641. Chinese Barbequed Spareribs 361
642. Chinese Broccoli 362
643. Chinese Cabbage Salad II 362
644. Chinese Chicken Casserole Surprise 363
645. Chinese Chicken Fried Rice I 363
646. Chinese Chicken Salad 364
647. Chinese Chicken Soup With Bok Choy ..364
648. Chinese Corn Soup 365
649. Chinese Dandelion Dumplings 365
650. Chinese Dong'an Chicken 366
651. Chinese Egg Dumplings 367
652. Chinese Glass Noodle Soup 368
653. Chinese Ham Stew 368
654. Chinese Homemade Watercress And Fish Ball Soup 369
655. Chinese Lemon Chicken 369
656. Chinese Lion's Head Soup 370
657. Chinese New Year Turnip Cake 370
658. Chinese Peppered Green Beans 371
659. Chinese Pork Buns (Cha Siu Bao) 371
660. Chinese Shrimp Wonton 372
661. Chinese Shrimp And Tofu Soup 373
662. Chinese Spareribs 373
663. Chinese Steamed Buns With Meat Filling 374
664. Chinese Steamed Cake 375
665. Chinese Steamed White Fish Fillet With Tofu (Cantonese Style) 375
666. Chinese Style Sesame Sauce 376
667. Chinese Sweet And Sour Spare Ribs 376
668. Chinese Take Out Shrimp With Garlic ...377
669. Chinese Tea Leaf Eggs 377
670. Chinese Yam Pudding 378
671. Crab Rangoon I 378
672. Crab Rangoon II 379
673. Crispy Baked Gau 379
674. Crispy Chinese Noodles With Eggplant And Peanuts 380
675. Crispy Ginger Beef 381
676. Deb's General Tso's Chicken 381
677. Duck Sauce 382
678. Easy Chinese Broccoli 383
679. Easy Fried Chinese Chicken Balls 383
680. Easy Moo Shu Pork 383
681. Easy Shrimp Lo Mein 384
682. Egg Drop Soup II 385
683. Eight Treasure Porridge Dessert 385
684. Ginger Chicken With Cashews 386
685. Hainanese Chicken Rice 386
686. Hakka Style Squid And Pork Belly Stir Fry 387
687. Hoisin Pork Stir Fry 388
688. Homemade Hainanese Chicken Rice 388
689. Honey Walnut Shrimp 389
690. Hong Kong Style Egg Tarts 389
691. Hong Kong Walnut Sweet Soup 390
692. Hot And Sour Soup With Tofu 390
693. Hot And Spicy Sichuan Chicken 391
694. Kerri's Szechuan Sauce 391
695. Lee's Incredible Momos 392
696. Lunar New Year Peanut Cookies 392
697. Mapo Doufu 393
698. Mongolian Beef And Spring Onions 394
699. One Egg Egg Drop Soup 394
700. Oriental Tea Leaf Eggs 395
701. Owen's Chicken Rice 395
702. Pineapple Fried Rice II 396
703. Popcorn Chicken (Taiwanese) 397
704. Pork Chop Suey 397
705. Pork Dumplings 398
706. Pork Lo Mein 398
707. Potstickers (Chinese Dumplings) 399
708. Prawn And Mussel Soup With Rice Noodles 400
709. Razor Clam In Sha Cha Sauce 400
710. Restaurant Style Beef And Broccoli 401
711. Roasted Szechuan Broccoli 401
712. Scallops A La Peking House 402
713. Sesame Chicken 402
714. Shrimp Egg Foo Young 403
715. Shrimp Stirfry 403
716. Shrimp With Broccoli In Garlic Sauce 404
717. Sichuan (Szechuan) Cold Noodle 404

718. Sichuan Cucumber Salad 405
719. Singapore Noodles 405
720. Slow Cooker Mongolian Beef 406
721. Spicy Beef Filet In Oyster Sauce 407
722. Spicy Crispy Beef 407
723. Spicy Orange Zest Beef 408
724. Spicy Szechuan Green Beans 408
725. Spicy Tan Tan Soup (Tantanmen Or Dan Dan Noodles) 409
726. Steamed Fish With Ginger 409
727. Steamed Garlic Prawns Chinese Style 410
728. Steamed Pork Spare Ribs 410
729. Stir Fried Chicken With Pineapple And Peppers 411
730. Stir Fried Chicken With Tofu And Mixed Vegetables 411
731. Stir Fried Mushrooms With Baby Corn .. 412
732. Stir Fried Pork With Sweet Bean Paste ... 412
733. Stir Fry Pork With Ginger 413
734. Sweet And Sour Pasta 413
735. Szechuan Beef 414
736. Szechuan Spicy Eggplant 414
737. Taiwanese Dumplings 415
738. Taiwanese Spicy Beef Noodle Soup 416
739. Taiwanese Style Three Cup Chicken 416
740. Ten Minute Szechuan Chicken 417

CHAPTER 7: VIETNAMESE CUISINE RECIPES 417

741. Amanda's Quick Pho 418
742. Asian Garlic Beef Cubes (Vietnamese Bo Luc Lac Or Shaking Beef) 418
743. Authentic Oxtail Pho 419
744. Authentic Pho 419
745. Banh Mi Burgers 420
746. Banh Mi Style Vietnamese Baguette 421
747. Beef Pho 422
748. Braised Green Beans With Fried Tofu 422
749. Cao Lau (Vietnamese Noodle Bowl) 423
750. Caramel Coated Catfish 424
751. Caramelized Pork Belly (Thit Kho) 424
752. Cha Gio Vietnamese Egg Rolls 425
753. Chicken Pho 426
754. Crabmeat And Asparagus Soup 426
755. Day After Thanksgiving Turkey Pho 427
756. Dragon Fruit Shake 427
757. Fried Squid With Pineapple (Muc Xao Thom) 428
758. Goi Cuon (Vietnamese Spring Roll With Pork And Prawns) 428
759. Grilled Shrimp Rice Noodle Bowl 429
760. Instant Pot® Beef Pho 429
761. Lemon Grass And Chicken Summer Rolls 430
762. Maho, Vietnamese Chicken Recipe 431
763. Minh Ai's Bitter Melon Soup 432
764. My Chicken Pho Recipe 432
765. Nuoc Cham (Vietnamese Dipping Sauce) 433
766. Nuoc Cham (Vietnamese Sauce) 433
767. Nuoc Cham (Vietnamese Spicy Dipping Sauce) 433
768. Nuoc Cham Sauce 434
769. Pasta With Vietnamese Pesto 434
770. Pho 435
771. Pho Ga Soup 435
772. Pickled Daikon Radish And Carrot 436
773. Roasted Pork Banh Mi (Vietnamese Sandwich) 436
774. Spicy Vietnamese Quick Pickled Vegetables 437
775. Steamed Vegan Rice Cakes (Banh Bo Hap) 437
776. Stir Fry Spicy Green Beans 438
777. Thai Chicken Spring Rolls 438
778. Thit Bo Xao Dau 439
779. Vegetarian Pho (Vietnamese Noodle Soup) 440
780. Vermicelli Noodle Bowl 440
781. Vietnamese Aromatic Lamb Chops 441
782. Vietnamese Beef And Lettuce Curry 442
783. Vietnamese Beef Noodle Soup 442
784. Vietnamese Beef Pho 443
785. Vietnamese Beef And Red Cabbage Bowl 443
786. Vietnamese Caramelized Pork 444
787. Vietnamese Chicken Cabbage Salad 444
788. Vietnamese Chicken Salad 445
789. Vietnamese Chicken And Long Grain Rice Congee 445
790. Vietnamese Coffee 446
791. Vietnamese Crispy Fish 446
792. Vietnamese Dipping Sauce 447
793. Vietnamese Eggplant With Spicy Sauce .. 447

794. Vietnamese Fresh Spring Rolls 448
795. Vietnamese Golden Chicken Wings 448
796. Vietnamese Grilled Lemongrass Chicken 449
797. Vietnamese Grilled Pork Skewers 449
798. Vietnamese Iced Coffee 450
799. Vietnamese Lemon Grass Chicken Curry 450
800. Vietnamese Meatballs..................................451
801. Vietnamese Pho Ga (Chicken).................451
802. Vietnamese Pickled Daikon Radish And Carrots 452
803. Vietnamese Pork And Five Spice 452
804. Vietnamese Rice Noodle Salad 453
805. Vietnamese Salad Rolls 453
806. Vietnamese Sandwich..................................454
807. Vietnamese Spring Rolls 454
808. Vietnamese Spring Rolls With Dipping Sauce 455
809. Vietnamese Steamed Buns (Banh Bao) ...456
810. Vietnamese Stir Fry......................................456
811. Vietnamese Style Vegetarian Curry Soup 457
812. Vietnamese Table Sauce.............................457
813. Vietnamese Style Shrimp Soup 458

CHAPTER 8: ASIAN DINNER CUISINE RECIPES 458

814. Apricot Chicken Stir Fry.............................458
815. Apricot Filled Pork Tenderloin 459
816. Asian Beef Noodle Toss 459
817. Asian Beef Ribbons 460
818. Asian Beef And Cauliflower Stew 460
819. Asian Pork Chops..461
820. Asian Pork Stir Fry......................................461
821. Asian Salmon Fillets 462
822. Asian Slow Cooker Pork............................462
823. Asian Steak..463
824. Asian Sweet And Sour Pork 464
825. Asparagus Mushroom Beef Stir Fry.........464
826. Beef Asparagus Stir Fry..............................465
827. Beef Pineapple Stir Fry...............................465
828. Beef Stir Fry On A Stick............................466
829. Calypso Pork Chops 467
830. Catfish In Ginger Sauce 467
831. Chicken Long Rice......................................468
832. Chicken Spareribs 468
833. Chicken Stir Fry With Noodles 469

834. Chicken And Rice Chow Mein 469
835. Chicken And Shrimp Satay.......................470
836. Chow Mein Chicken 471
837. Cranberry Turkey Stir Fry.........................471
838. Crunchy Curried Chicken 472
839. Curried Shrimp Stir Fry.............................472
840. Curried Tofu Stir Fry..................................473
841. Easy Marinated Sirloin Steak....................473
842. Easy Shrimp Stir Fry...................................474
843. Eckrich® Sweet And Sour Sausage 475
844. Egg Foo Yong With Sauce 475
845. Epiphany Ham 476
846. Firecracker Grilled Salmon.......................476
847. Garlic Chicken Kabobs...............................477
848. Glazed Shrimp & Asparagus For 2 477
849. Grilled Curried Salmon 478
850. Grilled Lime Teriyaki Shrimp 478
851. Grilled Mahi Mahi.......................................479
852. Grilled Marinated Pork Chops..................479
853. Grilled Marinated Pork Tenderloin..........480
854. Grilled Teriyaki Pork Tenderloin 481
855. Grilled Turkey Tenderloin..........................481
856. Ground Beef Lo Mein................................482
857. Hawaiian Stir Fry...482
858. Hoisin Shrimp & Broccoli 483
859. Hoisin Glazed Pork 483
860. Honey Citrus Chops 484
861. Honey Glazed Chicken Kabobs 484
862. Honey Grilled Pork Tenderloin 485
863. Indonesian Peanut Chicken 485
864. Lemon Plum Pork Roast 486
865. Marinated Beef Stir Fry..............................486
866. Orange Turkey Stir Fry 487
867. Orange Spiced Chicken..............................488
868. Pacific Rim Salmon.....................................488
869. Peanut Chicken Satay 489
870. Peanut Ginger Pasta 489
871. Pineapple Chicken Stir Fry 490
872. Pineapple Pork Stir Fry..............................490
873. Pineapple Red Pepper Beef Stir Fry.........491
874. Pineapple Shrimp Fried Rice....................491
875. Pineapple Shrimp Kabobs 492
876. Pineapple Teriyaki Chicken 493
877. Polynesian Sausage Supper.......................493
878. Pork 'n' Pea Pod Stir Fry...........................494
879. Pork Lo Mein With Spaghetti 494
880. Pork Tenderloin With Plum Sauce..........495

881. Pork With Sugar Snap Peas 495
882. Quick Almond Chicken Stir Fry 496
883. Quick Glazed Salmon 496
884. Quick Orange Chicken Stir Fry 497
885. Quick Pork Chow Mein 497
886. Ramen Chicken Stir Fry 498
887. Saucy Beef With Broccoli 498
888. Sesame Beef Stir Fry 499
889. Sesame Flank Steak 499
890. Sesame Pork Kabobs 500
891. Sesame Teriyaki Chicken 501
892. Sesame Crusted Pork Loin 501
893. Shrimp Fried Rice 502
894. Shrimp Lettuce Wraps 502
895. Shrimp Stir Fry 503
896. Simple Marinated Chicken Breasts 503
897. Sizzling Chicken Lo Mein 504
898. Slow Cooker Sweet And Sour Chicken ...504
899. Soy Ginger Grilled Swordfish 505
900. Spaghetti Hot Dish 506
901. Spareribs Cantonese 506
902. Spicy Beef & Pepper Stir Fry 507
903. Spicy Ginger Beef Stir Fry 507
904. Spicy Mongolian Beef Salad 508
905. Spicy Turkey Stir Fry 508
906. Steak Lo Mein 509
907. Steaks With Cucumber Sauce 510
908. Stir Fried Beef 'n' Beans 510
909. Stir Fried Beef On Lettuce 511
910. Sweet 'n' Tangy Shrimp 511
911. Sweet Beef Stew 512
912. Sweet Salsa Chicken 512
913. Sweet Spicy Asian Meatballs 513
914. Sweet And Sour Baked Chicken 514
915. Sweet And Sour Skewered Shrimp 514
916. Tangerine Cashew Snapper 515
917. Tangy Tropical Chicken 515
918. Tasty Tuna Steaks 516
919. Teriyaki Beef Stew 516
920. Teriyaki Beef Stir Fry For 2 517
921. Teriyaki Mushroom Chicken 517
922. Teriyaki Pork Tenderloin 518
923. Teriyaki Tangerine Ribs 518
924. Teriyaki Turkey Meatballs 519
925. Thai Barbecued Salmon 519
926. Thai Salmon Brown Rice Bowls 520
927. Thai Shrimp Linguine 520
928. Thai Shrimp Stir Fry 520
929. Thai Shrimp And Noodles 521
930. Tropical Turkey Meat Loaf 522
931. Turkey With Curried Cream Sauce 522
932. Vegetable Beef Stir Fry 523
933. Vegetarian Pad Thai 523

CHAPTER 9: SOUTHEAST ASIAN CUISINE RECIPES 525

934. Arroz Caldo (Chicken Rice Porridge) 525
935. Beef Stew With Curry And Lemongrass .525
936. Betel Leaf Wraps With Curried Squid And Cucumber Relish 526
937. Candy Pork 527
938. Chicken Curry 528
939. Chile Lime Sauce 529
940. Chili Crab 529
941. Coconut Chicken Soup 530
942. Coconut Tart 530
943. Coconut Marinated Short Rib Kebabs With Peanut Chile Oil 531
944. Crispy Fried Shallots 532
945. Cucumber Ajat 532
946. Curried Shrimp 533
947. Filipino Style Beef Steak With Onion And Bay Leaves (Bistek) 533
948. Filipino Style Roast Pork Belly With Chile Vinegar 534
949. Garlic Chile Ground Pork 535
950. Ginger Salad 536
951. Ginger And Honey Baby Back Ribs 536
952. Green Papaya Salad With Shrimp 537
953. Grilled Pork Chops With Sweet Lemongrass Marinade 538
954. Home Style Chicken Kebat 538
955. Indonesian Fried Noodles 539
956. Indonesian Fried Rice 540
957. Instant Pot Vietnamese Chicken Noodle Soup (Pho Ga) 541
958. Lamb Larb 541
959. Linguine With Shrimp And Scallops In Thai Green Curry Sauce 542
960. Lumpia Rolls 543
961. Malaysian Beef Curry 544
962. Marinated Thai Style Pork Spareribs 545
963. Massaman Chicken 545
964. Minted Eggplant Rounds 546

965. Ode To Halo Halo 547
966. Panang Vegetable Curry............................547
967. Penang Rice Salad 548
968. Pork Tenderloin With Turmeric, Squash, And Collard Greens Salad 549
969. Pork And Lemongrass Meatballs In Lettuce Cups 550
970. Pork Belly Buns...551
971. Red Curry Noodle Bowls With Steak And Cabbage 552
972. Rice Noodles..553
973. Rice Noodles With Garlic And Herbs......554
974. Roasted Brussels Sprouts............................554
975. Roasted Cauliflower Larb 555
976. Salt And Pepper Seasoning Mix................555
977. Salt And Pepper Tofu 556
978. Salt, Pepper, And Lemon Dipping Sauce 556
979. Saté Chicken Salad 557
980. Shredded Sweet Potato And Carrot Fritters (Ukoy) 557
981. Shrimp In Ginger Butter Sauce 558
982. Singaporean Chili Crab 558
983. Southeast Asian Rice Noodles With Calamari And Herbs 560
984. Southeast Asian Style Turkey Burgers With Pickled Cucumbers 561
985. Spicy Noodles With Ginger And Fresh Vegetables 561
986. Squid Salad With Tamarind Sauce............562
987. Squid And Pork Noodle Salad 562
988. Steak With Watercress Salad And Chile Lime Dressing...563
989. Thai Beef Salad..564
990. Thai Chile Herb Dipping Sauce................564
991. Thai Rice Curry With Herbed Chicken (Khao Mok Gai) 565
992. Thai Seafood Hot Pot 566
993. Thai Spiced Watermelon Soup With Crabmeat 566
994. Thai Style Chicken Soup With Basil 567
995. Thai Style Squid And Cucumber Salad....568
996. Toasted Coconut Sundaes With Candied Peanuts..569
997. Two Pepper Shrimp 569
998. Vegetable Summer Rolls 570
999. Vegetarian Dipping Sauce.........................571
1000. Vietnamese Chicken Soup With Rice 571
1001. Vietnamese Style Spring Rolls With Shrimp 572

INDEX **573**
CONCLUSION..**579**

Chapter 1: Thai Cuisine Recipes

***

1. Adrienne's Tom Ka Gai

Serving: 4 | Prep: 15mins | Cook: 45mins | Ready in:

Ingredients

- 2 teaspoons peanut oil
- 2 cloves garlic, thinly sliced
- 2 tablespoons grated fresh ginger root
- 1/4 cup chopped lemon grass
- 2 teaspoons crushed red pepper
- 1 teaspoon ground coriander
- 1 teaspoon ground cumin
- 1 skinless, boneless chicken breast halves - cut into thin strips
- 1 onion, thinly sliced
- 2 cups bok choy, shredded
- 4 cups water
- 1 (10 ounce) can coconut milk
- 1/4 cup fish sauce
- 1/4 cup chopped fresh cilantro

Direction

- Heat peanut oil in a big saucepan over medium heat. Mix in cumin, coriander, red pepper, lemon grass, ginger and garlic and cook for 2 minutes till fragrant. Mix in onion and chicken and cook for 5 minutes, mixing, till onion is translucent and chicken is white. Mix in bok choy and cook for 5 to 10 minutes till it starts to wilt. Mix in cilantro, fish sauce, coconut milk and water. Allow to simmer for half an hour till flavors are well incorporated and chicken is cooked through.

Nutrition Information

- Calories: 255 calories;
- Total Fat: 17.9
- Sodium: 1158
- Total Carbohydrate: 9.3
- Cholesterol: 34
- Protein: 17.2

2. Ajad (Authentic Thai Cucumber Salad)

Serving: 6 | Prep: 10mins | Cook: 5mins | Ready in:

Ingredients

- 1/2 cup white vinegar
- 1/4 cup water
- 4 tablespoons white sugar, or more to taste
- 1 1/2 teaspoons salt
- 6 cucumbers, peeled and thinly sliced
- 3 shallots, thinly sliced
- 2 Thai bird's eye chiles, halved lengthwise

Direction

- In a saucepan, mix salt, sugar, water, and vinegar together over medium heat. Boil it and cook for 3-5 minutes until salt and sugar dissolved. Taste and adjust the seasoning to make the pickling liquid slightly salty and nicely sour, sweet.
- In a big bowl, mix together chile peppers, shallots, and cucumbers. Fill with the pickling liquid. Chill for several hours for the flavors to blend.

Nutrition Information

- Calories: 93 calories;
- Total Carbohydrate: 22.9
- Cholesterol: 0
- Protein: 2.5

- Total Fat: 0.3
- Sodium: 590

3. Amazing Simple Thai Tofu

Serving: 4 | Prep: | Cook: | Ready in:

Ingredients

- 1 (14 ounce) package firm tofu, cut into 3/4 inch cubes
- 1/3 cup chopped green onion
- 1 1/2 teaspoons olive oil
- 1/2 teaspoon sesame oil
- 1 teaspoon soy sauce
- 2 teaspoons grated fresh ginger root
- 1/4 cup chunky peanut butter
- 3 tablespoons flaked coconut
- sesame seeds

Direction

- Over medium-high heat, heat sesame oil and olive oil in a skillet. Lower the heat to medium and then cook green onions for 1 minute. Place in tofu and continue to cook for 4 minutes longer. Drizzle with soy sauce when halfway through. Carefully mix in the ginger and peanut butter, taking care not to break tofu, until incorporated well.
- Take out from the heat and mix in coconut. Place onto a serving dish and scatter with sesame seeds.

Nutrition Information

- Calories: 285 calories;
- Cholesterol: 0
- Protein: 20.1
- Total Fat: 20.5
- Sodium: 179
- Total Carbohydrate: 10.6

4. Andrew's Tom Kha Gai

Serving: 6 | Prep: 15mins | Cook: 20mins | Ready in:

Ingredients

- 4 cups chicken stock
- 1 stalk lemongrass, cut into 2-inch pieces
- 4 ounces galangal, cut into 2-inch pieces
- 1/4 cup chopped fresh cilantro
- 3 tablespoons sliced green onion
- 10 kaffir lime leaves
- 3 pounds skinless, boneless chicken breasts, cut into 2-inch pieces
- 1/4 cup fish sauce
- 1 tablespoon white sugar
- 1/2 teaspoon red pepper flakes
- 3 (14 ounce) cans coconut milk
- 1 (8 ounce) package shiitake mushrooms, sliced
- 1 (8 ounce) package cremini mushrooms, sliced

Direction

- In a saucepan, boil chicken stock; put kaffir lime leaves, green onion, cilantro, galangal and lemon grass. Mix, lower heat, and allow to simmer for 5 minutes.
- Into stock mixture, mix red pepper flakes, sugar, fish sauce and chicken; mix and let simmer for 5 minutes. Put cremini mushrooms, shiitake mushrooms and coconut milk; mix and let simmer for 5 minutes.

Nutrition Information

- Calories: 707 calories;
- Total Fat: 47.8
- Sodium: 1535
- Total Carbohydrate: 16.8
- Cholesterol: 133
- Protein: 55.3

5. Authentic Pad Thai Noodles

Serving: 4 | Prep: 30mins | Cook: 20mins | Ready in:

Ingredients

- 2/3 cup dried rice vermicelli
- 1/4 cup peanut oil
- 2/3 cup thinly sliced firm tofu
- 1 large egg, beaten
- 4 cloves garlic, finely chopped
- 1/4 cup vegetable broth
- 2 tablespoons fresh lime juice
- 2 tablespoons soy sauce
- 1 tablespoon white sugar
- 1 teaspoon salt
- 1/2 teaspoon dried red chili flakes
- 3 tablespoons chopped peanuts
- 1 pound bean sprouts, divided
- 3 green onions, whites cut thinly across and greens sliced into thin lengths - divided
- 3 tablespoons chopped peanuts
- 2 limes, cut into wedges for garnish

Direction

- In a bowl filled with hot water, soak rice vermicelli noodles for half to a full hour until soft; drain. Set them aside.
- On medium heat, heat peanut oil in a big wok.
- Cook and stir tofu in the wok, turning the pieces until all sides are golden.
- Use a slotted spoon to place the tofu on a plate with lined paper towels; drain.
- In a small bowl, pour oil from the wok leaving only a tablespoon of used oil that will be used again for the later step.
- On medium heat, heat the remaining 1 tablespoon of oil in the pan until sizzling.
- Pour in beaten egg and lightly toss in the hot oil to scramble the egg.
- Take the egg out of the wok; let it stand.
- Pour the saved peanut oil in the small bowl back in the wok.
- Stir in drained noodles and toss garlic in the wok until covered in oil.
- Mix in sugar, vegetable broth, soy sauce, and lime juice. Softly toss and push the noodles around the wok to cover with sauce.
- Softly stir in 3tbsp peanuts, tofu, chili flakes, scrambled egg, and salt. Toss to mix all ingredients.
- Stir in green onions and bean sprouts, keeping a tablespoon of each to add on top later. Cook and stir for 1-2mins until the bean sprouts are a bit soft.
- On a warm serving dish, place noodles then top with the reserved green onion and bean sprouts, and 3tbsp peanuts. Arrange lime wedges around the sides of the platter.

Nutrition Information

- Calories: 397 calories;
- Total Fat: 23.3
- Sodium: 1234
- Total Carbohydrate: 39.5
- Cholesterol: 41
- Protein: 13.2

6. Authentic Thai Cashew Chicken

Serving: 4 | Prep: 15mins | Cook: 15mins | Ready in:

Ingredients

- 1 tablespoon canola oil
- 1 large yellow onion, chopped
- 1 large yellow bell pepper, chopped
- 3 tablespoons ketchup
- 2 tablespoons oyster sauce
- 1 tablespoon soy sauce
- 1/3 cup chicken broth
- 1 teaspoon white sugar
- 1 teaspoon Thai garlic chile paste
- 4 skinless, boneless chicken breast halves - cut into bite-size pieces
- 1 zucchini, chopped

- 1 yellow squash, chopped
- 6 ounces broccoli, chopped
- 8 ounces fresh mushrooms, quartered
- 1/2 cup unsalted cashew nuts

Direction

- Over medium heat, heat oil in a skillet, add the yellow bell pepper and onion and cook until tender. Stir in chile paste, sugar, chicken broth, soy sauce, oyster sauce and ketchup. Add the mushrooms, broccoli, squash, zucchini and chicken into the skillet. Continue cooking while stirring for 10 minutes until the chicken juices run clear and the vegetables are tender. Stir in cashews barely before you serve.

Nutrition Information

- Calories: 369 calories;
- Total Fat: 15.9
- Sodium: 506
- Total Carbohydrate: 25.8
- Cholesterol: 72
- Protein: 34.4

7. Barbequed Thai Style Chicken

Serving: 6 | Prep: 15mins | Cook: 30mins | Ready in:

Ingredients

- 1 bunch fresh cilantro with roots
- 3 cloves garlic, peeled
- 3 small red hot chile peppers, seeded and chopped
- 1 teaspoon ground turmeric
- 1 teaspoon curry powder
- 1 tablespoon white sugar
- 1 pinch salt
- 3 tablespoons fish sauce
- 1 (3 pound) chicken, cut into pieces
- 1/4 cup coconut milk

Direction

- Slice cilantro roots off the stem and mince well. Put several leaves aside for garnish. Mix salt, sugar, curry powder, turmeric, chile peppers, garlic, and cilantro leaves and roots together in a blender or a food processor. Blend until it forms a coarse paste. Add fish sauce and process until smooth.
- In a big shallow dish, put chicken. Rub cilantro paste on chicken. Put the cover on and put in the fridge to marinate for a minimum of 3 hours or overnight.
- Start preheating the grill to high heat.
- Lightly grease the grill grate. On the oiled grill, put the chicken and use coconut milk to brush it with generously. Grill the chicken for 8-15 minutes per side, depending on the pieces' size. Flip 1 time and baste from time to time using coconut cream. Cook until the juices run clear and the chicken is soft and turns brown.

Nutrition Information

- Calories: 324 calories;
- Total Fat: 18.3
- Sodium: 641
- Total Carbohydrate: 5.9
- Cholesterol: 100
- Protein: 32.8

8. California Thai Flank Steak

Serving: 8 | Prep: 30mins | Cook: 20mins | Ready in:

Ingredients

- 1/3 cup soy sauce
- 1/4 cup rice vinegar
- 1/4 cup rice wine
- 1/4 cup fresh lime juice
- 2 tablespoons dark sesame oil
- 1/2 small red onion, chopped

- 1/4 cup chopped fresh basil
- 1/4 cup chopped fresh mint
- 3 tablespoons sliced lemon grass
- 3 tablespoons crushed peanuts
- 3 tablespoons chile paste
- 1 tablespoon ground coriander
- 1/2 teaspoon garlic salt
- 2 pounds flank steak

Direction

- Mix together sesame oil, lime juice, rice wine, rice vinegar and soy sauce in a big bowl. Mix in crushed peanuts, lemon grass, mint, basil and onion. Spice with garlic salt, coriander and chile paste.
- Spread flank steak with marinade. Chill for 6 hours to overnight.
- Preheat outdoor grill for medium high heat, and grease grate gently with oil.
- Use non-stick cooking spray to coat a big sheet of aluminum foil. Remove liquid from marinade. Arrange meat on foil with the leftover non-liquid marinade ingredients. Fold edges of foil to secure, then grill for 20 minutes.

Nutrition Information

- Calories: 274 calories;
- Total Fat: 15.4
- Sodium: 826
- Total Carbohydrate: 7.1
- Cholesterol: 47
- Protein: 25.9

9. Carrie's Pad Thai Salad

Serving: 4 | Prep: 20mins | Cook: 8mins | Ready in:

Ingredients

- 1 (12 ounce) package dried rice noodles
- 1/2 cup white sugar
- 1/4 cup water
- 1/2 lime, juiced
- 2 tablespoons soy sauce
- 2 tablespoons fish sauce
- 1 teaspoon tamarind concentrate
- 1/4 cup peanut oil
- 1 clove garlic, minced
- 4 eggs
- 1 tablespoon paprika
- 1/4 teaspoon chili powder, or to taste (optional)
- 1 head lettuce, chopped, or as needed
- 2 tablespoons flaxseed oil
- 1/2 cup fresh bean sprouts, or to taste (optional)
- 1/2 cup chopped green onion
- 1/2 cup chopped fresh cilantro
- 1/2 cup chopped peanuts
- 1/2 lime, cut into wedges

Direction

- In a bowl, put in noodles and cover with enough hot water. Soak noodles for about 10 minutes until soft. Drain.
- Mix tamarind, fish sauce, soy sauce, lime juice, water, and sugar on medium heat in a big saucepan. Gently simmer, occasionally stirring, for 3-5 minutes until sauce thickens slightly.
- In a skillet, heat peanut oil on medium heat. Add garlic, stirring for 30 seconds to 1 minute until fragrant. Add eggs then stir and cook for 2-3 minutes until nearly set. Add strained noodles in egg mixture. Mix in half of the sauce. Keep cooking and stirring noodle mixture for another 2-3 minutes until hot, putting in extra sauce as you like. Sprinkle chili powder and paprika on noodles.
- In individual bowls or a serving dish, layer lettuce. Drizzle flaxseed oil on top. Put noodle mixture on top of lettuce. Garnish with peanuts, cilantro, green onion, and bean sprouts. Serve alongside lime wedges.

Nutrition Information

- Calories: 807 calories;
- Sodium: 1244
- Total Carbohydrate: 109.1
- Cholesterol: 186
- Protein: 16.6
- Total Fat: 35.3

10. Chicken Salad With Thai Flavored Dressing

Serving: 4 | Prep: | Cook: | Ready in:

Ingredients

- 4 cups rotisserie chicken, skinned and boned, meat shredded into bite-sized pieces
- 2 medium celery ribs, cut into small dice
- 2 medium green onions, sliced thin
- 1/4 cup chopped honey-roasted peanuts
- 2 tablespoons lime juice
- 2 tablespoons Asian fish sauce
- 1 teaspoon ground ginger
- 2 teaspoons white sugar
- 1/2 teaspoon hot red pepper flakes
- 2 tablespoons minced fresh cilantro leaves
- 2 tablespoons chopped fresh mint leaves
- To serve:
- Boston lettuce
- sliced cucumbers
- grated carrots
- chopped honey-roasted peanuts

Direction

- Mix peanuts, green onions, celery and chicken in a medium bowl. Whisk 2 tbsp. of water, mint, cilantro, red pepper, sugar, ginger, fish sauce and lime juice in a small bowl.
- Toss the chicken mixture with dressing. Serve with the recommended accompaniments on a Boston lettuce bed.

Nutrition Information

- Calories: 387 calories;
- Sodium: 792
- Total Carbohydrate: 16.8
- Cholesterol: 128
- Protein: 55.1
- Total Fat: 10.5

11. Chicken Satay

Serving: 12 | Prep: 2hours10mins | Cook: 20mins | Ready in:

Ingredients

- 2 tablespoons creamy peanut butter
- 1/2 cup soy sauce
- 1/2 cup lemon or lime juice
- 1 tablespoon brown sugar
- 2 tablespoons curry powder
- 2 cloves garlic, chopped
- 1 teaspoon hot pepper sauce
- 6 skinless, boneless chicken breast halves - cubed

Direction

- Mix together peanut butter, soy sauce, lime juice, garlic, hot pepper sauce, brown sugar, and curry powder in a mixing bowl. Toss the chicken breasts in and marinate in the refrigerator for 2 hours to overnight for the best flavor.
- Preheat grill to high.
- Skewer the chicken and grill for 5 minutes per side.

Nutrition Information

- Calories: 162 calories;
- Total Fat: 3
- Sodium: 694
- Total Carbohydrate: 4.1
- Cholesterol: 68
- Protein: 28.8

12. Chicken Satay With Peanut Sauce

Serving: 4 | Prep: 20mins | Cook: 20mins | Ready in:

Ingredients

- 1/2 cup unsweetened coconut milk
- 2 teaspoons yellow curry powder
- 1 teaspoon white sugar
- 1 teaspoon fish sauce
- 1/2 teaspoon granulated garlic
- 1 pound skinless, boneless chicken breasts, cut into strips
- 8 skewers
- 2 tablespoons olive oil
- 3/4 cup unsweetened coconut milk
- 1 tablespoon yellow curry powder
- 1/2 cup chicken broth
- 1/4 cup creamy peanut butter
- 1 tablespoon white sugar
- 1 tablespoon lime juice
- 1 tablespoon fish sauce

Direction

- In a bowl, mix together a teaspoon fish sauce, 1/2 cup coconut milk, a teaspoon of sugar, 2 teaspoons curry powder, and granulated garlic. Toss in the chicken pieces to coat well. Cover the bowl and let sit in refrigerator for at least 2 hours.
- Skewer the marinated chicken pieces.
- In a large skillet over medium-high heat, cook the chicken skewers in olive oil until browned and cooked through, about 3 to 4 minutes each side.
- Take a small saucepan or skillet and simmer 3/4 cup coconut milk over medium heat. Add a tablespoon of curry powder and let simmer for 4 minutes. Mix in peanut butter, 1 tablespoon fish sauce, chicken broth, lime juice, and 1 tablespoon sugar. Let simmer for a minute. Serve this dipping sauce with the chicken skewers.

Nutrition Information

- Calories: 466 calories;
- Total Fat: 33.9
- Sodium: 630
- Total Carbohydrate: 12.1
- Cholesterol: 70
- Protein: 31.7

13. Classic Pad Thai

Serving: 4 | Prep: 15mins | Cook: 15mins | Ready in:

Ingredients

- 8 ounces medium width rice vermicelli noodles
- 3 tablespoons vegetable oil
- 1/4 pound ground chicken
- 1 teaspoon hot pepper sauce
- 1 red pepper, thinly sliced
- 1/2 pound peeled, deveined raw shrimp
- 3 cloves garlic, minced
- 2 teaspoons freshly grated gingerroot
- 1/2 cup vegetable or chicken broth
- 1/2 cup Heinz Tomato Ketchup
- 1/4 cup lime juice
- 3 tablespoons granulated sugar
- 3 tablespoons fish sauce
- 1 1/2 cups bean sprouts
- 3 green onions, thinly sliced
- 1/4 cup fresh coriander or parsley leaves
- chopped peanuts

Direction

- Cook noodles in boiling water for 5mins, let it stand; drain well and set aside.
- On high heat, heat 1/2 of the oil in a deep pan or wok. Break the chicken in crumbles then pour in hot sauce; cook and stir-fry for 3-5mins

until brown. Transfer on a platter then set aside.
- Pour the remaining oil in the pan; cook and stir peppers for 3mins then put in shrimp. Cook and stir-fry the shrimp for 2mins. Mix in fish sauce, garlic, sugar, ginger, lime juice, broth, and ketchup; boil. Toss in the reserved meat and noodles until well combined. Heat completely.
- Gently toss in sprouts. Add peanuts, coriander, and onions on top.

Nutrition Information

- Calories: 553 calories;
- Total Fat: 18.2
- Sodium: 1298
- Total Carbohydrate: 70.2
- Cholesterol: 104
- Protein: 30.3

14. Coconut Rice Salad

Serving: 8 | Prep: 10mins | Cook: 2hours | Ready in:

Ingredients

- 2 cups basmati rice
- 1 (10 ounce) can unsweetened coconut milk
- 2 3/4 cups water
- 2 large limes, juiced
- 2 tablespoons peanut butter
- 1/4 cup sesame oil
- 1 teaspoon fish sauce
- 1 teaspoon curry paste
- 1 clove garlic, crushed
- 1/4 cup flaked coconut, toasted
- 1/2 cup raisins
- 1/4 cup slivered almonds, toasted

Direction

- Combine water, coconut milk and rice in a saucepan. Boil the mixture. Cover than saucepan, lower the heat to low. Simmer until rice completely absorbs all liquid, about 15-20 minutes. Set aside and let cool.
- Stir garlic, curry paste, fish sauce, sesame oil, peanut butter, lime juice together in a small bowl. Try it and adjust the dressing flavor if desired.
- Once the rice is cool, stir the dressing with the cooled rice, almonds, raisins and coconut. Put in the fridge for minimum of 1 hour and maximum of 1 day.

Nutrition Information

- Calories: 401 calories;
- Cholesterol: 0
- Protein: 6.8
- Total Fat: 18.8
- Sodium: 91
- Total Carbohydrate: 53.9

15. Curried Coconut Chicken

Serving: 6 | Prep: 20mins | Cook: 50mins | Ready in:

Ingredients

- 2 pounds boneless skinless chicken breasts, cut into 1/2-inch chunks
- 1 teaspoon salt and pepper, or to taste
- 1 1/2 tablespoons vegetable oil
- 2 tablespoons curry powder
- 1/2 onion, thinly sliced
- 2 cloves garlic, crushed
- 1 (14 ounce) can coconut milk
- 1 (14.5 ounce) can stewed, diced tomatoes
- 1 (8 ounce) can tomato sauce
- 3 tablespoons sugar

Direction

- Use the pepper and salt to season the chicken pieces.

- Heat the curry powder and oil on medium high heat in the big skillet for two minutes. Mix in the garlic and onions, and cook 60 seconds longer. Put in the chicken, coating with the curry oil by tossing lightly. Lower the heat to medium, and cook till the juices come out clear and the chicken is not pink in the middle anymore, or for 7-10 minutes.
- Add the sugar, tomato sauce, tomatoes and coconut milk to pan, and combine by mixing. Keep covered and let simmer, mixing once in a while, about 30-40 minutes.

Nutrition Information

- Calories: 375 calories;
- Total Carbohydrate: 16.7
- Cholesterol: 78
- Protein: 32.2
- Total Fat: 20.9
- Sodium: 807

16. Dad's Pad Thai

Serving: 4 | Prep: 20mins | Cook: 5mins | Ready in:

Ingredients

- 3/4 pound bean sprouts
- 6 ounces pad thai rice noodles
- 4 eggs
- salt
- 3 tablespoons lime juice
- 3 tablespoons ketchup
- 1 tablespoon brown sugar
- 1/4 cup fish sauce
- 3 tablespoons peanut oil
- 1 tablespoon minced garlic
- 1 1/2 teaspoons red pepper flakes
- 2 cups grated carrots
- 2/3 cup chopped peanuts
- 1 cup green onions cut into 1-inch pieces

Direction

- Boil a pot of water. Blanch bean sprouts for approximately 30 seconds in boiling water. Take out then drain well. Add noodles when water boils again. Cook for 3-5 minutes until firm yet tender. Drain then rinse with cold water.
- Beat a pinch of salt and eggs in a small bowl. Mix fish sauce, brown sugar, ketchup, and lime juice together in another bowl. Put aside.
- In a big skillet or wok, heat oil on medium-high heat. Fry garlic for several seconds. Add carrot and pepper flakes, cook for a minute, then take out. Add beaten egg and scramble gently. When eggs set, place in green onion, peanuts, noodles, bean sprouts, sauce, and carrots. Toss it altogether.

Nutrition Information

- Calories: 553 calories;
- Total Fat: 28
- Sodium: 1421
- Total Carbohydrate: 62.4
- Cholesterol: 186
- Protein: 18.4

17. Duck Legs In Green Curry

Serving: 4 | Prep: 15mins | Cook: 30mins | Ready in:

Ingredients

- 1 tablespoon vegetable oil
- 4 duck legs
- 1 small onion, minced
- 3 cloves garlic, minced
- 2 serrano peppers, seeded and minced
- 1 (1 inch) piece fresh ginger root, minced
- 3 (10 ounce) cans coconut milk
- 3 tablespoons yellow curry paste
- 2 kaffir lime leaves
- 2 green onions, minced
- 2 tablespoons Asian fish sauce
- 1 (12 ounce) package thin rice noodles

- 1/2 bunch cilantro leaves, coarsely chopped

Direction

- Warm a large skillet over medium-high heat, and then put the duck legs in. Be sure that the fat side of the duck legs is down, and then sear both sides, 3 minutes for each side, until golden. Afterwards, take the duck legs from the skillet set them aside. Prepare about 3 tablespoons of fat.
- In the skillet, add the reserved duck fat and onions. For five minutes, cook at medium heat until the onions are soft and translucent. You can then throw in garlic, ginger, and Serrano peppers. Take 3 minutes to cook.
- Take 1 can of coconut milk and skim the coconut cream from it. Stir the cream into the onion mixture. Then add curry paste and let cook for around 1 to 2 minutes, until the smells aromatic.
- Add the remaining 2 cans of coconut milk, fish sauce, green onions, and kaffir lime leaves in the skillet. Then take the duck legs to the pan. Leave to simmer on low heat for 15 minutes, until everything is just done. Note: if you need to reduce the curry sauce a little further, take the duck legs out of the skillet and place over to an oven set to low heat. Continue to cook the sauce over medium.
- Meanwhile, boil a large pot of lightly salted water. Take the noodles and cook them following the directions on the package. Once fully cooked, drain the water from the noodles, run them under clean cold water, and then set them aside.
- Mix noodles in the curry. Serve with chopped cilantro.

Nutrition Information

- Calories: 1488 calories;
- Total Carbohydrate: 81.1
- Cholesterol: 182
- Protein: 49.2
- Total Fat: 108.1
- Sodium: 1076

18. Easy Red Thai Curry With Chicken And Broccoli

Serving: 4 | Prep: 15mins | Cook: 11mins | Ready in:

Ingredients

- 1 teaspoon olive oil
- 2 skinless, boneless chicken breast halves, cut into strips
- 2 cloves garlic, minced
- 1 1/2 teaspoons Thai red curry paste
- 1 cup coconut milk
- 2 tablespoons white sugar
- 1 teaspoon salt
- 1 head broccoli, florets separated and stems chopped
- 3 green onions, chopped

Direction

- Over medium-high heat, heat oil in a deep skillet, add chicken and then sauté for 2 to 3 minutes until turned browned. Add curry paste and garlic and then cook for about 2 minutes until fragrant. Add coconut milk and then season with salt and sugar. Combine thoroughly. Place in broccoli, the cover skillet and let simmer for about 7 minutes until the broccoli is soft. Scatter with green onions.

Nutrition Information

- Calories: 281 calories;
- Protein: 13.4
- Total Fat: 18.8
- Sodium: 760
- Total Carbohydrate: 18
- Cholesterol: 34

19. Easy Spicy Thai Slow Cooker Chicken

Serving: 6 | Prep: 5mins | Cook: 4hours | Ready in:

Ingredients

- 1 (16 ounce) bottle Asian-style toasted sesame salad dressing (such as Kraft® Asian Toasted Sesame Dressing & Marinade)
- 1 tablespoon Thai chili paste, or more to taste
- 1 tablespoon ginger garlic paste
- 2 tablespoons peanut butter
- 6 pieces skinless, boneless chicken (such as breast halves and thighs)

Direction

- In a bowl, combine together the peanut butter, ginger garlic paste, Thai chili paste, and sesame salad dressing until the mixture is mixed well. Immerse the pieces of chicken into the mixture and then transfer to a slow cooker. Add remaining sauce on top of the chicken. Adjust the cooker to Low and then let cook for about 4 to 6 hours until chicken becomes very tender.

Nutrition Information

- Calories: 564 calories;
- Sodium: 1171
- Total Carbohydrate: 10.7
- Cholesterol: 48
- Protein: 17.5
- Total Fat: 51.1

20. Egg And Coconut Custard Jellies

Serving: 8 | Prep: 20mins | Cook: 10mins | Ready in:

Ingredients

- 2 eggs
- 1/4 cup palm sugar
- 1 1/2 cups unsweetened coconut cream
- 3 pandan leaves, cut into 1-inch pieces
- 1 tablespoon agar-agar powder
- 1 1/2 cups water
- 1/2 cup white sugar

Direction

- To prepare the custard, in a bowl, beat eggs together with pandan leaves, coconut cream and palm sugar. Ensure pandan aroma is imparted into the eggs. Sieve the mixture and reserve.
- Over medium heat, mix water and agar-agar powder in a small saucepan. Cook while stirring until powder is dissolved completely. Then whisk sugar into the mixture until it is dissolved but don't let to boil. Mix custard into the mixture and let cook for around 2 minutes. Transfer the mixture into one-cup molds. Keep in a fridge for about 2 hours to set. Take out the jellies from molds and serve.

Nutrition Information

- Calories: 233 calories;
- Sodium: 22
- Total Carbohydrate: 20.3
- Cholesterol: 46
- Protein: 3.2
- Total Fat: 16.8

21. Fabienne's Leeks And Monkfish

Serving: 4 | Prep: 10mins | Cook: 1hours5mins | Ready in:

Ingredients

- 2 tablespoons olive oil
- 2 cups chopped leeks, white and light green parts only
- 1/3 cup white wine

- 1 tablespoon lemon juice
- 1 teaspoon ground cumin
- 3/4 teaspoon hot Madras curry powder, or to taste
- 1/2 teaspoon ground turmeric
- 1/2 teaspoon ground paprika
- 1/4 teaspoon ground coriander
- 1/8 teaspoon ground ginger
- 1 pinch cayenne pepper, or to taste
- salt and ground black pepper to taste
- 1 (14 ounce) can coconut milk
- 1 pound monkfish fillets, cut into cubes

Direction

- In a stock pot, heat olive oil over medium heat. Add in pepper, salt, cayenne, ginger, coriander, paprika, turmeric, Madras curry powder, cumin, lemon juice, white wine, and leeks and stir well. Cover pot and lower heat to medium-low, frequently stirring till all liquid gets absorbed, about 30 minutes. Uncover pot, add coconut milk in and stir, and lower heat to low; allow to simmer, uncovered, for 30 minutes.
- In the pot, gently lay monkfish; pour leek mixture over monkfish. Cook and gently stir over low heat for about 5 minutes till fish easily flakes with a fork.

Nutrition Information

- Calories: 390 calories;
- Total Fat: 29.8
- Sodium: 83
- Total Carbohydrate: 10.8
- Cholesterol: 28
- Protein: 19.3

22. Fresh Spring Rolls With Thai Dipping Sauce

Serving: 6 | Prep: | Cook: | Ready in:

Ingredients

- 6 spring roll wrappers (available in Asian markets)
- 12 medium shrimp, cooked and shelled
- 1 cup shredded leaf lettuce
- 1/3 cup chopped cilantro
- 1/2 cup peeled, seeded, chopped cucumber
- 1 medium carrot, julienned
- Quick Thai Dipping Sauce:
- 1 tablespoon light soy sauce
- 1 tablespoon white-wine vinegar or rice vinegar
- 3 tablespoons mirin
- 1/4 teaspoon grated ginger root (optional)

Direction

- Submerge a wrapper in a bowl of cool water till limp. Spread the wrapper out evenly. Put 1/6 of every ingredient down the center of wrapper, beginning with lettuce. Fold every end on top and securely roll the wrapper surrounding the filling, like making a burrito. Dampen at seam; press to seal.
- Set on plate, cover using damp paper towel and chill till set to serve. Halve and serve along with peanut sauce or Quick Thai Dipping Sauce.
- For Quick Thai Dipping Sauce, mix every ingredient in a small bowl.

Nutrition Information

- Calories: 59 calories;
- Total Carbohydrate: 8.9
- Cholesterol: 20
- Protein: 3.4
- Total Fat: 0.3
- Sodium: 168

23. Fried Whole Tilapia With Basil And Chilies

Serving: 4 | Prep: 20mins | Cook: 15mins | Ready in:

Ingredients

- 1 whole (10 ounce) fresh tilapia, cleaned and scaled
- 1 quart oil for deep frying
- 2 tablespoons cooking oil
- 5 large red chili peppers, sliced
- 5 cloves garlic, chopped
- 1 yellow onion, chopped
- 2 tablespoons fish sauce
- 2 tablespoons light soy sauce
- 1/4 cup Thai basil leaves
- 1/4 cup chopped cilantro

Direction

- Heat 1-qt. oil to 175°C/350°F in big saucepan/deep fryer. Dip head of fish into oil if you don't have a thermometer; it's ready if it sizzles. If not, wait a few minutes then try again.
- Rinse fish; dry well. Create a few angled slits along the body of fish, cutting down to rib bones. Create 2 lateral slits along back of fish, beginning from heat towards tail, on either side of dorsal fin to guarantee maximum crispiness and fast cooking.
- Slip fish gently into oil; fry for 7-10 minutes till crispy. Remove fish carefully from oil; drain on paper towels. Put on big serving platter.
- Heat 2 tbsp. oil in big skillet as fish drains; mix and cook onion, garlic and chili peppers in hot oil for 5-7 minutes till lightly brown. Mix soy sauce and fish sauce into mixture; take off from heat. Fold cilantro and Thai basil into mixture. Put sauce on fish; serve.

Nutrition Information

- Calories: 368 calories;
- Total Fat: 30.1
- Sodium: 1033
- Total Carbohydrate: 9.2
- Cholesterol: 26
- Protein: 16.6

24. Gaeng Daeng Sai Fak Thong Lae Moo (Red Curry With Pork And Squash)

Serving: 2 | Prep: 15mins | Cook: 25mins | Ready in:

Ingredients

- 1 tablespoon vegetable oil
- 1 tablespoon red curry paste, or to taste
- 1/2 pound pork loin, thinly sliced
- 1 (14 ounce) can coconut milk
- 2 1/4 cups peeled, cubed butternut squash
- 2 1/4 cups cabbage, coarsely chopped
- 1 tablespoon fish sauce, or more to taste
- 1 tablespoon white sugar, or more to taste

Direction

- On medium heat, heat oil in a medium saucepan. Cook and stir in curry paste for 2-3 mins until aromatic; add in pork. Stir-fry for 3-5 mins until covered in curry paste and cooked through. Pour in coconut milk then boil; put in squash. Lower heat and let it simmer for 7-10 mins until the squash becomes nearly cooked through; put in cabbage. Let it simmer for another five minutes. Add sugar and fish sauce to season.

Nutrition Information

- Calories: 714 calories;
- Cholesterol: 54
- Protein: 26.3
- Total Fat: 55.3
- Sodium: 780
- Total Carbohydrate: 37.3

25. Goong Tod Kratiem Prik Thai (Prawns Fried With Garlic And White Pepper)

Serving: 4 | Prep: 5mins | Cook: 4mins | Ready in:

Ingredients

- 8 cloves garlic, chopped, or more to taste
- 2 tablespoons tapioca flour
- 2 tablespoons fish sauce
- 2 tablespoons light soy sauce
- 1 tablespoon white sugar
- 1/2 teaspoon ground white pepper
- 1/4 cup vegetable oil, divided, or as needed
- 1 pound whole unpeeled prawns, divided

Direction

- In a bowl, mix white pepper, garlic, sugar, tapioca flour, soy sauce, and fish sauce together; toss in prawns to coat.
- On high heat, heat 2tbsp oil in a heavy pan. Place half of the prawn in a single layer; cook for 1-2mins per side until crispy and golden brown. Repeat with the rest of the prawns and oil.

Nutrition Information

- Calories: 377 calories;
- Total Fat: 24.7
- Sodium: 1118
- Total Carbohydrate: 19.5
- Cholesterol: 157
- Protein: 20.5

26. Green Curry Lamb Balls

Serving: 4 | Prep: 15mins | Cook: 15mins | Ready in:

Ingredients

- 1/2 pound ground lamb
- 1/2 cup bread crumbs
- steak seasoning to taste
- 1 (10 ounce) can coconut milk
- 1 1/2 tablespoons green curry paste

Direction

- Combine steak seasoning, bread crumbs and ground lamb together in a medium bowl until well mixed. Shape into meatballs of about one inch in diameter. Over medium-high heat, heat a skillet that is greased and then fry lamb balls for about 5 minutes until they're a bit crusty and black. Take out the balls from the pan and reserve.
- Mix curry paste into hot skillet and then fry for about 1 minute. Add in the whole can of coconut milk and then decrease the heat. Allow mixture to simmer while stirring often for about 5 to 10 minutes. You can serve the curry sauce and meatballs on top of rice.

Nutrition Information

- Calories: 348 calories;
- Sodium: 249
- Total Carbohydrate: 12.6
- Cholesterol: 41
- Protein: 14.5
- Total Fat: 31.4

27. Green Curry Thai For Kings

Serving: 4 | Prep: 20mins | Cook: 25mins | Ready in:

Ingredients

- 2 tablespoons canola oil
- 3 shallots, finely chopped
- 3 cloves garlic, sliced
- 1 tablespoon finely chopped fresh ginger
- 1 1/2 tablespoons green curry paste

- 1 pound skinless, boneless chicken breast halves - cut into strips
- salt and pepper to taste
- 5 stalks lemon grass
- 1 (15 ounce) can baby corn, drained
- 1 (4 ounce) can water chestnuts, drained
- 1 (10 ounce) can coconut milk
- 1 bunch fresh Thai basil leaves, torn

Direction

- In a big skillet, over medium-high heat, heat the oil. In hot oil, cook and mix the ginger, garlic and shallots till shallots are soft for 3 to 4 minutes. Stir in the green curry paste. Cook and mix for a minute. Put pepper and salt on chicken to season, then in the skillet, put the lemon grass and chicken. Cook till chicken starts to brown for 5 minutes. Stir in the water chestnuts and baby corn. Cook and mix till juices run clear and the chicken is not pink anymore.
- Stir the coconut milk into the skillet, boil. Lower heat and allow to simmer till the coconut milk has thickened, mixing from time to time. Put basil leaves on top, serve.

Nutrition Information

- Calories: 395 calories;
- Total Fat: 27
- Sodium: 210
- Total Carbohydrate: 21.7
- Cholesterol: 59
- Protein: 27.7

28. Green Curry Tofu

Serving: 4 | Prep: 20mins | Cook: 25mins | Ready in:

Ingredients

- 1 1/2 cups water
- 1 cup uncooked basmati rice, rinsed and drained
- 3 tablespoons sesame oil
- 1 (14 ounce) package firm water-packed tofu, drained and cubed
- 1/4 teaspoon salt
- 1 (10 ounce) can coconut milk
- 2 tablespoons green curry paste

Direction

- Pour water into a medium saucepan and mix in rice. Heat to boil. Cover, lower the heat and let to simmer for 20 minutes. Take out from the heat, cool a bit and then fluff with a fork.
- Over medium heat, heat sesame oil in another medium saucepan and mix in tofu. Fry while stirring from time to time for about 20 minutes until lightly browned and evenly crisp. Add salt to taste.
- Heat coconut milk to boil in a small saucepan. Stir in the green curry paste. Lower the heat and let simmer for 5 minutes. Generously sprinkle over the rice and tofu before serving.

Nutrition Information

- Calories: 536 calories;
- Cholesterol: 0
- Protein: 23.2
- Total Fat: 37.9
- Sodium: 312
- Total Carbohydrate: 44.2

29. Grilled Mahi Mahi In Thai Coconut Sauce

Serving: 2 | Prep: 15mins | Cook: 15mins | Ready in:

Ingredients

- 1 1/2 cups coconut milk
- 2 tablespoons chopped fresh cilantro
- 2 tablespoons chopped green onion

- 2 tablespoons lime juice
- 4 teaspoons minced fresh ginger root
- 2 cloves garlic, minced
- 1 teaspoon fish sauce
- 2 (6 ounce) mahi mahi fillets
- 2 tablespoons chopped fresh cilantro
- 2 tablespoons chopped green onion

Direction

- At medium heat, put a grill pan on top until heated. In a saucepan, bring the stirred combination of fish sauce, garlic, ginger, lime juice, 2 tablespoons of green onion, 2 tablespoons of cilantro and coconut milk to a boil. Use an adequate amount of sauce to brush mahi-mahi fillers until well coated. At a boil, cook the rest of the sauce for 3 to 4 minutes until it thickens a little. In a grill pan, cook mahi-mahi for around 7 minutes on each side until you can use a fork to flake it off with ease. Move it on a serving platter. Over the top, put sauce then 2 tablespoons of green onion and 2 tablespoons of cilantro before serving.

Nutrition Information

- Calories: 496 calories;
- Total Carbohydrate: 8.9
- Cholesterol: 125
- Protein: 35.6
- Total Fat: 37.5
- Sodium: 360

30. Guay Diaw Lawd (Pork Belly, Chicken Wing, And Noodle Stew)

Serving: 5 | Prep: 40mins | Cook: 1hours | Ready in:

Ingredients

- 10 dried shiitake mushrooms
- 1/2 cup peeled and chopped cilantro root
- 1/4 cup coarsely chopped garlic
- 2 tablespoons black peppercorns
- 2 (32 ounce) cartons beef stock
- 9 ounces pork belly, cut into 3/4-inch pieces
- 1 pound chicken wings
- 9 ounces firm tofu, cut into 1/3-inch chunks
- 9 ounces pickled radish (jap chai), diced
- 2 tablespoons oyster sauce, or more to taste
- 2 tablespoons dark sweet soy sauce (pad se ew), or more to taste
- 1 dash fish sauce, or more to taste
- sea salt to taste
- 1 (16 ounce) package wide rice noodles
- 2 cups bean sprouts
- 1 cup green onions, sliced
- 1 cup chopped cilantro leaves

Direction

- In a small bowl, put shiitake mushrooms. Use hot water to cover and soak for about 20 minutes until tender. Drain and squeeze out extra water then slice.
- Pound black peppercorns, garlic, and cilantro root in a mortar and pestle to make a coarse paste. Place paste in a big pot.
- Place beef stock in the pot. Add chicken wings and pork belly. Simmer and cook for 10 minutes. Add pickled radish, tofu, and sliced shiitake mushrooms. Simmer the soup for about 45 minutes until chicken wings are cooked thoroughly. Mix in soy sauce and oyster sauce. Season with sea salt and fish sauce.
- Put a steamer basket in a big pot then pour in water to reach the bottom of the steamer. Boil water. Add noodles, then steam for about 5 minutes, covered, until tender.
- Put noodles in every serving bowl then place soup over it. Top with cilantro, green onions, and bean sprouts.

Nutrition Information

- Calories: 647 calories;

- Total Fat: 15.7
- Sodium: 1612
- Total Carbohydrate: 96.6
- Cholesterol: 34
- Protein: 28.7

31. Hot And Sour Prawn Soup With Lemon Grass

Serving: 4 | Prep: 15mins | Cook: 20mins | Ready in:

Ingredients

- 1 pound tiger prawns with shell
- 4 cups chicken stock
- 3 stalks lemon grass
- 3 tablespoons fish sauce
- 1/4 cup lime juice
- 2 tablespoons chopped green onion
- 10 kaffir lime leaves, torn in half
- 1 cup straw mushrooms
- 1 tablespoon chopped fresh cilantro
- 4 red chile peppers, seeded and chopped
- 2 green onions, chopped

Direction

- Devein and shell the prawns, set the shells aside. Wash the shells and in a big saucepan, put shells together with the chicken stock. Pound the lemon grass stalks, the put them to the broth together with half of the lime leaves. Boil, then turn heat to low, allow to simmer gently for 5 minutes till the stock becomes aromatic and the lemon grass changes color. Filter the stock and put back to the saucepan. Get rid of the solids.
- Bring the stock back to a simmer, the put the prawns and mushrooms. Cook till the prawns turned pink. Mix in the leftover lime leaves, red chilies, cilantro, 2 tablespoons green onion, lime juice and fish sauce. Taste, and if needed, adjust seasoning. The soup must be hot, spicy, salty and sour. Top with the rest of green onions.

Nutrition Information

- Calories: 182 calories;
- Total Fat: 2.3
- Sodium: 1688
- Total Carbohydrate: 15.2
- Cholesterol: 173
- Protein: 27

32. How To Make Peanut Dipping Sauce

Serving: 12 | Prep: 15mins | Cook: 5mins | Ready in:

Ingredients

- 3/4 cup smooth natural peanut butter
- 2 cloves garlic, minced
- 2 tablespoons brown sugar
- 1 tablespoon fish sauce
- 2 teaspoons soy sauce
- 2 teaspoons toasted sesame oil
- 1/2 lime, juiced
- 1 teaspoon chile-garlic sauce (such as Sriracha), or to taste
- 1 (5.6 ounce) can coconut milk
- 2 teaspoons chopped red bell pepper, or to taste
- 2 teaspoons chopped fresh cilantro, or to taste
- 2 teaspoons chopped peanuts, or to taste

Direction

- In a mixing bowl, put peanut butter. Whisk sesame oil, soy sauce, fish sauce, brown sugar and garlic into the peanut butter, then chile-garlic sauce and lime juice.
- Simmer the coconut milk over medium heat in a small saucepan; add onto peanut butter mixture. Whisk until they become smooth.
- Place into a serving bowl. Decorate with peanuts, cilantro and chopped red pepper.

Nutrition Information

- Calories: 126 calories;
- Total Fat: 10
- Sodium: 208
- Total Carbohydrate: 6.7
- Cholesterol: 0
- Protein: 4.4

33. Jet Tila's Tom Yum Goong Soup

Serving: 6 | Prep: 10mins | Cook: 15mins | Ready in:

Ingredients

- 6 whole Thai chiles
- 2 quarts Thai chicken broth
- 1 cup peeled and deveined medium shrimp
- 1 (15 ounce) can whole straw mushrooms, drained
- 6 tablespoons fish sauce
- 6 tablespoons lime juice
- 3 tablespoons Thai garlic chile paste
- 6 kaffir lime leaves
- 6 sprigs fresh cilantro

Direction

- Set the oven's broiler ready and start preheating; place the oven rack at around 6-in. from the heat source. Cover inside the baking sheet with aluminum foil. Put the peppers on the prepared baking sheet.
- Cook under the prepared broiler, turning around occasionally till the skin of peppers has become blackened and blistered, around 5 minutes. In a bowl, add the blackened peppers; firmly cover with plastic wrap. Keep the peppers steaming as they cool, approximately 20 minutes. Once cool, remove the stem, seeds and skin and throw them away. Cut the roasted chiles.
- Place a large saucepan on medium-high heat; pour in the chicken broth; simmer it. Mix in chopped roasted chiles, mushrooms and shrimp. Take back to the simmer; cook till the shrimps are not translucent in the middle anymore, about 1 minute. Mix in the chile paste, lime juice and fish sauce till the chile paste has melted. Ladle into bowls; dress with a sprig of cilantro and a lime leaf for each bowl.

Nutrition Information

- Calories: 66 calories;
- Cholesterol: 32
- Protein: 7
- Total Fat: 0.7
- Sodium: 1470
- Total Carbohydrate: 9.6

34. Kal Pot

Serving: 5 | Prep: 30mins | Cook: 30mins | Ready in:

Ingredients

- 2 cups water
- 1 cup uncooked white rice
- 2 pounds boneless pork loin, cut into 1 inch cubes
- 1 onion, chopped
- 4 tomatoes, cut into bite size pieces
- 2 teaspoons fish sauce
- 1 egg, beaten

Direction

- Heat water to boil in a saucepan and then stir in rice. Lower the heat, cover the rice and let simmer for 20 minutes.
- Heat the oil in a wok or large skillet and then add onion and pork. Stir-fry them until no pink is visible and done. Mix in the tomatoes and steam them until semi-soft. Take out from the heat and mix in cooked rice. Add beaten egg and fish sauce and mix thoroughly. Egg

should thicken the mixture. It's Kal Pot and ready to serve!

Nutrition Information

- Calories: 443 calories;
- Total Fat: 16.2
- Sodium: 218
- Total Carbohydrate: 37.3
- Cholesterol: 123
- Protein: 34.7

35. Khao Soi Soup

Serving: 6 | Prep: 30mins | Cook: 30mins | Ready in:

Ingredients

- 2 tablespoons vegetable oil
- 3 shallots, chopped
- 3 cloves garlic, minced
- 1/4 cup red curry paste
- 1 tablespoon curry powder
- 4 cups coconut milk
- 2 cups water
- 2 cups chopped cooked chicken, or more to taste
- 1 teaspoon sea salt
- 2 tablespoons fish sauce
- 2 tablespoons white sugar
- 1 tablespoon lime juice
- 1/2 cup vegetable oil
- 12 whole dried Thai chile peppers
- 6 small shallots, cut into quarters
- 1/2 head bok choy, chopped
- 1 (8 ounce) package rice noodles
- 1 cup pickled mustard cabbage, thinly sliced (optional)
- 1/2 cup coarsely chopped fresh cilantro
- 1 lime, cut into wedges

Direction

- In a big frying pan or a wok, heat 2 tablespoons of oil over medium heat, stir and cook garlic and chopped shallots for 2-4 minutes until garlic begins to turn golden. Add curry powder and red curry paste; stir and cook for 1-2 minutes until aromatic. Add sea salt, chicken, water, and coconut milk; boil. Lower the heat to medium-low and bring the soup to a simmer.
- Stir lime juice, sugar, and fish sauce into the soup and simmer for another 10 minutes until heated through.
- In a frying pan, heat 1/2 cup of oil over medium-high heat, add Thai chile peppers and fry for 2-4 minutes until turning brown. Move the chile peppers to the soup, saving the oil in the frying pan. Fry bok choy and quartered shallots in the hot oil for 2-4 minutes until turning brown; move to the saved oil and soup in the frying pan.
- In a big bowl, put noodles and cover with hot water. Put aside for 15 minutes until the noodles are tender. Drain and rinse well. Add 3/4 of the noodles to the soup. Fry the leftover rice noodles in the hot oil for 3-5 minutes until crunchy.
- Distribute the soup into 6 bowls and put lime wedges, cilantro, pickled cabbage, and fried noodles on top.

Nutrition Information

- Calories: 726 calories;
- Sodium: 1074
- Total Carbohydrate: 58.1
- Cholesterol: 35
- Protein: 20.5
- Total Fat: 48.5

36. Larb Gai Nikki Style

Serving: 4 | Prep: 20mins | Cook: 10mins | Ready in:

Ingredients

- Dressing:
- 2 lemons, juiced
- 1 lime, juiced
- 2 tablespoons fish sauce, or more to taste
- 1 tablespoon rice vinegar
- 1 teaspoon white sugar
- 1 teaspoon cayenne pepper
- 1 teaspoon lemon zest
- 1 pound ground turkey
- 1 clove garlic, minced
- 1 cup water to cover
- 1/2 red onion, thinly sliced
- 1 carrot, shredded
- 1/2 cup coarsely chopped chestnuts
- 3 Thai chile peppers, sliced
- 3 green onions, sliced
- 1/4 cup chopped fresh mint
- 1/3 cup chopped fresh Thai basil
- 2 tablespoons chopped fresh cilantro
- 3 tablespoons toasted rice powder
- 2 tablespoons Thai chile flakes

Direction

- In a bowl, mix lemon zest, cayenne, sugar, rice vinegar, fish sauce, lime juice and lemon juice till dressing is smooth in consistency.
- Spread ground turkey in a big skillet in a thin layer; add in garlic. Cover the turkey with enough water in the skillet; boil. Cook and stir turkey mixture, using fork to fluff meat apart, till turkey is crumbly and brown in color for 7 to 10 minutes. Drain liquid and transfer turkey into a big glass bowl.
- Combine cilantro, basil, mint, green onions, Thai chile peppers, chestnuts, carrot and red onion into turkey till combined well. Put in the refrigerator mixture till chilled for half an hour.
- Drizzle Thai chile flakes and rice powder on top of turkey mixture and combine well.

Nutrition Information

- Calories: 270 calories;
- Sodium: 630
- Total Carbohydrate: 22.3
- Cholesterol: 84
- Protein: 24.9
- Total Fat: 9.8

37. Mango With Sticky Coconut Rice (Kao Niaw)

Serving: 4 | Prep: 10mins | Cook: 25mins | Ready in:

Ingredients

- 1 tablespoon grapeseed oil
- 1 1/2 cups sweet rice
- 2 cups coconut milk
- 1/4 cup water
- 2 tablespoons palm sugar, or more to taste
- 1 pinch salt
- 1/2 cup unsweetened coconut cream (optional)
- 2 mangoes - peeled, seeded, and diced

Direction

- Over medium heat, heat oil in a saucepan, add rice and then gently cook while stirring for 2 to 3 minutes until toasted. Add salt, sugar, water, and coconut milk. Heat to boil. Decrease the heat, cover the saucepan and let simmer for 20 to 25 minutes until the rice has absorbed all the liquid and is tender. Mix the coconut cream into the rice.
- Ladle the rice into a serving bowl and then add mango on top.

Nutrition Information

- Calories: 701 calories;
- Total Carbohydrate: 86.1
- Cholesterol: 0
- Protein: 8.6
- Total Fat: 38.6
- Sodium: 64

38. Mild Thai Beef With A Tangerine Sauce

Serving: 4 | Prep: 20mins | Cook: 25mins | Ready in:

Ingredients

- 1 (8 ounce) package dry Chinese noodles
- 1/4 cup hoisin sauce
- 1/4 cup dry sherry
- 1 teaspoon tangerine zest
- 1/4 teaspoon ground ginger
- 4 teaspoons vegetable oil
- 1 pound flank beef steak, cut diagonally into 2 inch strips
- 2 teaspoons vegetable oil
- 1/2 small butternut squash - peeled, seeded, and thinly sliced
- 1 cup sliced fresh mushrooms
- 1 large red onion, cut into 2 inch strips
- 3 cups cabbage, thinly sliced
- 1 tangerine, sectioned and seeded

Direction

- On high heat, bring to a rolling boil a big pot of lightly salted water; once water is boiling, add noodles then boil again. Cook and stir pasta, uncovered, for 5mins until the pasta is completely cooked and firm to chew; stirring occasionally; drain and rinse pasta. Set aside.
- In a small bowl, combine ground ginger, hoisin sauce, tangerine zest, and sherry.
- On high heat, heat 2tbsp vegetable oil in a big pan or wok. Cook and stir 1/2 of the beef slices for 2-3mins until meat is nicely brown; stirring constantly. Using a slotted spoon, move meat to a plate. Cook the same with the rest of the beef.
- In the wok, heat the remaining 2tsp oil; mix in onion, mushrooms, and butternut squash. Cook and stir constantly for 5-7mins until the veggies are tender-crisp and the edges are lightly brown. Cook and stir in cabbage for another 2mins until a bit wilted.
- Turn to medium heat, mix in hoisin mixture, tangerine sections, and cooked beef into the vegetables. Cook for 2-3mins until completely heated. Serve on top of Chinese noodles.

Nutrition Information

- Calories: 506 calories;
- Total Fat: 13.6
- Sodium: 392
- Total Carbohydrate: 78.5
- Cholesterol: 26
- Protein: 23.9

39. Mung Beans Cooked In Sweet Syrup

Serving: 4 | Prep: 5mins | Cook: 35mins | Ready in:

Ingredients

- 1 cup skin-on, whole green mung beans
- 5 1/4 cups water
- 1 cup palm sugar

Direction

- Put mung beans in a large container and add cool water to cover by a few inches. Leave to sit for three hours to overnight. Drain the beans and then rinse before you use.
- Over medium heat, mix beans and 5 1/4 quart water in large pot and then cook for about 30 minutes until beans are tender. Mix sugar into the mixture and then cook while stirring until sugar is dissolved completely. Take out from the heat and then serve warm.

Nutrition Information

- Calories: 170 calories;
- Sodium: 137
- Total Carbohydrate: 38.9
- Cholesterol: 0

- Protein: 2
- Total Fat: 1.3

40. Nam Sod (Thai Pork Salad)

Serving: 10 | Prep: 1hours | Cook: | Ready in:

Ingredients

- Dressing:
- 2 cups fresh lime juice
- 12 fresh red or green Thai peppers, seeded and chopped, or to taste
- 1/4 cup fish sauce
- 2 tablespoons fish sauce
- 2 tablespoons dried chile flakes
- 6 shallots, sliced very thin, or more to taste
- 4 cups chopped fresh mint
- 1 cup unsalted roasted peanuts
- 1 onion, halved and sliced very thin
- 1 red onion, sliced very thin
- 6 green onions, coarsely sliced, or more to taste
- 1 cup finely chopped fresh ginger
- 2 pounds fresh ground lean pork, or more to taste
- 1 (10 ounce) package romaine lettuce hearts

Direction

- In a bowl, mix the dried chile flakes, 2 tablespoons plus 1/4 cup of fish sauce, fresh Thai peppers, and lime juice, then combine thoroughly. Put in ginger, green onions, red onion, onion, peanuts, cilantro, mint, and shallots. Combine thoroughly.
- Heat a non-stick skillet on medium-high. Put in pork; stir to break the pork while cooking for 3-5 minutes until the center is not pink anymore but not brown yet. Drain grease and discard. Let the pork cool briefly for 5 minutes.
- Place the pork into a bowl and put in the dressing mixture; combine very thoroughly. Before serving, allow the salad to sit for no less than 10 minutes. Scoop the mixture into lettuce leaves like stuffing a bun with a hot dog.

Nutrition Information

- Calories: 339 calories;
- Total Fat: 20.6
- Sodium: 715
- Total Carbohydrate: 19.3
- Cholesterol: 59
- Protein: 22.3

41. Nong's Khao Man Gai

Serving: 6 | Prep: 1hours | Cook: 45mins | Ready in:

Ingredients

- Chicken:
- 2 quarts water
- 1 (3 pound) whole chicken
- 1 head garlic
- 1 cup chopped fresh ginger root
- 1 teaspoon salt
- 1 tablespoon sugar
- Rice:
- 1 tablespoon coconut oil
- 1 tablespoon chopped garlic
- 1 tablespoon chopped shallots
- 4 pieces ginger, coarsely chopped
- 2 cups uncooked jasmine rice
- 2 cups chicken broth
- 3 pandan leaves (optional)
- Sauce:
- 1/3 cup peeled, roughly chopped ginger
- 4 red Thai chile peppers
- 1/2 cup fermented soybeans
- 1 head pickled garlic
- 1/3 cup white vinegar
- 1/3 cup thin soy sauce
- Garnish:
- fresh cilantro (optional)
- cucumber slices (optional)

Direction

- Boil a large pot of water. Add sugar, salt, ginger, garlic and chicken into the pot. Heat to boil and leave to simmer for 35 minutes. Take out the chicken, then cover to keep it warm and reserve.
- Into a heavy-bottomed pot with lid or rice cooker, heat the coconut oil, and then cook while stirring pandan leaves, ginger, shallots and garlic until aromatic and golden.
- Add the rice into the pot or rice cooker and mix to coat with oil. Mix in the chicken broth and switch to rice cooker cycle. In case you are using a pot, heat the rice to boil, then cover, decrease the heat to low and let simmer for 15 minutes.
- In a blender or food processor, mix soy sauce, white vinegar, pickled garlic, fermented soybeans, red Thai chilies and ginger. Then pulse until the resulting mix is liquefied but not smooth in texture.
- Debone the chicken and chop meat into 1-inch pieces.
- Put the chicken pieces on top of cooked rice and serve. Add sauce on top (or you can serve the sauce on the side) and stud with cilantro and cucumbers.

Nutrition Information

- Calories: 589 calories;
- Sodium: 2465
- Total Carbohydrate: 70.9
- Cholesterol: 63
- Protein: 31.2
- Total Fat: 19.2

42. Oriental Cold Noodle Salad

Serving: 8 | Prep: 15mins | Cook: 10mins | Ready in:

Ingredients

- 15 ounces dried soba noodles
- 1 1/2 teaspoons dark sesame oil
- 1/3 cup rice vinegar
- 1/3 cup soy sauce
- juice from one lime
- zest of one lime
- 2 tablespoons brown sugar
- 2 cloves garlic, minced
- 2 teaspoons red pepper flakes, or to taste (optional)
- 1 cup finely grated carrot
- 1/4 cup coarsely chopped salted peanuts
- 1/2 cup chopped fresh cilantro

Direction

- Cook soba noodles in a big pot as the package directs. Strain and rinse the noodles with cold water and put aside.
- In a big bowl, pour lime juice, soy sauce, rice vinegar, and sesame oil. Stir in red pepper flakes, garlic, brown sugar, and lime zest and mix until sugar is dissolved. Mix in cilantro, peanuts, and carrots.
- Chop noodles into 3-inch lengths. Combine with the dressing mixture. Put a cover on and put in the fridge for a minimum of 1 hour.
- Toss the salad again before eating. Splash with vinegar and soy sauce if dry. Enjoy cold.

Nutrition Information

- Calories: 242 calories;
- Total Fat: 3.7
- Sodium: 1068
- Total Carbohydrate: 47.2
- Cholesterol: 0
- Protein: 9.7

43. Pad Krapao (Thai Stir Fry Pork With Basil)

Serving: 3 | Prep: 10mins | Cook: 15mins | Ready in:

Ingredients

- 3 tablespoons vegetable oil
- 3 cloves garlic, chopped
- 3 large hot chile peppers, thinly sliced
- 1 1/2 cups sliced pork
- 1 tablespoon dark soy sauce
- 1 tablespoon sweet soy sauce
- 4 tablespoons fish sauce
- 1 tablespoon chile paste in soybean oil
- 1 1/2 cups sliced white onion
- 1/2 cup sliced green bell pepper
- 1 cup Thai basil leaves
- 1 teaspoon ground white pepper

Direction

- Over high heat, heat oil in a wok, then add chile peppers and garlic and cook for about 30 seconds until the garlic begins to brown. Place in pork and then stir-fry for about 3 minutes until turned browned. Add fish sauce, sweet soy sauce and dark soy sauce. Cook while stirring for about 3 minutes until the liquid is reduced by half.
- Add bell pepper, onion and chile paste. Stir-fry for 5 to 6 minutes until the pork is cooked through. Mix in the basil leaves and add pepper to taste. Mix until combined well.

Nutrition Information

- Calories: 369 calories;
- Total Fat: 18.4
- Protein: 28.9
- Sodium: 2110
- Total Carbohydrate: 24
- Cholesterol: 69

44. Pad Se Eew

Serving: 3 | Prep: 15mins | Cook: 20mins | Ready in:

Ingredients

- 1 tablespoon dark soy sauce
- 2 tablespoons soy sauce
- 1 tablespoon white sugar, or more to taste
- 1 teaspoon chile-garlic sauce (such as Sriracha®), or more to taste
- 1 tablespoon olive oil
- 1 tablespoon chopped garlic
- 6 ounces chicken tenders, cut into bite-size pieces
- 1 (16 ounce) package frozen broccoli
- 1 pound fresh flat rice noodles
- 1 egg, beaten
- 1/4 teaspoon sesame seeds
- 1 pinch crushed red pepper flakes

Direction

- In a small saucepan, mix the soy sauce, chile-garlic sauce, dark soy sauce and sugar together and heat it over medium-low heat. Let it simmer while stirring for about 5 minutes until the sugar dissolves. Remove the pan from heat and set aside.
- Heat a skillet with olive oil over medium heat. Sauté the chicken and garlic in hot oil for 7-10 minutes until the chicken is no longer pink inside. Add in the broccoli and cook and stir until the broccoli is well heated through. Put in the noodles and mix until all the ingredients are well combined. Put in the sauce and mix until everything is well coated with sauce then continue cooking until the sauce begins to thicken.
- Use a spatula to push the chicken mixture on one side of the skillet. Put in the egg on the other side of the skillet. Scramble and cook the egg all the way through. Mix cooked egg and chicken mixture together until well heated. Top with red pepper flakes and sesame seeds and serve.

Nutrition Information

- Calories: 758 calories;
- Total Fat: 9.9
- Sodium: 1353
- Total Carbohydrate: 140.1

- Cholesterol: 99
- Protein: 24.8

45. Peanut Butter Noodles

Serving: 4 | Prep: 15mins | Cook: 10mins | Ready in:

Ingredients

- 1/2 cup chicken broth
- 1 1/2 tablespoons minced fresh ginger root
- 3 tablespoons soy sauce
- 3 tablespoons peanut butter
- 1 1/2 tablespoons honey
- 2 teaspoons hot chile paste (optional)
- 3 cloves garlic, minced
- 8 ounces Udon noodles
- 1/4 cup chopped green onions
- 1/4 cup chopped peanuts

Direction

- Boil water in a big saucepan. Put the pasta and cook until al dente according to package instructions. Drain the pasta.
- Mix ginger, chicken broth, peanut butter, soy sauce, honey, garlic and chili paste in a little pot. Cook on moderate heat until peanut butter softens and is heated thoroughly. Put pasta and mix to coat. Top with peanuts and green onions.

Nutrition Information

- Calories: 330 calories;
- Total Fat: 12
- Sodium: 1188
- Total Carbohydrate: 46.8
- Cholesterol: 0
- Protein: 10.7

46. Poached Eggs In Ginger Syrup

Serving: 4 | Prep: 5mins | Cook: 15mins | Ready in:

Ingredients

- 3 cups water
- 1 cup white sugar
- 1 (2 inch) piece fresh ginger root, peeled and sliced
- 4 small eggs

Direction

- In a saucepan, mix together the sugar and water and then heat to boil. Decrease the heat to medium-low and add slices of ginger. Let cook for about 5 minutes until fragrant.
- Break eggs into individual bowls and then carefully place them in the syrup. Cook egg on one side for about 3 1/2 minutes until white is opaque and partially set. Gently flip over to cook another side for about 3 1/2 minutes longer or to the doneness desired until the yolk is still liquid and the egg white becomes opaque but not hard. Ladle the eggs into individual serving bowls and scoop the syrup on top of each egg. Stud with cooked ginger.

Nutrition Information

- Calories: 248 calories;
- Total Fat: 3.7
- Sodium: 116
- Total Carbohydrate: 50.8
- Cholesterol: 137
- Protein: 4.7

47. Potsticker Salad

Serving: 6 | Prep: 15mins | Cook: 20mins | Ready in:

Ingredients

- 1 (10 ounce) package egg noodles

- 12 frozen vegetable potstickers
- 2 tablespoons vegetable oil
- 2 tablespoons water
- 1/2 cup water chestnuts, drained and sliced
- 1/2 cup baby corn
- 1 carrot, shredded
- 1 (15 ounce) can straw mushrooms
- 1/2 cup Thai peanut sauce
- 1/4 cup chopped roasted peanuts

Direction

- Boil water in a large pot and cook egg noodles until al dente or in 5-7 minutes. Drain well and put it aside.
- On medium heat, put on a large frying pan and heat oil. Add potstickers to cook with 1 or 2 turns until they become golden brown. Pour water into the pan; decrease the heat to low and continue cooking with cover until the liquid has evaporated or for another 3 minutes. Put it under cold water to rinse; drain and cut into halves.
- Combine potstickers, noodles, peanut sauce, mushrooms, carrot, baby corn and water chestnuts in a large mixing bowl. Let it chill in 1 hour. Add peanuts on top to serve.

Nutrition Information

- Calories: 408 calories;
- Protein: 15.5
- Total Fat: 13.3
- Sodium: 804
- Total Carbohydrate: 59.9
- Cholesterol: 34

48. Pumpkin Coconut Curry

Serving: 4 | Prep: 30mins | Cook: 30mins | Ready in:

Ingredients

- 2 skinless, boneless chicken breast halves - cut into small chunks
- 1 teaspoon poultry seasoning
- 1 tablespoon olive oil
- 1 (2 pound) sugar pumpkin -- peeled, seeded and cubed
- 1 tablespoon butter
- 1 onion, chopped
- 2 cloves garlic, chopped
- 1 (1 inch) piece fresh ginger root, finely chopped
- 1 tablespoon ground coriander
- 1 tablespoon ground cumin
- 1 pinch ground turmeric
- 1 teaspoon red pepper flakes
- 1/2 cup canned coconut milk
- 1 1/2 cups chicken broth
- salt to taste

Direction

- Use the poultry seasoning to season the pieces of chicken and reserve. Over medium heat, heat olive oil in large skillet and then add chicken. Cook while stirring until the meat is cooked through and browned outside. Take out from heat and reserve.
- Over medium heat, melt butter in another skillet and add ginger, garlic, and onion. Cook while stirring until the onion is transparent. Then season with red pepper flakes, turmeric, cumin and coriander. Continue cooking while stirring until the spices become fragrant. Add chicken broth, coconut milk, cooked chicken and pumpkin. Add salt to taste. Let cook for about 15 to 20 minutes on medium heat. You can serve on top of noodles or rice.

Nutrition Information

- Calories: 266 calories;
- Sodium: 70
- Total Carbohydrate: 21.2
- Cholesterol: 42
- Protein: 17.5
- Total Fat: 14.1

49. Quick Red Curry Soup

Serving: 8 | Prep: 10mins | Cook: 35mins | Ready in:

Ingredients

- 1/4 cup red curry paste
- 2 tablespoons olive oil
- 3 cups coconut milk
- 3 cups chicken stock
- 2 limes, juiced
- 1 lime, zested
- 2 cups cherry tomatoes
- 1 tablespoon chopped fresh cilantro
- 1 pound shrimp
- 1 (14 ounce) can bean sprouts, drained
- 1 cup chopped cooked chicken
- salt and ground black pepper to taste

Direction

- Mix olive oil and red curry paste together in a saucepan. Turn on the heat to low. Cook for 5 minutes or until fragrant.
- Add the chicken stock, coconut milk, lime zest and lime juice. Let it boil then reduce the temperature to medium-low. Cook and let simmer for 10 more minutes.
- Add the cilantro and cherry tomatoes to the soup. Let it come to a simmer and cook for another 10 to 15 minutes, or until the tomatoes are tender.
- Throw in the cooked chicken, shrimp, and bean sprouts. Let it cook for 10 to 15 more minutes, until the meat's center is not transparent anymore and the shrimp is bright pink on the outside. Add salt and pepper to taste.

Nutrition Information

- Calories: 306 calories;
- Protein: 19.2
- Total Fat: 28.7
- Sodium: 557
- Total Carbohydrate: 8.1
- Cholesterol: 100

50. Satay Chicken Pizza

Serving: 4 | Prep: 15mins | Cook: 12mins | Ready in:

Ingredients

- 1 tablespoon vegetable oil
- 2 skinless, boneless chicken breast halves, chopped
- 1 cup prepared Thai peanut sauce
- 1 bunch green onions, chopped
- 4 small (4 inch) pita breads
- 4 slices provolone cheese

Direction

- In a skillet, heat oil on high heat; sauté chicken pieces for 6-7 minutes in hot oil. Don't overcook.
- Preheat an oven to 220°C/425°F.
- Assembling pizza: Spoon 1/4 of peanut sauce on each pita; sprinkle 1/4 scallions and 1/4 of the browned chicken on each. Top 1 cheese slice on each pizza. Put on lightly greased cookie sheet; bake for 10-12 minutes in the preheated oven till cheese is bubbly and melted. Let stand outside of oven for 1-2 minutes; cut using a pizza cutter.

Nutrition Information

- Calories: 554 calories;
- Protein: 34.9
- Total Fat: 28.3
- Sodium: 741
- Total Carbohydrate: 43.2
- Cholesterol: 54

51. Satay Sauce

Serving: 12 | Prep: 5mins | Cook: 5mins | Ready in:

Ingredients

- 1 (10 ounce) can coconut milk
- 1/2 cup crunchy peanut butter
- 1/2 small onion, grated
- 1 tablespoon dark soy sauce
- 2 teaspoons brown sugar
- 1/2 teaspoon red pepper flakes

Direction

- Over medium heat, mix pepper flakes, brown sugar, soy sauce, onion, peanut butter and coconut milk in a saucepan. Heat to boil while stirring often. Take out from the heat and keep the contents warm.

Nutrition Information

- Calories: 112 calories;
- Total Fat: 10.2
- Sodium: 128
- Total Carbohydrate: 3.9
- Cholesterol: 0
- Protein: 3.3

52. Scot's Thai Soup

Serving: 10 | Prep: 25mins | Cook: 4hours15mins | Ready in:

Ingredients

- 2 quarts vegetable broth
- 1 cup dried red beans
- 1 cup quinoa, or more to taste
- 1 cup pearl barley, or more to taste
- 1 stalk celery, chopped
- 1 tomato, diced
- 6 cloves garlic (or more to taste), peeled and chopped
- 1 red chile pepper, sliced
- 1/2 green bell pepper (or more to taste), cut into 1-inch pieces
- 1/2 cup chopped green onion, or more to taste
- 2 ounces Thai red curry paste
- 1 (1 inch) piece fresh ginger root, peeled and thinly sliced (or more to taste)
- 3 tablespoons chicken bouillon powder, or more to taste
- 2 tablespoons dried Italian seasoning, or more to taste
- 2 tablespoons ground black pepper
- 2 teaspoons dried chives
- 2 teaspoons onion powder
- 2 teaspoons garlic powder
- 1 (5.6 ounce) can coconut milk
- 2 tablespoons fresh lime juice

Direction

- In a large container, cover the red beans with a few inches of cool water; allow to soak for 8 hours to overnight.
- Drain and clean beans. In a slow cooker; pour beans and add garlic powder, onion powder, chives, black pepper, Italian seasoning, chicken bouillon, ginger, curry paste, green onion, green bell pepper, red chile pepper, garlic, tomato, celery, barley, and quinoa.
- Cook on High while sometimes stirring for 4 hours, till the barley and beans are softened. Blend lime juice and coconut milk into the soup then cook for 15 more minutes.

Nutrition Information

- Calories: 248 calories;
- Sodium: 821
- Total Carbohydrate: 45.5
- Cholesterol: < 1
- Protein: 11.1
- Total Fat: 3.1

53. Shrimp Fried Noodles Thai Style

Serving: 4 | Prep: 20mins | Cook: 10mins | Ready in:

Ingredients

- 1 pound dried rice vermicelli
- 2 cups bean sprouts, divided
- 3 tablespoons vegetable oil
- 1 teaspoon minced garlic
- 10 unpeeled, large fresh shrimp
- 1 tablespoon white sugar
- 1 tablespoon Asian fish sauce (nuoc mam or nam pla)
- 1 tablespoon Ketchup
- 2 eggs, beaten
- 1 tablespoon chopped dry roasted peanuts
- 1 tablespoon crushed dried shrimp
- 1 tablespoon chopped green onions
- 1 tablespoon chopped fresh cilantro
- 1 teaspoon chili powder
- 2 wedges fresh lemon

Direction

- Put noodles in a big bowl then cover with hot water. Soak noodles for 15 minutes. In cold water, soak bean sprouts. Drain prior to using.
- In a big skillet, heat oil on medium-high heat. Add garlic then fry until it's fragrant. Add shrimp then sauté for about 3 minutes. Mix in ketchup, fish sauce, and sugar. Pour eggs in and mix for 1 minute. Add noodles then stir fry until noodles are covered in sauce. Mix half of bean sprouts in, frying until soft.
- Put on a serving plate. Put lemon wedges, cilantro, and leftover bean sprouts on a different plate so people can put toppings on separate plates. Sprinkle noodles with chili powder, peanuts, and dried shrimp. Put green onion on top.

Nutrition Information

- Calories: 642 calories;
- Cholesterol: 175
- Protein: 20.1
- Total Fat: 15.6
- Sodium: 647
- Total Carbohydrate: 103.3

54. Shrimp Summer Rolls With Asian Peanut Sauce

Serving: 4 | Prep: 20mins | Cook: 5mins | Ready in:

Ingredients

- 1/4 pound medium shrimp - peeled and deveined
- 2 tablespoons olive oil
- salt and ground black pepper to taste
- 1/4 cup shredded napa cabbage
- 2 tablespoons shredded carrot
- 3 cloves garlic, minced
- 1 tablespoon grated fresh ginger
- 2 tablespoons teriyaki sauce
- 2 tablespoons fresh lime juice
- 4 (8 inch) round sheets rice paper
- 1/2 cup chunky peanut butter
- 2 tablespoons teriyaki sauce
- 2 tablespoons sesame oil
- 2 tablespoons hot sauce
- 3 cloves garlic, minced
- salt and ground black pepper to taste
- 1 tablespoon grated fresh ginger

Direction

- Preheat grill pan/outdoor grill to medium high heat.
- In a bowl, put shrimp. Toss with black pepper, salt and olive oil.
- On preheated grill, grill shrimp, 2 minutes per side, until opaque. Take off grill. Put aside.
- In a bowl, mix lime juice, teriyaki sauce, 1 tbsp. ginger, garlic, carrot and cabbage well.

- One at a time, use water to wet rice paper. Lay out onto clean surface. In the middle of the paper, put 1/4 of cabbage mixture. Put 1/4 of shrimp on top. Shape filling to a log shape. Roll rice paper around filling shaped into a log, tucking ends in while you go. Repeat process with remaining rice papers.
- Whisk pepper, salt, 1 tablespoon ginger, garlic, hot sauce, sesame oil, teriyaki sauce and peanut butter. Slice rolls, on an angle, in half. Serve with peanut sauce next to it.

Nutrition Information

- Calories: 388 calories;
- Total Carbohydrate: 17.2
- Cholesterol: 43
- Protein: 15.5
- Total Fat: 30.3
- Sodium: 1156

55. Spaghetti With Peanut Butter Sauce

Serving: 4 | Prep: | Cook: | Ready in:

Ingredients

- 1/2 cup creamy peanut butter
- 1/3 cup hot water
- 1 tablespoon light soy sauce
- 1 clove crushed garlic
- 1/3 cup heavy whipping cream
- 1 teaspoon sesame oil
- 1 dash chili sauce
- 12 ounces spaghetti
- 3 teaspoons chopped fresh cilantro

Direction

- Add peanut butter into a small-sized glass, and pour in hot water; whisk using fork till smooth. Stir in chili sauce, sesame oil, cream, garlic, and soy sauce till smooth. Put aside.
- Cook pasta in a big pot of boiling water till done. Drain off well.
- Put drained pasta into bowl. Whisk the reserved peanut butter mixture together one more time; put into cooked pasta. Toss them all together and use cilantro to decorate.

Nutrition Information

- Calories: 584 calories;
- Total Fat: 26.1
- Sodium: 294
- Total Carbohydrate: 70.2
- Cholesterol: 27
- Protein: 19.7

56. Spiced Thai Iced Tea

Serving: 4 | Prep: 5mins | Cook: 5mins | Ready in:

Ingredients

- 5 cups water
- 1/4 cup white sugar
- 5 pods star anise
- 1 cinnamon stick
- 4 pods cardamom, crushed
- 8 red rooibos tea bags
- 3/4 cup sweetened condensed milk
- ice

Direction

- In a saucepan, place cardamom, cinnamon stick, star anise, sugar and water then boil. Take away from the heat and place in tea bags. Allow tea to steep and cool for 1 hour to room temperature.
- Discard the tea bags then strain and discard the whole spices. Whisk in condensed milk. Transfer into a large pitcher then store in the fridge for at least 1 hour to combine the flavors.
- Add ice to fill 4 glasses. Pour over ice to serve.

Nutrition Information

- Calories: 251 calories;
- Total Carbohydrate: 48.2
- Cholesterol: 20
- Protein: 5
- Total Fat: 5.3
- Sodium: 84

---

57. Spicy Chicken Thai Noodle Soup

Serving: 12 | Prep: 20mins | Cook: 8hours10mins | Ready in:

Ingredients

- 5 cups chicken broth
- 1 cup white wine
- 1 cup water
- 1 onion, chopped
- 3 green onions, chopped
- 3 cloves garlic, chopped
- 4 large carrots, cut into 1 inch pieces
- 4 large stalks celery, cut into 1 inch pieces
- 1/2 teaspoon salt
- 1 teaspoon ground black pepper
- 1 tablespoon curry powder
- 1/2 tablespoon dried sage
- 1/2 tablespoon poultry seasoning
- 1/2 tablespoon dried oregano
- 1 teaspoon ground cayenne pepper
- 2 tablespoons vegetable oil
- 3 skinless, boneless chicken breast halves - cut into 1 inch cubes
- 1 fresh red chile pepper, seeded and chopped
- 1/2 (12 ounce) package dried rice noodles

Direction

- Mix chicken broth, poultry seasoning, wine, black pepper, water, oregano, onion, cayenne, green onion, carrots, salt, curry, garlic, sage, and celery in a slow cooker on low heat.
- Over medium heat, cook the chicken in oil in a skillet until brown. Mix into the slow cooker.
- Cook the soup for 5 hours on high or 8 hours on low.
- Mix in the red pepper about halfway through the cooking time. Mix in the noodles 15 minutes before serving.

Nutrition Information

- Calories: 131 calories;
- Total Fat: 3
- Sodium: 155
- Total Carbohydrate: 14.5
- Cholesterol: 17
- Protein: 7.9

---

58. Spicy Devil's Tom Yum Soup

Serving: 8 | Prep: 40mins | Cook: 30mins | Ready in:

Ingredients

- 2 pounds tiger prawns with heads and shells
- 4 cups water
- 2 tablespoons vegetable oil
- 1 tablespoon minced garlic
- 2 stalks fresh lemon grass, tough outer leaves removed and and white part slightly crushed
- 5 lime leaves
- 5 shallots, thinly sliced
- 5 slices galangal
- 10 chile padi (bird's eye chiles), thinly sliced
- 1 tablespoon Asian red chili paste
- 1 skinless, boneless chicken breast half - cut into cubes
- 1/4 cup lime juice
- 2 large squid, cleaned and sliced into rings
- 1/2 (15 ounce) can baby corn, drained
- 1/2 (6 ounce) can whole straw mushrooms, drained
- 3 fresh tomatoes, quartered

- 1/2 cup coconut milk
- salt to taste

Direction

- Wash prawns. Remove black veins, shells, and heads, but keep the heads. Put aside cleaned prawns. In a soup pot or big saucepan with water, boil prawns on high heat for about 15 minutes to concentrate flavor and reduce stock. Strain out prawn heads and throw away.
- In a big skillet, heat vegetable oil on medium heat. Sauté red chilies, galangal, shallots, lime leaves, lemon grass, and garlic for about 3 minutes until seasonings are fragrant and shallots are translucent. Mix in chili paste. Stir and cook for 1 minute. Add lime juice and chicken breast. Mix well to evenly mix chili paste in. Simmer mixture for 5 minutes. Pour seasoned chicken-lime juice mixture in prawn stock. Boil on medium-low heat.
- When soup boils, mix in tomatoes, cleaned prawns, straw mushrooms, baby corn, and squid rings. Bring heat to slow. Mix in coconut milk. Simmer soup for about 5 minutes until prawns are opaque and pink. Add salt. Serve.

Nutrition Information

- Calories: 224 calories;
- Sodium: 280
- Total Carbohydrate: 12.9
- Cholesterol: 180
- Protein: 25.3
- Total Fat: 8.3

59. Spicy Thai Basil Chicken (Pad Krapow Gai)

Serving: 2 | Prep: 15mins | Cook: 10mins | Ready in:

Ingredients

- 1/3 cup chicken broth
- 1 tablespoon oyster sauce
- 1 tablespoon soy sauce, or as needed
- 2 teaspoons fish sauce
- 1 teaspoon white sugar
- 1 teaspoon brown sugar
- 2 tablespoons vegetable oil
- 1 pound skinless, boneless chicken thighs, coarsely chopped
- 1/4 cup sliced shallots
- 4 cloves garlic, minced
- 2 tablespoons minced Thai chilies, Serrano, or other hot pepper
- 1 cup very thinly sliced fresh basil leaves
- 2 cups hot cooked rice

Direction

- In a bowl, combine the fish sauce, brown sugar, chicken broth, soy sauce, oyster sauce and white sugar together and mix well until combined.
- Place a big skillet over high heat setting and let it heat up. Pour in the oil. Put in the chicken and let it cook for 2-3 minutes until the meat no longer look raw. Add in the garlic, sliced chilies and shallots and give it a mix. Keep cooking the mixture for about 2-3 additional minutes over high heat setting until there are some juices at the bottom of the skillet that are beginning to caramelize. Put in about 1 tablespoon of the prepared sauce mixture and let the mixture cook for about 1 minute while stirring it until the sauce has caramelized.
- Add in all the remaining sauce mixture. Allow the mixture to cook while stirring it until the sauce deglazed the caramelized mixture at the bottom of the skillet. Keep cooking for another 1-2 minutes until the chicken is well-coated with the sauce. Remove the skillet away from the heat.
- Add in the basil. Stir the mixture and let the basil cook for about 20 seconds until it is wilted. Serve the chicken mixture with rice on the side.

Nutrition Information

- Calories: 715 calories;
- Protein: 49.8
- Total Fat: 30
- Sodium: 1182
- Total Carbohydrate: 58.6
- Cholesterol: 156

60. Spicy Thai Shrimp Pasta

Serving: 6 | Prep: 15mins | Cook: 5mins | Ready in:

Ingredients

- 1 (12 ounce) package rice vermicelli
- 1 large tomato, diced
- 4 green onions, diced
- 2 pounds cooked shrimp, peeled and deveined
- 1 1/2 cups prepared Thai peanut sauce

Direction

- Boil a big pot of water. Add the rice vermicelli. Cook until al dente or for 3-5 minutes; drain.
- Toss peanut sauce, shrimp, green onions, tomato, and rice vermicelli together in a medium bowl. Cover then chill in the fridge for eight hours or overnight.

Nutrition Information

- Calories: 564 calories;
- Total Carbohydrate: 52.4
- Cholesterol: 230
- Protein: 46.3
- Total Fat: 19.3
- Sodium: 375

61. Spicy Thai Vegetable Soup

Serving: 12 | Prep: 15mins | Cook: 1hours15mins | Ready in:

Ingredients

- 1 cup uncooked brown rice
- 2 cups water
- 3 tablespoons olive oil
- 1 sweet onion, chopped
- 4 cloves garlic, minced
- 1/4 cup chopped fresh ginger root
- 1 cup chopped carrots
- 4 cups chopped broccoli
- 1 red bell pepper, diced
- 1 (14 ounce) can light coconut milk
- 6 cups vegetable broth
- 1 cup white wine
- 3 tablespoons fish sauce
- 2 tablespoons soy sauce
- 3 Thai chile peppers
- 2 tablespoons chopped fresh lemon grass
- 1 tablespoon Thai pepper garlic sauce
- 1 teaspoon saffron
- 3/4 cup plain yogurt
- fresh cilantro, for garnish

Direction

- In a pot, boil the water and rice. Put cover, turn heat to low, and allow to simmer for 45 minutes.
- In a big pot over medium heat, heat the olive oil, and cook the carrots, ginger, garlic and onion for 5 minutes till tender. Add in saffron, garlic sauce, lemon grass, Thai chile peppers, soy sauce, fish sauce, wine, broth, coconut milk, red bell pepper and broccoli. Allow to simmer for 25 minutes.
- In batches, put soup into a food processor or blender, and blend till creamy and smooth. Put it back to the pot, add in cooked rice and yogurt. Atop with cilantro, serve.

Nutrition Information

- Calories: 183 calories;
- Sodium: 749
- Total Carbohydrate: 21.4
- Cholesterol: < 1
- Protein: 4.4
- Total Fat: 7.4

62. Steamed Lemon Grass Crab Legs

Serving: 2 | Prep: 15mins | Cook: 15mins | Ready in:

Ingredients

- 2 tablespoons vegetable oil
- 3 cloves garlic clove, pressed
- 1 (1 inch) piece fresh ginger root, crushed
- 1 stalk lemon grass, crushed
- 2 tablespoons fish sauce
- 1 tablespoon oyster sauce
- salt and pepper to taste
- 2 pounds frozen cooked Alaskan king crab legs, thawed

Direction

- Over medium-high heat, heat oil in a big pot and then add the lemon grass, crushed garlic, and ginger. Cook while stirring for about 5 minutes until brown. Mix in the fish sauce, pepper, salt, and oyster sauce until well blended. Put in the crab legs, cover and let to cook on medium heat while tossing from time to time for about 15 minutes until heated through.

Nutrition Information

- Calories: 586 calories;
- Protein: 89.1
- Total Fat: 20.7
- Sodium: 6018
- Total Carbohydrate: 5.3
- Cholesterol: 241

63. Sticky Rice With Coconut Milk And Mango

Serving: 4 | Prep: 20mins | Cook: 20mins | Ready in:

Ingredients

- 1 cup sweet (glutinous) rice
- 1 cup coconut milk
- 2 tablespoons white sugar
- 1/8 teaspoon salt
- 1 ripe mango - peeled, seeded, and sliced

Direction

- Rinse the sweet rice under water until the water is clear. Then soak the rice for about 2 to 4 hours in warm water. Strain.
- Put a steamer insert into saucepan and then add water to just below the steamer's bottom. Heat the water to boil. Line cheese cloth onto the steamer and scoop rice into the cheese cloth. Let steam for about 20 minutes until cooked thoroughly. Take out the steamer from heat and pour the rice into a bowl.
- In a saucepan, combine together the salt, sugar, and coconut milk. Heat to simmer. Spread 3/4 of coconut milk mixture on top of rice. Then cover the bowl and leave to stand for 5 minutes.
- Add the remaining coconut milk mixture on top of rice and add slices of mango over.

Nutrition Information

- Calories: 331 calories;
- Sodium: 84
- Total Carbohydrate: 52
- Cholesterol: 0
- Protein: 4.5
- Total Fat: 12.4

64. Stir Fried Sweet And Sour Vegetables

Serving: 4 | Prep: 30mins | Cook: 15mins | Ready in:

Ingredients

- 3 tablespoons palm sugar
- 2 tablespoons lime juice
- 1 tablespoon fish sauce
- 1 tablespoon oyster sauce
- 1 tablespoon light soy sauce
- 2 tablespoons vegetable oil
- 4 cloves garlic, minced
- 1 onion, cut into thin slivers
- 1/2 head cauliflower, chopped into bite-size pieces
- 1 carrot, peeled and sliced
- 1 cucumber, cut into bite-size pieces
- 8 baby corn, sliced
- 1 cup peas
- 1 large red bell pepper, sliced
- 1 tomato, cut into bite-size pieces
- 1/4 fresh pineapple, cut into bite-size chunks

Direction

- Over medium-low heat, mix soy sauce, oyster sauce, fish sauce, lime juice and palm sugar together in small saucepan until sugar dissolves completely. Heat to simmer and then reserve.
- In a large skillet, heat the oil and then in hot oil, fry garlic for 7 to 10 minutes until browned. Place in the onion and cook for a minute. Mix the carrot and cauliflower into the mixture. Cook while stirring for a minute. Combine peas, corn and cucumber into the mixture and then cook for one minute longer. Mix tomato and bell pepper into the mixture and let cook for 1 minute. Add the sauce on top of the mixture. Then add pineapple and mix to coat the whole mixture evenly with sauce. Let cook for 1 more minute. Serve while still hot.

Nutrition Information

- Calories: 231 calories;
- Total Fat: 7.5
- Sodium: 616
- Total Carbohydrate: 38.7
- Cholesterol: 0
- Protein: 6

65. Stir Fried Tofu With Cashews

Serving: 4 | Prep: 10mins | Cook: 10mins | Ready in:

Ingredients

- 1/2 (12 ounce) package extra-firm tofu, sliced
- 2 tablespoons whiskey
- 1 tablespoon fish sauce
- 1 tablespoon light soy sauce
- 1 tablespoon black soy sauce
- 1 tablespoon oyster sauce
- 2 tablespoons vegetable oil, or to taste
- 1 cup unsalted raw cashews
- 5 cloves garlic, chopped
- 1 onion, julienned
- 3 tablespoons palm sugar
- 2 fresh red chile peppers, sliced
- 3 tablespoons water
- 4 green onions, sliced

Direction

- In a bowl, mix black soy sauce, light soy sauce, oyster sauce, fish sauce, whiskey and tofu. Let the mixture marinate for 10 minutes.
- While the tofu mixture is marinating, heat a wok with oil over medium heat and fry the cashews for 3-5 minutes or until brown in color. Put the roasted cashews in a bowl and discard the oil.
- Put the garlic into the same wok and sauté for 1 minute. Add in the onions and marinated tofu and stir-fry for 1 minute. Put in the chile

peppers and palm sugar. Continue cooking the mixture for 2 more minutes. Mix in water and stir until fully mixed. Remove the wok from heat. Top with green onions and roasted cashews.

Nutrition Information

- Calories: 390 calories;
- Total Carbohydrate: 31.2
- Cholesterol: 0
- Protein: 12.3
- Total Fat: 24.4
- Sodium: 679

66. Sukhothai Pad Thai

Serving: 8 | Prep: 20mins | Cook: 10mins | Ready in:

Ingredients

- 1/2 cup white sugar
- 1/2 cup distilled white vinegar
- 1/4 cup soy sauce
- 2 tablespoons tamarind pulp
- 1 (12 ounce) package dried rice noodles
- 1/2 cup vegetable oil
- 1 1/2 teaspoons minced garlic
- 4 eggs
- 1 (12 ounce) package firm tofu, cut into 1/2 inch strips
- 1 1/2 tablespoons white sugar
- 1 1/2 teaspoons salt
- 1 1/2 cups ground peanuts
- 1 1/2 teaspoons ground, dried oriental radish
- 1/2 cup chopped fresh chives
- 1 tablespoon paprika
- 2 cups fresh bean sprouts
- 1 lime, cut into wedges

Direction

- Pad Thai sauce: Mix tamarind pulp, soy sauce, vinegar, and sugar on medium heat in a medium saucepan.
- Pad Thai: In cold water, soak rice noodles until soft then drain. On medium heat, warm oil in a wok or big skillet. Add eggs and garlic, scrambling the eggs. Stir in tofu until well combined. Add noodles and mix until cooked.
- Mix in 1 1/2 teaspoons salt, 1 1/2 tablespoon sugar, and Pad Thai sauce. Mix in ground radish and peanuts. Take off from heat then add paprika and chives.
- Serve with bean sprouts and lime on the side.

Nutrition Information

- Calories: 619 calories;
- Cholesterol: 93
- Protein: 19.5
- Total Fat: 34
- Sodium: 1010
- Total Carbohydrate: 64.1

67. Sweet Rice And Mango

Serving: 4 | Prep: 5mins | Cook: 20mins | Ready in:

Ingredients

- 1 1/2 cups uncooked short-grain white rice
- 2 cups water
- 3/4 cup white sugar, or to taste
- 2 mangos, peeled and sliced
- 1/2 cup cream of coconut (optional)

Direction

- In a saucepan, mix water and rice. Heat to boil, cover and then decrease the heat to low. Let to simmer for about 15 to 20 minutes until the water has been absorbed.
- Stir the amount of sugar desired into hot rice. Divide the rice into four bowls, add mango

slices on top and then spread some cream of coconut all over the top of every bowl.

Nutrition Information

- Calories: 588 calories;
- Sodium: 17
- Total Carbohydrate: 130.4
- Cholesterol: 0
- Protein: 5.8
- Total Fat: 5.6

68. Sweet Sticky Rice And Mango

Serving: 6 | Prep: | Cook: 30mins | Ready in:

Ingredients

- 8 cups water, divided
- 1 cup sweet rice
- 1 (15 ounce) can coconut milk
- 1/2 cup white sugar
- 3/4 teaspoon salt
- 1 ripe mango, peeled and sliced

Direction

- In a large bowl, mix rice and six cups of water and then soak for about 8 hours to overnight.
- Drain the rice and then rinse in fresh water. In a saucepan, mix rice and 2 cups of water and heat to boil. Decrease the heat to medium-low, then cover the pan and let simmer for 15 to 20 minutes until the water has been absorbed and the rice is tender. Place the cooked rice into a bowl.
- In a small saucepan, mix salt, sugar, and coconut milk and then heat barely until boiling. Add the mixture on top of cooked rice. Allow to sit for 30 minutes. Serve while warm along with sliced mango.

Nutrition Information

- Calories: 334 calories;
- Total Fat: 15.3
- Sodium: 312
- Total Carbohydrate: 48.1
- Cholesterol: 0
- Protein: 3.7

69. Sweet Sticky Rice With Mangoes

Serving: 6 | Prep: 15mins | Cook: 20mins | Ready in:

Ingredients

- 2 cups uncooked glutinous (sticky) white rice, rinsed
- 1 (13.5 ounce) can coconut milk, divided
- 1 cup white sugar
- 1 tablespoon white sugar
- 1/4 teaspoon salt
- 3/4 teaspoon cornstarch
- 2 ripe mangoes, peeled and cubed

Direction

- Cover rice with a few inches of fresh water and let the rice to sit for 30 minutes. Then drain off some water to submerge rice by 1/4 inch of water.
- Transfer the rice into a microwave oven, then cover and let cook on High for about 10 minutes until water has been mostly absorbed but rice is still wet. Mix and let cook for 4 minutes until almost dry.
- In a bowl, combine 1 cup of sugar and half the coconut milk and stir to dissolve the sugar. Add the mixture on top of rice and mix to coat the rice with the mixture. Then cover the rice and let to sit for 20 minutes at room temperature.
- Transfer remaining half can of coconut milk to a saucepan and then whisk in cornstarch, salt, and 1 tablespoon of sugar until smooth. Heat the mixture to simmer while whisking continuously on medium heat and let simmer

for about 2 minutes until thickened. Take out from the heat and cool.
- To serve, ladle rice into individual bowls and add several pieces of mango and about 2 tablespoons of coconut sauce on top of each serving.

Nutrition Information

- Calories: 525 calories;
- Sodium: 111
- Total Carbohydrate: 96.4
- Cholesterol: 0
- Protein: 5.7
- Total Fat: 14.1

70. Sweet Thai Style Chicken Bowl

Serving: 6 | Prep: 10mins | Cook: 40mins | Ready in:

Ingredients

- 3 cups water
- 1 1/2 cups jasmine rice
- 1 teaspoon salt
- 3 skinless, boneless chicken breast halves
- 1/2 cup soy sauce
- 1 tablespoon water, or as desired
- 1 (14 ounce) can coconut milk
- 1 cup white sugar
- 2 tablespoons curry powder
- 1 mango - peeled, seeded, and diced
- 2 cups clover sprouts, or to taste
- 1 cup finely chopped cashews
- 1 bunch fresh cilantro, finely chopped
- 4 green onions, chopped

Direction

- Bring together the salt, rice and 3 cups of water in the sauce pan; boil. Lower the heat to low, keep the sauce pan covered, and let it simmer roughly 15 minutes or till the liquid has been absorbed. Take the saucepan out of the heat and allow it to stand roughly 5 minutes longer or till the rice softens.
- Add the chicken breasts into the skillet and pour in 1 tbsp. of water and soy sauce; adjust the heat to medium high. Keep the skillet covered and cook the chicken, occasionally flipping, about 20 minutes or till middle is not pink anymore. Chop the chicken into cubes.
- Mix the curry powder, sugar and coconut milk in the sauce pan; simmer. Put the mango into the curry sauce and cook roughly 5 minutes till thoroughly heated.
- Scoop the rice into the bowl and add the chicken, green onions, cilantro, cashews and sprouts on top. Drizzle the mango curry sauce on top of the chicken.

Nutrition Information

- Calories: 669 calories;
- Total Carbohydrate: 90.5
- Cholesterol: 32
- Protein: 22.6
- Total Fat: 26.3
- Sodium: 1785

71. Tantalizing Pad Thai

Serving: 8 | Prep: 45mins | Cook: 30mins | Ready in:

Ingredients

- 8 cups water
- 1 (8 ounce) package dry flat rice noodles
- 1/2 cup fish sauce
- 2/3 cup fresh lime juice
- 2 teaspoons white sugar
- 1/3 cup oyster sauce
- 1/4 cup chile-garlic sauce (such as Sriracha®)
- 2/3 cup chicken stock
- 2 cloves garlic, minced
- 2 skinless, boneless chicken breast halves, cubed
- 2/3 cup vegetable oil

- 12 ounces edamame in the pod - thawed if frozen, shelled
- 12 green onions, sliced
- 1 cup finely diced eggplant
- 4 cloves garlic, minced
- 6 ounces mushrooms, diced
- 1 (4 ounce) can sliced water chestnuts, drained
- 1 pound fresh bean sprouts
- 1/4 cup chopped fresh cilantro
- 1/2 cup shredded carrot

Direction

- In a big saucepan, boil 8 cups water. Switch off the heat.
- Into the hot water, put the rice noodles and submerge for 20 minutes. Let the noodles drain and reserve.
- In a saucepan, mix 2 cloves minced garlic, chicken stock, chile-garlic sauce, oyster sauce, sugar, lime juice and fish sauce together.
- Boil; lower the heat to low, and while preparing other ingredients, allow the sauce to simmer.
- In a skillet with vegetable oil, cook and mix the chicken till juices run clear and not pink anymore in the middle for 5 to 10 minutes. Using a slotted spoon, take chicken off, and reserve.
- Into the same skillet, mix cooked chicken, carrots, cilantro, bean sprouts, water chestnuts, mushrooms, 4 cloves minced garlic, eggplant, green onions and shelled edamame, and cook and mix for 15 minutes till edamame and eggplant are soft and sauce has slightly thickened.
- Top on rice noodles and serve.

Nutrition Information

- Calories: 389 calories;
- Total Fat: 21.8
- Sodium: 1596
- Total Carbohydrate: 34.7
- Cholesterol: 16
- Protein: 15.6

72. Tapioca Pudding With Tender Coconut

Serving: 4 | Prep: 5mins | Cook: 30mins | Ready in:

Ingredients

- 4 cups water
- 3/4 cup small pearl tapioca
- 1 cup white sugar
- 1 cup fresh shredded coconut
- 1 cup unsweetened coconut cream
- 1 teaspoon salt

Direction

- Heat the water to boil in large pot, add tapioca pearls and let cook for 25 to 30 minutes until translucent. Mix coconut and sugar into the tapioca and then heat the mixture to boil. Remove right away from the heat. Distribute into four small bowls.
- Over medium-low heat, mix together the salt and coconut cream in a small saucepan. Cook for 5 to 10 minutes until warm yet do not allow to boil. Take out from the heat. Ladle about 1 to 2 tablespoons of the mixture on every serving of tapioca pudding.

Nutrition Information

- Calories: 564 calories;
- Total Fat: 27.5
- Sodium: 595
- Total Carbohydrate: 82.3
- Cholesterol: 0
- Protein: 2.9

73. Tender Taro Root Cooked In Coconut Milk

Serving: 4 | Prep: 10mins | Cook: 20mins | Ready in:

Ingredients

- 1 pound raw taro root, peeled and cut into 1/2-inch cubes
- 2 1/2 cups coconut milk
- 3/4 cup white sugar
- 1/4 cup palm sugar
- 1/2 teaspoon salt
- 1 cup unsweetened coconut cream

Direction

- Heat coconut milk to boil in saucepan and then decrease the heat to medium-low and maintain a simmer. Cook taro root for 15 to 20 minutes in simmering coconut milk until tender. Add salt, palm sugar and white sugar to the mixture and mix until sugars are dissolved entirely in the mixture. Mix coconut cream in the mixture and continue to cook barely until hot. Spoon into individual bowls and serve.

Nutrition Information

- Calories: 689 calories;
- Total Fat: 51
- Sodium: 585
- Total Carbohydrate: 62.6
- Cholesterol: 0
- Protein: 5.9

74. Thai Buffalo Wings

Serving: 15 | Prep: 10mins | Cook: 10mins | Ready in:

Ingredients

- 15 chicken wings
- 1/2 cup all-purpose flour
- oil for deep frying
- 1/4 cup butter
- 1/4 cup hot pepper sauce (such as Frank's RedHot®)
- 1 tablespoon chile-garlic sauce (such as Sriracha®)
- 1/2 teaspoon Thai red chile paste
- 2 tablespoons Asian sweet chile sauce (such as Mae Ploy® Sweet Chilli Sauce)
- 2 tablespoons honey

Direction

- Toss chicken wings in big nonporous bowl with flour to coat evenly; use plastic wrap to cover bowl. Refrigerate it for 60-90 minutes.
- Heat oil to 190°C/375°F in big saucepan/deep fryer.
- Mix honey, Asian sweet chile sauce, Thai red chile paste, chile-garlic sauce, hot pepper sauce and butter in small saucepan on low heat. Heat for 5 minutes till sauce is blended well and butter melts fully, occasionally mixing; put aside.
- Fry chicken wings in hot oil for 10-15 minutes till they're not pink anymore in center and golden brown. Transfer chicken wings into serving bowl.
- Put sauce on chicken wings; mix to coat.

Nutrition Information

- Calories: 181 calories;
- Total Fat: 14.1
- Sodium: 205
- Total Carbohydrate: 7.2
- Cholesterol: 27
- Protein: 6.5

75. Thai Cashew Chicken

Serving: 4 | Prep: 15mins | Cook: 45mins | Ready in:

Ingredients

- 1/4 cup soy sauce
- 1/4 cup fish sauce
- 1 1/2 tablespoons hot pepper sauce
- 3 cloves garlic, minced
- 1 tablespoon minced fresh ginger root
- 4 skinless, boneless chicken breast halves - cut into thin strips
- 1 cup dry jasmine rice
- 2 cups water
- 1 tablespoon sesame oil
- 3 tablespoons brown sugar
- 1 small onion, quartered then sliced
- 3/4 cup water
- 3 tablespoons creamy peanut butter
- 1 cup unsalted cashew nuts

Direction

- Combine ginger, garlic, hot pepper sauce, fish sauce and soy sauce in a resealable plastic bag. Add chicken into the bag, then seal and place in a fridge to marinate for at least 2 hours.
- Heat 2 cups water and jasmine rice to boil in a medium saucepan. Lower the heat, then cover and let simmer for 20 minutes.
- Over medium heat, heat sesame oil in a large skillet and then mix in brown sugar until it's dissolved. Mix in onion and then cook for about five minutes until tender. Setting the marinade mixture aside, put the chicken into skillet. Let cook for about ten minutes until browned.
- Mix 3/4 cup of water and the reserved marinade into skillet and heat to boil. Continue cook while stirring for about 10 minutes or until the juices run clear and the chicken is no longer pink. Blend in peanut butter thoroughly. You can serve on top of jasmine rice along with a sprinkling of cashews.

Nutrition Information

- Calories: 669 calories;
- Total Fat: 28.3
- Sodium: 2252
- Total Carbohydrate: 68.6
- Cholesterol: 61
- Protein: 37.2

76. Thai Chicken Dip

Serving: 24 | Prep: 10mins | Cook: 10mins | Ready in:

Ingredients

- 2 tablespoons vegetable oil
- 1 1/2 pounds ground chicken
- 2 small red chile peppers
- 2 cloves garlic, crushed
- 1/2 cup chunky peanut butter
- 1/3 cup lime juice
- 1 cup unsweetened coconut cream
- 1 1/2 tablespoons fish sauce
- 1 tablespoon finely chopped Vietnamese mint

Direction

- In a big skillet, heat oil on medium heat. Add chicken. Cool while mixing to crumble until it's not pink. Mix fish sauce, coconut cream, lime juice, peanut butter, garlic and chilies in. boil. Lower heat to low. Simmer for five minutes. Mix mint in. serve hot or warm. Top with a few mint leaves.

Nutrition Information

- Calories: 112 calories;
- Sodium: 110
- Total Carbohydrate: 2.5
- Cholesterol: 17
- Protein: 8.1
- Total Fat: 8.2

77. Thai Chicken Satay

Serving: 4 | Prep: 10mins | Cook: 10mins | Ready in:

Ingredients

- 1/2 cup canned coconut milk
- 1 1/2 teaspoons ground coriander
- 1 teaspoon yellow curry powder
- 1 teaspoon fish sauce
- 1/2 teaspoon chili oil
- 1 pound skinless, boneless chicken breast halves - cut into strips
- 1 tablespoon chopped fresh cilantro
- 1 tablespoon chopped unsalted peanuts
- 12 wooden skewers, soaked in water for 15 minutes
- 1 cup prepared Thai peanut sauce

Direction

- Stir together the fish sauce, chili oil, coconut milk, curry powder, and ground coriander. Toss in the chicken breast strips and stir to coat. Cover and refrigerate for at least half hour, or up to 2 hours, to marinate.
- Pre-heat an indoor or outdoor grill on high. Skewer the chicken strips, discarding its marinade.
- Grill for 2 to 3 minutes each side until chicken is cooked through and no longer pink. Grilling time is dependent on the thickness of your chicken strips. Transfer chicken skewer to a serving plate, and top with cilantro and peanuts. Put out some peanut sauce for dipping.

Nutrition Information

- Calories: 391 calories;
- Total Fat: 25
- Sodium: 315
- Total Carbohydrate: 9.3
- Cholesterol: 66
- Protein: 35.4

78. Thai Chicken Stock

Serving: 8 | Prep: 15mins | Cook: 1hours45mins | Ready in:

Ingredients

- 1 chicken carcass
- 3/4 cup thinly sliced galangal
- 2 kaffir lime leaves, or to taste
- 2 stalks lemon grass, crushed
- 2 chopped Thai chiles, or to taste
- 2 cloves peeled garlic
- 1 shallot, sliced
- 10 cups water

Direction

- In a big pot, put the chicken carcass and submerge in water. Boil over high heat, then lower heat to medium-low, allow to simmer for 5 minutes. Drain, and wash the carcass under running water. Put the carcass back to the pot with the shallots, garlic, chile peppers, lemon grass, lime leaves and galangal. Add 10 cups of water.
- Over high heat, bring back to a boil, then lower heat to medium-low. Without cover, allow to simmer for 1 1/2 hours, skimming the fat and foam frequently. Using cheesecloth, strain prior to use.

Nutrition Information

- Calories: 17 calories;
- Protein: 0.5
- Total Fat: 0.1
- Sodium: 11
- Total Carbohydrate: 4.1
- Cholesterol: 0

79. Thai Chicken Wings

Serving: 10 | Prep: | Cook: | Ready in:

Ingredients

- 5 pounds frozen chicken wings
- 1 cup chicken broth
- 1/2 cup white sugar
- 1/4 cup fish sauce
- 1/4 cup crushed garlic
- 1/4 cup finely chopped jalapeno chile peppers
- 2 tablespoons cornstarch
- 3 teaspoons paprika
- 1 tablespoon olive oil

Direction

- Preheat an oven to 200 degrees C (400 degrees F).
- Put the chicken wings onto a cookie sheet that is not greased. Then bake for about 45 minutes to 1 hour in prepped oven, flipping once until turned golden brown. Place onto a serving dish/platter.
- Sauté jalapeno peppers and garlic in olive oil in a medium skillet until they are soft. Add sugar, paprika, fish sauce and chicken broth. Pour in cornstarch and allow to thicken. Mix all contents together and then add on top of crispy chicken wings.

Nutrition Information

- Calories: 231 calories;
- Sodium: 485
- Total Carbohydrate: 13.3
- Cholesterol: 48
- Protein: 15.9
- Total Fat: 12.5

80. Thai Chicken With Basil Stir Fry

Serving: 6 | Prep: 15mins | Cook: 20mins | Ready in:

Ingredients

- 2 cups uncooked jasmine rice
- 1 quart water
- 3/4 cup coconut milk
- 3 tablespoons soy sauce
- 3 tablespoons rice wine vinegar
- 1 1/2 tablespoons fish sauce
- 3/4 teaspoon red pepper flakes
- 1 tablespoon olive oil
- 1 medium onion, sliced
- 2 tablespoons fresh ginger root, minced
- 3 cloves garlic, minced
- 2 pounds skinless, boneless chicken breast halves - cut into 1/2 inch strips
- 3 shiitake mushrooms, sliced
- 5 green onions, chopped
- 1 1/2 cups chopped fresh basil leaves

Direction

- Heat water and rice to boil in a pot. Then cover the pot, decrease the heat to low and let to simmer 20 minutes.
- Combine red pepper flakes, fish sauce, rice wine vinegar, soy sauce and coconut milk in a bowl.
- Over medium-high heat, heat the oil in a skillet or wok and the mix in garlic, ginger and onion. Cook until browned lightly. Stir in the chicken strips and let to cook for about 3 minutes until turned browned. Mix in coconut milk sauce. Continue to cook until the sauce is decreased to about 1/3. Stir in basil, green onions and mushrooms and then cook until heated through. You can serve on top of cooked rice.

Nutrition Information

- Calories: 506 calories;
- Total Fat: 12.1
- Sodium: 804
- Total Carbohydrate: 60
- Cholesterol: 78
- Protein: 36.9

81. Thai Chicken With Cashew Nuts

Serving: 4 | Prep: 10mins | Cook: 20mins | Ready in:

Ingredients

- 2 tablespoons sesame oil
- 4 ounces raw cashew nuts
- 2 fresh hot chile peppers, seeded and chopped
- 1 1/8 pounds boneless skinless chicken breasts, cut into cubes
- salt and pepper to taste
- 5 tablespoons light soy sauce
- 5 tablespoons fish sauce
- 1 tablespoon white sugar
- 1 bunch green onions, chopped

Direction

- In a wok, heat sesame oil and then add cashews. When browned, place the cashews in a bowl. Set aside.
- Add the chile peppers into the wok and then stir fry for around 20 seconds. Mix in chicken and add salt and pepper to taste. Cook the chicken until no pink color remains. Mix in sugar, fish sauce and soy sauce. Let to simmer for about five minutes or until the chicken is cooked through.
- Mix in green onions and cashews and then stir fry for two minutes.

Nutrition Information

- Calories: 443 calories;
- Total Fat: 25
- Sodium: 2114
- Total Carbohydrate: 20
- Cholesterol: 78
- Protein: 37

82. Thai Coconut Chicken

Serving: 4 | Prep: 10mins | Cook: 20mins | Ready in:

Ingredients

- 2 cups dry jasmine rice
- 3 cups water
- 1 1/2 pounds skinless, boneless chicken breast halves - cubed
- 1 tablespoon curry powder
- 2 cups 1 inch pieces asparagus
- 1 cup snow peas
- 1/2 cup shredded carrots
- 1 cup chopped green onions
- 1 (14 ounce) can light coconut milk

Direction

- Mix rice and water together in 2-qt. saucepan. Put a cover on and boil over high heat. Lower the heat and bring to a simmer for 20 minutes.
- Mix curry powder and chicken together in a medium-sized bowl, and blend by tossing.
- Spray cooking spray over a big nonstick skillet. Add chicken and cook for 4 minutes over medium-high heat, mixing often. Stir in green onions, carrots, snow peas, and asparagus; cook for 3 minutes. Add coconut milk, keep cooking until the chicken has thoroughly cooked and the sauce is hot. Enjoy with the hot, cooked rice.

Nutrition Information

- Calories: 697 calories;
- Total Fat: 12.1
- Sodium: 141
- Total Carbohydrate: 91.4
- Cholesterol: 99
- Protein: 50.9

83. Thai Coffee

Serving: 2 | Prep: 5mins | Cook: 5mins | Ready in:

Ingredients

- 2 tablespoons ground coffee beans
- 1/4 teaspoon ground cardamom
- water
- 2 tablespoons sweetened condensed milk

Direction

- Add cardamom and coffee in your coffee machine's filter. Add in the machine enough amount of water for 2 cups of coffee. Process the coffee machine.
- In 2 coffee cups, pour brewed coffee. Stir in 1 tbsp. of sweetened condensed milk into each cup to serve.

Nutrition Information

- Calories: 64 calories;
- Protein: 1.7
- Total Fat: 1.7
- Sodium: 27
- Total Carbohydrate: 11
- Cholesterol: 6

84. Thai Crab Rolls

Serving: 18 | Prep: 20mins | Cook: 10mins | Ready in:

Ingredients

- 1 pound crabmeat, drained and flaked
- 1 tablespoon mayonnaise
- 1 tablespoon tamarind paste
- 1 bird's eye chile, seeded and minced
- 2 pinches salt
- 1 (12 ounce) package spring roll wrappers
- 1 egg yolk, beaten
- 1 cup vegetable oil for deep-frying
- 1/4 cup rice vinegar
- 1 teaspoon soy sauce
- 1 clove garlic
- 2 tablespoons white sugar
- 15 butter lettuce leaves, rinsed

Direction

- Mix salt, chile pepper, tamarind paste, mayonnaise and crabmeat in a medium bowl. Put 2 tbsp. of the mixture in the middle of a spring roll square. Fold a corner up past the filling. Press it to seal. Brush egg yolk on the roll's open section to seal and make it crisp. Fold 2 corners on either side of folded corner to the middle. Tightly roll up the filling to the remaining point. Seal point with a bit more egg if needed. Repeat process with the remaining wrappers.
- In a heavy skillet, add the right amount of oil to cover rolls halfway. Heat on medium-high heat until oil becomes sizzling hot. Fry rolls for 45-50 seconds, several at a time, until golden. Drain on paper towels.
- Dipping sauce: in a food processor/blender, process sugar, garlic clove, soy sauce and rice vinegar until smooth.
- Line lettuce leaves on a serving platter. Put dipping sauce in a small bowl then place it in the middle of the platter. Put crab rolls over lettuce leaves around the dip. Serve.

Nutrition Information

- Calories: 108 calories;
- Sodium: 213
- Total Carbohydrate: 13.1
- Cholesterol: 36
- Protein: 7.4
- Total Fat: 2.7

85. Thai Cucumber Salad

Serving: 4 | Prep: 15mins | Cook: | Ready in:

Ingredients

- 3 large cucumbers, peeled, halved lengthwise, seeded, and cut into 1/4-inch slices
- 1 tablespoon salt
- 1/2 cup white sugar
- 1/2 cup rice wine vinegar
- 2 jalapeno peppers, seeded and chopped
- 1/4 cup chopped cilantro
- 1/2 cup chopped peanuts

Direction

- In a colander, use salt to toss cucumbers, and place in the sink for 30 minutes to strain. Rinse using cold water, then strain and use paper towels to pat dry.
- In a mixing bowl, whisk vinegar and sugar together till the sugar dissolves. Add cilantro, cucumbers, and jalapeno peppers; toss to combine. Before serving, use chopped peanuts to dredge on top.

Nutrition Information

- Calories: 238 calories;
- Sodium: 1751
- Total Carbohydrate: 37.1
- Cholesterol: 0
- Protein: 5.8
- Total Fat: 9.4

---

86. Thai Dipping Sauce

Serving: 16 | Prep: 10mins | Cook: | Ready in:

Ingredients

- 1/2 cup peanut butter
- 1/2 cup coconut milk, or more as needed
- 1/4 cup light soy sauce
- 3 tablespoons dark sesame oil
- 1 green onion, chopped
- 1 teaspoon red pepper flakes
- 1/2 teaspoon ground ginger

Direction

- Into a food processor, blend ground ginger, red pepper flakes, green onion, sesame oil, soy sauce, coconut milk and peanut butter until smooth. Transfer into a bowl and then encase with plastic wrap.
- Chill the sauce for at least 1 hour prior to serving.

Nutrition Information

- Calories: 87 calories;
- Protein: 2.5
- Total Fat: 8.2
- Sodium: 264
- Total Carbohydrate: 2.3
- Cholesterol: 0

---

87. Thai Fried Bananas

Serving: 20 | Prep: 20mins | Cook: 15mins | Ready in:

Ingredients

- 3/4 cup white rice flour
- 1/4 cup tapioca flour
- 2 tablespoons white sugar
- 1 teaspoon salt
- 1/2 cup shredded coconut
- 1 1/4 cups water
- 10 bananas
- 3 cups oil for frying

Direction

- Combine coconut, salt, sugar, tapioca and rice flour in a medium bowl. Mix in water, little by little and then stir to make a thick batter.
- Peel bananas and then chop each of them lengthwise into 3 or 4 slices. Heat the oil in a deep wok or deep-fryer to 190 degrees C (375 degrees F).
- Coat every slice of banana in batter completely, and then fry in the hot oil until

turned golden. Place on paper towels to drain and then serve right away.

Nutrition Information

- Calories: 129 calories;
- Sodium: 118
- Total Carbohydrate: 21.5
- Cholesterol: 0
- Protein: 1.2
- Total Fat: 5.1

88. Thai Fried Rice With Pineapple And Chicken

Serving: 6 | Prep: 10mins | Cook: 20mins | Ready in:

Ingredients

- 3 slices bacon, diced
- 3 shallots, sliced
- 4 ounces chicken breast, cut into small cubes
- 4 teaspoons curry powder, divided
- 3 egg yolks, beaten
- 1 teaspoon vegetable oil, or as needed (optional)
- 3 cups cooked jasmine rice
- 1 red Thai bird chile pepper, finely chopped
- 2 tablespoons whole cilantro leaves
- 1 tablespoon soy sauce
- 2 teaspoons fish sauce
- 1/2 teaspoon white sugar
- 4 ounces tiger prawns, peeled and deveined
- 1/4 cup chopped fresh pineapple
- 3 green onions, finely chopped

Direction

- On medium-high heat, cook and stir bacon in a big pan or wok for 10mins until crisp. Use a slotted spoon to take the bacon out of the pan; keep the bacon drippings in the pan. On medium-high heat, cook and mix shallots in the bacon drippings for 1-2mins until pale brown and aromatic.
- Combine chicken with the shallots; cook for 45secs to a minute. Avoid stirring until one side is brown; stir. Keep on cooking for a minute until the chicken is brown. Put in 2tsp curry powder; toss until the chicken is covered.
- Form a well in the middle of the chicken; pour in oil and egg yolks. Cook and stir for 1-2mins until the yolks set. Stir in rice, break up rice.
- In the rice mixture, stir in sugar, chile pepper, fish sauce, cilantro, remaining 2tsp curry powder, and soy sauce; put in shrimp. Cook for 2mins until the shrimp is pink and completely cooked. Mix in bacon, green onions, and pineapple into the rice mixture.

Nutrition Information

- Calories: 267 calories;
- Protein: 13.3
- Total Fat: 10.3
- Sodium: 441
- Total Carbohydrate: 29.7
- Cholesterol: 151

89. Thai Ground Chicken Basil

Serving: 4 | Prep: 15mins | Cook: 5mins | Ready in:

Ingredients

- 2 tablespoons peanut oil
- 1/4 cup minced garlic
- 1 pound ground chicken breast
- 12 Thai chiles, sliced into thin rings
- 2 teaspoons black soy sauce
- 2 tablespoons fish sauce
- 1 cup fresh basil leaves

Direction

- Over high heat, heat a wok until it's smoking. Add in peanut oil, then add garlic right away. Stir-fry the garlic for about 20 seconds until it starts to become golden brown. Stir in ground chicken and continue to cook while stirring for about 2 minutes until meat is no longer pink and is crumbly.
- Mix in fish sauce, soy sauce and sliced chilies. Let cook for around 15 seconds to soften chilies. Add basil and continue to cook until basil is wilted.

Nutrition Information

- Calories: 273 calories;
- Total Fat: 10.7
- Sodium: 769
- Total Carbohydrate: 16.5
- Cholesterol: 69
- Protein: 29.3

90. Thai Hot And Sour Soup

Serving: 6 | Prep: 10mins | Cook: 15mins | Ready in:

Ingredients

- 3 cups chicken stock
- 1 tablespoon tom yum paste
- 1/2 clove garlic, finely chopped
- 3 stalks lemon grass, chopped
- 2 kaffir lime leaves
- 2 skinless, boneless chicken breast halves - shredded
- 4 ounces fresh mushrooms, thinly sliced
- 1 tablespoon fish sauce
- 1 tablespoon lime juice
- 1 teaspoon chopped green chile pepper
- 1 bunch fresh coriander, chopped
- 1 sprig fresh basil, chopped

Direction

- Boil the chicken stock in a big saucepan. Mix in the garlic and tom yum paste, cook for approximately 2 minutes. Mix in the kaffir lime leaves and lemon grass. In the saucepan, put the chicken, and cook for 5 minutes till juices run clear and the chicken is not pink anymore.
- Stir in the mushrooms. Put in the green chile pepper, lime juice and fish sauce. Keep on cooking till well incorporated. Take away from heat, put the basil and coriander, serve warm.

Nutrition Information

- Calories: 71 calories;
- Total Fat: 1.8
- Sodium: 639
- Total Carbohydrate: 4.9
- Cholesterol: 21
- Protein: 9.1

91. Thai Monkfish Curry

Serving: 3 | Prep: 20mins | Cook: 20mins | Ready in:

Ingredients

- 1 tablespoon peanut oil
- 1/2 sweet onion, finely chopped
- 1 red bell pepper, chopped
- 3 tablespoons red Thai curry paste
- 1 (14 ounce) can coconut milk
- 12 ounces monkfish, cut into cubes
- 1 tablespoon fish sauce
- 2 tablespoons lime juice
- 2 tablespoons cilantro, chopped

Direction

- Over medium heat, heat peanut oil in a large sauce pan and then mix in chopped onion. Cook for 3 to 5 minutes until translucent and softened. Add the red bell pepper and continue cooking for about 3 to 5 more

minutes until it is softened. Mix in curry paste and then cook for a minute. Add in coconut milk and gently heat to a simmer.
- When the coconut milk starts to simmer, mix in the cubed monkfish and let simmer for about 7 to 10 minutes or until the center is no longer opaque and the fish is firm. Mix in cilantro, lime juice and fish sauce prior to serving.

Nutrition Information

- Calories: 418 calories;
- Sodium: 693
- Total Carbohydrate: 11
- Cholesterol: 28
- Protein: 20
- Total Fat: 34.2

92. Thai Peanut Butter Sauce

Serving: 8 | Prep: 5mins | Cook: |Ready in:

Ingredients

- 1/3 cup hot water
- 2/3 cup peanut butter
- 1/3 cup soy sauce
- 2 tablespoons lemon juice
- 1 teaspoon cayenne pepper
- 1/4 cup light corn syrup
- 1/4 cup dry sherry

Direction

- In a large bowl, mix all the ingredients and combine well. Pour into a serving bowl and then ladle on top of seafood that you like.

Nutrition Information

- Calories: 170 calories;
- Total Fat: 10.9
- Sodium: 751

- Total Carbohydrate: 14.5
- Cholesterol: 0
- Protein: 6.1

93. Thai Peanut Noodle Stir Fry

Serving: 4 | Prep: 15mins | Cook: 20mins |Ready in:

Ingredients

- 1 (8 ounce) package uncooked spaghetti
- 1 tablespoon cornstarch
- 1 cup vegetable broth
- 1/3 cup creamy peanut butter
- 3 tablespoons soy sauce
- 3 tablespoons honey
- 3 tablespoons brown sugar
- 1 teaspoon sesame oil
- 1 teaspoon ground ginger
- 1/4 teaspoon ground red pepper
- 2 tablespoons sake
- 2 tablespoons vegetable oil
- 2 cloves garlic, minced
- 1 onion, chopped
- 1 cup broccoli florets
- 1 cup carrots, sliced
- 1/2 cup red bell pepper, chopped
- 1/2 cup sugar snap peas

Direction

- Add lightly salted water into a large pot; bring to a rolling boil over high heat. When the water is boiling, mix the spaghetti in, and return to a boil. Allow pasta to cook, uncovered, occasionally stirring, for approximately 12 minutes till the pasta has thoroughly cooked yet is still firm to the bite. Strain well in a colander placed in the sink.
- In the meantime, whisk into the vegetable broth with cornstarch till dissolved. Mix red pepper, ground ginger, sesame oil, brown sugar, honey, soy sauce, and peanut butter in. Bring to a boil over medium-high heat; lower heat to medium-low, and let simmer for

approximately 5 minutes till thickened. Mix sake in and keep warm.
- In a large skillet, heat the vegetable oil over medium heat. Add onion and garlic in; cook and stir for approximately 5 minutes till the onion turns translucent and softened. Mix sugar snap peas, red bell pepper, carrots, and broccoli in. Lower heat, allow to steam, covered, for approximately 5 minutes till the vegetables get softened. Toss pasta and peanut sauce with vegetables, and it is ready to serve.

Nutrition Information

- Calories: 587 calories;
- Total Fat: 20.2
- Sodium: 930
- Total Carbohydrate: 87.1
- Cholesterol: 0
- Protein: 16.2

94. Thai Pork Satay

Serving: 4 | Prep: 45mins | Cook: 10mins | Ready in:

Ingredients

- 1/4 cup crunchy peanut butter
- 1/4 cup finely chopped green onions
- 2 tablespoons soy sauce
- 2 tablespoons lemon juice
- 1 1/2 tablespoons brown sugar
- 2 teaspoons minced garlic
- 1 teaspoon ground coriander
- 1/8 teaspoon ground cayenne pepper
- 1 pound pork tenderloin, cubed
- 1 (8 ounce) can water chestnuts, drained
- 1 medium green bell pepper, cut into 2 inch pieces
- 1 medium red bell pepper, cut into 2 inch pieces
- 1 small sweet onion, chopped
- skewers

Direction

- Combine cayenne pepper, coriander, garlic, brown sugar, lemon juice, soy sauce, green onions and peanut butter in a medium bowl. Place in pork and toss to coat. Cover the bowl and then marinate for at least 30 minutes in the fridge.
- Preheat the grill over high heat. Thread sweet onion, red bell pepper, green bell pepper, water chestnuts and marinated pork alternately onto skewers. Pour the remaining marinade into a small saucepan. Heat to boil and then cook for a few minutes.
- Coat the grate lightly with oil. Cook the skewers for about 10 minutes or to the doneness desired. Flip the skewers as you grill to cook evenly and brush with the boiled marinade on the last few minutes.

Nutrition Information

- Calories: 276 calories;
- Protein: 23.4
- Total Fat: 11
- Sodium: 578
- Total Carbohydrate: 22.7
- Cholesterol: 49

95. Thai Pork With Peanut Sauce

Serving: 4 | Prep: 7mins | Cook: 10mins | Ready in:

Ingredients

- 1/4 cup all-purpose flour
- 1 teaspoon ground cumin
- 1/4 teaspoon cayenne pepper
- 1/2 teaspoon salt
- 2 tablespoons vegetable oil
- 4 boneless pork chops, about 3/4-inch thick
- 1/3 cup chicken broth
- 1/2 cup coconut milk
- 2 tablespoons peanut butter

- 1 tablespoon honey
- 1 teaspoon ground ginger
- 1/4 teaspoon salt
- 1/4 cup chopped green onion
- 1/4 cup sliced red bell pepper
- 1/4 cup coarsely chopped dry roasted peanuts
- 1/4 cup chopped fresh cilantro

Direction

- Mix 1/2 teaspoon of salt, cayenne pepper, cumin and flour on a plate. Mix to distribute the spices. Use the flour mixture to coat the pork chops and then shake to remove any excess.
- Over medium-high heat, heat oil in a large skillet, add the pork chops and then fry for approximately 4 minutes on each side until cooked through.
- As pork chops cook, mix together 1/4 teaspoon of salt, ginger, honey, peanut butter, coconut milk and chicken broth. Transfer the pork chops onto a serving platter and keep them warm.
- Add the peanut sauce to skillet. Cook while stirring continuously for two minutes or until thickened. Add peanut sauce on top of the chops and stud with cilantro, peanuts, bell pepper and green onion.

Nutrition Information

- Calories: 366 calories;
- Total Fat: 26.9
- Sodium: 572
- Total Carbohydrate: 16.4
- Cholesterol: 31
- Protein: 17.3

96. Thai Pumpkin Soup

Serving: 4 | Prep: 10mins | Cook: 15mins | Ready in:

Ingredients

- 1 tablespoon vegetable oil
- 1 tablespoon butter
- 1 clove garlic, chopped
- 4 shallots, chopped
- 2 small fresh red chili peppers, chopped
- 1 tablespoon chopped lemon grass
- 2 1/8 cups chicken stock
- 4 cups peeled and diced pumpkin
- 1 1/2 cups unsweetened coconut milk
- 1 bunch fresh basil leaves

Direction

- Heat butter and oil in a medium saucepan on low heat; cook lemongrass, chilies, shallots and garlic in oil till fragrant. Don't burn the garlic. Mix pumpkin, coconut milk and chicken stock in; boil. Cook till pumpkin softens.
- Blend the soup till slightly chunky/smooth consistency, whichever you like, in batches in a blender; serve with basil leaves.

Nutrition Information

- Calories: 305 calories;
- Cholesterol: 8
- Protein: 5.4
- Total Fat: 25
- Sodium: 405
- Total Carbohydrate: 20.9

97. Thai Red Curry Paste

Serving: 4 | Prep: 15mins | Cook: | Ready in:

Ingredients

- 5 dried red chile peppers, or to taste
- 2 onions, cut into chunks
- 2 tablespoons chopped fresh cilantro
- 1 tablespoon vegetable oil, or more as needed
- 1 tablespoon chopped garlic
- 1 tablespoon ground coriander

- 2 teaspoons lemon zest
- 2 teaspoons ground cumin
- 2 teaspoons shrimp paste
- 2 teaspoons paprika
- 1 teaspoon whole black peppercorns
- 1 teaspoon lemon grass powder
- 1 teaspoon ground turmeric
- 1 teaspoon salt

Direction

- In a blender, combine salt, turmeric, lemon grass, peppercorns, paprika, shrimp taste, cumin, lemon zest, coriander, garlic, oil, cilantro, onions and chile peppers until making a smooth, paste-like, consistent mixture.

Nutrition Information

- Calories: 103 calories;
- Total Carbohydrate: 15
- Cholesterol: 2
- Protein: 2.6
- Total Fat: 4.3
- Sodium: 593

Direction

- Set oven to 400°F or 200°C to preheat.
- Start with preparing the dressing, combine lime juice, brown sugar, fish sauce and chopped chiles in a little bowl. Set the dressing on one side.
- Rub oil all over the salmon filet and arrange on a baking sheet. Bake in the oven for 20 or until salmon separates easily. Set aside and cool for 15 or more minutes.
- Transfer filet to a large bowl and break into big pieces using fork. Toss in basil, onion and tomato. Drizzle with dressing and toss lightly to mix well.
- When serving, place the mixture on lettuce leaves. Enjoy immediately.

Nutrition Information

- Calories: 249 calories;
- Protein: 26.8
- Total Fat: 10.8
- Sodium: 802
- Total Carbohydrate: 11.3
- Cholesterol: 77

98. Thai Salmon Salad

Serving: 6 | Prep: 20mins | Cook: 20mins | Ready in:

Ingredients

- 4 tablespoons fish sauce
- 4 tablespoons lime juice
- 2 teaspoons brown sugar
- 4 Thai chiles, chopped
- 1 1/2 pounds salmon fillet
- 1 teaspoon olive oil
- 1 onion, thinly sliced
- 1 large tomato, chopped
- 1 cup chopped fresh basil
- 1 head lettuce

99. Thai Shrimp And Clam Curry

Serving: 4 | Prep: 30mins | Cook: 15mins | Ready in:

Ingredients

- 2 tablespoons peanut oil
- 1 large onion, halved and sliced lengthwise
- 1 large red bell pepper, seeded and sliced lengthwise
- 1 tablespoon chopped fresh ginger
- 2 cloves garlic, minced
- 1 teaspoon red chile paste, or more to taste
- 1 (14 ounce) can coconut milk
- 4 large fresh cherrystone clams, scrubbed
- 1/4 cup chicken broth, or more as needed (optional)

- 1 fresh lime
- 1 teaspoon fish sauce
- 1 teaspoon brown sugar
- 3 tablespoons chopped fresh basil, divided, or more to taste
- 12 large shrimp, peeled and deveined

Direction

- Over medium-high heat, heat peanut oil in a large saucepan and add red bell pepper and onion. Sauté for about 4 minutes until softened. Decrease the heat to medium. Add garlic and ginger. Cook while stirring for 1 to 2 minutes until fragrant. Mix in coconut milk and red chile paste. Add in clams and simmer for 3 to 5 minutes until the flavors blend. In case the curry looks too thick, mix in chicken broth.
- Grate zest from lime finely. Mix half of zest into curry along with brown sugar and fish sauce. Press some juice of lime to the curry. Mix in shrimp and half of basil. Simmer the curry for 5 to 10 minutes until shrimp are cooked through and opaque. If necessary, you can thin the curry with additional chicken broth.
- Spoon out the clams from the curry, drain their juice back into saucepan and then discard. Stir in the remaining basil and lime zest prior to serving.

Nutrition Information

- Calories: 350 calories;
- Sodium: 291
- Total Carbohydrate: 13.4
- Cholesterol: 97
- Protein: 14
- Total Fat: 28.6

100. Thai Shrimp, Chicken, Grapefruit, And Coconut Salad

Serving: 6 | Prep: 30mins | Cook: |Ready in:

Ingredients

- 1/2 cup fresh lime juice
- 1 1/2 tablespoons fish sauce
- 2 teaspoons white sugar
- 2 cloves garlic, crushed
- 1 red grapefruit, peeled and sectioned
- 2 cups shelled cooked tiny shrimp, thawed if frozen
- 2 cups shredded precooked chicken breast meat
- 1 1/2 cups shredded coconut meat, unsweetened
- 6 shallots, thinly sliced
- 1 teaspoon chopped red chile pepper
- 1/2 cup fresh mint leaves
- 1 1/2 tablespoons finely chopped fresh cilantro
- 1 head iceberg lettuce, shredded

Direction

- In a bowl, mix together garlic, sugar, fish sauce and lime juice using a whisk for the dressing.
- In a large bowl, toss cilantro, mint, chile pepper, shallots, coconut, chicken breast, shrimp and grapefruit sections. Toss the grapefruit mixture with a drizzle of about 3/4 of the dressing to blend. Mix shredded lettuce with the rest of the dressing in a different bowl right before serving.
- Place the lettuce on a large serving plate. Add the grapefruit mixture in a layer on top.

Nutrition Information

- Calories: 364 calories;
- Total Fat: 16.9
- Sodium: 410
- Total Carbohydrate: 25.7
- Cholesterol: 108

- Protein: 30.3

101. Thai Steamed Banana Cake

Serving: 6 | Prep: 20mins | Cook: 20mins | Ready in:

Ingredients

- 1 (3.5 ounce) package flaked coconut
- 1/4 teaspoon salt
- 1/2 cup rice flour
- 3/4 cup tapioca flour
- 1/2 tablespoon arrowroot starch
- 1 cup unsweetened coconut cream
- 1/2 cup white sugar
- 1 pound ripe bananas, mashed
- 1/8 teaspoon salt
- 1/2 cup coconut milk

Direction

- In a bowl, mix the coconut together with 1/4 teaspoon of salt. Reserve.
- In a large bowl, sift together the arrowroot starch, tapioca flour and rice flour. Mix coconut cream into the mixture for at least 10 minutes until flours are blended into the cream. Mix sugar into the mixture until it dissolves completely. Pour in mashed banana and combine well. Add coconut milk and 1/8 teaspoon of salt and combine well one more. Transfer batter into individual aluminum foil cups or a square baking tin. Add the reserved coconut on top.
- Heat around 1-1/2 inches of water to boil in a steamer that is fitted with a large basket. Then steam the cake on top of boiling water for 20 to 25 minutes until cooked through.

Nutrition Information

- Calories: 508 calories;
- Cholesterol: 0

- Protein: 4.2
- Total Fat: 24.4
- Sodium: 212
- Total Carbohydrate: 73.9

102. Thai Sweet Sticky Rice With Mango (Khao Neeo Mamuang)

Serving: 4 | Prep: 10mins | Cook: 20mins | Ready in:

Ingredients

- 1 1/2 cups uncooked short-grain white rice
- 2 cups water
- 1 1/2 cups coconut milk
- 1 cup white sugar
- 1/2 teaspoon salt
- 1/2 cup coconut milk
- 1 tablespoon white sugar
- 1/4 teaspoon salt
- 1 tablespoon tapioca starch
- 3 mangos, peeled and sliced
- 1 tablespoon toasted sesame seeds

Direction

- Mix water and rice in a saucepan and then heat to boil. Cover the pan and decrease the heat to low. Let simmer for 15 to 20 minutes until water has been absorbed.
- As rice is cooking, over medium heat, combine together the 1/2 teaspoon salt, 1 cup sugar and 1 1/2 cups coconut milk in a saucepan. Heat to boil. Take out from the heat and reserve. Mix cooked rice into coconut milk mixture and then cover. Cool for 1 hour.
- Mix together the tapioca starch, 1/4 teaspoon salt, 1 tablespoon sugar and 1/2 cup coconut milk in a saucepan to make the sauce. Heat to boil.
- Put sticky rice onto a serving dish. Spread mangos over the rice. Spread the sauce on the rice and mangos. Scatter with sesame seeds.

Nutrition Information

- Calories: 817 calories;
- Protein: 8.4
- Total Fat: 26
- Sodium: 458
- Total Carbohydrate: 144.3
- Cholesterol: 0

103. Thai Tofu Soup

Serving: 4 | Prep: 25mins | Cook: 15mins | Ready in:

Ingredients

- 1 tablespoon vegetable oil
- 1 onion, chopped
- 2 tablespoons Thai red curry paste
- 1 tablespoon grated ginger
- 1 tablespoon grated garlic
- 1 (32 fluid ounce) container vegetable broth
- 1 (14 ounce) can coconut milk
- 1 tablespoon white sugar
- 1 (12 ounce) package extra-firm tofu, cut into small cubes
- 4 ounces broccoli, chopped into bite-sized pieces
- 4 ounces cauliflower florets, cut into bite-sized pieces
- 4 ounces mushrooms, cut into bite-size pieces
- 1 pinch salt and ground black pepper to taste

Direction

- In a big pot, heat oil over medium heat. Add garlic, ginger, curry paste, and onion. Toss continually for 2 minutes until the onion starts to get tender. Add coconut milk and vegetable broth. Add sugar. Boil it. Mix in mushrooms, cauliflower, broccoli, and tofu.
- Lower the heat and put a cover on the pot. Bring the soup to a simmer, about 5-8 minutes, until the vegetables are soft, whisking continually. Use pepper and salt to season.

Nutrition Information

- Calories: 385 calories;
- Sodium: 683
- Total Carbohydrate: 21.4
- Cholesterol: 0
- Protein: 14
- Total Fat: 30

104. Thai Dipped Beef Tri Tip

Serving: 8 | Prep: 15mins | Cook: 35mins | Ready in:

Ingredients

- 6 cloves garlic, crushed
- 1/3 cup chopped lemon grass
- 3 tablespoons grated fresh ginger root
- 2 tablespoons grated onion
- 1/3 cup fish sauce
- 1/4 cup seasoned rice vinegar
- 3 tablespoons soy sauce
- 2 tablespoons ground coriander
- 1 tablespoon ground cumin
- 2 teaspoons ground turmeric
- 1/2 teaspoon cayenne pepper
- 1/3 cup packed brown sugar
- 2 tablespoons vegetable oil
- 1 (2 1/2 pound) trimmed beef tri tip roast

Direction

- In a large mixing bowl, add vegetable oil, garlic, brown sugar, cayenne pepper, turmeric, cumin, coriander, soy sauce, rice vinegar, fish sauce, grated onion, grated gingerroot, and chopped/bruised lemon grass. Whisk together until mixed thoroughly.
- Place tri-tip roast in the marinade. Use a fork to poke the roast on both sides numerous times with the tines of a fork to help absorb

the marinade. Cover bowl with plastic wrap and refrigerate for 2 to 12 hours. Occasionally remove meat from fridge to poke more holes and turn during the marinade time.
- Transfer to a tray lined with paper towels to briefly drain. Reserve the marinade.
- Preheat covered grill to 325 degrees F (165 degrees C). Lightly brush oil on the grate.
- Place roast over indirect heat and cook with the grill closed. Brush marinade on roast and turn occasionally. Cook for 35 to 45 minutes, or adjust time depending on the heat of your grill. Insert an instant-read thermometer into the center of the meat, it should read 130 to 135 degrees F (54 degrees C). Transfer cooked roast to a cutting board. Let it cool for at least 20 minutes before slicing.
- In a saucepan, place any remaining marinade and bring to a boil. Then simmer for 1 to 2 minutes. Use as a serving sauce if you want.

Nutrition Information

- Calories: 362 calories;
- Total Carbohydrate: 14.9
- Cholesterol: 132
- Protein: 39.4
- Total Fat: 15.5
- Sodium: 1281

105. Thai Style Chicken Wings

Serving: 6 | Prep: | Cook: | Ready in:

Ingredients

- 3 pounds chicken wings
- 1 cup chicken broth
- 1 cup white sugar
- 1/4 cup fish sauce
- 2 tablespoons cider vinegar
- 1 tablespoon cornstarch
- 2 teaspoons paprika
- 1 tablespoon vegetable oil
- 1/3 cup minced garlic
- 3 tablespoons minced jalapeno peppers
- 1/4 cup sliced red bell peppers

Direction

- Preheat an oven to 200 degrees C (400 degrees F).
- Mix paprika, cornstarch, vinegar, fish sauce, sugar and broth in a large bowl. Reserve.
- Add chiles, garlic and oil in a hot skillet or wok and then stir fry for about 4 minutes on high heat until garlic is slightly golden. Stir in the broth mixture for about 10 to 15 minutes until it boils and has decreased to about 1 1/4 cups. Keep it warm.
- Put chicken wings into a baking dish of 10x15 inch and then bake with no cover for about 60 to 70 minutes (until crisp and browned). Flip from time to time. Then drain off the fat. Place the wings onto a platter using a slotted spoon and add garlic sauce mixture on top of them, combining thoroughly. If desired, stud with red bell pepper strips.

Nutrition Information

- Calories: 296 calories;
- Sodium: 911
- Total Carbohydrate: 38.4
- Cholesterol: 48
- Protein: 19.2
- Total Fat: 7.3

106. Thai Style Chicken With Noodles

Serving: 6 | Prep: 10mins | Cook: 30mins | Ready in:

Ingredients

- 1 tablespoon dark sesame oil
- 1 tablespoon vegetable oil
- 1 cup (1 small) chopped onion

- 1 teaspoon minced fresh ginger root
- 1 fresh red chile pepper, seeded and chopped
- 4 skinless, boneless chicken breast halves - cut into strips
- 1 1/2 tablespoons fresh lime juice
- 1 teaspoon dark soy sauce
- 1 tablespoon chopped fresh basil
- 1 tablespoon chopped fresh cilantro
- 1 (10 ounce) can coconut milk
- 1 tablespoon cornstarch
- 2 tablespoons water
- 1 (12 ounce) package dried rice noodles
- 1 tablespoon heavy cream
- 1 lime, cut into wedges

Direction

- In a big wok, heat vegetable oil and sesame oil on high heat. Fry chile pepper, ginger, and onion, constantly stirring, until onion is tender. Put in cilantro, basil, soy sauce, lime juice, and chicken strips. Cook, constantly stirring, until chicken pieces is cooked through and golden in color. Pour coconut milk in and boil. Mix water and cornstarch together then mix into sauce. Simmer until thick for 10 minutes.
- As it simmers, soak noodles for 3 minutes in hot water. Boil a big pot of water. Add soaked noodles and cook until tender or for 3 minutes. Drain.
- Serve chicken mixture on noodles. Top with a drizzle of cream and a twist of lime.

Nutrition Information

- Calories: 451 calories;
- Total Fat: 16.3
- Sodium: 212
- Total Carbohydrate: 54.1
- Cholesterol: 49
- Protein: 21.7

107. Thai Style Ground Pork Skewers

Serving: 8 | Prep: 20mins | Cook: 15mins | Ready in:

Ingredients

- 2 pounds ground pork
- 1/4 cup white sugar
- 2 tablespoons fish sauce
- 6 cloves garlic, minced
- 1 teaspoon sea salt
- 1 teaspoon ground black pepper
- 1 1/2 teaspoons baking powder
- 1 tablespoon water
- wooden skewers, soaked in water

Direction

- In a bowl, mix thoroughly the pork, fish sauce, garlic, sugar, salt, and pepper. Dissolve baking powder in a tablespoon of water and mix well into the pork mixture. Cling wrap the bowl and let sit in the refrigerator for 60 minutes.
- Preheat an outdoor grill on medium heat. Lightly grease the grate.
- Lightly oil your hands and skewer a fistful of pork through a skewer. Shape into a 1-inch thick meat loaf around the skewer. Do again with the remaining pork and skewers.
- Grill, turning as needed, until evenly browned and the meat is not pink in the center, about 15 minutes. Slice the sausages into bite sizes before serving.

Nutrition Information

- Calories: 262 calories;
- Total Carbohydrate: 7.5
- Cholesterol: 74
- Protein: 20.5
- Total Fat: 16.3
- Sodium: 643

108. Thai Style Steamed Pumpkin Cake

Serving: 6 | Prep: 10mins | Cook: 25mins | Ready in:

Ingredients

- 2 tablespoons tapioca flour
- 1/4 cup rice flour
- 1 1/2 teaspoons arrowroot powder
- 1/2 cup unsweetened coconut cream
- 1 cup white sugar
- 1 (2 pound) pumpkin - peeled, seeded, and grated
- 1 cup coconut milk
- 1/8 teaspoon salt

Direction

- Heat to boil approximately 1-1/2 inches of water in a steamer that is fitted with a basket big enough for a 9-inch square baking dish to lay flat.
- Sift together the arrowroot powder, rice flour and tapioca flour into a bowl. Slowly mix coconut cream into the mixture for about 10 minutes until smooth and incorporated completely. Mix the salt, coconut milk, pumpkin and sugar into the mixture. Ensure the sugar dissolves completely into batter and then transfer to a 9-inch square baking dish.
- Let steam on top of boiling water for about 25 minutes until cake is cooked through. Cool the cake before slicing into squares and serve.

Nutrition Information

- Calories: 344 calories;
- Protein: 3.4
- Total Fat: 15.2
- Sodium: 56
- Total Carbohydrate: 53.7
- Cholesterol: 0

109. Thai Style Steamed Tapioca Cake

Serving: 8 | Prep: 10mins | Cook: 25mins | Ready in:

Ingredients

- 1 cup white sugar
- 1/4 cup unsweetened coconut cream
- 1 tablespoon cornstarch
- 4 1/2 cups grated, peeled yucca root (tapioca root)
- 1 cup water
- 2 cups flaked coconut, divided
- 1/4 teaspoon salt

Direction

- In a bowl, combine together cornstarch, coconut cream and sugar to dissolve sugar completely. Add about 1/3 of the grated coconut, water and grated cassava. Combine thoroughly.
- Into a separate bowl, mix remaining coconut with salt and reserve.
- Heat to boil a few inches of water in a large pot or wok. Place eight 1-cup ramekins into large steamer insert and then put on top of boiling water for three minutes. Take out the insert and ladle cassava mixture into heated ramekins until filled. Scatter a coconut portion on top of every cake.
- Steam the cakes for 15 to 20 minutes on top of the boiling water until they're cooked through. You can do this in multiple batches depending on the size of steamer. Therefore, ensure there is sufficient water to continually boil.

Nutrition Information

- Calories: 395 calories;
- Total Carbohydrate: 80.1
- Cholesterol: 0
- Protein: 2.4
- Total Fat: 8.1
- Sodium: 143

110. The Best Thai Coconut Soup

Serving: 8 | Prep: 35mins | Cook: 30mins | Ready in:

Ingredients

- 1 tablespoon vegetable oil
- 2 tablespoons grated fresh ginger
- 1 stalk lemon grass, minced
- 2 teaspoons red curry paste
- 4 cups chicken broth
- 3 tablespoons fish sauce
- 1 tablespoon light brown sugar
- 3 (13.5 ounce) cans coconut milk
- 1/2 pound fresh shiitake mushrooms, sliced
- 1 pound medium shrimp - peeled and deveined
- 2 tablespoons fresh lime juice
- salt to taste
- 1/4 cup chopped fresh cilantro

Direction

- In a big pot, heat oil over medium heat. Stir and cook curry paste, lemongrass, and ginger in the hot oil for 1 minute. Gradually add chicken broth over the mixture, whisking continually. Mix in brown sugar and fish sauce; bring to a simmer for 15 minutes. Mix in mushrooms and coconut milk; stir and cook for about 5 minutes until the mushrooms are tender. Add shrimp, cook for about 5 minutes until the shrimp is not opaque anymore. Mix in lime juice; use salt to season and cilantro to garnish.

Nutrition Information

- Calories: 368 calories;
- Total Fat: 32.9
- Sodium: 579
- Total Carbohydrate: 8.9
- Cholesterol: 86
- Protein: 13.2

111. The Best Thai Curry Peanut Sauce

Serving: 28 | Prep: 10mins | Cook: 10mins | Ready in:

Ingredients

- 1 tablespoon vegetable oil
- 1 1/2 tablespoons minced garlic
- 2 tablespoons red curry paste
- 1 1/4 cups creamy peanut butter
- 3/4 cup brown sugar
- 1/2 teaspoon chili powder
- 1/2 teaspoon cayenne pepper
- 1/2 tablespoon fish sauce
- 1 teaspoon sesame oil
- 3 (13.5 ounce) cans coconut milk

Direction

- Over medium heat, heat oil in a large skillet, stir in garlic and then cook for about 1 minute until aroma of garlic has mellowed. Pour in red curry paste and mix for 1 minute longer. Whisk in coconut milk, sesame oil, fish sauce, cayenne pepper, chili powder, brown sugar and peanut butter. Heat to simmer while whisking from time to time until the sauce is smooth and has thickened.

Nutrition Information

- Calories: 179 calories;
- Cholesterol: 0
- Protein: 4.2
- Total Fat: 15.9
- Sodium: 101
- Total Carbohydrate: 9.6

112. Todd's Famous Thai Peanut Sauce

Serving: 8 | Prep: 10mins | Cook: 7mins | Ready in:

Ingredients

- 3 ounces roasted, salted peanuts
- 2 tablespoons canola oil
- 1 tablespoon Asian (toasted) sesame oil
- 1 teaspoon hot chili oil
- 2 tablespoons soy sauce
- 4 teaspoons fresh lime juice
- 1 tablespoon white sugar, or to taste
- 1 teaspoon Asian chili garlic sauce, or to taste

Direction

- Start preheating oven to 350°F (175°C).
- Transfer peanuts in single layer onto the dry baking sheet. Break whole nuts apart into halves. Toast peanuts for 7 to 10 mins until slightly darker in color and fragrant, watching carefully to avoid burning.
- Take the peanuts out of the oven, allow to cool, put into a work bowl of the food processor. Pulse 2-3 times to finely chop. Put in chili garlic sauce, sugar, lime juice, soy sauce, hot chili oil, toasted sesame oil and canola oil. Process until mixture becomes a fine paste with a little texture of the chopped peanuts, not a smooth paste totally. It will look a little grainy.

Nutrition Information

- Calories: 122 calories;
- Total Carbohydrate: 4.4
- Cholesterol: 0
- Protein: 2.8
- Total Fat: 11
- Sodium: 340

113. Tom Byoo (Sour Fish Soup)

Serving: 4 | Prep: 20mins | Cook: 30mins | Ready in:

Ingredients

- 3 cups fish stock
- 1 (1 inch) piece fresh ginger, peeled and sliced into disks, or more to taste
- 1 (1 inch) piece galangal, peeled and sliced into disks, or more to taste
- 5 Thai chile peppers, crushed
- 2 kaffir lime leaves, torn
- 2 stalks lemon grass, cut into 2-inch pieces and crushed
- 2 shallots, crushed
- 1 (10 ounce) trout, scales removed and fish cut into steaks
- 5 cherry tomatoes, halved
- 1/4 cup tamarind juice, or more to taste
- 2 tablespoons fish sauce, or more to taste
- 1/4 cup chopped fresh cilantro, or to taste

Direction

- Boil fish stock in a pot. Add shallots, lemon grass, kaffir lime leaves, Thai chile peppers, galangal and ginger. Lower heat. Simmer the stock for 20 minutes.
- Stir fish sauce, tamarind juice, tomatoes and trout in the stock. Simmer for 5 minutes until trout cooks through.
- Put trout in a bowl gently. Pour soup on fish. Put cilantro on top.

Nutrition Information

- Calories: 175 calories;
- Cholesterol: 37
- Protein: 18.3
- Total Fat: 5.2
- Sodium: 1144
- Total Carbohydrate: 13.8

114. Tom Ka Gai (Coconut Chicken Soup)

Serving: 6 | Prep: 15mins | Cook: 20mins | Ready in:

Ingredients

- 3/4 pound boneless, skinless chicken meat
- 3 tablespoons vegetable oil
- 2 (14 ounce) cans coconut milk
- 2 cups water
- 2 tablespoons minced fresh ginger root
- 4 tablespoons fish sauce
- 1/4 cup fresh lime juice
- 1/4 teaspoon cayenne pepper
- 1/2 teaspoon ground turmeric
- 2 tablespoons thinly sliced green onion
- 1 tablespoon chopped fresh cilantro

Direction

- Chop the chicken into thin strips and sauté it in oil till chicken turns white or for 2 - 3 minutes.
- In the pot, boil the water and coconut milk. Lower the heat. Put in the turmeric, cayenne powder, lime juice, fish sauce and ginger. Let it simmer for 10-15 minutes or till chicken is done.
- Drizzle with the fresh cilantro and scallions and serve when steaming hot.

Nutrition Information

- Calories: 433 calories;
- Total Fat: 41.1
- Sodium: 787
- Total Carbohydrate: 5.5
- Cholesterol: 38
- Protein: 14.8

115. Tom Kha Gai

Serving: 6 | Prep: 20mins | Cook: 25mins | Ready in:

Ingredients

- 3 cups chicken broth
- 1 (14 ounce) can coconut milk
- 1/4 cup sweet red chile sauce
- 3 tablespoons lime juice
- 2 tablespoons fish sauce
- 2 tablespoons brown sugar
- 1 (1 1/2 inch) piece fresh ginger, sliced
- 10 kaffir lime leaves, torn and bruised
- 1 1/2 pounds skinless, boneless chicken breast halves - cut into strips
- 1 (15 ounce) can straw mushrooms
- 1 cup coarsely chopped onion
- 1 zucchini, sliced
- 1 lemongrass stalk, chopped
- 1 bunch fresh basil, chopped

Direction

- Over medium heat, warm coconut milk and chicken broth together in a stockpot. Add kaffir lime leaves, ginger, brown sugar, fish sauce, lime juice and chile sauce. Heat the broth mixture to a low simmer for about 15 minutes until the flavors have combined.
- Take stockpot off heat and drain out lime leaves and ginger. Pour the broth mixture back into the stockpot and heat to simmer. Cook the chicken for about 5 minutes in the simmering broth until no pink color remains in the middle. Add basil, lemongrass, zucchini, onion and mushrooms. Simmer for about 3 minutes until the onion softens.

Nutrition Information

- Calories: 330 calories;
- Cholesterol: 61
- Protein: 26.7
- Total Fat: 17
- Sodium: 1318
- Total Carbohydrate: 20.8

116. Tom Yum Koong Soup

Serving: 5 | Prep: 10mins | Cook: 40mins | Ready in:

Ingredients

- 1/2 pound medium shrimp - peeled and deveined
- 12 mushrooms, halved
- 1 (4.5 ounce) can mushrooms, drained
- 4 cups water
- 2 lemon grass
- 4 kaffir lime leaves
- 4 slices galangal
- 4 chile padi (bird's eye chiles)
- 1 1/2 tablespoons fish sauce
- 1 1/2 limes, juiced
- 1 teaspoon white sugar
- 1 teaspoon hot chile paste
- 1 tablespoon tom yum soup paste (optional)

Direction

- Trim the lemongrass and chop into pieces similar to size of matchstick.
- To prepare the stock: Transfer shrimp shells and heads into water and cook for about 20 minutes. Switch off the fire. Let the heads and shells to soak for 20 more minutes prior to discarding.
- Trim the lemongrass and then chop into pieces that resemble size of matchstick.
- Add chili paste, sugar, lime juice, fish sauce, chili padi, galangal, kaffir lime leaves, lemon grass and stock into a pot and heat to boil. After boiling for five minutes, place in both mushrooms and shrimps. Then cook for 10 more minutes. Stud with coriander leaves.

117. Vegan Pad Thai With Baked Tofu

Serving: 4 | Prep: 25mins | Cook: 52mins | Ready in:

Ingredients

- 1 (12 ounce) package firm tofu
- Dual-Use Tofu Marinade:
- 1/2 cup soy sauce
- 1/4 cup rice vinegar
- 1/4 cup lime juice
- 1/4 cup coconut oil
- 2 tablespoons tamarind paste (optional)
- 2 tablespoons minced garlic
- 2 tablespoons minced fresh ginger root
- 1 tablespoon chile-garlic sauce, or to taste
- Vegetables:
- 1/2 head red cabbage, thinly shredded, or to taste (optional)
- 4 carrots, cut into matchsticks (optional)
- 1/2 daikon radish, peeled and cut into matchsticks, or to taste (optional)
- 1 red bell pepper, cut into matchsticks (optional)
- 1 onion, sliced
- 1/4 cup water, or as needed
- Sauce Ingredients:
- 1/4 cup roasted flaxseed meal
- 1 tablespoon peanut butter, or more to taste (optional)
- 2 teaspoons chili powder
- 1 large pinch Himalayan black salt (optional)
- 1 pinch stevia sugar substitute
- 2 (12 ounce) packages kelp noodles
- 2 (14.5 ounce) cans mung bean sprouts, drained, or more to taste
- 1 bunch green onions, sliced
- 1/4 cup peanuts
- 1/4 cup chopped fresh cilantro

Direction

- On a plate, put tofu and top with another plate. Put a 3-5 pound weight on it. Press the tofu for 20-30 minutes. Drain the discard accumulated liquid. Cut to 1/2-1-in. thick slabs that are wide to flip easily.
- In a square container, mix chili-garlic sauce, ginger, garlic, tamarind paste, coconut oil, lime juice, rice vinegar and soy sauce. Submerge tofu slabs in marinade. Marinade for a minimum of 15 minutes. Put tofu on a plate that's oven-proof. Keep marinade.

- Preheat oven to 175 degrees C/350 degrees F.
- In a skillet, mix onion, red bell pepper, daikon, carrots and cabbage on medium heat. Add 1/4 cup of water. Sauté veggies for 10-15 minutes until tender.
- Bake tofu in the preheated oven until dry, flipping when 15 minutes passes, for 30-40 minutes. Cut tofu to small pieces.
- Mix stevia, black salt, chili powder, peanut butter and flaxseed meal to marinade. Sit for 5 minutes until sauce is thick.
- Mix bean sprouts and kelp noodles in the skillet with cabbage. Stir and cook for 2 minutes until heated through and soft. Mix in sauce. Stir and cook for 5 minutes until sauce sticks to noodles and is thick. Add cilantro, peanuts, green onions and chopped tofu.

Nutrition Information

- Calories: 497 calories;
- Sodium: 2330
- Total Carbohydrate: 49.6
- Cholesterol: 0
- Protein: 20.7
- Total Fat: 28.2

118. Vegetarian Phad Thai

Serving: 8 | Prep: 20mins | Cook: 20mins | Ready in:

Ingredients

- 1 pound dried rice noodles
- 2 tablespoons vegetable oil
- 4 eggs, beaten
- 2 tablespoons peanut oil
- 1 1/2 cups peanut butter
- 1/3 cup water
- 1/3 cup soy sauce
- 1 cup milk
- 1 1/4 cups brown sugar
- 1/3 cup lemon juice
- 2 tablespoons garlic powder
- 1 tablespoon paprika
- cayenne pepper to taste
- 1 pound mung bean sprouts
- 1 cup shredded carrots
- 1/4 cup chopped green onions
- 1/2 cup chopped, unsalted dry-roasted peanuts
- 1 lime, cut into wedges

Direction

- In a big bowl with hot water, soak rice noodles for approximately 1 hour.
- Into a big skillet, put half tablespoon of oil, and put the eggs. Scramble into medium-sized portions, and put to a plate. Put aside.
- Combine lemon juice, brown sugar, milk, soy sauce, water, peanut butter and peanut oil in a saucepan. Add paprika and garlic powder to season. Heat till sauce turns smooth. Add cayenne pepper liberally to season.
- Drain noodles; noodles should be very flexible, but remain relatively firm. In a wok or big saucepan, heat the leftover 1 1/2 tablespoons of vegetable oil. In oil, cook the noodles for about 2 minutes, mixing continuously, till they are soft. Mix in scrambled eggs, ground peanuts, scallions, carrots, sprouts and peanut sauce. On low heat, keep cooking for about 5 minutes till vegetables are crisp-tender. Jazz up with wedges of lime and serve right away.

Nutrition Information

- Calories: 830 calories;
- Total Fat: 39.4
- Sodium: 999
- Total Carbohydrate: 103.6
- Cholesterol: 95
- Protein: 23.6

119. Yam Taeng (Spicy Cucumber Salad)

Serving: 4 | Prep: 15mins | Cook: |Ready in:

Ingredients

- 3 cucumbers - peeled, seeded, and grated
- 3 tablespoons crushed dried shrimp
- 2/3 pound long beans, sliced thin and mashed
- 5 cherry tomatoes, halved
- 5 Thai chilies, sliced thin
- 1 tablespoon palm sugar
- 2 tablespoons fish sauce
- juice of 1 lime, or more to taste
- 3 tablespoons roasted peanuts, chopped

Direction

- In a bowl, mix together tomatoes, beans, dried shrimp and cucumbers.
- In a small bowl, mix together the lime juice, fish sauce, palm sugar and Thai chilies. Add on top of cucumber mixture. Mix to combine and adjust the seasoning as desired. Scatter chopped peanuts on top of the mixture and serve.

Nutrition Information

- Calories: 347 calories;
- Total Carbohydrate: 57.9
- Cholesterol: 8
- Protein: 22.5
- Total Fat: 4.5
- Sodium: 625

120. Yellow Mung Bean Pudding With Coconut Cream

Serving: 4 | Prep: 10mins | Cook: 30mins |Ready in:

Ingredients

- 4 cups hulled yellow mung beans
- 3 1/2 cups water
- 3/4 cup white sugar
- 3/4 cup water
- 1/3 cup tapioca flour
- 1 cup unsweetened coconut cream
- 1/2 teaspoon salt

Direction

- Into a large container, add the mung beans and then add warm water to submerge by several inches. Leave to soak for two hours and then drain.
- Put a steamer insert in a saucepan and add sufficient water to reach just below the steamer's bottom. Cover the pan and heat the water to boil. Encase mung beans in cheesecloth and then put in the steamer insert. Cover the pan and let the beans steam for 25 to 30 minutes until tender.
- In a saucepan, mix together the sugar and 3 1/2 cups of water. Heat to boil. Mix the tapioca flour and 3/4 cup water together in a bowl until flour has been dissolved. Add the mixture to boiling water and mix until syrup is thickened and is clear. Carefully mix mung beans into syrup. Take out from the heat and distribute into four serving bowls.
- Over medium-low heat, heat salt and coconut cream together in small saucepan until cream is warmed. Do not boil. Ladle on top of the mung bean mixture and then serve.

Nutrition Information

- Calories: 1100 calories;
- Sodium: 332
- Total Carbohydrate: 180.7
- Cholesterol: 0
- Protein: 51.6
- Total Fat: 23.2

Chapter 2: Japanese Cuisine Recipes

***

121. Agedashi Esque Tofu

Serving: 2 | Prep: 10mins | Cook: 5mins | Ready in:

Ingredients

- 1 (12 ounce) package extra firm tofu
- 3 tablespoons cornstarch
- oil for frying
- 2 green onions, chopped
- 2 tablespoons hoisin sauce

Direction

- Slice the tofu, making 12 cubes. Put cornstarch in a shallow bowl or on a plate, dredge the tofu in it until thoroughly coated.
- Heat enough oil to submerge the tofu halfway through. Fry the tofu in the hot oil until crispy, about 3 to 5 minutes per side. Drain them on paper towels.
- Sprinkle green onions on top of tofu. Drizzle hoisin sauce on top. Immediately serve.

Nutrition Information

- Calories: 433 calories;
- Total Fat: 32.4
- Sodium: 275
- Total Carbohydrate: 22.5
- Cholesterol: < 1
- Protein: 17.5

122. Ashley's Chicken Katsu With Tonkatsu Sauce

Serving: 2 | Prep: 20mins | Cook: 10mins | Ready in:

Ingredients

- Sauce
- 1/2 cup Worcestershire sauce
- 1/4 cup ketchup
- 2 tablespoons soy sauce
- pepper to taste
- Chicken
- 2 cups vegetable oil, for deep-fat frying
- 1/2 cup all-purpose flour
- 1/2 cup panko bread crumbs
- salt and pepper to taste
- 1 egg, beaten
- 2 skinless, boneless chicken breast halves - pounded to 1/4 inch thickness
- 1 green onion, thinly sliced

Direction

- For sauce, combine together a pinch of pepper to taste, soy sauce, ketchup and Worcestershire sauce. Reserve.
- Heat the oil in a deep-fryer to 175 degrees C (350 degrees F).
- Put panko bread crumbs and flour into separate plates and then season with pepper and salt. Put beaten egg into a medium bowl. Dunk the flattened chicken pieces first into the flour, then dip in egg and finally dip in bread crumbs.
- Fry the breaded chicken breasts in the preheated hot oil for about 8 minutes until no longer pink in the middle and turned golden brown. Place onto a plate lined with paper towel to absorb the excess oil. Chop the chicken into thin strips and then top with a sprinkling of sliced green onions and a sprinkle of sauce. You can serve the rest of the sauce on the side for dipping.

Nutrition Information

- Calories: 718 calories;
- Cholesterol: 136
- Protein: 30.2
- Total Fat: 36.8
- Sodium: 2290
- Total Carbohydrate: 73.1

123. Asian Crab And Cuke Salad

Serving: 4 | Prep: 10mins | Cook: | Ready in:

Ingredients

- 1 cucumber, sliced
- salt and ground black pepper to taste
- 1 (8 ounce) package imitation crabmeat, coarsely chopped
- 1 tablespoon white wine vinegar
- 1 tablespoon soy sauce

Direction

- In a bowl put cucumber slices; season with pepper and salt. Toss imitation crabmeat in. In another bowl, whisk soy sauce and vinegar. Put on crab and cucumber mixture. Toss till coated.

Nutrition Information

- Calories: 63 calories;
- Total Fat: 0.3
- Sodium: 698
- Total Carbohydrate: 10.5
- Cholesterol: 11
- Protein: 4.9

124. Authentic Miso Soup

Serving: 4 | Prep: 15mins | Cook: 15mins | Ready in:

Ingredients

- 4 cups water
- 1/2 cup bonito flakes
- 1 (4 inch) piece dashi kombu (dried kelp)
- 1/2 (12 ounce) package tofu, cut into chunks
- 1 teaspoon dried wakame
- 3 tablespoons miso paste
- 1/4 cup chopped green onions

Direction

- On low heat, heat water in a big pot; cook in kombu until it just starts to simmer. Mix in bonito flakes until blended. Take pot out of heat then let it stand for 5 mins without a cover; strain. Set the dashi aside.
- On medium heat, heat 3 1/2 cups dashi in a pot; stir in wakame and tofu to combine. Take a cup of warm dashi then pour to a small bowl; stir in miso paste. Place the miso mixture back to the pot of remaining dashi; mix until completely warmed. Serve soup with chopped green onions on top.

Nutrition Information

- Calories: 65 calories;
- Total Fat: 2.8
- Sodium: 511
- Total Carbohydrate: 4.9
- Cholesterol: 0
- Protein: 6.2

125. Beef Bowl (Gyudon)

Serving: 4 | Prep: 15mins | Cook: 25mins | Ready in:

Ingredients

- 4 cups cooked rice
- 6 tablespoons mirin (Japanese sweet wine)
- 3 tablespoons soy sauce
- 2 tablespoons sake
- 1 onion, cut into wedges

- 10 ounces beef, thinly sliced
- 4 eggs
- 1 teaspoon pickled ginger (beni shoga), or to taste (optional)

Direction

- Evenly split the rice among four donburi bowls.
- On medium heat, boil sake, soy sauce, and mirin in a pot. Cook and stir onion into the mixture for 5 mins, or until onion becomes translucent. Mix in beef. Let it simmer for 5 mins, or until completely cooked and not pink anymore. Use a slotted spoon to move onion and beef onto top of the rice.
- Boil eggs in the pot; cook for 5-7 mins, or until soft boiled. Peel the eggs then place in the bowls. Top with pickled ginger.

Nutrition Information

- Calories: 448 calories;
- Sodium: 786
- Total Carbohydrate: 56.1
- Cholesterol: 223
- Protein: 24.7
- Total Fat: 9.5

126. Beef Short Ribs Rice Bowl (Gyu Kalbi Don)

Serving: 2 | Prep: 15mins | Cook: 5mins | Ready in:

Ingredients

- 1/3 bitter melon
- water to cover
- 1/4 cup dashi kombu (dried kelp)
- 2 tablespoons soy sauce
- 1 tablespoon sake
- 1 tablespoon mirin (Japanese sweet wine)
- 1 tablespoon white sugar
- 7 ounces beef short ribs
- 1/4 onion, chopped
- 2 ounces shredded konnyaku
- 1 teaspoon grated fresh ginger
- 1 garlic scape, cut into 5 pieces
- 2 teaspoons water
- 1 teaspoon cornstarch
- 2 cups steamed white rice
- 1 teaspoon minced myoga (Japanese ginger), or to taste

Direction

- Chop in lengthwise bitter melon in half. Use spoon to remove seeds. Slice deseeded bitter melon crosswise in thin slices and put in bowl. Cover slices with salted water For 5 minutes, soak then remove water.
- Prepare marinade mixture by stirring in a bowl soy sauce, dashi kombu, sake, mirin, and sugar; mix until well blended. In a microwaveable bowl, put beef short ribs and add marinade. Soak beef short ribs in marinade for 30 minutes.
- Add bitter melon, ginger, konnyaku, onion, and garlic scape into beef mixture then stir.
- For 4 minutes, cook beef in microwave.
- Prepare a small bowl, combine 2 teaspoon water and cornstarch; stir until dissolved then pour into beef mixture.
- Put back beef in microwave and cook for another 1 minute.
- Scoop rice into bowls and place beef and myoga over the rice, respectively.

Nutrition Information

- Calories: 556 calories;
- Total Fat: 18.6
- Sodium: 1470
- Total Carbohydrate: 73.8
- Cholesterol: 40
- Protein: 18

127. Black Sesame Pudding

Serving: 6 | Prep: 10mins | Cook: 3mins | Ready in:

Ingredients

- 6 tablespoons water
- 2 teaspoons powdered unflavored gelatin
- 1 1/2 cups milk
- 3 tablespoons white sugar
- 2 tablespoons black sesame paste

Direction

- Mix together gelatin and water in a bowl until gelatin dissolves.
- Mix black sesame paste, sugar, and milk in a saucepan over medium heat; stir and cook for 2 to 4 minutes, until sugar melts. Mix gelatin mixture into milk mixture; stir and cook the pudding for 1 to 2 minutes. Take away from heat.
- Chill the pudding in the saucepan for 5 minutes at room temperature. Place pudding into small bowls and keep in the refrigerator for about 2 hours, until set and chilled.

Nutrition Information

- Calories: 89 calories;
- Sodium: 28
- Total Carbohydrate: 10.4
- Cholesterol: 5
- Protein: 3.6
- Total Fat: 3.9

128. Broiled Mochi With Nori Seaweed

Serving: 8 | Prep: 10mins | Cook: 7mins | Ready in:

Ingredients

- 8 frozen mochi squares
- 1/2 cup soy sauce
- 1 sheet nori (dry seaweed)

Direction

- Preheat an oven to 275 degrees C (450 degrees F).
- Dunk the mochi into the soy sauce and put in a baking sheet. Bake for around five minutes or until heated through.
- As the mochi cooks, slice dried seaweed into eight strips. Put these strips into a large frying pan on medium heat. Remove them from heat when warmed after about 1 to 2 minutes.
- Encase every mochi cake with seaweed and then serve warm.

Nutrition Information

- Calories: 109 calories;
- Cholesterol: 0
- Protein: 3.1
- Total Fat: 0.2
- Sodium: 907
- Total Carbohydrate: 23.1

129. Butter Mochi

Serving: 24 | Prep: 15mins | Cook: 1hours | Ready in:

Ingredients

- 3 1/2 cups sweet rice flour (mochiko)
- 2 1/2 cups white sugar
- 2 tablespoons baking powder
- 5 eggs
- 1 teaspoon coconut extract
- 1 teaspoon vanilla extract
- 2 cups milk
- 1 (14 ounce) can coconut milk
- 1/2 cup melted butter

Direction

- Preheat the oven to 175 degrees C (350 degrees F). Coat a 9x13 inch baking dish with grease.

In a mixing bowl, whisk together baking powder, sugar and rice flour.
- In a mixing bowl, beat the vanilla extract, coconut extract, and eggs until eggs become smooth. Whisk in melted butter, coconut milk, and milk until blended. Mix in flour mixture little by little until there are no lumps that remain. Scrape into the prepared baking dish and then smoothen the top.
- Bake in the preheated oven for about 1 hour until mochi turns golden brown. Let cool to lukewarm temperature prior to chopping into 24 pieces. Serve.

Nutrition Information

- Calories: 256 calories;
- Total Fat: 9
- Sodium: 174
- Total Carbohydrate: 41.2
- Cholesterol: 51
- Protein: 3.9

130. California Roll

Serving: 5 | Prep: 1hours | Cook: 20mins | Ready in:

Ingredients

- 4 cups water
- 2 cups uncooked white rice
- 1/2 cup seasoned rice vinegar
- 1 teaspoon white sugar, or as needed
- 1 teaspoon salt, or as needed
- 1/4 pound cooked crab meat, drained of excess liquid and shredded
- 1 tablespoon mayonnaise
- 5 sheets nori (dry seaweed)
- 1 avocado, sliced
- 1/4 cup red caviar, such as tobiko
- 1 English cucumber, seeded and sliced into strips
- 2 tablespoons drained pickled ginger, for garnish
- 2 tablespoons soy sauce, or to taste
- 1 tablespoon wasabi paste

Direction

- Use a plastic wrap to wrap the entire sushi rolling mat, and put it aside.
- In a saucepan, put the rice and water and let it boil over high heat setting. Lower the heat setting to medium-low heat and allow it to simmer while covering for 20-25 minutes until the rice has softened the liquid is absorbed. Put the cooked rice into a bowl, then add the rice vinegar and use a wooden spoon or a rice paddle to cut. Add 1 teaspoon of salt and 1 teaspoon of sugar or to taste. Let the mixture cool down for about 30 minutes until it reaches room temperature.
- In a small bowl, mix the mayonnaise and crab meat.
- On a clean and flat work surface, put a sheet of nori then put a thin layer of the prepared rice over the nori sheet and spread it out evenly. Put the nori sheet with the rice side facing down onto the prepared sushi rolling mat. Put a layer of 2-3 slices of avocado over the nori sheet then put 2-3 tablespoons of the prepared crab mixture on top of the avocado slices. Scoop 1-2 teaspoons of tobiko lengthwise on one side of the avocado and crab, then put 2 strips of cucumber on the other side of the avocado and crab. Use the sushi rolling mat as a guide to carefully and tightly roll the California roll in the shape of a log. Remove the sushi rolling mat, then put additional tobiko over the top of the California roll; use a plastic wrap to cover the roll and gently press the tobiko onto the California roll top. Remove the plastic wrap and use a wet knife to slice the prepared California roll into 6 even-sized portions. Do the same procedure for the rest of the unused filling and nori sheets. Serve it garnished with soy sauce, wasabi paste and pickled ginger.

Nutrition Information

- Calories: 444 calories;
- Total Fat: 11.2
- Sodium: 1237
- Total Carbohydrate: 70.3
- Cholesterol: 94
- Protein: 15.3

131. Chicken Hekka

Serving: 8 | Prep: 30mins | Cook: 15mins | Ready in:

Ingredients

- 1 1/2 pounds skinless, boneless chicken breast meat
- 3/4 cup white sugar
- 3/4 cup soy sauce
- 3/4 cup mirin (Japanese sweet wine)
- 2 tablespoons vegetable oil
- 1 tablespoon grated fresh ginger
- 3 carrots, julienned
- 2 onions, thinly sliced
- 1 (14 ounce) can shredded bamboo, drained
- 1/2 pound fresh mushrooms, sliced
- 1 cup trimmed and coarsely chopped watercress
- 1 (8 ounce) package rice noodles, soaked and cut into 2 inch pieces

Direction

- Cut the chicken meat to bite-sized pieces. Mix mirin wine, soy sauce, and sugar in a medium-sized bowl. Combine well then put aside.
- In a wok or skillet, heat oil on medium-high heat. Squeeze grated ginger juice in the wok then add grated ginger, stir fry it until brown. Get rid of ginger fibers. Bring heat up to high then mix in chicken. Season with the soy sauce mixture then cook for another 2 minutes.
- Add watercress, mushrooms, bamboo shoots, onions, and carrots one at a time. Mix after every addition. Put in rice noodles and cook for another 3 minutes while stirring, or until done.

Nutrition Information

- Calories: 399 calories;
- Total Fat: 5
- Sodium: 1483
- Total Carbohydrate: 58.4
- Cholesterol: 49
- Protein: 24.6

132. Chicken Yakisoba

Serving: 4 | Prep: 20mins | Cook: 15mins | Ready in:

Ingredients

- 2 tablespoons canola oil
- 1 tablespoon sesame oil
- 2 skinless, boneless chicken breast halves - cut into bite-size pieces
- 2 cloves garlic, minced
- 2 tablespoons Asian-style chile paste
- 1/2 cup soy sauce
- 1 tablespoon canola oil
- 1/2 medium head cabbage, thinly sliced
- 1 onion, sliced
- 2 carrots, cut into matchsticks
- 1 tablespoon salt
- 2 pounds cooked yakisoba noodles
- 2 tablespoons pickled ginger, or to taste (optional)

Direction

- On medium-high heat, heat sesame oil and 2 tbsp. canola oil in a big pan; add garlic and chicken. Cook and stir for a minute, or until aromatic. Mix in chile paste; cook and stir for 3-4mins, or until the chicken is browned through. Pour in soy sauce then simmer for 2 mins; move to a bowl.
- On medium-high heat, heat a tablespoon of canola oil in a pan; cook and stir salt, cabbage,

carrots, and onion for 3-4 mins, or until the cabbage wilts.
- Mix the chicken mixture into the cabbage mixture; put in noodles. Cook and stir for 3-4 mins, or until the chicken is not pink in the center anymore and the noodles are hot. Add pickled ginger on top.

Nutrition Information

- Calories: 503 calories;
- Protein: 26.5
- Total Fat: 16.5
- Sodium: 3868
- Total Carbohydrate: 69.8
- Cholesterol: 29

133. Chicken And Sweet Potato Rice

Serving: 2 | Prep: 15mins | Cook: 10mins | Ready in:

Ingredients

- 1 cup Japanese sushi-style rice
- 1 cup water
- 1/4 pound ground chicken
- 3/4 teaspoon salt, divided
- 1/4 teaspoon ground black pepper
- 1 sweet potato, cubed
- 1/4 teaspoon ground black pepper

Direction

- In a large bowl, put rice and cover with water. Rinse rice by swirling water, then drain using a wire mesh strainer; repeat. Pour 1 cup of fresh water into a bowl and soak clean rice for 30 minutes.
- In a bowl, combine chicken, pepper, and 1/4 teaspoon of salt; set aside and let stand for 10 minutes.
- In a microwave pressure cooker, mix together rice and soaking water, sweet potato, chicken,

and 1/4 teaspoon of salt. Cover pressure cooker with lid and cook in the microwave for 10 minutes at 600W. Remove from the microwave and let stand 15 minutes.
- Release the pressure from the cooker by following instructions from the manual. Mix well, serve.

Nutrition Information

- Calories: 544 calories;
- Total Fat: 1.3
- Sodium: 992
- Total Carbohydrate: 108.1
- Cholesterol: 33
- Protein: 21.8

134. Coffee Gelatin Dessert

Serving: 5 | Prep: 10mins | Cook: 5mins | Ready in:

Ingredients

- 3/4 cup white sugar
- 3 (.25 ounce) envelopes unflavored gelatin powder
- 3 cups hot brewed coffee
- 1 1/3 cups water
- 1 tablespoon lemon juice
- 1 cup sweetened whipped cream for garnish

Direction

- Mix gelatin and sugar together in a saucepan. Stir in hot coffee and water. Then let cook while stirring frequently on low heat until sugar and gelatin have dissolved completely. Take out from the heat and mix in lemon juice. Transfer to a 4 1/2 cup mold. Chill for at least 6 hours or overnight until set. You can serve together with whipped cream.

Nutrition Information

- Calories: 215 calories;
- Cholesterol: 33
- Protein: 4.3
- Total Fat: 8.9
- Sodium: 22
- Total Carbohydrate: 30.9

135. Coffee Jelly

Serving: 4 | Prep: 5mins | Cook: 5mins | Ready in:

Ingredients

- 1 (.25 ounce) package unflavored gelatin
- 2 tablespoons hot water
- 3 tablespoons white sugar
- 2 cups fresh brewed coffee

Direction

- In a small bowl, allow the gelatin to dissolve in hot water. In a saucepan, put the coffee, sugar and dissolved gelatin mixture and let the mixture boil over high heat setting. You may either transfer the prepared coffee mixture into a big pan to be sliced into cubes afterwards or into glasses for individual servings. Keep it in the fridge for 6-7 hours until it becomes solid.

Nutrition Information

- Calories: 43 calories;
- Sodium: 6
- Total Carbohydrate: 9.4
- Cholesterol: 0
- Protein: 1.6
- Total Fat: 0

136. Cucumber And Avocado Sushi

Serving: 6 | Prep: 35mins | Cook: 25mins | Ready in:

Ingredients

- 1 1/4 cups water
- 1 cup uncooked glutinous white rice (sushi rice)
- 3 tablespoons rice vinegar
- 1 pinch salt
- 4 sheets nori (dry seaweed)
- 1/2 cucumber, sliced into thin strips
- 1 avocado - peeled, pitted and sliced

Direction

- Mix rice and water in a saucepan and make it boil. Then cover, minimize heat to low and simmer for 20 minutes, or until rice is soft and water has been absorbed. Separate from heat and add in a pinch of salt and vinegar. Reserve to cool.
- Use plastic wrap to cover a bamboo sushi mat to prevent the rice from sticking. Put a sheet of seaweed over the plastic. Spread the rice equally onto the sheet using your hands, keeping about 1/2 inch of seaweed empty at the bottom. Across the middle of the rice, lay out strips of cucumber and avocado. Raise the mat and roll over the vegetables once and push down. Unfold, then roll again towards the exposed end of the seaweed sheet to create a long roll. You may dampen a little water to help secure. Reserve and continue with remaining fillings, rice and nori sheets.
- Cut the rolls into 5 or 6 slices using a sharp wet knife. Then present/serve cut side up with your desired sushi condiments.

Nutrition Information

- Calories: 171 calories;
- Protein: 3
- Total Fat: 5.1
- Sodium: 6

- Total Carbohydrate: 28.7
- Cholesterol: 0

137. Dango (Sweet Japanese Dessert)

Serving: 3 | Prep: 30mins | Cook: 10mins | Ready in:

Ingredients

- 1 (12 ounce) package silken tofu
- 1 cup rice flour, or as needed
- 2 drops red food coloring
- 1/2 teaspoon matcha green tea powder, or as needed
- 3 bamboo skewers

Direction

- In a bowl, use your hands to mix the rice flour and tofu together until the texture of the mixture is slightly elastic and smooth. Check the texture of the dough by pulling the dough thinly; you'll know that it is ready if the texture is like your earlobe. Mix in additional rice flour or water if needed.
- Divide the dough into 3 equally-sized portions. Color 1 of the dough portions using a red food coloring then use your hand to knead the dough so that the color is evenly distributed. The color of the dango will intensify once they have been boiled. Use green tea powder to color another dough portion, and keep the last dough portion white.
- Divide each of the prepared dough portions into 3 equal portions then roll each of the dough portions in the shape of a ball to form the dango.
- Fill a big pot with water and let it boil. Drop the dango into the pot and let it boil for 3-5 minutes until the dango floats onto the surface of the water. Allow the floating dango to keep boiling for 2 more minutes.
- Use a slotted spoon to transfer the cooked dango into a bowl filled with room-temperature or cold water for 1 minute just until it is warm to touch. Thread the dango through skewers depending on your preferred order. Green, white and pink is the traditional order.

Nutrition Information

- Calories: 263 calories;
- Total Fat: 3.8
- Sodium: 40
- Total Carbohydrate: 45
- Cholesterol: 0
- Protein: 10.9

138. Dashi Stock (Konbudashi)

Serving: 8 | Prep: 5mins | Cook: 5mins | Ready in:

Ingredients

- 1 ounce dashi kombu (dried kelp)
- 1 quart water
- 1/2 cup bonito flakes

Direction

- Use a paper towel to clean any dirt from the kombu, but be careful not to scuff the white powdery deposits on seaweed. In a saucepan, put water and the kombu, allow to soak for about 30 minutes to get softened.
- Next, remove the seaweed from the water, trim some lengthways splits into the leaf. Put them back into the water and boil. When the water begins to boil, take the seaweed out to prevent the stock from getting bitter.
- Stir the bonito flakes into the kombu-flavored broth, boil again, then remove the pan from the heat. Let the water cool down. Once the bonito flakes have sunk to the bottom, use a

coffee filter or a strainer lined with cheesecloth to strain the dashi.

Nutrition Information

- Calories: 12 calories;
- Protein: 1
- Total Fat: 0
- Sodium: 111
- Total Carbohydrate: 2
- Cholesterol: 0

---

139. Dynamite Sauce

Serving: 12 | Prep: 5mins | Cook: | Ready in:

Ingredients

- 1 cup mayonnaise
- 1 tablespoon sugar
- 1 tablespoon chili garlic sauce

Direction

- Combine chili garlic sauce, sugar and mayonnaise together in a small bowl. Use right away or chill and use within a week.

Nutrition Information

- Calories: 136 calories;
- Total Fat: 14.6
- Sodium: 157
- Total Carbohydrate: 1.7
- Cholesterol: 7
- Protein: 0.2

---

140. Easy Japanese Okonomiyaki

Serving: 4 | Prep: 20mins | Cook: 10mins | Ready in:

Ingredients

- 1 cup whole wheat flour
- 3/4 cup prepared dashi stock
- 1 egg
- 1 small zucchini, grated
- 1/4 head cabbage, shredded
- 1 carrot, grated
- 2 green onions, chopped, divided
- 2 teaspoons vegetable oil, or as needed
- 3 slices bacon
- 1 tablespoon okonomiyaki sauce, or to taste
- 1 tablespoon mayonnaise, or to taste

Direction

- In a big bowl, combine one green onion, flour, carrot, dashi, cabbage, zucchini, and egg to make the batter.
- On medium heat, heat oil in a pan then add the batter. Put slices of bacon on top; cook for 5-15 mins on each side, or until golden brown. Add the remaining green onion and mayonnaise over the okonomiyaki on top to serve.

Nutrition Information

- Calories: 248 calories;
- Total Carbohydrate: 31.1
- Cholesterol: 56
- Protein: 10.8
- Total Fat: 10.2
- Sodium: 373

---

141. Easy Mochi

Serving: 8 | Prep: 30mins | Cook: 5mins | Ready in:

Ingredients

- 1 cup sweetened red bean paste
- 1 cup sweet rice flour (mochiko)
- 1 teaspoon green tea powder (matcha)
- 1 cup water

- 1/4 cup white sugar
- 1/2 cup cornstarch, for rolling out the dough

Direction

- Use aluminum foil to wrap the red bean paste; freeze for at least 3 hrs. In a microwave-safe ceramic or glass bowl, combine green tea powder and sweet rice flour well. Mix in water then sugar until smooth; use plastic wrap to cover.
- Microwave the rice flour mixture for 3 mins and 30 secs. In the meantime, take the red bean paste out of the freezer then equally split into eight balls; set aside. Mix the rice flour mixture then microwave for another 15-30 secs.
- Sprinkle cornstarch on a work surface. Start rolling still hot mochi into balls with around 2 tbsp. in size; flatten then put one frozen ball of red bean paste in the middle. Press the mochi over the red bean filling until the filling is totally covered. Scatter more cornstarch over then arrange the mochi on a paper muffin liner with the seam-side down to avoid sticking. Repeat with the rest of the red bean paste and mochi.

Nutrition Information

- Calories: 213 calories;
- Total Fat: 0.2
- Sodium: 82
- Total Carbohydrate: 49.8
- Cholesterol: 0
- Protein: 2.8

142. Eel Sauce

Serving: 6 | Prep: 5mins | Cook: 10mins | Ready in:

Ingredients

- 1/2 cup soy sauce
- 1/2 cup white sugar
- 1/2 cup mirin (Japanese sweet wine)

Direction

- In a small saucepan, put the sugar, mirin and soy sauce and let it heat up over medium heat setting. Allow the mixture to cook while stirring it until the mixture has reduced in volume to about 3/4 cup.

Nutrition Information

- Calories: 121 calories;
- Sodium: 1203
- Total Carbohydrate: 24.5
- Cholesterol: 0
- Protein: 1.4
- Total Fat: 0

143. Famous Japanese Restaurant Style Salad Dressing

Serving: 14 | Prep: 10mins | Cook: | Ready in:

Ingredients

- 1/2 cup minced onion
- 1/2 cup peanut oil
- 1/3 cup rice wine vinegar
- 2 tablespoons water
- 2 tablespoons minced fresh ginger root
- 2 tablespoons minced celery
- 2 tablespoons ketchup
- 4 teaspoons soy sauce
- 2 teaspoons white sugar
- 2 teaspoons lemon juice
- 1/2 teaspoon minced garlic
- 1/2 teaspoon salt
- 1/4 teaspoon ground black pepper

Direction

- Blend pepper, salt, garlic, lemon juice, sugar, soy sauce, ketchup, celery, ginger, water, rice vinegar, peanut oil and minced onion on high speed for 30 seconds till all ingredients are pureed well in blender.

Nutrition Information

- Calories: 82 calories;
- Total Fat: 7.7
- Sodium: 314
- Total Carbohydrate: 3.3
- Cholesterol: 0
- Protein: 0.2

144. Ginger Spiced Cucumbers

Serving: 4 | Prep: 45mins | Cook: | Ready in:

Ingredients

- 1/8 cup red wine vinegar
- 1/4 cup mirin (Japanese sweet wine)
- 1/8 cup packed brown sugar
- 3 teaspoons grated fresh ginger
- 1/8 cup fresh lime juice
- 1 large cucumber, thinly sliced
- 1/4 cup thinly sliced onion

Direction

- Combine lime juice, ginger, brown sugar, mirin, and red wine vinegar in a serving bowl. Add onion and cucumber, and mix lightly to blend. Refrigerate for 30 minutes for the flavors to blend before eating.

Nutrition Information

- Calories: 80 calories;
- Protein: 0.7
- Total Fat: 0.1
- Sodium: 4
- Total Carbohydrate: 16.4
- Cholesterol: 0

145. Glo's Sausage Fried Rice

Serving: 8 | Prep: 20mins | Cook: 20mins | Ready in:

Ingredients

- 1 pound ground pork sausage
- 5 eggs, beaten
- 3 tablespoons vegetable oil
- 1/2 head cabbage, cored and shredded
- 3 carrots, chopped
- 6 cups cooked white rice, cold
- 1/4 cup soy sauce, or to taste
- 1 (14.5 ounce) can bean sprouts, drained
- 1 (6 ounce) package frozen green peas, thawed
- ground black pepper to taste
- 3 green onions, chopped

Direction

- Over medium-high heat, cook sausage in a skillet until browned evenly. Then drain and remove the sausage from the pan. Into the same pan, scramble eggs while stirring often in the remaining coating of grease from sausage until cooked through. Reserve.
- Over medium-high heat, heat oil in an electric skillet or a very large skillet. Then stir fry carrots and cabbage until cabbage is wilted. Pour in cold rice and then fry while stirring to prevent clumps. Stir in sausage and add some soy sauce. Mix in eggs, peas, and bean sprouts. Combine well to prevent big chunks of egg. Add pepper to season and then mix in green onions before taking out from the heat. Adjust soy sauce to taste before serving.

Nutrition Information

- Calories: 540 calories;
- Protein: 17.3
- Total Fat: 31.7
- Sodium: 943
- Total Carbohydrate: 46.4
- Cholesterol: 155

146. Goya Champuru (Bitter Melon Stir Fry)

Serving: 4 | Prep: 10mins | Cook: 21mins | Ready in:

Ingredients

- 2 Asian bitter melon (goya)
- kosher salt as needed
- 2 tablespoons sesame oil
- 1 (1 pound) pork loin, cut into pieces
- 1 pinch garlic salt, or to taste
- 1 pinch garlic pepper, or to taste
- 2 eggs
- 1 tablespoon soy sauce, or to taste

Direction

- Use a sharp knife to slice the tip off the melons; halve lengthwise. Scoop out the seeds and white interior using a spoon; rinse melon then slice into very small portions. Put in a bowl then mix with a generous amount of kosher salt until completely covered; cover then chill for around 5 mins until the flavors blend.
- Rinse the melon to get rid of the excess salt. Put into a pot filled with water then boil while covering. Cook for about a minute until the melon is slightly soft. Take off the heat then drain.
- On medium-high heat, heat sesame oil in a skillet then put in pork. Sprinkle garlic pepper and garlic salt to season. Cook and stir for 7-10 mins until the pork is not pink anymore; put in melon. Cook for approximately 5 mins until soft.
- Turn to medium heat. Using a spatula, push the pork mixture to the edges of the skillet. Crack eggs into the middle of the skillet then scramble for 3-5 mins until firm. Mix the contents of the skillet together until blended. Add soy sauce to season.

Nutrition Information

- Calories: 259 calories;
- Sodium: 539
- Total Carbohydrate: 4.5
- Cholesterol: 147
- Protein: 24
- Total Fat: 15.8

147. Green Tea Kasutera (Green Tea Bread)

Serving: 6 | Prep: 15mins | Cook: 50mins | Ready in:

Ingredients

- 2/3 cup white sugar
- 4 eggs, separated
- 2 tablespoons grapeseed oil
- 2 tablespoons honey
- 2 tablespoons milk
- 1 cup all-purpose flour
- 2 teaspoons green tea powder (matcha)

Direction

- Preheat the oven to 160°C or 320°Fahrenheit. Oil lightly a small loaf pan.
- In a bowl, whisk egg whites and sugar with an electric mixer until it forms into stiff peaks. Mix in egg yolk, stir well. Into the egg mixture, mix milk, honey, and grapeseed oil.
- In a bowl, sift green tea powder and flour two times; stir in the egg mixture. Move batter to the greased pan.
- Bake for approximately 50 mins in the preheated oven until an inserted toothpick in the middle comes out clean.

Nutrition Information

- Calories: 274 calories;
- Sodium: 50
- Total Carbohydrate: 44.5

- Cholesterol: 124
- Protein: 6.6
- Total Fat: 8.2

148. Green Tea Mousse Cheesecake

Serving: 12 | Prep: 20mins | Cook: 1mins | Ready in:

Ingredients

- 1 (4.8 ounce) package graham crackers, crushed
- 2 tablespoons white sugar
- 3 tablespoons unsalted butter, melted
- 2 tablespoons green tea powder (matcha)
- 1/2 cup warm water
- 2 tablespoons unflavored gelatin
- 1/2 cup cold water
- 2 cups whipping cream
- 2 (8 ounce) packages cream cheese, at room temperature
- 1/2 cup white sugar
- 1 teaspoon vanilla extract
- 1/4 cup honey
- 2 eggs

Direction

- In a mixing bowl, mix 2 tbsp. sugar and graham cracker crumbs; stir in melted butter until moistened evenly. Press the mixture in a 9-in springform pan lined with waxed paper; set it aside.
- Mix tea powder into warm water; set aside. Scatter gelatin on top of cold water; set it aside.
- Beat the cream until it forms into stiff peaks, put aside. In a clean mixing bowl, mix honey, cream cheese, vanilla, and a half cup sugar. Stir in one egg at a time until well combined. Microwave the gelatin mixture for 45 secs, or until it melts. Mix the tea and gelatin into the cream cheese mixture; mix in whipped cream until the mixture is smooth. Move to the springform pan. Chill for 7 hrs to overnight. Unmold then serve.

Nutrition Information

- Calories: 417 calories;
- Total Fat: 32.6
- Sodium: 207
- Total Carbohydrate: 27.4
- Cholesterol: 134
- Protein: 5.7

149. Green Tea Muffins

Serving: 12 | Prep: 10mins | Cook: 25mins | Ready in:

Ingredients

- 1 2/3 cups all-purpose flour
- 1/2 teaspoon salt
- 1 teaspoon baking powder
- 1 tablespoon matcha green tea powder, or to taste
- 1/2 cup white sugar
- 1 egg
- 1/3 cup melted butter
- 1 cup milk
- 1/4 cup chopped walnuts (optional)

Direction

- Preheat the oven to 175°C or 350°F. Grease or put paper muffin liners on twelve muffin cups.
- In a mixing bowl, mix sugar, flour, matcha, salt, and baking powder; set aside. In a separate bowl, beat milk, melted butter, and egg; mix into the flour mixture until moistened. Fold in walnuts. Split the batter between the prepared muffin cups.
- Bake for 25 mins in the preheated oven, or until the tops bounce back when pressed lightly and the muffin is golden. Cool for 5 mins in the tin then move onto a wire rack to cool completely.

Nutrition Information

- Calories: 174 calories;
- Total Fat: 7.7
- Sodium: 189
- Total Carbohydrate: 23.1
- Cholesterol: 31
- Protein: 3.5

150. Gyoza (Japanese Potstickers)

Serving: 6 | Prep: 40mins | Cook: 14mins | Ready in:

Ingredients

- 1/2 pound ground pork
- 1/2 head napa cabbage, shredded
- 1 egg
- 3 green onions, thinly sliced
- 1 (2 inch) piece fresh ginger, grated
- 1 tablespoon soy sauce
- 1 teaspoon sriracha sauce, or more to taste
- 1 small clove garlic, minced
- 1/4 teaspoon sesame oil
- 30 gyoza wrappers, or as needed
- 1 tablespoon vegetable oil, or as needed
- 1 cup water
- Dipping Sauce:
- 2 tablespoons soy sauce
- 2 tablespoons seasoned rice vinegar
- 1 1/2 teaspoons sesame oil
- 1 dash sriracha sauce, or to taste

Direction

- In a bowl, mix together 1 teaspoon of sriracha sauce, egg, ginger, garlic, ground pork, 1 tablespoon of soy sauce, napa cabbage, 1/4 teaspoon of sesame oil and green onions.
- On a flat work surface, put the gyoza wrappers. Fill the center of each of the gyoza wrappers with 1 teaspoon of the pork mixture. Brush or use your finger to moisten the edges of the gyoza wrapper. Fold up the gyoza wrapper sides so that it is shaped in a semicircle, then pinch the edges together to seal.
- In a heavy skillet, put the oil and let it heat up over medium-high heat setting. Put in 12-15 pieces of the prepared gyoza and let it cook in the skillet for about 2 minutes until the bottom of each gyoza turns golden brown in color. Add 1/2 cup of water, then cover the skillet and allow the gyoza to cook for 5-7 minutes until the gyoza has absorbed the water. Place the cooked gyoza onto a plate. Do the same procedure with the rest of the uncooked gyoza.
- For the dipping sauce, combine 1 1/2 teaspoons of sesame oil, 2 tablespoons of soy sauce, 1 dash of sriracha sauce and rice vinegar. Serve the gyoza with the prepared dipping sauce on the side.

Nutrition Information

- Calories: 253 calories;
- Cholesterol: 59
- Protein: 12.8
- Total Fat: 10.6
- Sodium: 764
- Total Carbohydrate: 26.2

151. Hiyashi Chuka Noodles

Serving: 2 | Prep: 15mins | Cook: 5mins | Ready in:

Ingredients

- 3 tablespoons soy sauce
- 2 tablespoons white sugar
- 3 tablespoons white vinegar
- 5 tablespoons chicken stock
- 1 teaspoon sesame oil
- 1/2 teaspoon chili oil (optional)
- 2 (3 ounce) packages ramen noodles

- 1 egg, beaten
- 1/2 cucumber, julienned
- 1 carrot, grated
- 1 slice cooked ham, cut into thin strips
- 1/4 sheet nori, cut into thin slices
- 1 tablespoon hot Chinese mustard (optional)

Direction

- In a small bowl, mix chili oil, sesame oil, chicken stock, vinegar, sugar and soy sauce till sugar melts. Put aside.
- Boil water in a saucepan. Add ramen noodles. Cook for 2 minutes. Immediately drain. Keep noodles in fridge till cold. Meanwhile on medium heat, heat a small nonstick skillet. Put beaten egg in. Tilt pan to coat bottom thinly with egg. Fold egg in half when firm. Take out of pan. Cut to thin strips.
- Serving: Put cold noodles onto serving plates. Put ham, carrot, cucumber and egg in separate piles on top. Put sauce on top. Sprinkle crumbled nori. Serve with a bit of hot mustard on the side.

Nutrition Information

- Calories: 236 calories;
- Sodium: 2093
- Total Carbohydrate: 28.5
- Cholesterol: 101
- Protein: 9.3
- Total Fat: 10

152. Home Rice

Serving: 4 | Prep: 10mins | Cook: 30mins | Ready in:

Ingredients

- 1 cup uncooked white rice
- 2 cups water
- 1/2 cup diced carrots
- 1/2 cup diced onion
- 4 tablespoons butter or margarine, divided
- 4 eggs
- 2 tablespoons milk
- 1 cup ketchup
- salt and pepper to taste

Direction

- In a small saucepan, combine water and rice, and bring to a boil. Cover the saucepan, lower heat to low and simmer until tender, about 15-20 minutes.
- In a large skillet, melt 1 tablespoon butter over medium heat. Put in onion and carrots. Cook, stirring often, for about 5 minutes until onions are softened and lightly browned. Put in cooked rice and mix until well combined. Stir in the remaining butter. Turn heat down to medium-low, and mix in ketchup. Simmer the mixture for about 5 minutes to allow flavors to blend. Then turn the heat off.
- Beat milk and eggs in a small bowl. Heat a nonstick skillet over medium heat. Add 1/2 egg mixture. Cook until set, flipping over once halfway through. Take out of the skillet, and cut in half. Repeat the process with the remaining eggs.
- For each portion, put a scoop of rice on a plate, and shape into a flattened log. Put one of egg halves on top. You can add pepper, salt, and ketchup on top of the eggs when serving.

Nutrition Information

- Calories: 431 calories;
- Total Carbohydrate: 58.5
- Cholesterol: 217
- Protein: 11.8
- Total Fat: 17.3
- Sodium: 837

153. Homemade Japanese Curry

Serving: 8 | Prep: 50mins | Cook: 1hours10mins | Ready in:

Ingredients

- Curry Powder:
- 4 teaspoons coriander seeds
- 1 tablespoon fenugreek seeds
- 2 1/2 teaspoons cumin seeds
- 1 1/2 teaspoons green cardamom pods
- 1/4 teaspoon fennel seeds
- 1/2 teaspoon whole cloves
- 1/8 teaspoon ground star anise
- 1/8 teaspoon cinnamon stick
- 5 teaspoons ground turmeric
- 1/2 teaspoon white peppercorns
- 1/2 teaspoon black peppercorns
- 1/8 teaspoon ground allspice
- 1/8 teaspoon ground nutmeg
- Curry Paste:
- 3/4 cup butter
- 3/4 cup all-purpose flour
- 3 tablespoons Worcestershire sauce
- 3 tablespoons tomato paste
- 1/2 cup butter
- 2 large white onions, minced
- 2 pounds boneless, skinless chicken breasts, cut into 1-inch cubes
- 2 tablespoons minced garlic
- 1 teaspoon grated fresh ginger root
- 1 tablespoon soy sauce
- 1 teaspoon salt
- 6 cups chicken broth
- 2 cubes beef bouillon
- 8 carrots, peeled and cut into 1-inch cubes
- 4 potatoes, peeled and cut into 1-inch cubes, or more to taste
- 3 green bell peppers, cut into 1-inch cubes
- 2 Gala apples, peeled and grated

Direction

- In a large skillet, combine fennel seeds, cardamom pods, cumin seeds, fenugreek seeds, and coriander seeds on a low heat, toasting for 1 - 2 minutes until light gold. Add in the cinnamon sticks, star anise, and cloves, then toast for 1 - 2 minutes until fragrant. Remove the seeds from the cardamom pods and place back into the skillet, throwing away the pods.
- Transfer the toasted spice mixture into a blender or spice grinder. Add in nutmeg, allspice, black peppercorns, white peppercorns, and turmeric, then, grind into a fine curry powder.
- In a saucepan, melt 3/4 cup butter on medium heat, and whisk in the flour, cooking for 30 - 45 seconds until golden brown. Stir in tomato paste, Worcestershire sauce, and 4 tablespoons curry powder, then, take away from heat.
- In a large pot, melt 1/2 cup butter on low heat and add onions, cooking while stirring for 30 - 45 minutes until it turns golden brown. Turn the heat to high and add salt, soy sauce, ginger, garlic, chicken, and 2 tablespoons curry powder. Sauté for about 5 minutes until chicken is brown. Add bouillon cubes and chicken broth, then, bring to boil.
- Stir carrots into pot for about 5 minutes until soft. Add in the potatoes and cook for about 5 minutes until tender. Stir in apples and green bell peppers, for about 10 minutes until they turn soft. Stir in the curry paste and let it simmer for about 5 minutes until the sauce is thickened and the flavors have combined.

Nutrition Information

- Calories: 599 calories;
- Total Fat: 32.3
- Sodium: 1045
- Total Carbohydrate: 51.3
- Cholesterol: 135
- Protein: 28.7

154. Homemade Pickled Ginger (Gari)

Serving: 32 | Prep: 40mins | Cook: 5mins | Ready in:

Ingredients

- 8 ounces fresh young ginger root, peeled
- 1 1/2 teaspoons sea salt
- 1 cup rice vinegar
- 1/3 cup white sugar

Direction

- Cut the ginger into chunks; transfer them to a bowl. Use sea salt to sprinkle; toss until coated and let sit for half an hour. Prepare a clean jar and put the ginger in.
- Combine sugar and rice vinegar in a saucepan; stir to dissolve the sugar. Cook until it boils; transfer the boiling liquid to the jar with ginger root pieces.
- Let cool. Cover the jar with lid and put into the refrigerator to store for at least 1 week. The liquid will change into slight pink color in a few minutes due to the reaction of quality rice vinegar. The commercial pickled ginger will have red coloring added. Slice pieces of ginger into paper thin slices to serve.

Nutrition Information

- Calories: 14 calories;
- Total Carbohydrate: 3.3
- Cholesterol: 0
- Protein: 0.1
- Total Fat: 0.1
- Sodium: 83

155. Hoshi Shiitake Dashi

Serving: 4 | Prep: 5mins | Cook: 5mins | Ready in:

Ingredients

- 4 cups water
- 4 dried shiitake mushrooms

Direction

- In a saucepan, combine the water and mushrooms; let sit 10 minutes. Next, bring to a boil; remove from heat, let sit for another 20 minutes. Through a mesh strainer, filter the mixture before using.

Nutrition Information

- Calories: 11 calories;
- Total Carbohydrate: 2.7
- Cholesterol: 0
- Protein: 0.3
- Total Fat: 0
- Sodium: 8

156. Japanese Agedashi Deep Fried Tofu

Serving: 2 | Prep: 20mins | Cook: 20mins | Ready in:

Ingredients

- 1 (12 ounce) package medium-firm silken tofu
- vegetable oil for deep frying, or as needed
- 3 tablespoons potato starch
- Sauce:
- 2 tablespoons water
- 2 teaspoons potato starch
- 2 tablespoons sake
- 1 tablespoon soy sauce
- 1 tablespoon mirin (Japanese sweet wine)
- 1 tablespoon fish stock, or to taste
- 1 teaspoon salt
- 1/4 carrot, cut into matchsticks
- 3 dried shiitake mushrooms, sliced into long, thin strips, or more to taste
- 1/2 Welsh onion (shironegi), cut into matchsticks
- 1 (1 inch) piece fresh ginger, grated, or to taste

Direction

- Slice tofu into squares. Put on a microwave-safe plate and cover using paper towel. Microwave for 3 to 4 minutes till moisture is vaporized.
- In a big saucepan, heat vegetable oil over medium-high heat. Generously coat tofu squares with potato starch. In hot oil, fry for 3 to 5 minutes each side till golden brown. Put in a bowl.
- In a bowl, combine 2 teaspoons potato starch and water to create the thickening agent.
- In a saucepan, mix fish stock, mirin, soy sauce and sake over medium-high heat. Boil; put mushrooms and carrots. Cook and mix for about 5 minutes till carrots are soft. Mix in thickening agent. Let cook and mix for about 2 minutes longer till flavors incorporate and sauce is thickened.
- Put sauce on top of tofu. Put ginger and Welsh onion on top.

Nutrition Information

- Calories: 268 calories;
- Cholesterol: 0
- Protein: 13.2
- Total Fat: 10.2
- Sodium: 1708
- Total Carbohydrate: 25.8

---

157. Japanese Beef Rolls

Serving: 8 | Prep: 30mins | Cook: 10mins | Ready in:

Ingredients

- 1 tablespoon vegetable oil
- 12 shiitake mushrooms, sliced
- 24 spears fresh asparagus, trimmed
- 8 thin-cut top round steaks
- 1/4 cup soy sauce
- 1 bunch green onions, green parts only

Direction

- On medium heat, heat oil in a pan; put in mushrooms then cover. On low heat, let the mushrooms sweat until soft but avoid browning. In the meantime, boil water in a big pot or pan. Put the asparagus in a strainer then blanch in boiling water for half a minute, or until bright green; place in ice water to stop cooking. Set it aside.
- Place an oven rack approximately six inches from heat; preheat the broiler. Oil a broiling pan.
- To make the rolls, lay out the steaks flat. Pound the thick steaks until a quarter-inch thick. Slather soy sauce over the steak; add a couple of green onions and some mushrooms then three spears of asparagus at one end of every steak. Roll up to enclose towards the opposite end then secure with a toothpick. Arrange rolls on the broiling pan with the seam-side down.
- Roast for 3 mins in the preheated oven, or until the tops are brown. Turn then roast for 2-3 mins longer, or until the other side is brown. Do not overcook since it can burn or toughen the steak.

Nutrition Information

- Calories: 689 calories;
- Sodium: 583
- Total Carbohydrate: 5.9
- Cholesterol: 242
- Protein: 95.1
- Total Fat: 29.1

---

158. Japanese Beef Tongue Stir Fry

Serving: 4 | Prep: 15mins | Cook: 13mins | Ready in:

Ingredients

- 1 tablespoon salt, or as needed
- 1/2 pound beef tongue, very thinly sliced
- 1 1/2 teaspoons sesame oil, or as needed
- 2 cloves garlic, sliced
- 2 cups sliced spring onions
- 1 tablespoon sake (Japanese rice wine)
- 1/2 teaspoon dashi powder
- salt and ground black pepper to taste

Direction

- Rub a tablespoon of salt all over the beef tongue then put on a plate; let it sit for 5 mins for the flavors to meld.
- Boil water in a pot; submerge beef tongue for half a minute into boiling water using a slotted spoon. Take it out then drain the surplus water; move to a plate.
- On medium heat, heat sesame oil in a pan. Cook and stir garlic in hot oil for 1-2 mins, or until aromatic; mix in onions. Cook and stir for 2-3 mins, or until the onions are soft; put in beef tongue. Pour in additional sesame oil if necessary. Cook and stir for 3 mins, or until the beef tongue is brown.
- Mix in pepper, sake, salt, and dashi powder; let it simmer for 2-3 mins, or until the flavors meld.

Nutrition Information

- Calories: 141 calories;
- Sodium: 1777
- Total Carbohydrate: 4.7
- Cholesterol: 47
- Protein: 7.9
- Total Fat: 9.8

159. Japanese Deviled Eggs

Serving: 18 | Prep: 20mins | Cook: 20mins | Ready in:

Ingredients

- 9 eggs
- 2 tablespoons sesame seeds
- 1/2 cup mayonnaise
- 2 teaspoons soy sauce
- 2 teaspoons wasabi paste
- 2 teaspoons rice wine vinegar
- 2 tablespoons thinly sliced green onions
- 4 tablespoons panko bread crumbs

Direction

- In a saucepan, put eggs and cover with water. Boil it, take away from heat, and let eggs stay in hot water for 15 minutes. Take the eggs out of the hot water and put under cold running water to cool down. Remove the shells.
- In a dry frying pan, put sesame seeds, stir and cook over medium heat for 3 minutes until turning slightly brown. Move to a paper towel lined on a dish to cool down.
- Slice the eggs into two lengthwise. In a food processor with rice vinegar, wasabi paste, soy sauce, mayonnaise, put the egg yolks. Blend until smooth; add panko bread crumbs and green onion to the yolk mixture and pulse just enough to blend evenly.
- On a serving dish, put the egg white halves and put the yolk mixture in each white. Use toasted sesame seeds to drizzle.

Nutrition Information

- Calories: 91 calories;
- Cholesterol: 95
- Protein: 3.6
- Total Fat: 7.9
- Sodium: 122
- Total Carbohydrate: 2.1

160. Japanese Egg Yolk Sauce

Serving: 12 | Prep: 10mins | Cook: | Ready in:

Ingredients

- 3 egg yolks
- 1/2 teaspoon lemon juice
- 2 1/2 tablespoons white miso paste
- 1 cup vegetable oil
- salt to taste
- 1 pinch freshly ground white pepper
- 1/4 teaspoon grated yuzu (Japanese orange), lemon or lime peel

Direction

- Using a wooden spoon, whisk lemon juice and egg yolks in a medium bowl. Mix in vegetable oil, a few drops at a time, until the mixture starts to emulsify, mix well after every addition. Once all the oil is fully blended, mix in grated yuzu, miso, white pepper, and salt. Chill in a squeeze bottle for convenient application.

Nutrition Information

- Calories: 181 calories;
- Total Fat: 19.5
- Sodium: 137
- Total Carbohydrate: 1.2
- Cholesterol: 51
- Protein: 1.1

161. Japanese Fruitcake

Serving: 12 | Prep: 20mins | Cook: 25mins | Ready in:

Ingredients

- 1 cup all-purpose flour
- 1 pound raisins
- 1 cup butter
- 2 cups white sugar
- 6 eggs, separated
- 3 cups all-purpose flour
- 4 teaspoons baking powder
- 2 teaspoons ground cinnamon
- 1 teaspoon ground cloves
- 1 teaspoon ground nutmeg
- 1 cup milk
- 1 cup flaked coconut
- 1 cup chopped pecans
- 2 cups white sugar
- 1 1/2 cups hot water
- 4 teaspoons all-purpose flour
- 1 lemon -- peeled, seeded and minced
- 2 large orange, peeled, sectioned, and cut into bite-size
- 1 pound flaked coconut
- 1 cup pecan halves
- 1 cup maraschino cherries, halved

Direction

- In 1 cup flour, dredge raisins.
- Preheat oven to 175 degrees C/350 degrees F. Butter then flour 2 9-in. round pans.
- Mix nutmeg, clove, cinnamon, baking powder and flour.
- Cream sugar and margarine or butter in a big bowl. Add egg yolks. Beat it until smooth. In parts, stir in flour mixture alternately with the milk. Mix in raisins, pecans and coconut.
- Beat egg whites in a clean bowl to form stiff peaks. Fold in batter. Put batter in prepped pans.
- Bake until done for 25 minutes. Cool the layers on top of wire racks.
- Mix orange, lemon, flour, water and sugar in a medium saucepan. Cook until thick on medium heat. Mix in coconut. Cook for two minutes. Cool then ice cake. Alternate maraschino cherries and pecan halves on top of the cake to create a pinwheel.

Nutrition Information

- Calories: 1077 calories;
- Cholesterol: 135
- Protein: 13
- Total Fat: 44.4
- Sodium: 446
- Total Carbohydrate: 166.7

162. Japanese Ginger Pork

Serving: 4 | Prep: 10mins | Cook: 10mins | Ready in:

Ingredients

- 1 tablespoon grated fresh ginger root
- 2 tablespoons soy sauce
- 2 tablespoons sake
- 2 tablespoons mirin
- 1 pound thinly sliced pork loin
- 3 tablespoons vegetable oil

Direction

- Combine mirin, ginger, sake, and soy sauce together in a big bowl; add sliced pork. Marinate for an hour while covered.
- On high heat, heat oil in a wok or pan; fry in pork until it turns brown and has a dark crispy appearance. Do not cook the pork on medium or low heat or the juices won't be cooked quick enough to have a crispy texture. Get rid of the remaining marinade.

Nutrition Information

- Calories: 289 calories;
- Sodium: 491
- Total Carbohydrate: 3.6
- Cholesterol: 55
- Protein: 18.8
- Total Fat: 20.1

163. Japanese Green Tea Petits Fours

Serving: 12 | Prep: 30mins | Cook: 1hours | Ready in:

Ingredients

- 2 eggs
- 3 egg yolks
- 6 tablespoons white sugar
- 1/3 cup cake flour
- 2 tablespoons cornstarch
- 1 tablespoon powdered green tea
- 2 egg whites
- 1/8 teaspoon cream of tartar
- 2 tablespoons white sugar
- 1 cup heavy cream
- 2 teaspoons powdered green tea
- 4 teaspoons superfine sugar
- 6 tablespoons almond paste
- 1 teaspoon powdered green tea
- confectioners' sugar for dusting

Direction

- Preheat the oven to 230°C or 450°Fahrenheit. Oil an 11-in by 7-in. pan then put parchment paper on the bottom. Grease the parchment paper then flour. Sift a tablespoon of green tea, cornstarch, and flour together; set aside.
- Whisk 6 tbsp. sugar, yolks, and eggs in a bog bowl for 5 mins, or until it triples in volume; stir in flour mixture. Beat cream of tartar and egg whites in a metal mixing bowl or big glass until foamy. Put in 2 tbsp. sugar while continuously whisking until it forms into stiff peaks. Stir 1/3 of whites into the batter then stir in the rest of the whites quickly until there are no streaks. Spread batter over the prepared pan.
- Bake for 8-10 mins in the preheated oven, or until the middle of the cake bounces back when pressed lightly. Sprinkle confectioners' sugar over then turn to a flat surface. Cool.
- Prepare the Green Tea Whipped Cream. Beat 2 tsp. green tea, 4 tsp. superfine sugar, and heavy cream in a medium bowl until it forms into stiff peaks.
- Prepare the Decorative Green Tea Marzipan. Knead 1 tsp. green tea with almond paste; roll the mixture out between two plastic wrap sheets or roll with a light dust of confectioners' sugar.
- Once cool, get rid of the parchment paper from the base of the cake. Slice the cake horizontally downward the center to form 2

layers. Slather half of the whipped cream on the bottom layer then top with the cake layer; slather the remaining whipped cream on top. With decorative cutters or a knife, slice the assembled cake into twelve portions. Roll the marzipan out then slice into twelve portions to fit the cake shapes. Top the cake with the decorative marzipan pieces.

Nutrition Information

- Calories: 185 calories;
- Total Fat: 11.2
- Sodium: 32
- Total Carbohydrate: 18.3
- Cholesterol: 109
- Protein: 3.8

164. Japanese Gyudon (Beef Bowl)

Serving: 8 | Prep: 15mins | Cook: 42mins | Ready in:

Ingredients

- 4 cups Japanese sushi-style rice
- 1 1/3 cups dashi soup
- 5 tablespoons soy sauce
- 3 tablespoons mirin
- 2 tablespoons white sugar
- 1 teaspoon sake
- 1 onion, thinly sliced
- 1 pound thinly sliced beef sirloin, cut into 2-inch pieces

Direction

- In a saucepan, boil rice and water. Lower the heat to medium-low, put on the cover, and let it simmer for 20 to 25 minutes till rice is soft and liquid has been soaked in.
- In a big saucepan, mix sake, sugar, mirin, soy sauce and dashi on medium heat. Boil. Put in the onion; let it simmer for 6 to 8 minutes till softened. Put in the beef; let it simmer for approximately an additional of 6 minutes till not pink anymore.
- Among deep individual rice bowls, split hot rice equally. Put the mixture of simmered beef on top.

Nutrition Information

- Calories: 478 calories;
- Total Carbohydrate: 87.5
- Cholesterol: 25
- Protein: 18.2
- Total Fat: 4.1
- Sodium: 647

165. Japanese Minced Beef

Serving: 4 | Prep: 10mins | Cook: 6mins | Ready in:

Ingredients

- 3/4 pound ground beef
- 2 tablespoons freshly grated ginger
- 3 tablespoons soy sauce
- 3 tablespoons sake (Japanese rice wine)
- 2 tablespoons mirin (Japanese sweet wine)
- 1 tablespoon white sugar, or more to taste

Direction

- Heat the skillet on medium heat; cook and whisk the beef for 5-7 minutes or till thoroughly cooked. Put in the ginger and whisk them well. Whisk the sugar, mirin, sake and soy sauce into the beef mixture; boil and cook for 60 seconds longer.

Nutrition Information

- Calories: 232 calories;
- Cholesterol: 52
- Protein: 14.9
- Total Fat: 13.2

- Sodium: 726
- Total Carbohydrate: 7.4

166. Japanese Miso Glazed Cod

Serving: 6 | Prep: 10mins | Cook: 10mins | Ready in:

Ingredients

- 6 (6 ounce) fillets black cod, bones removed
- 1/3 cup white miso paste
- 1/4 cup dark brown sugar
- 2 tablespoons mirin (Japanese sweet wine)
- 1 teaspoon toasted sesame oil
- sesame seeds, for garnish (optional)
- scallions, chopped (optional)
- 1 teaspoon toasted sesame oil

Direction

- Wash fish fillets and pat dry using paper towels. In a bowl, mix sesame oil, mirin, brown sugar and miso. Mix well till dissolves completely brown sugar.
- Add cod into a baking sheet and brush on each fillet about 2 tbsp. of miso glaze. Let it marinate for half an hour to one hour.
- Place an oven rack about 6 in. away from the heat source and preheat the oven's broiler.
- Add fish under broiler till chars the top a bit and caramelizes the glaze for 3 to 4 minutes. Take fish out of oven and use leftover glaze to brush. Lower oven temperature to 190 degrees C (375 degrees F). Cook for 5 - 6 minutes longer till fish is flaky yet not overcooked.
- Drizzle with toasted sesame seeds and scallions prior to serving.

Nutrition Information

- Calories: 246 calories;
- Total Carbohydrate: 16.9
- Cholesterol: 62

- Total Fat: 4.6
- Protein: 32
- Sodium: 541

167. Japanese Okonomiyaki

Serving: 4 | Prep: 15mins | Cook: 30mins | Ready in:

Ingredients

- 12 ounces sliced bacon
- 1 1/3 cups water
- 4 eggs
- 3 cups all-purpose flour
- 1 teaspoon salt
- 1 medium head cabbage, cored and sliced
- 2 tablespoons minced pickled ginger
- 1/4 cup tonkatsu sauce or barbeque sauce

Direction

- On medium heat, fry bacon in a big pan until slightly crispy. Drain on paper towels then set aside.
- Whisk eggs and water together in a big bowl; stir in salt and flour gradually until smooth. Mix in ginger and cabbage until evenly blended.
- On medium heat, heat a pan then grease with cooking spray. Add a quarter of the batter in the middle of the pan; put four cooked bacon slices in the middle. Form the pancake into a circle using a spatula. Fry for 5 mins, or until dry on the edges. Turn, cook the other side until stable in the middle and both sides are brown. Take it out of the pan then drizzle tonkatsu sauce over to serve. Repeat with the rest of the bacon and batter.

Nutrition Information

- Calories: 659 calories;
- Cholesterol: 217
- Protein: 29.3

- Total Fat: 19.4
- Sodium: 1531
- Total Carbohydrate: 90.7

168. Japanese Onion Soup

Serving: 6 | Prep: 15mins | Cook: 45mins | Ready in:

Ingredients

- 1/2 stalk celery, chopped
- 1 small onion, chopped
- 1/2 carrot, chopped
- 1 teaspoon grated fresh ginger root
- 1/4 teaspoon minced fresh garlic
- 2 tablespoons chicken stock
- 3 teaspoons beef bouillon granules
- 1 cup chopped fresh shiitake mushrooms
- 2 quarts water
- 1 cup baby portobello mushrooms, sliced
- 1 tablespoon minced fresh chives

Direction

- Mix a few of the mushrooms, celery, garlic, onion, ginger, and carrot in a big stockpot or saucepan. Add water, beef bouillon, and chicken stock; let it come to a rolling boil on high heat. Cover once boiling then turn to medium heat; cook for 45 mins.
- Put all the rest of the mushrooms into another pot. Put a strainer on top of the mushroom pot once the boiling mixture is done. Strain the cooked soup into the mushroom pot; get rid of the strained materials.
- In small porcelain bowls, serve the broth along with mushrooms and sprinkle on top with fresh chives. To make it more elegant, Asian soup spoons.

Nutrition Information

- Calories: 25 calories;
- Sodium: 257
- Total Carbohydrate: 4.4
- Cholesterol: < 1
- Protein: 1.4
- Total Fat: 0.2

169. Japanese Pan Noodles

Serving: 4 | Prep: 25mins | Cook: 25mins | Ready in:

Ingredients

- 1 (10 ounce) package fresh udon noodles
- 1/2 teaspoon sesame oil, divided, or to taste
- 2 cups chopped broccoli
- 1/2 green bell pepper, cut into matchsticks
- 2 small carrots, cut into matchsticks, or to taste
- 1/2 zucchini, thinly sliced
- 2 tablespoons soy sauce
- 2 tablespoons mirin (Japanese sweet wine)
- 1 tablespoon chili-garlic sauce
- 3/4 teaspoon minced ginger

Direction

- Heat lightly salted water to boil in a large pot and add udon. Cook udon in boiling water while stirring often for 10 to 12 minutes until the noodles become tender but still firm to the bite. Drain the noodles and then rinse in cold water. Mix in some drops of sesame oil.
- Over medium heat, heat remaining sesame oil in a large skillet and then cook the broccoli for about 5 minutes until crunchy and bright green. Add carrots and green bell pepper. Cook while stirring for about 2 minutes until softened slightly. Place in zucchini and then cook for about 2 minutes more until softened slightly. Add ginger, chili-garlic sauce, mirin and soy sauce. Mix to blend. Stir in the noodles and then cook while stirring for 1 to 2 minutes more until the noodles absorb some of the sauce.

Nutrition Information

- Calories: 258 calories;
- Protein: 7.2
- Total Fat: 1.8
- Sodium: 1069
- Total Carbohydrate: 50.4
- Cholesterol: 0

170. Japanese Restaurant Cucumber Salad

Serving: 4 | Prep: 15mins | Cook: | Ready in:

Ingredients

- 2 tablespoons white sugar
- 2 tablespoons rice vinegar
- 1 teaspoon Asian (toasted) sesame oil
- 1 teaspoon chili paste (sambal oelek)
- salt to taste
- 2 large cucumbers - peeled, seeded, and cut into 1/4-inch slices

Direction

- In a bowl, combine salt, chile paste, sesame oil, rice vinegar, and sugar. Add cucumbers and mix to combine. Let the salad marinate for 30 minutes before eating at room temperature.

Nutrition Information

- Calories: 55 calories;
- Total Fat: 1.6
- Sodium: 14
- Total Carbohydrate: 10.5
- Cholesterol: 0
- Protein: 0.8

171. Japanese Scrambled Eggs With Pacific Saury

Serving: 2 | Prep: 5mins | Cook: 5mins | Ready in:

Ingredients

- 1/2 cup water
- 1 (5 ounce) can grilled Pacific saury
- 1 tablespoon mirin (sweet cooking rice wine)
- 1 tablespoon soy sauce, or more to taste
- 2 eggs, beaten
- 2 tablespoons chopped scallion

Direction

- Boil water in a pan; add soy sauce, mirin, and saury. Boil again then pour in beaten eggs slowly while mixing thoroughly. Cook for 2-3 mins, or until set and firm; add scallion on top.

Nutrition Information

- Calories: 266 calories;
- Total Fat: 16.2
- Sodium: 1000
- Total Carbohydrate: 10.1
- Cholesterol: 186
- Protein: 18.3

172. Japanese Spinach With Sweet Sesame Seeds

Serving: 6 | Prep: 5mins | Cook: 2mins | Ready in:

Ingredients

- 2 tablespoons sesame oil
- 1 tablespoon brown sugar
- 10 cups fresh spinach leaves
- 4 tablespoons black sesame seeds, toasted

Direction

- Over medium heat, heat sesame oil in a large skillet until it's hot. Place in spinach about 3 to 4 cups at a time. Then cook while stirring to wilt and add more spinach.
- Use a pestle and mortar to grind the sesame seeds into fine crumbs. Once spinach wilts, push it to the sides of pan and drizzle sugar in the middle. Once sugar melts, mix in spinach to coat.
- Place the spinach onto a serving plate and top with a drizzle of ground sesame seeds.

Nutrition Information

- Calories: 101 calories;
- Total Carbohydrate: 6.7
- Cholesterol: 0
- Protein: 3.4
- Total Fat: 7.9
- Sodium: 66

173. Japanese Tamago Egg

Serving: 6 | Prep: 15mins | Cook: 10mins | Ready in:

Ingredients

- 4 eggs
- 1/4 cup prepared dashi stock
- 1 tablespoon white sugar
- 1 teaspoon mirin (Japanese sweet wine)
- 1/2 teaspoon soy sauce
- 1/2 teaspoon vegetable oil, or more as needed

Direction

- In a bowl, whisk eggs well; mix in soy sauce, mirin, sugar and dashi stock till sugar has dissolve.
- Over medium heat, set an omelet pan or nonstick skillet. With vegetable oil, oil the pan. Into the hot pan, add a thin layer of the egg mixture and swirl to cover pan.
- Once egg layer is set on base yet remain lightly liquid on surface, using a spatula, pull approximately an-inch of omelet edge up and fold corner on top of the rest of egg layer; keep rolling omelet to end and move roll to corner of skillet. Oil skillet once more in case it seems dry; into the skillet, put one more thin egg layer and pull the roll up to allow the egg to stream beneath omelet roll. Fold omelet roll on top of the fresh layer of egg, proceeding to roll to last as earlier. Move the omelet to corner of skillet.
- Into the skillet, put a fresh egg layer, oiling pan if necessary. Turn omelet over to combine the following egg layer into roll. Put fresh layers and roll into omelet till the entire egg mixture has been used. Transfer omelet onto serving platter and slice into 6 even portions to serve.

Nutrition Information

- Calories: 63 calories;
- Sodium: 87
- Total Carbohydrate: 2.6
- Cholesterol: 124
- Protein: 4.4
- Total Fat: 3.8

174. Japanese Tofu Salad

Serving: 4 | Prep: 35mins | Cook: 5mins | Ready in:

Ingredients

- 1 (14 ounce) package firm tofu, drained
- 3 tablespoons soy sauce
- 1 tablespoon mirin (sweetened rice wine)
- 2 teaspoons sesame oil, or to taste
- 1 tablespoon rice vinegar
- 2 tablespoons vegetable oil
- 2 cloves garlic, minced
- 1 teaspoon minced fresh ginger
- 1 large tomato, seeded and chopped

- 1 small red onion, thinly sliced
- 1/4 cup chopped cilantro
- 1 tablespoon sesame seeds

Direction

- Put the tofu between two plates, and use a heavy book to weigh it down. Let the tofu drain for 1 hour, draining out the expelled liquid every 20 minutes. Mix rice vinegar, sesame oil, mirin, and the soy sauce in a small bowl. Put the oil in a small pan over medium heat, stir in the ginger and garlic, and cautiously cook until lightly golden; mix into the soy sauce mixture. Slice tofu into bite-sized portions, and toss with the cilantro, onion, and tomato. Add in the dressing and toss to coat. Dust with sesame seeds to decorate.

Nutrition Information

- Calories: 272 calories;
- Protein: 17.6
- Total Fat: 19.1
- Sodium: 695
- Total Carbohydrate: 11
- Cholesterol: 0

175. Japanese Style Deep Fried Chicken

Serving: 8 | Prep: 20mins | Cook: 20mins | Ready in:

Ingredients

- 2 eggs, lightly beaten
- 1/2 teaspoon salt
- 1/2 teaspoon black pepper
- 1/2 teaspoon white sugar
- 1 tablespoon minced garlic
- 1 tablespoon grated fresh ginger root
- 1 tablespoon sesame oil
- 1 tablespoon soy sauce
- 1/8 teaspoon chicken bouillon granules
- 1 1/2 pounds skinless, boneless chicken breast halves - cut into 1 inch cubes
- 3 tablespoons potato starch
- 1 tablespoon rice flour
- oil for frying

Direction

- Mix together bouillon, soy sauce, sesame oil, ginger, garlic, sugar, pepper, salt and eggs in big bowl. Add chicken pieces; mix to coat then cover the bowl. Refrigerate for 30 minutes.
- Take bowl out of fridge. Add rice flour and potato starch to meat; stir well.
- Heat oil to 185°C or 365°F in a deep fryer or big skillet. Put chicken in hot oil; fry till golden brown. Working in batches, cook meat to maintain oil temperature. Place on paper towels, briefly drain; serve hot.

Nutrition Information

- Calories: 256 calories;
- Total Fat: 16.7
- Sodium: 327
- Total Carbohydrate: 4.8
- Cholesterol: 98
- Protein: 20.9

176. Japanese Style Sesame Green Beans

Serving: 4 | Prep: 5mins | Cook: 15mins | Ready in:

Ingredients

- 1 tablespoon canola oil
- 1 1/2 teaspoons sesame oil
- 1 pound fresh green beans, washed
- 1 tablespoon soy sauce
- 1 tablespoon toasted sesame seeds

Direction

- Heat a large pan or wok on medium heat. Add sesame and canola oils once the pan is hot. Stir in whole green beans and cook until they are well coated with oil. Continue cooking for 10 minutes until turned bright green and slightly browned in spots. Turn off heat and add soy sauce; stir. Cover pan and allow to stand for 5 minutes. Transfer to a serving dish. Sprinkle with toasted sesame seeds on top.

Nutrition Information

- Calories: 97 calories;
- Total Carbohydrate: 8.9
- Cholesterol: 0
- Protein: 2.7
- Total Fat: 6.6
- Sodium: 233

177. Juicy Chicken

Serving: 5 | Prep: 20mins | Cook: 10mins | Ready in:

Ingredients

- 1/2 cup soy sauce
- 1/2 cup sherry or white cooking wine
- 1/2 cup chicken broth
- 1/4 teaspoon ground ginger
- 1 pinch garlic powder
- 1 bunch green onions, chopped
- 1 pound skinless, boneless chicken breast halves - cut into 2 inch pieces

Direction

- Mix green onions, garlic powder, ginger, chicken broth, sherry and soy sauce in a small saucepan. Heat to boil and then remove from heat immediately. Reserve.
- Preheat an oven's broiler. Then thread pieces of chicken onto bamboo or metal skewers. Spread on a broiler pan greased with cooking spray. Ladle about 1 or 2 tablespoons of sauce atop each chicken skewer.
- Put pan under the broiler and then broil for around 3 minutes until turned browned. Take out from oven, flip over and ladle some more sauce atop each one. Place back into the oven until the chicken is nicely browned and cooked through.

Nutrition Information

- Calories: 152 calories;
- Sodium: 1653
- Total Carbohydrate: 9.2
- Cholesterol: 53
- Protein: 23.5
- Total Fat: 1.2

178. Kasutera (Castella), The Japanese Traditional Honey Cake

Serving: 6 | Prep: 30mins | Cook: 50mins | Ready in:

Ingredients

- 1 teaspoon butter, softened, or as needed
- 1 1/3 cups superfine sugar
- 5 tablespoons honey, divided
- 3 1/3 fluid ounces milk
- 8 eggs
- 1 1/3 cups superfine sugar
- 1 5/8 cups all-purpose flour, sifted twice
- sweet bean paste (optional)

Direction

- Preheat the oven to 190°C or 375°Fahrenheit. Put parchment paper in a cake pan; spread butter on the paper then dust with a teaspoon of superfine sugar.
- Boil water in a pot then move to a big bowl.
- In a bowl, beat together milk and a quarter cup of honey until smooth.

- In a bowl set on top of hot water, use an electric mixer to beat eggs. Beat in 1 1/3 cup superfine sugar gradually until the mixture is warm and smooth. Take the bowl away from hot water; cool for 5 mins to room temperature. Place the egg mixture bowl back over the hot water then beat continuously. Repeat for a couple of times until the batter is thick and foamy.
- With a spatula, mix the milk mixture into egg mixture; mix in sifted flour until combined. Move batter to the prepared cake pan.
- Bake for 50 mins in the preheated oven, or until an inserted skewer in the middle of the cake comes out without residue. Slather remaining 1 tablespoon of honey over the cake's top. If desired, serve slices of cake with ice cream and sweet bean paste.

Nutrition Information

- Calories: 710 calories;
- Cholesterol: 251
- Protein: 14.7
- Total Fat: 8.1
- Sodium: 108
- Total Carbohydrate: 148.5

179. Kimchi Goya Champuru

Serving: 2 | Prep: 20mins | Cook: 6mins | Ready in:

Ingredients

- 1 bitter melon, seeded and thinly sliced
- 8 ounces deep-fried tofu, cut into bite-sized pieces
- 1/2 (12 ounce) can fully cooked luncheon meat (such as SPAM®), cut into bite-sized pieces
- 1/3 cup kimchi
- 1/3 mochi rice cake
- 2 eggs
- 2 tablespoons mayonnaise
- 1 1/2 teaspoons sesame oil
- 1 1/2 teaspoons soy sauce
- 1 teaspoon chicken stock powder

Direction

- Prepare salt water in a bowl and soak bitter melon in it for 5 minutes. Drain water.
- In a separate microwave-safe bowl, mix drained bitter melon, luncheon meat, tofu, mochi, and kimchi.
- In another bowl, mix eggs, soy sauce, sesame oil, mayonnaise, and chicken stock powder and whisk together. Pour the cream mixture on the bitter melon mixture. Use a microwave-safe cover to cover the bowl.
- Pop the bowl in the microwave for 6 minutes at 600W until eggs are completely set. Stir before serving.

Nutrition Information

- Calories: 811 calories;
- Protein: 38.9
- Total Fat: 65.2
- Sodium: 1898
- Total Carbohydrate: 24.4
- Cholesterol: 229

180. Kiyoko's Miso Sauce

Serving: 4 | Prep: 5mins | Cook: 15mins | Ready in:

Ingredients

- 5 tablespoons mirin (Japanese sweet wine)
- 3 tablespoons red miso paste
- 1 egg yolk
- 1 1/4 tablespoons cooking sake

Direction

- In a pot, mix sake, mirin, egg yolk, and miso paste well; boil while constantly mixing. Turn to low heat; let it simmer for 10-15 mins while constantly mixing, or until the sauce is jam-like.

Nutrition Information

- Calories: 87 calories;
- Cholesterol: 51
- Protein: 2.3
- Total Fat: 1.9
- Sodium: 487
- Total Carbohydrate: 9.7

181. Lucy's Quick Tonkatsu Sauce

Serving: 4 | Prep: 5mins | Cook: 1mins | Ready in:

Ingredients

- 1/2 cup ketchup
- 2 1/2 tablespoons reduced-sodium soy sauce
- 2 1/2 tablespoons Worcestershire sauce
- 1 1/2 tablespoons dry sherry
- 1 1/2 tablespoons white sugar
- 1/2 teaspoon garlic powder
- 1/2 teaspoon ground ginger

Direction

- In a microwave-safe mug or glass measuring cup, mix soy sauce, Worcestershire sauce, sherry, sugar, ketchup, garlic powder, and ginger. Stir mixture well with a fork. Microwave on high for 60 seconds. Stir mixture again. Set aside to cool.
- Let mixture sit for 60 minutes to allow flavors to fully combine together.

Nutrition Information

- Calories: 67 calories;
- Total Fat: 0.1
- Sodium: 771
- Total Carbohydrate: 15.6

- Cholesterol: 0
- Protein: 1.1

182. Manju (Japanese Sweet Bean Paste Cookies)

Serving: 50 | Prep: 45mins | Cook: 15mins | Ready in:

Ingredients

- 2 cups white sugar
- 1 cup butter, softened
- 4 eggs
- 1 teaspoon vanilla extract
- 5 cups all-purpose flour
- 2 tablespoons baking powder
- 1 (18 ounce) can koshi an (sweetened red bean paste)
- 1/4 cup evaporated milk, or as needed

Direction

- Preheat the oven to 190°C or 375°Fahrenheit. Oil two baking sheets lightly.
- In a big bowl, beat butter and sugar using an electric mixer until creamy and smooth. Whisk into the creamed butter with one egg at a time until smooth; beat in vanilla extract and whisk well.
- In a bowl, sift together baking powder and flour; mix flour into the butter mixture gradually, stirring well after each addition until smooth.
- Flour your hands generously. Form into walnut-sized dough balls then press into 4-in circles on a floured surface; the center of the circles should be thicker while the edges are thinner. Scoop around 1 1/2 tsp. koshi an in the middle of each circle. Gather together the edges of the dough then pinch around the filling until sealed. Arrange the dough balls on the greased baking sheets with the pinched-side down about 2-in apart from each other. Brush evaporated milk over the dough balls.

- Bake for approximately 15 mins in the preheated oven until light brown on top.

Nutrition Information

- Calories: 141 calories;
- Total Fat: 4.3
- Sodium: 114
- Total Carbohydrate: 23.4
- Cholesterol: 25
- Protein: 2.3

183. Marshmallow Cake

Serving: 24 | Prep: | Cook: | Ready in:

Ingredients

- 1/2 cup shortening
- 1 1/2 cups white sugar
- 1/2 cup milk
- 2 cups all-purpose flour
- 3 teaspoons baking powder
- 4 egg whites
- 1/4 teaspoon cream of tartar
- 1/8 teaspoon salt
- 1 teaspoon vanilla extract

Direction

- Set oven temperature to 350 degrees F (175 degrees C) and leave aside to preheat. Prepare 2 layer cake trays measuring 9 inches by greasing lightly.
- Cream shortening while adding sugar in small amounts.
- Sift flour, cream of tartar, baking powder, and salt by sifting. Alternate milk and flour mixture while combining with the creamed mixture.
- Beat egg whites until there is a formation of firm peaks. Incorporate vanilla and the beaten egg whites into the cake batter by folding them in. Fill the prepared pans with the batter.

- Bake for 30 minutes at 350 degrees F (175 degrees C).

Nutrition Information

- Calories: 130 calories;
- Sodium: 85
- Total Carbohydrate: 20.9
- Cholesterol: < 1
- Protein: 1.9
- Total Fat: 4.5

184. Marvel's Japanese Fried Oysters (Kaki Fuh Rai) With Lemony Tartar Sauce

Serving: 6 | Prep: 15mins | Cook: 10mins | Ready in:

Ingredients

- 1 cup mayonnaise
- 1/2 lemon, juiced and zested
- 1/4 dill pickle spear, seeded and minced
- 1/4 teaspoon cayenne pepper
- 1 cup panko (Japanese bread crumbs)
- 1/8 teaspoon cayenne pepper
- salt and ground black pepper to taste
- 2 cups canola oil
- 6 shucked oysters, or more if desired
- 1 egg, beaten

Direction

- For preheating, set the oven at 250 degrees Fahrenheit or 120 degrees Celsius.
- Tartar sauce: In a small bowl, stir together 1/4 tsp cayenne pepper, dill pickle, lemon zest, lemon juice, and mayonnaise until thoroughly combined, and set aside.
- In a shallow bowl, mix black pepper, salt, 1/8 tsp cayenne pepper, and panko crumbs.
- In a deep-fryer or saucepan, heat canola oil to 360 degrees Fahrenheit or 180 degrees Celsius.

For accuracy, measure the temperature with a deep frying thermometer.
- Dip oyster onto the beaten egg and press into the panko mixture to coat. Toss gently between your hands for the bread crumbs that aren't stuck would fall away. Place breaded oysters on a plate while breading the others, but do not stack.
- Cook oysters, 2 each time, into hot oil for about 1 minute per side until panko turns brown. Transfer fried oysters onto a baking sheet that is lined with paper towels. Place in oven to keep warm while you fry the remaining oysters. Serve along with the tartar sauce for dipping.

Nutrition Information

- Calories: 465 calories;
- Cholesterol: 77
- Protein: 6.8
- Total Fat: 42.8
- Sodium: 487
- Total Carbohydrate: 19.3

185. Matcha Green Tea Ice Latte

Serving: 3 | Prep: 5mins | Cook: | Ready in:

Ingredients

- 1 teaspoon green tea powder (matcha)
- 2 1/2 cups hot water
- 1/2 cup 2% milk
- 4 teaspoons honey

Direction

- In a bowl, whisk milk, water and green tea powder together. Add honey to sweeten then keep whisking to dissolve honey into the tea. Store in the fridge to chill completely. Pour over ice to serve.

Nutrition Information

- Calories: 52 calories;
- Total Fat: 0.8
- Sodium: 23
- Total Carbohydrate: 10.3
- Cholesterol: 3
- Protein: 1.5

186. Michelle's Chicken Yakitori

Serving: 4 | Prep: 25mins | Cook: 10mins | Ready in:

Ingredients

- 1/2 cup soy sauce
- 1/2 cup sake (Japanese rice wine)
- 1 tablespoon white sugar
- 1 tablespoon chopped fresh ginger
- 1 1/2 pounds skinless, boneless chicken breasts, cut into 24 cubes
- 4 green onions, cut into 2-inch pieces
- 8 (6-inch) wooden skewers, soaked in cold water for 2 hours

Direction

- In a bowl, combine ginger, soy sauce, sugar, and sake; put in chicken cubes then toss to coat. Refrigerate for 2-3hrs to marinate.
- Thread green onions and chicken cubes on the skewers.
- On medium heat, simmer marinade in a small pot. Turn to low heat and keep warm.
- Set the outdoor grill on medium-high heat to preheat; grease the grate lightly. Grill skewers for 3mins until the chicken is brown. Turn then brush with warm marinade. Cook for around another 3mins until the other side is brown.

Nutrition Information

- Calories: 263 calories;
- Sodium: 1891
- Total Carbohydrate: 8.4
- Cholesterol: 97
- Protein: 37.8
- Total Fat: 4.1

187. Miso Salmon

Serving: 6 | Prep: 20mins | Cook: 30mins | Ready in:

Ingredients

- 2 (1 1/2-pound) salmon fillets, skin removed
- 1 cup miso paste
- 1/4 cup sake
- 1/2 cup brown sugar
- 2 tablespoons sesame seeds
- 1 teaspoon sesame oil
- 1/4 cup water
- 1/2 cup prepared soy-ginger salad dressing
- 3 tablespoons seasoned rice vinegar

Direction

- Preheat oven to 200°C or 400°Fahrenheit. Boil an inch of water in a big skillet. Poach fish for approximately 2 mins on each side until the outside is cooked; move to a broiler pan.
- Combine rice vinegar, miso paste, salad dressing, sake, water, brown sugar, sesame oil, and sesame seeds in a small bowl; spread on top of the salmon fillets.
- Bake in the preheated oven for 15 mins or until nearly cooked through; turn the oven to broil. Broil for around another 5 mins until bubbly and brown on top. Slice fillet into pieces then serve.

Nutrition Information

- Calories: 719 calories;
- Total Fat: 40.5
- Sodium: 2247
- Total Carbohydrate: 34.9
- Cholesterol: 132
- Protein: 50.5

188. Miso Salmon (Sake Misozuke) With Spinach Sauce

Serving: 4 | Prep: 30mins | Cook: 25mins | Ready in:

Ingredients

- 1 1/2 pounds salmon fillet, cut into 4 portions
- 5 teaspoons salt
- 1 cup white miso paste
- 1/4 cup sake
- 1/4 cup mirin (Japanese sweet wine)
- 1/4 pound spinach leaves
- 1 tablespoon water, or as needed
- 1/2 cup white miso paste
- 1 tablespoon white sugar
- 2 egg yolks
- 2 tablespoons sake

Direction

- Sprinkle salt onto the salmon fillets to taste. Cover the seasoned salmon fillets and keep it in the fridge for 1 hour.
- Wipe any excess salt off the salmon fillets and use 2 layers of cheesecloth to wrap the salmon fillets. In a bowl, combine 1/4 cup of sake, mirin and 1 cup of miso. Spread over wrapped salmon fillets on both sides with the prepared miso mixture. In an airtight container, put in the salmon and keep it in the fridge for a minimum of 5 hours or overnight.
- Fill a small saucepan with water and let it heat up over medium-high heat setting. Put in the spinach and allow it to cook for 1-2 minutes until the spinach becomes wilted. Use a colander to drain the cooked spinach and let it cool down. Use a food processor to process the cooled-down spinach until it is smooth in

consistency, put in additional water in case the spinach gets too dry. Put it aside.
- In the top layer of a double boiler, combine the egg yolks, 2 tablespoons of sake and the remaining 1/2 cup of miso with sugar and let it cook over barely simmering water while stirring the mixture often and scraping down the sides using a rubber spatula until it is thick in consistency. Put it aside and let it cool down, then add the pureed spinach and mix everything together.
- Preheat the broiler on your oven and place the oven rack about 6 inches away from the source of heat. Coat a baking sheet with a little bit of oil. Unwrap the cheesecloth around the salmon fillets and scrape off excess miso mixture from the fillets. On the prepared baking sheet, put in the salmon fillets.
- Put it in the preheated oven and let it broil for about 4 minutes until the salmon fillets turn golden. Turn over the salmon fillet and brush with the prepared spinach sauce. Keep broiling the salmon fillets for about 4 more minutes until you could flake the fish easily using a fork and the fillets have been thoroughly cooked.

Nutrition Information

- Calories: 555 calories;
- Cholesterol: 197
- Protein: 48.1
- Total Fat: 19.3
- Sodium: 6852
- Total Carbohydrate: 37.6

189. Miso Soup With Shiitake Mushrooms

Serving: 4 | Prep: 10mins | Cook: 10mins | Ready in:

Ingredients

- 4 cups vegetable broth
- 4 shiitake mushrooms, thinly sliced
- 1/4 cup miso paste
- 4 teaspoons soy sauce
- 1/3 cup diced firm tofu
- 2 green onions, trimmed and thinly sliced

Direction

- Boil vegetable broth in a pot; put in mushrooms. Turn to low heat then simmer for 4 mins. In a small bowl, mix soy sauce and miso paste together; pour into the broth then add tofu. Cook continuously for another minute. Ladle soup in bowls then add green onions on top to serve.

Nutrition Information

- Calories: 92 calories;
- Total Fat: 2.5
- Sodium: 1406
- Total Carbohydrate: 11.8
- Cholesterol: 0
- Protein: 5.5

190. Miso And Soy Chilean Sea Bass

Serving: 4 | Prep: 10mins | Cook: 7mins | Ready in:

Ingredients

- 1/3 cup sake
- 1/3 cup mirin (Japanese sweet rice wine)
- 3 tablespoons soy sauce
- 1/4 cup packed brown sugar
- 1/3 cup miso paste
- 4 (4 ounce) fillets fresh sea bass, about 1 inch thick
- 2 tablespoons chopped green onion

Direction

- Prepare the marinade mixture by mixing together the soy sauce, sake, miso paste, mirin

and brown sugar in a bowl. In a big sealable plastic bag, put the sea bass then add in the prepared marinade mixture on top. Keep it in the fridge for 3-6 hours until chilled. Put the marinated sea bass fillets onto a baking sheet and throw away the marinade mixture.
- Preheat the broiler on your oven and place the oven rack about 6 inches away from the source of heat. Prop the door of the oven to keep ajar slightly.
- Put it under the oven broiler and bake for 7-9 minutes until you could flake the fish easily using a fork. Garnish the broiled sea bass with sprinkled chopped green onions and serve.

Nutrition Information

- Calories: 287 calories;
- Total Fat: 3.7
- Sodium: 1613
- Total Carbohydrate: 27.9
- Cholesterol: 47
- Protein: 24.7

191. Mizu Shingen Mochi With Strawberry Compote

Serving: 4 | Prep: 10mins | Cook: 16mins | Ready in:

Ingredients

- Mizu Shingen Mochi:
- 3/4 cup hot water
- 2 tablespoons white sugar
- 1 1/2 teaspoons agar-agar powder
- Strawberry Compote:
- 1/4 cup white sugar
- 1/4 cup water
- 1/4 teaspoon arrowroot powder
- 1 pound fresh strawberries, cut into quarters
- 1 lemon, zested and juiced

Direction

- In a saucepan, mix agar-agar, 2 tablespoons sugar and 3/4 cup of hot water. Heat to a low boil. Cook while stirring for 3 to 5 minutes until agar-agar and sugar are dissolved. Transfer the mochi mixture to a spherical mold and chill for 6 to 12 hours until set.
- Over medium heat, combine together 1/4 cup water and 1/4 cup of white sugar in a saucepan. Cook while stirring for 2 to 4 minutes until the sugar has dissolved. Stir in arrowroot for about 1 minute until dissolved. Add lemon juice, lemon zest and strawberries. Cook while stirring for 5 to 10 minutes on medium-low heat until the strawberries begin to release their juice and have soften. Place the strawberry compote in a storage container and let cool to lukewarm temperature. Put in the fridge for about 30 minutes until chilled.
- Put mochi in a serving dish and sprinkle strawberry compote on top of it.

Nutrition Information

- Calories: 116 calories;
- Sodium: 4
- Total Carbohydrate: 30.9
- Cholesterol: 0
- Protein: 1.1
- Total Fat: 0.4

192. My Fly Stir Fry

Serving: 4 | Prep: 20mins | Cook: 15mins | Ready in:

Ingredients

- 4 center cut pork chops, thinly sliced
- 1/4 cup mirin (Japanese sweet wine)
- 1/4 cup rice vinegar
- 1/2 cup soy sauce
- 1/2 cup mushrooms, sliced
- 1 green bell pepper, sliced
- 1 bunch green onions
- 1 clove garlic, minced

- 1 tablespoon minced fresh ginger root
- 1 tablespoon sesame oil

Direction

- Cut the pork as thin as possible. Slightly frozen chops are easier to slice. Combine soy sauce, pork, rice vinegar, and mirin in a medium bowl; cover. Chill to marinate as you prepare the rest of the ingredients.
- Chip the green part of the onions, green pepper, and mushrooms; set aside. Mince the ginger, garlic, and white part of the green onions.
- On medium heat, heat a big pan or wok; use sesame oil to coat. Sauté minced ginger, garlic, and green onion until aromatic. Turn to high heat. Press the marinade off the pork then place into the wok. Save the marinade. Cook and stir for 4 mins, or until the pork is not pink anymore. Mix in sliced green onion, green pepper, and mushrooms. Cook and stir for 4 mins, or until the veggies are tender. Mix in the reserved marinade; cook for 2 mins.

Nutrition Information

- Calories: 287 calories;
- Sodium: 1869
- Total Carbohydrate: 14.1
- Cholesterol: 76
- Protein: 28.2
- Total Fat: 11.5

193. Nigiri Sushi

Serving: 4 | Prep: 1hours | Cook: 35mins | Ready in:

Ingredients

- 4 cups water
- 2 cups uncooked white rice
- 1/2 cup seasoned rice vinegar
- 1 teaspoon white sugar, or as needed
- 1 teaspoon salt, or as needed
- 1/4 pound hamachi (yellowtail)
- 1/4 pound maguro (tuna)
- 1/4 pound cooked Ebi (shrimp), shelled and butterflied
- 6 eggs
- 1/2 teaspoon white sugar
- 1/8 teaspoon salt
- 1 teaspoon wasabi paste (optional)
- 1 sheet nori, cut into 1-inch strips

Direction

- On high heat, boil rice and water in a pot. Turn to medium-low heat; let it simmer for 20-25 mins, covered, or until the liquid is absorbed and the rice is tender; move to a bowl. Use a wooden spoon or rice paddles to cut in the rice vinegar. Sprinkle a teaspoon each of salt and sugar to season to taste. Cool rice for half an hour to room temperature.
- Thinly slice the fish across the grain to 2x10-in. portions to prepare it for wrapping. Chill until use.
- In a bowl, mix a quarter teaspoon salt, half teaspoon sugar, and eggs together. On medium heat, put a quarter of the mixture in a thin layer in a big greased pan. Cook for 2-3 mins without mixing or until completely cooked. Roll the egg like a log then put in one corner of the pan. Repeat with a quarter of the egg mixture then roll again to make a new log, to make one big log. Diagonally cut the omelette to half-in. thick portions.
- Hold a piece of shrimp or fish in your hands then lightly slather with wasabi paste if you wish. Grasp 1-2 tbsp. rice then roll in your hand to make a small nugget; put over the shrimp or fish then press gently to stick it. Set it aside while forming the rest of the shrimp or fish pieces.
- Hold one egg omelette slice in your hand, slather 1-2 tbsp. rice, then roll in your hand to make a small nugget; press over the egg gently to stick it.
- Wrap one nori strip around each; seal to join by moistening 1 end of each nori strip.

Nutrition Information

- Calories: 557 calories;
- Cholesterol: 351
- Protein: 35
- Total Fat: 10.3
- Sodium: 861
- Total Carbohydrate: 77.1

194. Nona's Tableside Homemade Soft Tofu

Serving: 4 | Prep: 15mins | Cook: 10mins | Ready in:

Ingredients

- 1 1/4 cups dried soybeans
- 14 fluid ounces water
- 1 1/2 teaspoons liquid nigari

Direction

- Put dry beans in water then soak for at least 12 hrs; drain. You should have 14-oz. soaked beans.
- In a bigger bowl, put a colander then cover the colander with a cotton towel or a few cheesecloth layers. Process 14 fluid oz. water and the beans in a blender; boil them in a non-stick pot while frequently mixing. Turn to low heat once boiling; let it simmer for 3 mins while stirring.
- In the lined colander, transfer the soybean mixture. Join the edges together then twist solids into a ball to squeeze the liquid out. You can use a can to assist in pressing out the soy milk. You need to have three cups or 24 fluid oz. of soy milk. You can add more hot water to the okara or soybean solids until you have the target amount.
- Heat soymilk in a pot until 75-80°C or 170-175°Fahrenheit.
- Prepare a container on a table that is 4-in. deep and 4- to 6-in. wide for making the tofu. Any container that is large enough to contain the milk is okay but it will be harder to form the tofu if it's too big.
- Gauge the nigari first in the container at the table; add the hot soy milk. You don't need to mix it since it will stir enough to make the tofu as you pour the liquid. Leave it for 3-5 mins to form the tofu. Serve right away or chill for future use.

Nutrition Information

- Calories: 259 calories;
- Protein: 21.2
- Total Fat: 11.6
- Sodium: 4
- Total Carbohydrate: 17.5
- Cholesterol: 0

195. Okonomiyaki (Japanese Pancake)

Serving: 4 | Prep: 25mins | Cook: 12mins | Ready in:

Ingredients

- 1 cup all-purpose flour
- 2/3 cup water
- 4 cups chopped cabbage
- 6 strips cooked bacon, crumbled
- 2 eggs
- 1 sausage, diced, or more to taste (optional)
- 1/2 cup chopped green onions
- 1/4 cup cooked shrimp (optional)
- 1/4 cup shredded cheese (optional)
- 1/4 cup tenkasu (tempura pearls)
- 1 tablespoon vegetable oil, or to taste
- Toppings:
- 2 tablespoons soy sauce
- 1 tablespoon ketchup
- 1 teaspoon white vinegar

- 1 tablespoon panko bread crumbs, or to taste
- 1 teaspoon mayonnaise, or to taste

Direction

- In a bowl, combine water and flour together until smooth; mix in tenkasu, cabbage, cheese, bacon, shrimp, eggs, green onions, and sausage.
- Preheat the griddle to 200°C or 400°Fahrenheit; grease with oil. Pour in dry mixture in the form of a pancake. Cook for 6 mins on each side, or until golden brown; move to a serving plate.
- In a small bowl, make the okonomiyaki sauce by mixing vinegar, ketchup, and soy sauce together; dribble all over the pancake. Add mayonnaise and panko on top.

Nutrition Information

- Calories: 507 calories;
- Total Carbohydrate: 33.8
- Cholesterol: 164
- Protein: 27.9
- Total Fat: 28.9
- Sodium: 1641

196. Okura And Sakura Shrimp Japanese Style Spaghetti

Serving: 2 | Prep: 10mins | Cook: 24mins | Ready in:

Ingredients

- 1 (7 ounce) package spaghetti
- 2 tablespoons olive oil, divided
- 1 red bell pepper, seeded and chopped
- 8 pods okra, cut into bite-sized pieces
- 2 tablespoons soy sauce
- 1 tablespoon sake
- 1 tablespoon mirin (Japanese sweet rice wine)
- 2 ounces sakura (cherry) shrimp

Direction

- Cook spaghetti in a big pot of boiling and lightly salted water for 12 mins while mixing from time to time, or until tender but firm to chew; drain. Save 3 tbsp. of the cooking water.
- On medium-low heat, heat a tablespoon of olive oil in a pan; add red bell pepper. Cook and stir for 5 mins, or until soft. Mix in mirin, okra, sake, and soy sauce; cook for a minute.
- Mix leftover 1 tbsp. olive oil, reserved cooking water, and spaghetti in the pan; stir in 1/2 of the shrimp then cook for a minute.
- Move the spaghetti mixture to a bowl then top with the rest of the shrimp.

Nutrition Information

- Calories: 578 calories;
- Total Fat: 15.5
- Sodium: 962
- Total Carbohydrate: 85.1
- Cholesterol: 42
- Protein: 20.1

197. Onigiri (Japanese Rice Balls)

Serving: 6 | Prep: 20mins | Cook: 25mins | Ready in:

Ingredients

- 2 cups water
- 1 cup jasmine rice
- salt
- 1 sheet nori (dry seaweed), cut into 1-inch strips, or as desired (optional)

Direction

- Mix a pinch of salt, rice, and two cups of water in a pot, boil; turn to medium-low then cover. Let it simmer for 20-25 mins, or until the liquid is absorbed and the rice is tender, mix from time to time to avoid rice sticking. Use a fork

- to fluff the rice then cool for 10 mins, or until easily handled.
- Pour water in a small bowl until full. Put 2 tbsp. salt in a separate small bowl.
- Submerge your hands in water then pat your hands in salt. Form a handful of warm rice into a ball then squish it gently using your hands to make a "C" or "L" form. Put gently pressure on the sides to form a triangle.
- Use a nori strip to wrap around the triangle, moisten with water if needed to help it adhere.

Nutrition Information

- Calories: 114 calories;
- Total Carbohydrate: 25.6
- Cholesterol: 0
- Protein: 2.2
- Total Fat: 0
- Sodium: 28

198. Orange Ponzu

Serving: 8 | Prep: 30mins | Cook: 5mins | Ready in:

Ingredients

- 1/4 cup soy sauce
- 1/2 cup rice vinegar
- 2 tablespoons bonito shavings (dry fish flakes)
- 1 (1 inch) square konbu (kelp)
- 1 orange, quartered

Direction

- Mix together orange quarters, konbu, bonito shavings, rice vinegar and soy sauce in a saucepan. Allow to stand for a half hour.
- Bring to a boil. Once it begins to boil, take away from the heat. Let it cool, then strain a sieve lined with cheesecloth.

Nutrition Information

- Calories: 15 calories;
- Sodium: 452
- Total Carbohydrate: 3.1
- Cholesterol: 0
- Protein: 0.8
- Total Fat: 0

199. Oyako Donburi

Serving: 4 | Prep: 20mins | Cook: 20mins | Ready in:

Ingredients

- 1 tablespoon vegetable oil
- 3/4 pound skinless, boneless chicken breast halves - cut into strips
- 1/2 onion, thinly sliced
- 1 cup chicken broth
- 6 dried shiitake mushrooms, soaked until soft, then sliced into strips
- 1 carrot, julienned
- 2 tablespoons white sugar
- 4 tablespoons soy sauce
- 1/2 teaspoon salt
- 1/2 cup chopped green onions
- 5 eggs, beaten

Direction

- In a big skillet set on medium-high heat, add oil. Stir-fry onion and chicken strips for approximately 5-7 minutes until chicken is cooked well. Strain off as much liquid as you can.
- Mix in chicken broth, and simmer for 2 minutes. Add the carrot and mushrooms and allow it to simmer for several minutes prior to stirring in the salt, soy sauce, and sugar. Simmer for 3 minutes longer. Add in half of green onions, stirring cautiously. Drop beaten eggs on chicken mixture, and simmer for approximately 10 minutes until the eggs are cooked well. Then pour on Japanese sticky rice to serve.

Nutrition Information

- Calories: 278 calories;
- Protein: 29.6
- Total Fat: 10.8
- Sodium: 1349
- Total Carbohydrate: 15.7
- Cholesterol: 282

200. Oyakodon (Japanese Chicken And Egg Rice Bowl)

Serving: 4 | Prep: 15mins | Cook: 25mins | Ready in:

Ingredients

- 2 cups uncooked jasmine rice
- 4 cups water
- 4 skinless, boneless chicken thighs, cut into small pieces
- 1 onion, cut in half and sliced
- 2 cups dashi stock, made with dashi powder
- 1/4 cup soy sauce
- 3 tablespoons mirin (Japanese rice wine)
- 3 tablespoons brown sugar
- 4 eggs

Direction

- Rinse rice in water 3 to 4 times until the water is almost clear. Drain rinse water off. In a pot, boil the rice and 4 cups water over high heat. Lower heat to medium-low, put on cover, and let simmer for 20 to 25 minutes or until rice is tender and the rice has absorbed the liquid.
- Use a nonstick skillet with a lid to stir and cook the chicken over medium heat for 5 minutes or until the chicken turns brown and is not pink in the center. Add the onion and stir for 5 minutes or until the onion is tender. Pour the stock in, and whisk in mirin, soy sauce, and brown sugar. Stir until sugar is dissolved. Heat to a boil. Simmer the mixture for 10 minutes until reduced slightly.
- Beat eggs in a separate bowl until beaten well. Pour on chicken and stock. For 5 minutes, cover the pan, decrease heat, and let the chicken steam until the egg is cooked. Remove skillet from heat.
- Place 1 cup of cooked rice into 4 separate bowls. Put 1/4 of the chicken and egg mixture on top of each. Add about 1/2 cup of soup into each bowl. Serve.

Nutrition Information

- Calories: 688 calories;
- Sodium: 1226
- Total Carbohydrate: 97.9
- Cholesterol: 208
- Protein: 35.3
- Total Fat: 14.6

201. Pan Roasted Beef Tenderloin With Ginger Shiitake Brown Butter

Serving: 4 | Prep: 25mins | Cook: 20mins | Ready in:

Ingredients

- 2 tablespoons olive oil
- 4 (8 ounce) beef tenderloin filets
- Kosher salt and freshly ground black pepper, to taste
- 3 tablespoons unsalted butter
- 2 tablespoons minced fresh ginger
- 1 tablespoon minced fresh garlic
- 1/2 cup thinly sliced fresh shiitake mushrooms
- 3 tablespoons sake
- 2 tablespoons mirin (sweetened rice wine)
- 1 tablespoon finely chopped garlic chives
- 3/4 cup unsalted butter

Direction

- Preheat oven to 200 °C or 400 °F.

- Over high heat, heat olive oil in a big ovenproof skillet until smoking lightly. Use pepper and salt to season filets to taste. Sear both sides for about 3 minutes per side until golden brown. Put into oven and cook for about 12 minutes for medium-rare to desired doneness. Once done, let it rest for 5 minutes out of the pan.
- Meanwhile, over medium-high heat, melt 3 tablespoons of butter in a saucepan. Stir garlic and ginger in. Cook for about 1 1/2 minutes until aromatic and translucent but not browned. Put shiitake mushrooms and cook until softened for 3 to 4 minutes. Put in mirin and sake. Allow to simmer until reduced by half. Melt the leftover 3/4 cup of butter, then, turn heat to medium-low. Cook for 6 to 8 minutes until the butter browns. Once done, add pepper and salt to taste, then, stir chives in. To serve, spoon sauce over steaks.

Nutrition Information

- Calories: 872 calories;
- Total Fat: 76.9
- Sodium: 189
- Total Carbohydrate: 5.2
- Cholesterol: 229
- Protein: 34.7

202. Pan Roasted Miso Marinated Sea Bass

Serving: 6 | Prep: 20mins | Cook: 15mins | Ready in:

Ingredients

- 1/4 cup white sugar
- 1 tablespoon dark corn syrup
- 1 1/2 teaspoons soy sauce
- 1/2 cup sake
- 1/4 cup hoisin sauce
- 1/4 cup white miso paste
- 1/4 cup red miso paste
- 1 1/2 teaspoons minced fresh ginger root
- 1 clove garlic, minced
- 1 shallot, minced
- 5 tablespoons canola oil, divided
- 6 (6 ounce) fillets sea bass

Direction

- In a bowl, whisk together 3 tablespoons canola oil, shallot, garlic, ginger root, red miso, white miso, hoisin sauce, sake, soy sauce, corn syrup and sugar until blended. Mix fillets with the marinade, then cover and place in the fridge to marinate for about 4 to 6 hours.
- Preheat an oven to 175 degrees C (350 degrees F).
- Take out the fillets from the marinade and then scrape off any excess. Then scrape marinade into a small saucepan and reserve. Over high heat, heat remaining two tablespoons canola oil in a large, heavy cast iron skillet. Then brown the fillets in hot oil for 1 minute per side. Transfer into the oven and let to bake for about 10 minutes until fish easily flakes with a fork.
- As the fish cooks in the oven, over medium-high heat, heat remaining marinade to a simmer and then decrease the heat to medium-low. Let simmer for ten minutes. Serve sea bass along with the miso sauce.

Nutrition Information

- Calories: 410 calories;
- Protein: 34
- Total Fat: 16.4
- Sodium: 1107
- Total Carbohydrate: 25.3
- Cholesterol: 69

203. Perfect Sushi Rice

Serving: 15 | Prep: 5mins | Cook: 20mins | Ready in:

Ingredients

- 2 cups uncooked glutinous white rice (sushi rice)
- 3 cups water
- 1/2 cup rice vinegar
- 1 tablespoon vegetable oil
- 1/4 cup white sugar
- 1 teaspoon salt

Direction

- Rinse rice in a colander or strainer until water runs clear. Then mix with water in a medium saucepan and heat to boil. Decrease heat to low, then cover and let to cook for 20 minutes. The rice will be tender and the water will be absorbed. Let cool until cooled enough to work with.
- Mix salt, sugar, oil, and rice vinegar in a small saucepan. Let cook on medium heat until sugar is dissolved. Let cool, and mix into the cooked rice. Once you add this to rice, it will look very wet. Continue stirring and rice should dry while it cools.

Nutrition Information

- Calories: 112 calories;
- Total Fat: 1
- Sodium: 158
- Total Carbohydrate: 23.5
- Cholesterol: 0
- Protein: 1.7

204. Pork Gyoza

Serving: 6 | Prep: 1hours | Cook: 8mins | Ready in:

Ingredients

- 12 ounces ground pork
- 1/4 head cabbage, shredded
- 1 egg
- 2 spring onions, sliced
- 1 tablespoon soy sauce
- 2 teaspoons sake
- 2 teaspoons mirin
- 2 teaspoons minced fresh ginger root
- 40 gyoza wrappers, or as needed
- 2 tablespoons vegetable oil
- 1/2 cup water
- Sauce:
- 1/4 cup rice wine vinegar
- 1/4 cup soy sauce

Direction

- In a big bowl, thoroughly mix together the sake, ginger, ground pork, spring onions, mirin, cabbage, 1 tablespoon of soy sauce and egg.
- Fill the middle of each of the gyoza wrappers with about 1-2 teaspoons of the prepared pork filling mixture. Damp your fingers in water and use it to rub around the edges of the filled gyoza wrappers. Fold in half the gyoza wrappers over the pork filling mixture so that it looks like a semi-circle. Take one side of the gyoza wrapper to make crimps along the edges so that it looks like the pleats of a skirt, then press it along the edges to seal the 2 sides together. Make sure that there's not a lot of excess air trapped inside each of the dumpling. Do the same procedure for the remaining pork filling mixture until all the filling have been used.
- In a big skillet, put the vegetable oil and let it heat up over medium-high heat setting. Put an even layer of as much of the prepared gyoza as you can on the bottom of the skillet and let it fry for about 3-5 minutes until the bottom of each gyoza turns brown in color. Pour in water and lower the heat setting. Cover the skillet and let the gyoza cook in steam for about 5 minutes until all of the water has already evaporated. Do the same procedure for the rest of the gyoza.
- To make the dipping sauce, combine the soy sauce and rice vinegar. Serve the cooked gyoza with the prepared dipping sauce on the side.

Nutrition Information

- Calories: 349 calories;
- Sodium: 1106
- Total Carbohydrate: 35.9
- Cholesterol: 69
- Protein: 17.8
- Total Fat: 14.2

205. Restaurant Style Shoyu Miso Ramen

Serving: 4 | Prep: 15mins | Cook: 4hours30mins | Ready in:

Ingredients

- 1/4 cup dried black fungus
- 2 cups mirin
- 1 1/4 cups soy sauce, divided
- 1/2 cup brown sugar
- 6 green onion bulbs, chopped, divided
- 1/2 onion, coarsely chopped
- 6 cloves garlic, peeled
- 2 pounds skin-on, boneless pork belly
- butcher's twine
- 4 eggs
- 2 tablespoons brown sugar
- 1/2 cup miso paste
- 4 (3 ounce) packages ramen noodles, or to taste
- 4 sheets nori (dry seaweed), quartered
- 1 naruto (fish paste stick with a red spiral pattern). sliced

Direction

- Preheat an oven to 135°C/275°F.
- In a big bowl, put black fungus and use water to fill.
- In an oven-safe pot, mix garlic, chopped onion, 3 green onion bulbs, 1/2 cup brown sugar, 1/2 cup soy sauce and mirin on high heat; boil.
- On flat work surface, put pork bell, skin-side down. Lengthwise, roll up. Use butcher's twine to wrap. In pot, put pork belly with the mirin mixture. Use a lid to partially cover.
- In preheated oven, bake for about 4 hours till an inserted instant-read thermometer in the middle reads 63°C/145°F and pork is tender.
- Boil another pot of water on high heat. Put eggs into pot gently. Cook for 8-10 minutes till yolks are barely set. Put eggs into bowl with ice water. Let eggs sit for about 1 minute. Take out of water; peel eggs.
- In a container, put 2 tbsp. brown sugar, 1/2 cup soy sauce, 1 cup water and eggs. Dampen a paper towel in mixture. Cover container with damp paper towel. Refrigerate for 4 hours up to overnight.
- Drain fungus. Put into liquid in pot with pork belly. Put lid on. Refrigerate for 4 hours to overnight.
- From top of pork belly mixture, skim fungus. Put into pot that has 8 cups water. The fungus has to be covered in pork belly fat. Put in miso paste and 1/4 cup soy sauce; boil.
- Use a knife to remove pork belly skin. Chop meat to pieces to your preferred thickness. Lengthwise, slice eggs in half.
- Boil another pot of water. In boiling water, cook ramen, occasionally mixing, for about 3 minutes till noodles are tender but firm to chew; drain.
- Diagonally in each bowl's corner, put 4 slices of nori. Put noodles on the top. In separate corners, put several pork belly slices and 2 egg halves. Use black fungus to cover. Put green onions on top. Put broth in. Put several naruto slices in every bowl. Before serving, let sit for about 3 minutes.

Nutrition Information

- Calories: 1104 calories;
- Protein: 47.1
- Total Fat: 43.5
- Sodium: 7959
- Total Carbohydrate: 103.1
- Cholesterol: 283

206. Seaweed (Nori) Soup

Serving: 6 | Prep: 15mins | Cook: 18mins | Ready in:

Ingredients

- 1 pound ground pork
- 2 quarts water
- 1 cube chicken bouillon
- 1 (8 ounce) can sliced water chestnuts
- 3 sheets nori (dry seaweed), broken into pieces.
- 1 egg, beaten
- 1/2 teaspoon salt
- 4 green onions, chopped
- 3/4 teaspoon sesame oil

Direction

- Over medium-high heat, cook the ground pork in a large saucepan until browned. Then drain off the excess fat and pour in water. Heat to boil, decrease the heat to medium and let to simmer while uncovered for about 15 minutes.
- Mix in bouillon cube until dissolved. Then add nori and water chestnuts. Mix in egg, and add salt. Take out from the heat and stir in sesame oil and green onions. Serve right away.

Nutrition Information

- Calories: 196 calories;
- Cholesterol: 80
- Protein: 15.2
- Total Fat: 12.4
- Sodium: 450
- Total Carbohydrate: 5.6

207. Semi Homemade Japanese Kare Pan (Curry Bread)

Serving: 12 | Prep: 25mins | Cook: 43mins | Ready in:

Ingredients

- 1 large potato, cut into 1/2-inch pieces
- 1 cup frozen peas
- 2 tablespoons butter
- 1 pound ground beef sirloin
- salt and ground black pepper to taste
- 1 onion, diced small
- 2 1/2 cups water, or as needed
- 3 cubes Japanese curry roux, or more to taste
- oil for frying
- 1 (11 ounce) can refrigerated French bread dough
- 1 egg
- panko bread crumbs

Direction

- Let a large pot of water come to a boil. Put in potatoes; cook for about 5 minutes or till mostly tender. Put in peas; keep cooking for 5-10 minutes or till potatoes are soft. Strain.
- Place a large skillet on medium heat and melt butter. Flavor the ground beef with pepper and salt and put into the skillet; add onion. Cook while stirring for about 5 minutes or till the beef is browned and the onion is translucent.
- Add 2 1/2 cups of water; let the mixture come to a boil. Turn the heat down to medium and mix in peas and potatoes. Simmer while skimming the scum off the surface till flavors mix together for about 15 minutes. Take it away from the heat and let it cool for around 5 minutes. Mix in curry roux cubes till dissolved.
- Let the curry mixture cool for around 20 minutes. Cover with the plastic wrap and chill in a refrigerator till thickened for 8 hours to overnight.

- Set a deep-fryer or a large saucepan to 350°F (175°C), heat oil.
- Cut the dough into 1/2-in. slices and roll out each slice to a 3-in. circle. Put a teaspoon chilled curry into the center of each circle. Fold sides of the circle over curry and press edges together to shape a round ball.
- Beat the egg in a small bowl. In a shallow dish, arrange panko bread crumbs. Dip each ball of the dough into the beaten egg. Press into the bread crumbs to coat, shake off excess.
- Fry in hot oil for 3-5 minutes or till evenly browned on all sides.

Nutrition Information

- Calories: 296 calories;
- Sodium: 273
- Total Carbohydrate: 27.1
- Cholesterol: 45
- Protein: 12.1
- Total Fat: 15.9

208. Sesame Crusted Mahi Mahi With Soy Shiso Ginger Butter Sauce

Serving: 6 | Prep: 20mins | Cook: 15mins | Ready in:

Ingredients

- 3 shallots, minced
- 2 teaspoons minced fresh ginger root
- 1 lemon, juiced
- 1/2 cup dry white wine
- 1/2 cup heavy cream
- 1/2 cup unsalted butter, chilled and cut into small cubes
- 3 tablespoons soy sauce
- 4 shiso leaves
- coarse kosher salt
- ground white pepper
- 2 tablespoons canola oil
- 6 (6 ounce) mahi mahi fillets
- 4 tablespoons sesame seeds
- 4 tablespoons black sesame seeds

Direction

- Mix white wine, lemon juice, ginger, and shallots in a saucepan set on medium heat. Then cook until liquid is lessened to about 2 tablespoons. Mix in heavy cream, then make it to a light boil. Lessen cream by half; keep from burning. Mix in soy sauce, then place to a blender. Then process on low while gradually adding butter, several cubes at a time, until all butter is blended. Then roughly tear or chop shiso, put in sauce, and process for approximately 10 seconds. Add pepper and kosher salt to season. Retain the sauce's warmth.
- Prepare the oven by preheating to 425°F (220°C).
- In a big sauté pan set on high heat, add oil. Put white pepper and kosher salt on both sides of fish fillets to season. Combine black and white sesame seeds, then transfer on a plate or flat dish. Push down the TOP side only of every fillet in the mixture, then let the seeds stick on fish by pressing. Once the oil is smoking, put the fish, with the sesame seed down on the pan, and be cautious of splattering oil. Brown fish for approximately 30-45 seconds each side. Transfer pan in the oven, or put the fish on the baking sheet, then cook in the oven for approximately 5-6 minutes. Present sesame crust up paired with ginger butter sauce.

Nutrition Information

- Calories: 502 calories;
- Total Carbohydrate: 11
- Cholesterol: 192
- Protein: 35.6
- Total Fat: 34.6
- Sodium: 776

209. Sesame Tuna With Soy Miso Dressing

Serving: 2 | Prep: 20mins | Cook: 4mins | Ready in:

Ingredients

- 3/4 cup sesame seeds, divided
- 1/2 teaspoon seasoning salt
- 1 teaspoon ground white pepper
- 1 teaspoon onion powder
- 1 tablespoon wasabi powder
- 1 teaspoon coarse kosher salt
- 1 cup all-purpose flour
- 2 eggs
- 3 fluid ounces milk
- 2 (4 ounce) tuna steaks (about 3/4 inch thick)
- 2 tablespoons vegetable oil
- 1 (1.12 ounce) package miso soup mix
- 1 tablespoon soy sauce

Direction

- Combine flour, half cup sesame seeds, kosher salt, seasoning salt, wasabi powder, white pepper, and onion powder in a shallow bowl; set aside. In another bowl, whisk milk and eggs together.
- Immerse tuna in egg mixture then roll in the flour mixture until both sides are well coated. Press and coat as much as sesame seeds as possible on the tuna until well covered. On medium-high heat, heat vegetable oil in a big and heavy pan. Fry steaks for 2mins on each side; take them away from heat immediately. The meat inside the fish should remain red.
- For the soy miso dressing, combine soy sauce and miso soup mix. Heat sauce in a microwave or small pot. Pour sauce over the tuna steaks.

210. Smoked Salmon Sushi Roll

Serving: 6 | Prep: 30mins | Cook: | Ready in:

Ingredients

- 2 cups Japanese sushi rice
- 6 tablespoons rice wine vinegar
- 6 sheets nori (dry seaweed)
- 1 avocado - peeled, pitted and sliced
- 1 cucumber, peeled and sliced
- 8 ounces smoked salmon, cut into long strips
- 2 tablespoons wasabi paste

Direction

- Soak rice in 4 hours. Drain; add the rice and 2 cups of water into the rice cooker and cook. As we will add vinegar later, the rice should be cooked dry. Add 6 tablespoons of rice vinegar into the hot rice right after cooking; mix well. Transfer the rice onto a plate and spread out for cooling.
- Put in a sheet of seaweed on the bamboo mat. Add cool rice and form it into a thin layer. Cover the seaweed but leave out 1/2 inch top and bottom edge for easier sealing. Use wasabi to dot on the rice. Place smoked salmon, avocado and cucumber on the rice, about 1 inch from the bottom edge. Wet the top edge of the seaweed. Use the bamboo mat and roll tightly from the bottom to top edge. Cut roll into 8 equal pieces to serve. The same with other rolls.

Nutrition Information

- Calories: 291 calories;
- Total Fat: 6.9
- Sodium: 405
- Total Carbohydrate: 45.1
- Cholesterol: 9
- Protein: 11.1

211. Spicy Chile Oil Squid

Serving: 4 | Prep: 10mins | Cook: 8mins | Ready in:

Ingredients

- 2 tablespoons soy sauce
- 2 cloves garlic, finely grated
- 1 teaspoon finely grated ginger root
- 4 drops chile oil, or more to taste
- 2 tablespoons butter, divided
- 2 pounds squid, cleaned and chopped
- 1 lemon, halved (optional)

Direction

- In a bowl, mix chile oil, ginger, garlic, and soy sauce until smooth.
- In a wok or skillet, heat 1 tablespoon butter on medium heat. Add squid and sauté squid for 8-10 minutes, adding soy-ginger sauce, until sauce thickens and reduces. Take off heat and mix in butter until combined.
- Squeeze halved lemons on squid then serve.

Nutrition Information

- Calories: 271 calories;
- Cholesterol: 544
- Protein: 36
- Total Fat: 9.4
- Sodium: 592
- Total Carbohydrate: 8.2

212. Spicy Japanese Crab Noodle Salad

Serving: 2 | Prep: 25mins | Cook: 8mins | Ready in:

Ingredients

- Dressing:
- 1 tablespoon red wine vinegar
- 1 tablespoon soy sauce, or more to taste
- 1 tablespoon sugar
- 1 1/2 teaspoons mirin (Japanese rice wine)
- 1 1/2 teaspoons sesame oil
- 1 teaspoon Chinese chili bean sauce (doubanjiang), or more to taste
- 1 teaspoon balsamic vinegar
- salt to taste
- Salad:
- 4 ounces instant ramen noodles (without flavor packet)
- 4 ounces cooked octopus, cut into bite-sized pieces (optional)
- 1/2 cucumber, thinly sliced
- 1/2 red bell pepper, sliced into rings
- 2 ounces cooked crab meat, broken up
- 2 ounces bean sprouts
- 2 scallions, sliced
- 1 tablespoon toasted nori (seaweed), crumbled, or more to taste

Direction

- Dressing: mix balsamic vinegar, chili bean sauce, sesame oil, mirin, sugar, soy sauce and red wine vinegar in a small bowl. Use salt to season.
- Boil a small pot with water. Cook instant noodles for about 3 minutes till tender. Drain. Put into a big bowl.
- Mix scallions with noodles, bean sprouts, crab meat, red bell pepper, cucumber and octopus. Add dressing. Stir to combine. Distribute onto serving plates. Drizzle crumbled nori on top.

Nutrition Information

- Calories: 465 calories;
- Total Fat: 14.6
- Sodium: 1303
- Total Carbohydrate: 52.2
- Cholesterol: 74
- Protein: 31

213. Spongy Japanese Cheesecake

Serving: 8 | Prep: 20mins | Cook: 1hours15mins | Ready in:

Ingredients

- 1 (8 ounce) package cream cheese, cubed
- 1/2 cup milk
- 3 tablespoons unsalted butter
- 10 tablespoons cake flour
- 2 tablespoons cornstarch
- 6 egg yolks
- 1 tablespoon fresh lemon juice
- 6 egg whites
- 1/4 teaspoon cream of tartar
- 1/8 teaspoon salt
- 10 tablespoons superfine sugar

Direction

- Preheat the oven to 325°F (165°C). Coat lightly an 8-inch round-shaped cake pan with oil and use a parchment paper to line on it.
- Allow the cream cheese to soak in a bowl filled with milk for 20 minutes.
- Put the butter and cream cheese along with the soaking milk in the top of a double boiler and let it heat up over simmering water for about 5 minutes while stirring often until the butter has melted and the mixture is smooth in consistency. Take away from the heat and allow it to fully cool down for no less than 15 minutes.
- Sift together the cornstarch and cake flour into a bowl. Sift the flour mixture again into the prepared cream cheese mixture and mix everything together. Put in the lemon juice and egg yolks and give it a thoroughly mix.
- In another bowl, use an electric mixer to whisk the cream of tartar, salt and egg whites together until it has a frothy consistency. Put in 2 tablespoons of sugar at a time and whisk it thoroughly before you add another sugar addition. Keep whisking on high speed setting until soft peaks are formed.
- Fold the prepared cream cheese mixture into the prepared egg white mixture and well-blended. Transfer the combined mixture into the prepared cake pan. Put the filled cake pan in a bigger baking dish filled with water extending up to half of the sides of the cake pan.
- Put it in the preheated oven and let it bake for about 1 hour and 10 minutes until the top of the cheesecake turns golden brown in color and the cheesecake mixture has already set. Switch off the oven and keep the baked cheesecake inside the oven for 1 hour with the oven door ajar. Place the baked cheesecake onto a wire rack and let it fully cool down.

Nutrition Information

- Calories: 301 calories;
- Total Fat: 17.8
- Sodium: 174
- Total Carbohydrate: 27.8
- Cholesterol: 197
- Protein: 8.2

214. Steamed Clams In Butter And Sake

Serving: 4 | Prep: 10mins | Cook: 10mins | Ready in:

Ingredients

- 4 teaspoons sake
- 4 teaspoons mirin (Japanese sweet wine)
- 2 teaspoons rice vinegar
- 1 1/4 pounds clams in shell, scrubbed
- 3 tablespoons butter
- 1 teaspoon soy sauce
- 1 green onion, chopped

Direction

- Brush and rinse the clams. Soak the rinsed

clams for 5 minutes in a big bowl of cold water. Drain the clams thoroughly.
- Heat a big saucepan or wok over high heat. Put in the mirin, rice vinegar and sake quickly. Put in the clams then cover the wok and cook the clams for 3-4 minutes until they open. Throw away the clams that didn't open.
- Use a paper towel or spoon to remove the scums that formed on top of the mixture. Add in the soy sauce, green onion and butter and mix well to fully coat the clams while the butter melts. Put the cooked clams on a serving plate and pour the sauce over the clams. Serve right away.

Nutrition Information

- Calories: 121 calories;
- Total Fat: 9
- Sodium: 155
- Total Carbohydrate: 3
- Cholesterol: 34
- Protein: 4.5

215. Sukiyaki

Serving: 6 | Prep: 10mins | Cook: 20mins | Ready in:

Ingredients

- 1 tablespoon vegetable oil
- 1 1/2 pounds beef sirloin strips
- 2/3 cup soy sauce
- 2 teaspoons monosodium glutamate (MSG)
- 1/3 cup chicken broth
- 1/3 cup white sugar
- 3 small onions, sliced
- 2 cups chopped celery
- 1 (14 ounce) can bamboo shoots, drained and chopped
- 4 green onions, sliced
- 1 (4.5 ounce) can mushrooms, drained
- 1 (8 ounce) can water chestnuts, drained
- 1 teaspoon cornstarch

Direction

- On medium-high heat, heat oil in a wok or big pot; cook in beef until brown. Mix in sugar, soy sauce, broth, and MSG. Stir in celery and onion until tender. Mix in water chestnuts, bamboo shoots, mushrooms, and green onions. Turn to medium heat then mix in cornstarch. Let it simmer until the sauce is thick.

Nutrition Information

- Calories: 311 calories;
- Cholesterol: 61
- Protein: 23.5
- Total Fat: 12.3
- Sodium: 1992
- Total Carbohydrate: 27

216. Sukiyaki Beef

Serving: 4 | Prep: 15mins | Cook: 20mins | Ready in:

Ingredients

- 1 tablespoon peanut oil
- 1 pound beef round steak, sliced diagonally into 3 inch pieces
- 1/2 cup beef stock
- 2 teaspoons soy sauce
- 1 tablespoon butter
- 3/4 cup onion, diced
- 3/4 cup celery, diced
- 1/4 pound mushrooms, chopped
- 1/4 pound fresh spinach, rinsed

Direction

- In a big and heavy skillet or a wok, put the oil and let it heat up over medium-high heat setting. Put in the beef and let it cook until it turns brown in color evenly on all sides. Add the soy sauce, butter and beef stock and mix everything together. Push the beef mixture onto one side then mix in the celery, mushrooms and onion and let it cook for about 4 minutes while stirring. Put in the spinach and allow it to cook for additional 2 minutes.

Nutrition Information

- Calories: 207 calories;
- Total Fat: 13.4
- Sodium: 254
- Total Carbohydrate: 5.5
- Cholesterol: 47
- Protein: 16.4

217. Sunomono (Japanese Cucumber And Seafood Salad)

Serving: 4 | Prep: 20mins | Cook: | Ready in:

Ingredients

- 1 large English cucumber, peeled and thinly sliced
- 1 teaspoon salt
- 1 (8 ounce) package imitation crab sticks, halved
- 2 tablespoons rice vinegar
- 1 tablespoon soy sauce
- 1 teaspoon sesame seeds, or to taste

Direction

- On a big plate, lay cucumber slices. Sprinkle both sides with salt. Put aside for 15 minutes till water gets drawn out. Scrape salt from cucumbers. Press paper towel on to get rid of extra moisture.
- In a glass dish bowl, mix soy sauce, rice vinegar, crabsticks and cucumber slices. Toss till coated. Use plastic wrap to cover bowl. Refrigerate for 1 hour minimum to 24 hours.
- Distribute cucumber salad to 4 plates. Sprinkle sesame seeds on every portion.

Nutrition Information

- Calories: 68 calories;
- Cholesterol: 11
- Protein: 5.1
- Total Fat: 0.7
- Sodium: 1279
- Total Carbohydrate: 10.6

218. Sushi Party

Serving: 12 | Prep: 3hours | Cook: 30mins | Ready in:

Ingredients

- Rice:
- 9 3/4 cups water
- 5 1/2 cups Japanese sushi-style white rice
- 5 1/2 tablespoons rice vinegar
- 5 1/2 tablespoons white sugar
- 2 3/4 tablespoons kosher salt
- Filling:
- 1 teaspoon vegetable oil
- 2 eggs, beaten
- 1 tablespoon vegetable oil
- 1 tablespoon sake
- 1 tablespoon soy sauce
- 2 tablespoons sesame oil
- 1 eggplant, sliced lengthwise into strips
- 1 carrot, sliced into thin strips
- 1 tablespoon rice vinegar
- 1 tablespoon soy sauce
- 8 spears fresh asparagus
- 1 avocado
- 1 tablespoon lemon juice, or as needed
- 12 sheets nori (dry seaweed)
- 1 (8 ounce) package imitation crabmeat strips, halved lengthwise
- 1 cucumber, seeded and sliced lengthwise into strips
- 1 (4 ounce) jar pesto
- 8 large cooked shrimp, coarsely chopped

Direction

- In a large pot, heat rice and water to boil. Decrease the heat to medium-low, cover the pot and let to simmer for about 25 minutes until the liquid has been absorbed and rice is tender. Take out the pot from the heat source, cover and keep for 10 minutes.
- In a microwave-safe bowl, mix together sugar, salt and 5 1/2 tablespoons of rice vinegar. Heat in microwave for 30 to 45 seconds until the vinegar mixture becomes warm. Combine thoroughly. Pour the vinegar mixture into the rice and mix well to coat each grain of rice. Let to cool completely.
- Over medium heat, heat one teaspoon of vegetable oil in a small skillet, add eggs and then cook for 3 to 5 minutes until firm. Place the eggs in a plate and slice into strips.
- Over medium heat, heat sesame oil, one tablespoon of soy sauce, one tablespoon of vegetable oil, and sake in a skillet. Then fry eggplant in the oil mixture for 5 to 10 minutes until lightly charred and softened. Place the eggplant onto a plate lined with paper towel.
- In a microwave-safe bowl, combine together carrot, one tablespoon of soy sauce and one tablespoon of rice vinegar. Heat in microwave for 1 to 2 minutes until the carrot becomes soft. Then drain.
- Bring lightly salted water to boil in a large pot, add asparagus and then cook for 2 to 3 minutes until turned bright green. Drain off water and then immediately dip the asparagus in ice water for a few minutes to halt the cooking process. Drain one again.
- Chop the avocado into eight slices and sprinkle lemon juice on top of the slices in a bowl.
- Onto a flat work surface, spread nori sheets, wet your hands and then add 3/4 to 1 cup of rice over each sheet. Spread the rice into a thin layer and leave half an inch exposed nori on one long side.
- To make California rolls, spread in a thin strip a layer of carrot, cucumber, crabmeat, and avocado on top of one another along the margin opposite the uncovered edge on three nori sheets.
- For the avocado and eggplant rolls, layer avocado and eggplant on top of one another in a thin strip along the margin opposite the uncovered margin on three nori sheets.
- For the egg and pesto rolls, arrange pesto in a thin strip along the margin opposite the uncovered margin and add slices of egg on three nori sheets.
- For the asparagus and shrimp rolls, spread a layer of asparagus and shrimp on top of one another in a thin strip along the margin opposite the uncovered margin on three nori sheets.
- Place one prepared nori onto a bamboo sushi mat. Fold the rice and nori around the filling towards the exposed nori margin using the mat and squeeze carefully. Wet the opened nori margin and then seal the roll. Cut every roll into eight pieces. Repeat this with the rest of the prepared nori.

Nutrition Information

- Calories: 516 calories;
- Sodium: 1738
- Total Carbohydrate: 87.9
- Cholesterol: 44
- Protein: 12.5
- Total Fat: 12.4

219. Sushi Roll

Serving: 8 | Prep: 45mins | Cook: | Ready in:

Ingredients

- 2/3 cup uncooked short-grain white rice
- 3 tablespoons rice vinegar
- 3 tablespoons white sugar
- 1 1/2 teaspoons salt
- 4 sheets nori seaweed sheets
- 1/2 cucumber, peeled, cut into small strips

- 2 tablespoons pickled ginger
- 1 avocado
- 1/2 pound imitation crabmeat, flaked

Direction

- Boil 1 1/3 cups water in a medium pot; stir in rice. Lower heat; let it simmer for 20 mins while covered. Combine salt, sugar, and rice vinegar in a small bowl; mix into the rice.
- Preheat the oven to 150°C or 300°Fahrenheit. Heat nori in a medium baking sheet for 1-2 mins in the preheated oven, or until warm.
- On a bamboo sushi mat, put one nori sheet in the center. Slather a thin layer of rice on the nori sheet using damp hands, and then press the rice. Put a quarter of the cucumber, imitation crabmeat, avocado, and ginger down in the middle of the rice. Lift and roll the end of the mat gently over the contents then gently press. Complete the roll by rolling forward. Repeat with the rest of the ingredients.
- Use a wet and sharp knife to slice each roll into 4-6 portions.

Nutrition Information

- Calories: 152 calories;
- Cholesterol: 6
- Protein: 3.9
- Total Fat: 3.9
- Sodium: 703
- Total Carbohydrate: 25.8

220. Sweet Miso Soup With Baby Turnips

Serving: 2 | Prep: 10mins | Cook: 14mins | Ready in:

Ingredients

- 2 cups warm water, or to taste
- 1 (4 inch) piece kombu (seaweed)
- 2 small baby white turnips, peeled, with leaves reserved
- 3 1/2 tablespoons miso paste
- 3 tablespoons white sugar
- 1 tablespoon sake (rice wine)
- 1 tablespoon mirin (sweet cooking rice wine)

Direction

- In a saucepan, mix together kombu and water. Let it sit for 20 minutes until kombu is tender.
- Boil water. Add turnips; bring to a simmer over medium heat for 10 minutes until soft. Move the turnips to 2 serving bowls. In the boiling water, put the reserved leaves. Cook for 1-2 minutes until wilted. Distribute the cooking water and leaves among the bowls. Remove the kombu.
- In a small pot, mix together mirin, sake, sugar, and miso paste over low heat. Cook until thickened, about 3-5 minutes, whisking continually. Add to the turnips in the bowls.

Nutrition Information

- Calories: 178 calories;
- Total Fat: 1.9
- Sodium: 1194
- Total Carbohydrate: 33.7
- Cholesterol: 0
- Protein: 4.2

221. Tamagoyaki With Mushroom And Mozzarella Cheese

Serving: 2 | Prep: 15mins | Cook: 10mins | Ready in:

Ingredients

- 2 teaspoons olive oil
- 6 button mushrooms, sliced very thin
- 3 eggs
- 2 1/2 tablespoons white sugar

- 1 pinch salt and ground black pepper to taste
- 1/4 teaspoon red chile powder, or to taste
- 2 tablespoons vegetable oil, divided
- 1 ounce mozzarella cheese, sliced very thin

Direction

- In a big frying pan, heat olive oil over medium heat. Add mushrooms, stir and cook for 5 minutes until the mushrooms let out their moisture and turn brown. Take away from heat, drain and pat dry.
- In a bowl, whisk together red chile powder, pepper, salt, sugar, and eggs.
- Use vegetable oil to coat the frying pan on medium heat. Add some of the whisked eggs; tip the frying pan so that the mixture spread into a thin layer. Cook for 1-2 minutes until nearly set. Run around the edges with a heatproof rubber spatula to loosen. Put some mushrooms to cover, roll up the egg and slide to the side of the frying pan.
- Use some vegetable oil to coat the frying pan. Add more eggs to make a second layer. Raise the first roll up so that the uncooked portions run underneath. Drizzle the top with mozzarella cheese; roll the second layer over the first.
- Continue to make the layers and rolling process with the rest of the mozzarella cheese, mushrooms, eggs, and oil. Cook the completed tamagoyaki for 30 seconds each side until turns slightly brown.
- Move the tamagoyaki to a cutting board. Let it cool down for 5-10 minutes before cutting.

Nutrition Information

- Calories: 380 calories;
- Total Fat: 28.3
- Sodium: 273
- Total Carbohydrate: 18.6
- Cholesterol: 288
- Protein: 14.6

222. Tempura Shrimp

Serving: 6 | Prep: 5mins | Cook: 10mins | Ready in:

Ingredients

- 32 vanilla wafers, crushed
- 1 egg, beaten
- 3/4 cup water
- 1/3 cup apricot nectar
- 2 teaspoons cornstarch
- 1/4 cup packed brown sugar
- 3 tablespoons red wine vinegar
- 1 tablespoon ketchup
- 2 cups vegetable oil
- 3/4 pound medium shrimp - peeled and deveined

Direction

- Combine water, egg, and vanilla wafers in a small bowl until well incorporated; chill for 1-2 hrs
- Prepare the dipping sauce: Combine cornstarch and nectar in a small sauce pan; mix in catsup, vinegar, and brown sugar. On medium heat, heat the mixture while constantly mixing until thick and reaches a boil; set aside.
- Heat two cups oil in a deep fryer or stockpot until 175°C or 375°Fahnrenheit. Submerge shrimp in vanilla wafer batter. Fry 4-6 shrimp at a time until golden brown; drain completely. Serve hot shrimp with dipping sauce.

Nutrition Information

- Calories: 920 calories;
- Total Fat: 81.4
- Sodium: 225
- Total Carbohydrate: 35.8
- Cholesterol: 117
- Protein: 14.1

223. Teriyaki Rib Eye Steaks

Serving: 2 | Prep: 10mins | Cook: 15mins | Ready in:

Ingredients

- 2 tablespoons soy sauce
- 2 tablespoons water
- 1 tablespoon white sugar
- 1 1/2 teaspoons honey
- 1 1/2 teaspoons Worcestershire sauce
- 1 1/4 teaspoons distilled white vinegar
- 1 teaspoon olive oil
- 1/4 teaspoon onion powder
- 1/4 teaspoon garlic powder
- 1/8 teaspoon ground ginger
- 2 (6 ounce) lean beef rib eye steaks

Direction

- Take a big bowl and whisk in ground ginger, garlic powder, onion powder, olive oil, vinegar, Worcestershire sauce, honey, sugar, water and soy sauce. Use a fork to piece steaks a few times. Dip steaks in the mixture and marinate for at least 2 hours.
- Cook the steaks in a wok, hibachi or a hot frying pan over medium heat for 7 minutes on each side for medium. An instant-read thermometer should read 60°C or 140°F when inserted into the middle of the steaks.

Nutrition Information

- Calories: 297 calories;
- Protein: 19.6
- Total Fat: 18.1
- Sodium: 992
- Total Carbohydrate: 13.5
- Cholesterol: 60

224. Teriyaki Sauce And Marinade

Serving: 8 | Prep: 10mins | Cook: 20mins | Ready in:

Ingredients

- 2/3 cup mirin (Japanese sweet rice wine)
- 1 cup soy sauce
- 4 1/2 teaspoons rice vinegar
- 1 teaspoon sesame oil
- 1/3 cup white sugar
- 7 cloves garlic, minced
- 1 tablespoon minced fresh ginger
- 1 dash red pepper flakes
- black pepper to taste

Direction

- Bring mirin in a saucepan to a boil on high heat. Lower heat to moderately low and simmer about 10 minutes. Add in sugar, sesame oil, rice vinegar and soy sauce, then season with black pepper, pepper flakes, ginger and garlic. Simmer for 5 minutes more. Transfer the mixture to a tightly sealed container and put in the fridge for storage.

Nutrition Information

- Calories: 105 calories;
- Total Carbohydrate: 18.2
- Cholesterol: 0
- Protein: 2.3
- Total Fat: 0.7
- Sodium: 1804

225. The Perfect Simplified Sushi Vinegar

Serving: 12 | Prep: 5mins | Cook: 10mins | Ready in:

Ingredients

- 2 cups rice vinegar (such as Marukan®)
- 1 1/2 cups white sugar
- 1 1/2 tablespoons salt
- 1/8 lemon, juiced

Direction

- In a saucepan, mix together the salt, rice vinegar, lemon juice and sugar until the salt and sugar have fully dissolved. Allow the mixture to get to an almost simmer over low heat setting but do not let it boil. Take the pan away from the heat and let it fully cool down. To store, keep it in the fridge.

Nutrition Information

- Calories: 97 calories;
- Total Carbohydrate: 25
- Cholesterol: 0
- Protein: 0
- Total Fat: 0
- Sodium: 872

226. Thick Kabocha Soup

Serving: 2 | Prep: 25mins | Cook: 18mins | Ready in:

Ingredients

- 1/4 cup cornmeal
- 1/4 cup all-purpose flour
- 1/2 teaspoon seasoned salt (such as LAWRY'S®)
- 1/2 teaspoon ground black pepper
- 1/4 onion, sliced
- vegetable oil, or as needed
- 2 cups cubed kabocha squash
- 1 small Japanese sweet potato, sliced
- 1 carrot, sliced
- 3 cloves garlic, minced
- 1 bay leaf
- 1/2 cup soy milk
- 1 teaspoon garam masala
- salt and ground black pepper to taste

Direction

- In a bowl, mix together pepper, seasoned salt, flour, and cornmeal. Dip slices of onion in the cornmeal mixture.
- In a big frying pan, heat oil over medium heat. Add the breaded onion and cook for 3-5 minutes until turning golden brown, flipping sometimes.
- Boil water in a big pot. Add bay leaf, garlic, carrot, sweet potato, and kabocha squash; cook for 10 minutes until the kabocha squash is soft. Strain nearly all of the water, remove the bay leaf.
- Using a potato masher, mash the kabocha squash mixture, pour in soy milk, until the consistency of the mixture resembles a thick soup. Mix in pepper, salt, and garam masala. Use fried onions to garnish.

Nutrition Information

- Calories: 523 calories;
- Cholesterol: 0
- Protein: 7.8
- Total Fat: 29.6
- Sodium: 405
- Total Carbohydrate: 59.4

227. Tofu Chanpuru

Serving: 6 | Prep: 20mins | Cook: 30mins | Ready in:

Ingredients

- 1 (12 ounce) package extra-firm tofu, drained
- 1 (12 ounce) can fully cooked luncheon meat (such as SPAM®), cubed
- 4 cloves garlic, chopped
- 1 tablespoon minced fresh ginger, or to taste
- 1/2 cup sake
- 1/2 cup miso paste

- 1/4 cup soy sauce
- 2 tablespoons white sugar
- 2 teaspoons vegetable oil, or as needed
- 4 eggs, slightly beaten
- 2 teaspoons vegetable oil, or as needed
- 1 large onion, chopped
- 1 head cabbage, cored and chopped
- 2 carrots, grated
- 8 mushrooms, sliced
- 1 tablespoon chopped green onion, or more to taste

Direction

- Use a paper towel to wrap the tofu, then put it in the microwave and allow it to cook for 1 minute. Squeeze the tofu to get rid of any excess water then use a dry paper towel to wrap. Allow it to rest for about 5 minutes to drain off any excess water. Remove the paper towel on the tofu and slice it into cubes.
- In a bowl, mix together the garlic, ginger and luncheon meat. In another bowl, beat the soy sauce, sake, sugar and miso paste.
- In a skillet, put 2 teaspoons of vegetable oil and let it heat up over medium heat setting. Put in the eggs and let it cook for about 5 minutes while stirring it until thoroughly cooked and is already scrambled. Put the scrambled eggs onto a plate. In the same skillet used for the eggs, put in the prepared tofu and allow it to cook for 5-10 minutes while stirring until it turns evenly brown on every side. Put the cooked tofu on the same plate with the eggs. Put the prepared luncheon meat mixture into the same skillet and let it cook for about 5 minutes while stirring until the garlic turns light brown in color and the mixture is thoroughly-cooked.
- In another skillet, put 2 teaspoons of vegetable oil and let it heat up over medium heat setting. Put in the carrots, onion, mushrooms and cabbage and allow it to cook for 10-12 minutes while stirring until the cabbage becomes soft and the onions turn translucent. Put in the cooked luncheon meat mixture, scrambled eggs, prepared sake mixture and cooked tofu into the veggies mixture and mix everything until well-coated. Allow the mixture to cook for about 1 minute until thoroughly heated. Top it with green onion to garnish.

Nutrition Information

- Calories: 463 calories;
- Cholesterol: 164
- Protein: 23.6
- Total Fat: 26.2
- Sodium: 2334
- Total Carbohydrate: 32.4

228. Tofu Hiyayakko

Serving: 1 | Prep: 10mins | Cook: |Ready in:

Ingredients

- 1 tablespoon soy sauce
- 1 teaspoon white sugar
- 1/2 teaspoon dashi granules
- 1/2 teaspoon water
- 1/4 (12 ounce) package silken tofu
- 1 1/2 teaspoons grated fresh ginger root
- 1/4 teaspoon thinly sliced green onion
- 1 pinch bonito shavings (dry fish flakes)
- 1 pinch toasted sesame seeds

Direction

- In small bowl, combine water, dashi granules, sugar and soy sauce to dissolve the sugar. On small plate, put the tofu and put green onion, bonito shavings and ginger on top. Sprinkle top with soy mixture, and scatter sesame seeds over.

Nutrition Information

- Calories: 100 calories;
- Total Fat: 4.5
- Sodium: 911

- Total Carbohydrate: 7.7
- Cholesterol: 0
- Protein: 8.8

229. Tonkatsu

Serving: 4 | Prep: 20mins | Cook: 20mins | Ready in:

Ingredients

- 4 (4 ounce) boneless pork chops
- salt and ground black pepper to taste
- 2 cups oil for frying, or as needed
- 1/4 cup all-purpose flour
- 1 egg, beaten
- 3/4 cup panko (Japanese-style bread crumbs)

Direction

- Put pork chops between 2 sheets of heavy plastic onto a solid, level surface (also works great with resealable freezer bags). Then use smooth side of a meat mallet to pound the pork firmly to a 1/4-inch thickness (about .75 cm). Add pepper and salt to season to taste.
- Add oil into a skillet until it reaches about 1/2 inch (1.25 cm) deep. Then heat the oil on medium-high heat to 190 degrees C (375 degrees F).
- Put panko crumbs, egg and flour in separate bowls. Then coat every cutlet in flour, followed by egg and lastly in bread crumbs. Tap off any loose crumbs.
- Fry the cutlets for about 4 minutes on each side until cooked through and golden brown. Then place on paper towels to drain.

Nutrition Information

- Calories: 290 calories;
- Total Fat: 17.4
- Sodium: 136
- Total Carbohydrate: 20.1
- Cholesterol: 77

- Protein: 17.4

230. Tonkatsu Asian Style Pork Chop

Serving: 8 | Prep: 25mins | Cook: 15mins | Ready in:

Ingredients

- 2 eggs
- 1 teaspoon milk
- 1/2 teaspoon minced garlic
- salt to taste
- 1/2 teaspoon pepper
- 1 cup vegetable oil for frying
- 8 thin cut boneless pork chops
- 1 1/2 cups panko crumbs

Direction

- Combine pepper, eggs, salt, garlic, and milk in a medium bowl. On medium-high heat, heat oil in a big heavy pan. In a shallow bowl, put panko crumbs. Wash pork chops in water, dredge in egg mixture. Cover with panko crumbs. Dredge again into egg mixture, then cover with an additional panko crumbs layer. Place the coated pork chops on a plate until the remaining are coated. Let it stand for 10 mins for the coating to set well if you have time. You can also freeze them now.
- Put pork chops in a pan with very hot oil; fry for 5 mins per side, or until golden brown.

Nutrition Information

- Calories: 276 calories;
- Sodium: 199
- Total Carbohydrate: 14.3
- Cholesterol: 109
- Protein: 28.4
- Total Fat: 13.2

231. Tonkatsu Shoyu Ramen (Pork Cutlet Soy Sauce Ramen)

Serving: 1 | Prep: 30mins | Cook: 41mins | Ready in:

Ingredients

- 1 egg
- 1 1/2 teaspoons spicy sesame oil
- 2 (1x3-inch) boneless pork chop slices
- 2 tablespoons olive oil, divided
- 1 tablespoon black sesame seeds, divided
- 2 leaves fresh basil, chopped, divided
- 1 leaf fresh sage, chopped, divided
- 1 (3 ounce) package instant ramen noodles (such as Shirakiku®), seasoning packet discarded
- 3 tablespoons shredded dried kombu
- 1 3/4 tablespoons bonito soup stock (such as Hondashi®)
- 1 3/4 tablespoons soy sauce (shoyu)
- 1/2 teaspoon white miso paste with dashi
- Toppings:
- 4 1/3-inch slices fish paste stick (naruto)
- 1 tablespoon tonkatsu sauce
- 1 tablespoon sushi ginger (shoga), finely chopped
- 1 green onion, thinly sliced
- 1 pinch ground black pepper

Direction

- Fill water in a small pot halfway; boil. Add egg; cook for 15 minutes then drain. Over egg, run cold water then cool.
- In a big skillet, put sesame oil. Add pork slices. Use 1/2 olive oil, sage, basil and sesame seeds to cover pork. Flip. Use leftover sage, basil, sesame seeds and olive oil to cover pork.
- On medium-low heat, cook pork for about 5 minutes, covered, until evenly brown in color on the bottom; flip. Continue cooking for about 5 more minutes until the other side turns brown in color. Take off heat.
- Boil a big pot with water. Add ramen noodles then cook for 3 minutes. In a colander in a sink, drain. Rinse noodles till water is clear. Put noodles into pot.
- Mix miso paste, soy sauce, bonito stock and kombu into noodles. Cook on medium heat, mixing with chopsticks, for 3-5 minutes till miso paste melts. Put noodles into bowl.
- Peel then cut egg in half lengthwise. Put fish paste slices, pork slices and egg over noodles. Use black pepper, green onion, ginger and tonkatsu sauce as a garnish.

Nutrition Information

- Calories: 1406 calories;
- Total Fat: 81.8
- Sodium: 3660
- Total Carbohydrate: 90
- Cholesterol: 321
- Protein: 75.6

232. Traditional Beef Sukiyaki

Serving: 4 | Prep: 25mins | Cook: 11mins | Ready in:

Ingredients

- Broth:
- 1 1/2 cups water
- 2/3 cup soy sauce
- 2/3 cup white sugar
- 1/3 cup sake
- Sukiyaki Ingredients:
- 1 pound thinly sliced beef
- 1 (12 ounce) package firm tofu, drained and cut into bite-size pieces
- 1/2 head Chinese cabbage, cut into bite-size pieces
- 1 (7 ounce) package yam noodles (shirataki), drained
- 7 shiitake mushrooms, sliced
- 1 enoki mustrooms, roots removed
- 1 green onion (negi), sliced

- 1 tablespoon vegetable oil
- 4 eggs

Direction

- In a bowl, mix sake, water, sugar, and soy sauce for the broth.
- On different plates on a table, put beef, green onion, tofu, enoki mushrooms, Chinese cabbage, shiitake mushrooms, and yam noodles.
- In a big pan or electric pan placed over a hot plate on the table, heat oil; cook and stir in beef slices for a minute, or until brown. Add some broth then boil. Mix in green onion, tofu, enoki mushrooms, cabbage, shiitake mushrooms, and noodles; simmer for 5 mins, or until soft.
- Scoop cooked sukiyaki mixture into serving bowls. Restock broth in the pan.
- Break each egg in a small bowl then lightly beat. Serve sukiyaki with beaten egg for dipping.

Nutrition Information

- Calories: 645 calories;
- Total Fat: 19.6
- Sodium: 2831
- Total Carbohydrate: 71.2
- Cholesterol: 235
- Protein: 40.3

233. Tuna Tartare

Serving: 6 | Prep: 10mins | Cook: | Ready in:

Ingredients

- 1 pound sushi grade tuna, finely diced
- 3 tablespoons olive oil
- 1/4 teaspoon wasabi powder
- 1 tablespoon sesame seeds
- 1/8 teaspoon cracked black pepper
- sliced French bread

Direction

- Stir together the cracked black pepper, sesame seeds, wasabi powder and olive oil in a bowl. Toss the tuna into the mixture until coated evenly. Modify the seasoning as preferred with more black pepper or wasabi powder. Serve it on a slice of French bread.

Nutrition Information

- Calories: 366 calories;
- Sodium: 514
- Total Carbohydrate: 42.6
- Cholesterol: 34
- Protein: 26.7
- Total Fat: 9.6

234. Vegan Edamame

Serving: 2 | Prep: 5mins | Cook: 10mins | Ready in:

Ingredients

- 2 tablespoons soy sauce
- 2 tablespoons rice vinegar
- 1 teaspoon finely grated ginger root
- 2 1/2 cups frozen edamame in the pod

Direction

- In a bowl, mix ginger, rice vinegar and soy sauce together; reserve dipping sauce.
- Boil a big saucepan of water. Put the edamame and let boil for 5 minutes till soft. Allow to drain and wash under cold water.
- Serve the pods along with sauce as dipping.

Nutrition Information

- Calories: 235 calories;
- Total Fat: 9.4

- Sodium: 921
- Total Carbohydrate: 18.3
- Cholesterol: 0
- Protein: 19.8

235. Vegan Japanese Spinach Salad

Serving: 2 | Prep: 5mins | Cook: 5mins | Ready in:

Ingredients

- 2 tablespoons toasted sesame seeds, divided
- 2 tablespoons water
- 1 1/2 tablespoons soy sauce
- 1/2 teaspoon white sugar
- 1/2 (8 ounce) package fresh spinach
- 1 pinch salt

Direction

- On a plate, place 1 1/2 tbsp. of sesame seeds then crush the seeds using the bottom of a heavy measuring cup or a pot. Place into a bowl. Stir in sugar, soy sauce and water.
- Boil water in a small pot and place in salt. Place in spinach and cook for up to 1 minute till wilted. Place spinach into a colander to drain and use cold water to rinse and make the cooking process stop. Use hands to squeeze spinach to discard the moisture. Cut the spinach into strips.
- In serving bowls, place cooked spinach. Drizzle over the top with dressing and garnish with the leftover sesame seeds.

Nutrition Information

- Calories: 75 calories;
- Total Carbohydrate: 6.1
- Cholesterol: 0
- Protein: 4
- Total Fat: 4.7
- Sodium: 800

236. Vegetarian Nori Rolls

Serving: 5 | Prep: 30mins | Cook: 30mins | Ready in:

Ingredients

- 2 cups uncooked short-grain white rice
- 2 1/4 cups water
- 1/4 cup soy sauce
- 2 teaspoons honey
- 1 teaspoon minced garlic
- 3 ounces firm tofu, cut into 1/2 inch strips
- 2 tablespoons rice vinegar
- 4 sheets nori seaweed sheets
- 1/2 cucumber, julienned
- 1/2 avocado, julienned
- 1 small carrot, julienned

Direction

- Cover rice with water in a large saucepan and leave it to sit for half an hour.
- Mix garlic, honey and soy sauce in a shallow dish. Marinate tofu for a minimum of half an hour in this mixture.
- Bring to boil the water and rice and then decrease the heat. Leave it to simmer for approximately twenty minutes or until sticky and thick. Mix rice vinegar with the cooked rice in a large glass bowl.
- Onto a bamboo mat, put a sheet of nori. Onto the nori, spread 1/4 of rice evenly with wet hands leaving approximately half inch at the top edge of nori. Put two strips of the marinated tofu end to end around one inch from bottom. Next to the tofu, put two strips of cuke, then avocado and carrot.
- Using the mat to help, fold the nori tightly from bottom to make a tight roll. Half inch at the top, seal by moistening with water. Repeat this with the ingredients remaining. Use a serrated knife to cut into slices of one inch thick.

Nutrition Information

- Calories: 289 calories;
- Total Fat: 4.8
- Sodium: 734
- Total Carbohydrate: 53.6
- Cholesterol: 0
- Protein: 8.1

237. Yakitori Chicken

Serving: 6 | Prep: 25mins | Cook: 20mins | Ready in:

Ingredients

- 1/2 cup sake
- 1/2 cup soy sauce
- 1 tablespoon sugar
- 1 clove garlic, crushed
- 1 (2 inch) piece fresh ginger root, grated
- 1 pound skinless, boneless chicken breast meat - cubed
- 3 leeks, white part only, cut into 1/2 inch pieces

Direction

- In a medium-sized plate, combine ginger, garlic, sugar, soy sauce and sake together. Put in the chicken, and let marinate for 15 minutes.
- Preheat the oven's broiler. Grease 6 metal skewers, and thread them alternately with 3 chicken pieces and 2 leek pieces. Add onto the baking sheet or broiling pan, and use marinade to brush.
- Broil for roughly 5 minutes, baste one more time, then broil till the chicken becomes thoroughly cooked or for 5 minutes more. Get rid of the leftover marinade.

Nutrition Information

- Calories: 159 calories;
- Sodium: 1261
- Total Carbohydrate: 11.5
- Cholesterol: 44
- Protein: 19.7
- Total Fat: 1.1

238. Yakitori Don

Serving: 4 | Prep: 20mins | Cook: 20mins | Ready in:

Ingredients

- 1 (3 pound) whole chicken, cut into pieces
- 1 tablespoon grated fresh ginger root
- 1 clove garlic, crushed
- 3 tablespoons white sugar
- 2/3 cup soy sauce
- 1 tablespoon sake
- 1/4 cup mirin (Japanese sweet wine)
- 2 tablespoons cooking oil

Direction

- Rinse and pat dry the chicken. Combine together mirin, sake, soy sauce, sugar, garlic, and ginger in a glass baking dish or bowl. Add chicken into the mixture so as to marinate. Chill while covered for a few hours or overnight.
- Over medium-high heat, heat oil in a large heavy skillet and then put the chicken pieces with the skin-side down into the pan. Set aside the marinade. Cook the meat until light brown. Turn and then brown the remaining side. Drain off the grease and add the marinade into the pan.
- Cover the pan and decrease the heat to low. Let it simmer for about 8 to 10 minutes. Uncover and continue to cook while shaking the skillet often until the chicken pieces are cooked fully and the marinade is decreased to a nice thick sauce.

Nutrition Information

- Calories: 587 calories;

- Cholesterol: 146
- Protein: 48.7
- Total Fat: 32.5
- Sodium: 2545
- Total Carbohydrate: 18

239. Yakitori Marinade

Serving: 24 | Prep: 5mins | Cook: | Ready in:

Ingredients

- 1/2 cup soy sauce
- 1/2 cup honey
- 1/2 cup sake
- 1 clove garlic, pressed (optional)

Direction

- In a medium-sized bowl, stir sake, honey, and soy sauce together, then mix in pressed garlic if using. Use as a marinade and/or basting sauce when grilling chicken.

240. Yummylicious Japanese Beef Croquettes

Serving: 10 | Prep: 10mins | Cook: 20mins | Ready in:

Ingredients

- 3 medium russet potatoes, peeled, and chopped
- 1 tablespoon butter
- 1 tablespoon vegetable oil
- 3 onions, chopped
- 3/4 pound ground beef
- 4 teaspoons light soy sauce
- all-purpose flour for coating
- 2 eggs, beaten
- panko bread crumbs
- 1/2 cup oil for frying

Direction

- Boil potatoes in a big pot of salted water; cook for 15 mins, or until tender. Drain the potatoes then move the potatoes to a big bowl. Mix in butter then mash using a potato masher or fork; set aside,
- On medium heat, heat 1 tbsp. oil in a big pan; cook and stir in onions until soft. Mix in soy sauce and beef. Cook while continuously mixing until all the liquid evaporates and the beef is brown. Mix beef with potatoes and onions, then combine well.
- On medium-high heat, heat a half cup oil in a wok or deep pan.
- Form the beef and potato mixture into ten even-sized balls then press into patties; dip in flour. Dip each patty in egg then cover in panko bread crumbs. Put into oil carefully then fry until each side is golden brown.

Nutrition Information

- Calories: 239 calories;
- Protein: 9.6
- Total Fat: 13.9
- Sodium: 196
- Total Carbohydrate: 20.4
- Cholesterol: 69

Chapter 3: Indian Cuisine Recipes

***

241. Alicia's Aloo Gobi

Serving: 4 | Prep: 10mins | Cook: 1hours20mins | Ready in:

Ingredients

- 1/4 cup olive oil
- 1 medium onion, chopped
- 1 tablespoon minced garlic
- 1 teaspoon cumin seeds
- 1 (15 ounce) can diced tomatoes
- 1 (15 ounce) can coconut milk
- 2 tablespoons ground coriander
- 1 tablespoon salt
- 1 tablespoon ground turmeric
- 1 tablespoon cayenne pepper
- 1 teaspoon ground cinnamon
- 1 teaspoon ground ginger
- 1 teaspoon ground cardamom
- 3 large Yukon Gold potatoes, peeled and cubed
- 1 medium head cauliflower, chopped into bite size pieces
- 1 (15 ounce) can garbanzo beans, drained
- 2 tablespoons garam masala

Direction

- In a big pot over medium high heat, heat the oil and put in onion. Cook for roughly 4 minutes or till becoming tender then mix in cumin and garlic. Keep cooking till onion starts to brown.
- Mix cardamom, ginger, cinnamon, cayenne pepper, turmeric, salt, coriander, coconut and tomatoes. Mix till mixture starts to boil, then add garbanzo beans, cauliflower and potatoes. Blend well. Lower the heat to low and cover up.
- Simmer for 45 minutes – 1 hour (based on the size of potato chunks), or till the potatoes become softened. Drizzle in the garam masala, mix, and cook for 5 minutes more.

Nutrition Information

- Calories: 622 calories;
- Sodium: 2172
- Total Carbohydrate: 64
- Cholesterol: 0
- Protein: 13.1
- Total Fat: 39.2

242. Aloo Gobi Masala (Cauliflower And Potato Curry)

Serving: 4 | Prep: 20mins | Cook: 15mins | Ready in:

Ingredients

- 1 head cauliflower, cut into 1-inch florets
- 3 potatoes, peeled and cut into 1-inch chunks
- 1 tablespoon olive oil
- 1 teaspoon cumin seeds
- 2 tomatoes, diced
- 1 onion, chopped
- 1 teaspoon salt
- 1 teaspoon curry powder

Direction

- In a big microwaveable dish, put cauliflower then microwave for 3mins on High; move to a bowl then set aside. Place the potatoes in the microwaveable dish; microwave for 4mins on High; move into the bowl with cauliflower.
- On medium-high heat, heat cumin seeds and olive oil in a big frying pan until the cumin is golden brown and swelling. Mix in onions then cook for 3mins. Put in tomatoes; cook and stir for 3mins more. Fold the potatoes and cauliflower into the mixture; sprinkle salt and curry powder to season. Cook for 3-5mins until completely heated. Serve hot.

Nutrition Information

- Calories: 228 calories;
- Sodium: 641
- Total Carbohydrate: 44.3
- Cholesterol: 0
- Protein: 7.5
- Total Fat: 4.1

243. Alu Baigan

Serving: 4 | Prep: 15mins | Cook: 45mins | Ready in:

Ingredients

- 1 eggplant
- 2 large potatoes, cut into 3/4 inch cubes
- 1/4 cup vegetable oil
- 3 teaspoons black mustard seed
- 1 medium onion, sliced
- 1/2 teaspoon chili powder
- 1 teaspoon ground dried turmeric
- 2 teaspoons ground cumin
- 2 teaspoons ground coriander
- 2 teaspoons minced garlic
- 2 teaspoons minced fresh ginger root
- 2 teaspoons garam masala
- 2 teaspoons caraway seed
- 1/4 cup soy sauce

Direction

- In a big bowl, fill with cold water. Slice eggplant to 3/4-in. cubes. Put into water immediately to avoid browning. In a pot, put mustard seeds and oil. Put on medium heat. Cook till seeds start to pop without burning. Mix onion in. cook till tender. Sprinkle caraway seed, garam masala, ginger, garlic, coriander, cumin, turmeric and chili powder in. Cook to release flavor for 1-2 minutes.
- Drain eggplant. Put into pot. Fry for several minutes. Put potatoes and soy sauce in. Use enough water to cover. Put heat on high; boil. Put heat on low. Simmer till potatoes are cooked for approximately 30 minutes.

Nutrition Information

- Calories: 349 calories;
- Cholesterol: 0
- Protein: 7.9
- Total Fat: 15.8
- Sodium: 926
- Total Carbohydrate: 48.2

244. Apple Chutney

Serving: 40 | Prep: 15mins | Cook: 30mins | Ready in:

Ingredients

- 15 tart apples - peeled, cored, and finely chopped
- 1 yellow onion, quartered
- 3 (1 inch) pieces fresh ginger root, peeled
- 1 cup white wine vinegar
- 1/2 cup white sugar
- 1/2 cup brown sugar
- 1/2 teaspoon cinnamon
- 1/2 teaspoon white pepper
- 1/2 teaspoon ground cardamom
- 1/4 teaspoon ground nutmeg

Direction

- Boil nutmeg, apples, cardamom, onion, white pepper, ginger, cinnamon, vinegar, brown sugar, and white sugar together on a pot; lower heat then cover. Let it simmer for half an hour until the apples are tender; mix constantly. If needed, stir in water to moisten the ingredients. Discard the ginger and onion. Refrigerate until ready to use.

Nutrition Information

- Calories: 49 calories;
- Sodium: 2
- Total Carbohydrate: 12.7
- Cholesterol: 0
- Protein: 0.2
- Total Fat: 0.1

245. Authentic South Indian Biryani

Serving: 4 | Prep: 15mins | Cook: 2hours | Ready in:

Ingredients

- 2 1/2 tablespoons vegetable oil
- 1 pod cardamom
- 1 clove
- 1 cinnamon stick
- 4 medium onions, chopped
- 3 tablespoons chopped fresh garlic
- 1/4 teaspoon chopped fresh ginger
- 1 pound boneless skinless chicken breasts, cut into cubes
- chili powder to taste
- 1 1/2 medium tomatoes, chopped
- 16 ounces plain yogurt
- 3 tablespoons water
- lemon juice, to taste
- 3 cups white rice
- 1 teaspoon butter
- salt to taste
- 1 bunch fresh mint, chopped
- 1 bunch chopped cilantro

Direction

- Turn on the oven to 400°F (200°C) to preheat.
- In a large oven-proof pot over medium heat, heat oil. Stir in cinnamon stick, clove and cardamom. Add chopped onions; fry with stirs until it is golden brown. Add in ginger and garlic; stir well. Add chicken pieces; fry for 3 minutes. Add chili powder; stir and cook for several minutes. Add tomatoes; cook for another 5 minutes. Combine lemon juice, 3 tablespoons of water and yogurt; add to the sauce and stir.
- Put into the oven to bake with cover for about 15 minutes until the sauce is slightly concentrated and thickened.
- At the same time, add rice and enough salted water to cover. Let it boil; cook for 7 minutes until it is half cooked. Drain rice; transfer it into the chicken and sauce and stir. Add butter and stir; use salt to taste. Bake for 1 hour with cover. Mix in cilantro and mint right away prior to serving.

Nutrition Information

- Calories: 860 calories;
- Sodium: 185
- Total Carbohydrate: 135.4
- Cholesterol: 75
- Protein: 44.9
- Total Fat: 14.1

246. Awadi Dahi Murg (Chicken In Yogurt Gravy)

Serving: 4 | Prep: 20mins | Cook: 35mins | Ready in:

Ingredients

- 1 (1 1/2 inch) piece fresh ginger root, chopped
- 1 tablespoon minced garlic
- 2 tablespoons ground turmeric
- 3 tablespoons chili powder
- 1/2 cup ground coriander
- 1/2 cup corn oil
- 1/2 teaspoon fenugreek seeds
- 1 (32 ounce) container plain yogurt
- 2 1/2 cups chopped fresh cilantro
- 2 tablespoons chopped green chiles
- 1 tablespoon salt
- 3 pounds skinless, boneless chicken breast halves - cut into cubes

Direction

- In a blender, put coriander, chili powder, turmeric, garlic, and ginger; process to form a smooth paste.
- In a large skillet, heat oil over medium heat. In the oil, cook the fenugreek seeds for 2-3 minutes until they are fragrant; mix in the paste, cook for about 20 minutes until the oil separates from the mixture. Stir in salt, chilies,

cilantro, and yogurt; cook for 5-6 minutes until thick. Add the chicken and cook for 10 minutes.

Nutrition Information

- Calories: 862 calories;
- Protein: 86.4
- Total Fat: 43
- Sodium: 2151
- Total Carbohydrate: 30.9
- Cholesterol: 208

247. Baingan Bharta (Eggplant Curry)

Serving: 4 | Prep: 15mins | Cook: 45mins | Ready in:

Ingredients

- 1 large eggplant
- 2 tablespoons vegetable oil
- 1 teaspoon cumin seeds
- 1 medium onion, thinly sliced
- 1 tablespoon ginger garlic paste
- 1 tablespoon curry powder
- 1 tomato, diced
- 1/2 cup plain yogurt
- 1 fresh jalapeno chile pepper, finely chopped
- 1 teaspoon salt
- 1/4 bunch cilantro, finely chopped

Direction

- Pre heat the oven to 230 degrees C (450 degrees F).
- Put the eggplant onto the medium-sized baking sheet. Bake in preheated oven till becoming soft or 20 - 30 minutes. Take out of the heat, let cool, remove the skin, and cut.
- Heat the oil on medium heat in the medium-sized sauce pan. Stir in the onion and cumin seeds. Cook and stir till the onion softens.
- Whisk the tomato, curry powder and ginger garlic paste to sauce pan, and cook roughly 60 seconds. Mix in the yogurt. Stir in the jalapeno pepper and eggplant, and use the salt to season. Keep covered, and cook on high heat for 10 minutes. Uncover, lower the heat to low, and keep cooking roughly 5 minutes. Use the cilantro to garnish and serve.

Nutrition Information

- Calories: 146 calories;
- Protein: 4
- Total Fat: 8
- Sodium: 739
- Total Carbohydrate: 15.2
- Cholesterol: 2

248. Banana Lassi

Serving: 2 | Prep: 10mins | Cook: | Ready in:

Ingredients

- 2 over-ripe bananas, broken into chunks
- 1 1/4 cups thick plain yogurt
- 1/3 cup milk, or more to taste
- 2 ice cubes
- 2 tablespoons white sugar

Direction

- In a blender, blend together sugar, ice cubes, milk, yogurt and bananas until smooth.

Nutrition Information

- Calories: 270 calories;
- Protein: 10.7
- Total Fat: 3.6
- Sodium: 126
- Total Carbohydrate: 52.1
- Cholesterol: 12

249. Best Potatoes Ever!

Serving: 4 | Prep: 15mins | Cook: 30mins | Ready in:

Ingredients

- 4 large potatoes, peeled and cubed
- 1 1/2 tablespoons ghee (clarified butter)
- 1 teaspoon cumin seeds
- 2 green chile peppers, chopped
- 1 (1 inch) piece fresh ginger root, finely chopped
- 1 teaspoon chili powder
- 1 teaspoon coriander, ground
- 1 teaspoon amchoor (dried mango powder)
- 1/2 teaspoon salt
- 1 bunch fresh cilantro, chopped

Direction

- In a saucepan, put potatoes then cover with enough water; boil. Cook for 10mins until the potatoes are tender; drain. Slightly cool.
- On medium heat, heat ghee in a big frying pan; toast cumin seeds lightly in the ghee. Stir in ginger and green chile peppers; sprinkle coriander and chili powder to season. Mix in potatoes then cook for 5mins. Sprinkle salt and amchoor to season, then keep cooking for 15mins. Place cilantro to decorate, then serve.

Nutrition Information

- Calories: 352 calories;
- Total Fat: 5.6
- Sodium: 320
- Total Carbohydrate: 71
- Cholesterol: 12
- Protein: 7.2

250. Bhuna Gosht

Serving: 6 | Prep: 15mins | Cook: 50mins | Ready in:

Ingredients

- 1/4 cup cooking oil
- 3 pods green cardamom
- 1 pod black cardamom
- 2 bay leaves
- 1 cinnamon stick
- 6 large onions, sliced thin
- 6 cloves garlic
- 1 (1/2 inch) piece fresh ginger root, peeled and julienned
- 2 teaspoons Kashmiri red chili powder
- 1 teaspoon ground cumin
- 1/2 teaspoon ground turmeric
- salt, to taste
- 2 tomatoes, pureed
- 2 pounds lamb chops, rinsed and patted dry
- 2 tablespoons water
- 3 green chile peppers, halved lengthwise
- 1/4 cup cilantro leaves, for garnish

Direction

- Put the oil in a big skillet and set over medium heat. Add the black cardamom pods, green cardamom pods, cinnamon stick and bay leaves in the hot oil, frying them until you smell the nice aroma. Mix in the ginger, garlic and onions in the mixture. Adjust the heat to low and continue to cook until the onions turned golden brown; spice it off using the salt, red chili powder, cumin and turmeric. Stir in the tomatoes and continue to cook for roughly additional 5 minutes until the oil separates from the gravy.
- Put the lamb chops with the mixture in the skillet and adjust the heat to medium-low. Stir while it cooks for roughly 20 minutes until the lamb is halfway done and the sauce produces a glaze on the outside of the meat. Drizzle the water over the mixture. Cook the lamb while covered for additional 15 to 20 minutes until it the meat is tender. Take the cover off and drop

the cilantro leaves and green chile peppers. Adjust the heat to high and allow to cook for additional 3 to 5 minutes. Serve while it is hot.

Nutrition Information

- Calories: 453 calories;
- Total Fat: 30.4
- Sodium: 90
- Total Carbohydrate: 20.5
- Cholesterol: 90
- Protein: 25.6

251. Biryani With Yogurt Marinated Chicken

Serving: 12 | Prep: | Cook: 45mins | Ready in:

Ingredients

- 1 (8 ounce) container whole milk yogurt
- 6 cloves garlic, crushed
- 2 teaspoons finely grated ginger root
- 1 1/2 teaspoons garam masala
- 1/2 teaspoon ground turmeric
- salt to taste
- 2 pounds skinless, boneless chicken breast halves
- 6 cups basmati rice
- 1 pinch saffron
- 7 3/4 cups water, divided
- 1/4 cup olive oil, divided
- 3 onions, sliced, separated into rings
- 3 tomatoes, sliced
- 6 whole cloves
- 5 cardamom pods
- 3 cinnamon sticks
- 1 tablespoon cumin seeds
- 2 tablespoons prepared masala curry sauce

Direction

- In a bowl, combine yogurt, salt, garlic, turmeric, garam masala, and ginger together. Place in chicken breast and mix to coat evenly. Cover the bowl and place the chicken in the fridge to marinate for at least 1 hour.
- Pour rice in a bowl and cover with enough water. Set aside to soften. In a small bowl containing 1/4 cup water, add in the saffron threads. Reserve to bloom.
- Preheat an oven to 200 degrees C (400 degrees F). Use 2 tablespoons olive oil to coat a baking dish.
- Spread a single layer of onions in the baking dish. Place the marinated chicken breast on top of onions and save the marinade. Pour 1/2 cup of water into the reserved marinade. Spread the marinade mixture atop chicken. Place slices of tomato on top.
- Bake for about 30 to 35 minutes in the oven until the juices run clear and the chicken breasts are no longer pink at the center. The temperature at the center should be at least 74 degrees C (165 degrees F).
- Bring to boil six cups of water in a large pot with cumin, cinnamon, cloves, and cardamom. Drain the rice and place into the pot. Heat to boil and then cook for 8 minutes until softened but still firm.
- Over medium heat, heat the remaining two tablespoons oil in a skillet and add masala curry sauce. Cook while stirring for 1 minute until fragrant. Place in parboiled rice and mix to combine for about 1 minute. Mix in 3/4 cup water and saffron-infused water. Cover the skillet, decrease the heat to low and let to simmer for 5 to 8 minutes until the liquid is absorbed. Take out from the heat source and allow to stand for 5 to 10 minutes until the rice becomes fluffy.
- Ladle the rice onto a serving platter and add tomatoes, onion, and chicken breasts on top.

Nutrition Information

- Calories: 506 calories;
- Total Carbohydrate: 83.3
- Cholesterol: 46
- Protein: 24.8

- Total Fat: 8.5
- Sodium: 79

252. Chai Tea Concentrate

Serving: 8 | Prep: 5mins | Cook: 10mins | Ready in:

Ingredients

- 4 cups water
- 15 whole cloves
- 3 cinnamon sticks
- 8 (1/4 inch thick) slices unpeeled fresh ginger
- 15 cardamom pods, split
- 15 whole black peppercorns
- 10 black tea bags
- 1/3 cup brown sugar
- 2 teaspoons vanilla extract

Direction

- In a saucepan, boil water then place in cloves and let boil for 1 minute. Add tea, peppercorns, cardamom pods, ginger and cinnamon sticks. Let steep for 6 minutes then strain the drink into a container. Add vanilla extract and brown sugar to tea then stir. Store in the fridge for at least 1 hour till chilled.

Nutrition Information

- Calories: 58 calories;
- Sodium: 13
- Total Carbohydrate: 13.7
- Cholesterol: 0
- Protein: 0.6
- Total Fat: 0.2

253. Chai Tea Ice Cream

Serving: 12 | Prep: 15mins | Cook: 20mins | Ready in:

Ingredients

- 3 cups whole milk, or more to taste
- 3 cups heavy whipping cream
- 3 cups white sugar
- 4 cinnamon sticks
- 4 tablespoons Indian-style plain black tea
- 3 tablespoons garam masala (Indian spice blend)
- 10 black peppercorns
- 6 cardamom pods
- 2 whole star anise pods
- 1 teaspoon ground nutmeg
- 1 tablespoon vanilla extract
- 1 cup chopped semisweet chocolate (optional)

Direction

- In a saucepan, combine nutmeg, anise pods, cardamom pods, peppercorns, garam masala, tea, cinnamon sticks, sugar, whipping cream and whole milk. Cook until it simmers; let it simmer for 20 minutes. Run the mixture into a large bowl through a colander to strain. Adjust sweetness and spice level as desired by adding up to 1 cup of milk.
- In an ice cream maker, add milk mixture; churn following the instructions of manufacturer.
- Combine churned milk and chocolate; stir well to combine. Freeze for 4-5 hours until it turns creamy and soft with occasional stirs.

Nutrition Information

- Calories: 523 calories;
- Total Carbohydrate: 65.5
- Cholesterol: 88
- Protein: 4.7
- Total Fat: 29
- Sodium: 52

254. Chef John's Chicken Tikka Masala

Serving: 4 | Prep: 25mins | Cook: 45mins | Ready in:

Ingredients

- 1 1/2 pounds skinless, boneless chicken thighs
- 1 tablespoon vegetable oil
- 2 teaspoons kosher salt
- 2 teaspoons garam masala
- 2 teaspoons ground cumin
- 1 teaspoon ground coriander
- 1 teaspoon smoked paprika
- 1 teaspoon ground turmeric
- 1/2 teaspoon ground black pepper
- 1/4 teaspoon cayenne pepper
- 1/8 teaspoon ground cardamom
- 2 tablespoons clarified butter (ghee), or more as needed
- 1 onion, chopped
- 1/4 cup tomato paste
- 4 cloves garlic, finely grated
- 1 tablespoon finely grated ginger, or more to taste
- 1 cup crushed tomatoes
- 1 (13 ounce) can coconut milk
- 1/2 cup chicken broth, or as needed
- 2 tablespoons chopped fresh cilantro
- 1/2 teaspoon red pepper flakes
- salt and ground black pepper to taste

Direction

- Put the chicken into a bowl and sprinkle vegetable oil atop the chicken. Mix to coat.
- In a small bowl, whisk together cardamom, cayenne pepper, black pepper, ground turmeric, smoked paprika, ground coriander, ground cumin, garam masala and kosher salt. Season the chicken with the spice mixture and then flip to coat evenly.
- Over high heat, melt the clarified butter in a large, heavy skillet and then cook the chicken thighs for 5 to 10 minutes in hot butter until they are browned on all sides. Place the chicken onto a plate. Once cooled enough to work on, slice the chicken into bite-size pieces.
- Decrease the heat under the skillet to medium-high. Mix onion into the skillet and then sauté for 5 to 6 minutes until the onion is translucent and soft. Stir in tomato paste. Sauté for about 5 minutes until the paste caramelizes. Mix ginger and garlic into the tomato-onion mixture and let it cook for about 1 minute until fragrant.
- Add crushed tomatoes into skillet and heat to a boil as you scrape off any browned bits of food from bottom of skillet using a wooden spoon. Add chicken broth and coconut milk, heat to a simmer. Decrease the heat to medium low and then cook while stirring from time to time for about 15 minutes until the sauce is slightly reduced and flavors blend.
- Mix the red pepper flakes, cilantro and chicken along with all the accumulated juices into the tomato mixture. Heat to a simmer. Decrease the heat to medium-low and let it cook for 10 to 15 minutes until the chicken is tender and cooked through. Add black pepper and salt to taste.

Nutrition Information

- Calories: 625 calories;
- Sodium: 1325
- Total Carbohydrate: 19.2
- Cholesterol: 122
- Protein: 33.5
- Total Fat: 48.2

255. Chef John's Tandoori Chicken

Serving: 6 | Prep: 5mins | Cook: 15mins | Ready in:

Ingredients

- 1/2 lime, juiced
- 1 1/2 tablespoons plain yogurt

- 1 1/2 tablespoons tandoori masala powder
- salt and freshly ground black pepper to taste
- 2 pounds boneless, skinless chicken thighs

Direction

- Stir together the yogurt, lime juice, tandoori powder, pepper and salt in a bowl. Put the mixture in the resealable plastic bag. Drop the chicken to coat with the marinade, release out excess air, and seal the bag to secure. Place inside the fridge for at least 2 hours to marinate.
- Set an outdoor grill for preheating to medium-high heat, and grease the grate lightly.
- Take the chicken out from the bag and put on a plate or baking sheet lined with paper towels. Pat them dry with extra paper towels.
- Grill the chicken with the lid open for roughly 2 minutes. Close the lid and continue grilling the chicken for about 6 minutes.
- Flip the chicken, close lid and let them grill for about 6 minutes until the chicken is browned nicely and meat is no longer pink in the middle. An instant-read thermometer poked in the thickest part of the thigh should reach 180°F (82°C).

Nutrition Information

- Calories: 215 calories;
- Sodium: 93
- Total Carbohydrate: 1.9
- Cholesterol: 94
- Protein: 25.8
- Total Fat: 11.1

256. Chicken Biryani

Serving: 7 | Prep: | Cook: | Ready in:

Ingredients

- 4 tablespoons vegetable oil
- 4 small potatoes, peeled and halved
- 2 large onions, finely chopped
- 2 cloves garlic, minced
- 1 tablespoon minced fresh ginger root
- 1/2 teaspoon chili powder
- 1/2 teaspoon ground black pepper
- 1/2 teaspoon ground turmeric
- 1 teaspoon ground cumin
- 1 teaspoon salt
- 2 medium tomatoes, peeled and chopped
- 2 tablespoons plain yogurt
- 2 tablespoons chopped fresh mint leaves
- 1/2 teaspoon ground cardamom
- 1 (2 inch) piece cinnamon stick
- 3 pounds boneless, skinless chicken pieces cut into chunks
- 2 1/2 tablespoons vegetable oil
- 1 large onion, diced
- 1 pinch powdered saffron
- 5 pods cardamom
- 3 whole cloves
- 1 (1 inch) piece cinnamon stick
- 1/2 teaspoon ground ginger
- 1 pound basmati rice
- 4 cups chicken stock
- 1 1/2 teaspoons salt

Direction

- Fry potatoes in 2 tbsp. of vegetable oil (or ghee) in a big skillet, till becoming brown, drain off and save the potatoes. Pour leftover 2 tbsp. of oil into the skillet and fry ginger, garlic and onion till onion becomes soft and golden. Put in tomatoes, salt, cumin, turmeric, pepper, and chili. Fry, mixing continuously for 5 minutes. Put in cinnamon stick, cardamom, mint, and yogurt. Keep it covered and cook on low heat, mixing once in a while till the tomatoes are cooked to a pulp. You may need to add a bit of hot water in if the mixture is too dry and begins to stick to the pan.
- Once the mixture becomes thick and smooth, put in the chicken pieces and mix them well to coat with the spice mixture. Keep it covered and cooked on very low heat for about 35-45 minutes or till the chicken turns soft. There

should only be a bit of very thick gravy remained when chicken is finished cooking. Cook while uncovered for several minutes to decrease the gravy amount if needed.
- Rinse the rice well and drain in the colander for no less than half an hour.
- Heat vegetable oil (or ghee) in a big skillet and fry the onions till they become golden. Put in rice, ginger, cinnamon stick, cloves, cardamom, and saffron. Mix constantly till the rice becomes coated with the spices.
- Heat salt and chicken stock in a medium-sized pot. Once the mixture becomes hot, add it on top of the rice and mix well. Put in potatoes and chicken mixture; lightly stir them into the rice. Boil. Cover the saucepan securely; switch on heat to very low and let steam for 20 minutes. Don't lift the lid or mix during cooking process. Scoop biryani onto a warm serving plate.

Nutrition Information

- Calories: 832 calories;
- Total Fat: 35.1
- Sodium: 1522
- Total Carbohydrate: 78.9
- Cholesterol: 134
- Protein: 47.8

257. Chicken Cauliflower Korma

Serving: 6 | Prep: 15mins | Cook: 30mins | Ready in:

Ingredients

- 2 tablespoons ghee (clarified butter)
- 1 onion, diced
- 4 cloves garlic, minced
- 1 1/2 tablespoons curry powder
- 2 1/2 teaspoons ground cumin
- 2 teaspoons minced fresh ginger root
- 1 1/2 teaspoons salt
- 1 1/4 teaspoons ground turmeric
- 3/4 teaspoon ground cardamom
- 1/4 teaspoon ground cinnamon
- 1/4 teaspoon cayenne pepper
- 1/8 teaspoon ground nutmeg
- 2 skinless, boneless chicken breast halves - cubed
- 3 carrots, cubed
- 1 (14 ounce) can coconut milk
- 1/4 cup ground cashews
- 2 tablespoons tomato paste
- 1 head cauliflower, chopped
- 1 cup frozen peas
- 1 red bell pepper, chopped
- 1/2 cup heavy whipping cream (optional)

Direction

- Over medium heat, heat ghee in a large pot, add onion and then cook while stirring for about 5 minutes until tender. Mix nutmeg, cayenne pepper, cinnamon, cardamom, turmeric, salt, ginger, cumin, curry powder and garlic into the onion. Cook while stirring for about 1 minute until fragrant.
- Mix chicken into the onion mixture and then let it cook for two minutes. Mix tomato paste, cashews, coconut milk and carrots into the chicken mixture. Let it simmer for five minutes. Mix cauliflower into the chicken mixture. Let it simmer while covering for about 5 minutes until chicken is cooked through and vegetables are tender.
- Mix cream, red bell pepper, and peas into the chicken mixture. Decrease the heat to low. Cover, and let it simmer for about 10 minutes until heated through.

Nutrition Information

- Calories: 402 calories;
- Total Fat: 29.5
- Sodium: 776
- Total Carbohydrate: 24.3
- Cholesterol: 60
- Protein: 15.3

258. Chicken Chicken Curry

Serving: 6 | Prep: 15mins | Cook: 1hours10mins | Ready in:

Ingredients

- 3 tablespoons olive oil
- 1 red onion, thinly sliced, divided
- salt to taste
- 1 bay leaf
- 1 tablespoon water
- 1 tablespoon ground turmeric
- 1/2 teaspoon chili powder
- 1/2 teaspoon paprika
- 2 tablespoons ground ginger
- 2 tablespoons minced garlic
- 1 tablespoon water
- 2 1/4 pounds skinless, boneless chicken breast, cut in bite-sized pieces
- 1 tomato, thinly sliced
- 1/4 teaspoon white sugar
- 3 cardamom pods, lightly crushed
- 3 whole cloves
- 1 (2 inch) cinnamon stick
- 1 tablespoon ghee (clarified butter)
- 1 tablespoon water
- 1 tablespoon ground coriander
- 1 bunch cilantro, chopped

Direction

- In a skillet, heat olive oil over high heat. Mix in 1/3 of the onion; cook and stir for 5 minutes, or until crisp and golden brown. Sprinkle salt to season. Transfer onion from the oil to a paper towel-lined plate to drain excess oil. Set aside.
- In the same skillet, add bay leaf and remaining 2/3 of onions over high heat. Cook and stir for 5 minutes, or until onions are golden brown. Stir 1 tablespoon of water into the skillet, then add garlic, paprika, ginger, chili powder, and turmeric. Lower heat to medium-high, continue to stir and cook until the liquid has decreased. Once the liquid has reduced, stir in another tablespoon of water.
- Add tomato slices and chicken to the onion mixture in the skillet. Add salt and sugar to season. Stir in 1 tablespoon of water, ghee, cinnamon stick, cloves, and cardamom pods. Cover with lid and simmer for 30 to 35 minutes over low heat until liquid has reduced. Add coriander and stir. Continue to simmer until liquid has evaporated. Garnish with a sprinkle of reserved fried onions and cilantro, then serve.

Nutrition Information

- Calories: 289 calories;
- Sodium: 84
- Total Carbohydrate: 7.8
- Cholesterol: 93
- Protein: 34.4
- Total Fat: 13

259. Chicken Chutney Sandwiches With Curry

Serving: 6 | Prep: 15mins | Cook: | Ready in:

Ingredients

- 1 roasted chicken, bones and skin removed, meat shredded
- 3/4 cup cranberry and apple chutney
- 1/4 cup whipped cream cheese
- 2 teaspoons curry powder
- 6 croissants, split

Direction

- Stir together the curry powder, cream cheese, chutney and chicken. Spread onto the split croissants. Serve.

Nutrition Information

- Calories: 450 calories;
- Total Fat: 20
- Sodium: 527
- Total Carbohydrate: 40.3
- Cholesterol: 109
- Protein: 26.9

260. Chicken Makhani (Indian Butter Chicken)

Serving: 4 | Prep: 10mins | Cook: 25mins | Ready in:

Ingredients

- 1 tablespoon peanut oil
- 1 shallot, finely chopped
- 1/4 white onion, chopped
- 2 tablespoons butter
- 2 teaspoons lemon juice
- 1 tablespoon ginger garlic paste
- 1 teaspoon garam masala
- 1 teaspoon chili powder
- 1 teaspoon ground cumin
- 1 bay leaf
- 1/4 cup plain yogurt
- 1 cup half-and-half
- 1 cup tomato puree
- 1/4 teaspoon cayenne pepper, or to taste
- 1 pinch salt
- 1 pinch black pepper
- 1 tablespoon peanut oil
- 1 pound boneless, skinless chicken thighs, cut into bite-size pieces
- 1 teaspoon garam masala
- 1 pinch cayenne pepper
- 1 tablespoon cornstarch
- 1/4 cup water

Direction

- Heat 1 tbsp. oil in a large pot over a medium-high flame. Sauté the shallots and the onions together until tender and translucent. Stir in the butter and the ginger-garlic paste. Squeeze over the lemon juice then add 1 tsp of garam masala, cumin and the chili powder, bay leaf; cook and stir for about a minute. Pour over the tomato sauce and allow to cook for another 2 minutes; stir occasionally. Mix in half-and-half together with the yoghurt. Adjust the heat to low and allow to simmer for 10 more minutes. Stir frequently. Season with salt and pepper. Remove from the flame, then set aside for a while.
- In a large pan, heat 1 tbsp. of oil over a medium heat. Cook the chicken for about 10 minutes or until lightly browned. Lower the heat and season with 1 tsp of garam masala together with cayenne. Stir in few spoonful of the sauce. Let it simmer until liquid evaporates and chicken is no longer pink. Mix together the cooked chicken with the sauce.
- Make a slurry by mixing cornstarch and water together, then stir into the sauce. Let it cook for roughly 5 to 10 minutes, or until the consistency turns thick.

Nutrition Information

- Calories: 408 calories;
- Total Fat: 27.8
- Sodium: 523
- Total Carbohydrate: 15.6
- Cholesterol: 107
- Protein: 23.4

261. Chickpea Coconut Salad

Serving: 4 | Prep: 15mins | Cook: | Ready in:

Ingredients

- 1 (15 ounce) can garbanzo beans (chickpeas), rinsed and drained
- 1/3 cup freshly grated coconut
- 1 teaspoon chopped green chile peppers (optional)

- 1/3 cup chopped fresh cilantro
- 2 teaspoons lemon juice
- 1/2 teaspoon salt

Direction

- In a big bowl, mix together the cilantro, green chile peppers, coconut and garbanzo beans, then stir in lemon juice and season with salt to taste. Before serving, chill for 2 hours for best flavor.

Nutrition Information

- Calories: 109 calories;
- Total Fat: 3.1
- Sodium: 503
- Total Carbohydrate: 17.3
- Cholesterol: 0
- Protein: 3.8

262. Coconut Chutney

Serving: 8 | Prep: 20mins | Cook: 5mins | Ready in:

Ingredients

- 1/2 fresh whole coconut, drained and grated
- 1/2 cup plain yogurt
- 1 tablespoon vegetable oil
- 3 fresh red chili peppers, chopped
- 1/2 teaspoon mustard seed
- 1/4 teaspoon cumin seeds

Direction

- In a food processor or blender, process yogurt and coconut until paste-like; move to a medium bowl.
- On medium heat, heat oil in a medium pot. Cook and stir cumin seeds, mustard seed, and chili peppers in hot oil until the mustard seeds pop; scoop on top the coconut mixture then cover. Place in the refrigerator until ready to serve.

Nutrition Information

- Calories: 121 calories;
- Sodium: 17
- Total Carbohydrate: 6.5
- Cholesterol: < 1
- Protein: 2
- Total Fat: 10.4

263. Coconut Curry Chili

Serving: 6 | Prep: 10mins | Cook: 1hours10mins | Ready in:

Ingredients

- 1/2 pound ground turkey
- 2 (10.75 ounce) cans tomato soup
- 1 1/4 cups water
- 1 tablespoon minced garlic
- 1 (15 ounce) can chickpeas (garbanzo beans), drained and rinsed
- 1 (15 ounce) can red kidney beans, drained and rinsed
- 1/2 cup chopped carrot
- 1/4 cup mango chutney
- 3 tablespoons curry powder
- 1 teaspoon onion powder
- salt and ground black pepper to taste
- 1/2 cup coconut milk, divided

Direction

- In a big skillet on medium heat, break ground turkey in small pieces. Continue to break stir and cook the turkey, breaking it in smaller pieces for 5-7 minutes until it becomes fully browned. Discard excess grease from the turkey as much as possible.
- In a big pot, mix water, minced garlic and tomato soup then let it boil. Put turkey in pot and let the mixture return to boiling; lowering heat to medium low. Mix salt, black pepper,

onion powder, curry powder, chutney, red kidney beans, chickpeas and carrot in the turkey mixture then let it simmer. Put cover on until chickpeas are soft, 15 minutes.
- Mix 1/4 cup coconut milk in the chili mixture then place the cover on and let it simmer for 15 minutes longer. Put the left1/4 cup coconut milk in chili, mix, and let it simmer for another half an hour.

Nutrition Information

- Calories: 312 calories;
- Sodium: 890
- Total Carbohydrate: 43.4
- Cholesterol: 28
- Protein: 16.4
- Total Fat: 9.7

264. Cod Curry

Serving: 4 | Prep: 15mins | Cook: 55mins | Ready in:

Ingredients

- 2 tablespoons vegetable oil
- 1 medium onion, chopped
- 1 teaspoon garlic paste
- 1 teaspoon ginger paste
- 2 teaspoons cumin
- 2 teaspoons coriander
- 1 teaspoon cardamom
- 1/2 teaspoon turmeric
- 1/2 teaspoon salt
- 2 fresh jalapeno peppers, seeded and diced
- 1/4 cup chopped cilantro
- 1 tablespoon lemon juice
- 1 (28 ounce) can diced tomatoes with juice
- 1 pound cod fillets, cut into chunks

Direction

- On medium heat, heat the oil in a skillet. Add onion into the skillet. Lower heat to low, and cook while mixing frequently till brown and soft for 15 minutes.
- Into the skillet, mix ginger paste and garlic paste. Cook for 60 seconds. Whisk in salt, turmeric, cardamom, coriander and cumin. Mix in tomatoes, lemon juice, cilantro and jalapeno with juice, scraping up any brown bits from the bottom of the skillet. Boil. Lower heat to low, keep it covered, and simmered for 20 minutes. Put the sauce aside for several hours at this point to let the flavors to blend if desired.
- Bring the sauce back to a boil, and add cod into the skillet. Lower heat to low, and cook till fish could be flaked easily using a fork, for 15 minutes.

Nutrition Information

- Calories: 227 calories;
- Total Carbohydrate: 11.4
- Cholesterol: 53
- Protein: 23.6
- Total Fat: 8.4
- Sodium: 757

265. Country Captain Chicken With Rice

Serving: 8 | Prep: 25mins | Cook: 1hours50mins | Ready in:

Ingredients

- 1 whole whole chicken, cut into 8 pieces
- 1 teaspoon ground thyme
- kosher salt and freshly ground black pepper to taste
- 1/4 cup canola oil
- 6 slices applewood smoked bacon, chopped
- 1 large yellow onion, diced small
- 3 ribs celery, chopped
- 2 green bell peppers, chopped
- 4 cloves garlic, minced

- 1 (28 ounce) can whole peeled tomatoes, drained and chopped, liquid reserved
- 1/4 cup dried currants, plus more for garnish
- 1/4 cup golden raisins, or to taste
- 3 tablespoons Madras curry powder
- 2 tablespoons unsalted butter
- 2 bay leaves
- 2 cups cooked basmati rice
- 2 tablespoons peanuts, or to taste
- 2 tablespoons chopped fresh parsley

Direction

- Use black pepper, kosher salt and thyme to season the chicken.
- In a 5-quart Dutch oven over high heat, heat oil. In hot oil, place chicken with skin-side down; cook for 2-5 minutes until golden brown. Put chicken on a plate; drain and get rid of oil.
- Lower the heat to medium; add bacon to the Dutch oven. Cook while stirring for 7-10 minutes until crispy and browned. Place bacon on a plate lined with paper towel. Chop into smaller pieces.
- In the Dutch oven over medium heat, cook while stirring garlic, bell peppers, celery and onion for about 10 minutes until soft. Add black pepper, salt, bay leaves, butter, curry powder, raisins, currants, 3/4 cup reserved tomato liquid and chopped tomatoes; bring to a simmer, lower the heat to medium-low, use a lid to cover the Dutch oven, then simmer for about half an hour until sauce becomes thickened.
- Set oven to 325°F (165°C) and start preheating.
- Put chicken back in the Dutch oven; scoop sauce over top. Use lid to cover the Dutch oven.
- Bake in the prepared oven for about an hour until chicken becomes tender. The inserted thermometer into the thickest part of the thigh near the bone should register 165°F (74°C).
- Press half cup rice into a small bowl; turn the cake upside down onto a plate to remove. Place 2 pieces of chicken on rice; scoop sauce on top. Do the same with the rest of sauce, chicken and rice. Decorate each with parsley, peanuts, currants and bacon.

Nutrition Information

- Calories: 783 calories;
- Sodium: 471
- Total Carbohydrate: 28.9
- Cholesterol: 106
- Protein: 28.2
- Total Fat: 62

266. Culture Blend Spaghetti

Serving: 8 | Prep: 10mins | Cook: 20mins | Ready in:

Ingredients

- 1 (16 ounce) package spaghetti
- 1 tablespoon oil
- 1 onion, chopped
- 1 bunch fresh parsley, stems removed and leaves chopped
- 3 cloves garlic, minced
- 9 cardamom pods
- 1 cinnamon stick
- 1/2 teaspoon ground turmeric
- 1/2 teaspoon cumin seeds
- 2 (14.5 ounce) cans Italian-style diced tomatoes
- 1 tablespoon white sugar
- 1/2 (7 ounce) container Greek yogurt
- kosher salt to taste

Direction

- Boil lightly salted water in a big pot. In the boiling water, cook spaghetti for 12 minutes until fully cooked yet firm to bite, tossing sometimes. Strain and put back into the pot.
- In a frying pan, heat oil over medium heat. In the hot oil, cook while stirring the onion for 5 minutes until tender. Add cumin seeds, turmeric, cinnamon stick, cardamom pods, garlic, and parsley to the onion; cook while

stirring for 2-3 minutes until the garlic is tender. Mix sugar and tomatoes into the onion mixture and cook for 5-10 minutes until aromatic and fully heated.
- Pour over the spaghetti with the tomato sauce mixture and stir thoroughly. Mix salt and yogurt into the spaghetti mixture.

Nutrition Information

- Calories: 288 calories;
- Sodium: 518
- Total Carbohydrate: 53.7
- Cholesterol: 3
- Protein: 9.7
- Total Fat: 4

267. Curried Celery

Serving: 8 | Prep: 20mins | Cook: | Ready in:

Ingredients

- 1/2 cup cream cheese, softened
- 1/2 cup raisins, finely chopped
- 2 tablespoons minced peeled apple
- 1 teaspoon medium curry powder, or to taste
- 1/2 teaspoon lemon juice
- 8 stalks celery, or as needed, cut into thirds

Direction

- Whisk the lemon juice, curry powder, apple, raisins, and cream cheese till becoming smooth. Spread onto the celery.

Nutrition Information

- Calories: 90 calories;
- Sodium: 76
- Total Carbohydrate: 10.2
- Cholesterol: 16
- Protein: 1.7
- Total Fat: 5.2

268. Curried Chicken With Rice

Serving: 4 | Prep: | Cook: | Ready in:

Ingredients

- 2 1/2 pounds cut up chicken pieces
- 3 tablespoons olive oil
- 3 tablespoons curry powder
- 1 (12 ounce) jar chutney
- 1 red bell pepper, thinly sliced
- 1 lime, cut into wedges
- 1/8 cup chopped green onion for topping
- 1/4 cup chopped peanuts

Direction

- Rinse the chicken and pat them dry. In the big skillet, heat the oil till becoming nearly hot. Place chicken, with skin-side facing downward. Brown the chicken till becoming browned a bit on both sides. Put in the red bell pepper, chutney and curry powder. Let it simmer half an hour on medium-low heat. Add the peanuts, chopped scallions and lime wedges on top of the chicken. Serve right away.

Nutrition Information

- Calories: 913 calories;
- Protein: 57.1
- Total Fat: 58.6
- Sodium: 220
- Total Carbohydrate: 41.7
- Cholesterol: 213

269. Curried Corn

Serving: 4 | Prep: 10mins | Cook: 10mins | Ready in:

Ingredients

- 3 tablespoons butter
- 2 cups frozen corn
- 2 tablespoons chopped green bell pepper
- 2 tablespoons chopped onion
- 1/2 teaspoon curry powder
- 1/2 cup sour cream
- salt and ground black pepper to taste

Direction

- Over medium heat, melt butter in a skillet and then stir in curry powder, onion, green pepper and corn. Cover skillet and let it cook for 8 to 10 minutes until the veggies are just tender. Mix sour cream into vegetable mixture. Add pepper and salt to season and continue to cook while stirring constantly for 2 to 3 minutes until hot. Serve right away.

Nutrition Information

- Calories: 214 calories;
- Total Fat: 15.3
- Sodium: 80
- Total Carbohydrate: 19.1
- Cholesterol: 36
- Protein: 3.6

270. Curried Cream Of Cauliflower Soup

Serving: 4 | Prep: 15mins | Cook: 50mins | Ready in:

Ingredients

- 1 head cauliflower, cut into florets
- 2 tablespoons vegetable oil
- 1 teaspoon salt
- 1 tablespoon butter, cut into small pieces
- 1 large yellow onion, diced
- 1 teaspoon chopped garlic
- 1 teaspoon curry powder
- 1 teaspoon cayenne pepper
- 1 teaspoon ground turmeric
- 1 quart chicken stock
- 1 cup heavy whipping cream
- salt and ground black pepper to taste
- 2 tablespoons chopped fresh parsley

Direction

- Preheat oven to 230 degrees C (450 degrees F).
- In a bowl, toss cauliflower florets with vegetable oil and 1 teaspoon salt; spread on a baking sheet. Roast cauliflower for 25 minutes in preheated oven, until it turns brown.
- Melt butter in a saucepan placed over medium-high heat. Sauté onions in heated butter for 5 minutes, until tender. Mix in garlic and cook for 2 minutes, until an aromatic; use ground turmeric, curry powder and cayenne pepper to season. Cook the mixture for 5 minutes, stirring continuously.
- Add roasted cauliflower to the mixture and stir. Spread stock over mixture. Boil the stock in a covered saucepan. Remove cover from the saucepan immediately, lower the heat to low, and let simmer for 10 minutes, until the liquid slightly decreases.
- Blend the mixture with an immersion blender, until desired consistency is achieved. Add cream to the soup; use pepper and salt to season. Divide soup into bowls and garnish with parsley.

Nutrition Information

- Calories: 359 calories;
- Total Carbohydrate: 15.1
- Cholesterol: 90
- Protein: 5.4
- Total Fat: 32.7
- Sodium: 1391

271. Curried Cumin Potatoes

Serving: 8 | Prep: 15mins | Cook: 20mins | Ready in:

Ingredients

- 2 pounds new potatoes, cut into 1/4 inch thick pieces
- 2 tablespoons olive oil
- 2 tablespoons cumin seed
- 2 teaspoons ground turmeric
- 2 teaspoons curry powder
- 2 teaspoons coarse sea salt
- 1 teaspoon ground black pepper
- 3 tablespoons chopped fresh cilantro

Direction

- Into a saucepan, put whole potatoes with water to submerge. Boil; let to cook till just soft. Allow to drain then slice potatoes in 4 portions. Put aside to retain warmth.
- In a big sauté pan, heat oil over medium-high heat. For a minute, sauté curry powder, turmeric and cumin. Put potatoes in and sauté till browned. Toss the potatoes with fresh cilantro, pepper and sea salt. Serve while hot.

Nutrition Information

- Calories: 128 calories;
- Total Fat: 4
- Sodium: 451
- Total Carbohydrate: 21.4
- Cholesterol: 0
- Protein: 2.7

272. Curried Scallops With Angel Hair Pasta

Serving: 2 | Prep: 10mins | Cook: 15mins | Ready in:

Ingredients

- 2 ounces whole-wheat angel hair pasta
- 1 teaspoon extra-virgin olive oil
- 1 onion, chopped
- 1 teaspoon curry powder
- 1/4 cup fat free, low-sodium chicken broth
- 1/4 cup evaporated skim milk
- 2 teaspoons low-sodium tomato paste
- 10 ounces fresh scallops
- 1/4 cup fat free, low-sodium chicken broth

Direction

- In a pot, let lightly salted water boil. In the boiling water, cook angel hair pasta 4 to 5 minutes until cooked through but firm to the bite. Distribute in two plates and keep it warm.
- Over medium heat, heat olive oil in a skillet. Cook and stir onion in the hot oil for about 3 minutes, until softened. In the onion, stir curry powder in. Cook and stir for another minute.
- Put the onion mixture into blender. Put 1/4 cup of chicken broth with tomato paste and evaporated milk.
- Put back skillet to medium heat. In the hot skillet, sear scallops for 2 to 3 minutes on per side. Over the angel hair pasta, put the scallops and keep it warm.
- In the pan, put in 1/4 chicken broth. Let it boil while using a wooden spoon to scrape the brown bits of food off at the bottom of the pan. Put contents of the skillet to the blender and blend until smooth. When done, put the mixture back to the skillet. Let the sauce simmer until warm. Put mixture over pasta and scallops. Serve.

Nutrition Information

- Calories: 413 calories;
- Total Fat: 15.9
- Sodium: 432
- Total Carbohydrate: 40.1
- Cholesterol: 91
- Protein: 27.2

273. Dal Makhani (Indian Lentils)

Serving: 6 | Prep: 15mins | Cook: 2hours | Ready in:

Ingredients

- 1 cup lentils
- 1/4 cup dry kidney beans (optional)
- water to cover
- 5 cups water
- 2 tablespoons salt
- 2 tablespoons vegetable oil
- 1 tablespoon cumin seeds
- 4 cardamom pods
- 1 cinnamon stick, broken
- 4 bay leaves
- 6 whole cloves
- 1 1/2 tablespoons ginger paste
- 1 1/2 tablespoons garlic paste
- 1/2 teaspoon ground turmeric
- 1 pinch cayenne pepper, or more to taste
- 1 cup canned tomato puree, or more to taste
- 1 tablespoon chili powder
- 2 tablespoons ground coriander
- 1/4 cup butter
- 2 tablespoons dried fenugreek leaves (optional)
- 1/2 cup cream (optional)

Direction

- In a big bowl, place kidney beans and lentils, pour in a large amount of water to cover. Allow to soak for no less than 2 hours or all night. Drain.
- In a pot on medium heat, cook salt, 5 cups water, kidney beans and lentils for 1 hour, mixing occasionally, until tender. Take away from heat; put aside. Leave any excess cooking water with kidney beans and lentils in the pot.
- In a saucepan on medium-high heat, heat vegetable oil. In the hot oil, cook cumin seeds 1-2 minutes till they start to pop. Put in cloves, bay leaves, cinnamon stick and cardamom pods; cook 1 minute till bay leaf turn brown. Decrease heat to medium-low; put in cayenne pepper, turmeric, garlic paste and ginger paste. Mix to coat.
- Mix tomato puree into the spice mixture; cook 5 minutes over medium heat until lightly reduced. Add in butter, coriander and chili powder; cook while stirring until butter melts.
- Mix any remaining cooking water along with kidney beans and lentils into the tomato mixture; boil, then decrease to low heat. Mix fenugreek into the lentil mixture. Put cover on the saucepan and allow to simmer 45 minutes, mixing occasionally, until heated through. Add in cream and cook 2-4 minutes until heated through.

Nutrition Information

- Calories: 375 calories;
- Sodium: 2718
- Total Carbohydrate: 34.2
- Cholesterol: 48
- Protein: 12.8
- Total Fat: 21.2

274. Easy Baked Indian Samosas

Serving: 16 | Prep: 30mins | Cook: 40mins | Ready in:

Ingredients

- 4 potatoes, peeled and cubed
- 1/4 cup oil
- 2 small onions, finely chopped
- 3 tablespoons coriander seed
- 1 tablespoon curry powder
- 1 (1 inch) piece fresh ginger, grated
- 1 teaspoon salt
- 1 teaspoon ground turmeric
- 1 teaspoon ground cumin
- 1/2 teaspoon ground allspice
- 1/2 teaspoon cayenne pepper
- 1/8 teaspoon ground cinnamon
- 2 roma (plum) tomatoes, finely chopped

- 1/2 cup frozen peas
- 4 prepared pie crusts
- 2 egg whites, beaten, or as needed

Direction

- In a big pot, put potatoes the pour salted water to cover; boil. Turn to medium-low heat; let it simmer for 20mins until tender. Drain the potatoes then mash coarsely in a bowl.
- Preheat the oven to 200°C or 400°Fahrenheit.
- On medium-high heat, heat oil in a frying pan. Cook and stir cinnamon, onions, cayenne pepper, coriander seed, allspice, curry powder, cumin, ginger, turmeric, and salt for 5mins until onion turns pale brown. Take skillet off heat. Mix peas and tomatoes into onion blend then stir into mashed potatoes and combine well. Completely cool.
- Slice each pie crust to eight equal triangles; scoop filling on the wide end of the triangles. Fold the sides over the filling to make a triangle hat figure. Seal by pinching the dough together. Slather egg white on top of each samosa then place on a baking sheet.
- Bake for 15mins in the preheated oven until samosas turn golden brown.

Nutrition Information

- Calories: 315 calories;
- Sodium: 396
- Total Carbohydrate: 32.7
- Cholesterol: 0
- Protein: 4.9
- Total Fat: 18.7

275. Easy Chickpea Curry

Serving: 4 | Prep: 15mins | Cook: 35mins | Ready in:

Ingredients

- 1 tablespoon butter
- 1 onion, chopped
- 3 cloves garlic, minced
- 3 teaspoons curry powder
- 2 teaspoons garam masala
- 1/2 teaspoon ground paprika
- 1/2 teaspoon white sugar
- 1/2 teaspoon ground ginger
- 1/4 teaspoon ground turmeric
- 1/4 teaspoon salt
- 1/4 teaspoon pepper
- 1 (15 ounce) can garbanzo beans, drained
- 2 potatoes, chopped
- 1 (14 ounce) can coconut milk
- 1 tomato, chopped
- 1/3 cup milk
- 2 tablespoons ketchup
- 2 tablespoons sour cream
- 2 cubes chicken bouillon
- 1/4 cup ground almonds, or as needed

Direction

- In a large saucepan, melt the butter over medium heat. Cook while stirring for about 5 minutes the garlic and onion in the melted butter, until onion becomes translucent. Scatter in pepper, salt, turmeric, ginger, sugar, paprika, garam masala and curry powder. Keep cooking and stirring for a further of 3 to 4 minutes, until spices are lightly toasted.
- Stir in bouillon cubes, sour cream, ketchup, milk, tomato, coconut milk, potatoes and the garbanzo beans. Simmer the curry for about 25 minutes over medium-low heat, until the potatoes get tender. Mix in ground almonds to thicken.

Nutrition Information

- Calories: 505 calories;
- Total Fat: 31.8
- Sodium: 1073
- Total Carbohydrate: 49.7
- Cholesterol: 13
- Protein: 11.9

276. Easy Curried Cauliflower

Serving: 6 | Prep: 20mins | Cook: 35mins | Ready in:

Ingredients

- 3 cups grated cauliflower
- 3 tablespoons vegetable oil
- 1/2 large onion, diced
- 2 cloves garlic
- 1 teaspoon cumin seeds
- 1 tomato, diced
- 1/2 teaspoon cayenne pepper
- 1 teaspoon salt, or to taste
- 1 teaspoon ground dried turmeric
- 2 teaspoons ground coriander seed
- 1 (12 ounce) can kidney beans, drained and rinsed
- 2 teaspoons garam masala

Direction

- In a large skillet, heat vegetable oil over medium heat. Stir in cumin seeds, garlic, and onions. Cook in a stirring motion for 10 minutes, or until onions are golden brown. Stir in coriander, turmeric, salt, cayenne pepper, and diced tomatoes. Cook for 2 minutes, then stir cauliflower in and lower to medium-low heat. Cook for 10 minutes, or until cauliflower is tender. Stir occasionally. Add kidney beans and cook in a stirring motion until heated through. Garnish with garam masala before serving.

Nutrition Information

- Calories: 139 calories;
- Total Carbohydrate: 14.8
- Cholesterol: 0
- Protein: 4.6
- Total Fat: 7.5
- Sodium: 528

277. Easy Curry Rice

Serving: 5 | Prep: 5mins | Cook: 15mins | Ready in:

Ingredients

- 2 cups uncooked white rice, rinsed
- 3 cups water
- 3 tablespoons mild curry powder

Direction

- In a rice cooker, mix together curry powder, water and rice. Let it cook for one full cycle about 15 to 20 minutes or until all water has been absorbed.

Nutrition Information

- Calories: 282 calories;
- Protein: 5.8
- Total Fat: 1
- Sodium: 10
- Total Carbohydrate: 61.4
- Cholesterol: 0

278. Easy Masoor Daal

Serving: 4 | Prep: 5mins | Cook: 30mins | Ready in:

Ingredients

- 1 cup red lentils
- 1 slice ginger, 1 inch piece, peeled
- 1/4 teaspoon ground turmeric
- 1 teaspoon salt
- 1/2 teaspoon cayenne pepper, or to taste
- 4 teaspoons vegetable oil
- 4 teaspoons dried minced onion
- 1 teaspoon cumin seeds

Direction

- Wash the lentils well and transfer to a medium saucepan with the turmeric, ginger, cayenne pepper and salt. Fill with about an inch of water enough to cover the lentils and let the mixture boil. Scoop off any foam on top of the lentils. Lessen the heat and let it simmer while occasionally stirring until beans becomes soupy and tender.
- Meanwhile, in a microwavable dish, mix together the oil, cumin seeds and dried onion. Set the microwave on high for 45 seconds up to 1 minute until the onions are browned yet avoiding them to get burnt. Mix in the lentil mixture.

Nutrition Information

- Calories: 185 calories;
- Protein: 11.1
- Total Fat: 5.2
- Sodium: 868
- Total Carbohydrate: 25
- Cholesterol: 0

279. Easy Paneer Tikka

Serving: 4 | Prep: 20mins | Cook: 7mins | Ready in:

Ingredients

- Marinade:
- 1 cup plain yogurt
- 1 tablespoon ginger-garlic paste
- 1 teaspoon lemon juice
- 1/4 teaspoon ground turmeric
- 1/4 teaspoon ground red chile pepper
- 1/4 teaspoon ground cumin
- 1/4 teaspoon garam masala
- salt to taste
- Skewers:
- 7 ounces paneer, cut into 1-inch cubes
- 1 large onion, cut into 1-inch squares
- 1 green bell pepper, cubed
- 1 tablespoon vegetable oil
- Serving:
- 1 onion, sliced into thin rings
- 1/2 cup green chutney

Direction

- Place a fine-mesh strainer that is lined with muslin or cheesecloth inside a small bowl. Pour in the yogurt and let liquid drain for 15 minutes. Dispose of the liquid.
- Take another bowl and stir together the drained yogurt, lemon juice, ginger-garlic paste, chile powder, turmeric, garam masala, cumin, and salt. Stir in onions, green bell peppers, and paneer to mix well. Let soak for an hour.
- Preheat grill on medium, and oil the grates lightly.
- Thread the marinated onions, paneer, and bell peppers onto metal skewers. Grill for 6 to 8 minutes, or until cheese is browned and the vegetables are tender. Oil the skewers with a brush and keep on the grill for 1 more minute.
- Mix green chutney and onion rings. Serve with the skewers.

Nutrition Information

- Calories: 218 calories;
- Total Carbohydrate: 27.8
- Cholesterol: 11
- Protein: 10.8
- Total Fat: 7
- Sodium: 419

280. Easy Veggie Samosas

Serving: 9 | Prep: 20mins | Cook: 25mins | Ready in:

Ingredients

- 1 tablespoon vegetable oil
- 1/2 cup chopped onion
- 3 (19 ounce) cans garbanzo beans, drained

- 2 tablespoons curry paste
- 1/2 cup apple juice
- 3 sheets frozen puff pastry, thawed
- 1/4 cup all-purpose flour for dusting

Direction

- Set the oven for preheating to 350 °F or 175 °C.
- In a big skillet, heat oil over medium-high heat. Sauté the onion for about 5 minutes or until browned. Lower the heat and add the garbanzo beans. Mix in the curry paste and apple juice till smooth and put into the skillet. Allow mixture to simmer for 10 minutes, stir occasionally. Add water or more apple juice if needed to moisten the dish as it cooks.
- Cut each pastry sheets into 3 equal rectangular sizes then cut each rectangle in half, to make 18 pieces. In a flat and lightly floured surface, roll each piece until it becomes double in size. Dust with flour as needed to prevent from sticking into the rolling pin. Take a spoonful amount of filling into the center of each pastry sheets, then fold in half. Press all edges to seal and then put on a non-stick baking sheet. Bake them in the preheated oven for about 25 minutes or until golden brown.

Nutrition Information

- Calories: 696 calories;
- Sodium: 803
- Total Carbohydrate: 82.5
- Cholesterol: 0
- Protein: 15.3
- Total Fat: 34.3

281. Faux Bombay Potatoes

Serving: 4 | Prep: 5mins | Cook: 20mins | Ready in:

Ingredients

- 3 turnips, diced
- 1/4 cup vegetable oil
- 1/2 teaspoon yellow mustard seed
- 1/2 teaspoon black mustard seed
- 1 1/2 teaspoons ground red pepper
- 1 teaspoon ground turmeric
- salt to taste

Direction

- Pour salted water over turnips to cover in a large pot. Bring to a boil over high heat, then turn heat to medium-low; simmer, covered for 15 to 20 minutes until tender. Drain off water and allow turnips to steam dry for 1 or 2 minutes.
- In a large skillet, heat oil over medium-high heat. Sauté turmeric, black mustard seeds, and yellow mustard seeds in hot oil until mustard seeds start to pop. Add turnips to the skillet. Cook, stirring for about 5 minutes until turnips is thoroughly heated. Sprinkle with salt to taste, and serve.

Nutrition Information

- Calories: 149 calories;
- Sodium: 262
- Total Carbohydrate: 5.7
- Cholesterol: 0
- Protein: 1
- Total Fat: 14.1

282. Four Seasons Chicken Curry

Serving: 8 | Prep: 15mins | Cook: 50mins | Ready in:

Ingredients

- 3 tablespoons vegetable oil
- 1 medium onion, chopped
- 3 cloves garlic, sliced
- 1 (1 inch) piece fresh ginger root, grated
- 1 (1 inch) piece stick cinnamon
- 3 bay leaves

- 1 tablespoon brown sugar
- 1 teaspoon coriander seeds
- 1 teaspoon fenugreek seeds
- 6 whole cloves
- 6 whole cardamom pods
- 1 teaspoon crushed red pepper flakes
- 10 whole black peppercorns
- 2 pounds skinless, boneless chicken breast halves - diced
- 3 tablespoons curry powder
- 1 1/2 cups water, or as needed
- 1 tablespoon lemon juice
- salt and pepper to taste
- 1/2 cup light cream

Direction

- In a wok on medium heat, heat oil, and cook the onion till becoming browned a bit. Whisk in peppercorns, red pepper, cardamom, cloves, fenugreek, coriander, brown sugar, bay leaves, cinnamon, ginger and garlic. Cook and stir approximately 3 minutes. Add chicken into the wok, and cook till becoming light brown. Whisk in curry powder. Add in water, and boil. Lower the heat to low, covered, and simmered for half an hour. Pour in extra water as needed to keep the chicken covered.
- Stir in lemon juice and use pepper and salt to season, and keep on cooking for no less than 15 minutes. Mix in cream and take the cinnamon stick and bay leaves out prior to serving.

Nutrition Information

- Calories: 194 calories;
- Cholesterol: 59
- Protein: 23
- Total Fat: 8
- Sodium: 344
- Total Carbohydrate: 7.5

283. Garam Masala Seared Salmon With Coconut Curry Butter

Serving: 8 | Prep: 15mins | Cook: 20mins | Ready in:

Ingredients

- 3/4 cup dry white wine
- 1/2 cup heavy cream
- 1/3 cup coconut milk
- 2 tablespoons curry powder
- 1 cup cold, unsalted butter, cut into pieces
- kosher salt to taste
- 1/4 cup vegetable oil
- 8 (6 ounce) fillets Alaskan king salmon
- 2 tablespoons garam masala
- kosher salt to taste

Direction

- Into a saucepan, add coconut milk, cream, and white wine. Add curry powder to taste. Over medium-high heat, heat to a light boil, then decrease the heat to medium-low and let to simmer for about 10 minutes until liquid is reduced to 1/2 cup.
- Once the liquid is reduced, switch the heat to low and then whisk in butter, a few cubes at a time, until all butter is incorporated. Avoid the mixture from boiling because it will separate. Once the butter is incorporated, add salt to taste and reserve keeping it warm.
- Over medium-high heat, heat oil in a sauté pan until oil starts to smoke. As the oil is heating, season lightly each side of the salmon with salt and garam masala.
- Sear salmon for about 3 to 4 minutes on one side in hot oil, flip over, and continue to cook for about 2 to 3 minutes until done. Drain briefly with paper towels to remove the excess oil. Serve right away along with curry butter sauce.

Nutrition Information

- Calories: 604 calories;

- Total Carbohydrate: 3.2
- Cholesterol: 156
- Protein: 36.9
- Total Fat: 47.7
- Sodium: 486

284. Garam Masala Spice Blend

Serving: 20 | Prep: 15mins | Cook: 2mins | Ready in:

Ingredients

- 2 tablespoons coriander seeds
- 1 tablespoon cumin seeds
- 1 tablespoon cardamom seeds
- 1 tablespoon whole black peppercorns
- 1 teaspoon fennel seed
- 1 teaspoon mustard seed
- 1/2 teaspoon whole cloves
- 2 dried red chile peppers, seeds discarded
- 2 tablespoons ground turmeric

Direction

- In a small skillet, mix red chile peppers, cloves, mustard seeds, fennel seeds, peppercorns, cardamom seeds, cumin seeds and coriander seeds on medium low heat. Toast until tangy, for about 2 minutes.
- In a spice mill or a clean coffee grinder, grind the toasted spices to a fine powder. Ladle in turmeric and process to combine. Use promptly or keep in a sealed jar for up to 1 month.

Nutrition Information

- Calories: 8 calories;
- Protein: 0.3
- Total Fat: 0.3
- Sodium: 1
- Total Carbohydrate: 1.4
- Cholesterol: 0

285. Goan Pork Vindaloo

Serving: 8 | Prep: 30mins | Cook: 1hours25mins | Ready in:

Ingredients

- 16 dried Kashmiri chile peppers, stemmed and seeded
- 1 (1 inch) piece cinnamon stick
- 1 teaspoon cumin seeds
- 6 whole cloves
- 1/2 teaspoon whole black peppercorns
- 1/2 teaspoon ground turmeric
- 1 tablespoon white vinegar
- salt to taste
- 2 pounds boneless pork loin roast, trimmed and cut into 1-inch cubes
- 1/4 cup vegetable oil
- 4 onions, chopped
- 10 cloves garlic, minced, or more to taste
- 1 (2 inch) piece fresh ginger root, minced
- 2 cups boiling water
- 2 green chile peppers, seeded and cut into strips
- 1/4 cup white vinegar

Direction

- Using an electric coffee grinder or a mortar and pestle, grind turmeric, peppercorns, clove, cumin, cinnamon stick and Kashmiri chills till spices is smoothly ground. To make a smooth paste, combine with a tablespoon white vinegar. Season with salt to taste.
- With the vinegar-spice paste, stir cubes of pork in a bowl till evenly coated. Put on plastic wrap to cover the bowl and refrigerate to marinate overnight.
- In a big pot or Dutch oven, heat vegetable oil over medium-high heat. Cook and mix ginger, garlic, and onions for about 10 minutes, till golden brown. Put in the pork marinade and the pork, and cook for approximately 5

minutes, mixing often, till cubes of pork have firmed. Add water, simmer, then lower the heat, place on the cover, and cook for about 40 minutes till pork is soft.
- Mix in a quarter cup of vinegar and strips of green chile pepper. Cook without a cover for an additional of half an hour till vindaloo thickens and green chile peppers softens. Season with salt to taste prior to serving.

Nutrition Information

- Calories: 264 calories;
- Total Fat: 16.4
- Sodium: 51
- Total Carbohydrate: 9.2
- Cholesterol: 54
- Protein: 19.7

286. Green Chutney

Serving: 4 | Prep: 15mins | Cook: | Ready in:

Ingredients

- 1 bunch fresh cilantro
- 1 clove garlic
- 1 tablespoon minced fresh ginger root
- 1 minced hot green chile peppers
- 1 tablespoon peanuts
- salt to taste
- 2 tablespoons lemon juice

Direction

- In a food processor, blend lemon juice, cilantro, salt to taste, garlic, peanuts, green chili, and ginger together until smooth. Blend in a few drops of water if the chutney is too dry.

Nutrition Information

- Calories: 25 calories;
- Sodium: 8
- Total Carbohydrate: 3.2
- Cholesterol: 0
- Protein: 1.2
- Total Fat: 1.2

287. Green Curry With Sweet Potato And Aubergine (Eggplant)

Serving: 5 | Prep: 20mins | Cook: 27mins | Ready in:

Ingredients

- 1 tablespoon vegetable oil
- 1 onion, chopped
- 1 tablespoon green curry paste, or more to taste
- 1 eggplant, quartered and sliced
- 1 (14 ounce) can coconut milk
- 1 cup vegetable stock
- 1 sweet potato, peeled and sliced
- 6 kaffir lime leaves
- 2 tablespoons lime juice
- 2 teaspoons lime zest
- 2 teaspoons soft brown sugar
- salt
- 1 shredded kaffir lime leaf for garnish
- 1 sprig chopped fresh cilantro for garnish

Direction

- Heat a skillet or big wok with oil over medium heat. Put in curry paste and onion then cook and stir for about 3 minutes until aromatic. Add in the eggplant and cook for 4-5 minutes until soft.
- Put in the vegetable stock and coconut milk into the eggplant mixture. Let it boil. Reduce the heat and let it simmer for about 5 minutes until the mixture is heated through. Add in the lime leaves and sweet potatoes. Cook and stir for 10 minutes or until the vegetables are soft. Add in the brown sugar, lime juice and lime

zest and mix everything until well combined. Add salt to taste and top with cilantro and shredded lime leaf.

Nutrition Information

- Calories: 277 calories;
- Total Fat: 19.8
- Sodium: 189
- Total Carbohydrate: 25.3
- Cholesterol: 0
- Protein: 4

288. Grilled "Tandoori" Lamb

Serving: 10 | Prep: 20mins | Cook: 15mins | Ready in:

Ingredients

- 1 cup plain yogurt
- 1/2 cup lemon juice
- 1/4 cup finely minced onion
- 2 cloves crushed garlic
- 1 tablespoon freshly grated ginger
- 2 teaspoons garam masala
- 2 teaspoons paprika
- 1 teaspoon ground cumin
- 1/2 teaspoon turmeric powder
- 1/2 teaspoon cayenne pepper
- 2 pounds boneless lamb shoulder, cut into 2 inch pieces
- 2 teaspoons kosher salt, divided
- 1 tablespoon vegetable oil
- chopped cilantro (optional)
- fresh lemon wedges (optional)
- medium red onion, sliced (optional)
- spicy cilantro chutney

Direction

- Whisk together yogurt, lemon juice, garlic, onion, ginger, paprika, garam masala, turmeric, cumin, and cayenne pepper in a bowl until well-blended.
- Toss the lamb in the marinade and season with salt, mixing until the lamb pieces are evenly coated. Cling wrap the bowl and marinate in the refrigerator for at least 4 hours.
- Cue the lamb with a small space in between pieces. Take off excess marinade by wiping with a paper towel, then brush the lamb pieces with vegetable oil. Sprinkle with salt.
- Set grill on medium to pre-heat, and lightly grease the grate.
- Grill the lamb skewers until the meat springs back when touched; this is about 5 to 7 minutes per side.
- Garnish the skewers with lemon wedges, red onions, and chopped cilantro, if desired.

Nutrition Information

- Calories: 194 calories;
- Total Fat: 11.8
- Sodium: 430
- Total Carbohydrate: 8.9
- Cholesterol: 58
- Protein: 15.7

289. Grilled Chicken Thighs Tandoori

Serving: 8 | Prep: 10mins | Cook: 45mins | Ready in:

Ingredients

- 2 (6 ounce) containers plain yogurt
- 2 teaspoons kosher salt
- 1 teaspoon black pepper
- 1/2 teaspoon ground cloves
- 2 tablespoons freshly grated ginger
- 3 cloves garlic, minced
- 4 teaspoons paprika
- 2 teaspoons ground cumin
- 2 teaspoons ground cinnamon
- 2 teaspoons ground coriander
- 16 chicken thighs
- olive oil spray

Direction

- Mix ginger, yogurt, cloves, pepper, and salt together in a medium bowl. Stir in coriander, garlic, cinnamon, cumin, and paprika; set aside.
- On cold water, rinse the chicken then use paper towels to pat dry; put chicken in a big resealable bag then add the yogurt mixture over chicken. Press the bag to release air then seal, flip the bag a few times to spread out the marinade. Put the bag in a bowl then place in the refrigerator for 8hrs to overnight; flip the bag from time to time.
- On direct medium heat, preheat the outdoor grill.
- Take the chicken out of the bag then discard the marinade; wipe off the extra marinade using paper towels. Put olive oil spray over the chicken pieces.
- Cook chicken on a grill for 2mins, flip then cook for another 2mins. Arrange chicken to receive indirect heat, cook the chicken for another 35-40mins until the internal temperature reaches 180°F.

Nutrition Information

- Calories: 349 calories;
- Sodium: 618
- Total Carbohydrate: 5.4
- Cholesterol: 120
- Protein: 34.2
- Total Fat: 20.5

290. Gujarati Carrot And Peanut Salad

Serving: 4 | Prep: 15mins | Cook: |Ready in:

Ingredients

- 2 cups grated carrots
- 1/2 cup chopped salted peanuts
- 3 tablespoons lemon juice
- 1/2 teaspoon salt
- 1 teaspoon white sugar
- 1 green chile pepper, seeded and diced
- 2 tablespoons finely chopped fresh cilantro

Direction

- Toss peanuts and carrots together in a medium serving bowl. Whisk cilantro, chile pepper, sugar, salt and lemon juice in another bowl. Pour over the carrots and gently stir to coat, then serve promptly.

Nutrition Information

- Calories: 141 calories;
- Total Carbohydrate: 12.3
- Cholesterol: 0
- Protein: 5.1
- Total Fat: 9.2
- Sodium: 479

291. Gujarati Kadhi

Serving: 4 | Prep: 5mins | Cook: 20mins |Ready in:

Ingredients

- 4 cups water
- 2 cups plain yogurt
- 2 tablespoons chickpea flour (besan)
- 4 green chile peppers, halved lengthwise
- 1 tablespoon minced fresh ginger root
- 1 tablespoon white sugar, or to taste
- 1/2 teaspoon ground turmeric
- salt to taste
- 1 tablespoon vegetable oil
- 1 tablespoon ghee
- 2 dried red chile peppers, broken into pieces
- 1 sprig fresh curry leaves
- 1/2 teaspoon cumin seeds
- 1/2 teaspoon mustard seed
- 1 pinch asafoetida powder

- 1/4 cup chopped cilantro leaves

Direction

- In a large saucepan, combine chickpea flour, yogurt and water together till smooth; include in salt, turmeric, sugar, ginger and green chile peppers. Boil the mixture; turn the heat down to low immediately; cook for 5-10 minutes on low.
- Set a small skillet over medium heat; heat ghee and oil together; fry in asafetida powder, mustard seed, cumin seeds, curry leaves and dried red chile peppers in the mixture till the seeds splutter. Combine the mixture into the saucepan with cilantro. Serve hot.

Nutrition Information

- Calories: 185 calories;
- Protein: 8.4
- Total Fat: 9.1
- Sodium: 100
- Total Carbohydrate: 18.9
- Cholesterol: 16

292. Hara Masala Murgh

Serving: 8 | Prep: 15mins | Cook: 40mins | Ready in:

Ingredients

- 1 whole chicken, cut into 8 pieces
- 1 teaspoon ginger paste
- 1 teaspoon garlic paste
- 1 teaspoon salt
- 1/2 cup vegetable oil
- 1 1/2 cups plain yogurt
- 1/4 cup ground almonds
- 1/2 teaspoon ground cumin
- 1/2 teaspoon ground coriander
- 1/2 teaspoon ground turmeric
- 6 green chile peppers, mashed into a paste
- 1 cup chopped fresh cilantro leaves
- 1/4 cup chopped fresh mint
- 1 cup shredded coconut
- salt to taste
- 1 cup water
- 1/4 cup heavy cream (optional)

Direction

- Thoroughly rub 1 teaspoon salt, garlic paste and ginger paste over the chicken pieces.
- In a kadhai or a big, deep saucepan, heat oil over medium-high heat. In the oil, fry both sides of the chicken pieces for 5 minutes until properly brown.
- In a bowl, combine turmeric, coriander, cumin, almonds and yogurt. Pour over the chicken with the yogurt mixture and flip to coat; cook for another 10 minutes. Mix mint, cilantro and mashed chile peppers into the pot; use salt to season. Pour in water, put a cover on, lower the heat to low, and keep cooking for another 20 minutes until the chicken is soft. Right before taking away from heat to enjoy, mix the cream into the sauce.

Nutrition Information

- Calories: 478 calories;
- Sodium: 467
- Total Carbohydrate: 15
- Cholesterol: 103
- Protein: 34.2
- Total Fat: 31.3

293. Indian Cabbage Patties

Serving: 20 | Prep: 20mins | Cook: 10mins | Ready in:

Ingredients

- 2 dried red chiles, stemmed and seeded
- 1 cup fresh grated coconut
- 1 cup rice flour
- 1/2 cup gram flour (chickpea flour)

- 1 tablespoon tamarind, or as needed
- 4 tablespoons coriander seeds
- 1 tablespoon skinned split black lentils (urad dal)
- 1 tablespoon asafoetida powder
- 1 medium head cabbage, shredded
- 1 pinch salt to taste
- 1 pinch white sugar, or to taste
- oil for frying

Direction

- On medium-high heat, heat a heavy pan. Toast chiles in the pan for 2-4 minutes, turning often, until fragrant, until fragrant. Put toasted chiles in a blender.
- In the blender with chiles, process tamarind, gram flour, rice flour and coconut to make a fine paste. Put a bit of water if needed.
- In a skillet, heat 2 tbsp. oil on high heat. Stir and cook asafoetida, urad dal and coriander for 30 seconds. Put this in the blender with tamarind mixture. Blend to incorporate.
- In a big bowl, put shredded cabbage and coriander-tamarind paste. Mix to combine. Season using sugar and salt.
- In a heavy, big skillet, heat oil to fry. Spread small cabbage mixture portions in hot pan. Fry patties for 2-3 minutes per side until brown.

Nutrition Information

- Calories: 126 calories;
- Total Carbohydrate: 13.1
- Cholesterol: 0
- Protein: 2.2
- Total Fat: 7.9
- Sodium: 19

294. Indian Chai Hot Chocolate

Serving: 1 | Prep: 2mins | Cook: 3mins | Ready in:

Ingredients

- 1/2 cup water
- 1/2 cup milk
- 1 chai tea bag
- 1 (.55 ounce) package instant hot chocolate mix

Direction

- In a microwave-safe mug, stir milk and water together. Cook for 1 1/2 minutes in the microwave on high. Take away and place in chai tea bag. Let the tea steep for 2 minutes. Discard the tea bag then add in hot chocolate mix and stir.

Nutrition Information

- Calories: 126 calories;
- Sodium: 131
- Total Carbohydrate: 19.3
- Cholesterol: 10
- Protein: 5.1
- Total Fat: 3

295. Indian Chicken Korma In The Slow Cooker

Serving: 4 | Prep: 20mins | Cook: 7hours15mins | Ready in:

Ingredients

- 2 onions, quartered
- 1 large green chile pepper, seeded
- 3 cloves garlic
- 1 1/2 inch piece fresh ginger root, peeled
- 1 tablespoon sunflower oil
- 8 boneless, skinless chicken thighs
- 2 tablespoons butter
- 1 teaspoon cumin seeds, crushed
- 1 teaspoon fennel seeds, crushed
- 4 cardamom pods, crushed
- 1 teaspoon paprika

- 1 teaspoon ground turmeric
- 1/4 teaspoon ground cinnamon
- 11 ounces chicken stock
- 1 tablespoon white sugar
- 1 pinch salt
- 5 tablespoons heavy cream
- 2 tablespoons ground almonds

Direction

- In a blender, combine ginger, garlic, chile pepper and onions, blend until smooth. Slice each chicken thigh into 4 pieces.
- In a large skillet over high heat, heat oil, place chicken breasts in skillet in batches and brown for about 5 minutes each batch until evenly browned. Move to a slow cooker.
- In the same skillet over medium heat, melt butter. When butter is melted, add onion mixture and cook for about 3 minutes until flavors are well blended. Stir in cinnamon, turmeric, paprika, cardamom, fennel and cumin and cook for another 1 minute. Mix in salt, sugar and chicken stock; bring to a boil. Pour contents of skillet on top of chicken in the slow cooker. Cover.
- Cook on LOW for about 7 hours until flavors are well incorporated and chicken is cooked through. Stir in ground almonds and heavy cream.

Nutrition Information

- Calories: 405 calories;
- Sodium: 384
- Total Carbohydrate: 15
- Cholesterol: 118
- Protein: 25.1
- Total Fat: 27.6

296. Indian Crepes

Serving: 6 | Prep: 10mins | Cook: 20mins | Ready in:

Ingredients

- 1 cup all-purpose flour
- 1 cup water
- 1 egg
- 2 tablespoons butter, melted
- 1 pinch salt
- 1 tablespoon caraway seeds

Direction

- Heat a non-stick crepe pan over medium high heat.
- In a bowl, mix water and flour. Stir in egg and blend well. Add caraway seeds, salt and butter into flour mixture to make a smooth batter.
- Place about 1/4 cup batter into heated pan. Swirl the pan around so that batter makes a fine round form. Then cook for 2 to 4 minutes until bubbles form throughout the batter. Turn the crepe with spatula to loosen it from the pan. Tap your wrist upwards to toss the crepe, turning it, and landing it back in the pan. Cook other side for about 30 seconds until lightly browned. Continue with remaining batter.

Nutrition Information

- Calories: 125 calories;
- Total Fat: 5
- Sodium: 41
- Total Carbohydrate: 16.5
- Cholesterol: 41
- Protein: 3.5

297. Indian Eggplant Bhurtha

Serving: 4 | Prep: 15mins | Cook: 50mins | Ready in:

Ingredients

- 1 eggplant
- 2 tablespoons vegetable oil
- 1/2 teaspoon cumin seeds
- 1 medium onion, sliced

- 1 teaspoon chopped fresh ginger
- 1 large tomato - peeled, seeded and diced
- 1 clove garlic, minced
- 1/2 teaspoon ground turmeric
- 1/2 teaspoon ground cumin
- 1/2 teaspoon ground coriander
- 1/4 teaspoon cayenne pepper
- 1/2 teaspoon salt, or to taste
- ground black pepper to taste
- 1/4 cup chopped fresh cilantro

Direction

- Prepare and preheat the broiler in the oven. Brush the eggplant on the outside with oil, or coat using cooking spray. Place the eggplant under the broiler, and cook for about 30 minutes, or until it becomes tender and the skin breaks out in blisters. Flip as necessary to thoroughly cook the eggplant. Slice in half lengthwise, scoop out the flesh from the skin and discard the skin. Chop up the eggplant flesh and then set aside.
- Heat the oil in a large skillet or in a big work over medium high heat. Then add the cumin seeds, allow to crackle for a few seconds or until color turns into golden brown. Be careful not to burn the seeds. Add and stir-fry the onions, garlic and ginger until tender, make sure that the onions don't get too brown. Mix in the tomatoes and seasonings of turmeric, grounded cumin and coriander, cayenne pepper, black pepper and salt. Continue to cook and stirring for a few minutes or until cooked.
- Set the eggplant pieces in the skillet, and allow to cook for 10 to 15 minutes, let its moisture to evaporate. Try tasting, and adjust seasoning as desired. Sprinkle with fresh cilantro before serving.

Nutrition Information

- Calories: 119 calories;
- Total Fat: 7.4
- Sodium: 300
- Total Carbohydrate: 13.4
- Cholesterol: 0
- Protein: 2.4

298. Indian Hot Curried Mangos With Tofu

Serving: 4 | Prep: 25mins | Cook: 20mins | Ready in:

Ingredients

- 1 tablespoon sesame oil
- 5 cloves garlic, minced
- 1 tablespoon minced ginger
- 1 firm mango, peeled and sliced
- 3 tablespoons yellow curry powder
- 2 tablespoons chopped cilantro
- 1 (14 ounce) can light coconut milk
- 1 (14 ounce) package extra firm tofu, cubed
- 1/4 teaspoon salt and pepper to taste

Direction

- Heat sesame oil on medium high heat in a big pan; cook ginger and garlic for 1-2 minutes till light brown and fragrant. Add mango; cook to slightly soften for 1 minute. Mix in cilantro and curry powder; cook to release curry flavor for 1 minute.
- Add coconut milk; simmer. Mix in tofu; season with pepper and salt to taste. Simmer for 5 minutes till liquid reduces by half, occasionally mixing.

Nutrition Information

- Calories: 323 calories;
- Sodium: 175
- Total Carbohydrate: 19.1
- Cholesterol: 0
- Protein: 17.7
- Total Fat: 21.6

299. Indian Onion Dipping Sauce

Serving: 10 | Prep: 10mins | Cook: | Ready in:

Ingredients

- 1 onion, chopped, or more to taste
- 1 1/2 tablespoons lemon juice
- 1 teaspoon ketchup, or more to taste (optional)
- 1/2 teaspoon cayenne pepper
- 1/2 teaspoon Hungarian paprika
- 1/2 teaspoon salt
- 1 pinch white sugar (optional)

Direction

- Pulse onion in a food processor until minced. Add sugar, salt, paprika, cayenne pepper, ketchup, and lemon juice and pulse until well combined. Pour the sauce into an airtight container. Chill in refrigerator for 2 to 3 hours for the flavors to combine.

Nutrition Information

- Calories: 11 calories;
- Sodium: 123
- Total Carbohydrate: 2.7
- Cholesterol: 0
- Protein: 0.3
- Total Fat: 0.1

300. Indian Salad

Serving: 4 | Prep: 15mins | Cook: 20mins | Ready in:

Ingredients

- 1 1/2 cups brown rice
- 4 cups water
- 1 (10 ounce) can asparagus tips, drained
- 1 red bell pepper, seeded and diced
- 2 red apples, cored and diced
- 1/4 cup golden raisins
- 1/2 cup heavy cream
- 1 teaspoon curry powder
- 1 teaspoon lemon juice
- salt and pepper to taste

Direction

- Combine water and rice in a saucepan. Boil, and lower the heat to low, cover the pan, keep simmering until rice is tender, about 30 minutes. If needed, drain. Let cool.
- While cooling the rice, in a bowl, put golden raisins and fill with sufficient hot water to cover. Let the rice soak in the water for 20 minutes until it plumps, then drain.
- Whip cream until it forms soft peaks in a medium bowl. Fold in pepper, salt, lemon juice and curry powder. In another bowl, stir raisins, apples, red pepper, asparagus, and brown rice together. Fold the mixture into the curry cream. Let chill and serve.

Nutrition Information

- Calories: 451 calories;
- Sodium: 218
- Total Carbohydrate: 76.9
- Cholesterol: 41
- Protein: 8.3
- Total Fat: 13.7

301. Indian Style Sheekh Kabab

Serving: 8 | Prep: 15mins | Cook: 10mins | Ready in:

Ingredients

- 2 pounds lean ground lamb
- 2 onions, finely chopped
- 1/2 cup fresh mint leaves, finely chopped
- 1/2 cup cilantro, finely chopped
- 1 tablespoon ginger paste

- 1 tablespoon green chile paste
- 2 teaspoons ground cumin
- 2 teaspoons ground coriander
- 2 teaspoons paprika
- 1 teaspoon cayenne pepper
- 2 teaspoons salt
- 1/4 cup vegetable oil
- skewers

Direction

- Mix together ground lamb, ginger paste, onions, cilantro, chile paste, and mint in a large bowl. Sprinkle with salt, cumin, cayenne, coriander, and paprika. Cover the bowl and let lamb marinate for 2 hours.
- Mold 1 cup of the lamb mixture to form sausages around the skewers. Even out the thickness all around the skewers. Keep in the fridge until ready to grill.
- Preheat grill on high.
- Generously oil the grates and arrange the kabobs, cooking for 10 minutes for well-done, and turning as necessary to cook evenly.

Nutrition Information

- Calories: 304 calories;
- Total Fat: 22.6
- Sodium: 665
- Total Carbohydrate: 4.7
- Cholesterol: 76
- Protein: 20.1

302. Indian Style Shrimp Fry

Serving: 4 | Prep: 20mins | Cook: 30mins | Ready in:

Ingredients

- 2 teaspoons paprika
- 1 teaspoon ground cumin
- 2 teaspoons ground turmeric
- 1/2 teaspoon salt
- 1/2 onion, minced
- 1 pound uncooked medium shrimp, peeled and deveined
- 2 tablespoons vegetable oil
- 1/2 teaspoon mustard seed
- 1 tablespoon garlic paste
- 3/4 teaspoon ginger paste
- 1 tablespoon water
- 1 tomato, diced
- 1 large green bell pepper, cut into 1-inch squares
- 1/2 teaspoon ground black pepper (optional)
- 1 teaspoon lemon juice (optional)

Direction

- Mix the cumin, paprika, salt and turmeric in a small bowl. Scatter 3/4 of the spice mixture on the shrimp in a bowl; put aside for roughly 10 minutes.
- Slightly crush the onion using a mortar and pestle. Make a few hard jabs for good consistency; it should be moist yet it should not be watery.
- Pour oil in a frying pan set over high heat; stir in the mustard seeds and allow to cook for a minute or two until the crackling has subsides. Adjust the heat to medium-high. Sauté the onion, ginger paste and garlic paste in the mustard seeds for 10 to 15 minutes until the onion turns brown.
- Mix the water in the remaining spice mixture and pour in the pan. Sauté the tomatoes in the onion mixture for about 5 minutes until tender. Add the green peppers and let it cook for 1 to 2 minutes.
- Adjust the heat to medium; add the shrimp and allow to cook for 3 to 5 minutes until no longer pink. Increase heat to medium-high and continue to stir until the entire liquid evaporates. Take off from heat. Top it off with black pepper and lemon juice.

Nutrition Information

- Calories: 191 calories;
- Total Fat: 8.5

- Sodium: 622
- Total Carbohydrate: 7.1
- Cholesterol: 173
- Protein: 19.9

303. Indian Tomato Chicken

Serving: 6 | Prep: 15mins | Cook: 2hours | Ready in:

Ingredients

- 1 large onion, chopped
- 4 cloves garlic, chopped
- 1 slice fresh ginger root
- 1 tablespoon olive oil
- 2 teaspoons ground cumin
- 1 teaspoon ground turmeric
- 1 teaspoon salt
- 1 teaspoon ground black pepper
- 1/2 teaspoon ground cardamom
- 1 (1 inch) piece cinnamon stick
- 1/4 teaspoon ground cloves
- 2 bay leaves
- 1/4 teaspoon ground nutmeg
- 6 skinless chicken thighs
- 1 (14.5 ounce) can whole peeled tomatoes, crushed

Direction

- In a food processor, process ginger, garlic and onion into a paste. In a big skillet, heat oil on medium heat. Add onion paste; sauté, continuously mixing, for 10 minutes.
- Mix nutmeg, bay leaves, cloves, cinnamon, cardamom, pepper, salt, turmeric and cumin in. Sauté for 1-2 minutes, mixing. Put chicken pieces into skillet; mix around with spice mixture till coated well.
- Sauté for additional 4 minutes. Put tomatoes with liquid in; mix. Lower heat to low. Simmer till oil separates from liquid, about 1-2 hours. Occasionally mix. Sauce will thicken if simmer without cover; add water or simmer while covered.

Nutrition Information

- Calories: 134 calories;
- Total Fat: 5.4
- Sodium: 547
- Total Carbohydrate: 6.9
- Cholesterol: 57
- Protein: 14.7

304. Indian Style Butter Chicken (Murgh Makhani)

Serving: 3 | Prep: 15mins | Cook: 25mins | Ready in:

Ingredients

- 2 teaspoons dried red chile pepper, crushed
- 1/4 teaspoon ground cinnamon
- 1/4 teaspoon ground nutmeg
- 1/4 teaspoon ground cloves
- 1 1/2 teaspoons garam masala
- 1 1/2 teaspoons salt
- 1 1/2 teaspoons minced ginger
- 2 cloves garlic, crushed
- 5 Roma tomatoes, seeded, diced
- 1/2 cup plain yogurt
- 1 pound skinless, boneless chicken breast, cut into 2-inch cubes
- 1/2 cup butter
- 2 red bell peppers, sliced
- 2 onions, thinly sliced
- 1/4 cup heavy whipping cream
- 2 tablespoons chopped fresh coriander

Direction

- In a large bowl, mix yogurt, tomatoes, garlic, ginger, salt, garam masala, cloves, nutmeg, cinnamon, and the ground red chile peppers. Put the chicken pieces into the yogurt mixture, stir and allow to marinate for 30-60 minutes in the fridge.

- In a large skillet, melt the butter on medium heat; cook onion and bell pepper slices for about 5-7 minutes, stirring from time to time, until the onion starts to turn transparent. Put the marinade and chicken into the skillet. Continue to cook for 5-10 minutes, constantly stirring, until the chicken firms and the center is not pink anymore.
- Set the heat to medium-high, mix in coriander and cream. Cook, stirring continuously, until the mixture just starts to boil. Serve immediately.

Nutrition Information

- Calories: 659 calories;
- Protein: 37.2
- Total Fat: 43
- Sodium: 1507
- Total Carbohydrate: 34.3
- Cholesterol: 189

305. Indian Style Chicken And Onions

Serving: 4 | Prep: 20mins | Cook: 40mins | Ready in:

Ingredients

- 3 tablespoons water
- 6 cloves garlic
- 2 serrano chile peppers, stemmed
- 1 (2 inch) piece fresh ginger, peeled and thinly sliced
- 1/4 cup ghee (clarified butter)
- 2 pounds chicken drumsticks
- salt and ground black pepper to taste
- 1 large white onion, sliced
- 1 tablespoon dried fenugreek leaves
- 2 teaspoons ground coriander
- 1 teaspoon garam masala
- 1/2 teaspoon ground turmeric
- 3 plum tomatoes, grated
- 3/4 cup milk
- 1/2 cup heavy whipping cream
- 1/3 cup finely chopped fresh cilantro

Direction

- In a food processor or a blender, purée together ginger, serrano chile peppers, garlic and water till smooth.
- Set a 6-qt. saucepan on medium heat; heat ghee. Season pepper and salt on chicken. Cook the chicken in the hot ghee for 3-4 minutes on each side, till browned. Move the chicken onto a plate.
- Cook while stirring the garlic purée in the 6-qt. saucepan for 2-3 minutes, or till golden. Include in onion; cook while stirring for 5-7 minutes, till golden. Include in turmeric, garam masala, coriander and fenugreek into the onion mixture; cook while stirring for around 1 minute, or till fragrant.
- Mix in tomatoes; cook while stirring for 4-6 minutes, or till the tomatoes lightly turn brown. Include in cream, milk and chicken; boil the mixture. Turn the heat down to medium; cook with a cover for 15-20 minutes, or till the chicken is tender and not pink in the center anymore. Using a slotted spoon, move the chicken onto a serving plate. Keep cooking the sauce for 5-7 more minutes, or till slightly reduced. Mix in cilantro; transfer the sauce over the chicken.

Nutrition Information

- Calories: 620 calories;
- Cholesterol: 216
- Protein: 45.6
- Total Fat: 42.4
- Sodium: 218
- Total Carbohydrate: 14.1

306. Kachori With Fresh Peas

Serving: 4 | Prep: 30mins | Cook: 15mins | Ready in:

Ingredients

- 1 tablespoon oil
- 2 fresh green chile peppers, chopped
- 1/2 teaspoon jeera (cumin seeds)
- 1 pinch hing (asafoetida powder)
- 2 cups fresh peas
- 1 teaspoon white sugar
- salt to taste
- 2 cups maida (refined white flour)
- 1 tablespoon oil
- 2 tablespoons water, or more as needed
- 1 tablespoon chopped fresh coriander (cilantro), or to taste
- 1 teaspoon lemon juice
- vegetable oil for frying

Direction

- Heat 1 tbsp. oil in skillet on medium heat then add hing, jeera and green chile peppers; mix and cook for 1 minute. Add salt, sugar and peas; mix and cook for 5 minutes on low heat till peas are soft. Take skillet off heat; cool the pea mixture.
- Mix salt, 1 tbsp. oil and maida in bowl; add sufficient water till dough forms. Rest for 2-3 minutes.
- Grind pea mixture with mortar and pestle to coarse paste. Add lemon juice and coriander; mix well.
- Shape dough to small balls; roll each with rolling pin to flat circle. Scoop pea mixture in the middle of every circle; roll dough around filling to fully enclose.
- Heat oil in big saucepan/deep fryer for frying; fry filled dough balls in batches for 3-5 minutes per batch till crisp. Put on paper towel-lined plate; drain.

Nutrition Information

- Calories: 382 calories;
- Total Carbohydrate: 59.9
- Cholesterol: 0
- Protein: 10.4
- Total Fat: 13.7
- Sodium: 45

307. Kashmiri Lamb

Serving: 6 | Prep: 35mins | Cook: 1hours30mins | Ready in:

Ingredients

- 4 dried red chile peppers (such as cayenne)
- 3 long, green fresh chile peppers (such as Indian Jwala)
- 1 teaspoon cumin seeds
- 1 teaspoon Kashmiri garam masala
- 1 (1 inch) piece fresh ginger root, peeled and grated
- 5 cloves garlic, crushed
- 1/4 cup dried unsweetened coconut
- 3 tomatoes, chopped
- 6 tablespoons vegetable oil
- 2 large onions, thinly sliced
- 2 pounds lamb meat, cut into 1 1/2-inch cubes
- salt to taste
- 1/2 teaspoon ground turmeric
- 1 cup plain yogurt
- 1/2 teaspoon saffron threads
- 20 whole blanched almonds
- 1/4 cup chopped fresh cilantro

Direction

- Put tomatoes, grated coconut, garlic, ginger, garam masala, cumin seeds, green chiles and red chiles in a blender; pulse a few times to chop, blend to smooth paste.
- Heat vegetable oil in big skillet/Dutch oven on medium heat. Mix onion in; mix and cook for 5 minutes till onion is translucent and soft. Lower heat to medium low; mix and cook for 10-15 minutes more till onion is golden brown and very tender.
- Mix spice paste into onion; mix and cook for 3 minutes till oil separates from mixture.
- Mix in salt and lamb pieces. Cook on medium

high heat for 8 minutes till lamb pieces are browned on all the sides, frequently mixing.
- Mix in blanched almonds, saffron and yogurt till combined well.
- Lower heat to low; simmer for 1 hour till gravy is thick and meat is tender, covered.
- Before serving, garnish curry using chopped cilantro.

Nutrition Information

- Calories: 489 calories;
- Protein: 28.1
- Total Fat: 35.4
- Sodium: 132
- Total Carbohydrate: 16.1
- Cholesterol: 88

308. Kashmiri Style Kidney Beans With Turnips

Serving: 4 | Prep: 30mins | Cook: 25mins | Ready in:

Ingredients

- 2 turnips, peeled and cubed
- 1 cup water
- 1/2 teaspoon salt
- 1 (14.5 ounce) can kidney beans, drained
- 3 tablespoons vegetable oil
- 1/2 teaspoon whole cumin seeds
- 1/2 teaspoon whole fennel seeds
- 1 cup finely chopped red onion
- 1/2 teaspoon minced fresh ginger root
- 1/2 teaspoon minced garlic
- 1 cup chopped tomatoes
- 1/2 teaspoon salt
- 1 teaspoon paprika
- 1/2 teaspoon turmeric powder
- 1/2 teaspoon ground ginger
- 2 tablespoons water
- 1/2 teaspoon Kashmiri garam masala

Direction

- Pour water into a saucepan and soak the turnips together with a half teaspoon of salt. Let it boil over high heat. Adjust the heat to medium-low and cover the saucepan. Simmer for 5 minutes until the turnip is soft. Add the kidney beans and cook for 5 more minutes.
- Meanwhile, put vegetable oil in a skillet and place it over medium-high heat to warm. Cook fennel and cumin for 60 seconds until the spices are fragrant and toasted. Add onion and cook for 5 more minutes until it turns golden brown. Add the garlic and minced ginger and cook and stir for 30 seconds. Stir in salt and tomatoes and let it cook until the mixture is pasty. Pour 2 tbsp. of water into the mixture together with the ground ginger, paprika, and turmeric. Allow it to cook for 2 more minutes.
- Pour the tomato mixture into the large saucepan with turnips. Bring it to simmer for 10 minutes. Before serving, flavor the dish with garam masala.

Nutrition Information

- Calories: 226 calories;
- Total Fat: 11.1
- Sodium: 852
- Total Carbohydrate: 26.6
- Cholesterol: 0
- Protein: 7.2

309. Keema Aloo (Ground Beef And Potatoes)

Serving: 8 | Prep: 20mins | Cook: 55mins | Ready in:

Ingredients

- 2 tablespoons extra-virgin olive oil
- 1 extra-large Spanish onion, chopped
- 2 tablespoons water (optional)
- 2 pounds lean ground beef
- 4 cloves garlic, minced
- 2 tablespoons grated fresh ginger root

- 1 serrano chile pepper, finely chopped
- 2 teaspoons chopped fresh cilantro
- 1 tablespoon ground coriander
- 1 1/2 teaspoons salt
- 1 1/2 teaspoons ground cumin
- 1 teaspoon ground cayenne pepper
- 1 teaspoon ground turmeric
- 1 (28 ounce) can diced tomatoes
- 3 potatoes, peeled and diced
- 1 cup frozen green peas
- 1 teaspoon garam masala

Direction

- Heat the olive oil on medium-high heat in the big saucepan. Cook and whisk the onion in hot oil for roughly 12 minutes or till tender and starting to brown. If the browned bits of the onion are stuck to pan's bottom, whisk the water to the onion and whisk to loosen browned bits.
- Combine the cilantro, Serrano chile, ginger, garlic and ground beef to the pan; cook and whisk for 10-15 minutes or till the beef becomes brown and crumbly. Lower the heat to medium-low. Whisk the turmeric, cayenne pepper, cumin, salt and coriander to beef; cook and whisk for roughly 5 minutes or till the flavors are blended. Put in the potatoes and tomatoes, keep the pot covered, and let simmer for roughly 15 minutes or till the potatoes soften.
- Stir the green peas to the dish and cook for 10-15 minutes or till the flavors are blended and the sauce becomes thick a bit. Drizzle the garam masala on dish, cover, and allow it to rest for 5 minutes prior to serving.

Nutrition Information

- Calories: 362 calories;
- Total Fat: 17.7
- Sodium: 687
- Total Carbohydrate: 23.4
- Cholesterol: 74
- Protein: 25.6

310. Keon's Slow Cooker Curry Chicken

Serving: 4 | Prep: 20mins | Cook: 3hours5mins | Ready in:

Ingredients

- 1 tablespoon butter
- 1 onion, chopped
- 1 (10.75 ounce) can condensed cream of mushroom soup
- 1 (10.75 ounce) can condensed cream of chicken soup
- 1 (14 ounce) can coconut milk
- 1 packet dry onion soup mix (such as Knorr® French Onion Soup Mix)
- 3 tablespoons curry powder, or to taste
- 1/2 teaspoon salt
- 1/2 teaspoon ground black pepper
- 2 teaspoons ground cayenne pepper, or to taste
- 3 large skinless, boneless chicken breast halves -- trimmed and cut into 1-inch pieces
- 1 cup green peas
- 2 cups sliced fresh mushrooms

Direction

- Switch a slow cooker to High setting.
- Over medium heat, heat butter in a skillet and then cook while stirring onion for 5 to 10 minutes until browned. Put aside the onion.
- Combine together cayenne pepper, pepper, salt, curry powder, dry soup mix, and coconut milk, cream of chicken soup and cream of mushroom soup in a large bowl until mixture is mixed thoroughly. Put chicken into the bottom of slow cooker and then spread mixture atop chicken. Mix in mushrooms, peas and onion.
- Cook for 1 1/2 hours on High setting, then decrease the heat to Low and let it cook for about 1 1/2 to 2 hours longer.

Nutrition Information

- Calories: 635 calories;
- Total Carbohydrate: 32
- Cholesterol: 111
- Protein: 45.2
- Total Fat: 37.9
- Sodium: 2231

311. Kheema Pulao

Serving: 6 | Prep: 30mins | Cook: 45mins | Ready in:

Ingredients

- 3 cups basmati rice
- 1/4 cup cooking oil
- 2 large onions, minced
- 1 tablespoon garlic paste
- 1 tablespoon ginger paste
- 1 teaspoon ground turmeric
- 1 teaspoon garam masala
- 1 teaspoon ground cumin
- 2 tomatoes, chopped
- 1 pound ground beef
- salt to taste
- 1/2 cup frozen green peas (optional)
- 4 green chile peppers, halved lengthwise
- 1 tablespoon ghee (clarified butter)
- 1 cinnamon stick
- 1 black cardamom pod
- 2 bay leaves
- 4 whole cloves
- 5 cups water
- 1/4 cup chopped fresh cilantro

Direction

- In a large container, put in basmati rice; pour in several inches of cool water to cover; allow to sit for 30 minutes; strain.
- In a large pan with a heavy bottom, heat oil; fry in ginger paste, garlic paste and onion for around 10 minutes, or till the onions are golden brown and caramelized. Mix in cumin, garam masala and turmeric; cook together for 30 seconds. Include in tomatoes; cook for around 10 minutes, or till the oil separates. Crumble in ground beef into the tomato mixture; season with salt; cook for around 15 minutes, or till the beef is not pink anymore. Stir in green chile peppers and frozen peas.
- Set a large skillet on medium heat; heat ghee. Cook in cloves, bay leaves, cardamom pod and cinnamon stick for around 1 minute, or till fragrant. Include in the rice; cook for 1-2 more minutes, or till the rice smells nutty. Transfer the rice with the spices over the beef mixture, spreading evenly, but do not combine. Transfer water gently over the rice; season with salt; boil the mixture for 2 minutes. Turn the heat down to low; cook with a cover for 12-15 minutes, till the rice becomes tender. Take away from the heat completely; let stand with a cover for 20 more minutes. Use cilantro for garnish. Serve.

Nutrition Information

- Calories: 636 calories;
- Protein: 22.4
- Total Fat: 21.8
- Sodium: 160
- Total Carbohydrate: 87.9
- Cholesterol: 51

312. Kobbari Annam (Coconut Rice)

Serving: 4 | Prep: 10mins | Cook: 15mins | Ready in:

Ingredients

- 2 tablespoons coconut oil
- 2 tablespoons ghee (clarified butter)
- 1/4 cup cashews
- 3 dried red chile peppers
- 2 tablespoons skinned split black lentils (urad dal)

- 1 tablespoon split Bengal gram (chana dal)
- 1 teaspoon mustard seeds
- 1 teaspoon cumin seeds
- 1 cup grated fresh coconut
- 4 green chile peppers, halved lengthwise
- 2 sprigs fresh curry leaves
- 1/4 teaspoon asafoetida powder
- 3 cups cold, cooked white rice
- salt to taste
- 2 tablespoons toasted sesame seeds (optional)

Direction

- In a large skillet, heat together the ghee and coconut oil over medium heat; fry the cashews in the hot mixture until they turn golden brown. Use a slotted spoon to move the cashews to a bowl; then put them aside. Put cumin seeds, mustard seeds, chana dal, urad dal, and red chile peppers into the remaining oil. Put in asafoetida powder, curry leaves, green chile peppers, and coconut once the seeds start spluttering; before putting in the rice, cook them together for a minute. Flavor with salt. Stir the mixture, using the back of the spoon to break the rice into separate grains; stir and cook for 8-10 minutes until the ice is reheated well. Add sesame seeds and cashews to decorate. Serve at room temperature or warm.

Nutrition Information

- Calories: 830 calories;
- Total Fat: 27.9
- Sodium: 74
- Total Carbohydrate: 129
- Cholesterol: 16
- Protein: 16.5

313. Lamb (Gosht) Biryani

Serving: 8 | Prep: 25mins | Cook: 1hours | Ready in:

Ingredients

- 2 1/2 cups basmati rice
- 1/4 cup cooking oil
- 8 whole cloves
- 4 black cardamom pods
- 4 cinnamon sticks
- 4 large onions, sliced thin
- 1 tablespoon garlic paste
- 1 tablespoon ginger paste
- 1/4 cup chopped fresh cilantro leaves
- 3 tablespoons chopped fresh mint leaves
- 1 pound lamb chops
- salt to taste
- 3 tomatoes, chopped
- 4 green chile peppers, halved lengthwise
- 2 teaspoons ground red pepper
- 2 tablespoons plain yogurt
- 2 tablespoons lemon juice
- 7 1/2 cups water
- 1 teaspoon salt
- 1 tablespoon vegetable oil
- 1 onion, sliced
- 1/2 teaspoon saffron
- 2 tablespoons warm milk

Direction

- In a big container, place basmati rice; pour in some inches of cool water to cover. Allow to stand for 30 minutes. Drain.
- In a big skillet, heat 1/4 cup oil on medium heat. In the hot oil, fry cinnamon sticks, cardamom pods and the cloves for 1 minute until fragrant. Put in onion, cook while stirring 5 minutes till onions are slightly browned. Mix ginger paste and garlic paste into onion mixture; cook 1 minute longer till ginger and garlic are fragrant. Sprinkle the mixture with mint and cilantro; cook 1 more minute.
- Put lamb chops in the skillet and season with salt. Cook while stirring the lamb 20 minutes until beginning to brown.
- Mix ground red pepper, green chile peppers and tomatoes into the mixture. Keep cooking 10 minutes till the oil starts to detach from the gravy. Put in lemon juice and yogurt. Put on

- cover and cook 15 minutes till lamb is tender. Add water if necessary to prevent the mixture from being too dry.
- In a saucepan, boil 1 teaspoon salt, 7 1/2 cups water, and rice until rice is almost done but a little chewy, about 10-15 minutes. Drain to remove excess water if there is.
- In a small skillet, heat 1 tablespoon oil. In the hot oil, fry sliced onion until slightly browned.
- In the bottom of a deep pot accompanied with a lid, layer about half of the rice. Scoop lamb masala over the rice. Spread lamb masala with fried onion. Layer the rest of rice atop. In a small bowl, combine warm milk and saffron; spread over the top rice layer. Put on lid to cover the pot. Place pot over low heat and cook 15 minutes till rice is well cooked.

Nutrition Information

- Calories: 544 calories;
- Total Fat: 25
- Sodium: 429
- Total Carbohydrate: 64.3
- Cholesterol: 43
- Protein: 16.5

314. Lamb Meatballs Over Tandoori Naan

Serving: 4 | Prep: 20mins | Cook: 30mins | Ready in:

Ingredients

- Lamb Meatballs:
- 1/4 cup Italian-seasoned bread crumbs
- 1/4 teaspoon garlic powder
- 1/4 teaspoon ground paprika
- 1/4 teaspoon dried mint
- 1/4 teaspoon dried basil
- 1/4 teaspoon dried parsley
- 1 pound ground lamb
- 1 egg
- 2 tablespoons finely chopped onion
- 2 cloves garlic, minced
- 1/2 teaspoon olive oil
- salt and ground black pepper to taste
- Sauce:
- 1 (26 ounce) jar tomato sauce
- 1 tablespoon capers
- 4 leaves fresh basil leaves, torn
- 1/4 teaspoon dried mint
- salt and ground black pepper to taste
- Remaining Ingredients:
- 4 pieces tandoori naan bread
- 8 slices Muenster cheese, or as needed

Direction

- Set the oven for preheating to 400°F (200°C). Prepare by greasing a baking sheet.
- Combine garlic powder, bread crumbs, paprika, a quarter teaspoon mint, parsley and dried basil together in a big bowl. Mix in the egg, ground lamb, onion, olive oil, garlic, pepper and salt together until equally distributed. Shape the lamb mixture into an inch balls and put on the prepared baking sheet, arranging them in a single layer.
- Let it bake inside the oven for 15 minutes. Turn the meatballs and continue to cook for additional 10 minutes until completely cooked. Take the meatballs out from the oven and adjust the oven temperature to 350°F (175°C).
- Put the tomato sauce in a saucepan placed over low heat; drop the fresh basil, capers, a quarter teaspoon mint, pepper and salt. Cook and occasionally stir the sauce for roughly 5 to 10 minutes, until heated completely and the flavors blended together.
- Put the naan bread on a baking sheet. Scoop the tomato sauce using a spoon and place the meatballs on the naan; cover with slices of Muenster cheese.
- Let it bake inside the oven for roughly 5 to 10 minutes until the cheese has melted.

Nutrition Information

- Calories: 771 calories;

- Total Fat: 38
- Sodium: 1885
- Total Carbohydrate: 61
- Cholesterol: 187
- Protein: 47.9

315. Lamb Shank Vindaloo

Serving: 4 | Prep: 30mins | Cook: 3hours50mins | Ready in:

Ingredients

- 4 lamb shanks
- 1/2 cup cider vinegar
- 1/4 cup vegetable oil
- 2 teaspoons salt
- 1 tablespoon tamarind concentrate
- 1 1/2 tablespoons garam masala
- 1 onion, chopped
- 8 cloves garlic, peeled
- 1/3 cup sliced fresh ginger
- 1 cup cherry tomatoes
- 1/2 cup water
- 1 1/2 teaspoons cayenne pepper
- 1 1/2 teaspoons paprika
- 1 teaspoon ground cinnamon
- 1 teaspoon ground cumin
- 1 teaspoon ground mustard
- 1 teaspoon ground black pepper
- 3 tablespoons ghee (clarified butter)
- 1 large onion, chopped
- salt and ground black pepper to taste
- 4 teaspoons brown sugar
- 1/2 cup fresh cilantro, for garnish (optional)

Direction

- In a big resealable plastic bag, put lamb shanks. In a bowl, mix garam masala, tamarind concentrate, salt, oil and cider vinegar. Put it in the bag. Squeeze excess air out. Seal bag. Marinade in the fridge for 8 hours to overnight.
- Preheat oven to 230 degrees C/450 degrees F. Get a foil-lined baking sheet and grease it.
- Take out marinated lamb shanks. Put on prepped baking sheet. Season salt on all sides. Roast in preheated oven for 15-20 minutes until well-browned. Keep marinade in bag.
- In a blender, pulse water, cherry tomatoes, ginger, garlic and 1 onion on and off until smooth. Put aside.
- In a small bowl, mix black pepper, dried mustard, cumin, cinnamon, paprika and cayenne pepper.
- In a big stockpot, melt clarified butter on medium-high heat. Sauté 1 onion for 30 minutes until well-browned and soft. Lower heat to medium. Put in cayenne pepper mixture. Stir and cook for 2 minutes until spices are aromatic.
- Put marinade from bag in stockpot. Mix in brown sugar and onion-tomato mixture. Simmer. Put lamb shanks in pan. Lower heat to low. Cook, covered, for 3-4 hours, occasionally turn, until meat is tender and pierced easily with a fork.
- Take lamb from pot. Cover with foil. Bring up heat. Simmer sauce for several minutes. Skim fat from top. Taste and put salt if needed. Put sauce spooned over the top of lamb shanks. Garnish using cilantro. Serve.

Nutrition Information

- Calories: 523 calories;
- Total Fat: 37
- Sodium: 1288
- Total Carbohydrate: 19.7
- Cholesterol: 114
- Protein: 28.7

316. Lemon Lentil Rice

Serving: 4 | Prep: 10mins | Cook: 30mins | Ready in:

Ingredients

- 1 tablespoon vegetable oil
- 1 teaspoon mustard seeds
- 1/2 cup chopped carrot
- 1/2 cup chopped fresh green beans
- 3 cups water
- 1 cup long grain white rice
- 1/2 cup dry brown lentils
- 1/4 cup fresh lemon juice
- 1 pinch salt, or to taste
- 1 teaspoon chili powder, or to taste

Direction

- In a big saucepan, heat the oil on medium-high heat. Put in mustard seeds and let it cook until it pops. When the seeds pop like a popcorn, add the green beans and carrot and sauté for around 2 minutes, just to blend the flavors.
- Put in lentils, rice and water. Lower the heat to low, put on cover and let it simmer for 20 minutes or until the lentils and rice become tender. Mix in lemon juice and sprinkle chili powder and salt to season. Prior to serving, allow to stand for 5 to 10 minutes with cover.

Nutrition Information

- Calories: 305 calories;
- Total Fat: 4.4
- Sodium: 23
- Total Carbohydrate: 56
- Cholesterol: 0
- Protein: 10.3

317. Lucy's Tomato And Peach Chutney

Serving: 64 | Prep: 35mins | Cook: 2hours | Ready in:

Ingredients

- 15 tomatoes, peeled and chopped
- 5 fresh peaches - peeled, pitted and chopped
- 5 red apples - peeled, cored and diced
- 4 medium onions, diced
- 4 stalks celery, diced
- 1 1/2 cups distilled white vinegar
- 1 tablespoon salt
- 1 cup pickling spice, wrapped in cheesecloth

Direction

- In a big stockpot, boil pickling spice, tomatoes, salt, peaches, vinegar, apples, celery, and onions together. Turn to low heat, let it simmer for about 2hrs until thick. Move to sterilized jars then refrigerate. You can also store it in plastic containers then freeze.

Nutrition Information

- Calories: 18 calories;
- Sodium: 113
- Total Carbohydrate: 4.3
- Cholesterol: 0
- Protein: 0.4
- Total Fat: 0.1

318. Makhani Chicken (Indian Butter Chicken)

Serving: 6 | Prep: 1hours | Cook: 15mins | Ready in:

Ingredients

- 1 3/4 pounds skinless, boneless chicken breast halves - cubed
- 1 tablespoon lemon juice
- 1 tablespoon chili powder
- salt to taste
- 1 cup yogurt
- salt to taste
- 2 tablespoons garlic paste
- 1/2 tablespoon garam masala
- 2 tablespoons melted butter
- 1 tablespoon chili powder
- 2 tablespoons ginger paste

- 2 tablespoons lemon juice
- 2 tablespoons olive oil
- 1 tablespoon butter
- 1 tablespoon garam masala
- 1 tablespoon ginger paste
- 1 tablespoon chopped garlic
- 1 tablespoon chopped green chile pepper
- 2 cups tomato puree
- 1 tablespoon chili powder
- salt to taste
- 1 cup water
- 1 tablespoon honey
- 1/2 teaspoon dried fenugreek leaves
- 1 cup heavy cream

Direction

- For marinating: In a bowl or nonporous glass dish, put in chicken, salt, 1 tbsp. chili powder and lemon juice. Coat by tossing. Chill in fridge for 1 hour to marinate, covered.
- Drain yogurt in a cloth, 15-20 minutes. Put in a moderate-sized bowl. Combine in oil, lemon juice, ginger paste, chili powder, butter, garam masala, garlic paste and salt. Put yogurt mixture over chicken, replace cover and chill in fridge to marinate for another 3-4 hours.
- Set oven to 200°C or 400°F.
- Put chicken on skewers. Arrange skewers in a 9x13 in. baking dish and bake until mostly cooked through in preheated oven, or for 20 minutes.
- For making sauce: In a medium saucepan, melt butter on medium heat. Stir in garam masala. Combine in green chile peppers, chopped garlic and ginger paste once masala starts to crackle. Sauté until softened then stir in water, salt, chili powder and tomato puree. Boil. Lower heat to low and simmer. Stir in fenugreek and honey.
- Put chicken in sauce mixture. Keep on cooking for another 5 more minutes or until chicken isn't pink inside anymore. Stir in fresh cream.

Nutrition Information

- Calories: 492 calories;
- Total Fat: 28.4
- Sodium: 666
- Total Carbohydrate: 19
- Cholesterol: 149
- Protein: 35.8

319. Mangalore Mutton Curry

Serving: 6 | Prep: 30mins | Cook: 51mins | Ready in:

Ingredients

- 1 teaspoon vegetable oil
- 15 whole black peppercorns
- 1 tablespoon white poppy seeds (khus khus)
- 4 whole cloves (lavang)
- 1 cinnamon stick (dalchini)
- 4 dried red chile peppers
- 1 teaspoon cumin seeds (jeera)
- 1 pod black cardamom (badi elaichi)
- 1/2 cup grated coconut
- 3 large onions, quartered
- 6 cloves garlic
- 1 (1 1/2 inch) piece ginger root, peeled
- 2 tablespoons vegetable oil
- 2 large tomatoes, pureed
- 1 teaspoon ground turmeric (haldi)
- salt to taste
- 1 pound boneless lamb, cut into small pieces
- 1/2 pound potatoes, quartered
- 1 cup water
- 1 tablespoon tamarind paste
- 1 teaspoon white sugar
- 1/4 cup fresh cilantro leaves, or to taste

Direction

- On medium heat, heat a teaspoon of vegetable oil in a small pan. Add and toast black cardamom, peppercorns, cumin seeds, poppy seeds, dried chile pepper, cloves, and cinnamon stick for 2-3 minutes until aromatic. Grind the mixture to a paste with grated coconut using a spice grinder.

- Grind the ginger, garlic, and onion to a paste using a food processor.
- Use a stovetop pressure cooker to heat 2 tbsp. of vegetable oil; mix in onion paste. Cook for 5 minutes until it's golden brown, stir. Add the pureed tomatoes and cook for 4-5 minutes until darkened, stir. Mix in salt and turmeric. Place in lamb, Cook for approximately 10 minutes until the lamb is coated and releases juice.
- Add sugar, coconut paste, tamarind paste, potatoes, and water in the pressure cooker; boil. Secure the lid and set the pressure on high as specified in the cooker's manual. Cook for approximately 10 minutes. Lower the heat and cook for another 15 minutes.
- Release the pressure as specified in the pressure cooker's manual. Garnish with cilantro leaves and serve.

Nutrition Information

- Calories: 277 calories;
- Total Fat: 14.4
- Sodium: 68
- Total Carbohydrate: 24.8
- Cholesterol: 36
- Protein: 14.8

320. Mango Lassi Come Home

Serving: 7 | Prep: 5mins | Cook: |Ready in:

Ingredients

- 2 cups lemon-flavored yogurt
- 1 cup vanilla yogurt
- 1/4 cup milk
- 2 cups pureed mango
- 3 tablespoons honey
- 1 (12.5 fl oz) can mango nectar
- 1/8 teaspoon ground cardamom

Direction

- In a blender, conflate cardamom mango nectar, honey, pureed mango, milk, vanilla yogurt and lemon yogurt till totally mixed. Serve right away.

Nutrition Information

- Calories: 207 calories;
- Total Fat: 3.1
- Sodium: 75
- Total Carbohydrate: 41.6
- Cholesterol: 9
- Protein: 5.9

321. Minty Cucumber Raita

Serving: 12 | Prep: 10mins | Cook: |Ready in:

Ingredients

- 1 cup plain yogurt
- 2 cups diced cucumber
- 2 tablespoons chopped fresh cilantro
- 1 tablespoon chopped fresh mint
- 1/2 teaspoon ground cumin
- salt and freshly ground black pepper to taste

Direction

- Mix cumin, mint, yogurt, cucumber and cilantro in a bowl until yogurt becomes smooth and creamy. Add black pepper and salt to taste. Cover the bowl and refrigerate before serving.

Nutrition Information

- Calories: 17 calories;
- Protein: 1.2
- Total Fat: 0.4
- Sodium: 15
- Total Carbohydrate: 2.3

- Cholesterol: 1

322. Mixed Grill Of Sausage, Chicken And Lamb With Tandoori Flavorings

Serving: 8 | Prep: | Cook: | Ready in:

Ingredients

- 2 pounds spicy or mild Italian pork sausage
- 1/4 cup olive oil
- 3 tablespoons ground cumin
- 1 tablespoon curry powder
- 1 1/2 teaspoons garlic powder
- 3/4 teaspoon ground ginger
- 3/4 teaspoon salt
- 1/2 teaspoon cayenne pepper
- 8 lamb loin chops
- 1/2 cup plain yogurt
- 3 tablespoons red wine vinegar
- 12 chicken drumsticks, skin removed

Direction

- In a big 12-inch skillet, add the sausage and 1/2 cup of water. Steam sausages with cover for 8 minutes until the raw color of sausages is gone throughout. Remove water and put to one side.
- Combine cumin, oil, curry powder, ginger, garlic powder, cayenne, and salt in a medium bowl. Transfer half of spice mixture in a separate medium bowl. Put the lamb chops in one of the bowls, tossing until well coated. Pour the vinegar and yogurt in the other bowl and put chicken legs in, tossing until well coated. Put on one side to marinate.
- 30 minutes before serving, set all the burners on high to preheat fully a gas grill for 10-15 minutes. Clean the grill rack with a wire brush and using the tongs, wipe a rag soaked in oil on the rack. Return the grill to correct temperature with the lid closed. Prepare water for extinguishing flare-ups.
- For all meats to finish at the same time, stagger the meat additions. Place the chicken on the grill and close the lid. Grill-roast for 20 minutes in total, 8 minutes each side (first side- 8 minutes and second- 8 minutes) and an additional 4 minutes, flipping as necessary towards the end of grilling to assure doneness. Put the lamb on and grill-roast for 8 minutes in total, 4 minutes on each side. Place the sausage on and grill-roast for 4 minutes in total, 2 minutes each side.
- Prepare a platter and transfer on it grilled, lamb, sausage, and chicken. Serve alongside couscous.

Nutrition Information

- Calories: 743 calories;
- Total Fat: 52.5
- Sodium: 1093
- Total Carbohydrate: 4.7
- Cholesterol: 214
- Protein: 59.8

323. Moong Dal

Serving: 6 | Prep: 30mins | Cook: 30mins | Ready in:

Ingredients

- 2 1/2 cups dried yellow split peas
- 2 1/2 cups water
- 1 1/2 teaspoons salt
- 1/2 teaspoon grated fresh ginger root
- 1 teaspoon diced jalapeno chile pepper
- 1/2 cup diced tomatoes
- 3 teaspoons lemon juice
- 1/2 teaspoon ground turmeric
- 2 teaspoons vegetable oil
- 1 teaspoon cumin seed
- 1/2 dried red chile pepper
- 1 pinch Asafoetida
- 2 cloves garlic, finely chopped
- 1/4 cup chopped fresh cilantro

Direction

- Rinse split peas; put in a saucepan with 2 1/2 cups of water. Soak split peas for 30 minutes.
- Heat salt, water and split peas till boiling; lower heat to medium low. Cook for 15-20 minutes till thick and tender; if needed, add more water to avoid drying out. Mix in turmeric, lemon juice, tomato, jalapeno pepper and ginger.
- Heat oil inside a small saucepan. Add red chile pepper and cumin seed; add garlic and Asafoetida powder when pepper is heated. Mix the mixture into the split peas. Add cilantro; stir well.

Nutrition Information

- Calories: 127 calories;
- Total Fat: 2.4
- Sodium: 656
- Total Carbohydrate: 20.4
- Cholesterol: 0
- Protein: 7.3

324. Mulligatawny Soup I

Serving: 6 | Prep: 20mins | Cook: 1hours | Ready in:

Ingredients

- 1/2 cup chopped onion
- 2 stalks celery, chopped
- 1 carrot, diced
- 1/4 cup butter
- 1 1/2 tablespoons all-purpose flour
- 1 1/2 teaspoons curry powder
- 4 cups chicken broth
- 1/2 apple, cored and chopped
- 1/4 cup white rice
- 1 skinless, boneless chicken breast half - cut into cubes
- salt to taste
- ground black pepper to taste
- 1 pinch dried thyme
- 1/2 cup heavy cream, heated

Direction

- In a big soup pot, sauté butter, carrot, celery. and onions. Add curry and flour then cook 5 minutes longer. Put in chicken stock, combine thoroughly; heat to a boil. Allow to simmer for 30 minutes.
- Put in thyme, pepper, salt, chicken, rice, and apple; let simmer until rice is done, about 15-20 minutes.
- Add hot cream when serving.

Nutrition Information

- Calories: 223 calories;
- Protein: 6.9
- Total Fat: 15.8
- Sodium: 734
- Total Carbohydrate: 13.5
- Cholesterol: 62

325. Mulligatawny Soup II

Serving: 6 | Prep: | Cook: | Ready in:

Ingredients

- 1 tablespoon ghee (clarified butter), or vegetable oil
- 1 onion, chopped
- 4 cloves garlic, minced
- 2 teaspoons grated fresh ginger
- 2 green chile peppers, chopped
- 1/4 teaspoon ground cinnamon
- 1/4 teaspoon ground cloves
- 2 teaspoons ground coriander seed
- 1 1/2 teaspoons ground cumin
- 1 teaspoon ground turmeric
- 4 pods cardamom, bruised
- 1 tablespoon chopped fresh curry
- 1 carrot, chopped

- 1 apple - peeled, cored, and chopped
- 1 large potato, peeled and diced
- 1 cup Masoor dhal (red lentils), rinsed, drained
- 8 cups chicken broth
- 1 tablespoon tamarind concentrate
- 1 tablespoon lemon juice
- 2 cups coconut milk
- 2 tablespoons chopped fresh cilantro

Direction

- In a big pan, heat vegetable oil/ghee on low heat. Cook curry leaves, spices, chilies, ginger, garlic and onion, mixing until fragrant and onion is lightly browned. Don't overbrown onion to avoid a burnt taste.
- Put chicken stock, dhal, potato, apple and carrot to pan. Simmer for 15 minutes, covered, until veggies are tender. Throw curry leaves and cardamom pods.
- Process/blend soup mixture until pureed in batches. Put back in pan. Add fresh coriander leaves, coconut milk, lemon juice and tamarind. Mix until heated through.

Nutrition Information

- Calories: 404 calories;
- Total Fat: 22
- Sodium: 29
- Total Carbohydrate: 43.8
- Cholesterol: 5
- Protein: 12.4

326. Nitya's Cauliflower

Serving: 6 | Prep: 15mins | Cook: 20mins | Ready in:

Ingredients

- 1/4 cup vegetable oil
- 1/8 teaspoon mustard seed
- 1 large head cauliflower, cut into bite-size pieces
- 1 baking potato, peeled and cut into 1/4-inch cubes
- 1 1/2 teaspoons salt
- 1/8 teaspoon ground turmeric
- 1 1/2 teaspoons white sugar
- 1/8 teaspoon cayenne pepper

Direction

- Pour the oil in a big, deep skillet and place over medium-high heat. Stir mustard seeds in hot oil and cook for 10 to 15 seconds until toasted and popping.
- Mix in the potato, cauliflower, turmeric and salt in the oil until well coated; cover the skillet with a lid, and adjust the heat to medium. Stir from every few minutes while it cooks for 15 to 20 minutes until the potato and cauliflower are softened. Spice it up with cayenne pepper and sugar; cook for additional 2 minutes for flavors to develop.

Nutrition Information

- Calories: 147 calories;
- Total Fat: 9.3
- Sodium: 626
- Total Carbohydrate: 14.7
- Cholesterol: 0
- Protein: 3.5

327. Nuvvu Podi (Sesame Seed Powder)

Serving: 192 | Prep: 5mins | Cook: 10mins | Ready in:

Ingredients

- 1 2/3 cups sesame seeds
- 1/2 teaspoon sesame oil
- 10 dried red chile peppers, or to taste
- salt to taste

Direction

- Place the sesame seeds in a skillet over medium-low heat and toast for about 5 minutes, until scented. Transfer to a baking sheet and spread to cool.
- Pu 1/2 teaspoon sesame oil in the skillet, again over medium-low heat. Place the red chile peppers in the hot oil and fry for about 5 minutes, until they start to change color. Let it cool on the baking sheet.
- Grind the salt, chile peppers, and sesame seeds into powder using a mortar and pestle. You can keep the Nuvvu podi for a few months on the shelf.

Nutrition Information

- Calories: 7 calories;
- Protein: 0.2
- Total Fat: 0.6
- Sodium: < 1
- Total Carbohydrate: 0.3
- Cholesterol: 0

328. Paneer (Home Made)

Serving: 4 | Prep: 2hours | Cook: 20mins | Ready in:

Ingredients

- 4 cups milk
- 1 tablespoon plain yogurt
- 1 teaspoon salt
- 1 teaspoon sugar
- 1 tablespoon fresh lemon juice

Direction

- Mix together the yogurt, milk, sugar and salt in a saucepan. Set the pan over medium heat and stir the mixture occasionally using a whisk. As the milk nearly boils (bubbles appear at the edges), add the lemon juice and stir.
- Take it off from heat and transfer in a sieve lined with cheesecloth. Bring together the four corners of the cheesecloth and tie them altogether. Hang the cheese in the cloth over the sink to let it drain. Draining would take half an hour to 1 hour. Once done, transfer the cheese, still in the cloth, in a bowl and keep in the fridge until about to use.
- Later, if you want to have the paneer sliced in firm fingers, you can use a spoon to press the paneer in a shape of a bowl before keeping it in the fridge.

Nutrition Information

- Calories: 129 calories;
- Total Fat: 4.9
- Sodium: 684
- Total Carbohydrate: 13.1
- Cholesterol: 20
- Protein: 8.3

329. Paneer Tikka Masala

Serving: 6 | Prep: 15mins | Cook: 40mins | Ready in:

Ingredients

- 1/4 cup butter
- 1 pound paneer, cut into 1/2-inch cubes
- 2 onions, finely chopped
- 1 green bell pepper, chopped
- 2 jalapeno peppers, chopped
- 1 tablespoon ground cashews
- 1 teaspoon garlic paste
- 1 teaspoon ginger paste
- 1 teaspoon cayenne pepper
- 1 teaspoon ground cumin
- 1 teaspoon ground coriander
- 1 teaspoon garam masala
- 1 (16 ounce) can tomato sauce
- 1 pint half-and-half
- 1 teaspoon salt, or to taste

Direction

- In a skillet, melt the butter on medium heat; stir and cook the paneer for 5 minutes until golden. Add garam masala, coriander, cumin, cayenne pepper, ginger paste, garlic paste, cashews, jalapeno peppers, green bell pepper, and onions to the paneer; stir and cook for a minute until coated evenly and fragrant.
- Combine salt, half-and-half, and tomato sauce into the paneer mixture; let it simmer for half an hour until thickened.

Nutrition Information

- Calories: 323 calories;
- Total Fat: 23
- Sodium: 1225
- Total Carbohydrate: 16.5
- Cholesterol: 66
- Protein: 14.4

330. Pork Vindaloo

Serving: 6 | Prep: 30mins | Cook: 1hours10mins | Ready in:

Ingredients

- 1 large onion, roughly chopped
- 1 (3 inch) piece fresh ginger, peeled and minced
- 3 cloves garlic, peeled and crushed
- 2 tablespoons mustard seeds
- 1 tablespoon cumin seeds
- 1 cinnamon stick
- 8 whole black peppercorns
- 4 whole cloves
- 1/2 cup vinegar, divided, or to taste
- 2 tablespoons water
- 1 pound lean pork, cut into cubes
- 3 tablespoons vegetable oil
- 8 fresh curry leaves
- 1 pound tomatoes, peeled and chopped
- 1 1/2 teaspoons ground turmeric
- salt to taste
- 4 cups pork stock, or as needed
- 3 sprigs cilantro

Direction

- In food processor or blender, grind cloves, peppercorns, cinnamon stick, cumin seeds, mustard seeds, garlic, ginger and onion with just sufficient vinegar to maintain the mixture moving till it forms a thick paste.
- In a big bowl, stir water and leftover vinegar together. Into the bowl, put the pork cubes and wash the meat well with vinegar mixture; let drain. Using paper towel, pat the pork dry.
- In clean bowl, combine pork cubes and paste together, ensuring pork cubes are covered in paste. Put plastic wrap on bowl to cover. Put in refrigerator to marinate for 8 hours to overnight.
- In a big skillet, heat the vegetable oil over moderately-high heat. In hot oil, let curry leaves fry for 2 to 3 minutes till golden brown. Put in the turmeric, tomatoes and marinated pork; cook and mix for about 10 minutes till tomatoes are totally softened.
- Add salt to pork mixture to taste. On the mixture, add sufficient pork stock to ensure all is at least 1/2 submerged. Simmer the stock, cover the skillet, lower heat to moderately-low, and let simmer for 1 to 2 hours till pork is fully softened.
- Uncover the skillet and keep simmering the mixture for about 10 minutes till sauce is extremely thick. Jazz up with cilantro.

Nutrition Information

- Calories: 209 calories;
- Total Fat: 11.5
- Sodium: 426
- Total Carbohydrate: 10.8
- Cholesterol: 43
- Protein: 16.8

331. Potato Cutlets

Serving: 10 | Prep: 20mins | Cook: 25mins | Ready in:

Ingredients

- 5 medium-size potatoes, washed thoroughly
- 2 teaspoons salt
- 2 tablespoons garam masala
- 2 tablespoons coriander powder
- 2 tablespoons black pepper
- 10 cilantro leaves, chopped
- 6 tablespoons bread crumbs
- oil for frying

Direction

- In a large saucepan, place unpeeled potatoes and fill with water, then place over high heat and bring to a boil. Cook potatoes until they are tender and soft. Drain off the water and let potatoes cool, then peel.
- Transfer potatoes to a large bowl. Add cilantro, pepper, coriander powder, garam masala, and salt. Use a potato masher or a large fork to mash the potatoes until smooth and no lumps. Shape potatoes into flat cutlets with a diameter of 2 or 3 inches and thickness of 1 inch. Lightly coat cutlets with bread crumbs and set aside.
- In a large skillet, heat 2 tablespoons of oil over medium heat. Fry cutlets in batches until every side is golden brown. Add oil between batches if necessary.

Nutrition Information

- Calories: 150 calories;
- Cholesterol: 0
- Protein: 2.2
- Total Fat: 9.1
- Sodium: 503
- Total Carbohydrate: 16.2

332. Potatoes Madras

Serving: 4 | Prep: 30mins | Cook: 30mins | Ready in:

Ingredients

- 3 tablespoons vegetable oil
- 1 1/2 pounds potatoes, cut into 1/2 inch dice
- 2 1/2 cups cauliflower florets
- 1 large onion, sliced
- 2 cloves garlic, crushed
- 1 tablespoon curry powder
- 1/2 tablespoon ground ginger
- 4 ounces dry red lentils
- 1 (14.4 ounce) can whole tomatoes, chopped
- 1 1/4 cups vegetable stock
- 2 tablespoons malt vinegar
- 1 tablespoon mango chutney
- salt and pepper to taste
- chopped fresh parsley for garnish

Direction

- On medium heat, warm oil in a big frying pan. Cook garlic, potatoes, onion, and cauliflower in hot oil until the garlic starts to brown. Mix in ginger and curry powder; cook for 3mins. Mix in chutney, lentils, vinegar, vegetable stock, and tomatoes; sprinkle pepper and salt to season then cover. Let it simmer for 20mins while mixing from time to time until the lentils are tender. Add parsley on top.

Nutrition Information

- Calories: 395 calories;
- Cholesterol: 0
- Protein: 14
- Total Fat: 11.4
- Sodium: 272
- Total Carbohydrate: 62.9

333. Pressure Cooker Sambar (Indian Lentil Curry)

Serving: 4 | Prep: 10mins | Cook: 30mins | Ready in:

Ingredients

- 6 1/2 cups water, divided
- 1 cup yellow lentils (tur daal)
- 1 cup chopped eggplant
- 1 teaspoon turmeric powder
- salt to taste
- 1 tablespoon tamarind paste
- 2 teaspoons ground red chile powder
- 1 teaspoon vegetable oil, or as needed
- 1 whole dried red chile
- 4 curry leaves, or more to taste
- 1 teaspoon whole cumin seeds
- 1 teaspoon mustard seeds
- 1 pinch asafoetida powder

Direction

- In a pressure cooker, mix salt, turmeric, eggplant, lentils and 4 cups water. Securely close cooker. Put pressure regular on vent following manufacturer's directions. Heat until a steady flow of steam escapes and creates a whistling noise, around 10 minutes. Adjust the temperature until the regulator rocks gently. Cook for about 3 minutes. Take off heat. Naturally release pressure following manufacturer's directions for 5-10 minutes. Unlock lid. Remove.
- In the pressure cooker, add chile powder, tamarind paste and 2 1/2 cups water. Securely close cooker. Put pressure regulator on vent following manufacturer's directions. Heat until a steady flow of steam escapes and creates a whistling noise, around 10 minutes. Take off heat. Release pressure naturally following manufacturer's directions for 5-10 minutes. Unlock lid. Remove.
- In a small saucepan on low heat, mix asafoetida powder, mustard seeds, cumin seeds, curry leaves, dried chile and oil. Cook for 1 minute until spices start to sputter a little.

Put spice mixture in pressure cooker with lentils. Season using salt.

Nutrition Information

- Calories: 238 calories;
- Total Fat: 2.4
- Sodium: 47
- Total Carbohydrate: 41
- Cholesterol: 0
- Protein: 14.8

334. Punjabi Chicken In Thick Gravy

Serving: 8 | Prep: 25mins | Cook: 1hours5mins | Ready in:

Ingredients

- 2 tablespoons vegetable oil
- 2 tablespoons ghee (clarified butter)
- 8 chicken legs, skin removed
- 1 teaspoon cumin seeds
- 1 onion, finely chopped
- 5 cloves garlic, minced
- 2 tablespoons minced fresh ginger root
- 1 small tomato, coarsely chopped
- 1 tablespoon tomato paste
- 1 tablespoon garam masala
- 1 tablespoon ground turmeric
- 1 teaspoon salt, or to taste
- 1 serrano chile pepper, seeded and minced
- 1 cup water
- 1/4 cup chopped fresh cilantro

Direction

- In a big pot, heat ghee and oil on medium heat. Cook cumin seeds in oil till seeds start to change in color.
- Mix chopped onion in; stir and cook for 5 minutes till onion is translucent and soft. Add

- ginger and garlic; cook for 5 more minutes till onions brown.
- Mix water, serrano pepper, salt, turmeric, garam masala, tomato paste and chopped tomato in; simmer for 5 minutes. Put chicken in sauce. Gently mix to coat legs; cover pan. Lower heat to medium-low. Cook for 40 minutes till chicken isn't pink near the bone. Use cilantro to garnish; serve.

Nutrition Information

- Calories: 325 calories;
- Total Fat: 21.5
- Sodium: 394
- Total Carbohydrate: 4.3
- Cholesterol: 102
- Protein: 27.7

335. Punjabi Sukha Urad Dal

Serving: 4 | Prep: 10mins | Cook: 45mins | Ready in:

Ingredients

- 1 cup skin-on, split black lentils (urad dal)
- 2 tablespoons cooking oil
- 1 onion, chopped
- 4 green chile peppers, cut into large chunks
- 4 cloves garlic, minced
- 1 tablespoon minced fresh ginger root
- 1 cup water
- salt to taste
- 1 large tomato, chopped
- 1 teaspoon garam masala
- 1/2 teaspoon ground turmeric
- 1/4 cup chopped fresh cilantro

Direction

- In a big container, put lentils then pour a few inches of cool water to cover; soak for 4hrs to overnight then drain. Rinse the lentils.
- On medium heat, heat oil in a heavy-bottomed saucepan; add ginger, onion, garlic, and green chile peppers. Cook for 5mins until the onions are golden brown. Mix a cup of water and the lentils into the onion mixture; sprinkle salt to season. Turn to low heat; let it simmer for half an hour until the lentils are tender. Mix in turmeric, garam masala, and tomato; cook for another 10mins until the lentils are completely cooked. Serve with cilantro on top.

Nutrition Information

- Calories: 277 calories;
- Cholesterol: 0
- Protein: 13.8
- Total Fat: 7.9
- Sodium: 31
- Total Carbohydrate: 39.8

336. Quick Cranberry Chutney

Serving: 12 | Prep: 15mins | Cook: 5mins | Ready in:

Ingredients

- 1 (16 ounce) can whole berry cranberry sauce
- 2 (8 ounce) cans crushed pineapple, drained and squeezed dry
- 2 tablespoons brown sugar replacement (such as Splenda® Brown Sugar Blend)
- 1/2 teaspoon ground ginger
- 1/4 teaspoon sea salt
- 3 green onions, chopped
- 1 jalapeno pepper, seeds and ribs removed, minced

Direction

- In a small pot, boil sea salt, cranberry sauce, ground ginger, pineapple, and brown sugar replacement together. Turn to low heat and let it simmer for about 5mins until thick; mix from time to time. Let it stand for 10mins to cool.

- Mix jalapeno pepper and green onion into the mixture; move to a bowl. Use a sheet of plastic wrap to cover.
- Refrigerate for half an hour until cold.

Nutrition Information

- Calories: 78 calories;
- Total Carbohydrate: 20.3
- Cholesterol: 0
- Protein: 0.2
- Total Fat: 0
- Sodium: 47

337. Quick And Savory Indian Peas

Serving: 2 | Prep: 5mins | Cook: 10mins | Ready in:

Ingredients

- 1 (16 ounce) package frozen peas
- 1 tablespoon vegetable oil
- 1 teaspoon cumin seeds
- 1 teaspoon ground cumin
- salt to taste
- 1/2 teaspoon dried mango powder (amchoor)
- 1 tablespoon chopped fresh cilantro

Direction

- Pour water over beans to cover in a bowl; let steep for 20 minutes. Drain off water.
- In a frying pan, heat oil over medium heat. Sauté cumin seeds in heated oil for about 1 minute until they begin to sputter. Add salt, cumin powder, and peas. Lower heat and put the lid on. Cook for about 10 minutes, stirring sometimes, until peas are softened and heated through.
- Turn off the heat. Mix in dried mango powder. Stir cilantro into peas and serve while still hot.

Nutrition Information

- Calories: 242 calories;
- Total Carbohydrate: 32.1
- Cholesterol: 0
- Total Fat: 8.1
- Protein: 12.1
- Sodium: 333

338. Ras Malai

Serving: 12 | Prep: 20mins | Cook: 35mins | Ready in:

Ingredients

- 1 (15 ounce) container whole-milk ricotta cheese
- 1/4 cup white sugar
- 3 cups half and half
- 1 cup white sugar
- 1/4 teaspoon ground cardamom
- 1/2 teaspoon rose water (optional)
- 1 pinch saffron
- 1 tablespoon chopped blanched almonds
- 2 teaspoons chopped pistachio nuts

Direction

- Preheat the oven to 350 degrees F (or 175 degrees C).
- Blend 1/4 cup of sugar with Ricotta cheese in a bowl using a hand mixer. Then divide the cheese mixture into 12 muffin cups.
- Bake in a preheated oven for about 35 to 40 minutes or until a toothpick inserted into the center comes out clean. Let it cool for 10 minutes inside the oven before taking out. Cool completely on a wire shelf. Place the cheese balls into a dessert serving dish.
- While baking the cheese, pour half and half into a pan and let it simmer over low heat, for about 10 minutes. Stir in 1 cup of sugar, add the saffron, cardamom and rose water. Then simmer for 2 minutes more. Remove the flame and let it cool completely. Sprinkle over the

cheese balls. Serve with almonds and pistachios on top.

Nutrition Information

- Calories: 216 calories;
- Total Fat: 10.4
- Sodium: 72
- Total Carbohydrate: 25.6
- Cholesterol: 33
- Protein: 6.1

339. Red Split Lentils (Masoor Dal)

Serving: 6 | Prep: 25mins | Cook: 1hours38mins | Ready in:

Ingredients

- 1 cup basmati rice
- 7 1/2 cups water, divided
- 1 cup red lentils (masoor dal), rinsed
- 1/2 cup finely chopped red onion (optional)
- 1 teaspoon ground cumin
- 1 teaspoon ground coriander
- 1 teaspoon salt, or to taste
- 1/2 teaspoon ground black pepper (optional)
- 1/2 teaspoon cayenne powder (optional)
- 1/2 teaspoon ground turmeric
- 1 cup broccoli florets (optional)
- 1 cup diced tomatoes (optional)
- 1 cup frozen peas (optional)
- 1 tablespoon olive oil, or as needed
- 1 cup sliced mushrooms (optional)
- 1 tablespoon peeled, finely grated fresh ginger
- 2 cloves garlic, finely grated

Direction

- Thoroughly rinse rice in a couple of changes of water and transfer to a container. Pour water in the container so that it covers the rice, and soak rice for 15 minutes to 1 hour at room temperature. Then drain.
- In a large pot, combine red lentils and 6 cups of water over medium heat. Simmer and skim off any scum that forms on surface. Stir in the turmeric, cayenne, black pepper, salt, coriander, cumin, and onion. Cover the pot partially with a lid, lower the heat to low and simmer on low heat for 30 minutes until lentils are tender.
- Stir salt, peas, tomatoes, and broccoli into the pot. Cook and frequently stir for 30 minutes until lentils are soft.
- In a separate pot, combine 1 1/2 cup of water and the drained rice. Bring to a boil, then reduce to very low heat. Cover with a tight-fitting lid and simmer for 20 minutes, until liquid is absorbed and rice is soft.
- In a small skillet, heat oil over medium heat. Add garlic, ginger, and mushrooms. Cook and stir for 3 to 5 minutes until fragrant. Pour and stir lentils in and distribute them. Cook for 5 minutes, or until flavor combines. Serve lentils with rice.

Nutrition Information

- Calories: 282 calories;
- Sodium: 437
- Total Carbohydrate: 50.8
- Cholesterol: 0
- Protein: 13.4
- Total Fat: 3.7

340. Restaurant Style Mango Lassi

Serving: 4 | Prep: 5mins | Cook: | Ready in:

Ingredients

- 2 (15.25 ounce) cans mango pulp, or mango slices with juice
- 1/2 cup plain yogurt

- 1/4 cup milk
- 2 cups ice cubes

Direction

- Simply combine the mangoes with milk and yogurt in a blender, and then add the ice. Blend all ingredients thoroughly until smooth.

Nutrition Information

- Calories: 121 calories;
- Sodium: 50
- Total Carbohydrate: 27.8
- Cholesterol: 3
- Protein: 2.3
- Total Fat: 1.2

341. Sabudana Khichdi (Tapioca With Potatoes And Peanuts)

Serving: 6 | Prep: 15mins | Cook: 30mins | Ready in:

Ingredients

- 2 cups tapioca pearls
- 5 medium potatoes, cut into 1-inch cubes
- 2 tablespoons vegetable oil, or to taste
- 1 teaspoon cumin seeds
- 1 cup chopped peanuts, divided
- 2 green chile peppers, chopped, or more to taste
- 7 fresh curry leaves, chopped, or more to taste
- salt to taste
- 1 teaspoon white sugar
- 1/4 cup chopped cilantro (optional)
- 2 tablespoons lime juice

Direction

- Wash tapioca thoroughly in a big container, drain and cover. Let it sit for not less than 8 hours to overnight.
- Rinse the tapioca again before you begin cooking. Drain, cover and then set it aside.
- In a big saucepan, bring the water to a boil then add the potatoes. Allow to cook and occasionally stir for 5 to 6 minutes or until tender but quite firm to the bite, then drain.
- In a large saucepan, heat oil on medium heat and cook the cumin seeds for about 30 seconds or until seeds turned darker in color. Then add the potatoes, the 3/4 cup of peanuts, green chili peppers and the curry leaves. Add salt to taste, and sauté for about 7 to 10 minutes or until all flavors are incorporated.
- Mix in sugar and stir. Then add in tapioca and the remaining 1/4 cup of peanuts. Lower the heat to low and allow to cook for about 10 to 15 minutes, or until tapioca looks transparent, while stirring occasionally. Mix in cilantro and lime juice. Mix them all well. Add salt as desired. This is good served while hot.

Nutrition Information

- Calories: 515 calories;
- Total Fat: 17
- Sodium: 41
- Total Carbohydrate: 84.4
- Cholesterol: 0
- Protein: 10.1

342. Saffron Rice With Raisins And Cashews

Serving: 4 | Prep: 5mins | Cook: 25mins | Ready in:

Ingredients

- 2 1/2 cups water
- 1 cup Basmati rice
- 1/4 cup white sugar
- 2 teaspoons clarified butter
- 1 pinch saffron
- 6 whole cloves
- 3 tablespoons raisins

- 1/4 cup cashews
- 1 teaspoon ground cardamom

Direction

- Boil water in saucepan. Add rice; boil for 5 minutes. Mix sugar in; lower heat, add clarified butter.
- Meanwhile, soak saffron in 1 tbsp. hot water for about 10 minutes.
- Add cashews, raisins, cloves and saffron to rice. Mix well, cover; cook for 5-10 minutes more on low heat till rice is cooked and all liquid is absorbed.
- Sprinkle cardamom; serve.

Nutrition Information

- Calories: 306 calories;
- Protein: 5.2
- Total Fat: 6.8
- Sodium: 60
- Total Carbohydrate: 57.9
- Cholesterol: 6

343. Savory Lassi

Serving: 2 | Prep: 10mins | Cook: | Ready in:

Ingredients

- 1 cup plain yogurt
- 1/2 cup water
- 1/2 cup milk
- 1 teaspoon ground cumin
- 1 teaspoon chopped cilantro leaves
- 2/3 teaspoon salt
- 1 pinch black pepper

Direction

- In a blender, combine pepper, salt, cilantro, cumin, milk, water and yogurt, blend until smooth. Serve plain or on top of ice.

Nutrition Information

- Calories: 113 calories;
- Total Carbohydrate: 12.3
- Cholesterol: 12
- Protein: 8.7
- Total Fat: 3.4
- Sodium: 890

344. Serena's Strawberry Lassi

Serving: 2 | Prep: 5mins | Cook: | Ready in:

Ingredients

- 2 cups plain whole-milk yogurt
- 2 cups strawberries
- 1 cup ice
- 1/2 cup white sugar

Direction

- In a blender, mix sugar, ice, strawberries and yogurt together then blend until smooth.

Nutrition Information

- Calories: 394 calories;
- Protein: 13.8
- Total Fat: 4.2
- Sodium: 177
- Total Carbohydrate: 78.3
- Cholesterol: 15

345. Shahi Tukra (Sweet Bread Dessert)

Serving: 6 | Prep: 10mins | Cook: 30mins | Ready in:

Ingredients

- 1 quart vegetable oil

- 15 slices white bread, cut into 2-inch squares
- 4 cups whole milk
- 2 cups white sugar
- 4 cardamom pods
- 4 whole cloves
- 2 cinnamon sticks
- 1 pinch saffron
- 1/2 cup toasted sliced almonds

Direction

- In a big saucepan or deep fryer, heat oil to 175°C or 350°Fahrenheit.
- In hot oil, fry the bread squares until brown and crispy; drain on a plate lined with paper towels.
- In a saucepan, mix and boil sugar and milk; turn to medium-low heat. Put in saffron, cardamom pods, cinnamon sticks, and cloves; simmer for 15mins. Get rid of the whole spices. Put the mixture aside to cool to room temperature.
- In a flat-bottomed serving dish, put the bread then pour the milk mixture gently to cover all pieces. Refrigerate for 2-3hrs. Serve with almonds on top.

Nutrition Information

- Calories: 705 calories;
- Total Fat: 26.1
- Sodium: 493
- Total Carbohydrate: 108.6
- Cholesterol: 16
- Protein: 11.8

346. Shahi Tukray (Indian Bread Pudding)

Serving: 8 | Prep: 15mins | Cook: 1hours31mins | Ready in:

Ingredients

- 1 quart half-and-half
- 2 cups white sugar
- 1 (14 ounce) can sweetened condensed milk
- 1 loaf sliced bread, crusts removed, divided
- oil for frying

Direction

- Gently boil condensed milk, sugar and half and half in big pot on medium low heat; simmer for 55 minutes till reduced by half.
- Dissolve 2 bread slices in half and half mixture; use immersion blender to blend mixture till thick.
- Preheat an oven to 200°C/400°F.
- Heat oil in big saucepan/deep fryer; in batches, fry leftover bread slices, 1 minute per side, till golden brown. Over paper towels, drain.
- Diagonally cut bread; layer slices in 9x12-in. baking dish. Put enough half and half mixture in to soak slices evenly.
- In preheated oven, bake for 20 minutes till bubbly. Flip bread slices; bake for 5 minutes.

Nutrition Information

- Calories: 707 calories;
- Sodium: 498
- Total Carbohydrate: 110.5
- Cholesterol: 61
- Protein: 11.8
- Total Fat: 25.5

347. Shahi Tukri (Sweet Fried Bread)

Serving: 10 | Prep: 5mins | Cook: 15mins | Ready in:

Ingredients

- 1 quart cooking oil
- 5 slices white bread, quartered
- 1 cup water

- 1/2 cup white sugar
- 1/2 teaspoon ground cardamom
- 2 tablespoons cream
- 2 tablespoons chopped pistachio nuts

Direction

- In a big saucepan or deep-fryer, heat oil to 175°C or 350°Fahrenheit.
- In batches, fry pieces of bread until deep golden brown; put aside to drain on a paper towel-lined plate.
- In a small pan, stir and boil sugar and water; mix in cardamom. Turn to low heat and let it simmer for 2-3mins more. Submerge the fried bread pieces in the liquid for 2-3mins; arrange in one layer on a flat-bottomed serving dish.
- Drizzle cream all over the bread pieces then add pistachio nuts on top. Refrigerate for at least 2hrs. Serve.

Nutrition Information

- Calories: 169 calories;
- Cholesterol: 4
- Protein: 1.4
- Total Fat: 11.1
- Sodium: 94
- Total Carbohydrate: 16.9

348. South Indian Style Okra Fritters

Serving: 5 | Prep: 15mins | Cook: 10mins | Ready in:

Ingredients

- 1/2 pound okra, finely chopped
- 1 green chile pepper, finely chopped
- 2 tablespoons finely chopped fresh cilantro leaves
- 1 tablespoon shortening
- 1 teaspoon salt, or to taste
- 1 teaspoon grated fresh ginger
- 3 tablespoons rice flour, or as needed
- 1 tablespoon chickpea (garbanzo bean) flour, or as needed
- 2 cups vegetable oil for frying, or as needed

Direction

- In a bowl, mix ginger, salt, shortening, cilantro, green chile pepper and okra. Knead chickpea flour and rice flour into okra mixture to make a stiff dough.
- In big saucepan/deep-fryer, heat oil to 175°C/350°F.
- Wet a hand; use to hold dough ball. From dough ball, break small marble-sized bits; drop into hot oil without overcrowding pan. Fry for 7-10 minutes till crisp and golden brown. Transfer fritters to paper towel-lined plate to drain. Keep cooking till you use all the dough. Refill and reheat oil if needed.

Nutrition Information

- Calories: 145 calories;
- Sodium: 470
- Total Carbohydrate: 9.6
- Cholesterol: 0
- Protein: 1.7
- Total Fat: 11.6

349. Spiced Chickpeas (Chole)

Serving: 4 | Prep: 30mins | Cook: 25mins | Ready in:

Ingredients

- 2 tablespoons vegetable oil
- 1 teaspoon ground cumin
- 1/2 teaspoon ground dried red chilies
- 2 serrano chile peppers, seeded and chopped
- 2 large onions, chopped
- 2 (15 ounce) cans garbanzo beans (chickpeas), drained
- 3 tablespoons lemon juice

- 2/3 cup water
- salt to taste
- 3 tablespoons minced fresh ginger root
- 2 large tomatoes, chopped
- 1/4 cup chopped fresh cilantro, for garnish

Direction

- In a big pot placed over medium heat, heat vegetable oil. Add ground red chili and cumin; cook and stir for a few seconds until fragrant. Add water, lemon juice, garbanzo beans, onions and serrano chiles; add salt to season. Increase the heat to high and bring to a boil, then lower the heat to medium-low and simmer for about 15 minutes until vegetables are softened and most of the liquid is evaporated. Add cilantro, tomatoes and ginger on top; serve.

Nutrition Information

- Calories: 285 calories;
- Cholesterol: 0
- Protein: 8.9
- Total Fat: 8.9
- Sodium: 431
- Total Carbohydrate: 44.7

350. Spiced Moong Beans

Serving: 8 | Prep: 15mins | Cook: 25mins | Ready in:

Ingredients

- 4 cups moong beans
- 2 tablespoons vegetable oil
- 1 1/2 teaspoons cumin seeds
- 1 onion, diced
- 1 (2 inch) piece fresh ginger, peeled and grated
- 4 cloves garlic, minced - or more to taste
- 2 teaspoons curry powder
- 1 teaspoon ground turmeric
- 1 teaspoon paprika
- salt to taste
- 2 tomatoes, chopped
- 1 jalapeno pepper, chopped
- water to cover
- 1 sprig fresh curry leaves
- 1 lime, juiced

Direction

- Place the moong beans into a large container and then add enough of cold water on top of the beans to cover by a few inches. Leave to soak for about 8 hours to overnight.
- Drain the beans and then rinse them. Put aside.
- Over medium-high heat, heat oil in a pressure cooker until it's smoking. Cook the cumin seeds in hot oil for about 90 seconds until they are sizzling. Put onion into pot. Cook while stirring for 2 to 5 minutes until they start to become translucent. Add salt, paprika, turmeric, curry powder, garlic and ginger into onion. Let it cook for about 1 minute longer until fragrant.
- Mix jalapeno pepper and tomatoes into onion mixture. Cook while stirring for about 5 minutes until tomatoes are softened. Put moong beans into the mixture. Add enough of water into pot to cover the contents by a minimum of 2 to 3 inches. Add lime juice and curry leaves.
- Lock the lid onto the pressure cooker, then bring cooker up to pressure and decrease the heat to maintain a steady pressure. Let it cook for about 15 to 20 minutes.
- Take cooker out of heat, put in the sink and then run cold water on top of the cooker's lid until pressure is released. Carefully take out the lid.

Nutrition Information

- Calories: 328 calories;
- Total Carbohydrate: 62.4
- Cholesterol: 0
- Protein: 9.6
- Total Fat: 4.8

- Sodium: 13

351. Spicy Banana Curry

Serving: 4 | Prep: 20mins | Cook: 20mins | Ready in:

Ingredients

- 1/3 cup sunflower seed oil
- 2 onions, diced
- 1/2 cup curry powder
- 1 1/2 tablespoons ground cumin
- 4 teaspoons ground turmeric
- 1 1/4 teaspoons salt
- 1 teaspoon white sugar
- 1 tablespoon ground ginger
- 1 teaspoon chili powder
- 1 1/4 teaspoons ground cinnamon
- 1 1/2 teaspoons ground black pepper
- 4 teaspoons curry paste
- 8 cloves garlic, pressed
- 1 (10 ounce) can tomato sauce
- 2/3 cup plain yogurt
- 2 bananas, diced
- 3 tomatoes, chopped
- 1/4 cup flaked coconut

Direction

- In a big saucepan, heat sunflower oil over medium heat. Mix in onions and cook for 5 minutes until the onions turn opaque and tender. Sprinkle black pepper, cinnamon, chili powder, ginger, sugar, salt, turmeric, cumin, and curry powder. Stir and cook for 1 minute until aromatic.
- Mix in pressed garlic and curry paste. Cook for 1 minute. Add yogurt and tomato sauce and simmer. Mix in diced banana and lightly simmer for 3 minutes. Stir in chopped tomatoes and keep simmering for another 1 minute. Mix in coconut flakes right before eating.

Nutrition Information

- Calories: 417 calories;
- Total Fat: 25.8
- Sodium: 1247
- Total Carbohydrate: 46.1
- Cholesterol: 2
- Protein: 8.4

352. Spicy Chicken In Tomato Coconut Sauce

Serving: 8 | Prep: 25mins | Cook: 45mins | Ready in:

Ingredients

- 2 cups uncooked basmati rice
- 1 quart water
- 1 teaspoon salt
- 1 teaspoon onion powder
- 1 teaspoon olive oil
- 4 chicken leg quarters
- 1 onion, chopped
- 2 fresh jalapeno peppers, seeded and chopped
- 1 (14 ounce) can coconut milk
- 1 cup water
- 1 (10 ounce) can diced tomatoes and green chiles
- 1 (6 ounce) can Italian-style tomato paste
- 2 tablespoons ground cumin
- 2 tablespoons garam masala
- 1 tablespoon brown mustard seed
- 2 tablespoons cayenne pepper
- 2 teaspoons salt
- 4 cubes chicken bouillon
- 8 wedges lime
- 1/2 cup sour cream

Direction

- Boil 1-qt. water and rice in pot; season with onion powder and 1 tsp. salt. Cover; lower heat to low. Simmer for 20 minutes.
- Heat oil in skillet; brown all sides of chicken. Put aside chicken; mix jalapenos and onion in.

Cook till tender. Add 1 cup water and coconut milk; mix tomato paste and diced tomatoes with green chilies in. Season with 2 tsp. salt, cayenne pepper, mustard seed, garam masala and cumin. Melt bouillon cubes in mixture; boil. Put chicken back in skillet; cook for 10 minutes till chicken juices are clear.
- Take chicken from skillet; cool enough to handle. Take meat from bones; put meat back in skillet. Serve the mixer on cooked rice; garnish using lime wedges. Put dollop of sour cream on top of each serving.

Nutrition Information

- Calories: 497 calories;
- Total Fat: 23.4
- Sodium: 1841
- Total Carbohydrate: 52.5
- Cholesterol: 54
- Protein: 21

353. Spicy Fried Shrimp

Serving: 4 | Prep: 20mins | Cook: 30mins | Ready in:

Ingredients

- 1 1/2 red onion, sliced
- 1 pound uncooked medium shrimp, peeled and deveined
- 1 teaspoon ground turmeric, or to taste
- salt to taste
- 1/4 cup water, or as needed
- olive oil for frying
- 1 tablespoon butter, or as needed
- 3 jalapeno peppers, thinly sliced
- 2 1/2 tablespoons ginger-garlic paste
- 2 1/2 teaspoons cayenne pepper
- 2 tablespoons ground coriander
- 1 tablespoon ground cumin
- 1 teaspoon ground black pepper
- 5 tablespoons lime juice
- 1 tablespoon white vinegar
- 1 teaspoon soy sauce
- 1/2 teaspoon red food coloring
- 1 cinnamon stick
- 2 teaspoons poppy seeds
- 1 teaspoon coconut milk powder
- 2 cardamom pods
- 2 whole cloves
- 1 star anise pod
- 1/2 teaspoon ground nutmeg
- 1/2 teaspoon dried oregano
- 1/2 teaspoon dried rosemary

Direction

- In a food processor or a blender, pulse red onion.
- Use salt and about half of the turmeric to season shrimp.
- Heat a skillet on medium heat. Put in water, the leftover turmeric and shrimp. Use salt to season; let it simmer for 6-8 minutes or till evaporating water.
- In another skillet on medium heat, heat butter and oil. Put in black pepper, cumin, coriander, cayenne pepper, garlic-ginger paste, jalapenos and pureed onions. Cook and stir for roughly 7 minutes or till becoming golden brown in color.
- In another saucepan on medium heat, mix rosemary, oregano, nutmeg, star anise, cloves, cardamom, coconut milk powder, poppy seeds and cinnamon stick. Cook while mixing often, for 5-7 minutes or till masala becomes aromatic.
- Add masala into the onion-jalapeno mixture; cook while covered, on medium heat for roughly 7 minutes or till flavors blend. Put in red food coloring, soy sauce, vinegar, lime juice and shrimp; cook and stir for roughly 5 minutes longer or till absorbing the flavors.

Nutrition Information

- Calories: 335 calories;
- Total Fat: 21
- Sodium: 663

- Total Carbohydrate: 11.9
- Cholesterol: 180
- Protein: 20.8

354. Spicy Indian Chicken Curry Yummy

Serving: 4 | Prep: 15mins | Cook: 1hours | Ready in:

Ingredients

- 3 tablespoons vegetable oil
- 4 boneless, skinless chicken thighs, cut into bite-size pieces
- 1 large white onion, finely chopped
- 2 tablespoons ginger garlic paste
- 2 tablespoons curry powder
- 1/2 (2 inch) stick cinnamon stick, broken into pieces
- 8 pods whole green cardamom pods
- 4 bay leaves
- 6 whole cloves
- 1 tablespoon red pepper flakes, or to taste
- 15 whole black peppercorns
- 2 teaspoons coriander seeds

Direction

- Over medium heat, put a small pot to heat oil. Stir in ginger garlic paste, onion and chicken. Use coriander seeds, black peppercorns, red pepper flakes, cloves, bay leaves, cardamom pods, cinnamon stick and curry powder to season. Let it simmer with cover and occasional stirs for about 30 minutes. The gravy should be runny. Take off the lid, continue cooking until the liquid reduces if you want thick curry.

Nutrition Information

- Calories: 248 calories;
- Cholesterol: 42
- Protein: 13.3

- Total Fat: 16
- Sodium: 300
- Total Carbohydrate: 10.8

355. Spicy Potato Noodles (Bataka Sev)

Serving: 8 | Prep: 45mins | Cook: 40mins | Ready in:

Ingredients

- For the Green Chile Paste:
- 1/4 cup chopped fresh green chile peppers
- 1 tablespoon coarsely chopped garlic
- 2 tablespoons fresh ginger, peeled and coarsely chopped
- 1 teaspoon salt
- 1/8 teaspoon ground turmeric
- 2 teaspoons vegetable oil
- For the Noodles:
- 1 pound potatoes, peeled
- 3 cups water
- 3 1/2 cups chickpea flour
- 2 1/2 teaspoons salt
- 1 teaspoon ground turmeric
- 2 tablespoons mustard oil
- vegetable oil for deep frying

Direction

- In a mortar and pestle or food processor, mix 2 teaspoons of vegetable oil, 1/8 teaspoon of turmeric, 1 teaspoon salt, ginger, garlic and chiles. Then process to form a fine paste. (If you need more liquid, pour in 1 tablespoon water). Put aside.
- Put potatoes in a saucepan along with water and then heat to a boil on high heat. Decrease the heat to low and cover the pan. Cook potatoes for about 15 minutes until soft and easily pricked with a fork. Save the cooking water.
- Mash potatoes while still warm and add some of the cooking water to have a smooth consistency. Stir in mustard oil, 1 teaspoon

turmeric, 2 1/2 teaspoons salt, chickpea flour and 1 tablespoon green chile paste. Pour in enough of the reserved potato-cooking water as needed to form a soft dough. Check the seasoning and heat lever of the dough (dough should taste raw but should be spicy and salty. Flavors will mellow slightly while cooking). If desired, add more chile paste and salt.

- Over medium-high heat, heat cooking oil in a deep pan. Press noodles into the oil with a potato ricer (or use sev machine, if lucky to have it). Fry for about 2 minutes until crisp and golden brown. Place noodles onto a bowl lined with paper towel with the help of a skimmer or slotted spoon. Repeat this until all of the noodles are fried. Keep in an airtight container for a maximum of 2 weeks.

Nutrition Information

- Calories: 336 calories;
- Total Fat: 18.4
- Sodium: 1024
- Total Carbohydrate: 35.2
- Cholesterol: 0
- Protein: 9.4

356. Spicy Tomato Chutney

Serving: 32 | Prep: 20mins | Cook: 40mins | Ready in:

Ingredients

- 4 pounds ripe tomatoes
- 1 (1 inch) piece fresh ginger root
- 3 cloves garlic
- 1 3/4 cups white sugar
- 1 cup red wine vinegar
- 2 onions, diced
- 1/4 cup golden raisins
- 2 teaspoons mixed spice
- 1 teaspoon chili powder
- 1 pinch paprika
- 1 tablespoon curry paste

Direction

- Boil a pot of water. Cook tomatoes in boiling water for 3-5mins until the skin starts to break and peel. Take the tomatoes out of the pot; cool then peel.
- In a blender or food processor, puree garlic, ginger, and the tomatoes together.
- In a big pot, put in golden raisins, tomato mixture, sugar, vinegar, and onions; add curry paste, mixed spice, paprika, and chili powder to season. On medium heat, let the mixture simmer until thick. Place in the refrigerator until ready serve.

Nutrition Information

- Calories: 63 calories;
- Total Fat: 0.2
- Sodium: 13
- Total Carbohydrate: 15.7
- Cholesterol: 0
- Protein: 0.7

357. Spicy Tomato Soup

Serving: 6 | Prep: 10mins | Cook: 20mins | Ready in:

Ingredients

- 2 tablespoons olive oil
- 1 onion, chopped
- 2 bay leaves
- 1 tablespoon all-purpose flour
- 1 tablespoon ginger-garlic paste
- 1 teaspoon garam masala
- 1/2 teaspoon ground turmeric
- 1 tablespoon Indian chili powder
- 1/2 cup water, or as needed
- 1 (28 ounce) can tomato puree
- 1 tablespoon white sugar
- salt to taste
- 1/3 cup heavy cream or half-and-half (optional)

Direction

- In a large saucepan, heat oil over medium heat; sauté bay leaves and onions in hot oil until onions start to soften, for 5 minutes. Add Indian chili powder, turmeric, garam masala, ginger-garlic paste, and flour. Sauté for about 1 minute until aromatic,
- Add water to the pan, bring to a boil while scraping the browned bits from the bottom of the pan using a wooden spoon. Add the pureed tomato into the mixture, add more water to get the desired consistency. Sprinkle with salt and sugar; cook for about 5 minutes until soup is hot and sugar is completely dissolved. Discard bay leaves; serve the soup with cream if desired.

Nutrition Information

- Calories: 167 calories;
- Sodium: 627
- Total Carbohydrate: 18
- Cholesterol: 18
- Protein: 3
- Total Fat: 10

358. Spicy Yogurt Dressing

Serving: 2 | Prep: 2mins | Cook: | Ready in:

Ingredients

- 1/4 cup chopped fresh cilantro
- 1 teaspoon lemon juice
- 1 pinch ground cumin
- 1/2 cup plain yogurt
- 1 teaspoon sweet chili sauce

Direction

- Combine the lemon juice, chili sauce, yogurt, cilantro, and cumin together in a small bowl. Keep in the fridge for a minimum of 1 hour or until it's time to use the dressing.

Nutrition Information

- Calories: 47 calories;
- Cholesterol: 4
- Protein: 3.4
- Total Fat: 1.1
- Sodium: 75
- Total Carbohydrate: 6.1

359. Steve's Chicken Korma

Serving: 4 | Prep: 15mins | Cook: 20mins | Ready in:

Ingredients

- 2 tablespoons cooking oil
- 1/2 teaspoon ground ginger
- 1/2 teaspoon red chile powder
- 1/2 teaspoon ground cinnamon
- 1/2 teaspoon ground turmeric
- 1/2 teaspoon ground white pepper
- 1 large onion, chopped
- 1 clove garlic, minced
- 1 cup chopped canned tomatoes
- 2 skinless, boneless chicken breast halves - cubed
- 1/4 cup chicken stock
- 2 tablespoons ground almonds
- 1/4 cup heavy cream
- 1/4 cup plain yogurt

Direction

- In a large skillet, heat oil on medium heat. Mix pepper, turmeric, cinnamon, chili powder, and ginger; add into the heated oil and stir, cook for 5 seconds. Add garlic and onion; cook and stir for 7 minutes until the onions turn transparent. Stir in the chicken and tomatoes and cook for 5-8 minutes until the chicken is not pink anymore.
- Mix the onion-chicken mixture with chicken stock; stir and cook for 3 minutes. Stir in

yogurt, cream, and almonds; carry on cooking for 2-4 minutes.

Nutrition Information

- Calories: 244 calories;
- Total Fat: 16.2
- Sodium: 181
- Total Carbohydrate: 9.5
- Cholesterol: 57
- Protein: 16

360. Stuffed Okra

Serving: 4 | Prep: 15mins | Cook: 5mins | Ready in:

Ingredients

- 2 tablespoons mango powder (amchur)
- 1 teaspoon ground ginger
- 1 teaspoon ground cumin
- 1 teaspoon ground turmeric
- 1/2 teaspoon chili powder (optional)
- 1/2 teaspoon salt
- 1/2 teaspoon vegetable oil
- 1 pound large okra
- 1/4 cup corn flour
- vegetable oil for frying

Direction

- In a bowl, mix 1/2 tsp. oil, salt, chili powder, turmeric, cumin, ginger and mango powder; put aside for 2 hours to merge flavors.
- In deep fryer/big saucepan, heat vegetable oil to 175°C/350°F.
- Trim okra; create a slit lengthwise down a side of each okra to make a pocket. Use spice mixture to fill each pocket.
- In resealable plastic bag, put corn flour; add filled okra. Shake till coated.
- In hot oil, fry okra for 5-8 minutes till golden brown. Use a slotted spoon to put fried okra on paper towel-lined plate.

Nutrition Information

- Calories: 200 calories;
- Sodium: 307
- Total Carbohydrate: 22.3
- Cholesterol: 0
- Protein: 3.2
- Total Fat: 12.2

361. Sweet Lentil Soup With Asparagus Tips

Serving: 8 | Prep: 15mins | Cook: 1hours15mins | Ready in:

Ingredients

- 3 tablespoons olive oil
- 1 medium head garlic
- 1/4 teaspoon dried basil
- 1 red bell pepper
- 2 1/2 cups dry lentils
- 2 (32 fluid ounce) containers chicken broth
- 1 1/2 large carrot, shredded
- 1 large onion, grated
- 1 cup asparagus tips
- 1 cup sweet peas
- 1/4 cup white sugar
- 2 tablespoons orange marmalade
- 2 tablespoons curry powder
- 1 pinch saffron
- 1 teaspoon kosher salt
- ground black pepper to taste

Direction

- Preheat an oven to 230°C/450°F.
- Cut off top head of garlic; put in shallow dish with 1-in. water. Drizzle 2 tbsp. olive oil and sprinkle basil; cover, put on baking sheet. Halve, then seed bell pepper; drizzle leftover 1 tbsp. olive oil and put on baking sheet.

- In preheated oven, bake pepper and garlic for 20-40 minutes till garlic is soft and pepper is browned. Remove from oven; remove pepper skin then chop when cool to handle. Squeeze garlic cloves out; mash in bowl to make paste.
- As pepper and garlic bakes, mix chicken broth and lentils in big pot on medium heat. Boil, lower heat; simmer till lentils are just tender for 40 minutes.
- Mix peas, asparagus, onion, carrots, bell pepper and garlic paste into lentil mixture; if needed, add extra broth to thin. Season with pepper, salt, saffron, curry powder, marmalade and sugar. Simmer till flavors blend well and veggies are tender for 30 minutes.

Nutrition Information

- Calories: 319 calories;
- Total Carbohydrate: 50.8
- Cholesterol: 6
- Protein: 17
- Total Fat: 6.6
- Sodium: 1367

362. Tamarind Date Chutney

Serving: 8 | Prep: 5mins | Cook: | Ready in:

Ingredients

- 5 pitted whole dates
- 1/2 cup water
- 1 tablespoon tamarind concentrate
- 1 tablespoon cayenne pepper
- 1 teaspoon salt

Direction

- In a blender, process salt, dates, cayenne pepper, tamarind concentrate, and water together until smooth.

Nutrition Information

- Calories: 17 calories;
- Total Carbohydrate: 4.3
- Cholesterol: 0
- Protein: 0.2
- Total Fat: 0.1
- Sodium: 291

363. Tandoori Chicken I

Serving: 4 | Prep: 20mins | Cook: 1hours | Ready in:

Ingredients

- 1 (2 to 3 pound) chicken, skinned and quartered
- 2 tablespoons lemon juice
- 1 teaspoon salt
- 4 teaspoons ground allspice
- 2 tablespoons plain yogurt
- 2 tablespoons lemon juice
- 2 tablespoons vegetable oil
- 2 tablespoons distilled white vinegar

Direction

- Create slits on the chicken flesh, almost to the bone. Put 2 tablespoons lemon juice over chicken then rub in salt.
- Mix the vinegar, oil, 2 tablespoons of the lemon juice, yogurt and tandoori spice. Coat mixture over the chicken and rub well into the cuts. Put chicken in a pan (about 13x9 inch), put foil on to cover and place in the refrigerator overnight, turning occasionally.
- Start preheating the oven to 350°F (175°C).
- Cover and bake the chicken for 60 mins at 350°F (175°C). In the final 15 mins of baking, discard the foil.

Nutrition Information

- Calories: 431 calories;
- Total Fat: 28.7

- Sodium: 703
- Total Carbohydrate: 3
- Cholesterol: 122
- Protein: 38.7

364. Tandoori Grilled Chicken

Serving: 8 | Prep: 30mins | Cook: 15mins | Ready in:

Ingredients

- 2 cups plain yogurt
- 3 tablespoons garam masala
- 2 pounds boneless, skinless chicken breasts
- 6 pita breads

Direction

- Start preheating the grill for medium heat.
- Mix tandoori and yogurt spice in large bowl. Save half cup for basting. Put chicken into the remaining sauce, marinate for 60 minutes in fridge.
- Brush the grate with oil to avoid sticking. Put the chicken on grill. Cook 5-6 mins on each side, frequently basting the reserved yogurt marinade over. Enjoy hot.

Nutrition Information

- Calories: 296 calories;
- Total Carbohydrate: 30.9
- Cholesterol: 68
- Protein: 31
- Total Fat: 4.7
- Sodium: 346

365. The Maharajah's Mulligatawny

Serving: 4 | Prep: 30mins | Cook: 45mins | Ready in:

Ingredients

- 4 fresh red chile peppers, or to taste
- 1 tablespoon coriander seeds
- 1 teaspoon cumin seeds
- 1 teaspoon ground turmeric
- 1/2 teaspoon grated nutmeg
- 4 whole cloves
- 10 whole black peppercorns
- 6 fresh curry leaves
- 2 cloves garlic, crushed
- 1 teaspoon grated ginger root
- 1 tablespoon ghee (clarified butter)
- 1 large onion, chopped
- 1 pound lamb meat, cut into small pieces
- 2 teaspoons salt
- 3 3/4 cups lamb stock
- 2 tablespoons tomato puree
- 1 large carrot, diced
- 1 large apple - peeled, cored, and diced
- 2 lemons, sliced

Direction

- With a blender or food processor, grind ginger, garlic, curry leaves, peppercorns, cloves, nutmeg, turmeric powder, cumin seeds, coriander seeds and red chile peppers into a smooth paste.
- In a big skillet, melt ghee over medium heat; in the melted ghee, let the onion fry for about 5 minutes till golden brown. To the skillet, put lamb and red chile pepper paste; cook and mix for approximately 5 minutes till lamb turns browned. Add salt to season. Into the lamb mixture, mix tomato puree and lamb stock; lower the heat to medium-low, put cover on skillet, and let it simmer for about half an hour till lamb is soft. Put in apple and carrot; cook for an additional of 15 minutes. Take off the heat and cool slightly.
- Take lamb out of the mixture and put aside. Into a blender, put the remaining soup. Using a folded kitchen towel, keep down the lid of blender and cautiously turn on the blender, with several quick pulses to make soup moving prior to leaving it on to puree.

Through a strainer with fine mesh, strain the soup back into skillet. You can press on the contents of the strainer. Take out and get rid of any big and tough pieces. Return lamb to skillet, set on medium heat, and cook for about 5 minutes till soup is well reheated. Serve in warmed bowls; jazz up with slice of lemon.

Nutrition Information

- Calories: 245 calories;
- Total Carbohydrate: 27.6
- Cholesterol: 62
- Protein: 20
- Total Fat: 8.8
- Sodium: 1255

366. Tim Perry's Soup (Creamy Curry Cauliflower And Broccoli Soup)

Serving: 4 | Prep: 15mins | Cook: 45mins | Ready in:

Ingredients

- 1 quart chicken broth
- 1 onion, finely chopped
- 1 head cauliflower, finely chopped
- 1/2 head broccoli, finely chopped
- 1 teaspoon curry powder
- 1 tablespoon chicken bouillon granules
- salt and pepper to taste
- 1/4 cup all-purpose flour
- 1/2 cup milk
- 2 cups shredded Cheddar cheese

Direction

- Stir in onion, broccoli, cauliflower and chicken broth to a stockpot. Boil and reduce heat to low. Continue simmering until vegetables become soft. Use pepper, salt, curry powder and chicken bouillon to season.
- Mix flour and 1/2 cup of the milk in a bowl. Mix until it is lump-free. Introduce the mixture into the soup, continually stir as the soup becomes thick. Mix in Cheddar cheese until it melts completely.

Nutrition Information

- Calories: 348 calories;
- Protein: 20.7
- Total Fat: 20
- Sodium: 838
- Total Carbohydrate: 24.1
- Cholesterol: 62

367. Tomato Cucumber Kachumbar

Serving: 4 | Prep: 25mins | Cook: | Ready in:

Ingredients

- 1 cup halved grape tomatoes
- 1 cup diced cucumber
- 1/2 cup chopped green onions
- 1/2 cup chopped fresh cilantro
- 1 tablespoon fresh lemon juice
- 1 tablespoon chopped fresh mint
- salt and ground black pepper to taste

Direction

- In a large bowl, add pepper, salt, mint, lemon juice, cilantro, green onions, cucumber, and grape tomatoes together then mix them well.

Nutrition Information

- Calories: 20 calories;
- Protein: 0.9
- Total Fat: 0.2
- Sodium: 48
- Total Carbohydrate: 4.6
- Cholesterol: 0

368. Traditional Chicken Curry

Serving: 6 | Prep: 20mins | Cook: 45mins | Ready in:

Ingredients

- 1 pound skinless, boneless chicken breast halves - cut into bite-size pieces
- 1 tablespoon fresh lemon juice
- salt and pepper to taste
- 3 tablespoons olive oil
- 1 teaspoon cumin seed
- 1 large onion, finely chopped
- 2 cloves garlic, minced
- 1 teaspoon minced fresh ginger
- 1 (8 ounce) can peeled, chopped tomatoes
- 1 teaspoon chili powder
- 1/2 teaspoon ground turmeric
- 1 teaspoon garam masala
- 1/2 teaspoon ground cumin
- 1 pinch ground coriander
- 1/2 teaspoon paprika
- 3 tablespoons plain yogurt
- 2 medium potatoes, peeled and cut into 1 inch cubes
- 1 1/2 cups water
- 1 (5.5 ounce) can tomato juice
- fresh chopped cilantro, for garnish

Direction

- Combine pepper, salt, lemon juice and chicken pieces in a large bowl; toss to coat. Set aside.
- In a heavy, large saucepan over medium heat, heat oil. Add cumin seed; cook and stir until it is toasted lightly for 1 minute. Stir in ginger, garlic and onion. Cook till onion has softened. Stir in tomatoes; use paprika, coriander, ground cumin, garam masala, turmeric and chili powder to season. Cook with stir for 2 minutes.
- Add yogurt to the saucepan and mix to well-blend. Stir in potatoes and chicken pieces. Pour in tomato juice and water. Lower the heat to medium-low; let it simmer with cover for about 40 minutes. Adjust seasonings to taste and use fresh cilantro to garnish. Serve.

Nutrition Information

- Calories: 234 calories;
- Total Fat: 9.2
- Sodium: 182
- Total Carbohydrate: 19.8
- Cholesterol: 44
- Protein: 18.8

369. Turmeric Milk

Serving: 1 | Prep: 10mins | Cook: 5mins | Ready in:

Ingredients

- 1 (1 1/2 inch) piece fresh turmeric root, peeled and grated
- 1 (1/2 inch) piece fresh ginger root, peeled and grated
- 1 tablespoon honey
- 1 cup unsweetened almond milk
- 1 pinch ground turmeric (optional)
- 1 pinch ground cinnamon (optional)

Direction

- In a bowl, combine honey, ginger root, and turmeric root, mashing ginger and turmeric root as much as possible.
- In a saucepan, heat almond milk over medium-low heat. Once milk starts bubbling around the edges, turn heat to low. Pour about 2 tablespoons milk to turmeric mixture to soften mixture and melt honey into a paste-like mixture.
- Transfer the turmeric paste into milk in the saucepan. Higher temperature to medium-low; cook and stir constantly until completely incorporated. Blend until texture is smooth using an immersion blender. Transfer turmeric

tea into a mug and sprinkle with cinnamon and ground turmeric on top.

Nutrition Information

- Calories: 143 calories;
- Sodium: 163
- Total Carbohydrate: 29.3
- Cholesterol: 0
- Protein: 1.5
- Total Fat: 2.9

370. Ullipaya (Onion) Tomato Chutney

Serving: 12 | Prep: 20mins | Cook: 10mins | Ready in:

Ingredients

- 1 tablespoon cooking oil
- 1 teaspoon skinned split black lentils (urad dal)
- 1 teaspoon mustard seed
- 4 dried red chile peppers
- 2 green chile peppers, chopped
- 1 pinch asafoetida powder
- 1 tablespoon cooking oil
- 1/2 onion, chopped
- 2 tomatoes, chopped
- salt to taste
- 1/4 cup chopped cilantro leaves

Direction

- On medium heat, heat oil in a small pan; cook in red chile peppers, mustard seed, and lentils until the seeds begin to burst. Take off from the heat then stir in asafoetida powder and green chile peppers. Let it cool for a bit. Pound the mixture with a mortar and pestle until it turns to a coarse powder.
- Turn on heat then heat a tablespoon of oil in the pan; add onion. Cook for about 5mins until soft. Mix in tomatoes and cook for about 3mins until most of the liquid evaporates; combine with the lentil mixture. Pound until the onions are thoroughly crushed and incorporated into the mixture; sprinkle salt. Mix in cilantro leaves. Serve.

Nutrition Information

- Calories: 34 calories;
- Sodium: 3
- Total Carbohydrate: 2.9
- Cholesterol: 0
- Protein: 0.6
- Total Fat: 2.4

371. Vankaya Pulusu Pachadi (Andhra Sweet And Sour Eggplant Stew)

Serving: 4 | Prep: 15mins | Cook: 45mins | Ready in:

Ingredients

- 1 eggplant
- 1 teaspoon vegetable oil
- 2 tablespoons vegetable oil
- 2 dried red chile peppers, broken into pieces
- 1 teaspoon cumin seeds
- 1 teaspoon mustard seed
- 1 pinch asafoetida powder
- 2 large onions, chopped
- 3 green chile peppers, chopped
- 2 sprigs fresh curry leaves
- 1 1/2 cups water
- 1 tablespoon tamarind paste
- 1/4 cup jaggery (palm sugar)
- 1 teaspoon white sugar
- 1/2 teaspoon ground turmeric
- 1/2 teaspoon ground red pepper
- salt to taste

Direction

- Preheat oven to 95 degrees C/200 degrees F.

- Coat 1 tsp. vegetable oil on the outside of eggplant. Put on baking sheet. Bake for 20-30 minutes in the oven until it's soft. Cool. Mash coarsely. Put aside.
- In a big skillet, heat 2 tbsp. vegetable oil. Fry asafoetida powder, mustard seed, cumin seeds and dried red chile peppers in hot oil until seeds begin to splutter. Add in and sauté curry leaves, green chile peppers and onion for 5 minutes until onions start to brown and are soft. Mix in salt, ground red pepper, turmeric, white sugar, jaggery, tamarind paste, water, and mashed eggplant. Boil for 5-10 minutes until mixture starts to thicken.

Nutrition Information

- Calories: 191 calories;
- Total Carbohydrate: 28.6
- Cholesterol: 0
- Protein: 2.3
- Total Fat: 8.6
- Sodium: 14

372. Veg Biryani

Serving: 4 | Prep: 20mins | Cook: 1hours | Ready in:

Ingredients

- 1/3 cup vegetable oil
- 1 large onion, cut lengthwise into 1/4-inch thick strips
- 5 fresh curry leaves
- 1 medium tomato, chopped
- 1 cup uncooked basmati rice
- 1/2 cup fresh green beans, cut into 2-inch pieces
- 1 medium carrot, peeled and cut into 2-inch pieces
- 1/2 cup frozen cut green beans, thawed
- 1 medium potato, peeled and cut into 2-inch pieces
- 1 teaspoon chili powder
- 1 teaspoon biryani masala powder
- 1 teaspoon salt
- 2 cups water
- 1/2 cup chopped cilantro

Direction

- Heat the oil on medium heat in a big pot till shimmering. Cook the curry leaves and onion, whisk once in a while, for 12-15 minutes till the onion turns dark brown. Put in the tomato and cook, whisk once in a while, for 3-5 minutes till becoming tender.
- At the same time, steep the rice in water to cover for 10 minutes. Drain it well.
- Put the salt, biryani masala powder, chile powder, potato, peas, carrots and beans into the onion mixture. Cook, whisk once in a while, for 2 minutes. Whisk in the water and drained rice and boil. Lower the heat to low and cook, while covering, for roughly half an hour till the water has been absorbed. Whisk in the cilantro and allow to rest, covered, for 10 minutes prior to serving.

Nutrition Information

- Calories: 412 calories;
- Sodium: 613
- Total Carbohydrate: 55.5
- Cholesterol: 0
- Protein: 6.3
- Total Fat: 19.4

373. Vegan Sweet Potato Chickpea Curry

Serving: 6 | Prep: 10mins | Cook: 20mins | Ready in:

Ingredients

- 3 tablespoons olive oil
- 1 onion, chopped
- 2 cloves garlic, minced

- 2 teaspoons minced fresh ginger root
- 1 (15 ounce) can chickpeas, drained
- 1 (14.5 ounce) can diced tomatoes
- 1 (14 ounce) can coconut milk
- 1 sweet potato, cubed
- 1 tablespoon garam masala
- 1 teaspoon ground cumin
- 1 teaspoon ground turmeric
- 1/2 teaspoon salt
- 1/4 teaspoon red chile flakes
- 1 cup baby spinach

Direction

- In a skillet, heat the oil on medium heat and cook the ginger, garlic and onion for about 5 minutes until softened. Add sweet potato, coconut milk, tomatoes and chickpeas, then boil. Lower the heat to low and let it simmer for around 15 minutes until it becomes tender.
- Sprinkle salt, chile flakes, turmeric, cumin and garam masala to season, then add spinach right before serving.

Nutrition Information

- Calories: 293 calories;
- Total Carbohydrate: 22.3
- Cholesterol: 0
- Total Fat: 21.6
- Protein: 5.1
- Sodium: 515

374. Vegetable Masala

Serving: 4 | Prep: 10mins | Cook: 20mins | Ready in:

Ingredients

- 2 potatoes, peeled and cubed
- 1 carrot, chopped
- 10 French-style green beans, chopped
- 1 quart cold water
- 1/2 cup frozen green peas, thawed
- 1 teaspoon salt
- 1/2 teaspoon ground turmeric
- 1 tablespoon vegetable oil
- 1 teaspoon mustard seed
- 1 teaspoon ground cumin
- 1 onion, finely chopped
- 2 tomatoes - blanched, peeled and chopped
- 1 teaspoon garam masala
- 1/2 teaspoon ground ginger
- 1/2 teaspoon garlic powder
- 1/2 teaspoon chili powder
- 1 sprig cilantro leaves, for garnish

Direction

- Place green beans, carrots and potatoes in the cold water. Let them soak while you prepare other vegetables; drain.
- Place the turmeric, salt, peas, green beans, carrots, and potatoes in a microwave-safe dish. Cook for 8 minutes.
- Place a large skillet over medium heat, heat oil. Cook cumin and mustard seeds; once seeds start to pop and sputter, put in the onion and sauté until transparent. Whisk in the chili powder, garlic, ginger, garam masala, and tomatoes; sauté in 3 minutes. Pour over the tomato mixture with the cooked vegetables and sauté 1 minute. Serve with cilantro leaves as garnish.

Nutrition Information

- Calories: 167 calories;
- Sodium: 641
- Total Carbohydrate: 29.8
- Cholesterol: 0
- Protein: 4.2
- Total Fat: 4.3

375. Vegetarian Splendor Chickpea Curry

Serving: 4 | Prep: 15mins | Cook: 35mins | Ready in:

Ingredients

- 2 tablespoons olive oil
- 1 teaspoon cumin seeds
- 3 whole cloves
- 1 white onion, halved and thinly sliced
- 3 ounces tomato paste
- 2 tablespoons curry powder
- 1 tablespoon all-purpose flour
- 1 tablespoon ground turmeric
- 1 teaspoon garlic powder
- 1 teaspoon ground ginger
- 1 teaspoon dried basil
- 1 pinch ground allspice
- 1 pinch salt
- 3 cups warm water, or as needed
- 1 (15 ounce) can garbanzo beans (chickpeas), drained
- 1/3 red bell pepper, chopped
- 2 cups fresh green beans, trimmed
- 1 cup frozen peas
- 1 teaspoon rice wine vinegar
- salt and ground black pepper to taste

Direction

- In a large pot, heat olive oil over medium-high heat. Sauté cloves and cumin seeds in hot oil for about 30 seconds until cumin seeds expand. Remove cloves. Add onion and sauté for about 5 minutes until it turns light golden.
- In a bowl, combine salt, allspice, basil, ginger, garlic powder, turmeric, flour, curry powder, and tomato paste. Pour in 1 cup warm water and stir well.
- Transfer tomato mixture into the pot with onion; stir gently until the mixture is incorporated and thickened. Add more water and stir well until a saucy consistency is reached. Mix in bell pepper and garbanzo beans. Lower heat and simmer curry for 5 minutes. Add peas and green beans; then season mixture with black pepper, salt, and rice wine vinegar. Simmer, and stirring occasionally the curry for 20 to 25 minutes until vegetables are softened. Add more water if the curry looks too thick.

Nutrition Information

- Calories: 253 calories;
- Protein: 8.8
- Total Fat: 8.8
- Sodium: 511
- Total Carbohydrate: 38.4
- Cholesterol: 0

376. Vendakka Paalu

Serving: 2 | Prep: 15mins | Cook: 20mins | Ready in:

Ingredients

- 2 tablespoons olive oil
- 1/2 bell pepper, seeded and sliced into strips
- 2 jalapeno peppers, seeded and sliced into strips
- 1 tablespoon minced fresh ginger root
- 1 tablespoon minced garlic
- 2 bay leaves
- 1 teaspoon ground coriander
- 1/2 teaspoon ground red pepper
- 1/4 teaspoon ground turmeric
- 1/4 teaspoon cumin seeds
- 1/8 teaspoon ground cardamom
- 1/8 teaspoon ground black pepper
- 1/8 teaspoon ground cinnamon
- 1 small tomato, sliced
- 1/4 cup golden raisins
- 1 cup sliced okra
- 1 cup coconut milk
- 1 tablespoon water
- salt to taste

Direction

- In a big skillet, heat the oil. Stir the bell pepper. Cook for about 3 minutes until it slightly softens. Add the bay leaves, garlic, ginger and jalapeno peppers into the bell pepper. For about 2 to 3 minutes more, cook

until fragrant. Season it with cinnamon, black pepper, cardamom, cumin seeds, turmeric, red pepper and coriander. For another 2 minutes, cook and stir it. Put the tomato slices and raisins into the mixture and continue cooking for 3 more minutes. Put the okra. Mix thoroughly into the mixture to coat with the spices.
- In a small bowl, stir the water and the coconut milk together. Put it into the mixture then, cover the skillet. Cook for 8 to 10 minutes until the okra is tender. To keep it moist, add water if needed. Season it with salt. Serve it warm.

Nutrition Information

- Calories: 456 calories;
- Cholesterol: 0
- Protein: 5.5
- Total Fat: 38.4
- Sodium: 27
- Total Carbohydrate: 30.5

377. Whole Wheat Chapati

Serving: 4 | Prep: 10mins | Cook: 2mins | Ready in:

Ingredients

- 1 cup whole wheat flour
- 1 pinch salt
- 1 tablespoon olive oil
- 1/4 cup water

Direction

- In a bowl, sift salt and flour together. Mix in water and olive oil then knead until pliable and firm; split into 4 balls. Use a rolling pin to roll the balls as flat as possible.
- On medium-high heat, heat a frying pan. Cook chapati for a minute on each side until golden brown on both sides. Sprinkle more olive oil before serving if desired.

Nutrition Information

- Calories: 132 calories;
- Total Fat: 3.9
- Sodium: 2
- Total Carbohydrate: 21.8
- Cholesterol: 0
- Protein: 4.1

378. Yogurt Samosas

Serving: 18 | Prep: 20mins | Cook: 15mins | Ready in:

Ingredients

- 1 tablespoon vegetable oil
- 2 onions, finely chopped
- 1 cup plain yogurt
- 1 teaspoon curry powder
- 1/2 teaspoon chili powder
- 2 tablespoons chopped fresh cilantro
- 1/4 cup chopped fresh cilantro
- 1 (16 ounce) package frozen phyllo dough, thawed
- 1/2 cup plain yogurt
- 3 tablespoons half-and-half cream
- 1/4 cup water
- 1 cup all-purpose flour
- 3 cups oil for frying, or as needed

Direction

- Place a skillet over medium heat and heat 1 tablespoon of oil. Cook onions in hot oil until browned. Stir in 2 tablespoons of cilantro, chili powder, curry powder, and 1 cup of yogurt. Stir while cooking until liquid is mostly evaporated. Remove from the heat and stir the rest of the cilantro in.
- Place one sheet of phyllo dough on a work surface, cover the remaining phyllo dough with a damp towel. On the corner of the dough, place 1 tablespoon of the onion mixture; do not place too close to the edge. Fold the dough in fourths towards the

opposite side, sealing the filling. From the filled end, fold dough towards the opposite end; dough should be shaped triangularly. Moisten fingers and press the dough edges together to seal. Repeat process with the rest of the filling and dough.
- Place a deep heavy skillet over medium-high heat. Pour in oil 3/4-inch-deep and heat to 185°C/365°F. Stir together water, half-and-half, and the rest of the yogurt in a small bowl. Dip the samosas into the yogurt mixture, then coat with flour and shake excess off.
- Fry samosas for 4 minutes; turn once while frying. Work in small batches to prevent samosas from touching each other. Place on a paper towels to drain oil. Serve hot.

Nutrition Information

- Calories: 161 calories;
- Total Fat: 6.6
- Sodium: 137
- Total Carbohydrate: 21.2
- Cholesterol: 2
- Protein: 3.8

379. Yogurt Marinated Salmon Fillets (Dahi Machhali Masaledar)

Serving: 4 | Prep: 15mins | Cook: 15mins | Ready in:

Ingredients

- 1 cup fat-free plain yogurt
- 1/2 tablespoon cayenne pepper
- 6 cloves garlic, minced
- 2 (2 inch) pieces fresh ginger root, minced
- 2 tablespoons cilantro, finely chopped
- 1 tablespoon ground coriander seed
- 1 teaspoon ground cumin
- 1 teaspoon salt
- 1/4 teaspoon ground turmeric

- 4 (6 ounce) skinless, boneless salmon fillets

Direction

- Combine turmeric, salt, cumin, ground coriander, cilantro, ginger, garlic, cayenne pepper, and yogurt in a resealable plastic bag. Seal the bag and turn to evenly combine everything. Put salmon into the bag and shake to coat well with marinade; allow to marinate overnight.
- Turn on the oven's broiler. Lightly oil a baking pan.
- Take salmon out of the marinade, dripping off excess; dispose the rest of the marinade. Arrange salmon on the greased baking pan; broil in the preheated oven, 5 to 7 minutes on each side, until salmon flesh is easily flaked using a fork.

Nutrition Information

- Calories: 365 calories;
- Total Fat: 18.9
- Sodium: 731
- Total Carbohydrate: 8.8
- Cholesterol: 100
- Protein: 37.8

380. Yummy Curd Rice

Serving: 2 | Prep: 5mins | Cook: 5mins | Ready in:

Ingredients

- 1 teaspoon clarified butter
- 1 teaspoon mustard seed
- 1 teaspoon chopped fresh ginger root
- 1 teaspoon chopped garlic
- 1 small cinnamon stick (optional)
- 1 teaspoon chopped green chile peppers
- 1 whole red chile pepper
- 7 leaves fresh curry
- 1 cup cooked basmati rice

- water as needed
- 1 cup plain lowfat yogurt

Direction

- In a heavy pan, heat the clarified butter on medium heat. Add in the mustard seeds; the heat should be hot enough for the seeds to crackle, not burn. Mix in curry leaves, red and green chile peppers, cinnamon, garlic, and ginger. Cook, stirring frequently, for 30 seconds.
- If the rice seems cold, add rice in the pan with a small amount of water, and close the lid. Let the steam separate rice. When rice is hot, or if adding in warm rice, blend rice with spices. Lower the heat, blend in yogurt, and heat thoroughly.

Nutrition Information

- Calories: 230 calories;
- Sodium: 90
- Total Carbohydrate: 36.4
- Cholesterol: 13
- Protein: 10.2
- Total Fat: 5

Chapter 4: Filipino Cuisine Recipes

***

381. Abalos Style Hamburger Soup (Picadillo Filipino)

Serving: 6 | Prep: 20mins | Cook: 45mins | Ready in:

Ingredients

- 1 tablespoon cooking oil
- 1 onion, diced
- 4 cloves garlic, minced
- 1 large tomato, diced
- 1 pound ground beef
- 4 cups water
- 1 large potato, diced
- 2 tablespoons beef bouillon
- 2 tablespoons fish sauce
- salt and pepper to taste

Direction

- In a large pot set on medium-high heat, add oil. Cook the garlic and onion in the hot oil until the onions are softened. Mix in the tomato; cook for approximately 3 minutes until soft. Break up the ground beef into the pan then cook for approximately 5 minutes until brown. Add the pepper, salt, fish sauce, beef bouillon, potato, and water; lower heat, cover, and simmer for approximately 30 minutes until the potatoes are softened, stirring occasionally.

Nutrition Information

- Calories: 233 calories;
- Cholesterol: 46
- Protein: 15.4
- Total Fat: 11.5
- Sodium: 862
- Total Carbohydrate: 16.9

382. Adobo Twist

Serving: 8 | Prep: 15mins | Cook: 20mins | Ready in:

Ingredients

- 2 tablespoons vegetable oil, or as needed
- 1 onion, chopped
- 1 head garlic, crushed
- 2 pounds pork belly, cut into 1-inch squares

- 3/4 cup soy sauce, or to taste
- 1/4 cup water
- 1 1/2 teaspoons whole black peppercorns
- 2 bay leaves
- 1/4 cup cane vinegar
- 3 tablespoons brown sugar, or more to taste
- 1 1/2 teaspoons dried basil leaves, or more to taste

Direction

- In a skillet set on high heat, add oil. Add garlic and onion; stir and cook for approximately 1 minute until scented. Place in pork; then cook for 2-3 minutes each side, until equally browned. Mix in bay leaves, peppercorns, water, and soy sauce. Lower heat and cover stockpot. Then cook for 1-2 minutes until liquid is at a simmer.
- Remove the stockpot's cover, put vinegar, and cook for 3-5 minutes without whisking until vinegar dissipates and the liquid turns thick. Mix in basil and brown sugar, cover stockpot, then cook for 10-15 minutes until pork is tender and cooking liquid has thickened to a consistency of a sauce.

Nutrition Information

- Calories: 288 calories;
- Cholesterol: 41
- Protein: 16.2
- Total Fat: 19.1
- Sodium: 2221
- Total Carbohydrate: 12.6

383. Adobong Pusit (Squid Adobo)

Serving: 5 | Prep: 20mins | Cook: 30mins | Ready in:

Ingredients

- 2 1/4 pounds squid, cleaned
- 1/2 cup white vinegar
- 1/2 cup water
- salt and ground black pepper to taste
- 2 tablespoons olive oil
- 1 small onion, minced
- 2 cloves garlic, minced
- 1 tomato, chopped
- 1 tablespoon soy sauce

Direction

- In a small pot set over medium heat, mix water, vinegar, and squid; add pepper and salt to taste. Then cook for ten minutes.
- In the meantime, add olive oil in a saucepan set on medium heat; stir and cook the garlic and onion in the hot oil for 5-7 minutes until softened. Mix the tomato and soy sauce into the mixture. Put the squid mixture into the saucepan and make it simmer; cook everything for 20 more minutes.

Nutrition Information

- Calories: 198 calories;
- Total Carbohydrate: 3.1
- Cholesterol: 0
- Protein: 28.4
- Total Fat: 7.4
- Sodium: 214

384. Atsara (Papaya Relish)

Serving: 10 | Prep: 20mins | Cook: 10mins | Ready in:

Ingredients

- 4 cups grated fresh green papaya
- 1/4 cup salt
- 1 carrot, peeled and sliced
- 1 red bell pepper, sliced into long strips
- 1 (2 inch) piece fresh ginger root, peeled and sliced
- 2 green chile peppers, sliced into thin rings

- 1 (1.5 ounce) box raisins
- 1 cup white vinegar
- 1 cup water
- 1 cup white sugar
- 1 teaspoon salt

Direction

- In a big bowl, toss the grated papaya with 1/4 cup salt; let it sit for 1 hour. Strain the liquid from the papaya and wash well. Put the papaya in the center of a big piece of cheesecloth and press to strain as much liquid from papaya as you can.
- In a clean big bowl, mix the raisins, green chile peppers, ginger, red bell pepper, carrot, and papaya; whisk. Place the mixture to dry jars that have lids.
- In a small saucepan, mix 1 teaspoon of salt, sugar, water, and vinegar; make it boil for around 5 minutes. Place vinegar mixture in the jars, ensuring the vegetables are fully covered in liquid. Let the vegetables to marinate in the liquid a minimum of 1 day prior to suing. Refrigerate between your uses.

Nutrition Information

- Calories: 112 calories;
- Sodium: 241
- Total Carbohydrate: 28.2
- Cholesterol: 0
- Protein: 1
- Total Fat: 0.2

385. Barbecued Pork Kebabs

Serving: 10 | Prep: 15mins | Cook: 15mins | Ready in:

Ingredients

- 1 cup white sugar
- 1 cup soy sauce
- 1 onion, diced
- 5 cloves garlic, chopped
- 1 teaspoon ground black pepper
- 1 (4 pound) boneless pork loin, cut into 1 1/2-inch cubes
- 10 bamboo skewers, soaked in water for 30 minutes

Direction

- In a large bowl, combine black pepper, garlic, onion, soy sauce, and sugar. Add in pork and coat by tossing. Keep in the refrigerator for at least 2 hours, covered. If possible, overnight would be best.
- Prepare and outdoor grill by preheating to high heat, and lightly oil the grate.
- Then onto the soaked sewers, thread the pork. Place on the preheated grill and cook for 3 to 5 minutes each side until the pork is not pink in the center.

Nutrition Information

- Calories: 369 calories;
- Total Carbohydrate: 24.7
- Cholesterol: 88
- Protein: 31.1
- Total Fat: 15.8
- Sodium: 1508

386. Barbecued Spareribs

Serving: 5 | Prep: 10mins | Cook: 1hours | Ready in:

Ingredients

- 1 (4 pound) package pork spareribs, rinsed and patted dry
- salt and ground black pepper to taste
- 1 cup water
- 1 cup sweet chili sauce

Direction

- Prepare the oven by preheating to 350°F (175°C).
- Add pepper and salt to the spareribs to season. Add the water into the bottom of a large baking dish then lay the spareribs in the dish; use aluminum foil to cover.
- Place in the preheated oven and bake for 30 minutes; add about half the chili sauce on top of the meat, cover, and put back to the oven. Every 5 minutes, sweep the ribs with more chili sauce and keep on cooking for approximately 30 minutes until the meat pulls away simply from the bone. Serve cold or hot.

Nutrition Information

- Calories: 710 calories;
- Sodium: 719
- Total Carbohydrate: 20.6
- Cholesterol: 192
- Protein: 46.1
- Total Fat: 48.4

387. Barquillos (Wafer Rolls)

Serving: 18 | Prep: 20mins | Cook: 5mins | Ready in:

Ingredients

- 1/2 cup butter
- 1/2 cup white sugar
- 1 teaspoon vanilla extract
- 2 egg whites
- 2/3 cup all-purpose flour

Direction

- Prepare the oven by preheating to 375°F (190°C). Prepare 2 baking sheets that are greased.
- In a large bowl, whisk vanilla, sugar, and butter using an electric mixer until smooth. Mix in the egg whites, one at a time, letting each to combine into the butter mixture prior to adding the next. Stir in the flour until just blended.
- Onto ungreased baking sheets, drop teaspoonfuls of the dough. Use a spatula or back of the spoon to spread thinly into a 3-inch circle.
- Place in the preheated oven then bake for approximately 5 minutes until browned along the edges.
- Use a spatula or a kitchen turner to take the baked wafers from the baking sheet one at a time. Around the handle of a wooden spoon, roll every wafer until the edges overlap. Place on a wire rack, seam-side down to cool until fully crisp.

Nutrition Information

- Calories: 86 calories;
- Total Fat: 5.2
- Sodium: 43
- Total Carbohydrate: 9.1
- Cholesterol: 14
- Protein: 0.9

388. Beef Asado

Serving: 6 | Prep: 25mins | Cook: 1hours40mins | Ready in:

Ingredients

- 1 (4 pound) beef chuck roast, quartered
- salt and pepper to taste
- 2 tablespoons cooking oil
- 1 onion, diced
- 2 cloves garlic, crushed
- 2 large tomatoes, chopped
- 1 tablespoon whole peppercorns, crushed
- 1 (5 ounce) jar pitted Manzanilla olives
- 1 onion, quartered
- 2 bay leaves
- 2 beef bouillon cubes
- 1/2 cup ketchup

- 1 large red bell pepper, sliced
- 4 small potatoes, peeled and quartered
- 1 tablespoon corn flour (optional)
- 1 teaspoon water (optional)

Direction

- Season the beef with pepper and salt; reserve.
- In a skillet set on medium heat, add the oil; cook the garlic and diced onion in the hot oil for approximately 5 minutes until softened. Place the garlic and onion to a 6-qt.pot. Separately brown the breed chunks on all sides in the skillet then put in the pot. Add the bouillon cubes, bay leaves, quartered onion, olives with their juice, crushed peppercorns, and tomatoes to the pot; make it boil. Mix the ketchup into the mixture, lower the heat to medium-low, and simmer for 1 hour.
- Take the beef from the pot and reserve. Put the red bell pepper to the mixture and keep on simmering for 30 minutes more.
- While the mixture keeps on simmering, add 2 tablespoons oil in the skillet to heat. Add the potatoes and cook in the oil until golden brown; instantly put to the simmering mixture.
- Cut the meat against the grain and put it to the pot; mix. Cook everything for 5 more minutes prior to serving. Combine the water and flour then mix into the sauce to thicken, if the sauce is too thin.

Nutrition Information

- Calories: 639 calories;
- Protein: 39.8
- Total Fat: 37.8
- Sodium: 1194
- Total Carbohydrate: 34.8
- Cholesterol: 138

389. Beef Nilaga

Serving: 5 | Prep: 30mins | Cook: 1hours30mins | Ready in:

Ingredients

- 4 1/2 pounds beef short ribs
- 1 quart water
- 1 tablespoon black peppercorns, crushed
- 2 onions, chopped
- 2 beef bouillon cubes
- 2 carrots, cut in chunks
- 2 stalks celery, quartered
- 1 chayote squash, peeled and quartered
- 2 potatoes, quartered
- salt to taste
- 1/4 head cabbage, cut into wedges

Direction

- In a large pot, put the beef ribs then cover with enough water. Make it boil over high heat, then boil for 5 minutes. Strain; get rid of the cooking water (the ribs will not be completely cooked).
- Put the beef back to the pot. Add in beef bouillon, onions, peppercorns, and 1 quart water. Make it boil, cover, lower the heat, and simmer for 1 hour.
- Remove any fat floating on the surface. Mix in the potatoes, chayote, celery, and carrots; then simmer for approximately 20 minutes, covered, until potatoes are softened. Add salt to taste. Mix in cabbage and cook for 5 more minutes.

Nutrition Information

- Calories: 983 calories;
- Total Fat: 75.4
- Sodium: 491
- Total Carbohydrate: 32.3
- Cholesterol: 168
- Protein: 43

390. Bringhe

Serving: 10 | Prep: 30mins | Cook: 40mins | Ready in:

Ingredients

- 2 tablespoons olive oil
- 1 onion, chopped
- 2 cloves garlic, minced
- 1 teaspoon curry powder
- 2 chicken leg quarters, meat removed and cut into bite-sized pieces
- 1/2 pound tiger prawns, peeled and deveined
- 1/2 pound cubed fully cooked ham
- 2 bay leaves
- salt and pepper to taste
- 1 (16 ounce) can coconut milk
- 1 cup uncooked glutinous white rice

Direction

- In a large skillet set on medium heat, add olive oil; stir and cook the garlic and onion for 5-7 minutes in the hot oil until glassy. Add the curry powder to season and mix to equally coat. Stir in the chicken. Cover then cook for 2 minutes. Stir the prawns into the mixture then cook for 2 more minutes. Add the bay leaves and ham; add pepper and salt to taste and stir well. Cover the skillet and cook for 2 more minutes.
- Add the coconut milk into the skillet. Stir in rice. Lower heat to low then cover; cook for approximately 30 minutes, occasionally stirring, until the rice is tender. Then serve hot.

Nutrition Information

- Calories: 291 calories;
- Total Fat: 19.1
- Sodium: 384
- Total Carbohydrate: 11.7
- Cholesterol: 77
- Protein: 18.4

391. Buko (Young Coconut) Chiller

Serving: 2 | Prep: 15mins | Cook: | Ready in:

Ingredients

- 2 fresh young coconuts
- 1 cup water
- 1 tablespoon white sugar, or to taste
- ice cubes

Direction

- Expose the soft meat inside of the coconuts by cutting the top. Transfer the juice into a large bowl. Cut the coconuts in half; take the meat from the coconuts using a spoon and place to the bowl with the juice. Add the sugar and water to the bowl; mix until the sugar fully dissolves. Split the ice between two tall glasses and add the mixture over the ice then serve.

Nutrition Information

- Calories: 1430 calories;
- Total Fat: 133
- Sodium: 87
- Total Carbohydrate: 66.7
- Cholesterol: 0
- Protein: 13.2

392. Buko (Young Coconut) Pie

Serving: 6 | Prep: 20mins | Cook: 1hours | Ready in:

Ingredients

- 1 fresh young coconut, drained with meat removed and chopped
- 2 (12 fluid ounce) cans evaporated milk
- 1 (14 ounce) can sweetened condensed milk

- 4 eggs, beaten
- 1/4 cup white sugar
- 1 pinch salt

Direction

- Prepare the oven by preheating to 350°F (175°C).
- In a bowl, mix the salt, sugar, eggs, sweetened condensed milk evaporated milk, and coconut; transfer into a round 3-qt. baking dish. Place the baking dish into a large roasting pan. Fill the bottom of the roasting pan with enough water about halfway up the side of the baking dish.
- Place carefully in the preheated oven and bake for approximately 1 hour, until a toothpick pricked into the middle comes out clean. Let it fully cool prior to serving.

Nutrition Information

- Calories: 693 calories;
- Sodium: 302
- Total Carbohydrate: 66.9
- Cholesterol: 183
- Protein: 20.1
- Total Fat: 40.7

393. Caldereta (Filipino Beef Stew)

Serving: 6 | Prep: 20mins | Cook: 1hours5mins | Ready in:

Ingredients

- 3 tablespoons vegetable oil
- 1 1/2 pounds cubed beef stew meat
- salt and ground black pepper to taste
- 3 cloves garlic, crushed
- 3 cups water
- 1/2 cup unsweetened pineapple juice
- 1 onion, chopped
- 1 (14 ounce) can tomato sauce
- 1/4 cup tomato paste
- 2 red potatoes, diced
- 1 red bell pepper, sliced
- 1 large carrot, sliced diagonally
- 1/2 pound miniature cocktail sausages
- 1 (8 ounce) can pineapple chunks, undrained
- 1 (6 ounce) can medium pitted ripe olives, drained
- 3 large bay leaves
- 1 tablespoon hot pepper sauce (such as Tabasco®) (optional)

Direction

- In a large pot set on medium heat, add vegetable oil. Dust beef with black pepper and salt then brown in the hot oil with garlic for approximately 10 minutes. Add in tomato paste and sauce, onion, pineapple juice, and water. Make it boil, lower the heat to low, and simmer for 35-45 minutes until the beef is just tender.
- Mix bay leaves, olives, pineapple chunks with their juice, mini sausages, carrot, red bell pepper, and potatoes into the stew. Make it boil again for approximately 20 more minutes until potatoes are tender. Add black pepper, salt, and hot pepper sauce to season.

Nutrition Information

- Calories: 518 calories;
- Total Fat: 35.7
- Sodium: 1168
- Total Carbohydrate: 25.2
- Cholesterol: 86
- Protein: 26

394. Caldereta (Filipino Beef And Chorizo Stew)

Serving: 6 | Prep: 20mins | Cook: 1hours20mins | Ready in:

Ingredients

- 2 pounds beef chuck, cubed
- 12 ounces chorizo sausage
- 1/4 cup garlic, minced
- 1/4 cup white vinegar
- 1/4 cup soy sauce
- 2 tablespoons olive oil, or as needed
- 1 onion, chopped
- 1 green bell pepper, chopped
- 3 cups tomato sauce
- 2 cups peeled and cubed potatoes
- 1 cup drained canned peas
- 1 teaspoon salt
- 1 teaspoon ground black pepper

Direction

- In a skillet set on medium heat, mix soy sauce, vinegar, garlic, chorizo, and beef chuck; stir and cook for approximately 20 minutes until the beef chuck is browned and liquid is lessened. Separate from heat.
- In a pot set on medium heat, add olive oil; stir and cook green bell pepper and onion in the hot oil for 5-10 minutes until the onion turns glassy. Mix in tomato sauce and boil for 3-5 minutes until liquid is slightly lessened.
- Mix the beef-chorizo mixture into tomato sauce mixture; make it boil. Minimize heat to medium-low, cover the pot, and simmer for 30-40 minutes.
- Mix pepper, salt, peas, and potatoes into stew; simmer for 20-30 minutes until the beef is tender and potatoes are cooked well. Put water if necessary.

Nutrition Information

- Calories: 641 calories;
- Protein: 37.2
- Total Fat: 42.6
- Sodium: 2409
- Total Carbohydrate: 27.5
- Cholesterol: 119

395. Cassava Cake

Serving: 10 | Prep: 20mins | Cook: 1hours | Ready in:

Ingredients

- 2 cups grated, peeled yucca
- 2 eggs, beaten
- 1 (12 ounce) can evaporated milk
- 1 (14 ounce) can sweetened condensed milk
- 1 (14 ounce) can coconut milk

Direction

- Preheat the oven to 175 degrees C (350 degrees F).
- In a bowl, mix the coconut milk, yucca, sweetened condensed milk, eggs, and evaporated milk together until combined thoroughly. Transfer to a baking dish.
- Bake for 1 hour in the preheated oven. Turn on the oven's broiler and then bake under the broiler for 2 to 3 minutes until the top of the cake turns brown. Leave it to cool completely in the fridge prior to serving.

Nutrition Information

- Calories: 329 calories;
- Sodium: 111
- Total Carbohydrate: 41.6
- Cholesterol: 60
- Protein: 8
- Total Fat: 15.5

396. Champorado

Serving: 6 | Prep: 5mins | Cook: 30mins | Ready in:

Ingredients

- 1 cup glutinous sweet rice
- 2 cups light coconut milk

- 1/2 cup cocoa powder
- 1 cup white sugar
- 1 teaspoon salt
- 1 cup thick coconut milk

Direction

- In a pot, mix light coconut milk and sweet rice; make it to a boil for 10 minutes, while whisking occasionally to prevent the rice from sticking to the bottom of the pot.
- Mix salt, sugar, and cocoa powder into the rice; lower the heat to low, then cover, and keep on cooking for approximately 10 more minutes, stirring occasionally until the rice is tender. Mix in the thick coconut milk to the mixture and combine well. Serve hot.

Nutrition Information

- Calories: 428 calories;
- Sodium: 407
- Total Carbohydrate: 53.4
- Cholesterol: 0
- Protein: 4.9
- Total Fat: 25.2

397. Chicken Adobo I

Serving: 5 | Prep: 15mins | Cook: 1hours | Ready in:

Ingredients

- 1 1/2 cups water
- 1 cup distilled white vinegar
- 4 tablespoons soy sauce
- 1 teaspoon whole peppercorns
- 4 cloves garlic, crushed
- 2 tablespoons salt, or to taste
- 1 (2 to 3 pound) whole chicken, cut into pieces
- 2 tablespoons vegetable oil

Direction

- Mix salt, garlic, peppercorns, soy sauce, vinegar, and water in a large pot. Stir together, mix in chicken pieces and simmer over low heat, without cover, until the chicken is cooked well and softened, for about 25-35 minutes.
- Take the chicken from pot and brown in oil in a large skillet set on medium-high heat.
- Put the chicken back to the pot, with oil/juices, with reserve sauce. Simmer over medium heat, covered, until sauced achieves desired consistency.

Nutrition Information

- Calories: 340 calories;
- Cholesterol: 100
- Protein: 32.5
- Total Fat: 21.5
- Sodium: 3600
- Total Carbohydrate: 2

398. Chicken Adobo II

Serving: 6 | Prep: 15mins | Cook: 30mins | Ready in:

Ingredients

- 1 (2 to 3 pound) whole chicken, cut into pieces
- 1/4 cup apple cider vinegar
- 1/4 cup soy sauce
- ground black pepper to taste
- 2 tablespoons olive oil
- 1 clove garlic, crushed
- 2 bay leaves

Direction

- In a big bowl, put the chicken pieces. Add soy sauce and vinegar on chicken, and ground black pepper to season and taste. Then coat by tossing.
- In a big skillet set on medium heat, add oil, then add the garlic until brown. Be cautious

not to scorch the garlic, because it will make the food taste bitter. Once the garlic is browned, take out of the oil.
- Put the marinated chicken in the hot oil. Add the rest of the marinade on everything, then the bay leaves. Lower heat, then cook chicken pieces for approximately 10 minutes on per side, or until not pink and juices are clear. The marinade will lessen and turn to a gravy. Take out bay leaves, then serve right away.

Nutrition Information

- Calories: 335 calories;
- Total Fat: 20.4
- Sodium: 691
- Total Carbohydrate: 4.6
- Cholesterol: 96
- Protein: 31.1

399. Chicken Adobo With Noodles Filipino Mexican Fusion

Serving: 4 | Prep: 15mins | Cook: 35mins | Ready in:

Ingredients

- 2 tablespoons extra-virgin olive oil, or as needed
- 8 large skinless, boneless chicken thighs
- 1/2 Spanish sweet onion, chopped
- 4 cloves garlic, crushed
- 1/2 cup rice wine vinegar
- 1/4 cup soy sauce
- 2 tablespoons ground cumin
- 2 bay leaves
- 2 tablespoons tomato paste
- 2 tablespoons chipotle sauce
- 1 1/2 tablespoons arrowroot powder, or as desired
- 1 (16 ounce) package dry flat rice noodles

Direction

- In a large pot set on medium heat, add olive oil. Add chicken thighs and cook in hot oil for 1-2 minutes each side, until not pink on the outside. Add onion and cook for 5-7 minutes until onion is translucent. Mix garlic into the chicken mixture; stir and cook for approximately 1 minute until scented. Add bay leaves, cumin, soy sauce, and vinegar to the pot. Mix chipotle paste and tomato paste into the liquid in the pot.
- Make the mixture simmer and cook for approximately 20 minutes until the chicken is not pink in the middle and the juices run clean. An instant-read thermometer poked into the middle should register at least 165°F (74°C). Mix arrowroot powder into the liquid at the bottom of the pot; keep on cooking for about 5 minutes, until the liquid turns thick.
- Place a lightly salted water in a large pot and make it boil. Add rice noodles in the boiling water and cook for about 4 minutes, whisking occasionally, until cooked well yet firm to the bite; strain. Scoop sauce and chicken over the noodles to serve.

Nutrition Information

- Calories: 1018 calories;
- Total Fat: 31.8
- Sodium: 1467
- Total Carbohydrate: 105.8
- Cholesterol: 232
- Protein: 70.5

400. Chicken Afritada (Filipino Stew)

Serving: 6 | Prep: 40mins | Cook: 48mins | Ready in:

Ingredients

- 1 tablespoon vegetable oil

- 3 cloves garlic, crushed and chopped
- 1 onion, chopped
- 1 cup seeded and chopped tomatoes
- 1 (3 pound) whole chicken, cut into pieces
- 3 cups water
- 1 cup tomato sauce (optional)
- 3 potatoes, quartered
- 1 green bell pepper, seeded and cut into matchsticks
- 1 carrot, chopped
- salt and ground black pepper to taste

Direction

- Heat a big wok with oil on medium heat then put in the garlic. Sauté the garlic for 3 minutes or until fragrant. Put in the onion and sauté for 5 minutes or until the onions are translucent. Mix in the tomatoes and cook and mash with a fork for 5 minutes until the skin and flesh separate from each other.
- Put chicken into the wok and stir-fry for about 5 minutes or until the chicken is slightly brown in color. Put in water. Cover the wok and let the mixture boil. Mix in the tomato sauce and let it simmer for 15 minutes or until all the flavors have combined.
- Add in the potatoes and let it simmer for 10 minutes until the potatoes are soft. Put in the carrots and bell pepper and let it simmer for 5 minutes or until the vegetables are soft. Put pepper and salt to taste.

Nutrition Information

- Calories: 596 calories;
- Total Fat: 44.7
- Sodium: 327
- Total Carbohydrate: 25.6
- Cholesterol: 80
- Protein: 22.9

401. Chicken Arroz Caldo (Chicken Rice Porridge)

Serving: 5 | Prep: 20mins | Cook: 30mins | Ready in:

Ingredients

- 2 tablespoons olive oil
- 1 onion, diced
- 2 cloves garlic, crushed
- 1 (2 inch) piece fresh ginger, peeled and thinly sliced
- 2 1/4 pounds chicken wings, split and tips discarded
- 1 tablespoon fish sauce
- 5 1/4 cups chicken broth
- 1 cup glutinous sweet rice
- salt and pepper to taste
- 1 green onion, chopped
- 1 lemon, sliced (optional)
- 1 teaspoon fish sauce for sprinkling, if desired (optional)

Direction

- In a big pot set on medium heat, add olive oil; stir and cook the ginger, garlic, and onion in the hot oil for approximately 5 minutes until fragrant. Mix in the chicken wings; stir and cook everything for 1 minute. Mix in fish sauce in the pot, then cook for 2 more minutes, covered.
- Add chicken broth in the pot. Stir in the sweet rice. Make mixture boil; cook for 10 minutes, covered, whisking occasionally to make sure the rice is not sticking to the bottom of the pot. Add pepper and salt to season. Decorate with the green onion, and serve with extra fish sauce and lemon slices, if wished.

Nutrition Information

- Calories: 294 calories;
- Total Fat: 14.9
- Sodium: 1586
- Total Carbohydrate: 24.6
- Cholesterol: 42

- Protein: 15.5

402. Chicken Binakol

Serving: 4 | Prep: 20mins | Cook: 25mins | Ready in:

Ingredients

- 2 tablespoons vegetable oil
- 2 small onions, quartered
- 3 lemon grass stalks, white parts only, cut into 1-inch pieces
- 1 (1 inch) piece fresh ginger, sliced
- 4 cloves garlic, chopped
- 1 (3 pound) whole chicken, cut into 4 pieces
- 2 young coconuts, liquid only
- 1 chayote squash, diced
- 1 tablespoon fish sauce

Direction

- In a large skillet set on medium-high heat, add vegetable oil; stir and cook garlic, ginger, lemongrass, and onions for approximately 5 minutes until tender. Fry in the chicken for approximately 10 minutes until lightly browned, flipping occasionally.
- Add coconut water into the skillet and mix in chayote squash. Add fish sauce to season. Keep on simmering for approximately 10 more minutes until the chicken is not pink in the middle and juices run clear.

Nutrition Information

- Calories: 820 calories;
- Total Fat: 70.5
- Sodium: 493
- Total Carbohydrate: 14.5
- Cholesterol: 121
- Protein: 31.4

403. Chicken Teriyaki

Serving: 4 | Prep: 15mins | Cook: 50mins | Ready in:

Ingredients

- 2 1/4 cups soy sauce
- 3/4 cup sugar
- 1 teaspoon ground black pepper
- 1 tablespoon cornstarch
- 1 (20 ounce) can pineapple chunks in juice, drained, juice reserved
- 1 onion, chopped
- 3 cloves garlic, minced
- 1 (2 inch) piece fresh ginger root, peeled and chopped
- 4 chicken thighs
- 4 chicken drumsticks
- 4 chicken wings
- salt and ground black pepper to taste

Direction

- Set oven to preheat at 350°F (175°C).
- Mix soy sauce, cornstarch, sugar, a teaspoon of black pepper, half cup of saved pineapple juice in a saucepan until sugar has dissolved completely. Add garlic, onion and ginger. Let it boil. Cook for 5 minutes, until sauce is thick.
- Rinse thighs, wings and drumsticks thoroughly. Pat dry with paper towels. Place on a baking dish. Season with salt and pepper.
- Bake in the preheated oven for 15 minutes. Put the pineapple chunks to surround the chicken. Baste generously with the sauce. Put back in the oven and bake for 30 more minutes. Baste every 10 minutes or so.

Nutrition Information

- Calories: 738 calories;
- Total Fat: 24.4
- Sodium: 8306
- Total Carbohydrate: 76.4
- Cholesterol: 154
- Protein: 54.5

404. Chicken With Chicharo (Snow Peas)

Serving: 6 | Prep: 20mins | Cook: 20mins | Ready in:

Ingredients

- 1 tablespoon olive oil
- 1 onion, chopped
- 2 cloves garlic, minced
- 1 tablespoon oyster sauce
- salt and pepper to taste
- 2 pounds bone-in chicken pieces, such as legs, thighs, and wings
- 1 tomato, diced
- 1 carrot, sliced
- 2 stalks celery stalks, sliced
- 1 pound fresh snow peas, trimmed
- 1 tablespoon cornstarch
- 1 teaspoon water

Direction

- In a large skillet set on medium heat, add oil; stir and cook the garlic and onion the olive oil for approximately 5 minutes until scented. Mix the oyster sauce into the mixture; add pepper and salt to taste. Mix in the chicken; cook for 10 minutes, covered. Add the celery, carrot, and tomato; cook for 5 more minutes, covered. Cook the chicken pieces until not pink at the bone and the juices run clear, an instant-read thermometer poked near the bone should register 165°F (74°C). Add the snow peas into the mixture then fold.
- In a small bowl, beat water and cornstarch until free from lumps; mix into the liquid in the skillet. Let the mixture simmer for approximately 5 minutes until the sauce has thickened. Then serve hot.

Nutrition Information

- Calories: 403 calories;
- Cholesterol: 127
- Protein: 29.1
- Total Fat: 25.6
- Sodium: 183
- Total Carbohydrate: 13

405. Chinky's Bibingka

Serving: 12 | Prep: 30mins | Cook: 10mins | Ready in:

Ingredients

- 4 cups grated fresh cassava
- 3 cups coconut milk
- 3 tablespoons melted butter
- 3 eggs
- 1 1/2 cups white sugar
- 1 teaspoon salt
- 1 teaspoon vanilla extract
- 1 teaspoon lemon zest
- 1/4 cup shredded mozzarella cheese
- 2 cups coconut milk
- 1 (14 ounce) can sweetened condensed milk
- 2 tablespoons all-purpose flour
- 1/2 cup shredded mozzarella cheese
- 2 egg yolks, beaten

Direction

- NOTE: Cassava, also known as yucca, tapioca, or Manioc, can be found in Latin American or Filipino food stores. Normally sold frozen and grated. Combine eggs, melted butter, coconut milk, and the cassava. Mix in the lemon rind, cheese, vanilla, salt, and white sugar.
- Place batter into a 9x5 inch loaf pan then bake for 30 to 35 minutes at 350°F (175°C) or until done.
- For the Topping: In saucepan, place some grated cheese, flour, condensed milk, and 2 cups coconut milk then boil, whisking constantly. Once thick, put the slightly beaten egg yolks. Then cook for 2 minutes. Scatter on top of the cooked cassava and bake for 10 minutes at 400°F (200°C) or until golden brown.

Nutrition Information

- Calories: 619 calories;
- Total Fat: 33.2
- Sodium: 343
- Total Carbohydrate: 75.9
- Cholesterol: 105
- Protein: 9.6

406. Chinky's Mango Bread

Serving: 20 | Prep: 20mins | Cook: 1hours | Ready in:

Ingredients

- 2 cups all-purpose flour
- 2 teaspoons ground cinnamon
- 2 teaspoons baking soda
- 1/2 teaspoon salt
- 1 1/4 cups white sugar
- 2 eggs
- 3/4 cup vegetable oil
- 2 1/2 cups mangos, peeled, seeded and chopped
- 1 teaspoon lemon juice
- 1/4 cup raisins

Direction

- Mix all of the dry ingredients. Whisks eggs with oil then mix to flour mixture. Add raisins, lemon, and mangoes.
- Transfer into two greased 8x4-inch loaf pans. Bake in the oven for approximately 60 minutes at 350°F (175°C), (325°F for glass pans) or until a toothpick comes out clean.

Nutrition Information

- Calories: 193 calories;
- Sodium: 192
- Total Carbohydrate: 27.2
- Cholesterol: 19
- Protein: 2.1
- Total Fat: 8.9

407. Chinky's Puto Bread

Serving: 24 | Prep: 10mins | Cook: 15mins | Ready in:

Ingredients

- 2 3/4 cups cake flour
- 1 1/4 cups white sugar
- 2 tablespoons baking powder
- 1/2 cup evaporated milk
- 1 cup water
- 2 eggs
- 1 cup margarine, softened

Direction

- Prepare the oven by preheating to 375°F (190°C).
- Combine baking powder, sugar, and cake flour. Add in the evaporated milk and water and mix well. Stir in the margarine or butter and eggs. Transfer the mixture in muffin cups or molds. Search for a baking pan that your muffin pan will fit in. Drag the oven rack out a bit (maybe 1/4 out of oven) and put the baking pan with the muffin pan inside it on the rack. Very cautiously put 4 cups of hot water in the baking pan that holds muffin cups. Next, very gradually and gently slide rack fully in the oven.
- Then bake for approximately 15 minutes at 375°F 9190°C) or until a toothpick pricked into the middle of a muffin exits clean. Be very cautious not to burn your hands with steam or hot water once you take the muffins from the oven. Put grated cheese on top.

Nutrition Information

- Calories: 181 calories;
- Total Fat: 8.6
- Sodium: 236

- Total Carbohydrate: 24.1
- Cholesterol: 17
- Protein: 2.3

408. Chocolate Orange Rice Pudding

Serving: 8 | Prep: 10mins | Cook: 40mins | Ready in:

Ingredients

- 5 1/2 cups milk
- 1 cup Arborio rice
- 2/3 cup white sugar
- 2 tablespoons orange juice
- 1 1/2 teaspoons grated orange zest
- 2 tablespoons orange liqueur
- 1 tablespoon unsweetened cocoa powder
- 1 cup semisweet chocolate chips

Direction

- In a heavy saucepan, mix orange zest and juice, sugar, rice, and milk; make it to a boil, lower heat to medium-low, and cook for 35-40 minutes, stirring frequently, until the rice is softened and the mixture turns thick.
- Separate the saucepan from heat. Mix cocoa powder and orange liqueur through the rice mixture; stir in chocolate chips until dissolved into the pudding.

Nutrition Information

- Calories: 356 calories;
- Sodium: 72
- Total Carbohydrate: 60.6
- Cholesterol: 13
- Protein: 8.3
- Total Fat: 9.7

409. Coconut Sauce

Serving: 10 | Prep: 5mins | Cook: 20mins | Ready in:

Ingredients

- 1 (14 ounce) can coconut milk
- 1 cup brown sugar

Direction

- In a heavy-bottomed pot, add together brown sugar and coconut milk; bring to a boil. Lower heat to medium low. While boiling, cook and stir for 20 minutes till thick and the volume reduce by about half.

Nutrition Information

- Calories: 161 calories;
- Total Fat: 8.4
- Sodium: 11
- Total Carbohydrate: 22.7
- Cholesterol: 0
- Protein: 0.8

410. Corned Beef Hash (Abalos Style)

Serving: 4 | Prep: 15mins | Cook: 30mins | Ready in:

Ingredients

- 1 tablespoon vegetable oil
- 4 cloves garlic, chopped
- 1 onion, diced
- 1 tomato, chopped
- 1 large potato, diced
- 1 (12 ounce) can corned beef
- salt and pepper to taste

Direction

- In a large skillet set on medium-high heat, add oil. Add garlic and onion then cook until scented. Mix in the potatoes and tomatoes, then cook for 7-10 minutes until potatoes are tender. Add in the corned beef, and flake into pieces. And cook for 10 more minutes, frequently stirring. Add pepper and salt to taste, then serve.

Nutrition Information

- Calories: 333 calories;
- Total Fat: 16.2
- Sodium: 853
- Total Carbohydrate: 21.1
- Cholesterol: 72
- Protein: 25.5

411. Crab Omelet

Serving: 6 | Prep: 15mins | Cook: 20mins | Ready in:

Ingredients

- 2 tablespoons olive oil
- 1 small potato, peeled and diced
- 1 onion, chopped
- 2 cloves garlic, minced
- 1/4 pound fresh crabmeat, drained and flaked
- salt and pepper to taste
- 1 small tomato, diced
- 1 (1.5 ounce) box raisins
- 1/4 cup peas
- 1 red bell pepper, chopped
- 3 eggs, beaten

Direction

- In a skillet set over medium heat, add olive oil. Add the potato and fry in the hot oil for 5-7 minutes until fork-tender. Place the potatoes to a plate lined with paper towels and reserve. Put the skillet back to medium heat. Cook the garlic and onion in the left oil for approximately 5 minutes until softened. Put the crab to the skillet and add pepper and salt to taste; mix. Then cover the skillet and cook for 2 minutes. Mix the tomatoes into the mixture and cook for 2 more minutes. Mix in the red bell pepper, peas, and raisins to the mixture; cook and stir for 2 more minutes.
- Place the eggs over the mixture. And cook for 2-3 minutes until the eggs are set. Turn the omelet over and cook for 1 more minute. Place to a serving plate then serve right away.

Nutrition Information

- Calories: 165 calories;
- Sodium: 104
- Total Carbohydrate: 17.5
- Cholesterol: 104
- Protein: 8.4
- Total Fat: 7.4

412. Dinengdeng

Serving: 6 | Prep: 30mins | Cook: 20mins | Ready in:

Ingredients

- 2 (8 ounce) fillets milkfish (bangus)
- 1 tomato, quartered
- 1 onion, chopped
- 2 tablespoons shrimp paste (bagoong)
- 1 cup water
- salt and pepper to taste
- 1/2 pound long beans, cut into bite-size pieces
- 1/2 pound zucchini, cut into bite-size pieces
- 1/2 pound fresh okra

Direction

- Prepare an outdoor grill by preheating to medium heat and lightly oil the grate.
- Place the milkfish fillet on the griller then grill for 2 to 3 minutes each side, until the flesh flakes simply with a fork.
- Mix water, shrimp paste, onion, tomato, and grilled fillet to the pot; make it boil for 5

minutes. Add pepper and salt to taste. Add the zucchini and long beans; mix. Then cover the pot and cook for 5 minutes on medium heat. Mix the okra into the mixture and cook for 5 more minutes. Serve right away.

Nutrition Information

- Calories: 288 calories;
- Total Fat: 5.8
- Sodium: 101
- Total Carbohydrate: 32.7
- Cholesterol: 43
- Protein: 27.5

413. Duck Adobo

Serving: 6 | Prep: 20mins | Cook: 2hours15mins | Ready in:

Ingredients

- 6 duck legs
- salt and freshly ground black pepper to taste
- 1 tablespoon vegetable oil
- 1 large onion, sliced
- 8 cloves garlic, minced
- 1 1/2 cups chicken broth
- 1 cup seasoned rice vinegar
- 1/2 cup soy sauce, or to taste
- 2 teaspoons sambal chili paste, or other hot pepper sauce to taste
- 2 bay leaves

Direction

- Season duck legs by sprinkling salt and black pepper.
- Prep a large deep skillet over medium-high heat. Pour in vegetable oil. Place duck legs, skin-side down. Cook for 3 – 4 minutes on each side until browned. Take duck legs out of pan and drain the duck fat. Leave about 1 tablespoon of duck fat.
- Cook over medium heat the onion in reserved duck fat. Cook for 3 – 4 minutes, or until onion starts to look see-through. Add garlic. Cook and stir for another 1 – 2 minutes until fragrant.
- Add rice vinegar, soy sauce, chicken broth, bay leaves, and sambal chili paste to the onion mixture. Bring to a simmer, then put the duck legs back in the skillet. Loosely cover pan and continue simmering until the duck legs are tender and easily pierced with fork. This should take 2 hours.
- Take cover off pan, increase heat to high and cook for 5 minutes, or until sauce has thickened. Add salt and black pepper to taste.

Nutrition Information

- Calories: 111 calories;
- Total Fat: 4.6
- Sodium: 1493
- Total Carbohydrate: 6.5
- Cholesterol: 34
- Protein: 11.3

414. Empanada Dough

Serving: 24 | Prep: 20mins | Cook: | Ready in:

Ingredients

- 2 cups all-purpose flour
- 1/2 teaspoon salt
- 1/3 cup white sugar
- 1 egg yolk
- 1/2 cup water
- 2 tablespoons all-purpose flour for dusting
- 2 tablespoons melted butter for brushing

Direction

- In a bowl, combine sugar, salt, and 2 cups flour until equally mixed; form a well in the middle of the mixture. In a small bowl, beat

water and egg yolk until smooth; add into the well and blend to make a stiff dough. Place the dough to a surface that is lightly floured then massage for approximately 8 minutes until elastic and smooth.
- Use a rolling pin to roll the dough until thin, dusting with flour to avoid from sticking. Use melted butter to brush with and roll it like a jelly roll. Use a sharp knife to cut into 1 1/2-inch slices. Turn every piece into a circle and stuff with about 1 tablespoon filling. Fold over into half moons and enclose.

Nutrition Information

- Calories: 62 calories;
- Total Fat: 1.3
- Sodium: 56
- Total Carbohydrate: 11.2
- Cholesterol: 11
- Protein: 1.3

415. Filipino Baked Milkfish (Baked Bangus)

Serving: 4 | Prep: 15mins | Cook: 1hours | Ready in:

Ingredients

- 2 pounds whole milkfish (bangus), or more to taste
- 1 tomato, diced
- 1 onion, chopped
- 1 (2 inch) piece ginger, thinly sliced crosswise, or to taste, divided
- salt and ground black pepper to taste
- 4 calamansi, juiced
- 1/2 cup soy sauce
- 2 cloves garlic, chopped

Direction

- Prepare the oven by preheating to 350°F (175°C). Use enough aluminum foil to line a roasting pan to cover the whole bangus.
- Take off the gills and scales from bangus. Rinse the innards. Use a paper towel to pat dry the fish.
- In a bowl, combine 1/3 of the ginger, onion, and tomato. Add pepper and salt to season. Slice open the front side of the fish then stuff with the tomato mixture. Put the fish in the prepared pan.
- In another bowl, whisk the rest of the ginger, garlic, soy sauce, and calamansi juice. Place over the fish in the pan. Turn foil over the fish then enclose all ends.
- Place in the preheated oven and bake for approximately 60 minutes until fish easily with a fork.

Nutrition Information

- Calories: 394 calories;
- Sodium: 2010
- Total Carbohydrate: 14.3
- Cholesterol: 119
- Protein: 49.8
- Total Fat: 15.5

416. Filipino Banana Blossoms Sisig

Serving: 4 | Prep: 20mins | Cook: 20mins | Ready in:

Ingredients

- 2 banana blossoms, sliced crosswise into fine strips
- salt to taste
- 2 tablespoons olive oil
- 2 cloves garlic, chopped
- 1 onion, chopped
- 1 (16 ounce) pork loin, diced
- salt and ground black pepper to taste
- 1/2 cup white vinegar

- 1/2 cup water

Direction

- Dust salt on banana blossoms and massage to release the juice. Get rid of juice. In a saucepan set on medium-high heat, add olive oil. Stir-fry garlic for approximately 1 minute until fragrant and browned slightly. Put onion; stir-fry for approximately 5 minutes until translucent. Add pepper, salt, and pork; stir well. Cook for approximately 5 minutes, covered until pork is a little pink at the center. Add the water, vinegar, and banana blossoms. Cook for approximately 5 more minutes, covered until flavors combined.

Nutrition Information

- Calories: 241 calories;
- Total Fat: 11.2
- Sodium: 185
- Total Carbohydrate: 12.5
- Cholesterol: 63
- Protein: 23.3

417. Filipino Beef Giniling (Afritada Style)

Serving: 6 | Prep: 25mins | Cook: 15mins | Ready in:

Ingredients

- 1 tablespoon oil, or as needed
- 1 clove garlic, minced
- 2 pounds ground beef
- 1 cup water, or as needed
- ground black pepper to taste
- 6 tablespoons soy sauce, divided
- 2 medium red potatoes
- 10 baby carrots, or more to taste, cubed
- 1/2 cup raisins, or more to taste
- 2 (6.5 ounce) cans tomato sauce with salt (such as Contadina®)
- 1/2 orange bell pepper, diced
- 4 tablespoons white sugar

Direction

- In a large saucepan set on medium heat, add oil. Cook in the garlic for about 1 minute until light golden brown. Add 1/2 cup of water and beef; stir and cook for 5 -7 minutes until crumble and browned. Add black pepper to season and add more water as necessary; keep the beef from drying out.
- Add carrots, potatoes, and 3 tablespoons soy sauce to the saucepan with the beef. Add more water as necessary to avoid drying out. Then cook for 4 minutes; mix in raisins. Then cook for another 2-3 minutes, adding water as necessary to ensure beef does not dry out.
- Mix 1 can of sauce to the saucepan with the beef mixture. Add water to fill the can, mix to get rid of excess sauce, and add water into the saucepan. Mix 1/2 of the rest of the can sauce to the saucepan; mix to blend. Add more water as necessary to make a sauce-like but not soupy consistency.
- Mix in sugar, remaining 3 tablespoons soy sauce, and bell pepper. Then cook for approximately 3-5 more minutes until all vegetables are soft, whisking occasionally and adding water as necessary to make sure the sauce does not dry out.

Nutrition Information

- Calories: 488 calories;
- Sodium: 1332
- Total Carbohydrate: 35.4
- Cholesterol: 93
- Protein: 28.6
- Total Fat: 26.1

418. Filipino Beef Stir Fry

Serving: 4 | Prep: 30mins | Cook: 30mins | Ready in:

Ingredients

- 2 (1/2 pound) New York strip steaks, sliced into thin strips
- 2 tablespoons cornstarch
- 2 tablespoons soy sauce
- 1 1/2 teaspoons white sugar
- 3 tablespoons olive oil
- 1 sweet onion, chopped
- 2 cloves garlic, crushed
- 1 tablespoon oyster sauce
- salt and pepper to taste
- 1 pound snow peas
- 3/4 cup green peas
- 1 carrot, sliced
- 2 stalks celery, sliced
- 1 red bell pepper, seeded and cut into chunks
- 1/4 cup oil for deep frying

Direction

- In a big bowl, put in steak slices. Drizzle cornstarch and coat over on beef. In a small bowl, blend sugar and soy sauce until the sugar melts. Pour on beef slices, stir, marinate, then place in the refrigerator for a minimum of 2 hours or overnight.
- In big skillet, heat 3 tbsps. of olive oil on medium heat. Let garlic and onion cook in oil for 5-7 minutes until it becomes tender. Mix in oyster sauce and add salt and pepper as seasoning. Mix in green peas, snow peas, red pepper, celery and carrot; stir and cook for 7-10 minutes. It should be somewhat tender but still crisp. Take skillet off heat.
- In another skillet, heat 2 tbsps. of oil. Take beef out of the marinade and shake out extra moisture, then dispose the marinade. In hot oil, fry sliced beef for 3-5 minutes until cooked to your preferred doneness. Mix in cooked beef and vegetable mixture well then serve warm.

Nutrition Information

- Calories: 452 calories;
- Total Carbohydrate: 26.5
- Cholesterol: 66
- Protein: 39.1
- Total Fat: 20.6
- Sodium: 652

419. Filipino Chicken Binakol

Serving: 4 | Prep: 15mins | Cook: 30mins | Ready in:

Ingredients

- 1 pound chicken, cut into pieces
- 1 cup water
- 1 tablespoon canola oil
- 1 red onion, finely chopped
- 1 tablespoon crushed fresh ginger root
- 3 cloves garlic, chopped
- 2 tomatoes, cut into wedges
- 2 fresh young coconuts, juice and meat
- 1 cup sliced bok choy
- 1 tablespoon fish sauce
- salt to taste

Direction

- In a pot, mix water and chicken pieces together and boil for 5 to 10 minutes or until the water has evaporated then take the chicken pieces out of the pot.
- In the same pot, heat up some oil to cook the garlic, ginger and onion for 3 minutes until it becomes fragrant and soft then mix tomatoes and chicken pieces in to cook for 5 minutes. Put the bok choy, coconut water and coconut meat in and let it simmer for 15 minutes until the chicken is thoroughly cooked. Add salt and fish sauce to season it. Serve.

Nutrition Information

- Calories: 881 calories;
- Total Fat: 72.5
- Sodium: 418
- Total Carbohydrate: 37.2

- Cholesterol: 59
- Protein: 30.2

420. Filipino Chicken Relleno

Serving: 12 | Prep: 35mins | Cook: 1hours10mins | Ready in:

Ingredients

- 1 (4.5 pound) whole chicken
- 2 tablespoons soy sauce
- 1 lemon, juiced
- 1 pound ground pork
- 1 onion, diced
- 1 tomato, diced
- 2 large eggs
- 1 carrot, cut into matchsticks
- 1 link chorizo de bilbao (spicy Spanish semi-cured sausage), finely chopped
- 1/2 cup shredded Cheddar cheese
- 1 (1.5 ounce) box raisins
- 2 cloves garlic, minced
- salt and ground black pepper to taste
- 1 cup chicken broth
- 1 tablespoon corn flour

Direction

- Prepare the oven by preheating to 350°F (175°C).
- Take the breast bones from chicken. Wash and use a paper towel to pat dry. Put the chicken in a roasting pan. Add lemon juice and soy sauce over chicken, rubbing the liquid into the cavity too.
- In a bowl, combine pepper, salt, garlic, raisins, Cheddar cheese, chorizo, carrot, eggs, tomato, and onion. Then fill the chicken with the mixture. Stitch the opening to enclose the filling.
- Place in the preheated oven then bake for approximately 60 minutes until the chicken is not pink at the bone and the juices run clear. Use aluminum foil to cover the chicken if it is turning brown too fast. An instant-read thermometer poked near the bone should register 165°F (74°C). Let it cool shortly prior to cutting crosswise.
- In a pot set on medium-high heat, place the drippings from the chicken and broth. Make it boil. Stir in corn flour; whisk constantly for 5-8 minutes, until the sauce turns thick. Then serve with the chicken.

Nutrition Information

- Calories: 597 calories;
- Total Fat: 48.8
- Sodium: 450
- Total Carbohydrate: 7.9
- Cholesterol: 145
- Protein: 30.6

421. Filipino Chicken Salad

Serving: 12 | Prep: 20mins | Cook: 30mins | Ready in:

Ingredients

- 1 skinless, boneless chicken breast
- 2/3 cup elbow macaroni
- 1 (20 ounce) can pineapple chunks, drained
- 1 apple, cored and diced
- 2 stalks celery, sliced
- 1 carrot, diced
- 2 (1.5 ounce) boxes raisins
- 1 cup mayonnaise
- 1 teaspoon white sugar
- 1 teaspoon seasoned salt

Direction

- Place water in a pot over low heat and let it simmer. Put the chicken breast into the water and cook for about 30 minutes until not pink in the middle and the juices run clear. The inserted instant-read thermometer in the middle should register at least 165°F (74°C).

Take the chicken from the water and let cool before shredding the meat into a big bowl.
- While cooking the chicken, place a lightly salted water in a pot and make it boil. Add the macaroni and cook at a boil for about 8 minutes until cooked through yet still firm to the bite. Strain and wash with cold water to stop the cooking process until the pasta is cool when touched. Place into the bowl with the chicken.
- Add raisins, carrot, celery, apple and pineapple into the bowl then mix to blend. Stir in the seasoned salt, sugar and mayonnaise; slowly whisk the mixture until equally coated. Keep in the refrigerator for at least 30 minutes prior to serving.

Nutrition Information

- Calories: 225 calories;
- Total Fat: 15
- Sodium: 196
- Total Carbohydrate: 20.9
- Cholesterol: 12
- Protein: 3.4

422. Filipino Fish Stew (Paksiw Na Bangus)

Serving: 6 | Prep: 20mins | Cook: 40mins | Ready in:

Ingredients

- 3 1/4 pounds whole milkfish (bangus)
- 1 eggplant, cut into chunks
- 1 onion, diced
- 1 (2 inch) piece ginger, thinly sliced crosswise, or to taste
- 2 large green chile peppers, chopped
- 1 teaspoon salt to taste
- 1 cup water
- 3/4 cup vinegar
- 1 green bell pepper, cut into chunks
- 1 small bitter melon, cut into chunks

Direction

- Get rid of guts, gills, and scales from fish. Wash and slice crosswise in 3 steak pieces. Then pat dry.
- In the bottom of a 1 1/2-qt pot, pile the ginger, onion, and eggplant. Put the fish on top. Put green chiles and dust with salt.
- Add vinegar and water in the pot with fish. Make it boil. Boil for 5 minutes; lower heat and simmer for approximately 20 minutes, until fish easily flakes with a fork. Mix in bitter melon and green bell pepper. Then cook for approximately 10 more minutes until bitter melon is soft.

Nutrition Information

- Calories: 419 calories;
- Total Fat: 16.9
- Sodium: 571
- Total Carbohydrate: 12.6
- Cholesterol: 129
- Protein: 52.6

423. Filipino Fried Chicken

Serving: 10 | Prep: 15mins | Cook: 15mins | Ready in:

Ingredients

- 1 cup cornstarch
- 1/2 cup white sugar
- 1/2 cup all-purpose flour
- 2 tablespoons salt
- 1 teaspoon monosodium glutamate (such as Ajinomoto®) (optional)
- 4 eggs, slightly beaten
- 1/2 bunch green onions, chopped
- 1/4 cup soy sauce (such as Aloha™ Shoyu)
- 10 cloves garlic, minced
- 5 pounds chicken wings
- vegetable oil for frying

Direction

- In a big bowl, mix monosodium glutamate, salt, flour, sugar, and cornstarch. Add garlic, soy sauce, green onions, and eggs. Then pat dry the chicken and mix in the sauce. Keep in the refrigerator for 8 hours or up to overnight, covered. In a big saucepan or deep-fryer, heat oil to 350°F (175°C). Add the chicken and fry in hot oil for 15-25 minutes until golden brown. An instant-read thermometer poked neat the bone should register 165°F (74°C).

Nutrition Information

- Calories: 364 calories;
- Total Carbohydrate: 35.1
- Cholesterol: 119
- Protein: 15.3
- Total Fat: 17.8
- Sodium: 2019

424. Filipino Leche Flan

Serving: 10 | Prep: 10mins | Cook: 2hours10mins | Ready in:

Ingredients

- 2 cups white sugar, divided
- 3/4 cup water
- 2 (11.3 ounce) cans evaporated milk
- 8 egg yolks
- zest of 1 lime

Direction

- Prepare the oven by preheating to 325°F (165°C).
- In a saucepan set on medium heat, mix water and 1 cup sugar. Heat for 7-10 minutes until sugar is melted and mixture turns thick and light brown. Put the caramel mixture to line the inside of a flan mold, slanting the mold to ensure the whole surface is coated.
- In a bowl, beat lime zest, egg yolks, evaporated milk, and the rest of 1 cup sugar. Cautiously combine, not beat, until yolks are all broken and mixed. Through a sieve, strain the custard to take off the zest. Place the mixture into the flan mold. Set the flan mold in a larger baking pan filled with water. Place in the preheated oven and bake for approximately 2 hours until firm.

Nutrition Information

- Calories: 293 calories;
- Protein: 7
- Total Fat: 8.9
- Sodium: 82
- Total Carbohydrate: 47.7
- Cholesterol: 185

425. Filipino Lechon (Roasted Pork Leg)

Serving: 10 | Prep: 10mins | Cook: 4hours | Ready in:

Ingredients

- 6 1/2 pounds pork leg with skin
- 3 tablespoons butter at room temperature, or as needed
- salt to taste
- 1 cup water

Direction

- Prepare the oven by preheating to 400°F (200°C).
- Wash pork; use paper towels to pat dry. Apply butter and rub it all over the skin. Dust salt over the skin.
- Put the pork leg on a rack in a roasting pan. Add water into the bottom of the pan. Use aluminum foil to cover the pan tightly so that steam will not escape.

- Place in the preheated oven and roast for 30 minutes. Take off the foil. Lower the heat to 320°F (160°C).
- Keep on baking for 3 1/2 hours, basting with drippings every 30 minutes, until skin turns crisp. An instant-read thermometer poked into the middle should register 176°F (80°C).
- Transfer pork leg on a serving platter. Cut into bite-sized pieces.

Nutrition Information

- Calories: 350 calories;
- Total Fat: 11.9
- Sodium: 1944
- Total Carbohydrate: 0
- Cholesterol: 170
- Protein: 60.9

426. Filipino Lumpia

Serving: 6 | Prep: 1hours | Cook: 10mins | Ready in:

Ingredients

- 1 lumpia wrappers
- 1 pound ground beef
- 1/2 pound ground pork
- 1/3 cup finely chopped onion
- 1/3 cup finely chopped green bell pepper
- 1/3 cup finely chopped carrot
- 1 quart oil for frying

Direction

- Be sure that the lumpia wrappers are fully thawed. On a clean dry surface, lay several lumpia wrappers and use a damp towel to cover. The edges will dry out fast and wrappers are super thin.
- Mix carrot, green pepper, onion, ground pork, and beef in a medium bowl. Put about 2 tablespoons of the meat mixture along the middle of the wrapper. The filling should no larger around than your thumb or the wrapper will burn prior the meat is done. Then fold one edge of the wrapper over to the other. Turn the outer edges in slightly, and keep on rolling into a cylinder. Damp your finger, and wet the edge to enclose. Continue with the rest of the wrappers and filling, leaving completed lumpias covered to avoid drying. This is a nice time to ask a loved one or a friend to make the job less repetitive!
- In a 9-inch skillet set at medium to medium-high heat, add oil and heat to 365-375°F (170-175°C). Then fry 3 to 4 lumpia at a time. It should only take approximately 2 to 3 minutes for each side. It will be browned nicely once done. Transfer to paper towels to drain on.
- You can slice every lumpia into thirds for parties if you want. We pair the lumpia with banana ketchup in the Philippines, yet I've never seen it promoted in America.

Nutrition Information

- Calories: 365 calories;
- Total Fat: 30.2
- Sodium: 60
- Total Carbohydrate: 2.3
- Cholesterol: 75
- Protein: 20.4

427. Filipino Menudo (Pork And Liver Stew)

Serving: 10 | Prep: 25mins | Cook: 50mins | Ready in:

Ingredients

- 2 1/4 boneless pork chops
- 1/2 pound pork liver
- 3 tablespoons olive oil
- 2 cloves garlic, minced
- 1 onion, diced
- salt and pepper to taste
- 2 tomatoes, diced

- 1 (15.5 ounce) can garbanzo beans, drained
- 1 (1.5 ounce) box raisins
- 2 potatoes, diced

Direction

- Place lightly salted water in a big pot and make it boil; put in the pork chops then bring back to a boil. Boil pork chops for 5 minutes, then remove, and reserve to cool. Take 1 cup of the broth from the pot and reserve for later use. When the chops are cooled to the touch, slice into bite-sized portions. Bring the water back to a boil; put the pork liver to the pot and boil for 7-10 minutes until tender. Strain and get rid of the liquid. Reserve the liver to cool; slice into bite-size portions.
- In a big skillet set on medium heat, add the olive oil; stir and cook the garlic and onion in hot oil for approximately 5 minutes until tender. Add the pork chops in the garlic and onion; stir and cook for 5 minutes. Add pepper and salt to season. Mix in the leftover broth and tomatoes; cook for 10 minutes, covered. Mix the potatoes, raisins, garbanzo beans, and pork liver into the mixture; then simmer for approximately 10 minutes, covered, until potatoes become fork tender.

Nutrition Information

- Calories: 194 calories;
- Total Carbohydrate: 24.7
- Cholesterol: 44
- Protein: 9.5
- Total Fat: 6.8
- Sodium: 164

428. Filipino Pancit Bihon With Canton

Serving: 6 | Prep: 30mins | Cook: 20mins | Ready in:

Ingredients

- 1/2 (8 ounce) package pancit bihon (rice noodles)
- 2 tablespoons olive oil
- 1 onion, chopped
- 2 cloves garlic, minced
- 1 cup chopped cooked chicken
- salt and ground black pepper to taste
- 2 cups fresh shrimp, peeled and deveined
- 2 tablespoons soy sauce
- 1 small head cabbage, shredded
- 2 stalks celery, sliced
- 1 carrot, peeled and cut into matchsticks
- 2 cups water
- 1/2 (8 ounce) package pancit canton (yellow Chinese noodles)

Direction

- In a bowl of warm water, soak bihon for approximately 5 minutes until soft. Strain the water off. In a large wok set on medium-high heat, add oil. Stir fry garlic and onion for approximately 5 minutes until onion is glassy. Add pepper, salt, and chicken. Stir and cook for approximately 3 minutes until flavors blend. Mix in shrimp; then cook for approximately 1 minute until they begin to change color. Mix in soy sauce; stir in carrot, celery, and cabbage. Then cook for approximately 2 minutes until well mixed. Put 2 cups of water; make it simmer. Cook for approximately 2 minutes until vegetables start to soften. Place the vegetables, shrimp, and chicken to a bowl, keeping the liquid behind in the wok. Add canton noodles and bihon to the liquid. Combine well then cover. Allow it to sit for approximately 5 minutes until softened. Put 1/2 the chicken-vegetable mixture back to wok; combine with noodles. Transfer soup into bowls; decorate with the rest of the chicken-vegetable mixture.

Nutrition Information

- Calories: 316 calories;
- Sodium: 486
- Total Carbohydrate: 40.1

- Cholesterol: 98
- Protein: 20.7
- Total Fat: 8.1

429. Filipino Pork Adobo

Serving: 6 | Prep: 20mins | Cook: 2hours30mins | Ready in:

Ingredients

- 1 cup distilled white vinegar
- 1 cup soy sauce
- 1/2 cup ketchup
- 1 tablespoon minced garlic
- 3 bay leaves
- 1 teaspoon fresh-ground black pepper
- 2 1/2 pounds lean pork, cut into 1 inch cubes
- 1 pound small green beans, trimmed (optional)

Direction

- In a large saucepan, mix bay leaves, garlic, ketchup, soy sauce, and vinegar. Mix in the cubed pork, and bring to a boil over high heat. Lower heat to medium-low, cover and simmer for approximately 2 1/2 hours until the pork is tender. Occasionally stir. Add the green beans (if using) during the last half hour of cooking.

Nutrition Information

- Calories: 337 calories;
- Total Fat: 15.5
- Sodium: 2687
- Total Carbohydrate: 14.4
- Cholesterol: 90
- Protein: 35.1

430. Filipino Pork Sinigang

Serving: 8 | Prep: 20mins | Cook: 1hours | Ready in:

Ingredients

- 2 1/2 pounds pork neck bones
- 2 pounds pork spareribs
- water to cover
- 1 tablespoon salt
- 1 1/2 onions, quartered
- 2 tomatoes, quartered, or more to taste
- 1 taro, peeled and cut into large chunks
- 1/2 cup fresh lemon juice
- 2 tablespoons fish sauce
- 1 pound bok choy, chopped
- 1 large leek, chopped
- 5 head-on shrimp

Direction

- In a stockpot, set the spare ribs and pork neck bones in and cover with water. Sprinkle some salt in and bring it to a boil then remove the layer of fat from the top of the broth. Lower the heat and add taro, tomatoes and onions in then continue boiling until the pork meat becomes extremely tender, about 30-40 minutes.
- Whisk fish sauce and lemon juice into the broth and continue boiling until flavors mix together, about 15 minutes. Put the shrimp, leek and boy choy in then cover it up. Lower the heat and let it simmer for 10 more minutes until the boy choy is tender and the shrimp is opaque.

Nutrition Information

- Calories: 546 calories;
- Sodium: 2200
- Total Carbohydrate: 11
- Cholesterol: 184
- Protein: 58.2
- Total Fat: 29

431. Filipino Rice (Arroz Valenciana)

Serving: 10 | Prep: 15mins | Cook: 45mins | Ready in:

Ingredients

- 3 tablespoons olive oil
- 1 onion, chopped
- 2 cloves garlic
- 2 teaspoons paprika
- 2 1/4 pounds chicken legs, thighs, and wings
- 1 1/2 cups sweet peas
- 1 (7 ounce) can olives
- 2 links chorizo de bilbao (spicy Spanish semi-cured sausage), or to taste
- salt and ground black pepper to taste
- 2 tomatoes, diced
- 1 cup water
- 2 cups glutinous sweet rice (malagkit)
- 1 (14 ounce) can coconut milk
- 1 red bell pepper, sliced lengthwise
- 2 hard-boiled eggs, sliced lengthwise

Direction

- In a skillet set on medium-high heat, add olive oil. Stir-fry garlic and onion for approximately 5 minutes, until the onion turns translucent. Mix in paprika. Add pepper, salt, chorizo, olives, sweet peas, and chicken; stir well. Cook for approximately 5 minutes, covered, until fragrant. Mix in tomatoes and cook for approximately 5 minutes until juices have released. Mix in water; cook for approximately 5 minutes until reduced slightly. Put in sweet rice; stir well. Cook for approximately 5 minutes, covered until flavors combined.
- Add coconut milk in the skillet and make it boil. Cook for approximately 5 minutes until reduced slightly. Stir in red bell pepper. Cook for another 10 minutes until the rice becomes tender and chicken is not pink. An instant-read thermometer poked near the bone should register 165°F (74°C). Decorate using hard-boiled eggs.

Nutrition Information

- Calories: 580 calories;
- Total Carbohydrate: 38.8
- Cholesterol: 89
- Protein: 17.8
- Total Fat: 39.5
- Sodium: 438

432. Filipino Spaghetti

Serving: 12 | Prep: 15mins | Cook: 40mins | Ready in:

Ingredients

- 2 pounds spaghetti
- 1 tablespoon vegetable oil
- 1 head garlic, minced
- 1 onion, chopped
- 1 pound ground beef
- 1 pound ground pork
- salt and pepper to taste
- 1 (26.5 ounce) can spaghetti sauce
- 1 (14 ounce) jar banana ketchup
- 1/4 cup white sugar
- 1/2 cup water
- 1 pound hot dogs, sliced diagonally
- 1/2 cup shredded Cheddar cheese

Direction

- Place lightly salted water in a large pot and make it to a rolling boil over high heat. When the water is boiling, mix in the spaghetti, and bring back to a boil. Then cook the pasta for approximately 12 minutes without cover, stirring occasionally, until the pasta has cooked well, yet still firm to the bite. Strain well in a colander set in the sink.
- In a skillet set on medium heat, add vegetable oil. Add in the onion and garlic; stir and cook

for approximately 5 minutes until the onion has softened and turned translucent. Mix in the pork and beef; add pepper and salt to taste. Stir and cook until the meat has browned. Add in the water, sugar, banana ketchup, and spaghetti sauce. Simmer for approximately 15 minutes until the sauce has thickened. Mix in hot dog slices and keep on cooking until hot dogs are heated well. Then pour over spaghetti and sprinkle with Cheddar cheese on top to serve.

Nutrition Information

- Calories: 708 calories;
- Total Carbohydrate: 82.9
- Cholesterol: 77
- Protein: 29.2
- Total Fat: 27.4
- Sodium: 1085

433. Filipino Stew (Caldereta)

Serving: 10 | Prep: 20mins | Cook: 1hours20mins | Ready in:

Ingredients

- 2 1/4 pounds beef stew meat, cut into 1 1/2-inch chunks
- 2 cups water
- 2 beef bouillon cubes
- 3 tablespoons olive oil, divided
- 1 onion, chopped
- 2 cloves garlic, minced
- 1 teaspoon paprika
- salt and ground black pepper to taste
- 3 tomatoes, diced
- 2 potatoes, quartered
- 2 carrots, cut in chunks
- 3/4 (6 ounce) package frozen peas
- 1 red bell pepper, cut into chunks
- 1 (3 ounce) can liver spread
- 1 tablespoon vinegar, or to taste
- 1 teaspoon white sugar

Direction

- In a pot, mix beef bouillon, water, and beef stew meat; make it to a Boil. Boil for 45 minutes to 1 hour until tender.
- In a large pot set on medium-high heat, add olive oil. Stir-fry garlic and onion for approximately 5 minutes until onion turns translucent. Add pepper, salt, and paprika. Add in tomatoes; make it to a boil then cook for approximately 5 minutes until tender. Place in the boiled beef and all but 1/2 cup broth.
- In a skillet set on medium-high heat, add the rest of the olive oil. Put in the potatoes; stir and cook for 5-7 minutes until browned. Add to the beef mixture. Add red bell pepper, peas, and carrots. Stir-fry for approximately 5 minutes until vegetables are tender.
- In a bowl, combine reserved beef broth, sugar, vinegar, and liver spread. Add mixture into the pot with the beef; mix in the sautéed vegetables. Combine and keep on cooking for approximately 5 more minutes until flavors are blended.

Nutrition Information

- Calories: 263 calories;
- Total Carbohydrate: 14.7
- Cholesterol: 75
- Protein: 22.3
- Total Fat: 12.5
- Sodium: 319

434. Filippino Lechon Kawali

Serving: 4 | Prep: 10mins | Cook: 45mins | Ready in:

Ingredients

- 1 1/2 pounds pork belly, cut into small pieces
- 3 cloves garlic, crushed

- 2 bay leaves
- 1/2 teaspoon salt
- 1/2 teaspoon ground black pepper
- water to cover
- oil for frying

Direction

- In a skillet, mix pepper, salt, bay leaves, garlic, and pork belly; add in enough water to cover. Make it boil, lower heat, and simmer for 35-45 minutes until skin is soft. Strain and allow to sit at room temperature until pork has air-dried.
- In a large saucepan or deep fryer, heat oil to 350°F (175°C).
- Add pork in the hot oil and fry in batches, for 3-5 minutes, until golden brown. Take the fried pork using a slotted spoon and place on a plate lined with a paper towel to drain.

Nutrition Information

- Calories: 502 calories;
- Sodium: 1587
- Total Carbohydrate: 1.8
- Cholesterol: 62
- Protein: 20.9
- Total Fat: 45.4

435. Fish Sinigang (Tilapia) Filipino Sour Broth Dish

Serving: 4 | Prep: 5mins | Cook: 10mins | Ready in:

Ingredients

- 1/2 pound tilapia fillets, cut into chunks
- 1 small head bok choy, chopped
- 2 medium tomatoes, cut into chunks
- 1 cup thinly sliced daikon radish
- 1/4 cup tamarind paste
- 3 cups water
- 2 dried red chile peppers (optional)

Direction

- Mix radish, tomatoes, bok choy, and tilapia in a medium pot. Mix water and tamarind paste; add into the pot. Mix in the chili peppers if you want. Make it boil then cook for 5 minutes, or just until the fish is cooked well. Even fish that is frozen will be cooked in less than ten minutes. Keep from overcooking or else the fish will fall apart. Scoop into bowls to serve.

Nutrition Information

- Calories: 112 calories;
- Total Carbohydrate: 13.4
- Cholesterol: 21
- Protein: 13.1
- Total Fat: 1
- Sodium: 63

436. Fresh Lumpia

Serving: 30 | Prep: 35mins | Cook: 25mins | Ready in:

Ingredients

- 2 tablespoons olive oil
- 1 onion, chopped
- 2 cloves garlic, crushed
- 3 (6 ounce) lean pork tenderloins, sliced into small pieces
- 4 cups uncooked medium shrimp, peeled and deveined
- 1/2 small jicama (singkamas or yambean), peeled and cut into matchsticks
- 1 1/2 cups bean sprouts
- 2/3 cup chickpeas, drained
- 1 cup fresh green beans, trimmed
- 2 stalks celery, diced
- 1 large carrot, minced
- 1 cup crushed salted peanuts
- 1 cup crushed salted peanuts, or to taste
- 1 head green leafy lettuce, or to taste

- 1 (16 ounce) package lumpia wrappers

Direction

- In a skillet set on medium heat, add olive oil. Add garlic and onion; stir-fry for 10-15 minutes until the onion turned brown and has softened. Place the garlic and onion on a plate.
- In the same skillet, cook shrimp and pork for 5-7 minutes until browned. Add back the garlic and onion; add pepper and salt to season. Mix in carrot, celery, green beans, chickpeas, bean sprouts, and jicama. Stir and cook for approximately 5 minutes until vegetables are softened. Transfer the filling mixture to a big bowl. Mix in peanuts.
- On top of a lumpia wrapper, put a lettuce leaf. Put 1 tablespoon of filling on the lettuce. Turn up wrapper, folding 1 end on the filling. Then put on a serving platter. Continue with the rest of the filling, lumpia, and lettuce.

Nutrition Information

- Calories: 156 calories;
- Sodium: 218
- Total Carbohydrate: 14.1
- Cholesterol: 35
- Protein: 10.5
- Total Fat: 6.7

437. Fresh Lumpia With Ubod

Serving: 30 | Prep: 50mins | Cook: 25mins | Ready in:

Ingredients

- 2 cups shrimp - deveined, cut into strips, heads reserved
- 2 tablespoons olive oil
- 2 cloves garlic, minced
- 1 medium onion, chopped
- 1/3 cup diced ham
- 1 chorizo de bilbao (spicy Spanish semi-cured sausage), cut into strips
- 1 (18.4 ounce) lean pork tenderloin, diced
- salt and ground black pepper to taste
- 1 tablespoon soy sauce
- 1 teaspoon white sugar
- 1/2 head cabbage, shredded
- 1 potato, cut into strips
- 2/3 cup chickpeas, drained
- 2 stalks celery, cut crosswise into slices
- 1 carrot, cut into strips
- 1 ubod (heart of palm), cut into strips
- 25 leaves lettuce
- 25 lumpia wrappers

Direction

- In a mortar, smash the shrimp heads until about 1/2 cup juice is released. Strain juice and set aside.
- In a skillet set on medium heat, add olive oil; put the garlic; stir and cook for 1-2 minutes until slightly brown; put the onion; then cook for approximately 5 minutes until glassy. Mix in chorizo and ham; cook for approximately 2 minutes until juices release. Put the pork; stir and cook for approximately 7 minutes until not pink. Add pepper and salt to season.
- Put the shrimp into the skillet; cook for approximately 3 minutes until opaque. Put in the reserved shrimp juice and combine well. Add sugar and soy sauce; stir and cook for approximately 2 more minutes mixed. Add ubod, carrot, celery, chickpeas, potato, and cabbage. Then cook for approximately 3 minutes until vegetables are softened. Allow the filling to cool for at least 10 minutes until safe to handle.
- On a lumpia wrapper, lay a lettuce leaf. Put about 2 tablespoons of the filling over the middle of the lettuce. Enclose the lower end by folding 1 end of the wrapper over the filling to secure the lower; then roll wrapper over to cover. Continue with the rest of the filling, wrappers, and lettuce.

Nutrition Information

- Calories: 92 calories;
- Total Fat: 2.9
- Sodium: 168
- Total Carbohydrate: 8.7
- Cholesterol: 27
- Protein: 7.6

---
438. Fried Rice (Sinangag)

Serving: 4 | Prep: 10mins | Cook: 20mins | Ready in:

Ingredients

- 2 teaspoons cooking oil
- 2 eggs, beaten
- 2 teaspoons cooking oil
- 2 cloves garlic, minced
- 4 cups cold, cooked white rice
- 1 tablespoon soy sauce
- 1/4 pound diced cooked ham

Direction

- In a skillet, add 2 teaspoons oil; add the eggs and cook in the hot oil for 3-5 minutes until set. Let it cool and cut into thin ribbons; reserve.
- In a large skillet, add 2 more teaspoons of oil; add the garlic and fry in the oil for approximately 5 minutes, mashing it while frying until almost crispy and light brown. Mix in the rice until it is well combined with the garlic. Mix in the soy sauce; then cook for 2 minutes. Mix the ham into the mixture; stir and cook for 5 more minutes. Add the sliced egg into the mixture and fold then cook for approximately 3 minutes until hot.

Nutrition Information

- Calories: 838 calories;
- Cholesterol: 116
- Protein: 22.2

- Total Fat: 14.8
- Sodium: 649
- Total Carbohydrate: 148.9

---
439. Fried Tulingan (Mackerel)

Serving: 4 | Prep: 10mins | Cook: 40mins | Ready in:

Ingredients

- 1 (3 1/2) pound whole mackerel, gutted and cleaned
- 2 cups water
- 1 tablespoon tamarind soup base
- 1 teaspoon fish sauce
- oil for frying

Direction

- In a pot set on medium heat, mix fish sauce, tamarind soup base, water, and mackerel. Cook at a simmer for about 15 minutes, covered. Turn over the fish, cover again, and boil for 15 more minutes. Separate from heat and let it set for 1 hour, covered.
- In a large saucepan or deep-fryer, add oil and heat to 350°F (175°C). Take the fish from the pot and use paper towels to pat dry to get rid as much excess moisture as possible.
- Then add the fish in the hot oil and fry for 7-10 minutes until golden brown. And serve immediately.

Nutrition Information

- Calories: 974 calories;
- Total Carbohydrate: 0.8
- Cholesterol: 222
- Protein: 77.6
- Total Fat: 70
- Sodium: 841

440. Garlic Rice

Serving: 4 | Prep: 5mins | Cook: 5mins | Ready in:

Ingredients

- 2 tablespoons vegetable oil
- 1 1/2 tablespoons chopped garlic
- 2 tablespoons ground pork
- 4 cups cooked white rice
- 1 1/2 teaspoons garlic salt
- ground black pepper to taste

Direction

- In a large skillet set on medium-high heat, add oil. Once the oil is hot, put the garlic and ground pork. Stir and cook until the garlic turns golden brown. For maximum flavor, this is the color you need, prevent it from burning, or the flavor will be bitter.
- Mix in the cooked white rice, and add pepper and garlic salt to season. Stir and cook for approximately 3 minutes until heated well and well combined. Serve and enjoy.

Nutrition Information

- Calories: 293 calories;
- Cholesterol: 6
- Protein: 5.9
- Total Fat: 9
- Sodium: 686
- Total Carbohydrate: 45.9

441. Ginataan

Serving: 8 | Prep: 5mins | Cook: 30mins | Ready in:

Ingredients

- 2 (14 ounce) cans coconut milk
- 3/4 cup white sugar
- 1 (20 ounce) can plantain bananas, drained
- 3/4 cup tapioca pearls
- 1 (15 ounce) can cut yams, drained
- 1/2 cup canned jackfruit, drained

Direction

- In a saucepan set on low heat, add coconut milk. Simmer for 5-10 minutes, covered, until gently bubbling. Mix in sugar until melted. Add tapioca pearls and plantain bananas. Simmer for 25-30 minutes until plantains and tapioca soften. Mix in jackfruit and yams.

Nutrition Information

- Calories: 456 calories;
- Sodium: 41
- Total Carbohydrate: 69.9
- Cholesterol: 0
- Protein: 3.1
- Total Fat: 21.2

442. Ginataang Manok (Chicken Cooked In Coconut Milk)

Serving: 6 | Prep: 10mins | Cook: 1hours5mins | Ready in:

Ingredients

- 3 tablespoons canola oil
- 1/2 cup sliced fresh ginger
- 1 (5 pound) whole chicken, cut into pieces
- salt and ground black pepper to taste
- 2 (14 ounce) cans coconut milk
- 1 (10 ounce) package frozen chopped spinach, thawed and drained

Direction

- In a large skillet set on medium heat, add canola oil then mix in the ginger slices. Stir and cook until lightly browned and scented.

Take the ginger out and reserve. Season chicken with pepper and salt. Put the chicken in the same skillet set on medium-high heat without crowding. Cook the chicken until all sides turn light brown. Put the ginger back to the skillet and add in coconut milk. Make it to a boil then close the skillet with a lid tilted to let the steam to escape. Lower heat to medium-low and simmer for approximately 30 minutes until the chicken is not pink at the bone, stirring occasionally.

- Mix in the spinach. Simmer for 8-12 minutes, without cover, until spinach is warmed well. Add pepper and salt to taste, as necessary.

Nutrition Information

- Calories: 709 calories;
- Sodium: 148
- Total Carbohydrate: 7
- Cholesterol: 103
- Protein: 39.4
- Total Fat: 59.7

443. Grandma Nena's Lumpia And Pancit

Serving: 10 | Prep: 30mins | Cook: 30mins | Ready in:

Ingredients

- 1 pound boneless, skinless chicken breast halves
- 1 pound boneless pork sirloin, cut into 1/2 inch cubes
- 1/2 head cabbage
- 4 carrots, diced
- 1/2 teaspoon salt, or to taste
- 1/2 teaspoon ground black pepper, or to taste
- 2 pinches monosodium glutamate (MSG) (optional)
- 1/8 cup all-purpose flour
- 1/8 cup water
- 30 spring roll wrappers
- 1 quart oil for frying
- 1 (8 ounce) package dry pancit (Canton) noodles
- 1 cup apple cider vinegar
- 4 cloves chopped garlic

Direction

- Put 2 quarts of water in a saucepan and make it boil. Cook in the chicken for 10-15 minutes, or until done. Set aside the chicken stock, and let the chicken cool. Slice chicken into small cubes.
- Stir-fry pork in a large skillet or a wok until equally brown. Mix in carrots, cabbage, and chicken. Then cook on medium heat until cabbage is soft. Separate from the heat, and let it slightly cool while you separate the wrappers.
- Mix water and enough flour in a small bowl to form a paste about the consistency of glue. Scoop meat mixture into a thin line on every wrapper, and roll up, enclosing the edge with a dab of the flour paste. Leave every lumpia thin; the wrapper will break if you overfill them. Keep about 1/2 to 1/4 of the filling in the pot for the pancit.
- In a large skillet, add 1/2 to 1 inch of oil to heat. Add the lumpia, one at a time, then fry until it turns golden brown. Strain, standing every piece upright, in a bowl or a pot lined with a paper towel.
- Place the rest of the filling to the stove, and cautiously stir in the pancit noodles. Slowly add the chicken stock, and cook until noodles are tender.
- To make the sauce: crush the garlic using a mortar and pestle or back of a spoon then stir into the vinegar. Serve in small bowls with spoons. You can use the sauce as a dip, or to scoop into the lumpia.

Nutrition Information

- Calories: 349 calories;
- Total Fat: 12
- Sodium: 346

- Total Carbohydrate: 38.7
- Cholesterol: 45
- Protein: 21.9

444. Grilled Chicken Adobo

Serving: 8 | Prep: 15mins | Cook: 35mins | Ready in:

Ingredients

- 1 1/2 cups soy sauce
- 1 1/2 cups water
- 3/4 cup vinegar
- 3 tablespoons honey
- 1 1/2 tablespoons minced garlic
- 3 bay leaves
- 1/2 teaspoon black pepper
- 3 pounds skinless, boneless chicken thighs

Direction

- Prepare an outdoor grill by preheating to high, then oil the grate lightly.
- Combine pepper, bay leaves, garlic, honey, vinegar, water, and soy sauce in a big pot. Make the mixture to a boil and add the chicken into the pot. Lower heat, cover, then cook for 35-40 minutes.
- Take the chicken to paper towels to drain on and reserve. Get rid of bay leaves. Bring the mixture back to a boil, then until it reduced to approximately 1 1/2 cups. Put the chicken on the prepared grill, approximately 5 minutes per side, until crisp and brown. Serve with the rest of the soy sauce mixture.

Nutrition Information

- Calories: 255 calories;
- Total Fat: 6.7
- Sodium: 2854
- Total Carbohydrate: 10.8
- Cholesterol: 141
- Protein: 36.6

445. Guinataan Chicken Adobo

Serving: 6 | Prep: 10mins | Cook: 55mins | Ready in:

Ingredients

- 4 1/2 pounds chicken leg quarters
- 3/4 cup white vinegar
- 3/4 cup water
- 1 teaspoon white sugar
- 1/4 cup soy sauce
- 2 bay leaves
- 1 teaspoon whole black peppercorns, crushed
- 1 onion, chopped
- 2 cloves garlic, crushed
- salt to taste
- 1 (14 ounce) can coconut milk

Direction

- In a large pot, mix garlic, onion, crushed peppercorns, bay leaves, soy sauce, sugar, water, vinegar, and chicken; mix and make the mixture boil for 2 minutes. Lower the heat to medium-low and cook at a simmer for 30 minutes.
- Take the chicken to a large serving platter and reserve. Change the heat under the pot to medium then cook for approximately 10 minutes until the liquid lessens by about 1-qt. Add salt to taste; mix the coconut milk into the mixture. Cook for approximately 10 minutes, covered until the coconut milk looks oil. Drop the mixture over the chicken then serve.

Nutrition Information

- Calories: 657 calories;
- Total Carbohydrate: 7.4
- Cholesterol: 192
- Protein: 57.6
- Total Fat: 43.5

- Sodium: 805

446. Halo Halo Especial

Serving: 4 | Prep: 15mins | Cook: | Ready in:

Ingredients

- 1 (12 ounce) can jackfruit, drained and diced
- 1 (12 ounce) jar sweetened white kidney beans
- 1 (12 ounce) jar red (adzuki) beans, drained
- shaved ice
- 1/2 cup evaporated milk, or to taste
- 1/2 cup vanilla ice cream, or to taste

Direction

- In a bowl, out jack fruit. Add red and white beans then blend well. Put 2 tablespoons of the jackfruit mixture in a tall glass. Add shaved ice to the glass, about 2/3 full. Add evaporated milk over the shaved ice. Use a teaspoon to mix. Put 2 tablespoons vanilla ice cream on top. Continue layering the halo halo in 3 more glasses.

Nutrition Information

- Calories: 462 calories;
- Total Carbohydrate: 94.6
- Cholesterol: 16
- Protein: 11.7
- Total Fat: 4.9
- Sodium: 241

447. Ham Hocks With Lima Beans

Serving: 5 | Prep: 15mins | Cook: 35mins | Ready in:

Ingredients

- 4 ounces dried lima beans
- 2 1/2 pounds ham hocks
- 1 (2 inch) piece fresh ginger root, sliced
- 1 large tomato, diced
- 1 onion, chopped
- 2 fresh green chile peppers
- 1 tablespoon tamarind soup base
- 3 cups water
- salt to taste
- 1 bunch fresh spinach

Direction

- In a large container, put the lima beans then add warm water to cover, about a few inches; allow it to stand for 1 hour. Drain.
- Place lightly salted water in a large pot then make it to a rolling boil over high heat. Put in the ham hocks then bring back to a boil, and cook at a boil for 1 minute. Drain and wash.
- In a stockpot, mix ham hocks and lima beans; add the 3 cups water, tamarind powder, green chile pepper, onion, tomato, and ginger. Add salt to season and taste. Make the mixture to a boil; lower heat to medium-low then simmer for approximately 20 minutes until the pork is tender and the lima beans are soft and bursting from their skins. Put the spinach to the soup then cook until the spinach has just wilted.

Nutrition Information

- Calories: 725 calories;
- Sodium: 494
- Total Carbohydrate: 25
- Cholesterol: 154
- Protein: 46.7
- Total Fat: 48.3

448. Healthier Crema De Fruta

Serving: 10 | Prep: 20mins | Cook: 20mins | Ready in:

Ingredients

- 1 1/2 cups 2% evaporated milk
- 1 1/2 cups 2% milk
- 3/4 cup white sugar
- 1/2 cup water
- 1/4 cup all-purpose flour
- 5 egg yolks
- 1 1/4 cups water
- 1 (16 ounce) can fruit cocktail in heavy syrup, syrup drained and reserved
- 3 (1 ounce) packages unflavored gelatin
- 2 tablespoons lemon juice, or to taste
- 2 (5.3 ounce) packages ladyfingers

Direction

- In a tempered glass bowl (like Pyrex®), whisk egg yolks, flour, 1/2 cup water, sugar, milk, and evaporated milk.
- Add ice water into a large bowl to fill, making an ice bath.
- In a large saucepan of boiling water, put the milk mixture; cook for 10 to 15 minutes, stirring constantly, until custard turns thick and achieves a temperature of 170°F (77°C). Then place to ice bath to cool the custard.
- In another saucepan set on medium heat, combine lemon juice, gelatin, 1 cup heavy syrup from fruit cocktail, and 1 1/4 cup water; stir and cook for 10 to 12 minutes until gelatin melts. Keep the gelatin mixture in the refrigerator for approximately 30 minutes until cooled.
- In the bottom of a deep 9x13-inch dish, layer ladyfingers; put custard layer and fruit cocktail layer on top. Keep on layering with the rest of the ingredients, finishing with gelatin mixture covering the last fruit layer. Keep in the refrigerator for 8 hours or overnight, until set.

Nutrition Information

- Calories: 336 calories;
- Protein: 16
- Total Fat: 8.6
- Sodium: 124
- Total Carbohydrate: 49.9
- Cholesterol: 183

449. Karioka Sweet Rice Balls

Serving: 5 | Prep: 10mins | Cook: 10mins | Ready in:

Ingredients

- 1 cup rice flour
- 1 cup shredded coconut
- 3/4 cup coconut milk
- 2 cups vegetable oil for frying
- Coating:
- 1/2 cup coconut milk
- 1/4 cup brown sugar

Direction

- In a bowl, whisk 3/4 cup coconut milk, shredded coconut, and rice flour until the dough is well blended. Turn dough into balls, approximately 1 tablespoon each ball.
- In a pot set on medium heat, add oil.
- Then add the dough balls and fry in the hot oil for approximately 5 minutes until lightly browned. Separate from heat and place balls to a plate lined with a paper towel.
- Put 1/2 cup coconut milk into a saucepan; make it boil. Mix brown sugar into hot coconut milk for 2-3 more minutes until liquid turns thick. Separate the saucepan from heat, let the coconut cool, coating slightly, and sink balls into the coating. Slightly cool prior to serving.

Nutrition Information

- Calories: 414 calories;
- Cholesterol: 0
- Protein: 3.5
- Total Fat: 25.4
- Sodium: 53
- Total Carbohydrate: 45.4

450. Leyley's Spicy Chicken Adobo Wings

Serving: 24 | Prep: 30mins | Cook: 1hours | Ready in:

Ingredients

- 3 pounds chicken wings, separated at joints, tips discarded
- 1 cup distilled white vinegar
- 1/2 cup water
- 2 bay leaves
- 1 teaspoon whole or cracked black peppercorns
- 1 medium onion, chopped
- 2 jalapeno peppers
- 1/2 cup soy sauce, or to taste
- 1 whole head garlic, minced

Direction

- Add water into a large pot and make it boil. Place in the wings, and boil for 5 to 8 minutes. Strain in a colander and run under warm water. Put back to the dry pot and add jalapenos, onion, peppercorns, bay leaves, water, and vinegar. Simmer for 20 minutes, over low heat.
- Add soy sauce to season the chicken, and simmer for another 10-15 minutes, or until the sauce has lessened by half. Take the wings to a colander, and reserve. Put a few garlic cloves to the liquid in the pan, and simmer until the consistency of the sauce turn syrupy, and the jalapenos have burst open releasing all of their seeds into the reduction.
- Prepare a large nonstick skillet by preheating on medium heat. Add the rest of the garlic and chicken wings. Stir and cook for approximately 10 minutes, until the wings have browned and the garlic is tender. Put the wings back to the sauce to coat prior to serving.

Nutrition Information

- Calories: 50 calories;
- Sodium: 313
- Total Carbohydrate: 1.7
- Cholesterol: 12
- Protein: 4.4
- Total Fat: 2.8

451. Lipardo's Puto Seco

Serving: 12 | Prep: 10mins | Cook: 10mins | Ready in:

Ingredients

- 1 egg
- 1/3 cup white sugar
- 1/4 cup butter, softened
- 1 cup all-purpose flour
- 1 cup cornstarch
- 1/2 cup powdered milk
- 1/2 teaspoon baking powder
- 1 dash salt

Direction

- Prepare the oven by preheating to 375°F (190°C). Prepare a baking sheet that is greased. In a bowl, mix salt, baking powder, powdered milk, cornstarch, flour, butter, white sugar, and egg. Massage for several few minutes to form a soft dough. Split the dough in 12 pieces. Then turn each piece in a ball and slightly flatten. Set 1 inch apart on prepared baking sheet.
- Place in preheated oven and bake for approximately 10 minutes until light brown. Let it fully cool and keep in an airtight container.

Nutrition Information

- Calories: 166 calories;
- Total Carbohydrate: 25.4
- Cholesterol: 31

- Protein: 3.1
- Total Fat: 5.8
- Sodium: 101

452. Lisa's Adobo

Serving: 8 | Prep: 20mins | Cook: 1hours30mins | Ready in:

Ingredients

- 1 tablespoon vegetable oil
- 2 pounds cubed pork meat
- 4 cloves garlic, chopped
- 1 (32 fluid ounce) container chicken broth
- 1/4 cup dark soy sauce
- 1/4 cup apple cider vinegar
- 5 bay leaves
- 1 (14 ounce) can unsweetened coconut milk
- 2 tablespoons all-purpose flour

Direction

- In a Dutch oven set on medium heat, add oil, then add the pork and cook until equally brown.
- Add the garlic into the Dutch oven then cook for 1 minute, until softened. Add in the cider vinegar, soy sauce, and chicken broth. Add the bay leaves into the mixture. Make it boil. Lower heat to medium-low, then cook for 1 hour, or until the pork is simply shredded with a fork. (Mix a small amount of flour with coconut milk, water, or chicken broth, then mix into the sauce for a thicker consistency.) Be sure the meat remains moist and coated with the liquid. Put a bit more water or chicken broth if the meat looks like it's drying out.
- Mix flour into coconut milk and place to the Dutch oven. Keep on cooking until heated well.

Nutrition Information

- Calories: 231 calories;
- Total Fat: 16.8
- Sodium: 1017
- Total Carbohydrate: 4.7
- Cholesterol: 42
- Protein: 15.5

453. Lolah's Chicken Adobo

Serving: 8 | Prep: 10mins | Cook: 1hours10mins | Ready in:

Ingredients

- 3 tablespoons vegetable oil
- 3 pounds boneless, skinless chicken thighs, rinsed and patted dry
- 6 cloves garlic, peeled and thinly sliced
- 1/2 cup soy sauce
- 1/2 cup apple cider vinegar
- 1/2 cup water
- 2 tablespoons pickling spice, wrapped in cheesecloth

Direction

- In a large pot set on medium heat, add oil until oil is shimmering. Add garlic and cook in oil for not more than 30 seconds. Put all of the chicken to the pot; then cook, whisking frequently, until chicken turns white all over. Keep from turning into brown. Add in water, vinegar, and soy sauce, then add in the pickling spice. Ensure the spice ball is submerged. Make it boil, lower the heat once boils, and put the lid on the pot so that some steam can get out. Simmer for 1 hour, or until chicken is very tender.

Nutrition Information

- Calories: 265 calories;
- Total Fat: 11.8
- Sodium: 1050
- Total Carbohydrate: 2.6

- Cholesterol: 141
- Protein: 34.6

454. Lumpia

Serving: 10 | Prep: 40mins | Cook: 15mins | Ready in:

Ingredients

- 3 cloves garlic, minced
- 1 cup chopped onions
- 2 tablespoons vegetable oil
- 1/2 teaspoon ground black pepper
- 1 tablespoon soy sauce
- 1 cup water
- 1/2 cup diced carrots
- 1/2 cup green beans, French cut
- 1/2 cup diced celery
- 1 (10 ounce) can bamboo shoots, julienned
- 1 (8 ounce) can water chestnuts, drained and julienned
- 1/2 cup jicama, peeled and julienned
- 1/2 cup bean sprouts
- 1 (16 ounce) package egg roll wrappers
- 1 quart vegetable oil for frying

Direction

- Stir-fry onions and garlic in hot oil in a skillet or a work until the onions are translucent. Mix in the soy sauce and pepper then stir-fry further.
- Strain the excess oil put the water and make it boil. Mix in carrots then simmer for 5 minutes. Add the jicama, water chestnuts, bamboo shoots, celery, and green beans. Simmer for 5 more minutes. Separate the pan from heat and mix in the bean sprouts. Let it cool at room temperature.
- Put 3 heaping tablespoons of filling diagonally near a corner of every wrapper, keeping a 1 1/2-in room at both ends. Then fold the side along the length of the filling on the filling, enclose both ends, and neatly roll. Maintain the roll tight as you assemble. Dampen the other side of the wrapper with water to enclose the edge. Use plastic wrap to cover the rolls to keep the moisture.
- Set a wok on medium heat, put oil to 1/2-inch depth, then heat for 5 minutes. Put 3 or 4 egg rolls in oil, cautiously. Then fry the rolls until golden brown on all sides. Transfer to paper towels to drain on. Serve right away.

Nutrition Information

- Calories: 262 calories;
- Total Carbohydrate: 32.4
- Cholesterol: 4
- Protein: 5.7
- Total Fat: 12.4
- Sodium: 391

455. Lumpia (Shanghai Version)

Serving: 20 | Prep: 1hours | Cook: 20mins | Ready in:

Ingredients

- 1 pound ground pork
- 1 pound ground beef
- 1 medium onion, finely chopped
- 1 carrot, grated
- 1/4 cup soy sauce
- 2 1/2 teaspoons black pepper
- 1 1/2 tablespoons garlic powder
- 2 tablespoons salt
- 1 (16 ounce) package spring roll wrappers
- 1 1/2 quarts oil for frying

Direction

- Mix carrot, onion, and ground beef and pork in a large bowl. Make sure to fully blend everything. I recommend using your hands, getting down and dirty. Massage the meat in the bowl if you must. Slowly mix in the salt,

garlic powder, black pepper, and soy sauce until everything are equally distributed.
- On a flat surface, lay out a few wrappers at a time, and put about 2 tablespoons of the filling in a line down the middle of the wrapper. Be sure the filling is not thicken than your thumb, or the wrapper will cook faster than the meat. Fold the bottom and top edges of the wrapper towards the center Grab the right and left sides, then fold them towards the middle. Dampen the last edge of the wrapper to enclose. Now continue with the rest of the wrappers, and have the children or hubby to help you out.
- In a heavy skillet or deep fryer, add oil to heat to 375°F (190°C). Cook lumpia, 3 or 4 at a time. Then fry for approximately 3 or 4 minutes, flipping once. Once the lumpia floats, they are cooked, and the wrapper turns golden brown. Slice in half, or serve as is paired with dipping sauce. We like banana ketchup, soy sauce with lemon, or sweet and sour sauce.

Nutrition Information

- Calories: 261 calories;
- Total Fat: 17.8
- Sodium: 1037
- Total Carbohydrate: 14.6
- Cholesterol: 38
- Protein: 10.2

456. Lumpia Filipino Shrimp And Pork Egg Rolls

Serving: 75 | Prep: 1hours | Cook: 30mins | Ready in:

Ingredients

- 1 pound ground pork
- 1 cup finely chopped raw shrimp
- 1/2 cup finely chopped onion
- 1/2 cup grated carrots
- 1/4 cup finely chopped green onions
- 3 tablespoons soy sauce
- 1 teaspoon salt
- 1/2 teaspoon black pepper
- 1 teaspoon monosodium glutamate (MSG) (optional)
- 1 (16 ounce) package spring roll wrappers
- 1 egg white, beaten
- 1 quart vegetable oil for frying

Direction

- In a bowl, combine MSG, pepper, salt, soy sauce, green onions, carrots, onion, shrimp, and ground pork until well blended.
- Take a wrapper off the pile, and use a damp cloth to cover the rest of the wrappers. On a work surface, put the wrapper. Put a thin line, about the width of your little finger, across one side of the wrapper, 1/2-inch from the edge of the wrapper. Then roll tightly the wrapper around the filling, and enclose the edges with egg white. Continue making rolls with the rest of filling and wrappers, and slice the rolls into thirds.
- In a heavy pan or deep fryer, add oil and heat to 375°F (190°C). Add 3 or 4 lumpia at a time then deep-fry for approximately 3 minutes, flipping once, until the rolls float and turn golden brown. Serve hot.

Nutrition Information

- Calories: 43 calories;
- Total Fat: 2.1
- Sodium: 115
- Total Carbohydrate: 3.7
- Cholesterol: 7
- Protein: 2.1

457. Lumpia Mollica

Serving: 25 | Prep: 30mins | Cook: 45mins | Ready in:

Ingredients

- 1 tablespoon vegetable oil
- 1 yellow onion
- 1 large stalk celery, finely chopped
- 1 large carrot, finely chopped
- salt to taste
- 2 pounds ground pork
- 1 tablespoon minced fresh garlic
- 1 teaspoon red pepper flakes
- 1 teaspoon garlic powder
- 1/2 teaspoon ground turmeric
- 1/2 teaspoon ground ginger
- 1/2 teaspoon ground cumin
- 1/2 teaspoon ground coriander
- 1/4 teaspoon celery seed
- 2 (16 ounce) packages lumpia wrappers
- 1 quart vegetable oil for frying

Direction

- In a big skillet set on medium-low heat, add 1 tablespoon vegetable oil; stir and cook carrot, celery, and onion for 5-7 minutes until onion is translucent and tender. Carrot and celery may still be crisp; add salt to taste. Add garlic and ground pork. Keep on cooking and stirring until pork is not pink. Add more salt to taste. Strain any extra grease and mix in celery seed, coriander, cumin, ginger, turmeric, garlic powder, and red pepper flakes. Reserve to cool.
- Put about 1 tablespoon pork mixture on a lumpia wrapper with one corner that is facing you. Then fold corner nearest to you on the filling, and fold 2 sides corners toward the middle and keep on rolling the wrapper around the pork. Use a small amount of water to brush on top corner and pinch to enclose. Continue with the rest of the wrappers and filling.
- In a big saucepan or deep fryer, add 1-qt vegetable oil and heat to 350°F (175°C).
- Fry in rolls in batches for 4-6 minutes until they are golden brown. Transfer to a plate lined with paper towels to drain on.

Nutrition Information

- Calories: 214 calories;
- Total Carbohydrate: 22.3
- Cholesterol: 29
- Protein: 9.6
- Total Fat: 9.2
- Sodium: 229

458. Maja Blanca (Coconut Pudding)

Serving: 10 | Prep: 15mins | Cook: 10mins | Ready in:

Ingredients

- 1/2 cup water
- 1/2 cup cornstarch
- 1 cup coconut milk
- 3/4 cup water
- 1/2 cup white sugar
- 1/4 cup fresh sweet corn kernels
- 1/4 cup sweetened flaked coconut

Direction

- Prepare an 8-inch baking dish or pie pan that is buttered, and reserve. In a bowl, combine 1/2 cup of water with the cornstarch, and mix until smooth.
- In a saucepan set on low heat, mix sugar, 3/4 cup water, and coconut milk, and whisk until sugar is melted. Make the mixture boil, mix in the corn kernels, then the cornstarch mixture, whisking quickly to prevent lumps as it turns very thick. Return mixture to a boil, and simmer for approximately 2 minutes until smooth and completely thickened, whisking constantly. Transfer the Maja Blanca in the prepared dish, and reserve to cool for approximately 2 hours until firm.
- In a dry skillet set on medium heat, add the coconut flakes, then stir to toast. Check them cautiously so they don't scorch. Take the toasted coconut flakes to a bowl, allow it to cool, and dust over the pudding prior to serving.

Nutrition Information

- Calories: 119 calories;
- Total Fat: 5.4
- Sodium: 10
- Total Carbohydrate: 18.2
- Cholesterol: 0
- Protein: 0.7

459. Maja Blanca Maiz (Corn Pudding)

Serving: 10 | Prep: 5mins | Cook: 30mins | Ready in:

Ingredients

- 1 2/3 cups coconut milk
- 1 (14.5 ounce) can cream-style corn
- 1 cup rice flour
- 1 cup white sugar

Direction

- In a nonstick pot set on medium heat, combine well the sugar, rice flour, cream-style corn, and coconut milk. Whisk frequently while cooking for approximately 30 minutes until thick. Transfer into a serving platter with a tray, or ridges, and allow it to fully cool prior to serving.

Nutrition Information

- Calories: 239 calories;
- Sodium: 121
- Total Carbohydrate: 41.1
- Cholesterol: 0
- Protein: 2.4
- Total Fat: 8.4

460. Melon Chiller

Serving: 10 | Prep: 20mins | Cook: | Ready in:

Ingredients

- 1 cantaloupe, halved and seeded
- 1 gallon water
- 2 cups white sugar
- ice cubes, as needed

Direction

- Use a melon baller or a spoon to scrape the cantaloupe meat lengthwise then put in a punch bowl; add sugar and water. Combine well until all sugar is melted. Let it chill with the addition of lots of ice cubes.

Nutrition Information

- Calories: 174 calories;
- Total Fat: 0.1
- Sodium: 23
- Total Carbohydrate: 44.5
- Cholesterol: 0
- Protein: 0.5

461. Mongo Guisado (Mung Bean Soup)

Serving: 6 | Prep: 20mins | Cook: 1hours | Ready in:

Ingredients

- 1/2 pound raw mung beans
- 2 cups water
- 2 tablespoons olive oil
- 1 onion, chopped
- 2 cloves garlic, minced
- 1/4 pound boneless pork loin, cut into 1-inch cubes
- salt and ground black pepper to taste
- 1/4 pound peeled and deveined prawns

- 1 small tomato, diced
- 3 cups chicken broth, or more as needed
- 1/2 pound fresh spinach leaves

Direction

- Place water and mung beans in a pot then make it boil; boil for approximately 40 minutes until the beans are tender. Smash the beans; reserve.
- In a big pot, add olive oil; stir and cook the garlic and onion in the hot oil for 5-7 minutes until softened. Put in the pork; add pepper and salt to taste. Keep on cooking the mixture for 3 more minutes. Cautiously mix the prawns in the mixture; cook for 2 more minutes. Stir in the tomatoes; cook for 3 more minutes. Lower heat and add the chicken broth over the mixture; let the mixture to simmer in the broth for 5 minutes.
- Mix the mashed beans to the soup; stir well. Cook for 5 more minutes, whisking frequently to avoid any of the mixture from sticking to the bottom of the pot. Put more water or chicken broth if the soup turns too thick. Mix spinach leaves in the soup then cook for 2 more minutes prior to serving hot.

Nutrition Information

- Calories: 202 calories;
- Total Carbohydrate: 22
- Cholesterol: 40
- Protein: 14.7
- Total Fat: 6.5
- Sodium: 896

462. Paksiw Na Pata (Pig's Feet Stew)

Serving: 5 | Prep: 10mins | Cook: 1hours10mins | Ready in:

Ingredients

- 3 1/4 pounds pig's feet, rinsed and patted dry
- 1 1/2 cups vinegar
- 1 1/2 cups water
- 1/3 cup soy sauce
- 1 onion, diced
- 2 cloves garlic, crushed
- 1 tablespoon whole black peppercorns, crushed
- 3 bay leaves
- 1 tablespoon white sugar
- salt to taste

Direction

- In a stockpot, mix salt, sugar, bay leaves, peppercorns, garlic, onion, soy sauce, water, vinegar, and pig's feet; make it simmer for 2-3 minutes. Lower heat to medium-low; let the stew to simmering, whisking occasionally, until the meat pulls simply from the bones and the liquid has thickened, approximately 1 hour. Then serve hot.

Nutrition Information

- Calories: 342 calories;
- Sodium: 1092
- Total Carbohydrate: 9.2
- Cholesterol: 138
- Protein: 30
- Total Fat: 20.8

463. Pan De Sal I

Serving: 20 | Prep: | Cook: | Ready in:

Ingredients

- 2 cups warm water (110 degrees F/45 degrees C)
- 2 teaspoons active dry yeast
- 1/3 cup white sugar
- 1/4 cup vegetable oil
- 1 1/2 teaspoons salt

- 6 cups all-purpose flour

Direction

- In a small mixing bowl, place the warm water and add 1 teaspoon sugar and yeast; mix to dissolves. Allow it to stand for approximately 10 minutes until creamy. Mix the rest of 15 teaspoons sugar and the oil in a large mixing bowl until smooth. Add the yeast mixture, 1 cup of flour, and salt; blend well. Mix in the rest of 5 cups flour, a half cup at a time, until the dough pulls away from the sides of the bowl.
- Roll the dough out onto a surface that is lightly floured and massage until elastic, supple, and smooth; approximately 10 minutes. Prepare a large mixing bowl that is lightly oiled, put the dough in it and flip to coat the dough with oil. Use a damp towel or plastic wrap to cover and allow it to sit in a warm place until the dough has twice in size; approximately 1 hour.
- Roll the dough out onto a surface that is lightly floured and split into 4 equal portions. Turn every piece into a cylinder and roll out into a log that is 1/2 inch in diameter. Slice each log with a sharp knife into 1/2 inch pieces. Then transfer the pieces onto two baking sheets that are lightly greased, flat side down. Cautiously press every roll down to flatten.
- Prepare the oven by preheating to 375°F (190°C).
- Use a damp cloth to cover the rolls and allow it to rise for approximately 30 minutes until twice in size.
- Bake in the preheated oven for approximately 20 minutes at 375°F (190°C), until golden brown.

Nutrition Information

- Calories: 175 calories;
- Total Fat: 3.1
- Sodium: 176
- Total Carbohydrate: 32.1
- Cholesterol: 0
- Protein: 4

464. Pan De Sal II

Serving: 15 | Prep: 2hours | Cook: 20mins | Ready in:

Ingredients

- 2 cups milk
- 3/4 cup white sugar
- 1/2 cup butter
- 1 (.25 ounce) package active dry yeast
- 1 1/2 teaspoons salt
- 1/2 teaspoon baking soda
- 1/2 teaspoon baking powder
- 6 cups all-purpose flour
- 2 tablespoons dry bread crumbs for topping

Direction

- In a small saucepan, heat the milk until it bubbles; separate from heat. Add the sugar and butter; whisk until dissolved. Allow it to cool until lukewarm. Transfer the cooled milk mixture into a large mixing bowl. Stir in the yeast until melt. Add 4 cups of the flour, baking powder and soda, and salt; whisk well to mix. Add the rest of the flour, 1/2 cup at a time, whisking well after every addition. Once the dough has pulled together, roll it out onto a surface that is lightly floured and massage for approximately 8 minutes until supple and smooth.
- Prepare a large mixing bowl that is lightly oiled, then put the dough in the bowl and roll to coat with oil. Use a damp cloth to cover and allow it to rise in a warm place for approximately 1 hour until twice in size.
- Prepare the oven by preheating to 375°F (190°C).
- Flatten the dough and roll it out onto a surface that is lightly floured. Split the dough into 12 equal portions and make into rounds. Put the rolls on 2 baking sheets that are lightly

greased. Use a damp cloth to cover and allow it to rise for approximately 40 minutes until twice in size.
- Dust with bread crumbs and place in the preheated oven then bake for approximately 15-20 minutes at 375°F (190°C) or until golden brown on tops.

Nutrition Information

- Calories: 296 calories;
- Sodium: 355
- Total Carbohydrate: 50.5
- Cholesterol: 19
- Protein: 6.6
- Total Fat: 7.3

465. Pan De Sal Filipino Bread Rolls

Serving: 20 | Prep: 3hours | Cook: 8mins | Ready in:

Ingredients

- 2 1/2 teaspoons active dry yeast
- 3 1/4 cups bread flour
- 3/4 teaspoon bread improver
- 1/4 cup sugar
- 1/4 teaspoon salt
- 2 tablespoons margarine
- 2 eggs
- 1 cup canned evaporated milk
- 1 cup canned evaporated milk
- 1/2 cup dry bread crumbs

Direction

- In a bread machine, put the yeast, bread flour, bread improver, sugar, salt, margarine, eggs, and 1 cup of evaporated milk in the order suggested by the manufacturer. Choose the Dough Cycle, and push start.
- Once the cycle has finished, take the dough out from the machine, and turn into 2 inch balls. Then dip every ball in the rest of evaporated milk, and next in the dry bread crumbs. Transfer the rolls on a baking sheet, crumb-side up. Use plastic or cloth to cover loosely, and allow it to rise for approximately 30 minutes until twice in volume.
- Prepare the oven by preheating to 350°F (175°C). Then place the rolls inside and bake for 8 minutes, or until the top and bottom are golden brown.

Nutrition Information

- Calories: 72 calories;
- Total Fat: 3.6
- Sodium: 95
- Total Carbohydrate: 7.2
- Cholesterol: 26
- Protein: 2.9

466. Pancit

Serving: 4 | Prep: 10mins | Cook: 50mins | Ready in:

Ingredients

- 1 (8 ounce) package thin rice noodles
- 1/2 pound skinless, boneless chicken legs, cut into bite-size pieces
- 1/2 pound pork tenderloin, cut into bite-size pieces
- 1/2 cup soy sauce
- ground black pepper to taste
- 1/2 medium head cabbage, shredded
- 2 carrots, shredded
- 2 green onions, chopped into 1 inch pieces
- 1/2 pound shrimp, peeled and deveined

Direction

- In a large bowl, put the rice noodles, then add warm water to cover. Once soft, cut into 4-inch lengths, strain, and reserve.

- Brown the pork and chicken in a skillet set on medium heat, until not pink. Add pepper and soy sauce to season. Take from the skillet and reserve. Stir-fry the carrots and cabbage until tender. Mix in shrimp, green onions, and noodles then cook for 4-5 minutes. Mix in the pork and chicken, then cook for 5 minutes longer.

Nutrition Information

- Calories: 484 calories;
- Protein: 40
- Total Fat: 8.4
- Sodium: 2109
- Total Carbohydrate: 59.6
- Cholesterol: 169

467. Pancit Luglug

Serving: 8 | Prep: 15mins | Cook: 35mins | Ready in:

Ingredients

- 1 (16 ounce) package dried rice vermicelli noodles
- 2 1/4 pounds small shrimp, peeled and deveined
- 1 tablespoon olive oil
- 1 onion, chopped
- 2 cloves garlic, minced
- 1 1/2 teaspoons achiote powder
- 2 1/4 pounds ground pork
- salt and ground black pepper to taste
- 2 (10.75 ounce) cans cream of chicken soup
- 3 1/4 cups chicken broth
- 3 hard-boiled eggs, crumbled (optional)
- green onions, chopped (optional)

Direction

- In a bowl with warm water, add the noodles to soak for 5 minutes. Place water in a big pot and put it on a rolling boil. Mix in noodles and return to a boil. Cook for 4-5 minutes until tender. Strain.
- Place water in a saucepan and make it to a boil. Mix in the shrimp then simmer for 2-3 minutes until opaque. Strain.
- In a skillet set on medium heat, add oil. Add garlic and onion; stir and cook for approximately 5 minutes until onions turn translucent. Place half of the mixture to a bowl and reserve. Mix achiote powder in the skillet with the rest of the garlic and onion mixture. Mix in the prawns; lower heat and allow to boil for approximately 2 minutes until thoroughly coated.
- Set a big pot over medium-high heat. Stir-fry the pork for 5-7 minutes until not pink, crumbly, and browned. Add the rest of 1/2 of the onion-garlic mixture; add pepper and salt to season. Mix in cream of chicken soup; whisk until well combined. Mix in chicken broth; stir for approximately 5 minutes until it turns to a thick sauce.
- Put a portion of the noodles on a plate, scoop a portion of sauce on, and put a small portion of shrimp mixture on top. Decorate with hard-boiled eggs and green onions.

Nutrition Information

- Calories: 698 calories;
- Cholesterol: 365
- Protein: 50.5
- Total Fat: 28
- Sodium: 1408
- Total Carbohydrate: 56

468. Pandesal

Serving: 16 | Prep: 30mins | Cook: 15mins | Ready in:

Ingredients

- 1 1/2 cups warm milk
- 3/4 cup white sugar, divided

- 1 (.25 ounce) package active dry yeast
- 4 cups bread flour
- 2 teaspoons salt
- 1/4 cup vegetable oil
- 1 cup bread crumbs

Direction

- In a large bowl, mix yeast, 2 teaspoons sugar, and milk; mix for about 5 minutes until the yeast and sugar are completely melted.
- In a large bowl, combine salt, flour, and the rest of the sugar. Add in vegetable oil and milk mixture. Whisk until dough comes together.
- Onto a flat work surface, roll dough. Massage until smooth. Form into a ball and put back into the bowl. Use a damp cloth to cover and allow it to rise for at least 1 hour, until twice in volume.
- Use a bench knife to split the dough into 4 even portions. Turn every portion into a log; cut diagonally into 1-inch pieces.
- Place bread crumbs onto a large plate. Then roll every piece of dough in bread crumbs and put on a baking sheet lined with parchment paper. Allow it to rise for 30-45 minutes until puffy.
- Prepare the oven by preheating to 375°F (190°C).
- Then place in the preheated oven and bake for 15-20 minutes until golden brown.

Nutrition Information

- Calories: 106 calories;
- Total Fat: 4.2
- Sodium: 350
- Total Carbohydrate: 15.5
- Cholesterol: 2
- Protein: 1.8

469. Party Pancit

Serving: 8 | Prep: 15mins | Cook: 15mins | Ready in:

Ingredients

- 1/2 tablespoon sesame oil
- 2 cloves garlic, minced
- 2 teaspoons minced fresh ginger root
- 1 bunch green onions, chopped into 1 inch pieces
- 2 hot chile peppers, minced
- 1 (8 ounce) package fresh mushrooms, sliced
- 1 cup chopped cooked chicken breast
- 1 cup peeled, chopped shrimp
- 3 links spicy pork sausage, sliced
- 1/2 cup sake
- 1/4 cup soy sauce
- 7 cups chicken broth
- 1 (12 ounce) package rice noodles
- 1/2 pound fresh bean sprouts
- 1/2 pound snow peas

Direction

- Sauté sausage, shrimp, chicken, mushrooms, chile peppers, green onion, ginger, and garlic in the hot oil in a large Dutch oven or wok until the sausage is lightly browned and shrimp turns pink. Mix in the soy sauce and sake and simmer for 2-3 minutes. Cover and reserve.
- Add chicken broth in a large saucepan then make it to a rolling boil. Put in the noodles then cook for 2 minutes over high heat. Drain instantly and rinse with cold water.
- Put the shrimp mixture over medium heat and put the bean sprouts; stir-fry for 2 minutes. Mix in the snow pear and stir-fry for 2 minutes. Mix in noodles and toss until well combined. Serve right away.

Nutrition Information

- Calories: 261 calories;
- Sodium: 568
- Total Carbohydrate: 35.9

- Cholesterol: 41
- Protein: 13.6
- Total Fat: 5.2

470. Philippine Longanisa De Eugenio (Sweet Sausage)

Serving: 12 | Prep: 45mins | Cook: 28mins | Ready in:

Ingredients

- 1/2 cup white sugar
- 1 teaspoon dried oregano
- 1/4 teaspoon ground ginger
- 1/2 teaspoon ground pepper
- 4 1/2 teaspoons fine salt
- 1/2 teaspoon curing salt (Prague powder #1)
- 1 tablespoon minced garlic
- 2 pounds ground pork
- 1 pound coarse ground pork back fat
- 1/4 cup distilled white vinegar
- Hog casing, rinsed well

Direction

- Mix curing salt, salt, pepper, ginger, oregano, and sugar in a small bowl until equally blended; reserve. In a large bowl, combine ground pork fat, ground pork, and garlic until mixed. Dust with spice mixture, add in white vinegar and blend well.
- Wash the sausage casings very thoroughly until all of the salt or brine is gone; at one end of the casing, tie a knot, and thread the other end onto a sausage filling tube. Fill the casing with the sausage mixture, rotating the filled casing every 2 1/2-4 inches to make links. Tie the end of the last link once all of the sausage mixtures have been used.
- Tie the ends of every sausage link securely with fine cotton kitchen twine, then slice between every link separate. Put into a plastic or glass container, cover, and let it mature for 4 days in the refrigerator, after which point they may be frozen.
- For cooking the longanisa, add 1/2 to 3/4 inches of water in a skillet then put thawed sausages. Simmer for approximately 20 minutes on medium-high heat until the water evaporates. Remove the cover, and let the sausages dry to fry in their own oil for approximately 8 more minutes until golden brown.

Nutrition Information

- Calories: 496 calories;
- Sodium: 1011
- Total Carbohydrate: 8.7
- Cholesterol: 71
- Protein: 14.6
- Total Fat: 44.4

471. Pinoy Chicken Adobo

Serving: 6 | Prep: 15mins | Cook: 45mins | Ready in:

Ingredients

- 5 pounds chicken legs and thighs, rinsed and patted dry
- 3/4 cup water
- 3/4 cup white vinegar
- 1/4 cup soy sauce
- 1 teaspoon white sugar
- 1 onion, chopped
- 2 cloves garlic, crushed
- 1 teaspoon whole black peppercorns, crushed
- 2 bay leaves
- salt to taste

Direction

- In a 6-qt pot, put the chicken. Add soy sauce, vinegar, and water on the chicken. Add the bay leaves, peppercorns, garlic, onion, and sugar to the pot; make the mixture boil for 2 minutes. Lower heat; simmer for approximately 30 minutes until the chicken is

not pink and the juices are clear. An instant-read thermometer poked in the thickest part of the thigh, near the bone should register 180°F (82°C). Take the chicken from the pot and keep on cooking the sauce for approximately 10 minutes until it thickens; add salt to taste.
- Put the chicken back to the pot, ensuring the chicken is entirely coated by the sauce. Then cook together for approximately 3 minutes until the chicken is reheated.

Nutrition Information

- Calories: 584 calories;
- Protein: 62.4
- Total Fat: 32.8
- Sodium: 815
- Total Carbohydrate: 5.6
- Cholesterol: 213

472. Plantain Egg Rolls (Turon)

Serving: 20 | Prep: 20mins | Cook: 4mins | Ready in:

Ingredients

- 1 cup white sugar
- 1/4 cup water
- 20 spring roll wrappers
- 5 plantains, peeled and quartered
- 1/3 cup brown sugar
- 1 1/2 cups vegetable oil

Direction

- In individual bowls, put water and sugar. Then separate spring roll wrappers; pile them. And peel plantains; slice in half then half again in lengthwise.
- On a clean work surface, put 1 wrapper with 1 corner fronting you. Cover 1 plantain piece in sugar; put 1 inch from the near corner of the wrapper. Turn corner over the plantain; fold up halfway. Then roll in 2 side corners; keep on rolling until almost to the top. Wet the top corner with damp fingers; complete rolling. Continue with the rest of the wrappers.
- In a deep-fryer or large saucepan, heat oil to 350°F (175°C). Put egg rolls in one layer; then fry for 2-3 minutes until the bottom turns golden brown. Turn over; dust with brown sugar. And fry for 2-3 more minutes. Place the egg rolls to a plate.

Nutrition Information

- Calories: 145 calories;
- Protein: 1.4
- Total Fat: 1.9
- Sodium: 49
- Total Carbohydrate: 32.5
- Cholesterol: < 1

473. Pochero

Serving: 6 | Prep: 20mins | Cook: 50mins | Ready in:

Ingredients

- 3 tablespoons olive oil
- 2 plantains, peeled and quartered
- 2 small potatoes, quartered
- 1 onion, chopped
- 2 cloves garlic, minced
- 4 pounds chicken legs, thighs, and wings
- 2 (4 ounce) links chorizo de bilbao (spicy Spanish semi-cured sausage), quartered
- salt and pepper to taste
- water to cover
- 2 tomatoes, diced
- 1 (15.5 ounce) can garbanzo beans, drained
- 1 small head cabbage, chopped

Direction

- In a large pot set on medium heat, add olive oil; add the potatoes and plantains then fry for

5-7 minutes in the hot oil until crisp on the outside. Take from the pot and reserve, leaving the oil in the pot.
- Stir and cook the garlic and onion in the hot oil for 5-7 minutes until the onion is glassy. Add the chorizo and chicken; add pepper and salt to taste. Then cover the pot and cook for 5 minutes.
- Add enough water over the chicken to fully cover; make it simmer and cook for 10 minutes. Mix in the tomatoes, then cook for 10 more minutes, covered. Mix the cabbage, garbanzo beans, potatoes, and plantains into the mixture. Cook for approximately 5 more minutes, covered until the cabbage is wilted and everything is hot.

Nutrition Information

- Calories: 959 calories;
- Cholesterol: 203
- Protein: 64.1
- Total Fat: 52.3
- Sodium: 886
- Total Carbohydrate: 58.9

474. Pork Afritada

Serving: 10 | Prep: 30mins | Cook: 30mins | Ready in:

Ingredients

- 2 1/4 pounds boneless pork, cut into bite-sized pieces
- 2 tablespoons soy sauce
- 1/2 lemon, juiced
- 2 pounds pork liver
- 3 tablespoons olive oil
- 2 potatoes, quartered
- 2 tablespoons olive oil
- 1 onion, chopped
- 2 cloves garlic, minced
- 2 large tomatoes, diced
- 1 green bell pepper, cut into chunks
- salt and ground black pepper to taste

Direction

- In a big pot, put the pork; then cover pork with enough water in the pot. Mix the lemon juice and soy sauce in the water. Make the mixture boil for 5 minutes. Take the meat out and reserve. Get rid of the liquid. Use fresh water to refill the pot; put the pork liver and make it boil for approximately 5 minutes. Take the liver and let it cool; slice into bite-sized portions. Reserve.
- In a big skillet set on medium-high heat, add 3 tablespoons olive oil; add the potatoes and fry in the hot oil for 7-10 minutes until cooked well and golden brown. Take the potatoes to a plate lined with paper towels. Put 2 more tablespoons olive oil to the skillet and let it get hot. Stir and cook the garlic and onion in the hot oil for 3-5 minutes until fragrant. Add the pork liver and pork to the skillet; cook for 5 minutes, covered. Mix the tomatoes into the mixture; then cook together for 5 more minutes, whisking occasionally. Put potatoes back to the skillet with green bell pepper. Add pepper and salt to season. Stir and cook for 5 more minutes.

Nutrition Information

- Calories: 324 calories;
- Total Fat: 16.9
- Sodium: 250
- Total Carbohydrate: 14.1
- Cholesterol: 189
- Protein: 28.6

475. Pork Sinigang

Serving: 4 | Prep: 15mins | Cook: 1hours | Ready in:

Ingredients

- 1 tablespoon vegetable oil

- 1 small onion, chopped
- 1 teaspoon salt
- 1 (1/2 inch) piece fresh ginger, chopped
- 2 plum tomatoes, cut into 1/2-inch dice
- 1 pound bone-in pork chops
- 4 cups water, more if needed
- 1 (1.41 ounce) package tamarind soup base (such as Knorr®)
- 1/2 pound fresh green beans, trimmed

Direction

- In a skillet set on medium heat, add vegetable oil. Mix in the onion; stir and cook for approximately 5 minutes until the onion has softened and turned glassy. Add salt to taste. Mix in the pork chops, tomatoes, and ginger. Then cover and lower heat to medium-low. Flip the pork occasionally, until browned. Add in the tamarind soup base and water. Make it boil, then lower heat. Keep on simmering for approximately 30 minutes until the pork is tender and cooked well. Mix in green beans and cook until softened.

Nutrition Information

- Calories: 240 calories;
- Total Carbohydrate: 12.2
- Cholesterol: 64
- Protein: 26.5
- Total Fat: 9.1
- Sodium: 2598

476. Pork Tocino (Sweet Cured Pork)

Serving: 10 | Prep: 20mins | Cook: 10mins | Ready in:

Ingredients

- 4 1/2 pounds boneless pork shoulder
- 2 1/4 cups brown sugar
- 3 tablespoons seasoned salt
- 1 tablespoon garlic salt
- 1 tablespoon ground black pepper
- 1 teaspoon curing salt (Prague powder #1)
- cooking oil

Direction

- Slice the pork into thin cuts measuring about 4-inch square; smaller portions are ok.
- In a bowl, mix curing salt, pepper, garlic salt, seasoned salt, and brown sugar; dust every pork slices with the mixture. In a large container with a cover, lay the pork slices flat. Allow it to sit in the refrigerator for 3 to 4 days prior to using it.
- To make the tocino, mix the desired portion of pork with enough water to cover in a large nonstick skillet and make it boil for approximately 5 minutes. Strain and get rid of the water. Then fully dry the pan.
- In a skillet set on medium heat, add oil; then fry the pork slices in the hot oil for 1-2 minutes each side, until lightly browned.

Nutrition Information

- Calories: 440 calories;
- Cholesterol: 81
- Protein: 24.9
- Total Fat: 15.6
- Sodium: 1672
- Total Carbohydrate: 50.1

477. Pork And Chicken Adobo

Serving: 4 | Prep: 20mins | Cook: 55mins | Ready in:

Ingredients

- 1 1/4 pounds boneless pork loin roast, cut into 2-inch pieces
- 1 1/4 pounds boneless, skinless chicken thighs, trimmed and cut into 2-inch pieces
- 2 teaspoons salt, or amount to taste

- 1/2 tablespoon black peppercorns, coarsely ground
- 2 tablespoons crushed garlic
- 2 bay leaves, torn
- 1 cup white vinegar
- 1/4 cup soy sauce
- 1 tablespoon vegetable oil
- 2 cloves garlic, smashed

Direction

- Season chicken and pork with pepper and salt then put in a stock pot. Knead with torn bay leaf and crushed garlic, then coat using soy sauce and vinegar. Keep in the refrigerator to marinate, covered, for a minimum of 2 hours or up to overnight. Place the marinating liquid and meat in a Dutch oven or cast-iron casserole then boil. Lower heat to simmer and cook for approximately 30 minutes until meat is tender. If needed, put water to avoid the sauce from getting dry.
- Drain liquid from the meat and reserve; get rid of bay leaves. In a big skillet set on medium-high heat, add 1 tablespoon oil. Brown the chicken and pork on all sides; lower heat and mix in the rest of 2 cloves of smashed garlic. Stir and cook for 2 more minutes. Add in the leftover cooking liquid and keep on boiling until the sauce turns slightly thickened. Then serve hot.

Nutrition Information

- Calories: 251 calories;
- Total Fat: 14.9
- Sodium: 2106
- Total Carbohydrate: 3.7
- Cholesterol: 67
- Protein: 24.3

478. Prawns In Peanut Soup

Serving: 6 | Prep: 15mins | Cook: 30mins | Ready in:

Ingredients

- 2 cups water
- salt to taste
- 2 1/4 pounds peeled and deveined prawns
- 1/2 pound fresh green beans, trimmed
- 1 large eggplant, diced
- 1/2 pound bok choy, chopped
- 2 tablespoons olive oil
- 1 onion, chopped
- 2 cloves garlic, minced
- 1 teaspoon achiote powder
- 3 tablespoons smooth peanut butter

Direction

- Place salt and water in a big pot then boil. Then put prawns in the water and boil; boil for 5 minutes. Take the prawns using a strainer and reserve.
- Cook the bok choy, eggplant, and beans in the water for approximately 3 minutes until they are slightly tender. Strain and set aside the liquid. Reserve the vegetables. In a big skillet set on medium heat, add the olive oil; stir and cook the garlic and onion in the hot oil for approximately 5 minutes until fragrant. Dust the achiote powder over the mixture; mix until you make an even orange-red hue. Mix in peanut butter and keep on whisking until the peanut butter has dissolved evenly in the mixture. Mix the reserved water into the mixture and make it boil; boil for 3 minutes prior to stirring in the vegetables and prawns. Keep on boiling everything for 2 more minutes prior to serving.

Nutrition Information

- Calories: 280 calories;
- Sodium: 396
- Total Carbohydrate: 15.5
- Cholesterol: 259
- Protein: 32.7
- Total Fat: 10.4

479. Puto

Serving: 18 | Prep: 20mins | Cook: 30mins | Ready in:

Ingredients

- 4 cups all-purpose flour
- 2 cups white sugar
- 1 tablespoon baking powder
- 6 eggs
- 1 (12 fluid ounce) can evaporated milk
- 1 1/2 cups water
- 2 1/4 cups Edam cheese, shredded

Direction

- Grease ramekins, puto molds, or small cake for use in a steamer. In a bowl, combine baking powder, sugar, and flour. In another large bowl, whisk the eggs with the water and evaporated milk. Add the dry ingredients mixture into the eggs then fold until equally combined. Then stuff the prepared mold 2/3 of the way up with the batter and put shredded cheese on top.
- Add a few inches of water into a saucepan or a wok to fill that will hold a steamer basket. Make the water boil over medium-high heat. Set the molds into a steamer basket and put over the boiling water and cover.
- Steam for approximately 30 minutes until a toothpick pricked in the middle of one of the putos comes out clean. Transfer to a wire rack to cool and serve at room temperature or warm.

Nutrition Information

- Calories: 290 calories;
- Sodium: 265
- Total Carbohydrate: 46.1
- Cholesterol: 81
- Protein: 9.9
- Total Fat: 7.5

480. Quick And Easy Pancit

Serving: 6 | Prep: 20mins | Cook: 20mins | Ready in:

Ingredients

- 1 (12 ounce) package dried rice noodles
- 1 teaspoon vegetable oil
- 1 onion, finely diced
- 3 cloves garlic, minced
- 2 cups diced cooked chicken breast meat
- 1 small head cabbage, thinly sliced
- 4 carrot, thinly sliced
- 1/4 cup soy sauce
- 2 lemons - cut into wedges, for garnish

Direction

- In a large bowl, put the rice noodles, and add warm water to cover. Once soft, drain, and reserve.
- In a large skillet or a wok set over medium heat, add oil. Stir-fry garlic and onion until soft. Mix in soy sauce, carrots, and chicken cabbage. Then cook until the cabbage starts to soften. Mix in noodles, and cook, whisking constantly, until heated well. Place the pancit to a serving dish and decorate with quartered lemon.

Nutrition Information

- Calories: 369 calories;
- Total Fat: 4.9
- Sodium: 789
- Total Carbohydrate: 65.1
- Cholesterol: 35
- Protein: 18.1

481. Rumaki

Serving: 12 | Prep: 20mins | Cook: 15mins | Ready in:

Ingredients

- 1 1/2 cups teriyaki sauce
- 1/2 teaspoon minced garlic
- 1/2 teaspoon minced fresh ginger root
- 12 ounces fresh chicken livers, halved
- 1 (4 ounce) can water chestnuts, drained and sliced
- 12 slices bacon, cut in half
- 1 quart oil for frying

Direction

- Combine ginger root, garlic, and teriyaki sauce in a medium bowl. Add water chestnuts and chicken livers in the mixture. Keep in the refrigerator to marinate, at least 2 hours.
- In a large, heavy saucepan, heat oil to 375°F (190°C).
- Then wrap every half of bacon slice around one chicken liver half and a slice of water chestnut. Enclose by skewering with toothpicks or small skewers. Gently lower skewered wraps into the hot oil in small batches. Then deep fry for 3-4 minutes, or until the bacon is equally brown and of achieved the crispness you want. Separate from heat and transfer to paper towels to drain.

Nutrition Information

- Calories: 259 calories;
- Total Fat: 21.3
- Sodium: 1633
- Total Carbohydrate: 6.1
- Cholesterol: 116
- Protein: 10.1

482. Salmon Sarciado

Serving: 2 | Prep: 10mins | Cook: 30mins | Ready in:

Ingredients

- 2 salmon steaks
- salt and pepper to taste
- 3 tablespoons cooking oil, divided
- 1 onion, chopped
- 2 cloves garlic, crushed
- 2 tomatoes, diced
- 1 egg, beaten

Direction

- Season each side of salmon steaks with pepper and salt.
- Over medium heat, heat two tablespoons of cooking oil in a skillet and then briefly fry salmon in the hot oil for about 2 minutes on each side until cooked lightly. Take out from the skillet and reserve.
- Into the skillet, pour in 1 tablespoon of cooking oil and let it get hot before placing in garlic and onion. Cook while stirring in the hot oil for about 5 minutes until fragrant. Mix diced tomatoes into the mixture and then add pepper and salt to taste. Continue to cook for about 5 minutes until moisture from tomatoes makes a sauce. Place the salmon back into the skillet and let to simmer in the sauce for about 10 minutes until fish easily flakes with a fork. Mix beaten egg into the sauce until integrated well. Serve while still hot.

Nutrition Information

- Calories: 537 calories;
- Sodium: 195
- Total Carbohydrate: 17.6
- Cholesterol: 169
- Protein: 42.1
- Total Fat: 33.3

483. Salmon Stew (Abalos Style)

Serving: 4 | Prep: 10mins | Cook: 25mins | Ready in:

Ingredients

- 1 tablespoon olive oil
- 4 cloves garlic, minced
- 1 onion, diced
- 1 tomato, diced
- 1 (14.75 ounce) can pink salmon
- 2 1/2 cups water
- bay leaf (optional)
- salt and ground black pepper to taste
- 1 teaspoon fish sauce (optional)

Direction

- In a skillet set on medium heat, add olive oil. Mix in the onion and garlic; stir and cook for approximately 5 minutes until the onion has softened and turned glassy. Mix in tomato and cook until tender, then put in the salmon. Flake the salmon and keep on cooking for 3 minutes. Mix in fish sauce, pepper, salt bay leaf, and water. Make it to a simmer. Cook for 20 minutes, covered.

Nutrition Information

- Calories: 223 calories;
- Cholesterol: 45
- Protein: 24.9
- Total Fat: 11
- Sodium: 466
- Total Carbohydrate: 4.8

484. Salpicao Jalisco

Serving: 10 | Prep: 15mins | Cook: 15mins | Ready in:

Ingredients

- 3 tablespoons extra-virgin olive oil
- 4 bulbs garlic, peeled and sliced
- 3 pounds beef sirloin or top round, cut into 3/4 inch cubes
- salt and pepper to taste
- 1 dash hot pepper sauce (e.g. Tabasco™)
- 2 tablespoons all-purpose flour

Direction

- In a large skillet set on medium heat, add oil. Add garlic and fry until just starting to turn golden; use a slotted a spoon to take the garlic out and reserve. Put the beef to the oil, then fry until the outside turned brown. While the beef is browning, add hot pepper sauce, pepper, and salt generously to season. Put the garlic back to the pan, then cook until the meat has achieved the degree of doneness that you wished. It's great at medium to medium-well. Use a slotted spoon to take the beef out to a serving dish.
- Combine about 1 cup of water and flour, then place over the drippings in the pan. Use a fork to mix until smooth. Boil over medium heat until thickened. Then place over the beef in the serving dish.

Nutrition Information

- Calories: 491 calories;
- Total Fat: 33.5
- Sodium: 89
- Total Carbohydrate: 8.6
- Cholesterol: 120
- Protein: 36.9

485. Sati Babi

Serving: 8 | Prep: 15mins | Cook: 15mins | Ready in:

Ingredients

- 3 pounds pork butt roast, cut into 1 1/2 inch cubes
- 3/4 teaspoon salt
- 1/8 teaspoon ground black pepper
- 1 tablespoon ground coriander
- 1 tablespoon cumin seed
- 1/2 teaspoon vegetable oil
- 1/2 cup sliced onions
- 1 tablespoon brown sugar

- 1/3 cup soy sauce
- 1/4 teaspoon ground ginger
- 3 limes, cut into wedges

Direction

- Combine vegetable oil. Cumin seed, coriander, pepper, and salt in a glass bowl. Put in pork cubes and mix to coat. Allow it to stand for 20 minutes. Add ginger, soy sauce, brown sugar, and onion; whisk to combine. Keep in the refrigerator for a minimum of 1 hour, covered, but preferably overnight.
- Prepare an outdoor grill by preheating to high, then put oil on the grate lightly. Onto skewers, thread the pork cubes.
- Place on the grill and cook, frequently basting with the rest of the marinade. Flip occasionally until cooked well, approximately 15 minutes. Serve drizzled with lime juice to taste. Get rid of any marinade that is not used.

Nutrition Information

- Calories: 224 calories;
- Total Carbohydrate: 6.6
- Cholesterol: 71
- Protein: 20.2
- Total Fat: 13
- Sodium: 873

486. Savory Mussels

Serving: 4 | Prep: 20mins | Cook: 20mins | Ready in:

Ingredients

- 2 tablespoons olive oil
- 1 onion, chopped
- 2 cloves garlic, minced
- 1 carrot, sliced
- 1 stalk celery, sliced
- 3 1/4 cups chicken broth
- 2 1/4 pounds mussels, cleaned and debearded
- 1 bunch fresh spinach, leaves torn in half

Direction

- In a large pot set on medium heat, add olive oil. Cook the garlic and onion in the hot oil for 5-7 minutes until tender. Mix the celery and carrot into the mixture and keep on cooking for 7-10 more minutes until the celery and carrot have also softened.
- Add the chicken broth into the pot and make it boil; cook at a simmer for 5 minutes. Stir in the mussels; then close the pot and let the mussels to simmer in the broth mixture for approximately 5 minutes just until they start to open. Get rid of any mussels which do not open. Mix the spinach into the broth just prior to serving hot.

Nutrition Information

- Calories: 335 calories;
- Protein: 34.4
- Total Fat: 13.4
- Sodium: 1763
- Total Carbohydrate: 18.3
- Cholesterol: 76

487. Singkamas (Jicama) Salad

Serving: 10 | Prep: 30mins | Cook: | Ready in:

Ingredients

- 1 large jicama, peeled and cut into matchsticks
- 1 red bell pepper, cut into long thin strips
- 1 green bell pepper, cut into long thin strips
- 1 small red onion, sliced into thin lengthwise slivers
- 2 green chile peppers - halved lengthwise, seeded, and cut into strips
- 1 (2 inch) piece fresh ginger root, thinly sliced
- 1 carrot, cut into matchsticks
- 1 cup water

- 2/3 cup vinegar
- 2/3 cup white sugar
- 1 teaspoon salt

Direction

- Mix carrot, ginger, green chile peppers, red onion, green bell pepper, red bell pepper and jicama together in a big bowl. In a separate bowl, whisk salt, sugar, vinegar and water together. Spread over the vegetable mixture; toss to coat. Leave in the fridge at least 1 hour then serve.

Nutrition Information

- Calories: 113 calories;
- Sodium: 244
- Total Carbohydrate: 27.5
- Cholesterol: 0
- Protein: 1.4
- Total Fat: 0.2

488. Sinigang (Pork Spare Ribs In Sour Soup)

Serving: 6 | Prep: 30mins | Cook: 1hours | Ready in:

Ingredients

- 2 1/4 pounds pork spareribs
- 3 pounds raw taro root, peeled and cut into 1/2-inch cubes
- 2 cups water
- 1 onion, chopped
- 1 small white radish, peeled and chopped
- 2 large green chile peppers, chopped
- 1 small tomato, quartered
- 1 tamarind pod
- 1 (1/2 inch) piece fresh ginger root, peeled and chopped
- salt to taste
- 3 pounds fresh green beans, trimmed
- 1 small eggplant, chopped

Direction

- Add water in a large pot and make it boil; add spareribs and boil for 15 minutes; strain. Wash well the spareribs with cold water. Wash the pot and put it back to the stovetop.
- Put the spareribs back to the pot; add salt, ginger, tamarind, tomato, green chiles, radish, onion, 2 cups of water, and taro. Make the soup boil. Then cook for approximately 30 minutes, until vegetables and pork are tender. An instant-read thermometer poked near the rib bone should register 145°F (63°C).
- Add the eggplant and green beans into the soup. Then cook for 5-7 more minutes until tender. Drain soup into bowls. And pile the vegetables and pork on a serving platter while hot.

Nutrition Information

- Calories: 623 calories;
- Total Fat: 40.5
- Sodium: 195
- Total Carbohydrate: 34.8
- Cholesterol: 136
- Protein: 34.5

489. Sinigang Na Bangus (Filipino Milkfish In Tamarind Broth)

Serving: 5 | Prep: 20mins | Cook: 15mins | Ready in:

Ingredients

- 5 cups water
- 2 onions, sliced
- 2 tomatoes, sliced
- 1 pound milkfish (bangus), cut into 5 pieces
- 2 small eggplants, sliced 1/8-inch thick
- 1 cup fresh green beans, cut into 1-inch pieces
- 2 white radishes (labanos), sliced
- 5 pods okra, sliced

- 3 small green chile peppers
- 1 cup watercress (kangkong) leaves and stems
- 1/2 cup tamarind powder
- salt to taste (optional)

Direction

- Add water into a pot. Add tomatoes and onions, and make it boil, covered. Add in green chile peppers, okra, radishes, beans, eggplants, and milkfish. Boil for 5 minutes. Mix in tamarind powder and watercress. Then cover, lower the heat, and add salt to taste. Boil for 5 minutes until the fish is cooked well.

Nutrition Information

- Calories: 291 calories;
- Sodium: 126
- Total Carbohydrate: 38.1
- Cholesterol: 47
- Protein: 23.2
- Total Fat: 6.8

490. Sinigang Na Isda Sa Miso (Fish Stew With Miso)

Serving: 4 | Prep: 30mins | Cook: 20mins | Ready in:

Ingredients

- 2 tablespoons vegetable oil
- 1 onion, sliced
- 3 cloves garlic, crushed
- 1 (1 inch) piece fresh ginger, sliced
- 2 tomatoes, sliced
- 3 tablespoons miso paste, or more to taste
- 1 teaspoon patis (fish sauce), or to taste
- 5 cups water
- 2 pounds red snapper fillets
- 1 white (daikon) radish, sliced
- 3 green chile peppers, or more to taste
- 1 bunch Chinese mustard greens with stalks
- 2 tablespoons kalamansi (Filipino lemon) juice, or more to taste

Direction

- In a pot set on medium heat, add oil. Add ginger, garlic, and onion; stir and cook for approximately 5 minutes until onions become translucent. Mix in tomatoes; stir and cook for approximately 5 minutes until mushy. Mix in fish sauce and miso paste; boil for approximately 2 minutes until flavors blend.
- Add water in the pot; boil. Add the radish and fish fillets; then boil for approximately 2 minutes until radish softens slightly. Mix in calamansi juice, mustard, greens, and chile peppers. Boil for 1-2 minutes, without cover, until greens have wilted.

Nutrition Information

- Calories: 404 calories;
- Total Fat: 11.2
- Sodium: 730
- Total Carbohydrate: 23.6
- Cholesterol: 83
- Protein: 52.8

491. Siopao (Filipino Steamed Buns)

Serving: 16 | Prep: 30mins | Cook: | Ready in:

Ingredients

- 3 1/3 cups all-purpose flour
- 1/2 cup white sugar
- 1/2 teaspoon salt
- 1 (.25 ounce) package active dry yeast
- 1 cup lukewarm water
- 1/4 cup vegetable oil
- 1 teaspoon vegetable oil, or as needed

Direction

- In a large bowl, combine yeast, salt, sugar, and flour. Add 1/4 cup oil and water; stir into a dough. Massage for at least 10 minutes until elastic and smooth. Sprinkle with extra flour if needed.
- Warm up the oven for 1 minute. Switch off the oven.
- Put in a large bowl; put the dough inside and use cheesecloth to cover. Put in the warmed oven for approximately 1 hour, until twice in volume.
- Smash down the dough. Place in the oven for at least 15 more minutes until risen. Onto a flat work surface, massage the dough and split into 12 golf-sized balls. Turn out every ball and stuff with choice of filling (look at footnote for my chicken and pork filling). Collect and tiwst the edges together to enclose the filling.
- Put every siopao on a 3x3-inch piece of wax paper.
- Put the siopao in a steamer then steam for 30 minutes.

Nutrition Information

- Calories: 153 calories;
- Total Fat: 4
- Sodium: 74
- Total Carbohydrate: 26.3
- Cholesterol: 0
- Protein: 2.9

492. Siopao (Filipino Steamed Dumplings)

Serving: 15 | Prep: 45mins | Cook: 30mins | Ready in:

Ingredients

- 1 tablespoon active dry yeast
- 1 1/2 cups lukewarm water
- 1/4 cup white sugar
- 4 1/2 cups rice flour, divided
- 1/2 cup solid vegetable shortening, divided
- 1 teaspoon vegetable oil
- 1 large onion, diced
- 1 clove garlic, chopped, or to taste
- 1 1/2 pounds shredded cooked chicken meat
- 1/4 cup soy sauce
- 2 teaspoons white sugar
- 1/2 cup diced green onion
- 1 pinch salt and black pepper to taste
- 1 teaspoon cornstarch, if needed (optional)

Direction

- Melt the yeast in the water; mix in the sugar and whisk in 2 1/2 cups of rice flour to form a soft sponge. Reserve in a warm place to twice in bulk, approximately 40 minutes. Stir in 1/4 cup shortening and another 2 cups rice flour then put the dough on a work surface that is greased; massage in the rest of 1/4 cup of shortening to form a smooth dough. Slice the dough in 15 equal-sized portions; turn each piece into a ball.
- In a skillet set on medium heat, add vegetable oil; stir and cook garlic and onion in the hot oil for approximately 5 minutes until translucent. Mix in the pepper, salt, green onion, 2 teaspoons of sugar, soy sauce, and chicken. Add cornstarch to thicken the mixture if it's juicy.
- Working on a work surface that is lightly greased, use the heel of your hand to flatten a dough ball in a circle approximately 4-inches in diameter. Put about 1 tablespoon of filling into the middle of the dough ball, take the edges of the dough together at the top, then pinch and spin to enclose the filling. Put every filled dumpling on waxed paper with the pinched seal at the bottom while you complete the rest of the dumplings.
- Use cooking spray to coat a multi-layered bamboo steamer, set the steamer on top of a big saucepan, and add in water to a few inches below steamer. Make the water boil.
- Working in a few batches, put 3 or 4 filled buns into every steamer layer without allowing the buns touch each other or the edge

of the steamer, then close the steamer, and allow the buns steam on medium-low heat until the dough is springy and puffy, approximately 15 minutes each batch. Then serve warm.

Nutrition Information

- Calories: 346 calories;
- Sodium: 270
- Total Carbohydrate: 43.9
- Cholesterol: 34
- Protein: 16
- Total Fat: 11.2

493. Siopao Chicken And Pork Filling

Serving: 16 | Prep: 20mins | Cook: 20mins | Ready in:

Ingredients

- 2 tablespoons olive oil
- 1 onion, chopped
- 2 cloves garlic, minced
- 2 1/4 pounds pork loin, diced
- 2 1/4 pounds chicken thighs, deboned and diced
- 1/4 cup soy sauce
- 1 tablespoon white sugar
- salt and ground black pepper to taste

Direction

- In a wok set on medium-high heat, add olive oil. Stir-fry garlic and onion for approximately 5 minutes until the onion turns translucent. Add chicken and pork; mix and cook for approximately 5 minutes until browned lightly. Mix in sugar and soy sauce. Combine well; add pepper and salt to season. Boil for approximately 10 more minutes until the mixture is almost dry and chicken and pork

are not pink. Allow it cool prior to filling siopao dough.

Nutrition Information

- Calories: 183 calories;
- Sodium: 292
- Total Carbohydrate: 1.9
- Cholesterol: 74
- Protein: 22.3
- Total Fat: 8.9

494. Slow Cooker Adobo Chicken With Bok Choy

Serving: 4 | Prep: 10mins | Cook: 8hours5mins | Ready in:

Ingredients

- 2 onions, sliced
- 4 cloves garlic, smashed
- 2/3 cup apple cider vinegar
- 1/3 cup soy sauce
- 1 tablespoon brown sugar
- 1 bay leaf
- ground black pepper to taste
- 8 skinless, bone-in chicken thighs
- 2 teaspoons paprika
- 1 large head bok choy, cut into 1-inch strips
- 2 green onions, sliced thinly

Direction

- In a slow cooker, mix bay leaf, brown sugar, soy sauce, garlic, onions and apple cider vinegar then season it with black pepper. Set the chicken thighs on top of the mixture and scatter paprika all over it. Cover it up and leave it cooking on a low setting for 8 hours then switch it to high after. Mix the bok choy and continue cooking for 5 more minutes. Decorate with green onion and serve.

Nutrition Information

- Calories: 458 calories;
- Total Fat: 23.1
- Sodium: 1394
- Total Carbohydrate: 20.8
- Cholesterol: 128
- Protein: 40.4

495. Slow Cooker Chicken Afritad

Serving: 6 | Prep: 10mins | Cook: 3hours | Ready in:

Ingredients

- 1 pound skinless, boneless chicken breast halves, cut into cubes
- 1/2 cup soy sauce, or to taste
- 1/2 cup olive oil, or to taste
- 1 lemon, juiced
- 3 cloves garlic, minced
- ground black pepper to taste
- 2 tomatoes, cubed
- 2 carrots, chopped
- 3 red potatoes, cubed
- 1 onion, sliced (optional)
- 1 green bell pepper, sliced
- 1 red bell pepper, sliced
- 1 yellow bell pepper, sliced
- 1 cup green peas

Direction

- In a slow cooker, mix black pepper, garlic, lemon juice, olive oil, soy sauce, and chicken; let it marinate for 10-15 minutes.
- Mix peas, red, green, and yellow bell pepper, onion, red potatoes, carrots, and tomatoes into chicken mixture.
- Then cook for 3-4 hours on high heat or on low heat for 7-8 hours.

Nutrition Information

- Calories: 332 calories;
- Total Fat: 20
- Sodium: 1260
- Total Carbohydrate: 19.9
- Cholesterol: 39
- Protein: 19.4

496. Squash And Coconut Milk Stew

Serving: 4 | Prep: 40mins | Cook: 40mins | Ready in:

Ingredients

- 1 tablespoon butter
- 1 (1 inch) piece fresh ginger, minced
- 1 clove garlic, minced
- 1 small onion, chopped
- 1 acorn squash, peeled and cut into 1-inch cubes
- 1 (14 ounce) can coconut milk
- 8 ounces green beans, cut into 3-inch pieces
- 8 ounces cooked shrimp, peeled and deveined
- 1 (14 ounce) package extra-firm tofu, cut into 1/2-inch cubes
- Salt and pepper to taste
- 2 tablespoons white sugar

Direction

- In a large skillet set on medium heat, add butter to dissolve. Add onion, garlic, and ginger. Cook for approximately 5 minutes until garlic starts to brown.
- Add green beans, coconut milk, and squash to skillet. Make it boil over high heat, then change heat to medium, cover, and simmer for 30 minutes until squash is softened, whisking occasionally. Mix in tofu and shrimp, and add sugar, pepper, and salt to season and taste.

Nutrition Information

- Calories: 449 calories;

- Total Carbohydrate: 30.1
- Cholesterol: 117
- Protein: 23.9
- Total Fat: 29.3
- Sodium: 174

497. Stuffed Filipino Fish (Bangus Relleno)

Serving: 4 | Prep: 40mins | Cook: 20mins | Ready in:

Ingredients

- 1 (8 ounce) fillet whole milkfish (bangus), or to taste
- 1 lemon
- 1 tablespoon soy sauce
- 2 tablespoons olive oil
- 1 onion
- 2 cloves garlic, crushed
- 6 1/2 tablespoons green peas
- 1 carrot, diced
- 1 stalk celery, diced
- 1/4 cup raisins, or more to taste
- salt and ground black pepper to taste
- vegetable oil for frying

Direction

- Get rid of the gills, scales, and insides of milkfish; slice off part of the tail. Loosen it up by smashing the fish firmly. Slice fish open lengthwise from the backside. Drag the meat out into a saucepan set on medium-high heat, being cautious not to tear the skin.
- Press 1/2 the lemon into the fish meat; add in soy sauce. Make it boil; then cook for approximately 2 minutes, until the liquid is absorbed. Separate from heat and allow it to cool for 5-10 minutes. Take the fish bones from the meat.
- In a skillet set on medium-high heat, add olive oil. Add garlic and onion; stir-fry until the onion turns glassy. Add the pepper, salt, raisins, celery, carrot, peas, and fish meat. Then cook for approximately 5 minutes until fish is opaque and flavors are mixed. Allow the filling to cool for at least 7 minutes until safe to handle. Fill the fish skin with the filling. Stitch up any openings to enclose in the filling. In a deep saucepan, heat vegetable oil. Then add the stuffed fish whole and fry for 5-7 minutes, flipping as necessary, until crisp and golden brown. Transfer on a plate or flat work surface and cut fish crosswise.

Nutrition Information

- Calories: 264 calories;
- Sodium: 344
- Total Carbohydrate: 18.4
- Cholesterol: 30
- Protein: 14
- Total Fat: 16.3

498. Tokneneng (Filipino Street Food)

Serving: 4 | Prep: 20mins | Cook: 20mins | Ready in:

Ingredients

- 12 eggs
- oil for deep frying
- 4 tablespoons cornstarch, plus more as needed
- bamboo skewer
- Sauce:
- 1/4 cup rice vinegar
- 1/4 cup ketchup
- 1/4 cup brown sugar
- 2 teaspoons soy sauce
- Batter:
- 1 cup all-purpose flour
- 1/2 cup water
- salt and freshly ground black pepper to taste
- red and yellow food coloring

Direction

- In a saucepan, put the eggs and add water to cover. Make it boil, separate from the heat, and allow the eggs to stand in hot water for 15 minutes. Take the eggs from hot water, let cool under cold running water, and remove the skin.
- In a saucepan, mix soy sauce, brown sugar, ketchup, and rice vinegar. Set on medium heat while whisking until sugar has melted, approximately 5 minutes. Whisk sauce and allow it to cool.
- Ready the batter by putting a few drops of yellow and red food coloring to the water to get a deep orange color. In a bowl, mix pepper, salt, and flour; add in orange water and mix until free from lumps.
- In a wok, heat oil to 375°F (190°C).
- Cautiously roll eggs in cornstarch to coat and jiggle off extra cornstarch. Then sink into the orange batter so they are completely covered. Use a bamboo skewer to poke eggs and put into the hot oil. Then deep fry for approximately 2 minutes each side, until the batter turns crispy. Use a slotted spoon to take the eggs out and transfer to paper towels to drain.

Nutrition Information

- Calories: 790 calories;
- Total Fat: 57.5
- Sodium: 546
- Total Carbohydrate: 49.7
- Cholesterol: 491
- Protein: 20.3

499. Traci's Adobo Seasoning

Serving: 21 | Prep: 5mins | Cook: | Ready in:

Ingredients

- 2 tablespoons salt
- 1 tablespoon paprika
- 2 teaspoons ground black pepper
- 1 1/2 teaspoons onion powder
- 1 1/2 teaspoons dried oregano
- 1 1/2 teaspoons ground cumin
- 1 teaspoon garlic powder
- 1 teaspoon chili powder

Direction

- Mix chili powder, garlic powder, cumin, oregano, onion powder, black pepper, paprika, and salt in a bowl. Keep a sealed jar set in a dry, cool place.

Nutrition Information

- Calories: 4 calories;
- Total Carbohydrate: 0.7
- Cholesterol: 0
- Protein: 0.2
- Total Fat: 0.1
- Sodium: 666

500. Turon (Caramelized Banana Triangles)

Serving: 15 | Prep: 30mins | Cook: 15mins | Ready in:

Ingredients

- Filling:
- 1 tablespoon butter
- 1 banana, halved lengthwise
- 1/4 cup brown sugar
- 1 dash ground cinnamon
- Paste:
- 1 tablespoon water
- 1 tablespoon all-purpose flour
- Sprinkle:
- 1 tablespoon white sugar
- 1/4 teaspoon ground cinnamon
- 5 lumpia wrappers, cut into thirds, or more as needed
- vegetable oil for frying

Direction

- In a skillet set over medium-high heat, add butter to dissolve. Add in 1 dash cinnamon and brown sugar then stir. Combine thoroughly until bubbles begin to form. Mix in banana; cook for approximately 5 minutes, whisking cautiously, until it begins to brown. Place banana to a bowl; use a spoon to roughly cut into 1/4-inch chunks. Allow the filling to cool briefly.
- In a small bowl, mix flour and water to form the paste. In a separate small bowl, combine 1/4 teaspoon cinnamon and white sugar.
- On a flat work surface, lay 1 lumpia strip. Put 3/4- to 1 teaspoon of filling in the lower corner of the wrapper; then fold 1 corner over the filling and secure, making a triangle. Fold over the edges to complete the triangle, smearing with the paste to secure the last fold. On a plate, set the triangle, seam-side down. Continue with the rest of paste, filling, and wrappers.
- In a skillet set over medium-high heat, add 2 inches of oil. Cook the triangle in batches for 4 minutes every batch, until golden brown. Transfer to a paper towel to drain on and dust cinnamon sugar over the warm triangles.

Nutrition Information

- Calories: 67 calories;
- Cholesterol: 2
- Protein: 0.4
- Total Fat: 3.8
- Sodium: 22
- Total Carbohydrate: 8.3

Chapter 5: Korean Cuisine Recipes

***

501. Awesome Korean Steak

Serving: 6 | Prep: 20mins | Cook: 10mins | Ready in:

Ingredients

- 2 pounds thinly sliced Scotch fillet (chuck eye steaks)
- 1/2 cup soy sauce
- 5 tablespoons white sugar
- 2 1/2 tablespoons sesame seeds
- 2 tablespoons sesame oil
- 3 shallots, thinly sliced
- 2 cloves garlic, crushed
- 5 tablespoons mirin (Japanese sweet wine)

Direction

- Mix mirin, garlic, shallots, sesame oil, sesame seeds, sugar, and soy sauce in a big bowl. Add meat, mixing to coat. Cover then keep in fridge for 12-24 hours.
- Heat a big skillet on medium heat. Fry meat until it's not pink for 5-10 minutes. Serve with fried rice or salad.

Nutrition Information

- Calories: 376 calories;
- Sodium: 1249
- Total Carbohydrate: 21.4
- Cholesterol: 69
- Protein: 20.6
- Total Fat: 21.9

502. Baechu Kuk (Napa Cabbage And Soya Bean Paste Soup)

Serving: 4 | Prep: 20mins | Cook: 55mins | Ready in:

Ingredients

- 8 dried anchovies, or more to taste
- 8 cups cold water
- 1/2 pound bean sprouts
- 15 leaves napa cabbage
- 3 tablespoons Korean soy bean paste
- 1 tablespoon crushed garlic
- 1 teaspoon Korean red pepper powder
- 1/2 teaspoon salt
- 4 green onions, diagonally cut into 2-inch pieces
- 1/2 teaspoon dashi granules (Korean soup stock)

Direction

- Transfer the dried anchovies to a large pot and then pour in cold water. Soak for 20 minutes. Heat the liquid to boil, decrease the heat to medium and allow to simmer for 20 minutes. Take out the anchovies.
- Clean the bean sprouts with cold water about 3 or 4 times and get rid of any bad or brown heads of bean sprouts. Clean the cabbage and slice into bite-size pieces.
- Cook the cabbage for 5 minutes in a pot containing boiling water. Rinse with cold water and then squeeze out any excess liquid.
- Combine cabbage and bean sprouts in anchovy broth. Then add the soy bean paste while stirring until the soy bean paste has dissolved. Add salt, red pepper powder and garlic. Cook while stirring for 15 minutes on medium-high heat.
- Mix dashi and green beans into the soup, decrease the heat to medium and let to cook for 15 minutes.

Nutrition Information

- Calories: 81 calories;
- Total Carbohydrate: 11.3
- Cholesterol: 17
- Protein: 7.5
- Total Fat: 1.8
- Sodium: 957

503. Baek Kimchi (Korean White Non Spicy Kimchi)

Serving: 12 | Prep: 1hours | Cook: | Ready in:

Ingredients

- 1/2 cup coarse salt
- 1 napa cabbage, cut into chunks
- 2 jujube (Chinese dates), or more to taste (optional)
- 5 1/2 cups water, divided
- 3 tablespoons salted fermented shrimp (saewujeot)
- 2 scallions, cut into 1-inch pieces
- 6 cloves garlic, sliced
- 2 tablespoons sliced fresh ginger
- 1/2 Korean radish, cut into matchsticks
- 5 chestnuts, cut into thin strips
- 1/2 pear, cut into matchsticks
- 2 carrots, cut into matchsticks
- 1 red chile pepper, seeded and thinly sliced, or more to taste
- 1 green chile pepper, seeded and thinly sliced, or more to taste
- 4 teaspoons brown sugar
- 2 teaspoons salt

Direction

- In a large bowl, dissolve half cup of coarse salt in water. Immerse the cabbage into salty water and soak for about 12 to 24 hours. Drain off the water. Then rinse thoroughly and drain again pressing out any excess water.
- In a small bowl, soak jujube in water for about 10 to 15 minutes. Then drain, pit, and slice into thin pieces.
- In a food processor, mix ginger, garlic, scallions, 1/2 cup water, and salted shrimp. Puree until the resulting mix is smooth.
- Transfer the puree into large bowl. Add 2 teaspoon salt, brown sugar, green chile pepper, red chile pepper, carrots, pear,

chestnuts, radish and jujube. Mix in the remaining five cups of water. Stir in cabbage until coated well.
- Transfer the cabbage mixture into an airtight jar and then add in any liquid left in bowl.
- Seal the jar and allow to stand for 1 to 2 days at room temperature until beginning to ferment. Place in the fridge.

Nutrition Information

- Calories: 52 calories;
- Protein: 1.8
- Total Fat: 0.3
- Sodium: 4201
- Total Carbohydrate: 11.3
- Cholesterol: 2

504. Baek Kimchi (White Kimchi)

Serving: 10 | Prep: 30mins | Cook: | Ready in:

Ingredients

- 1 head napa cabbage
- 3 tablespoons salt
- water to cover
- 1 cup water
- 1 cup thinly grated white (daikon) radish
- 2 green onions, sliced diagonally into thin strips
- 4 cloves garlic, minced
- 2 slices fresh ginger
- 1 teaspoon white sugar
- 1 teaspoon salt
- 1 teaspoon white vinegar
- 3 pinches dried Korean red pepper threads

Direction

- Chop the cabbage lengthwise into quarters and ensure the leaves are still attached to the core. Rinse the cabbage under cold water and then liberally drizzle three tablespoons of salt in between the leaves. Transfer the cabbage into a large bowl and then add enough water to cover. Reserve for 4 to 5 hours until the leaves are soft.
- Rinse salted cabbage for about 3 or 4 times in cold water and then drain for about 20 minutes in a colander.
- In a bowl, mix red pepper threads, vinegar, 1 teaspoon salt, sugar, ginger, garlic, 1 cup water, green onions and radish. Drizzle the radish mixture in between all the cabbage leaves apart from the large outer leaf of each quarter. Save the liquid from radish mixture.
- Then peel back large outer leaf of every quarter and do not remove it from the core. Fold inner leaves in half. Enclose outer leaf around inner leaves and then pack cabbage quarters into 1/2-gallon jar that is clean. Add in reserved liquid from the radish mixture and seal the jars. Allow to stand for 1 day at room temperature. Chop wrapped cabbage quarters into 1 1/2-inch slices.

Nutrition Information

- Calories: 27 calories;
- Total Fat: 0.3
- Sodium: 2343
- Total Carbohydrate: 5.6
- Cholesterol: 0
- Protein: 1.7

505. Barbecued Korean Ribs

Serving: 4 | Prep: | Cook: | Ready in:

Ingredients

- 4 pounds beef short ribs, 2-1/2 inches long
- 2/3 cup Kikkoman Teriyaki Marinade & Sauce
- 1 tablespoon sesame seeds, toasted
- 1 teaspoon sugar
- 2 teaspoons hot pepper sauce

- 2 large cloves garlic, pressed

Direction

- Score the rib's meat side, opposite the bone, 1/2 inch deep and apart, crosswise and lengthwise. Put ribs in a big plastic food storage bag.
- Mix garlic, pepper sauce, sugar, sesame seeds, and teriyaki sauce. Pour on ribs. Press out air from bag. Securely close bag. Turn bag over a few times to coal everything. Refrigerate for 4 hours, occasionally turning bag.
- Take out ribs, throw out marinade.
- Broil or grill 4 inches from hot coals/heat source for 15-18 minutes until ribs are crisp and brown. Occasionally turn ribs over.

Nutrition Information

- Calories: 995 calories;
- Protein: 46
- Total Fat: 84.4
- Sodium: 1788
- Total Carbohydrate: 7.8
- Cholesterol: 186

---

506. Beef Bulgogi

Serving: 4 | Prep: 10mins | Cook: 5mins | Ready in:

Ingredients

- 1 pound flank steak, thinly sliced
- 5 tablespoons soy sauce
- 2 1/2 tablespoons white sugar
- 1/4 cup chopped green onion
- 2 tablespoons minced garlic
- 2 tablespoons sesame seeds
- 2 tablespoons sesame oil
- 1/2 teaspoon ground black pepper

Direction

- In a shallow dish, put beef. Mix ground black pepper, sesame oil, sesame seeds, garlic, green onion, sugar, and soy sauce in a small bowl. Pour on beef. Cover then keep in a fridge for at least 1 hour up to overnight.
- Preheat outdoor grill to high heat. Oil grate lightly.
- Grill beef quickly on hot grill for 1-2 minutes on each side until cooked through and slightly charred.

Nutrition Information

- Calories: 232 calories;
- Sodium: 1157
- Total Carbohydrate: 12.4
- Cholesterol: 27
- Protein: 16.2
- Total Fat: 13.2

---

507. Beef Bulgogi Lettuce Wraps

Serving: 6 | Prep: 10mins | Cook: 15mins | Ready in:

Ingredients

- 1 1/2 pounds beef flank steak
- 1/3 cup reduced-sodium soy sauce
- 4 green onions, cut in 1-inch pieces
- 1 tablespoon sake
- 1 tablespoon sesame oil
- 4 teaspoons white sugar
- 3 cloves garlic, minced
- 2 teaspoons grated ginger root
- 1 teaspoon ground black pepper
- 1 tablespoon gochujang (Korean hot pepper paste)
- 1 teaspoon soy sauce
- 1 teaspoon sesame oil
- 1 tablespoon sesame seeds, toasted
- 4 cups hot cooked short-grain rice
- 1/2 English cucumber, sliced

- 1 head Boston lettuce, separated into leaves

Direction

- Freeze the beef partially for about 1 hour until firm. Chop across the grain into half-inch pieces.
- In a large bowl, mix black pepper, ginger, garlic, sugar, 1 tablespoon sesame oil, sake, green onions and 1/3 cup soy sauce. Place in beef and toss to coat. Cover using plastic wrap and chill for 1 to 3 hours until the flavors of sauce are absorbed.
- In a bowl, mix together 1 teaspoon sesame oil, 1 teaspoon of soy sauce and gochujang.
- Assemble the oven rack to about six inches away from the heat and then preheat oven's broiler. Spread the marinated beef in a rimmed baking sheet.
- Broil the beef while stirring often for 15 to 20 minutes until its dark brown, glazed and almost all the marinade has evaporated. Drizzle with sesame seeds.
- Assemble cucumber, rice, and cooked beef in serving bowls. Then enclose portions of each in lettuce and dunk into gochujang sauce.

Nutrition Information

- Calories: 369 calories;
- Protein: 18.2
- Total Fat: 12.3
- Sodium: 582
- Total Carbohydrate: 44.6
- Cholesterol: 36

508. Best Bulgoki Korean Barbeque Beef

Serving: 4 | Prep: 15mins | Cook: 9mins | Ready in:

Ingredients

- 6 scallions, chopped
- 1/2 cup coarsely grated pear
- 3 tablespoons dark soy sauce
- 3 tablespoons sesame oil
- 1 tablespoon mirin (Japanese sweet wine)
- 1 tablespoon brown sugar, or more to taste
- 4 cloves garlic, grated
- 1 teaspoon lime juice
- 1 teaspoon grated fresh ginger
- 1/2 teaspoon ground black pepper
- 1/4 teaspoon red pepper flakes
- 1 pound beef top sirloin, thinly sliced
- Sauce:
- 1/4 cup soy sauce
- 3 tablespoons water
- 2 tablespoons gochujang (Korean chile paste)
- 1 teaspoon brown sugar
- 1 teaspoon mirin (Japanese sweet wine)

Direction

- In a bowl, whisk together red pepper flakes, black pepper, ginger, lime juice, garlic, 1 tablespoon of brown sugar, 1 tablespoon of mirin, sesame oil, dark soy sauce, pear and scallions. Transfer into a plastic bag that is resealable. Place in beef and then coat with the marinade. Squeeze out the excess air and then seal the bag. Place in the refrigerator to marinate for 8 hours to overnight.
- Preheat the outdoor grill over medium-high heat and coat the grate lightly with oil.
- Transfer slices of beef from the marinade to the preheated grill and save the marinade. Cook for about 3 minutes on each side until no pink color remains in the middle. Transfer the beef into a serving dish.
- Transfer the marinade into a saucepan along with 1 teaspoon of mirin, 1 teaspoon of brown sugar, gochujang, water and soy sauce. Heat to a boil and cook for 3 to 5 minutes until thickened to sauce consistency. Spread the sauce on top of beef.

Nutrition Information

- Calories: 298 calories;

- Sodium: 1942
- Total Carbohydrate: 14.3
- Cholesterol: 49
- Protein: 21.4
- Total Fat: 16.8

509. Best Korean Bulgogi

Serving: 4 | Prep: 20mins | Cook: 30mins | Ready in:

Ingredients

- 2 1/2 cups soy sauce
- 1 bunch green onions, chopped
- 4 tablespoons toasted sesame seeds
- 1/2 tablespoon sesame oil
- 1 (12 fluid ounce) can or bottle beer
- 2 pounds thinly sliced beef chuck roast
- 1 cup uncooked long grain rice
- 2 cups water
- 1 tablespoon Vegetable oil
- 1 head lettuce leaves - rinsed and dried

Direction

- Mix together sesame oil, sesame seeds, green onion, soy sauce and beer in a medium bowl. Put the meat in the marinade and chill overnight for best result.
- Mix rice and water in a pot and make it boil. Adjust the heat to low, without cover, and simmer for 20 minutes until the rice is tender.
- In a large skillet, heat oil on medium heat. Fry beef strips for about 5 minutes per side or to your preferred doneness.
- Serve with rice and lettuce leaves on the side. Scoop rice and beef into the lettuce leaf and fold in sides and roll up to the top to make a bag of bulgogi. No need to use silverware.

Nutrition Information

- Calories: 759 calories;
- Total Fat: 35.6

- Sodium: 9118
- Total Carbohydrate: 60.5
- Cholesterol: 103
- Protein: 43.7

510. Bibimbap With Beef

Serving: 4 | Prep: 15mins | Cook: 4mins | Ready in:

Ingredients

- 1/2 pound beef top sirloin steak
- 2 tablespoons soy sauce
- 1 tablespoon sesame oil
- 2 teaspoons honey
- 2 teaspoons dry sherry
- 4 cups hot cooked rice
- 2 teaspoons vegetable oil
- 1 carrot, thinly sliced
- 1 1/2 cups bean sprouts
- 1/2 cup peeled and matchstick-cut daikon radish
- 1/4 teaspoon salt
- ground black pepper to taste
- 1/8 teaspoon cayenne pepper, or to taste
- 1 cup fresh spinach

Direction

- Slice the steak across grain into pieces of about two inches long and 1/4-inch wide. Then stack the pieces and chop lengthwise into 1/4-inch strips.
- In a bowl, mix sherry, honey, sesame oil and soy sauce. Place in beef strips and stir. Then marinate for 15 minutes at room temperature.
- Over high heat, heat a nonstick wok and then add the marinade and beef. Cook while stirring for about 2 minutes until the beef is browned slightly.
- Distribute the rice into four individual serving bowls. Distribute the beef mixture atop rice and keep it warm.
- Over medium-high heat, heat oil in the same wok and then add cayenne pepper, black

pepper, salt, daikon, bean sprouts and carrot. Cook while stirring for about 1 minute until slightly tender. Place in spinach and cook for about 1 minutes until wilted. Distribute the vegetable mixture atop the rice and beef.

Nutrition Information

- Calories: 363 calories;
- Sodium: 655
- Total Carbohydrate: 52.5
- Cholesterol: 24
- Protein: 15.8
- Total Fat: 9.5

511. Bill's Kimchi

Serving: 10 | Prep: 20mins | Cook: | Ready in:

Ingredients

- 2 heads bok choy, cut into 2-inch squares
- 1/2 cup pickling salt, divided, or more to taste
- 1/4 cup Korean chile powder
- 6 green onions, chopped
- 4 large carrots, cut into 1/4-inch-thick slices
- 3 serrano chile peppers, thinly sliced, or more to taste (optional)
- 4 cloves garlic, minced, or more to taste
- 1 tablespoon fish sauce (optional)
- 2 1/2 teaspoons minced fresh ginger, or more to taste

Direction

- Put bok choy in a big bowl. Add 1/4 cup of pickling salt then mix. Cover using a flipped plate. Let salted cabbage stand for 2-3 days until liquid releases and it's soft. Rinse cabbage inside a colander; drain.
- Place cabbage in a clean bowl. Add ginger, fish sauce, garlic, serrano chile peppers, carrots, green onions, Korean chile powder, and 1/4 cup of pickling salt. Mix well.
- In clean jars, pack cabbage mixture to reach an inch of the top. Secure lids tightly on every jar.
- Keep in fridge for at least 2 weeks until cabbage ferments and flavors merge.

Nutrition Information

- Calories: 40 calories;
- Total Fat: 0.8
- Sodium: 5757
- Total Carbohydrate: 7.8
- Cholesterol: 0
- Protein: 2.4

512. Bulgogi (Korean BBQ)

Serving: 4 | Prep: 25mins | Cook: 10mins | Ready in:

Ingredients

- 1 cup soy sauce
- 1/2 cup pear juice or white wine
- 3 tablespoons white sugar
- 2 tablespoons chopped garlic
- 1 teaspoon sesame oil
- 1 teaspoon sesame seeds
- 1 tablespoon ground black pepper
- 1 teaspoon monosodium glutamate
- 1 (2 pound) beef rump roast, sliced into thin strips
- 1 onion, cut into thin strips

Direction

- Mix monosodium glutamate, black pepper, sesame seeds, sesame oil, garlic, sugar, pear juice, and soy sauce in a big bowl. Stir in onions and beef to mixture until coated. Cover and keep in fridge for 1 hour.
- Preheat grill pan on high heat. Brush oil on grill pan. Add onions and beef. Cook for 3-6 minutes, turning to evenly brown, until done.

Nutrition Information

- Calories: 439 calories;
- Total Carbohydrate: 24.3
- Cholesterol: 101
- Protein: 44.2
- Total Fat: 17.5
- Sodium: 3820

513. Chinese Korean Cucumber Kimchi

Serving: 10 | Prep: 25mins | Cook: 5mins | Ready in:

Ingredients

- 5 cucumbers, peeled and cut into 1/2 x1 1/2 inch sticks
- 1/2 cup sea salt
- 1/2 cup white sugar
- 1/2 cup white vinegar
- 1 cup water
- 2 tablespoons chili bean sauce (toban djan)
- 1 tablespoon hot chili oil
- 2 (4 inch) fresh hot red chile peppers, sliced
- 1 small onion, sliced
- 5 cloves garlic, sliced and crushed

Direction

- In a bowl, combine sea salt and cucumbers together and allow to sit for half an hour to soften the cucumbers. Drain and then rinse under fresh water.
- As the cucumbers stand in salt, in a saucepan, whisk together the water, vinegar and sugar. Heat to boil. Decrease the heat and mix in the hot chili oil and chili bean sauce.
- In a heatproof airtight container, combine the cucumbers with garlic, onion and sliced chiles. Then add hot vinegar mixture on top of the veggies. Cover and chill for about 2 to 3 hours to blend flavors. You can serve while chilled.

Nutrition Information

- Calories: 80 calories;
- Sodium: 4415
- Total Carbohydrate: 17.4
- Cholesterol: 0
- Protein: 1.8
- Total Fat: 1.3

514. Chompchae Deopbap (Korean Spicy Tuna And Rice)

Serving: 2 | Prep: 10mins | Cook: 40mins | Ready in:

Ingredients

- 1 cup uncooked white rice
- 2 cups water
- 1 tablespoon olive oil
- 3 cloves garlic, minced
- 1 (1/2 inch) piece fresh ginger, minced
- 1/2 onion, coarsely chopped
- 1 cup kim chee
- 1/2 cup sliced cucumber
- 1/4 cup sliced carrots
- 2 tablespoons soy sauce
- 2 tablespoons rice vinegar
- salt and pepper to taste
- 1 tablespoon Korean chile powder, or to taste
- 1 tablespoon water, or as needed
- 1 (5 ounce) can tuna, drained

Direction

- Over high heat, heat 2 cups of water and rice to boil in a saucepan. Decrease the heat to medium-low, then cover and simmer for 20 to 25 minutes until the liquid is absorbed and the rice is tender.
- Over medium heat, heat olive oil in a skillet and then mix in the onion, ginger and garlic. Cook while stirring for about 5 minutes until the onion has turned translucent and is softened. Mix in the carrot, cucumber, and Kim chee. Add in the rice vinegar and soy

sauce. Season with chile powder, pepper and salt. In case the mix is too thick, pour in one tablespoon of water. Slowly mix in tuna and continue to cook until fish is heated through. Can serve together with rice.

Nutrition Information

- Calories: 538 calories;
- Total Fat: 8.8
- Sodium: 1574
- Total Carbohydrate: 87.5
- Cholesterol: 19
- Protein: 26.4

515. Daeji Bulgogi (Pork Bulgogi)

Serving: 6 | Prep: 20mins | Cook: 15mins | Ready in:

Ingredients

- 3 tablespoons soy sauce
- 2 tablespoons Korean barbeque sauce
- 2 tablespoons Korean hot pepper paste
- 1 tablespoon white sugar
- 1 tablespoon minced ginger root
- 2 teaspoons red pepper flakes
- 1/2 teaspoon sesame seeds
- 1/4 teaspoon ground black pepper
- 1 1/2 pounds boneless pork shoulder, thinly sliced
- 1 onion, sliced

Direction

- In a small bowl, whisk together black pepper, sesame seeds, red pepper flakes, ginger root, sugar, hot pepper paste, barbeque sauce and soy sauce.
- Put the pork into a large bowl and then add the soy sauce mixture on top of pork. Toss to coat. Place in the fridge to marinate for at least three hours and up to overnight.
- Over medium-high heat, preheat a grill pan or large skillet and then add pork. Get rid of the marinade. Cook while stirring often for about 5 minutes until the pork starts to brown. Mix in the onion and then cook for about 10 minutes until soft.

Nutrition Information

- Calories: 150 calories;
- Total Fat: 5.1
- Sodium: 583
- Total Carbohydrate: 10
- Cholesterol: 43
- Protein: 15.4

516. Dak Bulgogi (Korean Barbeque Chicken)

Serving: 4 | Prep: 10mins | Cook: 15mins | Ready in:

Ingredients

- 2 pounds bone-in chicken thighs
- 1/2 cup soy sauce
- 1/2 apple - peeled, cored, and chopped
- 1 tablespoon brown sugar
- 3 cloves garlic
- 1 teaspoon sesame oil
- 1 teaspoon gochugaru (Korean chile powder)
- 1 teaspoon minced fresh ginger root
- 1 teaspoon sesame seeds

Direction

- Peel skin off chicken thighs, trimming off extra fat. Cut every piece to a flat 'steak' slicing around the bone. Keep any small pieces for cooking as well. Rinse thighs in cold water, getting rid of film. Put in a big bowl.
- In a food processor, pulse ginger, gochugaru, sesame oil, garlic, sugar, apple, and soy sauce until marinade becomes smooth.

- Place marinade in the bowl with chicken and mix to coat. Use a skewer to pierce chicken to absorb more if you want. Cover using plastic wrap. Keep in fridge for 6-12 hours.
- Heat skillet on medium heat. Take chicken out of marinade and place in the skillet. Sauté for 15-20 minutes until it's not pink in the middle. An inserted instant-read thermometer in the middle will say at least 74 degrees C/165 degrees F.
- Place thighs on a serving plate. Top with sesame seeds.

Nutrition Information

- Calories: 435 calories;
- Sodium: 1940
- Total Carbohydrate: 9.5
- Cholesterol: 141
- Protein: 40.5
- Total Fat: 25.3

517. Dak Dori Tang (Spicy Korean Chicken Stew)

Serving: 4 | Prep: 15mins | Cook: 31mins | Ready in:

Ingredients

- 1/4 cup soy sauce
- 3 tablespoons gochujang (Korean hot pepper paste)
- 1 tablespoon brown sugar
- 1 tablespoon minced garlic
- 2 teaspoons sesame oil
- 1 1/2 teaspoons minced fresh ginger root
- 1/2 teaspoon chile powder
- 2 tablespoons vegetable oil, divided, or as needed
- 2 skinless, boneless chicken breasts, cut into 1-inch cubes
- 3 carrots, peeled and thickly sliced
- 2 potatoes, peeled and diced
- 1 leek, trimmed and thinly sliced
- 1 small onion, cut into 8 wedges
- 1 habanero pepper, seeded and minced
- 2 cups water, or as needed

Direction

- For the marinade, in a bowl, mix chile powder, ginger, sesame oil, garlic, brown sugar, gochujang and soy sauce.
- Over medium heat, heat one tablespoon of vegetable oil in a stockpot and add chicken. Cook for ten minutes until browned evenly. Place the chicken into a bowl containing the marinade and toss to coat.
- Heat the remaining vegetable oil in a stockpot and then mix in onion, leek, potatoes and carrots. Cook while stirring for about 10 minutes until the onion becomes translucent. Mix in the habanero pepper and let to cook for about 1 minute until fragrant.
- Add water into the stockpot, then mix in marinade and chicken. Heat to boil. Decrease the heat and let to simmer for about 10 minutes while adding extra water as needed until the veggies are tender.

Nutrition Information

- Calories: 316 calories;
- Total Carbohydrate: 40.6
- Cholesterol: 29
- Protein: 15.4
- Total Fat: 10.8
- Sodium: 1081

518. Dak Galbi (Korean Spicy Chicken Stir Fry)

Serving: 8 | Prep: 20mins | Cook: 30mins | Ready in:

Ingredients

- 1 tablespoon vegetable oil

- 2 pounds skinless, boneless chicken breast halves, cut into bite-size pieces, or more as needed
- 1/4 cup gochujang (Korean hot pepper paste)
- 2 tablespoons soy sauce
- 2 tablespoons gochugaru (Korean red pepper flakes)
- 1 tablespoon mirin (Japanese sweet wine)
- 1 tablespoon brown sugar
- 1 tablespoon sesame oil
- 4 cloves garlic, minced
- 1/4 teaspoon ground black pepper
- 1/4 teaspoon ground ginger
- 2 cups Korean-style glutinous rice cakes (tteok)
- 1/4 large head cabbage, sliced into strips
- 1 sweet potato, sliced into rounds
- 1/2 onion, chopped
- 3 scallions, sliced into 1-inch pieces, divided
- 4 leaves perilla leaves, sliced, or to taste
- 1/2 cup water
- 1 tablespoon sesame seeds

Direction

- Heat the oil in large nonstick saucepan, add the chicken pieces and then cook while stirring for 4 to 7 minutes until almost opaque.
- In a bowl, mix ginger, black pepper, garlic, sesame oil, brown sugar, mirin, gochugaru, gochujang, and soy sauce. Transfer to saucepan containing the chicken. Cook while stirring for 3 to 5 minutes until the chicken pieces are well coated and browned.
- Mix onion, sweet potato, cabbage, and rice cakes into the skillet containing chicken mixture. Cook for about 10 minutes until the sweet potato changes color. Add perilla leaves and 2 to 2 1/2 scallions and then cook for about 3 minutes until wilted. You can add extra water in case the sauce looks to be drying up. Garnish with sesame seeds and the remaining scallions.

Nutrition Information

- Calories: 386 calories;
- Total Fat: 7.3
- Sodium: 384
- Total Carbohydrate: 52.8
- Cholesterol: 59
- Protein: 25.8

519. Dakdoritang (Korean Spicy Chicken Stew)

Serving: 4 | Prep: 20mins | Cook: 45mins | Ready in:

Ingredients

- 1 1/2 cups water
- 1/4 cup soy sauce
- 2 tablespoons rice wine
- 2 tablespoons Korean red chili pepper paste (gochujang)
- 2 tablespoons Korean red chili pepper flakes (gochugaru)
- 1 tablespoon honey
- 1 tablespoon white sugar
- 1 pinch ground black pepper
- 3 pounds bone-in chicken pieces, trimmed of fat and cut into small pieces
- 10 ounces potatoes, cut into large chunks
- 2 carrots, cut into large chunks
- 1/2 large onion, cut into large chunks
- 4 large garlic cloves, or more to taste
- 2 slices fresh ginger, or more to taste
- 2 scallions, cut into 2-inch lengths
- 1 tablespoon sesame oil
- 1 teaspoon sesame seeds

Direction

- In a big pot, mix and boil black pepper, sugar, honey, red chili pepper flakes, red chili pepper paste, rice wine, soy sauce, and water. Add chicken and boil. Bring heat to medium, cover pot, and cook at a simmer for 15 minutes until chicken is brown.

- Mix ginger, garlic, onion, carrots, and potatoes in chicken mixture. Replace cover atop the pot, cook, occasionally stirring, for 15 minutes until potatoes are soft. Uncover, cooking for another 10 minutes until liquid slightly thickens and chicken becomes tender. An inserted instant-read thermometer inserted into a piece of the chicken near the bone will say 74 degrees C/165 degrees F.
- Mix sesame seeds, sesame oil, and scallions on the stew. Take pot off heat.

Nutrition Information

- Calories: 896 calories;
- Total Fat: 69.1
- Sodium: 1111
- Total Carbohydrate: 36.1
- Cholesterol: 121
- Protein: 33.4

520. Dakdoritang (Spicy Chicken Stew)

Serving: 8 | Prep: 20mins | Cook: 35mins | Ready in:

Ingredients

- 1 (3 pound) whole chicken, cut into 10 pieces and fat trimmed
- water to cover
- 3 slices fresh ginger
- 1 1/2 cups water
- 3 tablespoons soy sauce
- 1 tablespoon white sugar
- 1 tablespoon Korean hot pepper paste
- 1 tablespoon Korean hot pepper powder
- 2 teaspoons sesame oil
- 1 teaspoon crushed garlic
- 3 potatoes, peeled and cut into 1x2-inch pieces
- 1 carrot, peeled and cut into 1x2-inch pieces
- 1 yellow onion, peeled and cut into 1x2-inch pieces
- 1/2 teaspoon salt
- 1/4 teaspoon ground black pepper
- 3 green onions, chopped
- 1 teaspoon sesame seeds

Direction

- Transfer pieces of chicken into a large pot and then cover with enough water. Place in ginger and then heat the water to boil. Decrease the heat to medium and let to simmer for ten minutes. Drain off water and get rid of ginger.
- Combine garlic, sesame oil, hot pepper powder, hot pepper paste, soy sauce, 1 1/2 cups water, and sugar into the chicken. Cook while stirring for 10 minutes over medium heat.
- Mix carrot and potatoes into the chicken mixture, let to cook for five minutes. Add black pepper, salt and onion. Combine thoroughly. Cook the stew for about 5 minutes until the chicken is no longer pink in the center and it's heated through. The temperature of an instant-read thermometer inserted near the bone should be 74 degrees C (165 degrees F). Garnish the stew with sesame seeds and green onions.

Nutrition Information

- Calories: 332 calories;
- Total Fat: 14.4
- Sodium: 600
- Total Carbohydrate: 21.8
- Cholesterol: 102
- Protein: 28.3

521. Dol Sot Bi Bim Bap

Serving: 6 | Prep: 1hours | Cook: 1hours | Ready in:

Ingredients

- 1/2 cup soy sauce
- 1/2 cup white sugar
- 1/2 cup brown sugar

- 1/4 cup minced garlic
- 1/3 cup chopped green onion
- 4 tablespoons toasted sesame seeds
- 20 ounces rib-eye steak, sliced thin
- salt and pepper to taste
- 3 cups uncooked glutinous (sticky) white rice, rinsed
- 6 1/2 cups water
- 4 dried shiitake mushrooms
- 1 pound fresh spinach, washed and chopped
- 12 ounces cucumber, julienned
- 12 ounces carrots, julienned
- sesame oil
- 8 ounces fresh bean sprouts
- 6 eggs
- 6 sheets nori, crumbled
- 6 tablespoons sesame oil
- 1/4 cup chili bean paste (Kochujang)

Direction

- Make the beef marinade. In a big bowl, mix green onions, sesame seeds, soy sauce, garlic and sugar then put in the sliced beef strips into the marinade, add pepper and salt to taste. Cover the bowl and keep the marinated beef strips in the fridge for not less than 2 hours.
- Put water and rice in a saucepan and let it boil over high heat. Lower the heat setting to medium-low then cover the saucepan and let the rice simmer for 20-25 minutes or until the rice is soft and the water has been absorbed by the rice.
- Preheat the oven at 425°F (220°C) and put 6 Korean stone bowls in the oven. In a small bowl, soak the shiitake mushrooms in 1/2 cup of hot water for about 10 minutes until the mushrooms are flexible. Cut and throw away the stems. Cut the mushroom caps into thin slices. Set aside.
- Boil water in a saucepan. Put the spinach into the boiling water and let it sit until the leaves have wilted. Drain the spinach and pat dry. Set aside. In a bowl, mix the carrot and cucumbers, add pepper and salt to taste. Set aside.
- Preheat the wok over medium-high heat. Put the seasoned carrots and cucumbers into the wok with a little bit of sesame oil. Cook and stir often until the vegetables are soft. Remove the cooked carrots and cucumbers from the wok and set aside. Add a little bit more of sesame oil in the same wok and stir-fry the spinach for about 1-2 minutes. Remove the spinach from the pan and set aside. Put in the marinated beef strips into the wok along with the marinade then cook and stir often for about 4-5 minutes or until the liquid has reduced.
- Take the stone bowls out of the oven and put them on a heat resistant surface. Coat each bowl with sesame oil. Divide the cooked rice and gently press into the bottom of each of the stone bowls (you'll hear sizzles as you put the rice into each bowl). Place the bean sprouts, shiitake mushrooms, greens, beef mixture and cucumbers and carrots over each portion of the rice. Put one raw egg yolk on top of each bowl right before serving and finish off with a drizzle of about a tablespoon of sesame oil and nori on top. Serve with Kochujang sauce on the side.

Nutrition Information

- Calories: 937 calories;
- Protein: 35.8
- Total Fat: 37.6
- Sodium: 1517
- Total Carbohydrate: 120.8
- Cholesterol: 220

522. Dubu Jeon (Korean Pan Fried Tofu)

Serving: 2 | Prep: 15mins | Cook: 6mins | Ready in:

Ingredients

- 1 (14 ounce) package firm tofu, cut into 1/4-inch slices
- 1 teaspoon salt
- 1 teaspoon vegetable oil
- 2 tablespoons soy sauce
- 2 green onions, chopped
- 1 tablespoon water
- 1 teaspoon sesame seeds
- 1/2 teaspoon sesame oil
- 1/2 teaspoon Korean red pepper powder
- 1 pinch ground black pepper
- 1 pinch Korean red pepper flakes

Direction

- Season the tofu with salt.
- Over medium heat, heat vegetable oil in a skillet and then add a single layer of tofu. Allow to cook for about 3 minutes until easily released from the bottom of the skillet and turned golden brown. Turn and continue to cook for about 3 more minutes until turned golden brown on the other side.
- In a small bowl, combine together black pepper, red pepper powder, sesame oil, sesame seeds, water, green onions and soy sauce. Pour onto the cooked tofu and spread out. Decorate with red pepper flakes.

Nutrition Information

- Calories: 195 calories;
- Protein: 17.8
- Total Fat: 12.6
- Sodium: 2098
- Total Carbohydrate: 7
- Cholesterol: 0

523. Easy And Simple Korean BBQ Ribs

Serving: 4 | Prep: 15mins | Cook: 15mins | Ready in:

Ingredients

- 1 cup soy sauce
- 1 cup white sugar
- 1 teaspoon ground black pepper
- 5 cloves garlic, chopped
- 3 green onions, chopped
- 2 tablespoons Asian (toasted) sesame oil
- 1 teaspoon sesame seeds
- 2 pounds Korean-style short ribs (beef chuck flanken, cut 1/3 to 1/2 inch thick across bones)

Direction

- In a bowl, whisk together sugar and soy sauce until sugar is dissolved. Mix in sesame seeds, black pepper, sesame oil, garlic, and green onions.
- In a large bowl, put the ribs and then add the marinade on top of the ribs. Mix to coat the ribs with marinade and then refrigerate for an hour. Mix the marinade and ribs again and chill for one more hour.
- Preheat the outdoor grill over medium-high heat and coat the grate lightly with oil.
- Take out the ribs from the marinade, get rid of marinade and then grill ribs for about 5 minutes on each side until turned brown and no pink color remains in the center. Be sure to have a spray bottle of water available if the ribs flare up.

Nutrition Information

- Calories: 771 calories;
- Total Carbohydrate: 57.4
- Cholesterol: 93
- Protein: 26
- Total Fat: 49
- Sodium: 3660

524. Eunah's Korean Style Seaweed Soup

Serving: 4 | Prep: 10mins | Cook: 20mins | Ready in:

Ingredients

- 1 ounce dried wakame (brown) seaweed
- 2 teaspoons sesame oil
- 1/2 cup extra lean ground beef
- 1 teaspoon salt, or to taste
- 1 1/2 tablespoons soy sauce
- 1 teaspoon minced garlic
- 7 cups water

Direction

- Soak seaweed in room temperature water for about 15 minutes until soft. Drain off water. Then rinse the sheets and slice into two inch long pieces. Reserve.
- Over medium-high heat, heat sesame oil in a saucepan. Mix in the 1/3 of the soy sauce, beef, and salt. Cook while stirring for about 4 minutes until beef is no longer pink and is crumbly. Add the remaining soy sauce and the seaweed. Cook while stirring for one minute. Mix in garlic and add in water. Heat to boil, decrease the heat to medium-low and let to simmer for about 15 minutes until the seaweed and beef become tender.

Nutrition Information

- Calories: 49 calories;
- Sodium: 991
- Total Carbohydrate: 1.3
- Cholesterol: 9
- Protein: 3.8
- Total Fat: 3.2

525. Fiery Red Pepper Potatoes

Serving: 4 | Prep: 15mins | Cook: 10mins | Ready in:

Ingredients

- 1 1/2 tablespoons soy sauce
- 1 pinch cayenne pepper, or to taste
- 1 1/2 tablespoons vegetable oil
- 3 potatoes, cut into bite sized pieces
- 4 green onions, chopped
- 1 large red bell pepper, chopped
- 2 teaspoons sesame seeds

Direction

- In a small bowl, mxi cayenne pepper and soy sauce until cayenne pepper melts. Put aside.
- In a big skillet, heat vegetable oil on medium-high heat. Cook potatoes in hot oil for 5 minutes until golden brown. Mix in sesame seeds, bell pepper, and onions, cook for another minute. Pour soy sauce mixture on potatoes. Stir and cook for 1-2 minutes until liquid is absorbed completely.

Nutrition Information

- Calories: 198 calories;
- Sodium: 352
- Total Carbohydrate: 32.3
- Cholesterol: 0
- Protein: 4.6
- Total Fat: 6.2

526. Fried Kimchi

Serving: 4 | Prep: 5mins | Cook: 15mins | Ready in:

Ingredients

- 1 cup kimchi, chopped into bite-sized pieces, or to taste
- 1/2 teaspoon sesame oil, or to taste
- 1 1/2 teaspoons white vinegar
- 1 tablespoon white sugar, or to taste

Direction

- Heat nonstick skillet over medium-high heat, add kimchi and then sauté kimchi for about 5 minutes until slightly yellow and fragrant. Pour in sesame oil and then cook for 2 to 3 minutes until the kimchi is coated. Add in vinegar to coat the skillet's bottom. Raise the heat a bit and heat the vinegar to boil. Pour in sugar. Decrease the heat to low and then cook for about 3 minutes until kimchi is browned and sugar has dissolved.

Nutrition Information

- Calories: 25 calories;
- Total Fat: 0.7
- Sodium: 249
- Total Carbohydrate: 4.7
- Cholesterol: 0
- Protein: 0.6

527. Galbitang (Korean Beef Short Rib Soup)

Serving: 4 | Prep: 20mins | Cook: 57mins | Ready in:

Ingredients

- 2 pounds beef short ribs
- 3 tablespoons soy sauce
- 4 cloves garlic, minced
- 2 teaspoons sesame oil
- 1 teaspoon ground black pepper
- 1/2 Korean radish (mu), cut into 1-inch slices
- 1/2 onion
- 2 cloves garlic
- 1 slice fresh ginger
- 4 ounces Korean glass noodles (dangmyun)
- 2 scallions, sliced into 1-inch pieces
- 1 tablespoon cooked egg strips (optional)
- 1/2 teaspoon toasted sesame seeds (optional)

Direction

- In a big bowl with cold water, soak ribs to drain leftover blood for an hour, changing water when needed. Drain.
- In a bowl, mix pepper, sesame oil, 4 cloves minced garlic, and soy sauce. Add the sliced radish.
- In a big pot, cover ribs with water. Add ginger, 2 cloves garlic, half an onion, and boil for 15 minutes. Skim any foam that floats at the top. Drain. Throw out ginger, garlic, and onion.
- Rinse ribs and put back in pot. Cover using fresh water. Boil, reduce the heat, then simmer for 20 minutes until tender.
- Mix radish mixture into pot. Cook for 10 minutes until flavors merge. Add scallions and noodles. Cook for 2-4 minutes until noodles are tender.
- Place soup in bowls. Top with toasted sesame seeds and egg strips.

Nutrition Information

- Calories: 610 calories;
- Sodium: 912
- Total Carbohydrate: 23.8
- Cholesterol: 105
- Protein: 25.5
- Total Fat: 45.1

528. Gluten Free Kalbi Beef

Serving: 10 | Prep: 10mins | Cook: 20mins | Ready in:

Ingredients

- Kalbi marinade:
- 2 tablespoons sesame seeds
- 1 1/2 cups gluten-free soy sauce (tamari)
- 2/3 cup white sugar
- 1/2 cup chopped green onions
- 1/4 cup sesame oil
- 2 tablespoons minced garlic
- 1/2 teaspoon red pepper flakes
- 5 pounds Korean short ribs (cut flanken-style into 1/2-inch slices across the bones)

Direction

- Over medium heat, toast sesame seeds in a small skillet for 3 to 5 minutes until browned lightly.
- In a saucepan, mix red pepper flakes, garlic, sesame oil, green onions, sugar, sesame seeds, and soy sauce. Let to simmer on medium-low heat while stirring continuously for about 10 minutes until the flavors have combined. Take out from the heat and leave the marinade completely cool for 15 minutes.
- Transfer the short ribs into large plastic bags that are sealable and then cover with the cooled marinade. Seal the bags and place in the fridge to marinate for at least one hour or overnight for maximum flavor.
- Preheat the grill over medium heat and coat the grate lightly with oil.
- Drain the short ribs and get rid of the marinade. Let to cook on the preheated grill for about 5 minutes on each side until browned.

Nutrition Information

- Calories: 608 calories;
- Sodium: 2444
- Total Carbohydrate: 17.1
- Cholesterol: 93
- Protein: 26.4
- Total Fat: 48.1

529. Gochujang Barbeque Sauce

Serving: 24 | Prep: 10mins | Cook: 10mins | Ready in:

Ingredients

- 1/2 white onion, chopped
- 3 pounds heirloom tomatoes, chopped
- 1/2 cup apple cider vinegar
- 1/4 cup firmly packed light brown sugar
- 3 tablespoons Worcestershire sauce
- 3 tablespoons gochujang (Korean hot pepper paste)
- 2 tablespoons soy sauce
- 1 tablespoon molasses
- 4 cloves garlic, crushed
- 1 1/2 teaspoons lime juice

Direction

- Heat the big saucepan on medium heat. Add in onion, cook and stir for 5 minutes until translucent. Put in lime juice, garlic, molasses, soy sauce, gochujang, Worcestershire sauce, brown sugar, vinegar and tomatoes. Bring to a simmer. Take away from heat and let the sauce cool at least 15 minutes.
- Fill the sauce in a blender then puree until smooth.
- Using a sieve to strain sauce through and transfer it into sterilized Mason jars.

Nutrition Information

- Calories: 31 calories;
- Protein: 0.6
- Total Fat: 0.1
- Sodium: 116
- Total Carbohydrate: 7.1
- Cholesterol: 0

530. Gochujang Pulled Pork In The Slow Cooker

Serving: 12 | Prep: 15mins | Cook: 8hours10mins | Ready in:

Ingredients

- 2/3 cup gochujang (Korean hot pepper paste)
- 1 large onion, thinly sliced
- 1/2 cup apple cider vinegar
- 1/2 cup chicken stock
- 1/4 cup honey

- 1/4 cup brown sugar
- 2 tablespoons fresh ginger
- 1 tablespoon soy sauce
- 1 tablespoon yellow mustard
- 3 cloves garlic, minced
- 1 tablespoon ground cinnamon
- 1 teaspoon salt
- 5 sprigs thyme, stemmed
- 1/2 teaspoon ground black pepper
- 1 (4 pound) boneless pork shoulder roast, trimmed
- 1/4 cup butter, divided
- 1 tablespoon all-purpose flour
- 8 hamburger buns, split
- 3 green onions, thinly sliced

Direction

- Mix mustard, garlic, black pepper, thyme, salt, cinnamon, soy sauce, ginger, brown sugar, honey, chicken stock, vinegar, onion, and gochujang in a big bowl well.
- Dredge pork in gochujang sauce all over the sides. Pour sauce in a slow cooker, add pork. Spoon some sauce on pork's surface. Cook then cook on low for 8 hours until pork easily shreds with a fork.
- Preheat oven to 175 degrees C/350 degrees F.
- In a big bowl. Place and shred meat using 2 forks. Pour sauce from slow cooker in a pot on medium-high heat. Cover then boil. Uncover, lower heat to simmer.
- Mix flour and 1 tablespoon butter in a small bowl. Mix with sauce in the pot well. Cook for 5 minutes until slightly thickened and heated through. Take off heat and mix again.
- Spread leftover 3 tablespoons butter inside buns. Put on a baking sheet.
- Toast in preheated oven for 5-7 minutes until golden brown.
- Pour sauce into the shredded pork bowl then mix. Top with green onions. Spoon pork on toasted buns.

Nutrition Information

- Calories: 341 calories;
- Total Carbohydrate: 35.1
- Cholesterol: 67
- Protein: 22.5
- Total Fat: 11.8
- Sodium: 627

531. Gochujang Sauce

Serving: 4 | Prep: 10mins | Cook: | Ready in:

Ingredients

- 2 tablespoons gochujang (Korean chile paste)
- 2 tablespoons diagonally sliced green onions
- 1 tablespoon soy sauce
- 1 tablespoon rice vinegar
- 2 cloves garlic, minced
- 2 teaspoons toasted sesame seeds
- 2 teaspoons white sugar
- 2 teaspoons grated ginger
- 1 teaspoon sesame oil

Direction

- Mix sesame oil, ginger, sugar, sesame seeds, garlic, rice vinegar, soy sauce, green onions, and gochujang in a bowl until its smooth.

Nutrition Information

- Calories: 38 calories;
- Cholesterol: 0
- Protein: 0.7
- Total Fat: 1.9
- Sodium: 544
- Total Carbohydrate: 4.3

532. Godeungeo Jorim (Korean Braised Mackerel With Radish)

Serving: 4 | Prep: 20mins | Cook: 35mins | Ready in:

Ingredients

- 1 red chile pepper, seeded and minced (optional)
- 1 green chile pepper, seeded and minced (optional)
- 2 tablespoons cooking wine
- 2 tablespoons gochugaru (Korean red pepper flakes)
- 1 tablespoon gochujang (Korean chile paste)
- 2 tablespoons soy sauce
- 1 tablespoon brown sugar
- 5 cloves garlic, minced
- 1/2 teaspoon minced fresh ginger
- 2 cups water
- 1 daikon radish, halved lengthwise and sliced into 1/2-inch thick pieces
- 2 whole mackerel - gutted, cleaned, and cut into 3-inch pieces
- 2 green onions, sliced on the bias into 1/2-inch pieces

Direction

- Mix ginger, garlic, brown sugar, soy sauce, gochujang, gochugaru, cooking wine, green chile pepper, and red chile pepper in a small bowl, combine well to create sauce.
- Boil daikon radish and water in a big pot for 5 minutes until radish becomes tender.
- Mix mackerel pieces in the pot. Pour sauce on mackerel. Cook on high heat for 10 minutes, spooning sauce occasionally on mackerel without stirring the mixture until cooking liquid reduces to half. Reduce heat then simmer for 15 minutes until sauce thickens, partially covered.
- Sprinkle green onions on mackerel.

Nutrition Information

- Calories: 178 calories;
- Total Fat: 7.7
- Sodium: 776
- Total Carbohydrate: 13.9
- Cholesterol: 32
- Protein: 13.4

533. Grilled Korean Style Beef Short Ribs

Serving: 4 | Prep: 10mins | Cook: 10mins | Ready in:

Ingredients

- 1 large Asian pear, peeled, cored and sliced
- 1/3 cup sherry wine
- 1/3 cup soy sauce
- 1/4 cup rice vinegar
- 1/8 cup brown sugar
- 3 cloves garlic, peeled
- 5 slices fresh ginger, peeled and thinly sliced
- 1 tablespoon hoisin sauce
- 1 tablespoon hot chile paste (such as sambal oelek)
- 1 teaspoon sesame oil
- 4 pounds beef short ribs, trimmed
- 1 chopped green onion for garnish

Direction

- In ab lender, mix sesame oil, hot chili paste, hoisin sauce, garlic, ginger, brown sugar, rice vinegar, soy sauce, sherry wine, and pear slices for 4 minutes until smooth.
- Place short ribs in a 9x13-inch baking dish. Completely coat with marinade. Use plastic wrap to cover baking dish. Place in fridge for 8-12 hours to marinate.
- Place short ribs on a plate. Blot dry using a paper towel to get rid of excess marinade.
- Preheat outdoor grill to medium-high heat. Oil grate lightly.
- Grill short ribs for 4 minutes per side until a little pink in the middle, hot and firm. An inserted instant-read thermometer in the

middle should say 60 degrees C/140 degrees F.

Nutrition Information

- Calories: 1054 calories;
- Protein: 44.8
- Total Fat: 85.3
- Sodium: 1522
- Total Carbohydrate: 24.1
- Cholesterol: 186

---

534. Haemoolpa Jun (Pan Fried Seafood And Green Onion Pancake)

Serving: 4 | Prep: 15mins | Cook: 1hours40mins | Ready in:

Ingredients

- 1/4 cup chopped green onions
- 1 tablespoon vegetable oil, or as needed
- 32 green onions
- 2 1/2 cups all-purpose flour
- 1 cup water
- 1 teaspoon salt
- 10 ounces frozen seafood mix, defrosted
- 6 eggs
- Seasoned Soy Sauce:
- 2 tablespoons soy sauce
- 1/2 teaspoon Korean red pepper powder
- 1/2 teaspoon vinegar
- 1/2 teaspoon sesame oil
- 1/2 teaspoon sesame seeds
- 1/4 teaspoon ground black pepper

Direction

- Trim the ends from the green onions and then chop off the roots. Clean 2 to 3 times with cold water and then slice into eight inches from the white part. Then drain the green onions using a colander.
- Over medium heat, heat approximately one teaspoon of vegetable oil in large skillet. Put one green onion in one direction and one in the opposite direction. Repeat this until eight are used up for each serving batch.
- In a bowl, combine together salt, water and flour until the batter is smooth. Transfer 1/4 of the batter atop the green onions in the skillet. Add 1/4 of seafood mix on top. Cook for about 10 minutes until the pancake is browned lightly on the bottom and the seafood is cooked through.
- In a bowl, whisk the eggs together. Spoon 1/4 of eggs atop the pancake. Cook for about 5 minutes until mostly cooked. Turn the pancake with 1 or 2 spatulas and then cook for 10 more minutes. Repeat this with remaining egg, batter, oil, and green onions.
- In a bowl, whisk together black pepper, sesame seeds, sesame oil, vinegar, Korean red pepper powder and soy sauce. Serve together with pancakes for dipping.

Nutrition Information

- Calories: 545 calories;
- Protein: 35.1
- Total Fat: 13.5
- Sodium: 1321
- Total Carbohydrate: 70.4
- Cholesterol: 416

---

535. Herb Samgyupsal (Korean Grilled Pork Belly)

Serving: 6 | Prep: 25mins | Cook: 17mins | Ready in:

Ingredients

- 1 teaspoon dried thyme
- 1 teaspoon dried dill weed
- 1 teaspoon dried rosemary
- 1 teaspoon garlic powder
- 2 pounds pork belly strips

- 1 cup chopped kimchi
- 1 bulb garlic, cloves separated and peeled
- 3 scallions (pajori), chopped
- Ssamjang Dipping Sauce:
- 2 tablespoons doenjang (Korean soybean paste)
- 2 tablespoons gochujang (Korean hot pepper paste), or more to taste
- 1 tablespoon sesame oil
- 2 cloves garlic, minced
- 1 1/2 teaspoons sesame seeds
- 1 teaspoon rice wine
- 1 teaspoon brown sugar

Direction

- In a small bowl, combine together garlic powder, rosemary, dill and thyme. Brush onto each side of every pork belly strip. Allow to sit for about 15 minutes at room temperature.
- Over medium-high heat, heat a large skillet and then cook the pork belly strips about 7 minutes per side until browned well. Place onto a plate lined with paper towel. Save some grease in skillet. Slice the strips into bite-sized pieces.
- Over medium-high heat, sauté scallions, garlic cloves and kimchi in the reserved grease for about 3 minutes until beginning to brown. Then drain on a plate lined with paper towel.
- In a bowl, combine brown sugar, rice wine, sesame seeds, minced garlic, sesame oil, gochujang and doenjang to prepare the ssamjang sauce.
- Serve the pork belly strips together with ssamjang sauce, scallions, garlic and kimchi.

Nutrition Information

- Calories: 349 calories;
- Cholesterol: 55
- Protein: 20.9
- Total Fat: 24.1
- Sodium: 1594
- Total Carbohydrate: 11.5

536. Hobak Namul (Zucchini Side Dish)

Serving: 2 | Prep: 15mins | Cook: 10mins | Ready in:

Ingredients

- 12 ounces zucchini, halved and cut into 1/4-inch sliced
- 1 teaspoon salt
- 2 teaspoons olive oil
- 2 teaspoons minced garlic
- 1 teaspoon salted fermented shrimp
- 1/2 yellow onion, sliced
- 1 teaspoon sesame seeds
- 1/4 teaspoon ground black pepper

Direction

- Put slices of zucchini in a bowl and then drizzle salt at the top. Allow to sit for ten minutes. Then drain off the excess moisture.
- Over medium heat, heat olive oil in a skillet and then add salted shrimp, garlic and zucchini. Cook while stirring for about 5 minutes until the zucchini softens. Add black pepper, sesame seeds and onion. Cook while stirring for about 5 minutes until the onion becomes translucent.

Nutrition Information

- Calories: 109 calories;
- Total Fat: 5.9
- Sodium: 1185
- Total Carbohydrate: 12.9
- Cholesterol: 2
- Protein: 3.6

537. Hotteok

Serving: 10 | Prep: 30mins | Cook: 10mins | Ready in:

Ingredients

- 2 1/2 cups all-purpose flour
- 1 tablespoon instant dry yeast
- 2 teaspoons white sugar
- 1 cup milk
- 1/4 cup water
- 3/4 teaspoon salt
- 3/4 cup packed brown sugar
- 1/4 cup white sugar
- 1/4 cup finely chopped walnuts
- 1/4 cup black sesame seeds, ground
- 2 teaspoons ground cinnamon
- 2 tablespoons margarine, or as needed

Direction

- In a bowl, mix together 2 tsp white sugar, yeast, and flour.
- In a microwaveable bowl, mix together water and milk, heat in the microwave for 20 seconds until lukewarm. Whisk together the flour mixture and milk mixture with a fork until well blended.
- Knead dough for 2 minutes on a floured surface until sticky. Add in salt and knead for another 2 minutes until the dough is smooth. Form into a ball and put on a floured surface and use a wet paper towel to cover. Set aside for 10 minutes to let it rise.
- In a resealable plastic bag, mix together cinnamon, brown sugar, sesame seeds, quarter cup white sugar, and walnuts. Seal and shake until filling is well combined.
- Form dough into a cylinder and slice into 10 parts; shape each part into a ball. Use a rolling pin to roll each ball into 5-in circles. Place the circles in your palm and scoop 2 tbsp. filling in the center. Fold dough around the filling and shape into a ball by pinching four edges together in the center. Pinch another 4 edges together to close it entirely. On a floured surface, put the dough balls seam-side down.
- Use a rolling pin to spread every ball into 5-in rounds while keeping the filling inside the dough.
- Spread margarine around in a skillet using a paper towel, heat margarine on low heat. Cook the dough in the skillet for 5-10 minutes each side until golden brown.

Nutrition Information

- Calories: 275 calories;
- Cholesterol: 2
- Protein: 5.6
- Total Fat: 6.7
- Sodium: 216
- Total Carbohydrate: 49.1

---

538. Jab Chae (Korean Noodles)

Serving: 4 | Prep: 20mins | Cook: 20mins | Ready in:

Ingredients

- 3 cups water
- 1/2 pound sweet potato vermicelli noodles
- 1 tablespoon vegetable oil, divided, or as needed
- 3 1/2 ounces beef tenderloin, cut into strips
- 1 clove garlic, crushed
- salt and ground black pepper to taste
- 1 onion, thinly sliced
- 1 carrot, cut into matchstick-size pieces
- 2 spring onions, cut into 2-inch pieces
- Sauce:
- 2 tablespoons soy sauce
- 2 teaspoons white sugar
- 1/2 teaspoon sesame seeds
- 1/2 teaspoon sesame oil

Direction

- Boil water in a pot. Add the vermicelli noodles. Cook for 10-12 minutes until soft and clear. Drain noodles inside a colander, sitting for 10 minutes. Rinse noodles under cold water. Cut noodles 2-3 times.

- In a skillet, heat 1 teaspoon oil on medium-high heat. Sauté pepper, salt, garlic, and beef for 3-4 minutes until beef is cooked through. Place beef in a big bowl.
- In the same skillet, heat 1 teaspoon oil. Sauté pepper, salt, and onion for 2-3 minutes until slightly tender. Add onion to the beef. In the same skillet, heat 1 teaspoon of oil. Sauté pepper, salt, and carrot for 2-3 minutes until slightly tender. Put carrot in beef mixture. In the same skillet, heat 1 teaspoon oil. Sauté pepper, salt and spring onions for a minute until slightly tender. Add spring onions to beef mixture.
- Combine noodles with the beef mixture.
- In a bowl, mix sesame oil, sesame seeds, sugar, and soy sauce. Pour on noodle mixture. Mix well.

Nutrition Information

- Calories: 320 calories;
- Total Fat: 7
- Sodium: 523
- Total Carbohydrate: 58.6
- Cholesterol: 14
- Protein: 5.7

539. Jajangmyeon (Vegetarian Korean Black Bean Noodles)

Serving: 2 | Prep: 10mins | Cook: 20mins | Ready in:

Ingredients

- 1/2 tablespoon canola oil
- 1 clove garlic, minced, or more to taste
- 1/2 cup cubed carrots
- 1/2 cup peeled and cubed potatoes
- salt and ground black pepper to taste
- 1/2 cup peeled and cubed zucchini
- 1/2 cup chopped onion
- 1 tablespoon cornstarch
- 1 tablespoon water
- 1 cup water
- 4 tablespoons black bean paste (chunjang)
- 1 tablespoon white sugar, or to taste
- 1/2 (7 ounce) package jaa jang myun noodles

Direction

- Over medium heat, heat oil in a wok and then add potato, carrot, and garlic. Mix and then add pepper and salt. Cook for 5 to 7 minutes until softened. Stir in onion and zucchini.
- In a bowl, mix water and cornstarch together until combined fully.
- Add sugar, black bean paste and water into the wok and mix. Slowly pour the starch mixture into the wok while stirring. Let to cook for 3 to 5 minutes until the sauce becomes thick.
- Bring lightly salted water to boil in a large pot, add noodles and then cook while stirring often for about 3 minutes until the noodles become tender and still firm to bite. Drain off water.
- Serve the noodles in a pasta bowl and then top with black bean mixture. Combine thoroughly.

Nutrition Information

- Calories: 315 calories;
- Cholesterol: 0
- Total Fat: 5.9
- Protein: 9.5
- Sodium: 401
- Total Carbohydrate: 55.6

540. Jang Jorim With Hard Boiled Eggs (Korean Soy Beef Strips)

Serving: 8 | Prep: 45mins | Cook: 1hours5mins | Ready in:

Ingredients

- 2 pounds hanger steak

- 6 cups water
- 1 cup soy sauce
- 2 green chile peppers
- 1/2 onion, quartered
- 2 green onions, trimmed and cut into thirds
- 6 cloves garlic, halved, or more to taste
- 2 tablespoons white sugar
- 1 tablespoon light corn syrup (optional)
- 1 tablespoon rice wine
- 1/2 teaspoon Korean red chile pepper, or to taste
- 4 hard-boiled eggs, peeled, or more to taste

Direction

- In a cold water, soak hanger steak in a big bowl to drain leftover blood for 30 minutes-1 hour, changing water as necessary. Drain.
- Boil and mix red chile pepper, rice wine, corn syrup, sugar, garlic, green onions, onion, green chile peppers, soy sauce, and 6 cups water to create broth. When boiling, add steak. Reduce the heat then simmer for 45 minutes until steak is nearly tender. Place eggs in broth. Keep cooking for another 15 minutes until steak becomes tender.
- Take steak out of broth. Rinse in cold water for 2-3 minutes until cool to touch. Slice steak to bite-size strips. Place in an airtight container. Add the eggs.
- Throw out garlic, green onions, onion, and chile peppers from broth. Skim broth to get rid of oily residue. Strain broth throw a mesh strainer lined with paper towels into a bowl. Repeat process a few times, changing paper towels when needed, until you remove all oily residue.
- Pour broth on eggs and steak in the container. Cover then chill prior to serving for an hour.

Nutrition Information

- Calories: 223 calories;
- Protein: 19.2
- Total Fat: 10.9
- Sodium: 1881
- Total Carbohydrate: 11.4
- Cholesterol: 142

541. Jap Chae Korean Glass Noodles

Serving: 2 | Prep: 20mins | Cook: 20mins | Ready in:

Ingredients

- 1/2 pound Korean dang myun noodles
- 1 teaspoon sesame oil
- 2 tablespoons soy sauce
- 2 teaspoons white sugar
- 1 tablespoon vegetable oil
- 2 cloves garlic, minced
- 3/4 cup thinly sliced onions
- 2 carrots, cut into match-stick size pieces
- 1/2 pound asparagus, thinly sliced
- 3 green onions cut into 1-inch pieces
- 1/2 cup dried shiitake mushrooms, soaked until soft, then sliced into strips
- 1 tablespoon sesame seeds
- 1 1/2 teaspoons sesame oil

Direction

- Add lightly salted water into a large pot until filled and then heat rolling to a boil on high heat. When water is boiling, mix in dang myun noodles and heat to boil. Cook noodles while uncovered and stirring often for 4 to 5 minutes until noodles are cooked through and still firm to bite. Then rinse under cold water and drain thoroughly in a colander that is set in a sink. Toss the noodles with one teaspoon sesame oil and reserve. In a small bowl, whisk sugar and soy sauce and reserve.
- Over medium-high heat, heat vegetable oil in a skillet and then mix in the asparagus, carrots, onion and garlic. Cook while stirring for about 5 minutes until veggies have softened. Mix in shiitake mushrooms and green onions and continue to cook while stirring for 30 seconds. Add in soy sauce

mixture, followed by noodles. Cook while stirring for 2 to 3 minutes until noodles are warmed through. Take out from the heat and toss with the remaining 1 1/2 teaspoon of sesame oil and sesame seeds.

Nutrition Information

- Calories: 673 calories;
- Sodium: 1639
- Total Carbohydrate: 117.2
- Cholesterol: 0
- Protein: 17.3
- Total Fat: 17.3

542. Japchae

Serving: 8 | Prep: 30mins | Cook: 15mins | Ready in:

Ingredients

- Sauce:
- 3 tablespoons soy sauce
- 2 1/2 tablespoons white sugar
- 2 tablespoons sesame oil
- 2 teaspoons minced garlic
- Stir Fry Ingredients:
- 8 ounces sweet potato noodles
- 4 ounces lean beef, cut into 2-inch long strips
- 6 ounces fresh spinach
- salt and ground black pepper to taste
- 1 tablespoon vegetable oil, divided
- 1 small sweet onion, thinly sliced
- 4 mushrooms, stemmed and sliced
- 1 small carrot, cut into matchsticks

Direction

- In a bowl, mix garlic, sesame oil, sugar, and soy sauce until sugar melts into sauce.
- Boil a big pot of lightly salted water. In boiling water, cook sweet potato noodles for 6-7 minutes, occasionally stirring until firm to the bite but cooked through. Rinse noodles in cold water then drain. Place noodles in a bowl, add 2 tablespoons of sauce, then toss until coated.
- Squeeze beef in running water until juices are clear. Mix 1 tablespoon sauce and beef in a bowl together.
- Boil a pot of water. In boiling water, cook spinach for 1 minutes until wilted. Quickly drain and place spinach in a bowl with cold water to stop cooking process. Squeeze extra water out of spinach. Place in a big bowl. Season with pepper and salt.
- In a big skillet, heat 1 tablespoon oil on medium-high heat. Cook onion for 1-2 minutes until crisp and fragrant. Place onion in bowl with the spinach. In the same skillet, heat another 1 teaspoon of oil. Cook mushrooms in hot oil for 1-2 minutes until light brown and still firm. Add into onion mixture. Heat leftover 1 teaspoon of oil in the skillet. Cook carrot in hot oil for 1-2 minutes until crisp and light brown. Add to the onion mixture.
- Sauté beef for 1-2 minutes in the same skillet until its brown. Add into onion mixture. Stir and cook noodles for 1-2 minutes in the same skillet until they're heated through. Add to onion-beef mixture. Add leftover sauce on noodles-beef mixture. Coat by tossing with your hands.

Nutrition Information

- Calories: 201 calories;
- Total Fat: 7
- Sodium: 368
- Total Carbohydrate: 31.5
- Cholesterol: 7
- Protein: 3.6

543. Kalbi (Korean BBQ Short Ribs)

Serving: 4 | Prep: 15mins | Cook: 15mins | Ready in:

Ingredients

- 3/4 cup soy sauce
- 3/4 cup brown sugar
- 3/4 cup water
- 1 garlic clove, minced
- 2 green onions, chopped
- 1 tablespoon Asian (toasted) sesame oil
- 2 pounds Korean-style short ribs (beef chuck flanken, cut 1/3 to 1/2 inch thick across bones)

Direction

- Mix together the sesame oil, green onions, garlic, water, brown sugar and soy sauce in a bowl until sugar is dissolved.
- Transfer the ribs into a large plastic zipper bag and then add the marinade on top of the ribs. Squeeze out the air and chill for three hours to overnight.
- Preheat the outdoor grill over medium-high heat and coat the grate lightly with oil. Take out the ribs from bag, then shake off excess marinade and get rid of the marinade. Grill ribs over the grill 5 to 7 minutes per side until meat is still pink and not bloody closest to the bone.

Nutrition Information

- Calories: 1096 calories;
- Sodium: 2831
- Total Carbohydrate: 44.9
- Cholesterol: 172
- Protein: 35.9
- Total Fat: 85.6

544. Kalbi (Korean Marinated Short Ribs)

Serving: 10 | Prep: 20mins | Cook: 8mins | Ready in:

Ingredients

- 3 pounds beef short ribs
- 1/2 cup soy sauce
- 1 Asian pear, cored and diced
- 1/2 small onion
- 2 tablespoons finely chopped garlic
- 1 tablespoon chopped ginger
- 2 green onions, thinly sliced
- 2 tablespoons sesame oil
- 2 tablespoons brown sugar
- 2 tablespoons toasted sesame seeds
- 1 tablespoon honey
- 1/4 teaspoon ground black pepper

Direction

- In a bowl, cover ribs with water. Soak for an hour until water becomes pink. Drain; rinse with cold water.
- In a food processor, pulse ginger, garlic, onion, Asian pear, and soy sauce until smooth.
- In a big bowl, mix black pepper, honey, sesame seeds, brown sugar, sesame oil, and green onions well. Add ribs and thoroughly coat with marinade. Cover using plastic wrap. Keep in fridge for 8 hours to overnight.
- Preheat outdoor grill to high heat. Oil grate lightly.
- Cook ribs on grill for 4 minutes on each side until tender and slightly charred.

Nutrition Information

- Calories: 347 calories;
- Cholesterol: 56
- Protein: 14.2
- Total Fat: 28.6
- Sodium: 753
- Total Carbohydrate: 8

545. Kalbi (Marinated Beef Short Ribs)

Serving: 6 | Prep: 10mins | Cook: 30mins | Ready in:

Ingredients

- 3/4 cup white sugar
- 3/4 cup soy sauce
- 1/4 cup sesame oil
- 4 cloves garlic, minced
- 3 green onions, chopped
- 2 tablespoons sesame seeds
- 5 pounds beef short ribs

Direction

- Mix sugar into soy sauce inside a bowl until sugar melts completely. Mix in sesame seeds, green onions, garlic, and sesame oil. Put short ribs in a sealable, big bag and pour marinade on meat. Marinate in the fridge for 8 hours to overnight.
- Preheat outdoor grill to medium heat, oiling grate lightly. Take ribs out of bag, throw out marinade.
- On preheated grill, cook short ribs for 15 minutes on each side until they are hot, very firm, and grey in the middle. An instant-read thermometer poked in the middle will say 70 degrees C/160 degrees F.

Nutrition Information

- Calories: 995 calories;
- Total Fat: 80
- Sodium: 1888
- Total Carbohydrate: 29.3
- Cholesterol: 155
- Protein: 38.5

546. Kim Chee Squats

Serving: 8 | Prep: 25mins | Cook: | Ready in:

Ingredients

- 2 pounds coarsely chopped Chinese cabbage
- 1 tablespoon salt
- 2 tablespoons chopped green onion
- 1 clove garlic, crushed
- 1 tablespoon chili powder
- 2 teaspoons minced fresh ginger root
- 1/2 cup light soy sauce
- 1/2 cup white wine vinegar
- 2 teaspoons white sugar
- 1 dash sesame oil

Direction

- In a big dish, put cabbage and dust with salt. Set aside for 3-4hours until the cabbage wilts.
- Use your hands to massage the cabbage until it softens more; drain. Stir in sugar, green onion, vinegar, garlic, soy sauce, chili powder, and ginger. Move into a big glass jar and let it chill for a day before serving. It can last for a week when refrigerated. Drizzle with sesame oil. Serve.

Nutrition Information

- Calories: 36 calories;
- Total Carbohydrate: 6.8
- Cholesterol: 0
- Protein: 2.6
- Total Fat: 0.5
- Sodium: 1796

547. Kimchi (Korean Fermented Spicy Cabbage)

Serving: 14 | Prep: 1hours | Cook: 10mins | Ready in:

Ingredients

- 3 heads napa cabbage
- 3 cups water
- 4 cups coarse sea salt
- 3 cups water
- 3 tablespoons sweet rice flour
- 1 yellow onion
- 12 cloves garlic, peeled
- 2 tablespoons minced fresh ginger root
- 1 tablespoon water, or as needed

- 4 cups Korean red chile flakes (gochugaru)
- 1/2 cup fish sauce
- 1/4 cup dried salted shrimp (saeujeot)
- 2 tablespoons brown sugar
- 1 tablespoon sesame seeds, or more to taste
- 2 cups Korean radish, cut into matchstick-size pieces
- 3 green onions, cut into 2-inch pieces

Direction

- Remove the discolored and bruised outer leaves of cabbage and then rinse the cabbage with cold water. Slice the cabbage head into two-inch pieces.
- Distribute three cups of water between three bowls. Mix one cup of sea salt into each bowl containing water. Drizzle remaining one cup of sea salt atop cabbage.
- Transfer the salted cabbage into the three bowls of salted water until they are partially submerged. Leave to stand for about 6 to 12 hours.
- Thoroughly rinse the cabbage with cold water a few times. Then squeeze the cabbage to get rid of the excess water. The cabbage will have a rubbery texture. Place the cabbage into a basket or colander to drain the cabbage thoroughly for at least 2 hours.
- In a saucepan, mix rice flour and three cups of water and then heat to boil. Whisk the mixture for 5 to 10 minutes until a glue-like consistency. Take out the saucepan from heat and then cool the rice mixture to room temperature.
- In a food processor, mix 1 tablespoon water, ginger, garlic, and onion and then pulse until smooth. You can add more water if necessary.
- Transfer the chile flakes into a large bowl. Then mix in sesame seeds, brown sugar, shrimp, fish sauce, cooled rice flour mixture and onion-garlic mixture until combined well. Add green onions and radish and combine well.
- Use your hands to coat every cabbage piece with the chile mixture. (It's best if you use a rubber gloves). Pack the coated cabbage leaves into air-tight containers or glass jars. Then tightly cover each with a lid. Keep jars at room temperature for fermentation to occur, about 2 days. Chill the kimchi after two days.

Nutrition Information

- Calories: 88 calories;
- Total Fat: 1.2
- Sodium: 24796
- Total Carbohydrate: 17.9
- Cholesterol: 3
- Protein: 3.9

548. Kimchi Fried Rice With Bell Pepper

Serving: 4 | Prep: 15mins | Cook: 24mins | Ready in:

Ingredients

- 1 cup kimchi, finely chopped, juice reserved
- 1 tablespoon gochujang (Korean hot pepper paste)
- 1 1/2 teaspoons soy sauce
- 2 teaspoons sesame oil
- 3 cups cooked white rice
- 1 1/2 tablespoons sesame oil, divided
- 2 large eggs, beaten
- 2 green onions, chopped, white and green parts separated
- 1/2 red bell pepper, diced
- 1 1/2 teaspoons Korean red pepper powder (optional)

Direction

- In a bowl, whisk together soy sauce, gochujang and kimchi juice until gochujang is dissolved.
- Sprinkle two teaspoons of sesame oil over white rice and combine together in a bowl and break up any clumps.

- Over medium-high heat, heat 1 1/2 teaspoons of oil in a large skillet and then add eggs into the skillet. Cook while stirring for about 4 minutes until set. Place the scrambled eggs into a bowl.
- Over medium heat, heat the remaining one tablespoon of sesame oil in the same skillet until it's shimmering. Place in kimchi and then cook for about 5 minutes until fragrant and browned. Mix in whites of green onions and bell pepper and then cook for about 5 minutes until softened. Pour in rice and then cook for about 5 minutes while stirring and pushing down on any clumps, until the mixture forms a uniform color.
- Spread the kimchi juice mixture over rice and stir. Raise the heat to high and then let to cook for about 5 minutes until the rice doesn't stick together and is browned. Mix in the eggs. Add red pepper powder and the remaining green onions on top.

Nutrition Information

- Calories: 284 calories;
- Sodium: 441
- Total Carbohydrate: 39.4
- Cholesterol: 93
- Protein: 7.5
- Total Fat: 10.6

549. Kimchi Jigae (Kimchee Soup)

Serving: 4 | Prep: 15mins | Cook: 25mins | Ready in:

Ingredients

- 2 cups chopped kimchi
- 1 cup water
- 1 tablespoon brown sugar
- 4 cloves garlic, minced
- 1/2 pound pork belly, cut into bite-size pieces
- 1 (12 ounce) can fully cooked luncheon meat (such as SPAM®), cubed (optional)
- 1/4 cup kochujang (Korean hot sauce) (optional)
- 1 (12 ounce) package silken tofu
- 1 (3 ounce) package enoki mushrooms

Direction

- Over medium-high heat, mix garlic, sugar, water and kimchi in a large skillet. Heat to a boil. Mix in kochujang, luncheon meat and pork belly. Add mushrooms and tofu. Mix gently to prevent breaking up the tofu. Decrease the heat to medium-low. Cook for 20 to 30 minutes until the pork becomes slightly pink in the middle and the kimchi becomes softened.

Nutrition Information

- Calories: 477 calories;
- Total Fat: 35.1
- Sodium: 2733
- Total Carbohydrate: 14.9
- Cholesterol: 80
- Protein: 26.9

550. Kimchi Jun (Kimchi Pancake) And Dipping Sauce

Serving: 4 | Prep: 15mins | Cook: 15mins | Ready in:

Ingredients

- 1 cup kimchi, drained and chopped
- 1/2 cup reserved juice from kimchi
- 1 cup all-purpose flour
- 2 eggs
- 1 green onion, chopped
- 1 tablespoon vegetable oil
- salt to taste
- 1 tablespoon rice vinegar
- 1 tablespoon soy sauce

- 1/2 teaspoon sesame oil
- 1/2 teaspoon Korean chili pepper flakes (optional)
- 1/2 teaspoon toasted sesame seeds (optional)

Direction

- Mix green onion, eggs, flour, kimchi juice, and kimchi in a bowl.
- In a big skillet, heat vegetable oil on medium heat. Use 1/4 cup batter for every pancake. Pour in skillet, spreading as thinly as you can. Cook pancakes for 3-5 minutes on each side until light brown and set, flipping once. Season with salt to taste.
- Whisk toasted sesame seeds, chili pepper flakes, sesame oil, soy sauce, and rice vinegar. Serve with pancakes.

Nutrition Information

- Calories: 199 calories;
- Protein: 7.4
- Total Fat: 7.1
- Sodium: 552
- Total Carbohydrate: 26.5
- Cholesterol: 93

551. Kimchi Jun (Kimchi Patty)

Serving: 4 | Prep: 10mins | Cook: 40mins | Ready in:

Ingredients

- 2 cups chopped kimchi
- 1/2 yellow onion, sliced
- 1 1/2 cups all-purpose flour
- 2 cups water
- 1 tablespoon vegetable oil, or as needed
- Dipping Sauce:
- 1/4 cup chopped green onions
- 2 tablespoons soy sauce
- 1/2 teaspoon sesame seeds
- 1/2 teaspoon Korean red pepper powder
- 1/2 teaspoon sesame oil

Direction

- In a big bowl, mix onion and kimchi. Add flour then combine well for a minute. Pour water on kimchi mixture. Mix until batter combines evenly.
- Heat skillet on medium heat. Add 1 teaspoon vegetable oil. Scoop 1/4 cup batter in hot skillet, making a 1/4-inch thick pancake. Smoothen and flatten edges with a spatula. Cook pancake for about 3 minutes. Flip, lightly pressing, and cooking for another 2 minutes. Repeat process with leftover batter and vegetable oil.
- In a bowl, mix sesame oil, red pepper powder, sesame seeds, soy sauce, and green onion. Serve with pancakes.

Nutrition Information

- Calories: 242 calories;
- Total Fat: 4.9
- Sodium: 959
- Total Carbohydrate: 42.8
- Cholesterol: 0
- Protein: 7.1

552. Kkakdugi (Korean Radish Kimchi)

Serving: 30 | Prep: 20mins | Cook: | Ready in:

Ingredients

- 2 daikon radishes, cubed
- 6 tablespoons kosher salt
- 5 tablespoons Korean red pepper paste (gochujang)
- 3 tablespoons minced fresh ginger
- 2 2/3 tablespoons Korean red pepper powder (gochukaro)

- 2 tablespoons fish sauce
- 7 teaspoons white sugar
- 6 cloves garlic, minced

Direction

- Transfer the cubed daikon into a bowl and then add kosher salt. Toss to coat. Gently pour water down the side of bowl to the level of radishes. Be sure not to rinse off all of salt. Then cover with plastic wrap and transfer to cool spot for about 12 to 24 hours.
- Drain radishes and then rinse properly. Add sugar, garlic, fish sauce, Korean red pepper powder, ginger and Korean red pepper paste. Combine well. Then cover container with lid or plastic wrap and place it in a cold spot. Let to ferment for about 4 to 6 weeks.

Nutrition Information

- Calories: 13 calories;
- Total Carbohydrate: 2.9
- Cholesterol: 0
- Protein: 0.3
- Total Fat: 0.1
- Sodium: 1343

553. Kongnamool (Korean Soybean Sprouts)

Serving: 4 | Prep: 10mins | Cook: 5mins | Ready in:

Ingredients

- 1 pound soybean sprouts
- 2 tablespoons soy sauce
- 1/4 cup sesame oil
- 2 tablespoons Korean chile powder
- 1 1/2 teaspoons garlic, minced
- 2 teaspoons sesame seeds
- 1/4 cup chopped green onion
- 2 teaspoons rice wine vinegar, or to taste

Direction

- Boil a big pot of lightly salted water. Add bean sprouts, cooking for 15 seconds, uncovered, until crisp-tender. Drain in a colander then immerse immediately in ice water for a few minutes to stop cooking process until they're cold. When bean sprouts become cold, drain them well and put aside.
- In a big bowl, mix sesame seeds, garlic, chile powder, sesame oil, and soy sauce. Mix in bean sprouts, tossing until coated well with sauce. Sprinkle green onions and season using rice wine vinegar. Keep in fridge before serving.

Nutrition Information

- Calories: 288 calories;
- Sodium: 508
- Total Carbohydrate: 14.8
- Cholesterol: 0
- Protein: 16.3
- Total Fat: 22.7

554. Korean BBQ Chicken Marinade

Serving: 48 | Prep: 10mins | Cook: 15mins | Ready in:

Ingredients

- 1 cup white sugar
- 1 cup soy sauce
- 1 cup water
- 1 teaspoon onion powder
- 1 teaspoon ground ginger
- 1 tablespoon lemon juice (optional)
- 4 teaspoons hot chile paste (optional)

Direction

- Mix and boil ground ginger, onion powder, water, soy sauce, and sugar in a medium

saucepan on high heat. Reduce heat down to low then simmer for 5 minutes.
- Take mixture off heat. Cool and mix in hot chile paste and lemon juice. Put chicken in mixture. Cover then marinate in the fridge for at least 4 hours prior to making chicken as desired.

Nutrition Information

- Calories: 20 calories;
- Total Fat: 0.1
- Sodium: 304
- Total Carbohydrate: 4.9
- Cholesterol: 0
- Protein: 0.3

555. Korean BBQ Galbi

Serving: 6 | Prep: 1hours30mins | Cook: 10mins | Ready in:

Ingredients

- 5 pounds beef short ribs, cut flanken style
- 5 cloves garlic
- 1 onion, coarsely chopped
- 1 Asian pear, cored and cubed
- 1 cup soy sauce (such as Kikkoman®)
- 1 cup brown sugar
- 1/4 cup honey
- 1/4 cup sesame oil
- black pepper to taste

Direction

- In a big stock pot, cover ribs with cold water. Soak ribs for an hour in the fridge to pull any blood out. Drain.
- In a blender, puree Asian pear, onion, and garlic. Place in a big bowl. Mix in black pepper, sesame oil, honey, brown sugar, and soy sauce. Marinade ribs in soy mixture overnight, covered.

- Preheat an outdoor grill to high heat. Oil grate lightly.
- Grill ribs for 5-10 minutes per side until outside is crusty and meat is tender.

Nutrition Information

- Calories: 1092 calories;
- Cholesterol: 155
- Protein: 39.1
- Total Fat: 78.6
- Sodium: 2501
- Total Carbohydrate: 57.5

556. Korean BBQ Short Ribs (Gal Bi)

Serving: 5 | Prep: 15mins | Cook: 10mins | Ready in:

Ingredients

- 3/4 cup soy sauce
- 3/4 cup water
- 3 tablespoons white vinegar
- 1/4 cup dark brown sugar
- 2 tablespoons white sugar
- 1 tablespoon black pepper
- 2 tablespoons sesame oil
- 1/4 cup minced garlic
- 1/2 large onion, minced
- 3 pounds Korean-style short ribs (beef chuck flanken, cut 1/3 to 1/2 inch thick across bones)

Direction

- In a big, non-metallic bowl, put in vinegar, water, and soy sauce. Mix in onion, garlic, sesame oil, pepper, white sugar, and brown sugar until sugars melt. Submerge ribs in marinade, covering with plastic wrap. Keep in fridge for 7-12 hours. It's better if you leave them for a long time.
- Preheat outdoor grill to medium-high heat.

- Take ribs out of marinade, shaking excess off, then throw out marinade. Cook on preheated grill for 5-7 minutes on each side until meat isn't pink.

Nutrition Information

- Calories: 710 calories;
- Sodium: 2231
- Total Carbohydrate: 23.2
- Cholesterol: 112
- Protein: 28.8
- Total Fat: 55.5

557. Korean BBQ Inspired Short Ribs

Serving: 4 | Prep: 10mins | Cook: 15mins | Ready in:

Ingredients

- 1/4 cup rice wine vinegar
- 1/4 cup soy sauce
- 1/4 cup sriracha hot sauce, or to taste
- 2 tablespoons olive oil
- 1/4 cup brown sugar
- 2 green onions, chopped (optional)
- 3 cloves garlic, minced, or more to taste
- 1 tablespoon ground black pepper
- 1 tablespoon toasted sesame seeds
- 1 tablespoon minced fresh ginger
- 1 pinch Chinese five-spice powder
- 2 pounds beef short ribs, cut 1/3-inch-thick across the bones

Direction

- In a large bowl, whisk together olive oil, vinegar, sriracha hot sauce, and soy sauce. Stir in brown sugar until dissolved. Into the vinegar mixture, combine green onions, five-spice powder, garlic, ginger, black pepper, and sesame seeds until the marinade is combined evenly.
- Transfer short ribs into a large bag that is resealable and add marinade on top of ribs. Then coat ribs with marinade, press out the excess air and seal the bag. Place in a refrigerator to marinate for at least 3 hours.
- Preheat the grill over medium heat and then coat the grate lightly with oil.
- Take out the ribs from the marinade and transfer onto the grill. Let cook for about 6 to 7 minutes. Turn the ribs and ladle the marinade on top of the second side. Cook for 6 to 7 more minutes until the pink color of meat disappears. Switch the grill heat to high and let ribs cook for one more minute per side. Take out the ribs from the heat and transfer onto a plate. Allow to stand for five minutes.

Nutrition Information

- Calories: 619 calories;
- Total Carbohydrate: 19.5
- Cholesterol: 93
- Protein: 23.3
- Total Fat: 49.6
- Sodium: 1593

558. Korean Barbequed Beef

Serving: 8 | Prep: 15mins | Cook: 7mins | Ready in:

Ingredients

- 1 1/2 pounds beef sirloin
- 1/2 cup soy sauce
- 1/2 cup rice wine
- 2 tablespoons white sugar
- 2 tablespoons minced garlic
- 1 1/2 teaspoons toasted sesame oil
- 1/4 teaspoon freshly ground black pepper
- 1 teaspoon hot chile paste
- 8 green onions, chopped into 1 inch pieces
- 1 cup Bibb lettuce

Direction

- Slice beef with grain to long strips that are 1 1/2-inch wide. Put in a bowl. In a small bowl, mix chile paste, pepper, sesame oil, garlic, sugar, rice wine, and soy sauce. Pour 1/3 of it on beef, tossing to coat. Marinade for at least an hour in room temperature or for longer in the fridge. Simmer leftover sauce and green onions for a minute in a small saucepan. Pour in a serving dish. Let cool.
- Wash then dry lettuce. Trim off any big stems. Flatten leaves gently with a big knife or side of a cleaver. Place on serving dish.
- Preheat a grill to medium-high heat. Oil grate lightly.
- Put grate 3 inches above coals. Cook meat to preferred doneness, 3 minutes on each side to get medium rare. Slice against grain to thin strips.
- To serve, place some sauce and beef in a lettuce leaf to each diner, folding it to a bundle and eating with your fingers.

Nutrition Information

- Calories: 166 calories;
- Cholesterol: 37
- Protein: 16.4
- Total Fat: 5.9
- Sodium: 942
- Total Carbohydrate: 7.4

559. Korean Bean Curd (Miso) Soup

Serving: 4 | Prep: 15mins | Cook: 20mins | Ready in:

Ingredients

- 3 1/2 cups water
- 3 tablespoons denjang (Korean bean curd paste)
- 1 tablespoon garlic paste
- 1/2 tablespoon dashi granules
- 1/2 tablespoon gochujang (Korean hot pepper paste)
- 1 zucchini, cubed
- 1 potato, peeled and cubed
- 1/4 pound fresh mushrooms, quartered
- 1 onion, chopped
- 1 (12 ounce) package soft tofu, sliced

Direction

- Over medium heat, combine gochujang, dashi, water, garlic paste and denjang in a large saucepan. Heat to boil and boil for two minutes. Mix in onions, mushrooms, potato and zucchini. Boil for about 5 to 7 minutes. Mix in tofu and then cook until the veggies become tender and the tofu has expanded.

Nutrition Information

- Calories: 158 calories;
- Total Fat: 4.1
- Sodium: 641
- Total Carbohydrate: 21.6
- Cholesterol: 0
- Protein: 9.1

560. Korean Beef Simmered In Soy Sauce (Jangjorim)

Serving: 6 | Prep: 20mins | Cook: 1hours5mins | Ready in:

Ingredients

- 1/2 pound beef brisket, cut into 2-inch pieces
- 1/2 cup soy sauce
- 1/4 cup white sugar
- 5 cloves garlic
- ground black pepper to taste
- 3 shishito peppers, or more to taste (optional)
- 3 hard boiled eggs, sliced, or more to taste (optional)

Direction

- Add water into a large pot until filled and then place in beef. Heat to boil. Decrease the heat and let to simmer for about half an hour until the meat can be pierced with a fork. Mix in ground black pepper, garlic, white sugar and soy sauce. Cook while stirring for about 15 minutes until the flavors have combined.
- Mix eggs and shishito peppers into beef mixture. Cook while stirring for about 15 minutes until the liquids have been decreased to a third of the original amount and the meat is easily pulled apart with a fork.

Nutrition Information

- Calories: 159 calories;
- Cholesterol: 122
- Protein: 9
- Total Fat: 7.9
- Sodium: 1246
- Total Carbohydrate: 13.3

561. Korean Crab Cakes

Serving: 4 | Prep: 15mins | Cook: 35mins | Ready in:

Ingredients

- 1/4 cup mayonnaise
- 2 tablespoons chopped fresh cilantro
- 1 tablespoon chopped fresh ginger
- 2 teaspoons Asian fish sauce (nuoc mam or nam pla)
- 1 (6 ounce) can crabmeat - drained, flaked and cartilage removed
- 3 ounces chopped shrimp
- 1 1/2 cups fresh breadcrumbs, made from crustless French bread
- salt and pepper to taste
- 1 1/2 tablespoons peanut oil

Direction

- Mix fish sauce, fresh ginger, cilantro, and mayonnaise in a medium bowl. Mix in 1/2 cup of breadcrumbs, shrimp, and crab. Season with pepper and salt to taste.
- Put leftover 1 cup of breadcrumbs in a shallow bowl or plate. Drop 1/4 crab mixture on breadcrumbs. Turn to coat. Form to an oval or circle. Repeat with leftover crab mixture.
- In a heavy skillet, heat oil on medium heat. Cook cakes in oil until cooked through and golden brown, for 5 minutes on each side.

Nutrition Information

- Calories: 254 calories;
- Total Fat: 17.4
- Sodium: 620
- Total Carbohydrate: 9.6
- Cholesterol: 75
- Protein: 14.5

562. Korean Cucumber Salad

Serving: 2 | Prep: 20mins | Cook: 5mins | Ready in:

Ingredients

- 1/4 cup white vinegar
- 1/4 teaspoon black pepper
- 1/2 teaspoon red pepper flakes
- 1 teaspoon vegetable oil
- 2 tablespoons sesame seeds
- 1 cucumber, thinly sliced
- 1/2 green onion, sliced
- 1/2 carrot, julienned

Direction

- Mix red pepper flakes, black pepper, and vinegar in a medium bowl.
- In a saucepan, heat oil on medium-high heat. Mix in sesame seeds. Reduce the heat to medium. Cook for 5 minutes until seeds become brown. Take seeds out using a slotted

spoon. Mix into the vinegar mixture. Stir in carrot, green onions, and cucumber. Cover then keep in fridge for at least five minutes.

Nutrition Information

- Calories: 98 calories;
- Total Fat: 7
- Sodium: 14
- Total Carbohydrate: 8.1
- Cholesterol: 0
- Protein: 2.6

563. Korean Egg Roll Triangles

Serving: 6 | Prep: 45mins | Cook: 15mins | Ready in:

Ingredients

- 1/2 (8 ounce) package dry thin Asian rice noodles (rice vermicelli)
- 1/2 medium head cabbage, cored and shredded
- 1 (12 ounce) package firm tofu
- 2 small zucchini, shredded
- 4 green onions, finely chopped
- 4 cloves garlic, finely chopped
- 1 tablespoon ground black pepper
- 2 tablespoons Asian (toasted) sesame oil
- 2 eggs, slightly beaten
- 2 teaspoons salt
- 1 (12 ounce) package round wonton wrappers
- 1/2 cup vegetable oil for frying

Direction

- Boil a pot of water and put in rice noodles. Boil for 3-5 minutes until noodles become soft yet not mushy, occasionally stirring. Rinse using cold water then drain into a colander in the sink. Chop noodles to small pieces then put aside.
- In a length of cheesecloth or kitchen towel, wrap shredded cabbage. Squeeze extra moisture out. Put chopped rice noodles, salt, eggs, sesame oil, black pepper, garlic, green onions, zucchini, tofu, and cabbage in a big bowl. Use your hands to mix until it's evenly distributed and tofu gets broken to very small chunks.
- On a work surface, put a round wonton wrapper. Place 1-2 teaspoons of the filing in the middle of the wrapper. Put your finger in water then moisten the wrapper's edge about halfway around. Fold wrapper over, covering the filling. Pinch edges together to create a half-moon shape. Put completed rolls onto a cookie sheet as you do the rest.
- In a heavy skillet, heat vegetable oil. Work in batches to fry rolls for 2-3 minutes on each side until golden brown.

Nutrition Information

- Calories: 534 calories;
- Total Carbohydrate: 56.9
- Cholesterol: 67
- Protein: 14.6
- Total Fat: 28.4
- Sodium: 1177

564. Korean Fried Chicken

Serving: 4 | Prep: 15mins | Cook: 10mins | Ready in:

Ingredients

- Marinade:
- 1 pound skinless, boneless chicken thighs, quartered
- 1/2 yellow onion, grated
- 4 cloves garlic, minced
- 1 teaspoon fine salt
- 1/2 teaspoon freshly ground black pepper
- Batter:
- 3/4 cup cornstarch

- 1/2 cup self-rising flour
- 1 teaspoon white sugar
- 1/2 teaspoon ground black pepper
- 1/4 teaspoon salt
- 1 cup very cold water, or as needed
- oil, or as needed

Direction

- In a bowl, mix 1/2 teaspoon black pepper, fine salt, garlic, onion, and chicken until chicken is coated. Use plastic wrap to cover bowl. Keep in fridge for 4 hours up to overnight.
- In a big saucepan or deep-fryer, heat oil to 171 degrees C/340 degrees F.
- In a big bowl, mix 1/4 teaspoon salt, 1/2 teaspoon black pepper, sugar, flour, and cornstarch. Slowly mix ice water in flour until it looks like a smooth pancake batter. Place chicken in batter. Stir to completely coat.
- In batches, cook chicken for 4 minutes in preheated oil. Place cooked chicken on a cooling rack.
- Bring up oil temperature in big saucepan or a deep-fryer to 190 degrees C/375 degrees F.
- In batches, cook chicken in hot oil again for 3-4 minutes until outside is crispy and golden brown. Transfer and drain on a wire rack.

Nutrition Information

- Calories: 476 calories;
- Sodium: 1150
- Total Carbohydrate: 45.4
- Cholesterol: 71
- Protein: 18.6
- Total Fat: 23.8

565. Korean Fried Chicken Sauce

Serving: 6 | Prep: 10mins | Cook: 5mins | Ready in:

Ingredients

- 1/2 cup ketchup
- 2 green onions, minced
- 4 cloves garlic, minced
- 1 lemon, juiced, or more to taste
- 2 tablespoons honey
- 1 tablespoon chile-garlic sauce (such as sambal), or to taste
- 1 teaspoon red pepper flakes, or to taste
- 1/2 teaspoon freshly ground black pepper, or to taste
- 1/4 cup water, or as needed
- 1 pinch salt, or to taste

Direction

- In a saucepan, mix black pepper, red pepper flakes, chile-garlic sauce, honey, lemon juice, garlic, green onion, and ketchup on medium-high heat. Add enough water to reach your preferred sauce consistency. Simmer sauce, reduce heat down to medium-low. Simmer for 5 minutes until flavors merge and it's thick. Cool down to room temperature. Season with salt.

Nutrition Information

- Calories: 50 calories;
- Total Fat: 0.2
- Sodium: 356
- Total Carbohydrate: 13.1
- Cholesterol: 0
- Protein: 0.7

566. Korean Fusion Chicken Burrito

Serving: 4 | Prep: 15mins | Cook: 15mins | Ready in:

Ingredients

- Meat:
- 6 cloves garlic, minced
- 2 tablespoons Korean chile paste (gochujang)

- 1 tablespoon soy sauce
- 2 teaspoons white sugar
- 1 teaspoon sesame oil
- 2 (10 ounce) cans chicken chunks, drained
- Everything Else:
- 4 (10 inch) flour tortillas
- 2 tablespoons vegetable oil
- 2 teaspoons butter, softened (optional)
- 1 cup fresh cilantro leaves
- 1/2 cup chopped kimchi, squeezed dry (optional)
- 2 tablespoons shredded sharp Cheddar cheese
- 1 tablespoon salsa

Direction

- Preheat oven to 182 degrees C/360 degrees F.
- In a bowl, mix sesame oil, sugar, soy sauce, chile paste, and garlic until sugar melts in liquid. Add chicken then mix to coat.
- Wrap aluminum foil on tortillas, baking in the preheated oven for 10 minutes until soft and hot.
- As tortillas are warming, heat vegetable oil on a skillet. Sauté chicken in the skillet for 10 minutes until sauce thickens and it's hot.
- Spread half a teaspoon of butter on one side of every warm tortilla. Distribute chicken between tortillas. Top equal portions of salsa, cheddar cheese, kimchi, and cilantro on chicken.
- Fold opposite ends of every tortilla towards each other, partially covering filling. Pull a leftover edge on the filling then roll it out so the tortilla completely surrounds filling.

Nutrition Information

- Calories: 597 calories;
- Sodium: 1635
- Total Carbohydrate: 45.6
- Cholesterol: 97
- Protein: 38.5
- Total Fat: 29.1

567. Korean Hot Wings

Serving: 6 | Prep: 15mins | Cook: 30mins | Ready in:

Ingredients

- 1 cup low-sodium soy sauce
- 3/4 cup dark brown sugar
- 1/4 cup ketchup
- 3 tablespoons barbeque sauce
- 2 tablespoons minced garlic
- 1 tablespoon rice wine vinegar
- 1 tablespoon chile-garlic sauce (such as Sriracha) (optional)
- 1 1/2 teaspoons ground black pepper
- 1 teaspoon Asian (toasted) sesame oil
- 1 teaspoon grated fresh ginger
- 1 tablespoon cornstarch
- 1 tablespoon water
- 1 quart peanut oil for frying, or as needed
- 4 pounds chicken wings
- 2 tablespoons lemon-pepper seasoning, or to taste (optional)

Direction

- Boil and mix ginger, sesame oil, pepper, chile-garlic sauce, vinegar, garlic, barbeque sauce, ketchup, brown sugar, soy sauce in a saucepan.
- Mix water and cornstarch in a small bowl, mixing into sauce. Take off heat. Put aside to thicken and cool.
- In a big saucepan or deep-fryer, heat oil to 182 degrees C/360 degrees F.
- Season lemon-pepper seasoning on chicken wings.
- Fry chicken wings 6-8 pieces at one time in batches. Cook in hot oil for 6-8 minutes for each batch until juices are clear and it's not pink near the bone. An inserted instant-read thermometer pierced in the meatiest part of the wing next to the bone will say 74 degrees C/165 degrees F.
- Put cooked wings in a big mixing bowl. Put sauce on wings, tossing to coat.

Nutrition Information

- Calories: 459 calories;
- Total Fat: 22.5
- Sodium: 2260
- Total Carbohydrate: 39.1
- Cholesterol: 64
- Protein: 25.5

568. Korean Kalbi Jjim (Braised Beef Short Ribs)

Serving: 6 | Prep: 30mins | Cook: 1hours25mins | Ready in:

Ingredients

- 2 pounds beef short ribs, or more to taste
- 1 onion, quartered
- 1 (1 inch) piece fresh ginger, sliced
- 2 cloves garlic
- 5 tablespoons soy sauce
- 1/4 cup brown sugar
- 2 tablespoons Korean red pepper flakes (gochugaru)
- 4 cloves garlic, minced
- 1 tablespoon rice vinegar
- 1 tablespoon sesame oil
- 2 potatoes, peeled and cut into 2-inch pieces
- 2 carrots, peeled and cut into 2-inch pieces
- 1/2 cup Japanese beech mushrooms
- 7 chestnuts (bam), or more to taste
- 7 dried Korean dates (daechu)
- 1 tablespoon corn syrup (mulyeot)
- 2 green onions, sliced

Direction

- Soak the beef short ribs for about 30 minutes in a large bowl containing cold water to get rid of residual blood.
- Transfer 2 cloves garlic, ginger, onion and short ribs into a large pot and then add water to cover. Heat to boil for 20 to 30 minutes while skimming the foam that rises to the top. Then measure out two cups of broth and set aside. Drain the short ribs and then rinse with cold water. Get rid of garlic, ginger, and onion. Let to cool until easy to handle.
- Form slits in each short rib to get rid or chop away the excess fat.
- Place the short ribs back into the pot. Add sesame oil, rice vinegar, 4 minced garlic cloves, red pepper flakes, brown sugar, soy sauce and reserved broth. Let to simmer for about 45 minutes on low heat until the flavors have combined. Add dates, chestnuts, mushrooms, carrots and potatoes. Continue to simmer for about 10 minutes until the sauce thickens and the potatoes are tender.
- Mix the corn syrup into sauce. Then simmer for about 5 minutes until the sauce has a slightly syrupy consistency. Garnish with slices of green onion before serving.

Nutrition Information

- Calories: 547 calories;
- Protein: 18.7
- Total Fat: 31
- Sodium: 841
- Total Carbohydrate: 50.2
- Cholesterol: 62

569. Korean Kebabs

Serving: 6 | Prep: 35mins | Cook: 30mins | Ready in:

Ingredients

- 1/4 cup vegetable oil
- 1/4 cup soy sauce
- 1 tablespoon peanut butter
- 2 tablespoons finely chopped spring onion
- 1 teaspoon sesame seeds
- 1 clove garlic, crushed
- 1/8 teaspoon red chile powder, or to taste

- salt and freshly ground black pepper to taste
- 1 1/2 pounds pork tenderloin, cut into cubes
- 1 onion, cut into chunks, or to taste
- 1 (8 ounce) package fresh mushrooms, or to taste
- 1 large red bell pepper, cut into chunks, or to taste
- 1 zucchini, cut into chunks, or to taste

Direction

- Mix soy sauce, oil, and peanut butter until well-blended and creamy. Stir in garlic, salt, pepper, spring onion, sesame seeds, and red chile powder. Toss in the pork to coat.
- Let the pork soak in the marinade for 2 to 4 hours.
- Set oven to 400 degrees F (200 degrees C). Use enough aluminum foil to line a rimmed baking sheet.
- Thread pork, red bell pepper, mushrooms, onion, and zucchini onto skewers. Arrange on foil-lined baking sheet and pour the marinade over them.
- Bake until pork is nicely browned and tender, about half an hour.

Nutrition Information

- Calories: 237 calories;
- Total Fat: 13.4
- Sodium: 685
- Total Carbohydrate: 8.9
- Cholesterol: 49
- Protein: 21.2

570. Korean Kimchi

Serving: 20 | Prep: 20mins | Cook: | Ready in:

Ingredients

- 3 heads napa cabbage, cored and cut into quarters lengthwise
- 1/2 cup salt
- 3 heads garlic, minced
- 1 bunch green onions, cut into 2 inch pieces
- 1 1/2 tablespoons monosodium glutamate (MSG)
- 2 teaspoons red pepper flakes, or to taste

Direction

- Cut cabbage leaves to 2-inch long pieces. Spread a quarter of leaves in a big, non-metallic bowl. Sprinkle 1/4 of salt. Repeat layers until all cabbage is salted. Let stand in room temperature for 3-4 hours until a lot of liquid has been pulled from the leaves and cabbage is soft. Drain. Rinse cabbage with 2-3 changes of water. Drain again very well. Put cabbage back in mixing bowl.
- Sprinkle red pepper flakes, MSG, green onions, and minced garlic on cabbage. Season with extra salt to taste. Toss until combined evenly. Pack mixture to sterilized gallon sized glass jar. Cover jar using wax paper and a loose-fitting lid so the seal is not airtight.
- Let cabbage ferment in room temperature for 2-5 days until it gets your preferred degree of sourness. Keep in an airtight jar in the fridge.

Nutrition Information

- Calories: 30 calories;
- Total Carbohydrate: 6
- Cholesterol: 0
- Protein: 1.6
- Total Fat: 0.3
- Sodium: 114

571. Korean Marinated Flank Steak

Serving: 6 | Prep: 15mins | Cook: 15mins | Ready in:

Ingredients

- 4 cloves garlic
- 1 teaspoon minced fresh ginger
- 1 onion, roughly chopped
- 2 1/2 cups low sodium soy sauce
- 1/4 cup toasted sesame oil
- 3 tablespoons Worcestershire sauce
- 2 tablespoons unseasoned meat tenderizer
- 1 cup white sugar
- 2 pounds beef flank steak, trimmed of excess fat

Direction

- In a blender bowl, put onion, ginger, garlic, sugar, meat tenderizer, Worcestershire sauce, sesame oil, and soy sauce. Puree it until smooth.
- Pour marinade in a resealable plastic bag or a glass bowl. Score flank steak and put in marinade. Marinate overnight in the fridge.
- Preheat grill to medium-high heat.
- Grill steak on preheated grill, 7 minutes on each side for medium, to your preferred doneness.

Nutrition Information

- Calories: 417 calories;
- Protein: 24.1
- Total Fat: 15.4
- Sodium: 3661
- Total Carbohydrate: 46.5
- Cholesterol: 34

572. Korean Oxtail Soup

Serving: 6-8 serving(s) | Prep: 45mins | Cook: 3hours | Ready in:

Ingredients

- Soup
- 1 1/2 kg oxtails, jointed
- 8 cups water
- 2 slices fresh ginger
- 1 teaspoon salt
- Sauce
- 3 tablespoons light soy sauce
- 1 tablespoon sesame oil
- 1 tablespoon toasted crushed sesame seeds
- 1/4 teaspoon ground black pepper
- 3 tablespoons finely chopped spring onions
- 3 teaspoons finely chopped garlic
- 1 teaspoon finely chopped gingerroot

Direction

- In a big pan with water, put salt, ginger, water, and oxtail.
- Boil, reduce heat, then simmer until meat becomes tender.
- Take out scum and any froth on the surface.
- This can take up to 2 hours.
- It will take 45 minutes if you use a pressure cooker.
- Liquid should reduce to around 6 cups.
- Mix leftover ingredients and serve alongside soup as a dip sauce for oxtail pieces.

Nutrition Information

- Calories: 38.1
- Protein: 1.4
- Sodium: 897.7
- Cholesterol: 0
- Saturated Fat: 0.4
- Fiber: 0.4
- Sugar: 0.3
- Total Carbohydrate: 1.8
- Total Fat: 3

573. Korean Pizza

Serving: 8 | Prep: 10mins | Cook: 30mins | Ready in:

Ingredients

- 2 cups all-purpose flour

- 2 eggs
- 4 cups water
- 1/2 teaspoon salt
- 1 shallot, chopped
- 1 green onion, chopped
- 1/2 cup minced crabmeat
- 1/2 cup chopped cooked pork
- 1/2 cup diced firm tofu
- 1 cup bean sprouts
- 1 cup frozen mixed vegetables, thawed
- 1/2 cup shredded cabbage
- 4 teaspoons canola oil
- 1/4 cup soy sauce
- 2 tablespoons rice vinegar
- 1 tablespoon sesame oil
- 1 chile pepper, chopped (optional)

Direction

- Combine salt, water, eggs, and flour in a large bowl; stir. It will be super watery, as the pizza is like a crepe. Mix in the cabbage, mixed vegetables, bean sprouts, tofu, pork, and crab meat until well combined.
- In a large skillet set on medium heat, put some of the oil to heat. Your pizzas will be the size of the skillet. Scoop in enough of the vegetable batter to cover the pan's bottom. Then cook for approximately 8 minutes, or until the underside turns golden brown. Turn, and cook the second side for approximately 3 minutes, until browned. You should have crispy edges. Keep on cooking with the rest of the batter. Serve pizzas with dipping sauce.
- For the dipping sauce, combine in a sealable container the chile pepper, sesame oil, rice vinegar, and soy sauce. Then seal, and shake until well mixed. Then shake again before serving.

Nutrition Information

- Calories: 233 calories;
- Total Fat: 7
- Sodium: 663
- Total Carbohydrate: 30.1
- Cholesterol: 63
- Protein: 12.7

574. Korean Pork Curry

Serving: 6 | Prep: 20mins | Cook: 50mins | Ready in:

Ingredients

- 1/4 cup olive oil, divided
- 1 1/2 pounds boneless pork chops, cut into cubes
- 1 large yellow onion, cut into cubes
- 2 large russet potatoes, peeled and cut into cubes
- 3 large carrots, peeled and cut into cubes
- 4 cups water
- 1 tablespoon Korean-style curry powder (such as Assi® mild curry powder), or more to taste

Direction

- Over medium heat, heat two tablespoons of olive oil in a large skillet and then cook while stirring the pork in hot oil for 5 to 7 minutes until browned completely.
- Heat two tablespoons of olive oil in a large pot and then cook while stirring carrots, potatoes and onion in hot oil for 5 to 7 minutes until the veggies start to soften. Mix the pork into vegetable mixture.
- Add water into pot, decrease the heat to low and cover the pot. Let to cook at a simmer for about 20 minutes until potatoes become tender but not falling apart.
- Take out the pot from the heat and mix the curry powder into pork mixture until dissolved completely. Place the pot back to heat and continue to cook for 20 to 30 minutes until the onions are translucent and the sauce is thick.

Nutrition Information

- Calories: 303 calories;

- Total Fat: 13.6
- Sodium: 60
- Total Carbohydrate: 27.9
- Cholesterol: 36
- Protein: 17.6

575. Korean Rice Cake (Tteok)

Serving: 16 | Prep: 15mins | Cook: 1hours | Ready in:

Ingredients

- 2 teaspoons oil, or as needed
- 1 1/2 cups milk
- 1 egg
- 2 cups glutinous rice flour
- 1/4 cup white sugar
- 1 teaspoon baking powder
- 1/2 teaspoon salt
- 2 cups chopped dried mixed fruit

Direction

- Preheat an oven to 175 degrees C (350 degrees F). Generously coat a 9x13-inch baking pan with oil.
- In a bowl, whisk together egg and milk.
- In a separate bowl, sift together, salt, baking powder, sugar and rice flour. Stir in the milk mixture until combined well. Fold in the dried fruit. Spread the batter into the prepared baking pan.
- Bake for about 1 hour in oven until the edges begin to brown. Allow to cool completely for about 20 to 30 minutes prior to slicing.

Nutrition Information

- Calories: 153 calories;
- Total Carbohydrate: 32.5
- Cholesterol: 13
- Protein: 2.8
- Total Fat: 1.7

- Sodium: 120

576. Korean Rice Cakes And Lentils With Gochujang

Serving: 4 | Prep: 15mins | Cook: 35mins | Ready in:

Ingredients

- 1 cup dry lentils
- 2 cups water
- 2 cloves garlic
- 1 (1 inch) piece fresh ginger, peeled and chopped
- salt and ground black pepper to taste
- 1/2 pound bok choy, leaves and stalks separated
- 1/2 cup water
- 3 tablespoons black bean sauce
- 1 tablespoon gochujang (Korean hot pepper paste), or more to taste
- 1 tablespoon sweet soy glaze (such s Kikkoman®)
- 1 tablespoon reduced-sodium soy sauce
- 1 pound Korean rice cakes
- 2 tablespoons raw cashews (optional)
- 1/4 cup water
- 1 green onion, green parts only, thinly sliced

Direction

- Rinse the lentils properly. Mix two cups of water and lentils in a pot. Heat to boil. Decrease to a simmer. Let to cook for about 20 to 30 minutes and check after 20 minutes, until they are chewy but still firm. Drain off water.
- Pour the lentils into a wok or frying pan along with pepper, salt, ginger and garlic. Cook while stirring for 2 to 3 minutes on medium heat until aromatic. Add soy sauce, soy glaze, gochujang, black bean sauce, 1/2 cup water and bok choy. Cook for 3 to 4 minutes until thickened.
- Heat water in a pot to boil and then add rice

cakes. Cook for 2 to 3 minutes until chewy. Drain off water and transfer to lentil mixture.
- In a blender, blend cashews with 1/4 cup of water. Then pour into the lentil mixture and let to cook for 1 to 2 minutes until the flavors have combined. You can serve together with chopped green onion.

Nutrition Information

- Calories: 543 calories;
- Total Fat: 4.4
- Sodium: 456
- Total Carbohydrate: 106.1
- Cholesterol: 0
- Protein: 18.5

577. Korean Seafood Tofu Soup (Soondubu Jjigae)

Serving: 4 | Prep: 30mins | Cook: 39mins | Ready in:

Ingredients

- 6 cups chicken broth
- 4 (1 inch) pieces kelp
- 6 dried anchovies
- 6 ounces sliced pork belly
- 2 tablespoons Korean red pepper flakes (gochugaru)
- 1 zucchini, cubed
- 1/2 cup chopped onion
- 1/2 cup kimchi
- 2 serrano chile peppers, chopped (optional)
- 1 tablespoon minced fresh ginger root
- 1 tablespoon fish sauce
- 1 teaspoon white sugar
- 2 (12 ounce) packages extra-soft tofu
- 10 shrimp, peeled
- 5 mussels
- 5 clams
- 1/2 cup sliced button mushrooms
- 1 tablespoon minced garlic
- 4 eggs (optional)
- 2 tablespoons chopped green onion, or to taste (optional)

Direction

- Ina large pot, bring dried anchovies, kelp and chicken stock to boil. Cover the pot and then cook for about 10 minutes on medium heat. Then strain the broth and get rid of anchovies and kelp.
- Cook the pork belly over medium heat in a large pot for 3 to 5 minutes until turned browned. Place in a small bowl and save the drippings in the pot. Pour in red pepper flakes and the cook while stirring for about 30 seconds until sizzling. Place the pork belly back into the pot. Add sugar, fish sauce, ginger, serrano chile peppers, kimchi, onion, zucchini, and the strained broth. Cover and simmer the soup for about 15 minutes until the flavors have combined.
- Mix garlic, mushrooms, clams, tofu, mussels and shrimp into the soup. Let simmer for about 5 minutes until the clams and mussels have opened.
- Gently cut the tofu into chunks. Spoon the boiling soup into the serving bowls and then crack an egg onto each. Stud with green onions.

Nutrition Information

- Calories: 375 calories;
- Sodium: 2606
- Total Carbohydrate: 17.5
- Cholesterol: 266
- Protein: 35
- Total Fat: 19.5

578. Korean Short Ribs (Kalbi Jjim)

Serving: 4 | Prep: 35mins | Cook: 2hours | Ready in:

Ingredients

- 6 dried shiitake mushrooms
- 2 pounds beef short ribs
- 2 cups water
- 1 onion, sliced
- 2 tablespoons soy sauce
- 7 cloves garlic, minced
- 1 1/2 tablespoons brown sugar
- 1 tablespoon rice wine
- 1 Korean radish, peeled and cut into chunks
- 2 carrots, cut into chunks
- 6 roasted and peeled chestnuts (optional)
- 6 hard-boiled eggs, peeled (optional)
- 2 tablespoons corn syrup (mulyeot)
- 1 tablespoon sesame oil
- 1 teaspoon ground black pepper
- 1 green onion, chopped

Direction

- Soak the shiitake mushrooms for about 3 hours in bowl containing very warm water until softened. Drain off water and chop into strips.
- Soak the short ribs for 20 minutes in a bowl containing cold water and change water several times. Drain off the water and bring the ribs to room temperature for about half an hour.
- Heat water to boil in a large pot and then add short ribs. Cook for about 10 minutes until no pink color remains. Drain the ribs and then rinse under cold water. Take out any loose particles and the excess fat. Place in a large pot.
- In a bowl, combine rice wine, brown sugar, garlic, soy sauce, sliced onion and 2 cups of water. Spread on top of ribs in pot. Heat to boil. Cook for about 20 to 25 minutes. Mix in carrot, radish, and shiitake mushrooms. Decrease the heat to low and let to simmer while stirring often for about 1 hour until the short ribs become tender.
- Mix black pepper, sesame oil, corn syrup and eggs into the pot. Raise the heat to medium-high and cook while stirring often for about 15 minutes until most of the cooking liquid is evaporated. Place the short ribs onto a serving platter and then add chopped green onion on top.

Nutrition Information

- Calories: 782 calories;
- Sodium: 652
- Total Carbohydrate: 40.3
- Cholesterol: 411
- Protein: 34.2
- Total Fat: 53.5

---

579. Korean Soft Tofu Stew (Soon Du Bu Jigae)

Serving: 2 | Prep: 5mins | Cook: 15mins | Ready in:

Ingredients

- 1 teaspoon vegetable oil
- 1 teaspoon Korean chile powder
- 2 tablespoons ground beef (optional)
- 1 tablespoon Korean soy bean paste (doenjang)
- 1 cup water
- salt and pepper to taste
- 1 (12 ounce) package Korean soon tofu or soft tofu, drained and sliced
- 1 egg
- 1 teaspoon sesame seeds
- 1 green onion, chopped

Direction

- In a big saucepan, heat vegetable oil on medium heat. Mix in ground beef and Korean chile powder. Sauté until beef is not pink, evenly browned, and crumbly. Mix in soy bean paste to coat beef. Pour in water and boil. Season with pepper and salt. Drop tofu gently into soup. Keep cooking for 1-2 minutes until tofu is heated through. Take off heat. Add egg quickly into soup, gently stirring to break it. Garnish with green onion and sesame seeds.

Nutrition Information

- Calories: 242 calories;
- Protein: 20
- Total Fat: 16.5
- Sodium: 415
- Total Carbohydrate: 7
- Cholesterol: 99

---

580. Korean Soybean Noodles (Kong Kook Su)

Serving: 2 | Prep: 10mins | Cook: 10mins | Ready in:

Ingredients

- 1 cup dried soybeans
- hot water to cover
- 2 1/2 cups water
- sea salt to taste
- 1 (9 ounce) package Korean noodles
- 2 tomato wedges
- 1 cucumber, thinly sliced
- 1 teaspoon black sesame seeds, or to taste (optional)

Direction

- Put the soybeans in a bowl and then add enough hot water to cover. Soak the soybeans for about 1 to 2 hours and then drain.
- Pour the soybeans into a pot and pour in enough water to cover. Heat to boil. Drain off water and then rinse properly with cold water.
- Heat water to boil in a pot and then add noodles. Cook for 3 to 4 minutes until tender but still firm to bite. Drain off water.
- In a blender, mix 2 1/2 cups water and soybeans and then blend until smooth. Pour in water or strain the water until the consistency desired is reached.
- Pour the noodles into a bowl and then top with sesame seeds, cucumber, tomato, and pureed soybeans. Add salt to taste.

Nutrition Information

- Calories: 804 calories;
- Total Fat: 21.2
- Sodium: 944
- Total Carbohydrate: 106.9
- Cholesterol: 0
- Protein: 44

---

581. Korean Spicy Chicken And Potato (Tak Toritang)

Serving: 4 | Prep: 15mins | Cook: 45mins | Ready in:

Ingredients

- 2 1/2 pounds chicken drumettes
- 2 large potatoes, cut into large chunks
- 2 carrots, cut into 2 inch pieces
- 1 large onion, cut into 8 pieces
- 4 cloves garlic, crushed
- 1/4 cup water
- 1/2 cup soy sauce
- 2 tablespoons white sugar
- 3 tablespoons gochujang (Korean hot pepper paste)

Direction

- Mix garlic, sugar, onion, carrots, potatoes, and chicken in a big pot on medium heat. Place soy sauce and water. Mix in hot pepper paste and sugar.
- Boil, bring heat to low, then simmer for 45 minutes until liquid thickens, veggies are soft, and chicken juices are clear. Serve alongside hot cooked rice.

Nutrition Information

- Calories: 447 calories;
- Protein: 25.6
- Total Fat: 14.1
- Sodium: 1994
- Total Carbohydrate: 54.7
- Cholesterol: 59

582. Korean Squash

Serving: 6 | Prep: 20mins | Cook: 20mins | Ready in:

Ingredients

- 5 medium zucchini, sliced
- 1 bunch green onions, sliced
- 1/4 cup white vinegar
- 1/2 cup soy sauce
- 1/4 cup water
- 2 tablespoons sugar
- 2 tablespoons sesame oil
- ground black pepper to taste

Direction

- Mix sesame oil, zucchini, vinegar, green onions, soy sauce, sugar and water in a large pot. Add black pepper to taste. Stir to blend, cover and allow to cook on medium heat for about 20 minutes until the zucchini becomes tender.

Nutrition Information

- Calories: 106 calories;
- Protein: 4
- Total Fat: 4.9
- Sodium: 1225
- Total Carbohydrate: 14
- Cholesterol: 0

583. Korean Style Salad Dressing

Serving: 12 | Prep: 5mins | Cook: | Ready in:

Ingredients

- 1/4 cup low-sodium soy sauce
- 2 tablespoons white sugar
- 1/4 cup water
- 3 tablespoons rice vinegar
- 3 tablespoons sesame oil
- 1 tablespoon ground red chile pepper

Direction

- In a bowl, whisk together red chile pepper, sesame oil, rice vinegar, water, sugar and soy sauce.

Nutrition Information

- Calories: 44 calories;
- Total Fat: 3.5
- Sodium: 177
- Total Carbohydrate: 3
- Cholesterol: 0
- Protein: 0.4

584. Korean Sushi

Serving: 6 | Prep: 30mins | Cook: 30mins | Ready in:

Ingredients

- 2 cups uncooked short-grain white rice
- 2 cups water
- 2 tablespoons cider vinegar
- 2 leaves chard
- 2 eggs, well beaten
- 2 tablespoons soy sauce, divided
- 3 tablespoons water
- 1 onion, diced
- 1 tablespoon vegetable oil

- 3/4 pound beef tenderloin, minced
- 1 (5 ounce) can tuna, drained
- 1 carrot, julienned
- 1 cucumber, julienned
- 6 sheets nori (dry seaweed)

Direction

- Boil cider vinegar and 2 cups water in a medium saucepan. Add rice then stir. Reduce heat, simmer for 20 minutes, covered, until rice grains are soft and sticky.
- Cover chard with enough water in a medium saucepan then boil. Cook until tender. Slice to thin strips.
- Whisk eggs with 3 tablespoons water and soy sauce. Place in medium skillet on medium heat. Cook until thick. Take off heat. Slice to strips.
- In a medium saucepan heat vegetable oil on medium-high heat. Slowly sauté onion until tender. Mix beef in with 1 tablespoon soy sauce. Cook until browned evenly. Drain then put aside.
- Preheat oven to 175 degrees C/350 degrees F. Put nori sheets onto a medium baking sheet. Heat in the preheated oven for 1-2 minutes until a little crisp.
- One by one, put nori sheets on the bamboo rolling mat. Evenly line nori sheets with approximately 3/4-inch/2 cm depth of rice. Be sure rice doesn't cover nori edges. Start with one nori sheet end, top rice with a line of beef, a cucumber slice, a line of tuna, and a stick of carrot, repeat process until you food reaches approximately the middle of the nori sheet. Carefully roll sheets tightly. Seal with one or two grains of sticky rice. Slice every roll to approximately 4 pieces then serve.

Nutrition Information

- Calories: 492 calories;
- Total Fat: 17.6
- Sodium: 409
- Total Carbohydrate: 58
- Cholesterol: 109
- Protein: 23.1

585. Korean Take Out Rice Noodles (Vegan)

Serving: 4 | Prep: 15mins | Cook: 20mins | Ready in:

Ingredients

- 1 tablespoon diced ginger root
- 1 clove garlic, chopped
- 1/4 cup palm sugar
- 1/3 cup water
- 1/4 cup tamari
- 1/4 cup almond butter
- 3 tablespoons sesame oil, divided
- 2 tablespoons vegan Worcestershire sauce (such as Annie's®)
- 1 tablespoon rice vinegar
- 1/2 teaspoon red pepper flakes
- 1 (8 ounce) package spaghetti-style rice noodles (such as Tinkyada®), or more to taste
- 2 small heads baby bok choy, trimmed and chopped
- 2 large carrots, peeled and cut into matchsticks
- 1 large zucchini - peeled, seeded, and cut into matchsticks
- 1 bunch scallions, chopped
- 1 tablespoon toasted sesame seeds (optional)

Direction

- Using a food processor or blender, mix in garlic, ginger, and sugar together. Put in tamari, almond butter, water, Worcestershire sauce, red pepper flakes, rice vinegar, and 2 tablespoons of sesame oil. Blend again to a smooth texture. Put sauce into a small bowl. Seal it with plastic wrap and set in the refrigerator for at least an hour to let the flavors intensify.
- Boil water with a bit of salt in a large pot. When the water starts boiling, cook the noodles and stir occasionally for around 14 minutes or until firm to the bite and tender.

Mix the bok choy in and cook for 1 minute to a slightly wilted consistency. Using cold water, drain and rinse the noodles to chill. Mix with the remaining 1 tablespoon of sesame oil in a bowl.
- Put a skillet on medium heat. Mix in the carrots, stirring for 3 minutes until a slightly tender texture.
- Put in zucchini and cook for 5 minutes or until it becomes tender without getting mushy.
- Combine noodles with the chilled sauce into the bowl, then serve with scallions, sesame seeds, carrots and the zucchini mixture.

Nutrition Information

- Calories: 530 calories;
- Total Fat: 21.4
- Sodium: 1327
- Total Carbohydrate: 78.5
- Cholesterol: 0
- Protein: 9.7

586. Korean Tofu And Vegetable Soup

Serving: 4 | Prep: 20mins | Cook: 15mins | Ready in:

Ingredients

- 3 cups beef stock
- 1/4 cup toenjang (fermented soybean paste)
- 1 (4 inch) piece dashi kombu (dried kelp) (optional)
- 5 cloves garlic, chopped
- 1 (16 ounce) package medium-firm tofu, cut into 1 1/2 x 1/4 inch dominoes
- 1 pound napa cabbage, thickly sliced
- 1 pound daikon radish cut into 1 1/2x1/4 inch pieces
- 1 pound yellow squash, cut into 1 1/2x1/4 inch dominoes
- 2 large green onions, white and pale green part only, sliced diagonally into 1 1/4 inch pieces
- 1 hot red pepper, seeded and sliced diagonally into 1/4 inch pieces

Direction

- Over medium-high heat, add beef stock into a large deep skillet or stock pot and mix in toenjang until dissolved. Add the garlic and kelp and heat to boil. Add in the yellow squash, daikon, cabbage and tofu. Cover and heat to boil. Gently cook for 5 minutes. Add the hot pepper and green onions and then boil for 1 minute or until the pepper and onion are brightly colored and fragrant. The cook time should not be more than 15 minutes. Take out and get rid of kelp. Serve right away.

Nutrition Information

- Calories: 289 calories;
- Total Fat: 12.3
- Sodium: 661
- Total Carbohydrate: 24.7
- Cholesterol: 0
- Protein: 26.4

587. Korean Tteokguk (Rice Cake Soup)

Serving: 6 | Prep: 30mins | Cook: 16mins | Ready in:

Ingredients

- 1 tablespoon olive oil, divided
- 2 eggs, separated
- 1 sheet nori (dry seaweed)
- 5 cups thinly sliced garae tteok (Korean glutinous rice cakes)
- 32 fluid ounces Korean beef bone stock (such as Ottogi®)
- 2 cloves garlic, minced, or more to taste

- 2 green onions, thin sliced
- salt and ground black pepper to taste

Direction

- In a nonstick skillet, heat 1 1/2 teaspoon olive oil on medium-low heat. In a small bowl, beat egg yolks and pour in skillet. Tilt skillet to spread egg yolks thinly and evenly. Cook for 1 minute per side until set. Place on a cutting board, slicing to thin strips. Repeat process with egg whites.
- In another skillet, put nori on medium heat. Toast for 30 seconds on each side until crispy and bright green. Slice to thin strips.
- Rinse rice cakes under cold water then drain.
- Boil beef stock in a big pot. Add garlic and rice cakes. Simmer for 5 minutes until rice cake slices become tender. Add green onions, keep cooking for 3-5 minutes until they begin floating to the top. Season with pepper and salt,
- Place soup in serving bowls. Top with nori strips and egg.

Nutrition Information

- Calories: 553 calories;
- Cholesterol: 62
- Protein: 9.4
- Total Fat: 6.2
- Sodium: 567
- Total Carbohydrate: 111.5

588. Korean Style Braised (Slow Cooker) Baby Back Ribs

Serving: 4 | Prep: 15mins | Cook: 3hours11mins | Ready in:

Ingredients

- 2 pounds baby back pork ribs
- 1 teaspoon salt, or to taste
- 1 tablespoon canola oil
- 1/2 cup soy sauce
- 1/2 cup light soy sauce
- 1/2 cup rice wine
- 1/2 onion, cut into quarters
- 1/4 cup orange juice
- 1 head garlic, chopped
- 1/4 cup minced fresh ginger root
- 1 jalapeno pepper, chopped (optional)
- 1 bunch scallions, trimmed and chopped

Direction

- Clean the ribs and then pat dry. Then season the ribs with salt liberally.
- In a skillet place over high heat, heat the oil, add the ribs and then cook while turning from time to time for 6 to 8 minutes until turned browned on all sides.
- Transfer the browned ribs into a 3-quart slow cooker.
- Into a blender, put jalapeno, ginger, garlic, orange juice, rice wine, light soy sauce, soy sauce and onion. Cover the blender and then blend until mixed. Add the sauce on top of ribs in the slow cooker. Cover the cooker and cook on High for 3 to 4 hours until the meat easily pulls away from the bone.
- Assemble the oven rack to around six inches from the heat and then preheat the oven's broiler. Transfer the ribs into a roasting pan or baking sheet.
- Bake the ribs under the broiler for about 5 minutes until charred nicely but not burned. Stud with scallions.

Nutrition Information

- Calories: 533 calories;
- Cholesterol: 117
- Protein: 30.3
- Total Fat: 33.1
- Sodium: 3562
- Total Carbohydrate: 20.8

589. Korean Style Seaweed Soup

Serving: 4 | Prep: 15mins | Cook: 30mins | Ready in:

Ingredients

- 1 (1 ounce) package dried brown seaweed
- 1/4 pound beef top sirloin, minced
- 2 teaspoons sesame oil
- 1 1/2 tablespoons soy sauce
- 1 teaspoon salt, or to taste
- 6 cups water
- 1 teaspoon minced garlic

Direction

- Cover seaweed in water to soak. When soft, drain then cut to 2-inch pieces.
- Heat a saucepan on medium heat. Add a little salt, 1/2 tablespoon soy sauce, sesame oil, and beef. Cook for a minute. Mix in leftover 1 tablespoon soy sauce and seaweed. Cook for a minute, frequently stirring. Place in 2 cups of water and boil. Mix in leftover 4 cups of water and garlic. Boil, put a cover, then reduce heat. Simmer it for 20 minutes. Season with salt to taste.

Nutrition Information

- Calories: 65 calories;
- Sodium: 940
- Total Carbohydrate: 1
- Cholesterol: 17
- Protein: 6.8
- Total Fat: 3.7

590. Las Vegas Galbi (Korean Style Beef Ribs)

Serving: 8 | Prep: 20mins | Cook: 16mins | Ready in:

Ingredients

- 2 1/2 pounds beef short ribs, cut flanken-style
- 1/2 large Asian pear, cored and cubed
- 1 white onion
- 1 kiwi, peeled and diced
- 5 cloves garlic
- 1 cup soy sauce
- 1 cup brown sugar
- 1/4 cup honey
- 1/4 cup sesame oil
- 1/4 teaspoon ground black pepper

Direction

- In a big bowl, place ribs in and cover with water. Soak for 1 hour before draining the ribs and placing it back in the bowl.
- Puree garlic, kiwi, onion and Asian pear in a food processor then put it in a bowl. Stir black pepper, oil, sesame, honey, brown sugar and soy sauce in. Place marinade on the ribs. Use plastic wrap to cover it and let it marinate in the fridge for a minimum of 8 hours or overnight. During this process, flip it over once. Strain the marinade and throw it away.
- Preheat a grill on medium heat and oil the grate lightly then put the ribs on the grill. Grill until the meat is not pink anymore and the exterior is crispy, around 8 minutes on each side.

Nutrition Information

- Calories: 383 calories;
- Cholesterol: 58
- Protein: 21.6
- Total Fat: 18.2
- Sodium: 1846
- Total Carbohydrate: 34.1

591. Mae's Kimchi Stew

Serving: 4 | Prep: 15mins | Cook: 31mins | Ready in:

Ingredients

- 1 teaspoon sesame oil
- 1/2 pound pork belly, cut into bite-size pieces
- 2 cloves garlic, chopped
- 2 cups prepared dashi stock
- 1 cup kimchi, cut into bite-size pieces
- 2 tablespoons gochujang (Korean chile paste)
- 1 tablespoon gochugaru (Korean chile powder)
- 1/2 (12 ounce) package tofu, cut into 1/2-inch squares
- 1 cup zucchini, cut into bite-size pieces
- 1 small onion, sliced
- 2 green chile peppers, sliced
- 2 green onions, sliced

Direction

- Over medium-high heat, heat sesame oil in large saucepan and then add pork. Cook for 5 to 7 minutes until no pink color remains in the center. Mix the garlic into the pork mixture. Cook for about 1 minute until fragrant.
- Mix kimchi and dashi stock into pork mixture and heat to boil. Mix in gochugaru and gochujang. Let to simmer for about 20 minutes until the stew is thickened a bit.
- Mix green chile peppers, onion, zucchini and tofu into the stew. Cook for about 5 minutes until tender. Take out from heat and garnish with green onion.

Nutrition Information

- Calories: 206 calories;
- Protein: 15
- Total Fat: 12.4
- Sodium: 1205
- Total Carbohydrate: 10.3
- Cholesterol: 22

592. Maple Syrup Korean Teriyaki Chicken

Serving: 5 | Prep: 15mins | Cook: 1hours | Ready in:

Ingredients

- 1/4 cup soy sauce
- 1 cup water
- 1/3 cup maple syrup
- 3 tablespoons dark sesame oil
- 2 cloves garlic, crushed
- 1 tablespoon minced fresh ginger root
- 2 teaspoons ground black pepper
- 5 skinless, boneless chicken breast halves
- 1 cup brown rice
- 2 cups water
- 2 tablespoons cornstarch

Direction

- Combine soy sauce, maple syrup, 1 cup water, sesame oil, ginger, garlic, and pepper in a big resealable plastic bag. Save 1/3 cup of the mixture for later. Put chicken in the bag. Seal and chill to marinate for minimum 2 hours.
- Put rice in a saucepan with 2 cups of water. Boil. Put lid on. Lower heat to Low. Let simmer for 45 minutes.
- Set oven broiler to preheat. Grease a baking dish lightly.
- Transfer marinade from bag to the saucepan. Let it boil. Add cornstarch. Mix and cool until thick.
- Put chicken in the prepared baking dish. Baste often with the saved 1/3 cup of marinade. Broil until juices run clear, 8 minutes on each side. Put chicken on top of cooked rice. Add boiled marinade on top when serving.

Nutrition Information

- Calories: 388 calories;
- Sodium: 785
- Total Carbohydrate: 41.5
- Cholesterol: 67
- Protein: 27.7

- Total Fat: 11.9

593. Mom's Kimchi Egg

Serving: 2 | Prep: 5mins | Cook: 5mins | Ready in:

Ingredients

- 2 tablespoons vegetable oil
- 1 cup kimchi, or to taste
- 2 large eggs, beaten

Direction

- Over medium heat, heat oil in a wok or skillet and then cook kimchi in the hot oil for about 2 minutes until softened. Place in the eggs. Cook while stirring the kimchi and eggs for 2 to 3 minutes until eggs are set.

Nutrition Information

- Calories: 208 calories;
- Total Carbohydrate: 3.5
- Cholesterol: 186
- Protein: 7.5
- Total Fat: 18.8
- Sodium: 568

594. Moose's Close Enough Bulgogi

Serving: 4 | Prep: 20mins | Cook: 6mins | Ready in:

Ingredients

- 1 tablespoon sesame seeds
- 1/2 onion, coarsely chopped
- 1/4 Asian pear, peeled and coarsely chopped
- 3 tablespoons dark soy sauce
- 2 tablespoons light soy sauce
- 1 1/2 tablespoons Shaoxing rice wine
- 1 1/2 tablespoons Asian (toasted) sesame oil
- 1 (1 inch) piece fresh ginger, peeled
- 2 cloves garlic, peeled
- 1/4 teaspoon ground black pepper
- 1 pound beef, sliced 1/4-inch thick

Direction

- In a small skillet, toast sesame seeds on medium heat for 3-5 minutes until light brown.
- In a blender, puree black pepper, garlic, ginger, sesame oil, rice wine, light soy sauce, dark soy sauce, Asian pear, and onion to make a smooth marinade. Add sesame seeds, briefly blending on low to combine.
- Spread marinade thinly on the bottom of a big container. Add one single layer of beef. Evenly cover beef with a second thin layer of marinade. Repeat process with leftover marinade and beef. Cover container and keep in fridge for at least 3 hours up to overnight to merge flavors.
- Heat a skillet or big grill pan on high heat. Add all marinade and beef, cooking for 3-4 minutes, constantly stirring, until majority of marinade evaporates, and beef begins to brown. An instant-read thermometer pierced in a slice should say 60 degrees C/140 degrees F.

Nutrition Information

- Calories: 232 calories;
- Sodium: 988
- Total Carbohydrate: 5.5
- Cholesterol: 49
- Protein: 21
- Total Fat: 12.9

595. My Auntie's Real Bulgogi

Serving: 8 | Prep: 25mins | Cook: 15mins | Ready in:

Ingredients

- 1 Asian pear, peeled and seeded
- 1 kiwi, peeled
- 3 tablespoons soy sauce
- 3 pounds beef top sirloin, thinly sliced
- 3/4 cup brown sugar
- 3 (1 inch) pieces fresh ginger root, peeled
- 10 slices fresh ginger root
- 5 cloves garlic, minced
- 3 1/2 tablespoons chili oil
- 2 tablespoons sesame oil
- 2 tablespoons honey
- 2 teaspoons red pepper flakes
- 1/8 teaspoon salt
- 1/8 teaspoon ground black pepper

Direction

- In a blender, add soy sauce, kiwi and Asian pear and then puree until smooth. Pour the puree into a large plastic bag that is resealable. Place in beef slices and then shake to coat well.
- Transfer the beef mixture into a large bowl and then add black pepper, salt, red pepper flakes, sesame oil, honey, chili oil, garlic, ginger slices, peeled ginger root and brown sugar. Then cover using plastic wrap and transfer to the fridge to marinate for at least three hours.
- Preheat the outdoor grill over high heat and then cover the grate with aluminum foil.
- Take out the beef from bowl and get rid of the marinade. Cook while covered over the grill for about 10 minutes until turned browned. Flip the beef slices and then cook for about 5 minutes until the second side turns browned.

Nutrition Information

- Calories: 414 calories;
- Total Fat: 22.7
- Sodium: 444
- Total Carbohydrate: 23
- Cholesterol: 91
- Protein: 29.3

596. Nabak Kimchi (Water Kimchi)

Serving: 10 | Prep: 20mins | Cook: 10mins | Ready in:

Ingredients

- 1/2 napa cabbage, cut into 1-inch pieces
- 1 teaspoon sea salt
- 1/2 teaspoon Korean red pepper powder
- 5 cups water
- 1 tablespoon sweet rice flour (glutinous rice flour)
- 1/2 yellow onion, cut into chunks
- 1/2 Asian pear - peeled, cored, and thinly sliced
- 3 green onions, cut into 1-inch pieces
- 6 cloves garlic, sliced
- 3 slices fresh ginger
- 1 (1 gram) packet granular sucralose sweetener (such as Splenda®)

Direction

- Transfer the cabbage into a large bowl and then scatter red pepper powder and salt on top. Toss well and allow to sit for about 1 hour until the cabbage seems wilted.
- Bring to boil rice flour and water in a large pot and let simmer for five minutes. Take out from the heat and cool for about 10 to 15 minutes.
- Mix green onions, Asian pear and onion in a half-gallon jar. Add sweetener, ginger, garlic and wilted cabbage. Add the water mixture on top. Seal the jar and store at room temperature for 1 to 2 days to ferment. Transfer into the fridge.

Nutrition Information

- Calories: 17 calories;
- Total Carbohydrate: 3.8
- Cholesterol: 0
- Protein: 0.7
- Total Fat: 0.1

- Sodium: 184

597. Oi Sobagi (Korean Cucumber Kimchi)

Serving: 20 | Prep: 25mins | Cook: 5mins | Ready in:

Ingredients

- 10 Kirby cucumbers, trimmed and halved
- 8 cups water
- 1 cup coarse sea salt
- Sauce Mixture:
- 1 cup Korean red pepper flakes (gochugaru)
- 1/2 cup water
- 1/4 cup fish sauce
- 2 tablespoons white sugar
- 2 tablespoons minced garlic
- 2 teaspoons minced ginger
- 1 tablespoon salted fermented shrimp (saewujeot)
- 2 cups garlic chives, cut into 1/2-inch pieces
- 1 radish, cut into matchstick-size pieces, or to taste
- 1 pinch sesame seeds, or to taste

Direction

- Put cucumbers on one end. Slice half down the length to make an x shape. Leave the final 1/4 inch uncut. Put in a bowl. Boil sea salt and 8 cups of water on medium heat. Pour the brine mixture on cucumbers. Brine for an hour until flavors combine.
- In a bowl, mix fermented shrimp, ginger, garlic, sugar, fish sauce, 1/2 cup of water, and red pepper flakes. Mix until sauce is combined thoroughly.
- Rinse cucumbers with cold water. Drain in a colander. Let sit for 10 minutes until semi-dry.
- Slather cucumbers, inside and out, with sauce. Be sure you get the x-shape cut as well. Put sesame seeds, radish, chives, and cucumbers in an air-tight container. Let rest in room temperature for 1-2 days until flavors merge. Keep in fridge until serving time.

Nutrition Information

- Calories: 41 calories;
- Cholesterol: < 1
- Protein: 1.7
- Total Fat: 1.4
- Sodium: 4451
- Total Carbohydrate: 7.9

598. Pine Nut Rice Soup

Serving: 6 | Prep: | Cook: | Ready in:

Ingredients

- 1 cup pine nuts
- 2 cups cooked long-grain white rice
- 6 cups water
- 1 tablespoon pine nuts
- 1 cup dates, pitted and chopped
- 1/2 teaspoon white sugar
- salt to taste

Direction

- Finely blend 2 cups of water, rice and 1 cup pine nuts with a food processor or a blender.
- Transfer the blended pine nut mixture into a saucepan with a thick bottom. Then pour in four cups of water. Heat to boil while stirring often. Once it boils, decrease the heat to low and cook for about 10 minutes or until heated through. Keep stirring when it's heating through to prevent burning.
- Before you serve, garnish with diced dates and pine nuts. Add salt and sugar to taste.

Nutrition Information

- Calories: 275 calories;
- Sodium: 9

- Total Carbohydrate: 37
- Cholesterol: 0
- Protein: 7.8
- Total Fat: 12.5

599. Quick And Easy Kimchi Salad

Serving: 6 | Prep: 10mins | Cook: | Ready in:

Ingredients

- 1 small head cabbage, shredded
- 1/4 cup rock salt
- 1 small carrot, cut into thin strips
- 3 tablespoons vinegar
- 2 tablespoons vegetable oil
- 1 tablespoon white sugar, or to taste
- 1 teaspoon sesame oil
- 1 teaspoon toasted sesame seeds, ground
- 1/2 teaspoon cayenne pepper, or to taste
- 1/4 teaspoon salt

Direction

- Mix rock salt and cabbage in a bowl. Let it stand for 15 minutes, mixing often. Lightly rinse then drain.
- In a bowl, mix salt, cayenne pepper, sesame seeds, sesame oil, sugar, vegetable oil, vinegar, carrot, and cabbage. Keep in fridge for at least 30 minutes until chilled.

Nutrition Information

- Calories: 92 calories;
- Total Fat: 5.8
- Sodium: 4736
- Total Carbohydrate: 10
- Cholesterol: 0
- Protein: 1.7

600. Quick And Simple Korean Doenjang Chigae (Bean Paste/Tofu Soup)

Serving: 6 | Prep: 15mins | Cook: 25mins | Ready in:

Ingredients

- 3 cups vegetable stock
- 3 cups water
- 2 cloves garlic, coarsely chopped
- 2 tablespoons Korean soy bean paste (doenjang)
- 4 green onions, chopped
- 1 zucchini, halved and cut into 1/2-inch slices
- 1/2 (16 ounce) package firm tofu, drained and cubed
- 1 jalapeno pepper, sliced

Direction

- Boil water and vegetable stock in a saucepan on high heat. Mix in soy bean paste and garlic. Mix until paste melts. Mix in jalapeno, tofu, zucchini, and green onion. Let soup return to boil, reduce heat to low, then simmer for 15 minutes.

Nutrition Information

- Calories: 59 calories;
- Total Fat: 2.7
- Sodium: 378
- Total Carbohydrate: 5
- Cholesterol: 0
- Protein: 4.9

601. Refreshing Korean Cucumber Salad

Serving: 6 | Prep: 10mins | Cook: | Ready in:

Ingredients

- 3 pounds seedless cucumber, sliced paper-thin
- 1 1/2 tablespoons sea salt
- 1/2 cup rice vinegar
- 1 tablespoon rice wine
- 2 tablespoons sesame oil
- 2 tablespoons honey
- 2 tablespoons freshly squeezed lemon juice
- 1 green onion, sliced
- 1 tablespoon toasted sesame seeds
- 2 walnut halves, finely chopped (optional)
- 1 clove garlic, minced
- 1 1/2 teaspoons Korean red pepper powder
- freshly ground black pepper to taste

Direction

- In a big bowl, evenly sprinkle sea salt on sliced cucumbers. Let liquid drain from cucumbers for 15 minutes. Spoon cucumbers to a sheet of paper towels. Wrap the paper towels around the cucumbers then wring out a lot of liquid, as much as you can.
- In a bowl, mix ground black pepper, Korean red pepper powder, garlic, walnuts, sesame seeds, green onion, lemon juice, honey, sesame oil, rice wine, and rice vinegar. Add cucumber then toss. Use plastic wrap to cover the bowl then keep in fridge for a minimum of 30 minutes until flavors merge.

Nutrition Information

- Calories: 117 calories;
- Total Carbohydrate: 15.8
- Cholesterol: 0
- Protein: 2.1
- Total Fat: 6.1
- Sodium: 1332

602. Russian Carrot Salad (Korean Style)

Serving: 8 | Prep: 30mins | Cook: 10mins | Ready in:

Ingredients

- 1 pound carrots, peeled and julienned (preferably with a mandoline)
- 3 cloves garlic, minced
- 1/4 cup vinegar
- 1 tablespoon white sugar
- 2 1/2 teaspoons salt
- 1/3 cup vegetable oil
- 1/2 onion, minced
- 1 teaspoon ground coriander
- 1/2 teaspoon cayenne pepper

Direction

- Put the carrots in a large bowl and then drizzle garlic on top of carrots.
- In a small bowl, combine together salt, sugar and vinegar.
- Over medium heat, heat oil in a skillet and add onion. Cook while stirring for 5 to 7 minutes until translucent and soft. Mix cayenne pepper and coriander into the onion. Transfer to the carrot mixture and toss. Add the vinegar dressing atop the carrot mixture and toss to coat.
- Pour the carrot salad into a dish that has a tight-fitting lid. Then cover and chill for 4 to 24 hours and toss the salad a few times as it marinates.

Nutrition Information

- Calories: 119 calories;
- Sodium: 767
- Total Carbohydrate: 8.9
- Cholesterol: 0
- Protein: 0.8
- Total Fat: 9.3

603. Samgyetang (Chicken Soup With Ginseng)

Serving: 4 | Prep: 10mins | Cook: 55mins | Ready in:

Ingredients

- 1/2 cup glutinous rice (chapssal)
- 3 chestnuts (bam)
- 2 pieces ginseng root (insam)
- 2 dried Korean dates (daechu)
- 1 Cornish hen, giblets removed
- 8 cups water
- 4 cloves garlic, or more to taste
- 2 green onions, diced
- 1 pinch salt and ground black pepper to taste

Direction

- Soak the rice in a bowl containing water for half an hour. Then drain.
- Stuff dates, ginseng root, chestnuts, and drained rice into the hen. Use a cotton kitchen twine to sew up the cavity. Transfer the hen into a large pot and add in eight cups of water. Place in garlic cloves.
- Heat the water to boil and let to simmer on medium heat for about 40 minutes while skimming off any scum that floats on the surface until the juices run clear and the hen is no longer pink at the bone.
- Mix the green onions into pot and let to simmer for about 10 minutes until the hen becomes very tender. The temperature one the instant-read thermometer inserted at the thickest part of the thigh, close to the bone, should be 74 degrees C (165 degrees F). Season to taste with pepper and salt.

Nutrition Information

- Calories: 281 calories;
- Total Carbohydrate: 29.5
- Cholesterol: 75
- Protein: 15.1
- Total Fat: 10.8
- Sodium: 94

604. Simple Slow Cooked Korean Beef Soft Tacos

Serving: 8 | Prep: 15mins | Cook: 8hours | Ready in:

Ingredients

- 1 (3 pound) beef chuck roast, trimmed
- 1/2 onion, diced
- 1/2 cup dark brown sugar
- 1/3 cup soy sauce
- 10 cloves garlic
- 1 jalapeno pepper, diced (optional)
- 1 (1 inch) piece fresh ginger root, peeled and grated
- 2 tablespoons seasoned rice vinegar
- 1 tablespoon sesame oil
- salt and ground black pepper to taste
- 16 (6 inch) corn tortillas (optional)

Direction

- Transfer the chuck roast into the crock of a slow cooker. Add onion, jalapeno pepper, brown sugar, sesame oil, soy sauce, rice vinegar, garlic, ginger root, pepper, and salt.
- Cook on Low for 10 hours or on High for 8 hours. Use a pair of forks to shred the meat and then mix into the liquid in the slow cooker.
- You can serve with toppings you like and corn tortillas.

Nutrition Information

- Calories: 456 calories;
- Total Carbohydrate: 40.3
- Cholesterol: 77
- Protein: 23.9
- Total Fat: 22.4
- Sodium: 697

605. Soondubu Jjigae (Korean Soft Tofu Stew)

Serving: 2 | Prep: 10mins | Cook: 18mins | Ready in:

Ingredients

- 1 teaspoon crushed garlic
- 1/2 teaspoon vegetable oil
- 1/2 teaspoon Korean red pepper powder
- 1/4 pound ground beef
- 21 ounces soft tofu
- 1 1/3 cups water
- 1/2 teaspoon salt
- 1/4 teaspoon ground black pepper
- 1 egg
- 3 green onions, chopped

Direction

- Put clay pot on medium-high heat. Add red pepper powder, oil, and garlic. Stir and cook for 2 minutes until fragrant. Mix in ground beef. Cook for 3-5 minutes until brown.
- Scoop tofu into pot with a spoon. Add pepper, salt, and water. Boil, reduce heat, then simmer for 5 minutes.
- Crack egg in the middle of the pot. Put green onions on soup. Simmer for 3 minutes until eggs begin to set.

Nutrition Information

- Calories: 340 calories;
- Sodium: 688
- Total Carbohydrate: 8.2
- Cholesterol: 127
- Protein: 32.7
- Total Fat: 21.4

606. Spicy Korean Chicken

Serving: 4 | Prep: 15mins | Cook: 10mins | Ready in:

Ingredients

- 1 pound skinless, boneless chicken thighs
- 2 tablespoons soy sauce
- 2 tablespoons vegetable oil
- 1 1/2 tablespoons Korean chile paste (gochujang)
- 1 tablespoon sesame oil
- 3 cloves garlic, minced
- 1 (1 inch) piece ginger, peeled and minced
- 1 teaspoon Korean red chile flakes (gochugaru)

Direction

- If you want, pound chicken thighs. In a big bowl, mix red chile flakes, ginger, garlic, sesame oil, chile paste, vegetable oil, and soy sauce. Mix to dissolve chile paste completely. Add chicken and coat by stirring. Cover using plastic wrap. Keep in fridge for at least 30 minutes to 2 hours.
- Preheat grill to medium heat. Oil grate lightly.
- Grill chicken for 5-8 minutes per side until center isn't pink and it's slightly charred. An inserted instant-read thermometer in the middle will say at least 74 degrees C/165 degrees F.

Nutrition Information

- Calories: 257 calories;
- Cholesterol: 70
- Protein: 19.8
- Total Fat: 18.3
- Sodium: 755
- Total Carbohydrate: 2.3

607. Spicy Korean Ribs

Serving: 8 | Prep: 15mins | Cook: 2hours12mins | Ready in:

Ingredients

- 4 racks baby back pork ribs
- salt and ground black pepper to taste
- 1 small onion, sliced
- 1 cup kochujang (Korean hot sauce)
- 1/4 cup white vinegar
- 1/4 cup minced garlic
- 3 tablespoons sesame oil
- 2 tablespoons soy sauce
- 1 (1 1/2 inch) piece fresh ginger root, minced, or to taste
- 1 (1 1/2 inch) piece fresh ginger root, sliced, or to taste
- 1 (12 fluid ounce) bottle pilsner-style lager
- 1 1/2 teaspoons toasted white sesame seeds
- 1 1/2 teaspoons toasted black sesame seeds

Direction

- Take membrane out of the back of the ribs or use a sharp knife to score. In a shallow dish, put in ribs and season with pepper and salt.
- In a food processor or blender, puree onion. Add minced ginger, soy sauce, sesame oil, garlic, vinegar, and kochujang and puree to a sauce. Generously rub 1/3 on ribs, keeping the leftover sauce. Use plastic wrap to cover ribs. Keep in fridge for 5 hours up to overnight.
- Preheat oven to 165 degrees C/325 degrees F.
- Place sliced ginger root on the bottom of a roasting pan. Put ribs, meat-side down, on top of the ginger slices. Pour lager on ribs. Cover with aluminum foil or a lid.
- Bake in the preheated oven for 2 to 2 1-2 hours until meats are loose but don't fall off the bone. Cool for 5-10 minutes.
- Preheat an outdoor grill to 200 degrees C/400 degrees F. Oil grate lightly. Put ribs on grill, cooking for 6 minutes per side until browned. Coat with half of leftover sauce during final 2 minutes of cooking every side. Garnish with black and white sesame seeds.

Nutrition Information

- Calories: 645 calories;
- Protein: 37

- Total Fat: 49.7
- Sodium: 1668
- Total Carbohydrate: 6.9
- Cholesterol: 176

608. Spicy Korean Rice Cakes (Ddeokbokki Or Tteokbokki)

Serving: 6 | Prep: 15mins | Cook: 14mins | Ready in:

Ingredients

- 1 1/2 quarts water
- 1 (24 ounce) package thinly sliced tteok (Korean rice cakes), drained
- 1 (14 ounce) package eomuk (Korean fish cakes), sliced
- 3 tablespoons simple syrup
- 3 tablespoons gochujang (Korean hot pepper paste), or more to taste
- 2 tablespoons red chile powder, or more to taste
- 1 tablespoon minced garlic
- 1/2 teaspoon salt
- 1/2 teaspoon ground black pepper
- 1 cup diced white onion
- 1 cup chopped green onions

Direction

- Heat water until it boils in a saucepan and then add fish cakes and rice cakes. Heat to boil again. Add pepper, salt, garlic, chile powder, gochujang and simple syrup. Let to cook for about 1 to 2 minutes. Add green onion and onion. Let to simmer for about 5 minutes until the sauce becomes red, thick and silky.

Nutrition Information

- Calories: 441 calories;
- Total Fat: 2.1
- Sodium: 311
- Total Carbohydrate: 89.6

- Cholesterol: 32
- Protein: 13.3

609. Spicy Mandoo (Korean Dumpling)

Serving: 8 | Prep: 45mins | Cook: 17mins | Ready in:

Ingredients

- 1 (8 ounce) package sweet potato noodles
- 1 pound ground pork
- 1/2 cup finely chopped onion
- 1/2 cup finely chopped napa cabbage
- 3 tablespoons soy sauce
- 2 tablespoons chile-garlic sauce
- 1 tablespoon sesame oil
- 3 cloves garlic, minced
- 1 teaspoon salt
- 1 teaspoon ground black pepper
- 40 gyoza wrappers
- 1 tablespoon vegetable oil

Direction

- Bring lightly salted water to boil in a large pot, add noodles and then cook at a boil for about 3 minutes until softened but still firm to bite. Drain the noodles and rinse with cold water for one minute. Place the noodles onto a flat work surface and then slice into small pieces.
- In a bowl, mix together garlic, sesame oil, chile-garlic sauce, soy sauce, napa cabbage, noodles, onion, pork, pepper and salt. Mix the filling together by mashing with hand or with a spoon.
- Put 3/4 tablespoon of the filling in the middle of each wrapper. Make your fingers wet and then move them along the margins of the wrapper. Fold over filling and use a fork to press the ends together. Turn and then repeat this with the other side to strengthen the seal. Repeat the process of filling and shaping with remaining wrappers and filling.
- Over medium heat, heat one tablespoon of oil in a skillet and then add mandoo. Cook for 4 to 5 minutes until crispy and lightly browned. Pour in about half inch water. Cook while covered for about 5 minutes until the liquid has been absorbed.

Nutrition Information

- Calories: 374 calories;
- Total Fat: 12.2
- Sodium: 1049
- Total Carbohydrate: 50
- Cholesterol: 40
- Protein: 14.7

610. Stewed Korean Short Ribs (Kalbi Jim)

Serving: 6 | Prep: 20mins | Cook: 1hours | Ready in:

Ingredients

- 2 pounds beef short ribs, trimmed
- 1 green onion, chopped
- 2 carrots, peeled and chopped
- 4 cloves garlic, minced
- 1 (1 inch) piece fresh ginger root, chopped
- 1/2 cup reduced-sodium soy sauce
- 1/4 cup brown sugar
- 2 cups water to cover

Direction

- Score surface of every beef short rib to a diamond pattern. In a big skillet, mix brown sugar, soy sauce, ginger, garlic, carrots, green onion, and beef. Cover beef with enough water. Boil on medium-high heat, reducing heat to medium low. Simmer for 1 hour until beef becomes tender. Skim excess oil then serve.

Nutrition Information

- Calories: 647 calories;
- Sodium: 805
- Total Carbohydrate: 14.1
- Cholesterol: 115
- Protein: 23.3
- Total Fat: 54.9

611. Sweet And Spicy Shrimps

Serving: 2 | Prep: 30mins | Cook: 7mins | Ready in:

Ingredients

- Marinade:
- 1/2 cup light soy sauce
- 3 scallions, minced, divided
- 3 cloves garlic, minced
- 1 tablespoon toasted sesame seeds
- 1 tablespoon cornstarch
- 1 tablespoon finely minced ginger
- 1 1/2 teaspoons mirin
- 1 1/2 teaspoons white sugar, or more to taste
- 1 teaspoon red pepper flakes (optional)
- 1/2 teaspoon sesame oil
- 1 pound fresh shrimp, peeled and deveined
- 1/2 tablespoon gochujang (Korean red hot chile paste)

Direction

- Make the marinade by mixing together sesame oil, soy sauce, red pepper flakes, two minced scallions, sugar, garlic, mirin, sesame seeds, ginger, and cornstarch in a bowl.
- In a big ziploc/resealable plastic bag, put in shrimp and marinade; seal. Shake the bag to cover the shrimp. Let it chill in the refrigerator for 15- 20 minutes to marinate.
- On medium-high heat, heat pan and put in shrimp. Cook for 5-7 minutes while flipping and basting the shrimp several times with the remaining marinade; move shrimp into a bowl. Keep the oil in the pan.
- On medium heat, pour gochujang and 3 tbsp. of marinade in the pan. Cook and mix for about 2 minutes until thick. Use the glaze as a dip or slather over the cooked shrimp. Top with the leftover minced scallion.

Nutrition Information

- Calories: 304 calories;
- Sodium: 2554
- Total Carbohydrate: 17
- Cholesterol: 345
- Protein: 42.3
- Total Fat: 5.7

612. Toasti

Serving: 1 | Prep: 10mins | Cook: 10mins | Ready in:

Ingredients

- 1/2 cup shredded cabbage
- 1/2 carrot, shredded
- 1 egg
- 1/2 teaspoon soy sauce
- 2 tablespoons butter
- 2 slices bread, toasted

Direction

- In a bowl, mix carrot and cabbage. Mix in soy sauce and egg into the vegetables until combined.
- In a big skillet, heat butter on medium heat. Create a patty with veggie mixture to the size of a bread slice. Place patty in the skillet. Cook for 3 minutes on each side until both sides are brown. Put patty between two toasted bread slices then serve.

Nutrition Information

- Calories: 431 calories;
- Cholesterol: 247

- Protein: 11.2
- Total Fat: 29.8
- Sodium: 751
- Total Carbohydrate: 30.9

613. Tteokbokki (Korean Spicy Rice Cakes)

Serving: 2 | Prep: 5mins | Cook: 25mins | Ready in:

Ingredients

- 3 cups water
- 2 dried anchovies, or more to taste
- Sauce:
- 3 tablespoons chile paste
- 2 tablespoons white sugar
- 1 tablespoon soy sauce
- 1 tablespoon corn syrup
- 2 Korean fish cakes, sliced
- 1/2 onion, thickly sliced
- 1 spring onion, thickly sliced

Direction

- In a saucepan, mix anchovies and water and then heat to boil. Let to cook for ten minutes and then take out the anchovies.
- To make the sauce, in a bowl, mix corn syrup, chile paste, soy sauce and sugar.
- Add onion and rice cakes to anchovy water in the saucepan. Pour in sauce and heat to a boil. Let to cook while stirring from time to time for five minutes. Place in spring onion and then allow to boil for three more minutes.

Nutrition Information

- Calories: 183 calories;
- Total Carbohydrate: 41.6
- Cholesterol: 16
- Protein: 4.4
- Total Fat: 3.3
- Sodium: 733

614. Umma's Kimchi Jigeh

Serving: 4 | Prep: 30mins | Cook: 35mins | Ready in:

Ingredients

- 1 tablespoon canola oil
- 5 cloves garlic, minced, or more to taste
- 1 teaspoon minced ginger
- 1/2 pound boneless pork loin, sliced
- 1 teaspoon ground black pepper
- 1/2 teaspoon salt
- 2 cups kimchi, large slices, juice reserved
- 1 small onion, quartered
- 1 tablespoon kochu jang (Korean red pepper paste)
- 1 teaspoon beef dashida (bouillon granules)
- 4 cups water, or as needed
- 1 Korean green chile pepper, sliced
- 1 (12 ounce) package firm tofu, cubed
- 1 bunch scallions, cut into 1-inch pieces

Direction

- Over medium heat, heat a large saucepan and then add ginger, garlic, and oil. Cook while stirring for about 1 minute until the garlic is soft. Place in pork and then season with salt and black pepper. Stir-fry for about 3 to 5 minutes until the pork is golden brown and crisp. Add onion and kimchi and then stir-fry for about 3 to 5 minutes until the onion becomes soft.
- Add dashida and kochu jang to the veggies in the saucepan. Add in enough water to cover all the ingredients and then heat to boil. Add 1/4 cup reserved kimchi juice and green pepper. Cover the pot, decrease the heat and let to simmer for 15 minutes.
- Place in tofu and let to simmer for 10 minutes. Pour in scallions and mix to combine.

Nutrition Information

- Calories: 221 calories;
- Sodium: 1101
- Total Carbohydrate: 13.7
- Cholesterol: 27
- Protein: 19.5
- Total Fat: 11.1

615. Vegan Korean Kimchi Fried Rice

Serving: 2 | Prep: 10mins | Cook: 8mins | Ready in:

Ingredients

- 1 tablespoon vegetable oil
- 1/4 cup diced red onion
- 1 tablespoon minced garlic
- 1 1/2 teaspoons minced ginger (optional)
- 1/2 cup finely chopped kimchi
- 1 tablespoon rice wine vinegar
- 1 cup day-old cooked white rice
- 2 tablespoons white sugar
- 2 tablespoons reduced-sodium soy sauce
- 2 tablespoons kimchi brine
- 1/2 tablespoon sesame oil
- salt to taste
- ground black pepper to taste

Direction

- Over medium heat, heat oil in a large nonstick skillet and then add ginger, garlic, and red onion. Cook while stirring often for about 3 minutes until the onion softens. Raise the heat to high and then add vinegar and chopped kimchi. Mix in sesame oil, kimchi brine, soy sauce, sugar and cooked rice. Cook while stirring for about 5 minutes until heated through. Ensure you scrape the skillet's bottom to prevent sticking. Add pepper and salt.

Nutrition Information

- Calories: 275 calories;
- Protein: 4.1
- Total Fat: 10.6
- Sodium: 861
- Total Carbohydrate: 41.6
- Cholesterol: 0

616. Vegan Korean Tofu And Leek Barbeque

Serving: 8 | Prep: 20mins | Cook: 8mins | Ready in:

Ingredients

- 1 (16 ounce) package firm tofu, cubed
- Marinade:
- 1 cup cored and quartered apples
- 1/4 cup soy sauce
- 1/4 cup sesame oil
- 2 tablespoons maple syrup
- 2 tablespoons gochujang (Korean hot pepper paste)
- 1 tablespoon toasted sesame seeds
- Skewers:
- 8 skewers, or as needed
- 1 leek, cut into thick wedges
- cooking spray
- 1 tablespoon toasted sesame seeds

Direction

- Put tofu in a big bowl. In a blender, puree 1 tablespoon sesame seeds, hot pepper paste, maple syrup, sesame oil, soy sauce, and apples until smooth. Pour marinade on tofu. Cover using plastic wrap. Keep in fridge for 8 hours up to overnight.
- Drain tofu and throw out marinade. Thread leek pieces and tofu on skewers alternately.
- Heat a grill pan on high heat. Spray using cooking spray. Grill the skewers for 2 minutes on each side until all 4 sides are brown. Top with sesame seeds.

Nutrition Information

- Calories: 154 calories;
- Sodium: 493
- Total Carbohydrate: 11.3
- Cholesterol: 0
- Protein: 5.7
- Total Fat: 10.4

617. Vegetarian Bibimbap

Serving: 3 | Prep: 30mins | Cook: 20mins | Ready in:

Ingredients

- 2 tablespoons sesame oil
- 1 cup carrot matchsticks
- 1 cup zucchini matchsticks
- 1/2 (14 ounce) can bean sprouts, drained
- 6 ounces canned bamboo shoots, drained
- 1 (4.5 ounce) can sliced mushrooms, drained
- 1/8 teaspoon salt to taste
- 2 cups cooked and cooled rice
- 1/3 cup sliced green onions
- 2 tablespoons soy sauce
- 1/4 teaspoon ground black pepper
- 1 tablespoon butter
- 3 eggs
- 3 teaspoons sweet red chili sauce, or to taste

Direction

- Take a big skillet and heat sesame oil on medium heat. Stir and fry zucchini and carrot for 5 minutes until vegetables soften. Add in mushrooms, bamboo shoots and bean sprouts. Stir and fry for 5 minutes until carrots become tender. Dash a bit of salt for added taste then set aside.
- Use the same skillet to stir fry cooked rice, black pepper, soy sauce and green onions until rice becomes hot. Use another skillet to melt butter on medium heat, then fry eggs gently for 3 minutes each, until egg whites are firm, but the yolks are still a bit runny. Turn eggs once.
- Split cooked rice mixture among three serving bowls. For each bowl, top with 1/3 of vegetable mixture plus a fried egg. On the side, serve sweet red chili sauce for mixing in bibimbap.

Nutrition Information

- Calories: 395 calories;
- Total Fat: 18.8
- Sodium: 1086
- Total Carbohydrate: 45
- Cholesterol: 196
- Protein: 13.6

618. Vegetarian Kimchi

Serving: 30 | Prep: 25mins | Cook: | Ready in:

Ingredients

- 1 head napa cabbage, chopped
- 1/4 cup salt, divided
- 6 cloves garlic
- 1 (1 inch) piece fresh ginger root, peeled and chopped
- 1 small white onion, peeled and chopped
- 2 tablespoons water
- 3 green onions, minced
- cayenne pepper to taste
- 1 ripe persimmon, chopped
- 1 small radish, shredded
- 1 cucumber, diced (optional)

Direction

- Thoroughly rinse the cabbage then put in a bowl. Add a generous amount of salt then toss to mix; set aside for an hour.
- Stir cabbage with more salt; set aside for an hour more. Rinse then drain the cabbage. In a

blender on high speed, combine water, garlic, onion, and ginger together until smooth.
- Mix cucumber, rinsed drained cabbage, radish, garlic-ginger mixture, persimmon, cayenne pepper, and minced green onions together until well combined; move to airtight containers. Place in the refrigerator for three days then serve.

Nutrition Information

- Calories: 6 calories;
- Cholesterol: 0
- Protein: 0.3
- Total Fat: 0
- Sodium: 2
- Total Carbohydrate: 1.5

619. Yaki Mandu

Serving: 25 | Prep: 30mins | Cook: 15mins | Ready in:

Ingredients

- 1 pound ground beef
- 1 1/2 cups vegetable oil for frying
- 1/2 cup finely chopped green onions
- 1/2 cup finely chopped cabbage
- 1/2 cup finely chopped carrot
- 1/2 cup minced garlic
- 4 teaspoons sesame oil, divided
- 1 tablespoon toasted sesame seeds
- 1/2 teaspoon monosodium glutamate (such as Ac'cent®)
- salt and ground black pepper to taste
- 2 eggs
- 1 (16 ounce) package wonton wrappers
- 3 tablespoons soy sauce
- 2 teaspoons rice wine vinegar
- 1 teaspoon toasted sesame seeds, or more to taste

Direction

- Over medium-high heat, heat a large skillet and then cook while stirring the beef in hot skillet for 5 to 7 minutes until crumbly and browned. Drain the beef and get rid of the grease.
- Over medium heat, heat the vegetable oil in a separate skillet.
- Combine monosodium glutamate, 1 tablespoon sesame seeds, 1 tablespoon sesame oil, garlic, carrot, cabbage, green onions, pepper and salt into the ground beef mixture. Cook while stirring for 5 to 10 minutes until vegetables are tender and the liquid has evaporated. Place the beef mixture into a bowl and stir in one egg.
- Crack the second egg into a bowl and then beat thoroughly.
- Place one wonton wrapper in palm of your hand and then brush a thin layer of beaten egg on one edge. Spoon approximately one teaspoon of the beef mixture into the middle of wrapper. Fold the wrapper in half, from corner to corner, to form a triangle and then pinch the edges shut. Crimp using your fingers to form a seal. Press out the air by cupping the fingers over dumpling in the palm and press lightly.
- Fry the wontons in hot oil for 2 to 3 minutes until one side is browned. Turn and let to cook for 2 to 3 minutes until the remaining side is browned. Use a slotted spoon Place the wontons onto a plate lined with paper towel to drain.
- In a bowl, whisk together 1 teaspoon sesame seeds, 1 teaspoon sesame oil, vinegar, rice wine and soy sauce until the dipping sauce is smooth. You can serve together with wontons.

Nutrition Information

- Calories: 125 calories;
- Sodium: 246
- Total Carbohydrate: 12.1
- Cholesterol: 28
- Protein: 5.7
- Total Fat: 5.8

620. Yummy Korean Glass Noodles (Jap Chae)

Serving: 4 | Prep: 15mins | Cook: 5mins | Ready in:

Ingredients

- 1 pkg. (8 serving size) sweet potato vermicelli
- 1/2 cup reduced-sodium soy sauce
- 1/4 cup brown sugar
- 1/2 cup boiling water
- 3 tablespoons vegetable oil
- 1 teaspoon toasted sesame seeds

Direction

- Break vermicelli to small pieces. Put in a deep-sided dish. Cover and soak in hot tap water for 10 minutes. Drain.
- Mix boiling water, brown sugar, and soy sauce. Pour on drained noodles. Let soak for 2 minutes.
- Pour vegetable oil in a skillet on medium heat. Add soy sauce mixture and noodles in the skillet. Stir and cook for 5 minutes until hot. Top sesame seeds on noodles prior serving.

Nutrition Information

- Calories: 363 calories;
- Sodium: 1073
- Total Carbohydrate: 65.2
- Cholesterol: 0
- Protein: 1.9
- Total Fat: 10.7

Chapter 6: Chinese Cuisine Recipes

***

621. 8 Treasures

Serving: 10 | Prep: 15mins | Cook: 25mins | Ready in:

Ingredients

- 1 tablespoon vegetable oil
- 2 1/3 cups ground beef
- 2 1/3 cups peeled and deveined medium shrimp (30-40 per pound)
- 1 cup cubed fully cooked ham
- 4 sliced fresh mushrooms
- 2 leeks, chopped
- 8 cups water
- 2 (12 ounce) packages firm tofu, drained and cubed
- 1 (14.75 ounce) can cream-style corn
- 1/2 cup cornstarch
- 1 cup water
- 4 egg whites, beaten

Direction

- Put oil in a large soup pot and heat it over medium-high heat. Add the shrimp, ground beef, ham, leeks, and mushroom and cook them in the oil for about 10 minutes until the ground beef is browned. Add 8 cups of water and until it starts to simmer, cook for 10 more minutes.
- Add the creamed corn and tofu into the soup while stirring. Mix together 1 cup water and cornstarch and whisk then stir this mixture into the pot. Bring the soup into a simmer and continue to cook for about 5 minutes until the soup has thickened. Add the egg whites slowly into the thickened soup while stirring until they are ribbon-like in form.

Nutrition Information

- Calories: 288 calories;
- Total Fat: 15.3

- Sodium: 391
- Total Carbohydrate: 17.7
- Cholesterol: 77
- Protein: 21.3

622. Adriel's Chinese Curry Chicken

Serving: 4 | Prep: 25mins | Cook: 25mins | Ready in:

Ingredients

- 1 tablespoon yellow curry paste
- 1/2 cup chicken broth, divided
- 1 teaspoon white sugar
- 1 1/2 teaspoons curry powder
- 1/2 teaspoon salt
- 4 1/2 teaspoons light soy sauce
- 1 (5.6 ounce) can coconut milk
- 1 tablespoon canola oil
- 3 skinless, boneless chicken breast halves, sliced
- 2 teaspoons minced garlic
- 1 teaspoon minced fresh ginger
- 1 onion, sliced
- 2 potatoes - peeled, halved, and sliced

Direction

- Smash yellow curry paste in a large bowl together with 2 tbsp. of chicken broth to dissolve the paste. Stir in the remaining chicken broth, light soy sauce, salt, coconut milk, sugar, and curry powder into the bowl. Set aside.
- Warm skillet over high heat for 30 seconds. Add oil and allow it to heat until glistening, approximately half a minute. Cook and stir ginger, garlic, and chicken for about 2 minutes until garlic and ginger are fragrant and the chicken starts to brown. Add potatoes and onion and toss to combine. Pour in the sauce mixture and let it boil. Lower the heat and cover the skillet. Let it simmer for 20-25 minutes until the potatoes are tender and the chicken is completely cooked.

Nutrition Information

- Calories: 241 calories;
- Cholesterol: 46
- Protein: 20.1
- Total Fat: 7.1
- Sodium: 864
- Total Carbohydrate: 24.1

623. Adzuki Mooncake

Serving: 8 | Prep: 30mins | Cook: 1hours50mins | Ready in:

Ingredients

- Pastry:
- 1/3 cup golden syrup
- 3 tablespoons peanut oil
- 1 cup cake flour
- 1/2 teaspoon baking soda
- 1 pinch salt
- Adzuki Bean Filling:
- 1 1/2 cups dry adzuki beans
- 4 cups water
- 1/4 cup peanut oil
- 1/4 cup white sugar, or more to taste
- 2 tablespoons wheat starch
- 1/2 cup all-purpose flour
- 1 egg yolk, beaten

Direction

- In a small saucepan, put in 3 tablespoons of peanut oil and golden syrup and mix it together over low heat setting for about 3 minutes until the golden syrup is a lot easier to mix and the mixture is really warm in temperature. While finishing up the golden syrup and peanut oil mixture, combine the baking soda, salt and cake flour together in a mixing bowl. Add the golden syrup mixture into the flour mixture and mix everything together until you get a dough that has a smooth texture. Use a plastic wrap to wrap the dough securely then keep it in the fridge for not less than 4 hours.

- While the dough is resting in the fridge, fill a big saucepan placed over high heat setting with water then put in the adzuki beans. Let the mixture boil then lower the heat to medium-low setting and allow the mixture to simmer with cover for about 1 hour until the beans soften. Drain the cooked beans and let it cool down for 10 minutes. Use a food processor or a blender to puree the cooked beans.
- In the same saucepan used for the adzuki beans, put in 1/4 cup of peanut oil and let it heat up over medium heat setting. Mix in the white sugar and the pureed adzuki beans. Let the mixture cook in hot oil for 10-20 minutes while stirring it until bean paste mixture that adheres to the stirring spoon. Add in the wheat starch and give it a mix. Scrape off the mixture into a mixing bowl and keep it in the fridge until the mixture is cold in temperature.
- Preheat the oven to 375°F (190°C). Coat a baking sheet with oil.
- Separate the prepared filling and the dough both into 8 even portions, and shape each of the dough and filling portions into balls. Flatten each of the dough balls using your palms to create a flat circle where you could fit the filling ball. Put 1 filling ball in the middle of each of the flattened dough circles then enclose the filling ball with the dough, and press together the edges. Roll the formed mooncakes in the all-purpose flour until it is coated with flour then give it a shake to remove any excess flour. Put the floured mooncakes on the prepared baking sheet with the seam side facing down then flatten each of the mooncakes a little bit.
- Lightly spray the mooncakes with water. Put it in the preheated oven and let it bake for 8 minutes. Take the mooncakes out from the oven then lower the temperature of the oven to 300°F (150°C).
- Use a brush to coat the mooncakes with beaten egg yolk, coating the top part more than the sides of the mooncakes. Put the mooncakes back in the preheated oven and bake it for about 15 more minutes until they turn golden brown in color. Allow it to fully cool down first before serving.

Nutrition Information

- Calories: 396 calories;
- Protein: 10
- Total Fat: 12.8
- Sodium: 113
- Total Carbohydrate: 61.7
- Cholesterol: 26

624. Ahi Tuna Spice Rub

Serving: 14 | Prep: 5mins | Cook: | Ready in:

Ingredients

- 3 tablespoons Chinese five-spice powder
- 3 tablespoons white sesame seeds
- 2 tablespoons white sugar
- 1 tablespoon ground white pepper
- 1 tablespoon salt
- 1 tablespoon ground ginger
- 1 tablespoon garlic powder
- 1 1/2 teaspoons Sichuan pepper powder
- 1 1/2 teaspoons ground anise seed
- 1 1/2 teaspoons ground black pepper
- 3/4 teaspoon red pepper flakes

Direction

- In a jar, combine together red pepper flakes, black pepper, ground anise, Sichuan pepper powder, garlic powder, ground ginger, salt, white pepper, sugar, sesame seeds and

Chinese five-spice powder. Close and shake to blend

Nutrition Information

- Calories: 31 calories;
- Total Carbohydrate: 5
- Cholesterol: 0
- Protein: 0.7
- Total Fat: 1.3
- Sodium: 499

625. Anise Wine Chicken

Serving: 4 | Prep: 30mins | Cook: 25mins | Ready in:

Ingredients

- 1 small onion, chopped
- 2 inch piece fresh ginger root, minced
- 2 cloves garlic, minced
- 2 whole star anise pods
- 1/2 cup dry white wine
- 1 teaspoon salt
- 1/4 teaspoon ground black pepper
- 2 tablespoons vegetable oil
- 1 teaspoon rice vinegar
- 1/2 pound skinless, boneless chicken breast meat - cut into bite-size pieces
- 20 new potatoes
- 1 tablespoon vegetable oil
- 1 cup cherry tomatoes
- 1 tablespoon cornstarch
- 2 tablespoons water
- 1/4 cup minced fresh Thai basil leaves

Direction

- Combine chicken, 2 tbsp. of vegetable oil, star anise, salt, onion, white wine, rice vinegar, garlic, pepper, and ginger together in a large mixing bowl. Cover the bowl and place it inside the refrigerator to marinate for 4-6 hours. While waiting, cover potatoes with salted water inside a large pot. Let it boil over high heat. Adjust the heat to medium-low and cover the pot to simmer for 15 minutes until the potatoes are tender. Drain the potatoes and cool before cutting them into halves.
- Spread 1 tbsp. of vegetable oil into a large skillet and heat it over high heat. Take the chicken out of the marinade, squeezing off any excess, and cook it into the heated oil for 5 minutes until the center is no longer pink in the middle and the sides are all browned. Reserve the marinade for the next step. Discard star anise from the reserved marinade. Pour the marinade all over the chicken and bring it to boil. Stir in halved potatoes and cherry tomatoes and cook for 3 minutes until the potatoes are hot and the cherry tomatoes start to burst. Dissolve cornstarch in the water and add it into the chicken mixture together with Thai basil. Cook for 1 more minute, stirring it frequently until thick.

Nutrition Information

- Calories: 562 calories;
- Total Carbohydrate: 87.8
- Cholesterol: 33
- Protein: 23.3
- Total Fat: 11.6
- Sodium: 653

626. Asian Beef With Snow Peas

Serving: 4 | Prep: 5mins | Cook: 10mins | Ready in:

Ingredients

- 3 tablespoons soy sauce
- 2 tablespoons rice wine
- 1 tablespoon brown sugar
- 1/2 teaspoon cornstarch
- 1 tablespoon vegetable oil
- 1 tablespoon minced fresh ginger root

- 1 tablespoon minced garlic
- 1 pound beef round steak, cut into thin strips
- 8 ounces snow peas

Direction

- Put together the rice wine, soy sauce, cornstarch, and brown sugar in a small bowl then put aside.
- Pour oil in a cooking pan or wok and heat it on medium-high heat. Add the garlic and ginger to the oil and stir-fry for 30 seconds. Add the steak and stir-fry until it's browned evenly for 2 minutes. Add the snow peas in then stir-fry for 3 more minutes. Pour in the soy sauce mixture and boil with constant stirring. Reduce the heat and allow to simmer until the sauce has become smooth and thick. Serve right away.

Nutrition Information

- Calories: 203 calories;
- Total Carbohydrate: 9.7
- Cholesterol: 39
- Protein: 16
- Total Fat: 10
- Sodium: 711

627. Authentic Chinese Egg Rolls (from A Chinese Person)

Serving: 20 | Prep: 1hours | Cook: 20mins | Ready in:

Ingredients

- 4 teaspoons vegetable oil
- 3 eggs, beaten
- 1 medium head cabbage, finely shredded
- 1/2 carrot, julienned
- 1 (8 ounce) can shredded bamboo shoots
- 1 cup dried, shredded wood ear mushroom, rehydrated
- 1 pound Chinese barbequed or roasted pork, cut into matchsticks
- 2 green onions, thinly sliced
- 2 1/2 teaspoons soy sauce
- 1 teaspoon salt
- 1 teaspoon sugar
- 1/2 teaspoon monosodium glutamate (MSG)
- 1 (14 ounce) package egg roll wrappers
- 1 egg white, beaten
- 4 cups oil for frying, or as needed

Direction

- On medium heat, heat a teaspoon of vegetable oil in a big skillet or wok; add beaten eggs. Cook until the eggs are firm, avoid stirring. Turn the eggs and cook for another 20secs until the opposite side is firm; let them cool. Cut the egg pancakes in thin strips.
- On high heat, heat the left vegetable oil in a big skillet or wok; add carrot and cabbage. Cook and stir for 2 minutes until wilted. Put in MSG, bamboo, sugar, mushroom, salt, pork, soy sauce, and green onions. Cook for 6 minutes until the veggies are soft; mix in sliced eggs. Fan out the mixture in a pan and let it chill in the refrigerator for an hour until cold.
- Prepare the egg rolls by laying a wrapper in a diamond on a work surface. Scoop 3 tbsp. of the chilled filling on the base third of wrapper. Slather beaten egg whites on the top sides of wrapper, fold the base portion to cover filling; firmly roll up to the middle point. Join the right and left corners tightly over egg roll. Keep on rolling until the top portions close the egg roll with egg white. Repeat with the left filling and wrappers. Use a plastic wrap to cover the finished rolls and to prevent them from getting dry.
- In a deep fryer or wok, heat 6-in oil to 175°C or 350°F.
- Cook egg rolls for 5-7 minutes until golden, fry 3-4 rolls at a time. Place on paper towels to drain.

Nutrition Information

- Calories: 169 calories;
- Sodium: 315
- Total Carbohydrate: 16
- Cholesterol: 46
- Protein: 9.9
- Total Fat: 7.4

628. Authentic Chinese Steamed Fish

Serving: 6 | Prep: 15mins | Cook: 15mins | Ready in:

Ingredients

- 1 (4 pound) whole rockfish, dressed
- 1/4 cup vegetable oil
- 1 green onion, thinly sliced diagonally
- 1 (1 inch) piece fresh ginger, peeled and cut into matchstick strips
- 1/2 cup soy sauce

Direction

- Pour water in a big pot, filling it 1/2 full then on top of the pot, put a bamboo steamer with a lid. Bring the water to a rolling boil. Clean the fish by scouring off its scales then wash it off using cold water. Move the fish to a small metal plate with its belly side down.
- Place it in the steamer then cover and cook for 10-12 minutes until the fish is already flaky and not opaque. Avoid taking the pot lid off until it is finished steaming to make sure that the fish is completely tender and cooked.
- While steaming the fish, put together the vegetable oil, ginger, and green onions in a small cooking pan. Cook them on medium-high heat until the ginger starts to bubble. Pour the hot oil carefully on the steamed fish then dribble with soy sauce and serve.

Nutrition Information

- Calories: 379 calories;

- Protein: 58.1
- Total Fat: 13.8
- Sodium: 1385
- Total Carbohydrate: 2
- Cholesterol: 104

629. Beefy Chinese Dumplings

Serving: 10 | Prep: 30mins | Cook: 5mins | Ready in:

Ingredients

- 1 1/2 pounds ground beef
- 2 cups shredded Chinese cabbage
- 1 carrot, shredded
- 1 onion, minced
- 1 egg
- 1 teaspoon sugar
- 1 teaspoon salt
- 1 tablespoon soy sauce
- 1 tablespoon vegetable oil
- 1 (14 ounce) package wonton wrappers

Direction

- Whisk carrot, onion, beef, and cabbage in a big bowl. Add the soy sauce, vegetable oil, sugar, salt, and egg.
- Spoon a big teaspoonful of the filling and place it on the middle of the dumpling skin. Drop water into the edges of the wonton to moisten it. Fold the dumpling in half and pinch its edges to secure the filling. Make a ripple pattern along the pinched edge by pinching and pushing small parts of it. Do the same with the rest of the dumplings.
- Boil dumplings in the water for 5 minutes until they float.

Nutrition Information

- Calories: 356 calories;
- Total Fat: 20.6

- Sodium: 606
- Total Carbohydrate: 25.4
- Cholesterol: 80
- Protein: 16.2

630. Broccoli And Carrot Stir Fry

Serving: 5 | Prep: 10mins | Cook: 16mins | Ready in:

Ingredients

- 5 1/2 cups broccoli florets
- 1 carrot, thinly sliced
- 2 teaspoons water
- 1 teaspoon cornstarch
- 1 teaspoon chicken bouillon granules, or to taste
- salt to taste
- 2 tablespoons peanut oil

Direction

- Boil a big pot with slightly salted water. Put in the broccoli and cook for 2 minutes with no cover till bright green. Use slotted spoon to turn broccoli into bowl with ice water and soak for a few minutes to halt cooking. Strain.
- In same big pot, return water to boil; put in and cook sliced carrot, about a minute. Strain.
- In bowl, combine cornstarch and water till smooth. Put in the salt and chicken granules and combine thoroughly.
- In a big skillet or a wok, heat the peanut oil on high heat; sauté carrots and broccoli, about 2 minutes. Put in mixture of cornstarch; cook and mix to evenly coat the vegetables, for a minute or 2.

Nutrition Information

- Calories: 90 calories;
- Cholesterol: < 1
- Protein: 2.9

- Total Fat: 5.8
- Sodium: 147
- Total Carbohydrate: 8.4

631. Cantonese Barbecued Pork

Serving: 6 | Prep: 6mins | Cook: 1hours | Ready in:

Ingredients

- 2 tablespoons dry sherry
- 2 slices fresh ginger root
- 1 tablespoon oyster sauce
- 1/2 teaspoon Chinese five-spice powder
- 4 1/2 teaspoons soy sauce
- 1 tablespoon white sugar
- 2 tablespoons hoisin sauce
- 2 tablespoons ketchup
- 1/2 teaspoon ground cinnamon
- 1 1/2 pounds pork shoulder roast
- 1 tablespoon honey

Direction

- Combine the sherry, oyster sauce, ginger root, soy sauce, five-spice powder, white sugar, hoisin sauce, sugar, cinnamon, and ketchup in a bowl.
- Slice the pork into strips, 5x2 inches. In a shallow baking dish, lay the strips flat. Pour the marinade over the strips of pork and let the pork marinate in the refrigerator for at least 6 hours.
- Strain the pork and set the marinade aside. In a small bowl, mix together 3 tablespoons of the reserved marinade and honey, then set it aside. Prepare the oven by preheating it to 350° F (175° C).
- Put water in a shallow roasting pan, filling it, then place the pan in the bottom of the oven. Place the pork strips carefully on a roasting rack above the roasting pan so that all sides are exposed to heat. In case you don't have a roasting rack, you can use an S-shaped hook,

drapery hook, or paper clip, insert its curved end on the pork strips and then hang them from the top shelf of the oven.
- Roast the pork for 30 minutes. Brush honey mixture on the pork strips to baste them. Roast them again for another 15 minutes then brush again with honey mixture. Allow to roast for another 10 minutes until the pork strips are golden brown and are crispy. Take them out of the oven and leave them to cool.

Nutrition Information

- Calories: 158 calories;
- Total Carbohydrate: 10.2
- Cholesterol: 45
- Protein: 13.1
- Total Fat: 6.9
- Sodium: 451

632. Cantonese Style Pork And Shrimp Dumplings

Serving: 10 | Prep: 30mins | Cook: 20mins | Ready in:

Ingredients

- 1/4 pound ground pork
- 1 cup chopped watercress
- 1/2 (8 ounce) can water chestnuts, drained and chopped
- 1/4 cup chopped green onions
- 1 tablespoon oyster sauce
- 1 1/2 tablespoons sesame oil
- 1 teaspoon minced garlic
- 1 teaspoon soy sauce
- 1/8 teaspoon ground white pepper
- 1/8 teaspoon salt
- 1 (16 ounce) package round dumpling skins
- 1 pound peeled and deveined medium shrimp

Direction

- Mix thoroughly pork, oyster sauce, soy sauce, watercress, garlic, green onion, salt, ground white pepper, water chestnuts, and sesame oil in a large bowl.
- Spoon a half teaspoonful of filling into each dumpling skin. Add one shrimp into the filling. Wet the edge of the dumpling skin slightly and then fold it over. Pinch the skin with your finger to seal the fillings all over.
- To cook: Heat oil in a large skillet over medium heat and cook the dumplings for 15 minutes, flipping it over halfway through. You can also cook the dumplings by placing them in a pot with boiling water for 10 minutes. Let them drain and serve them together with hot chicken broth.

Nutrition Information

- Calories: 234 calories;
- Protein: 15.8
- Total Fat: 5.9
- Sodium: 402
- Total Carbohydrate: 28.2
- Cholesterol: 81

633. Chi Tan T'ang (Egg Drop Soup)

Serving: 6 | Prep: 10mins | Cook: 10mins | Ready in:

Ingredients

- 8 cubes chicken bouillon
- 6 cups hot water
- 2 tablespoons cornstarch
- 2 tablespoons soy sauce
- 3 tablespoons distilled white vinegar
- 1 green onion, minced
- 3 eggs, beaten

Direction

- Melt bouillon in a big pot with hot water. Stir a little water and cornstarch together; pour mixture in bouillon, Mix in green onion, soy sauce, and vinegar; boil. Let it simmer while stirring from time to time. Pour in beaten eggs slowly while continuously stirring. Serve immediately.

Nutrition Information

- Calories: 62 calories;
- Total Fat: 2.8
- Sodium: 1872
- Total Carbohydrate: 4.7
- Cholesterol: 94
- Protein: 4.5

634. Chicken Broccoli Ca Unieng's Style

Serving: 6 | Prep: 10mins | Cook: 25mins | Ready in:

Ingredients

- 12 ounces boneless, skinless chicken breast halves, cut into bite-sized pieces
- 1 tablespoon oyster sauce
- 2 tablespoons dark soy sauce
- 3 tablespoons vegetable oil
- 2 cloves garlic, chopped
- 1 large onion, cut into rings
- 1/2 cup water
- 1 teaspoon ground black pepper
- 1 teaspoon white sugar
- 1/2 medium head bok choy, chopped
- 1 small head broccoli, chopped
- 1 tablespoon cornstarch, mixed with equal parts water

Direction

- Mix oyster sauce, soy sauce, and chicken in a large bowl. Let it sit for 15 minutes.
- Pour oil into a large heavy skillet or wok and heat it over moderate heat. Cook garlic and onion until translucent and tender. Adjust the heat to high and stir in chicken together with marinade. Cook and stir for 10 minutes until golden brown. Stir in pepper, sugar, water, bok choy, and broccoli. Cook and stir for 10 minutes until the bok choy and broccoli are tender. Drizzle over cornstarch mixture and cook for 5 more minutes until the sauce is thickened.

Nutrition Information

- Calories: 170 calories;
- Sodium: 418
- Total Carbohydrate: 9.8
- Cholesterol: 33
- Protein: 16.2
- Total Fat: 7.9

635. Chicken Vicious

Serving: 4 | Prep: 15mins | Cook: 30mins | Ready in:

Ingredients

- 2 teaspoons vegetable oil
- 4 skinless, boneless chicken breast halves - cut into 1 inch pieces
- 1 1/2 cups distilled white vinegar
- 1 cup white sugar
- 1/2 cup soy sauce
- 1 tablespoon red pepper flakes, or to taste
- 2 tablespoons garlic powder, or to taste
- 1 tablespoon onion powder, or to taste
- 1/2 teaspoon ground ginger
- 1 (8 ounce) package button mushrooms, sliced
- 1 cup frozen green peas
- 3 green onions, chopped
- 3 teaspoons cornstarch
- 2 tablespoons cold water

Direction

- Place the big and heavy skillet on high heat and heat the oil. Cook the chicken pieces in the hot oil until all gets browned. Stir in soy sauce, sugar, and vinegar and cook until the sugar dissolves completely. Flavor the mixture with red pepper flakes, ginger, garlic powder, and onion powder. Adjust the heat to low and cover the skillet. Let it simmer for 15 minutes. Adjust the seasoning according to your taste (it should be very sweet). If it's too sweet, you can add extra vinegar, while if it's too tart, you can add extra sugar.
- Stir in green onions, peas, and mushrooms and simmer for 5 minutes on low heat. Once the mushrooms shrink, pour in water and cornstarch. Bring the mixture to simmer until the preferred thickness was achieved.

Nutrition Information

- Calories: 442 calories;
- Total Fat: 4.6
- Sodium: 1931
- Total Carbohydrate: 67.9
- Cholesterol: 68
- Protein: 34.3

636. Chicken And Chinese Vegetable Stir Fry

Serving: 6 | Prep: 20mins | Cook: 25mins | Ready in:

Ingredients

- 14 ounces skinless, boneless chicken breast meat - cut into bite-size pieces
- 1/2 cup oyster sauce
- 2 tablespoons soy sauce
- 3 tablespoons vegetable oil
- 2 cloves garlic, minced
- 1 large onion, chopped
- 1/2 cup water
- 1 teaspoon ground black pepper
- 1 teaspoon white sugar
- 1 (8 ounce) can sliced water chestnuts, drained
- 1 cup snow peas
- 1 small head broccoli, cut into florets
- 3 tablespoons cornstarch
- 1/4 cup water

Direction

- Use a mixing bowl to combine the oyster sauce, chicken, and soy sauce to coat the chicken evenly with sauce. Let rest.
- Set the heat to high, then use a wok or large skillet to heat some vegetable oil. Add in the garlic and onion, then cook while stirring for a minute or until onion is limp. Cook in the chicken and marinade. Stir the chicken around for 10 minutes, until it turns a nice brown color.
- Add half a cup of water, then season with sugar and pepper. Mix in the snow peas, water chestnuts, and broccoli. Put the cover on, then let the vegetables boil for 5 minutes until soft. Use 1/4 cup of water to dissolve cornstarch, then add it to the boiling pot. Let it cook to a thick consistency until it has no more cloudiness.

Nutrition Information

- Calories: 217 calories;
- Total Carbohydrate: 16.8
- Cholesterol: 40
- Protein: 17.5
- Total Fat: 9.2
- Sodium: 500

637. Chicken And Cold Noodles With Spicy Sauce

Serving: 4 | Prep: | Cook: | Ready in:

Ingredients

- 6 cups water

- 1 whole bone-in chicken breast, with skin
- 6 ounces dry Chinese noodles
- 1 teaspoon sesame oil
- 1/4 cup tahini
- 3 tablespoons water
- 1 tablespoon sesame oil
- 2 teaspoons chili oil (optional)
- 3 tablespoons soy sauce
- 2 tablespoons red wine vinegar
- 1/4 cup peanut oil
- 2 tablespoons minced garlic

Direction

- Boil 6 cups of water in a large saucepan over medium-high heat. Stir in chicken breast and boil. Adjust the heat to low, and let it simmer uncovered for 15 minutes. Remove the meat from the pan once it's done. Set aside to cool.
- Boil broth again then stir in the noodles. Cook the noodles for 5-7 minutes while stirring it from time to time. Drain the noodles and reserve the broth for another use if desired. Wash and chill the noodles under cold running water. Transfer the drained noodles in a serving bowl. Stir in 1 tsp. of sesame oil and toss them lightly.
- Cut chicken meat into fine shreds and remove its bone and skin. Set it aside.
- Stir in 3 tbsp. of water and tahini. Blend them well before adding 1 tbsp. of sesame oil, garlic, soy sauce, chili oil, vinegar, and peanut oil. Mix them until well-blended.
- Garnish the noodles with chicken and drizzle the sauce all over.

Nutrition Information

- Calories: 542 calories;
- Total Fat: 35.6
- Sodium: 752
- Total Carbohydrate: 37.2
- Cholesterol: 46
- Protein: 23.3

638. Chicken In Garlic And Black Bean Sauce

Serving: 6 | Prep: 15mins | Cook: 15mins | Ready in:

Ingredients

- Marinade:
- 1 tablespoon cornstarch
- 1 tablespoon water
- 1 tablespoon soy sauce
- 1 1/2 teaspoons white sugar
- 1 teaspoon salt
- 6 skinless, boneless chicken breast halves, sliced
- 1 cup bean sprouts
- 1/4 cup water
- Sauce:
- 2 teaspoons oyster sauce
- 1 teaspoon white sugar
- 1 tablespoon vegetable oil
- 3 tablespoons black bean sauce with garlic
- 1 tablespoon chopped garlic
- 1 onion, finely sliced
- 1/2 teaspoon salt
- 1/2 bell pepper, chopped
- 2 teaspoons cornstarch
- 1 tablespoon water

Direction

- In a bowl, mix together a tablespoon each of water and cornstarch. Mix in a teaspoon salt, sugar, and soy sauce; put in chicken. Mix well to blend. Set aside for 20 minutes to marinate.
- Boil water in a pot; put in bean sprouts. Cook for half minute until just blanched; drain.
- In a small bowl, mix together sugar, oyster sauce, and quarter cup water.
- On high heat, heat vegetable oil in a pan; add garlic and black bean sauce. Sauté and stir for 2-3 minutes until aromatic; add half teaspoon salt and onion. Cook for 3-4 minutes while stirring until soft; put in marinated chicken. Stir-fry for 3-4 minutes until the chicken is

cooked through and opaque. Mix oyster sauce in and cook 1-2 minutes until cooked through; cover. Let it simmer for 3 minutes until the flavors are blended. Cook and stir bell pepper for 1-2 minutes until soft. Melt 2 tsp cornstarch in a tablespoon water. Fold bean sprouts and cornstarch mixture in. Cook for another 2-3 minutes until the sauce is thick.

Nutrition Information

- Calories: 175 calories;
- Sodium: 849
- Total Carbohydrate: 8.2
- Cholesterol: 59
- Protein: 23.1
- Total Fat: 5

639. Chicken With Green Peppers In Black Bean Sauce

Serving: 4 | Prep: 30mins | Cook: 15mins | Ready in:

Ingredients

- 2 tablespoons toasted sesame oil
- 4 cloves garlic cloves, peeled and sliced
- 6 tablespoons black bean sauce
- 1 teaspoon salt
- 3/4 pound skinless, boneless chicken breast half - cut into cubes
- 1 cube chicken bouillon dissolved in
- 1/2 cup boiling water
- 1 large onion, peeled and sliced
- 1 bunch green onions, chopped
- 2 green bell pepper, diced
- 1 1/2 tablespoons dark soy sauce
- 1 teaspoon black pepper
- 4 teaspoons cornstarch dissolved in
- 3 tablespoons water
- 4 tablespoons chopped fresh cilantro

Direction

- Place the wok over medium heat and heat it until it's hot then add in the toasted sesame oil and wait 30 seconds for it to heat up. Add the black bean sauce and garlic into the oil while stirring then add salt to season. Mix in the chicken into the wok with frequent stirring, until the chicken is well cooked. Add the dissolved chicken bouillon, cover the wok and let it cook for 6 minutes.
- Add the green onions, onions, and bell pepper while stirring then add black pepper and soy sauce to season. Cover the wok again and let it cook for 8 minutes. Add the cornstarch mixture, stirring it in until the sauce is thickened. Add the cilantro while stirring then serve.

Nutrition Information

- Calories: 253 calories;
- Sodium: 1421
- Total Carbohydrate: 17.2
- Cholesterol: 43
- Protein: 18.7
- Total Fat: 12.6

640. Chinese Barbeque Pork (Char Siu)

Serving: 6 | Prep: 10mins | Cook: 2hours | Ready in:

Ingredients

- 2/3 cup soy sauce
- 1/2 cup honey
- 1/2 cup Chinese rice wine (or sake or dry sherry)
- 1/3 cup hoisin sauce
- 1/3 cup ketchup
- 1/3 cup brown sugar
- 4 cloves garlic, crushed
- 1 teaspoon Chinese five-spice powder
- 1/2 teaspoon freshly ground black pepper
- 1/4 teaspoon cayenne pepper

- 1/8 teaspoon pink curing salt (optional)
- 1 (3 pound) boneless pork butt (shoulder)
- 1 teaspoon kosher salt, or to taste

Direction

- Put together in a cooking pan the soy sauce, rice wine, honey, hoisin sauce, brown sugar, ketchup, garlic, black pepper, five-spice powder, curing salt, and cayenne pepper. Bring this to a boil over high heat then lower the heat to medium-high. Cook for another minute before turning the heat off. Let it cool to room temperature.
- Slice the pork roast in half lengthwise then each half, cut in lengthwise as well to form 4 long and thick pork pieces.
- Move to a big mixing bowl the sauce that's been cooled. Add red food coloring while stirring. Put the pork pieces into the sauce, coating each piece. Use a plastic wrap to cover the pork and leave it refrigerated for 4-12 hours.
- Prepare the grill by preheating it to medium heat, 275° to 300° F (135° to 150° C and grease the grate lightly. Use parchment paper to line a baking sheet.
- Take the pieces of pork from the marinade and let the excess sauce drip off. Put the pork pieces on the baking sheet that you prepared then drizzle with kosher salt to taste.
- Place the pork pieces to the grate over indirect heat on the grill. Cover the grill and cook for about 45 minutes. Brush the pork with marinade then turn and continue to cook for about 1hr and 15 minutes more. Use an instant-read thermometer and insert it into the center of the pork and it should read 185° to 190° F to indicate that it's cooked. Do not any more marinade on the cooked pork after boiling it.
- Boil the remaining marinade in the cooking pan and let it simmer for a minute. Turn off the heat. Now it can be used to brush over the cooked pork.

Nutrition Information

- Calories: 513 calories;
- Total Fat: 21.9
- Sodium: 2421
- Total Carbohydrate: 49.1
- Cholesterol: 90
- Protein: 26

641. Chinese Barbequed Spareribs

Serving: 6 | Prep: 1hours20mins | Cook: 1hours | Ready in:

Ingredients

- 1/2 cup hoisin sauce
- 1/4 cup jellied cranberry sauce
- 3 tablespoons reduced sodium soy sauce
- 2 tablespoons white wine
- 2 tablespoons honey
- 1/2 teaspoon red food coloring
- 1/2 teaspoon garlic salt
- 1/4 teaspoon Chinese five-spice powder
- 4 pounds pork spareribs, cut into 1-inch pieces
- 2 cups water

Direction

- Combine honey, red food coloring, hoisin sauce, soy sauce, cranberry sauce, and white wine in a large bowl. Add Chinese five-spice powder and garlic salt and mix well. Arrange the ribs in the marinade; cover with cling wrap and leave to marinate in the refrigerator for at least an hour.
- Preheat the oven to 350°F or 175°C.
- Fill the bottom of a big roasting pan with water. Place the ribs on the pan rack, and cook for half an hour in the preheated oven. Coat the ribs with the remaining sauce, and continue to cook for another half an hour until the internal temperature reaches 160°F or 70°C.

Nutrition Information

- Calories: 932 calories;
- Cholesterol: 243
- Protein: 48
- Total Fat: 71.5
- Sodium: 1009
- Total Carbohydrate: 20.5

642.   Chinese Broccoli

Serving: 4 | Prep: 10mins | Cook: 10mins | Ready in:

Ingredients

- 1 bunch Gai Lan (Chinese broccoli), trimmed
- 2 tablespoons white sugar
- 1 tablespoon cornstarch
- 2 tablespoons soy sauce
- 1 tablespoon rice vinegar
- 1 tablespoon sesame oil
- 3 tablespoons hoisin sauce
- 1 teaspoon minced fresh ginger root
- 2 cloves garlic, minced

Direction

- Boil water that is lightly salted in a big pot. Place in the Chinese broccoli and cook for 4 minutes, uncovered, until the broccoli is tender. Drain then set aside for a while.
- In a small saucepan, mix sesame oil, ginger, garlic, vinegar, cornstarch, sugar, hoisin sauce, and soy sauce. Cook the mixture on medium heat for 5-7 minutes until it's thick and not cloudy. Toss with broccoli. Serve.

Nutrition Information

- Calories: 130 calories;
- Sodium: 705
- Total Carbohydrate: 21.5
- Cholesterol: < 1
- Protein: 3
- Total Fat: 4.3

643.   Chinese Cabbage Salad II

Serving: 5 | Prep: 15mins | Cook: 10mins | Ready in:

Ingredients

- 3 tablespoons red wine vinegar
- 2 tablespoons white sugar
- 1/2 teaspoon salt
- 1/4 teaspoon ground black pepper
- 1 (3 ounce) package chicken flavored ramen noodles, crushed, seasoning packet reserved
- 1/2 cup vegetable oil
- 1 (16 ounce) package broccoli coleslaw mix
- 1/2 cup chopped green onions
- 4 ounces toasted slivered almonds
- 1/4 cup sesame seeds, toasted

Direction

- Pour sugar and vinegar into a small saucepan. At moderate heat, cook them until they start dissolving. Move it away from the heat then add oil, ramen seasoning packet, pepper and salt. After stirring, leave it cooling on one side.
- Mix the green onions, broccoli coleslaw mix and the uncooked ramen noodles together in a big bowl. Empty the dressing out into the big bowl, tossing with salad until everything is equally coated. Keep it chilling in the fridge.
- When ready to serve, scatter sesame seeds and almonds over the top.

Nutrition Information

- Calories: 481 calories;
- Total Fat: 37.4
- Sodium: 472
- Total Carbohydrate: 28.9
- Cholesterol: 0
- Protein: 9.6

644. Chinese Chicken Casserole Surprise

Serving: 6 | Prep: 30mins | Cook: 45mins | Ready in:

Ingredients

- 2 skinless, boneless chicken breasts - cooked and cubed
- 1 cup chicken broth
- 1 (10.75 ounce) can condensed cream of mushroom soup
- 1 (5 ounce) can evaporated milk
- 1 cup sliced almonds
- 1 (4.5 ounce) can sliced mushrooms, drained
- 1 (8 ounce) can water chestnuts, drained and minced
- 1 (5 ounce) can crispy chow mein noodles
- 2/3 cup shredded Cheddar cheese
- 1 cup diced celery (optional)

Direction

- Prepare the oven by preheating it to 350° F (175° C).
- Put together the broth, chicken, milk, soup, almonds, water chestnuts, mushroom pieces, celery (if you're using it), noodles and cheese in a 9x13 baking dish that's been lightly coated with oil. Combine well and make sure it's evenly spread in the baking dish.
- Put it in the oven and bake for 45 minutes.

Nutrition Information

- Calories: 434 calories;
- Cholesterol: 47
- Protein: 21.8
- Total Fat: 27
- Sodium: 664
- Total Carbohydrate: 28.7

645. Chinese Chicken Fried Rice I

Serving: 7 | Prep: 25mins | Cook: 15mins | Ready in:

Ingredients

- 1/2 tablespoon sesame oil
- 1 onion
- 1 1/2 pounds cooked, cubed chicken meat
- 2 tablespoons soy sauce
- 2 large carrots, diced
- 2 stalks celery, chopped
- 1 large red bell pepper, diced
- 3/4 cup fresh pea pods, halved
- 1/2 large green bell pepper, diced
- 6 cups cooked white rice
- 2 eggs
- 1/3 cup soy sauce

Direction

- In a big cooking pan, heat the oil on medium heat. Sauté the onion in the hot oil until it's soft then add 2 tablespoons of soy sauce and the chicken and stir-fry it for 5-6 minutes.
- Add the celery, carrots, pea pods, green bell pepper, and red bell pepper while stirring then stir-fry for 5 more minutes. Add the rice and mix well.
- Add 1/3 soy sauce and scrambled eggs while stirring, heat it through and serve while it's hot.

Nutrition Information

- Calories: 425 calories;
- Protein: 34.7
- Total Fat: 9.5
- Sodium: 1060
- Total Carbohydrate: 47.5
- Cholesterol: 134

646. Chinese Chicken Salad

Serving: 6 | Prep: | Cook: | Ready in:

Ingredients

- 3 1/2 boneless chicken breast halves, cooked and diced
- 1 head lettuce, torn into small pieces
- 4 green onions, sliced
- 4 stalks celery, sliced thin
- 1/2 cup walnuts, chopped
- 2 tablespoons sesame seeds, toasted
- 6 ounces Chinese noodles, heated briefly to crisp
- 6 tablespoons seasoned rice vinegar
- 4 tablespoons white sugar
- 1 teaspoon salt
- 1/2 cup peanut oil

Direction

- Mix noodles, seeds, nuts, celery, green onion, lettuce, and chicken together in a big salad bowl. Put aside.
- Dressing: place vinegar into a small bowl. Melt salt and sugar in vinegar then add oil. Beat/shake well.
- Put dressing on salad then toss until coated then serve.

Nutrition Information

- Calories: 517 calories;
- Total Fat: 31.6
- Sodium: 757
- Total Carbohydrate: 38.8
- Cholesterol: 48
- Protein: 23.9

647. Chinese Chicken Soup With Bok Choy

Serving: 4 | Prep: 15mins | Cook: 26mins | Ready in:

Ingredients

- 6 cups chicken broth
- 1 bunch green onions, sliced
- 4 cups chopped bok choy
- 1/4 cup soy sauce
- 1 small carrot, cut into 1/4-inch dice
- 1 small stalk celery, cut into 1/4-inch dice
- 2 tablespoons ginger root, peeled and minced
- 1 tablespoon creamy peanut butter
- 2 teaspoons sriracha sauce
- 3 cloves garlic, minced
- 1 teaspoon white sugar
- 1 cup chopped cooked chicken
- 1 (12 ounce) package ramen noodles

Direction

- In a stock pot, heat up the chicken broth on medium high until it begins to boil. Place in green onions and bring down the heat to a simmer so the flavors can merge for a minute or two. Put in bok choy, carrots, celery, soy sauce, peanut butter, ginger, garlic, sugar, and sriracha. Simmer them until the veggies become tender, 10 minutes.
- Put a big pot that's full of water lightly salted and let it come a rolling boil; put in the ramen and bring it back to a boil. Let it cook without a cover and mix it occasionally until the noodles become soft but still are firm to chew around 2-5 minutes. Drain the noodles and put them into bowls.
- Put chicken in the broth pot and let the chicken simmer for about 4 minutes until it's fully cooked. Put the soup on top of the noodles in the bowls.

Nutrition Information

- Calories: 225 calories;
- Total Fat: 8.3
- Sodium: 3165
- Total Carbohydrate: 20.8
- Cholesterol: 35
- Protein: 17.1

648. Chinese Corn Soup

Serving: 5 | Prep: 15mins | Cook: 15mins | Ready in:

Ingredients

- 5 cups chicken broth
- 1 (14.75 ounce) can cream-style corn
- 1/4 cup butter
- 1 stalk celery, cut into bite-size pieces
- 1 onion, cut into bite-size pieces
- 1 1/2 tablespoons all-purpose flour
- 1 teaspoon ground nutmeg, or to taste
- 1 egg, or more as desired
- fresh ground pepper (optional)

Direction

- Place saucepan over medium heat and pour in the chicken broth to heat. Stir in the can of corn and bring the mixture to boil while stirring it occasionally. Adjust the heat and simmer the mixture.
- Melt butter in a skillet over medium-low heat. Stir in onion and celery and cook for 5 minutes until tender. Add the flour, and cook and stir for 2 more minutes to remove any raw taste from the flour. Stir in vegetable mixture, beating the flour frequently to avoid lumps, and add the nutmeg. Bring the soup to simmer.
- In a bowl, beat the egg thoroughly. Stir the soup in a clockwise circular motion and gently pour the beaten egg into the moving soup. Use a fork to gently stir the egg that is in the soup to create egg strands. Season the soup with black pepper. Serve.

Nutrition Information

- Calories: 177 calories;
- Sodium: 322
- Total Carbohydrate: 19.6
- Cholesterol: 62
- Protein: 3.4
- Total Fat: 10.8

649. Chinese Dandelion Dumplings

Serving: 10 | Prep: 1hours10mins | Cook: 50mins | Ready in:

Ingredients

- 2 pounds ground pork
- 2 cups minced dandelion greens
- 3 cups minced napa cabbage
- 1/2 cup minced bok choy leaves
- 4 green onions, white and light green parts only, minced
- 1 tablespoon minced fresh ginger root
- 3 cloves garlic, minced
- 1 (8 ounce) can bamboo shoots, drained and minced
- 3 tablespoons soy sauce
- 1 teaspoon white pepper
- 1 teaspoon kosher salt
- 1 teaspoon white sugar
- 4 teaspoons sesame oil
- 1 egg whites
- 1 tablespoon water
- 100 wonton wrappers
- 1/2 cup vegetable oil
- 2 teaspoons chili oil, or to taste
- 3 tablespoons hoisin sauce
- 1/2 cup soy sauce
- 4 teaspoons sesame oil
- 1 teaspoon white sugar
- 3 tablespoons balsamic vinegar
- 1 teaspoon minced fresh ginger root
- 2 tablespoons chopped green onion
- 2 cloves garlic, minced

Direction

- Combine pork, napa cabbage, dandelion greens, 4 minced green onions, bok choy, 3 cloves of garlic, 1 tablespoon of ginger,

- bamboo shoots, 1 teaspoon of sugar, 3 tablespoons of soy sauce, white pepper, salt, and 4 teaspoons of sesame oil. Leave it refrigerated to chill for 6-8 hours, or overnight.
- Combine egg white with the water in a small bowl, whisk them together and set it aside. Get 1 tablespoon of the pork mixture and place it into a wonton wrapper. Work one wonton wrapper at a time. While working on one, cover the remaining wonton wrappers with a damp towel to prevent them from drying. Using the egg white mixture, brush the edges of the wrapper then fold the wrapper and seal its edges using a fork that's been moistened.
- Coat a large cooking pan using cooking spray. Pour 2 tablespoons of vegetable oil on it and heat over medium-high heat. Place the dumplings into the pan with the seam side up; work in batches. Cook them for 30 seconds to 1 minute, until the dumplings have slightly browned. Add 1/2 cup of water into the pan then cover it. Steam the dumplings gently for 7-8 minutes, until the water and oil start to sizzle. Flip the dumplings once the water is cooked off and cook for 3-5 minutes until their bottom begins to brown. Do this by batch with the rest of the dumplings, water, and oil. Serve with the dipping sauce.
- To make dipping sauce: Put and mix together in a bowl the hoisin sauce, chili oil, 1/2 cup soy sauce, 1 teaspoon of sugar, 4 teaspoons of sesame oil, balsamic vinegar, 2 tablespoons of green onion, 1 teaspoon of ginger, and 2 cloves of garlic.

Nutrition Information

- Calories: 602 calories;
- Sodium: 1787
- Total Carbohydrate: 55.2
- Cholesterol: 66
- Protein: 26.8
- Total Fat: 30.1

650. Chinese Dong'an Chicken

Serving: 4 | Prep: 30mins | Cook: 27mins | Ready in:

Ingredients

- 1 (2 pound) whole chicken
- 1 tablespoon cornstarch
- 1 tablespoon cold water
- 6 tablespoons peanut oil
- 1 1/2 tablespoons grated fresh ginger
- 2 teaspoons finely chopped dried chile peppers
- 3 tablespoons vinegar
- 1 1/2 tablespoons rice wine
- 20 Szechuan peppercorns, crushed
- salt to taste
- 2 spring onions, chopped, or more to taste
- 1/8 teaspoon monosodium glutamate (MSG)
- 2 teaspoons sesame oil

Direction

- Soak the chicken in a stockpot with water then let it boil and cook for not less than 20 minutes until the juices run clear. Insert an instant-read thermometer into the thick part of the thigh close to the bone to check the temperature, the thermometer should read 165°F (74°C). Remove the cooked chicken from the pot then allow it to cool down on the side. Reserve 1/2 cup of the cooking liquid.
- Separate the chicken meat from the bone and cut the meat into 1/2 x 2-inch strips. In a small bowl, combine cold water and cornstarch. Put in the chicken meat in 1/2 of the cornstarch mixture then mix until evenly coated.
- Heat a big skillet or wok with peanut oil over high heat. Put in the chiles, chicken mixture and ginger then stir-fry for 2-3 minutes until fragrant. Mix in the vinegar, rice wine, reserved cooking liquid, salt and peppercorns. Let it boil. Cook and stir for about 3 minutes until most of the liquid has been absorbed. Add in the remaining cornstarch mixture, spring onions and monosodium glutamate.

Cook for 2-3 more minutes until the sauce has thick consistency. Drizzle some sesame oil on top.

Nutrition Information

- Calories: 697 calories;
- Total Carbohydrate: 6.5
- Cholesterol: 80
- Protein: 20.2
- Total Fat: 65
- Sodium: 130

651. Chinese Egg Dumplings

Serving: 5 | Prep: 35mins | Cook: 30mins | Ready in:

Ingredients

- 4 eggs
- 2 teaspoons cornstarch
- 1 teaspoon water
- 1/4 teaspoon salt
- 3 ounces ground pork
- 3 water chestnuts, minced
- 1 1/2 teaspoons finely chopped green onions
- 1 teaspoon cornstarch
- 1/2 teaspoon finely shredded fresh ginger
- 1/2 teaspoon white sugar
- 1/2 teaspoon salt
- 1/4 teaspoon toasted sesame oil
- 3/4 cup chicken broth
- 1 tablespoon soy sauce
- 1/2 teaspoon dry sherry
- 1/4 teaspoon salt
- 1/2 teaspoon white sugar
- 1/4 teaspoon black pepper

Direction

- In a bowl, beat a quarter teaspoon salt, eggs, water, and 2 teaspoon cornstarch; set aside for 25 minutes.
- In another bowl, combine toasted sesame oil, pork, half teaspoon salt, green onions, half teaspoon sugar, a teaspoon cornstarch, water chestnuts, and ginger knead until it is blended well; cover with plastic wrap. Let it chill in the refrigerator until ready to use.
- Start making wrappers by greasing the non-stick pan with cooking spray, placing it on medium heat. Gradually pour a tablespoon egg mixture in pan, tilt pan to spread batter making a 3-in flat circle. Let it cook for a minute until the bottom is firm but the surface is moist. Stack the wrappers on the plate with wax paper, cool.
- On medium-low heat, combine and heat black pepper, chicken broth, half teaspoon sugar, soy sauce, quarter teaspoon salt, and sherry in a pot.
- Scoop a teaspoon of pork filling in the middle of every wrapper. Make a half-moon shape by folding the wrapper over; seal by softly pressing it together. Place the dumplings in the chicken broth mix and let it simmer for 10-15 minutes until the filling is cooked. Serve dumplings with broth.

Nutrition Information

- Calories: 114 calories;
- Total Fat: 7.5
- Sodium: 720
- Total Carbohydrate: 3.6
- Cholesterol: 136
- Protein: 7.5

652. Chinese Glass Noodle Soup

Serving: 4 | Prep: 10mins | Cook: 25mins | Ready in:

Ingredients

- 2 ounces uncooked bean threads (cellophane noodles)

- 3 (14.5 ounce) cans chicken broth
- 1 large clove garlic, minced
- 2 tablespoons thin strips fresh ginger root
- 4 2-inch pieces fresh lemongrass, minced
- 2 skinless, boneless chicken breast halves, cut into 1/2-inch strips
- 6 large shrimp, peeled and deveined
- 2 tablespoons lime juice
- 2 tablespoons fish sauce
- 1 jalapeno pepper, cut into 8 thin slices
- 1/4 cup chopped fresh cilantro

Direction

- Put hot water in a big bowl and soak the bean threads in it for 15 minutes, until soft. Drain it then slice them into bite-size lengths. Distribute the noodles into 4 separate bowls.
- In a big cooking pan, combine the chicken broth, ginger, lemongrass, and garlic and boil. Lower the heat to medium-low then allow to simmer for 15 minutes until the mixture is fragrant. Toss in the shrimp and chicken into the soup and allow it to simmer for 3-5 minutes more until the chicken pieces are cooked through. Pour in the fish sauce and lime juice while stirring. Pour soup on the noodles then add cilantro and jalapeno pepper slices as toppings before you serve.

Nutrition Information

- Calories: 166 calories;
- Total Carbohydrate: 16.7
- Cholesterol: 84
- Protein: 18.2
- Total Fat: 2.2
- Sodium: 1933

653. Chinese Ham Stew

Serving: 8 | Prep: | Cook: | Ready in:

Ingredients

- 1 (5 pound) pork leg, cut into bite size pieces
- 4 ounces dried wood ear mushrooms
- 5 tablespoons soy sauce
- 10 cloves minced garlic
- 4 cups water

Direction

- Wash garlic, leaving skin intact; wash the mushrooms and allow to sit in water until tender.
- In a large pot, place garlic, soy sauce, mushrooms and pork. Add water, set the heat to low and allow to simmer for 60 to 90 minutes or until a thermometer inserted in the center of pork shows 160°F (70°C)

Nutrition Information

- Calories: 437 calories;
- Protein: 55.9
- Total Fat: 17.4
- Sodium: 686
- Total Carbohydrate: 12.4
- Cholesterol: 172

654. Chinese Homemade Watercress And Fish Ball Soup

Serving: 4 | Prep: 10mins | Cook: 3hours20mins | Ready in:

Ingredients

- 2 pounds pork chops
- water to cover
- 4 dried pitted dates
- 1 (2 inch) piece fresh ginger root, peeled
- 2 bunches fresh watercress
- 8 fried fish balls, or to taste
- 1 pinch salt to taste

Direction

- In a stockpot, put the pork chops and add enough water to cover them. Bring it to a boil then turn off the heat. Wash off residue on the pork chops with cold water.
- Put the pork chops back to the stock pot and add enough cold water to fill twice the space as the pork chops. Bring the water again to a boil then lower the heat to low, cover the pan and allow it to simmer for 3 hours.
- In a bowl, put the dates and enough water to cover them. Soak for 5 minutes then drain.
- Add ginger and dates into the stockpot while stirring. Mix in fish balls and watercress and allow 10 minutes for it to simmer. Remove any residue from the top of the soup then add salt to taste.

Nutrition Information

- Calories: 545 calories;
- Total Fat: 22
- Sodium: 485
- Total Carbohydrate: 39
- Cholesterol: 142
- Protein: 49.6

655. Chinese Lemon Chicken

Serving: 4 | Prep: 10mins | Cook: 20mins | Ready in:

Ingredients

- 3 skinless, boneless chicken thighs
- 3 tablespoons oyster sauce
- 1 teaspoon sesame oil
- 1 teaspoon white sugar
- 1 egg, beaten
- salt and pepper to taste
- 1/8 cup corn flour
- 1/2 cup water
- 3 tablespoons white sugar
- 1/2 lemon, juiced
- 1 (3.4 ounce) package instant lemon pudding mix
- water as needed
- 2 tablespoons toasted sesame seeds

Direction

- To marinate: In a nonporous glass dish or bowl, lay the chicken and set aside. Combine oyster sauce, egg, pepper, salt, sugar, and sesame oil together in a small bowl. Pour the mixture all over the chicken and cover the dish. Allow it to marinate for a minimum of 60 minutes.
- Coat the marinated chicken with corn flour. Cook it in a large skillet until cooked through, its color is golden brown, and its juices run clear.
- To make the sauce, boil 1/2 cup of water in a small saucepan. Stir in sugar and dissolve first before adding lemon juice and pudding mix to thicken the sauce.
- Slice chicken into bite-size pieces. Drizzle sauce over chicken and sprinkle toasted sesame seeds on top. Serve.

Nutrition Information

- Calories: 279 calories;
- Total Fat: 8.5
- Sodium: 450
- Total Carbohydrate: 39.7
- Cholesterol: 82
- Protein: 12.6

656. Chinese Lion's Head Soup

Serving: 4 | Prep: 15mins | Cook: 20mins | Ready in:

Ingredients

- 1 pound ground pork
- 1 egg
- 1 tablespoon cornstarch
- 2 teaspoons sesame oil

- 1 tablespoon minced fresh ginger root
- 1/4 teaspoon monosodium glutamate (MSG) (optional)
- 1 teaspoon salt
- 2 green onions, chopped and divided
- 1 tablespoon vegetable oil
- 1 head napa cabbage, cored and cut into chunks
- 2 cups low-sodium chicken broth
- 2 cups water, or as needed
- 1 tablespoon soy sauce
- 2 teaspoons sesame oil

Direction

- In a bowl, combine ground pork, monosodium glutamate, cornstarch, egg, ginger, 1/2 chopped green onions, salt, and 2 tsp. of sesame oil. Mix them well using your hands and then set aside.
- Place a large skillet over high heat and heat vegetable oil. Fry napa cabbage in hot oil for 2-3 minutes, stirring frequently until it begins to wilt. Add water, soy sauce, and chicken broth and then bring them to boil. Adjust the heat to moderate.
- Form the meat mixture into 1-inch balls using a spoon. Slowly put the balls into the boiling soup and then cover the skillet. Simmer the soup for 10 minutes. Season it with salt to taste. Before serving, drizzle sesame oil over the soup and garnish it with the remaining chopped onions.

Nutrition Information

- Calories: 431 calories;
- Total Carbohydrate: 7.1
- Cholesterol: 130
- Protein: 24.1
- Total Fat: 34
- Sodium: 991

657. Chinese New Year Turnip Cake

Serving: 6 | Prep: | Cook: | Ready in:

Ingredients

- 2 tablespoons vegetable oil
- 8 ounces Chinese dried mushrooms, soaked overnight in water
- 1/3 cup dried shrimp, soaked in water overnight and drained
- 1 pound pork sausage, sliced
- 1 tablespoon vegetable oil
- 2 slices fresh ginger root
- 3 turnips, shredded
- 1 1/2 teaspoons Chinese five-spice powder
- 2 teaspoons salt
- 1/2 teaspoon chicken bouillon granules
- 1 tablespoon ground white pepper
- 2/3 pound white rice flour

Direction

- In a large skillet or wok, heat 2 tablespoons oil over high heat. Sauté sausages, shrimp, and mushrooms in heated oil for 30 seconds. Take out of the skillet/wok and put to one side. Heat another 1 tablespoon oil in the same skillet/wok. Sauté ginger a bit. Add shredded turnips and sauté for about 3 minutes (reserve turnip water). Add white pepper, chicken bouillon, salt, and five-spice powder and stir until evenly distributed. Take ginger slice out of the mixture.
- Turn off the heat. Add rice flour on top of turnip mixture and mix flour evenly using chopsticks. Stir in reserved sausage mixture and stir to combine. Transfer the mixture from the skillet/wok to a 9x2-inch deep round cake pan.
- Clean skillet/wok. Add water and bring to a boil: Set the cake pan on a round wide rack over boiling water. Turn heat down to low; simmer and steam the batter for 45 minutes. (A large bamboo steamer can be used in this situation). Once cake is steamed through, cut

into pieces and serve right away or allow to cool on a wire cooling rack before wrapping tightly using plastic wrap and chilling in the fridge.

Nutrition Information

- Calories: 629 calories;
- Sodium: 1504
- Total Carbohydrate: 74.7
- Cholesterol: 62
- Protein: 19.1
- Total Fat: 29.9

658. Chinese Peppered Green Beans

Serving: 6 | Prep: 10mins | Cook: 3mins | Ready in:

Ingredients

- 2 tablespoons green peppercorns, drained
- 1 cup coarsely chopped cilantro
- 1 tablespoon olive oil
- 1 pound Chinese yardlong beans
- 4 cloves garlic, finely chopped
- 2 teaspoons brown sugar
- 1 small red chile pepper, seeded and chopped fine
- 2 tablespoons water

Direction

- Using the bottom of a glass or jar, mash the peppercorns into a rough pulp in a small bowl then add the cilantro, stirring them together.
- In a large cooking pan or wok, heat the oil over medium-high heat then add the beans, brown sugar, garlic, chile pepper, cilantro, and peppercorns, stir-frying them for 45 seconds. Add the water and cover the pan to allow to steam for about 2 minutes. Serve right away.

Nutrition Information

- Calories: 69 calories;
- Total Carbohydrate: 9.9
- Cholesterol: 0
- Protein: 2.3
- Total Fat: 2.4
- Sodium: 144

659. Chinese Pork Buns (Cha Siu Bao)

Serving: 24 | Prep: | Cook: | Ready in:

Ingredients

- 6 cups all-purpose flour
- 1/4 cup white sugar
- 1 3/4 cups warm water (110 degrees F/45 degrees C)
- 1 tablespoon active dry yeast
- 1 tablespoon baking powder
- 2 tablespoons shortening
- 1 pound finely chopped pork
- 1 1/2 tablespoons light soy sauce
- 1 1/2 tablespoons hoisin sauce
- 1 teaspoon soy sauce
- 1 1/2 tablespoons white sugar
- 1 1/2 tablespoons soy sauce
- 1 1/2 tablespoons oyster sauce
- 1 cup water
- 2 tablespoons cornstarch
- 2 1/2 tablespoons water
- 2 tablespoons shortening
- 1 1/2 teaspoons sesame oil
- 1/4 teaspoon ground white pepper

Direction

- Stir 1/4 cup sugar into 1 3/4 cups warm water until dissolved, then add the yeast. Allow to sit until mixture becomes frothy, about 10 minutes. Sift baking powder and flour together into a large mixing bowl. Mix in the

yeast mixture and 2 tablespoons shortening; stir well.
- Knead dough until elastic and smooth. Position dough in an oiled bowl; cover the dough using a sheet of cling wrap. Allow dough to rise for 2 hours in a warm area until tripled in size.
- Cut pork into thick strips about 2 inches. Pierce all over the pork with a fork. Allow pork to marinate in a mixture made with 1 teaspoon sweet soy sauce, 1 1/2 tablespoons hoisin sauce, and 1 1/2 tablespoons light soy sauce, for 5 hours. Grill marinated pork until cooked thorough inside and charred outside. Divide roasted pork into cubes about 1/2 inch.
- Combine 1 cup water, oyster sauce, 1 1/2 tablespoons soy sauce, and 1 1/2 tablespoons sugar in a saucepan. Bring to a boil. Stir together 2 1/2 tablespoons water and cornstarch; pour into the saucepan; and whisk until thickened. Stir in white pepper, sesame oil, and 2 tablespoons shortening or lard. Allow to cool, and stir in roasted pork.
- Take the dough out of the bowl, and knead it until elastic and smooth on a work surface lightly coated with flour. Roll dough into a long roll, and cut into 24 portions. Press each portion into a thin circle using the palm of your hand. Edges of the circle should be thinner than the center. Put 1 portion of pork filling in the middle of each circle. Wrap the dough over the filling to enclose. Pinch edges to shape the bun. Allow buns to rest to 10 minutes.
- Steam buns for 12 minutes until done. Serve right away.

Nutrition Information

- Calories: 191 calories;
- Sodium: 196
- Total Carbohydrate: 28.3
- Cholesterol: 12
- Protein: 7.3
- Total Fat: 5.2

660. Chinese Shrimp Wonton

Serving: 12 | Prep: 1hours | Cook: 10mins | Ready in:

Ingredients

- 3 green onions, chopped
- 5 slices fresh ginger
- 3/4 cup water
- 1 pound ground pork
- 3 tablespoons Chinese rice wine, divided
- 2 tablespoons soy sauce
- 3 teaspoons salt, divided
- 1 teaspoon sesame oil
- 1 teaspoon ground white pepper
- 40 shrimps, minced
- 1/2 cup diced mushrooms
- 1 stalk celery, finely chopped
- 100 (3.5 inch square) wonton wrappers
- 1 (14.5 ounce) can chicken stock

Direction

- Fill a bowl with water, and mash ginger and green onion. Add in white pepper, pork, soy sauce, 2 tablespoons of rice wine, 2 teaspoons of salt, and sesame oil.
- In a bowl, mix mushrooms, shrimp, celery, a tablespoon of rice wine, and a teaspoon of salt. Mix the mushroom mixture to the pork mixture until well combined.
- Carefully separate the wonton wrappers and place them on your work surface. Place a tablespoon of the shrimp-pork mixture at the center of each wrapper. Lightly moisten the edges of the wrappers with water with your finger or a pastry brush. Pull a corner of the wrapper over the filling and pull up to form a triangle and press the edges to seal. Boil the chicken stock and cook the wontons for about 5 minutes or until they float to the top.

Nutrition Information

- Calories: 302 calories;

- Total Carbohydrate: 39.9
- Cholesterol: 61
- Protein: 17
- Total Fat: 7.1
- Sodium: 1275

661. Chinese Shrimp And Tofu Soup

Serving: 6 | Prep: 30mins | Cook: 8mins | Ready in:

Ingredients

- 1 tablespoon vegetable oil
- 2 cloves garlic, minced
- 1 (1/2 inch) piece fresh ginger root, minced
- 6 ounces raw small shrimp, shelled and deveined
- 1 quart chicken stock
- 8 ounces tofu, diced small
- 1/3 cup frozen peas, thawed
- 1 teaspoon salt
- 1/2 teaspoon black pepper
- 1 tablespoon cornstarch

Direction

- Place a large cooking pan or work over high heat and heat the oil in it. Put the ginger and garlic in and cook until they have lightly browned and fragrant. Add the shrimp while stirring and stir fry until it's cooked then remove it from the pan and set it aside. Pour the chicken stock into the pan and bring it to a boil then lower the heat to medium. Toss in the peas and tofu then add salt and pepper to season. Return the soup to a simmer. Combine cornstarch and a bit of water until it forms a thin paste then stir in the mixture into the soup. Let the soup simmer for 1 more minute until it's clear and thickened. Put the shrimp back into the soup while stirring then serve.

Nutrition Information

- Calories: 99 calories;
- Cholesterol: 43
- Protein: 9.6
- Total Fat: 5
- Sodium: 896
- Total Carbohydrate: 4.5

662. Chinese Spareribs

Serving: 2 | Prep: 5mins | Cook: 40mins | Ready in:

Ingredients

- 3 tablespoons hoisin sauce
- 1 tablespoon ketchup
- 1 tablespoon honey
- 1 tablespoon soy sauce
- 1 tablespoon sake
- 1 teaspoon rice vinegar
- 1 teaspoon lemon juice
- 1 teaspoon grated fresh ginger
- 1/2 teaspoon grated fresh garlic
- 1/4 teaspoon Chinese five-spice powder
- 1 pound pork spareribs

Direction

- Mix together five-spice powder, hoisin sauce, garlic, ketchup, ginger, honey, lemon juice, soy sauce, rice vinegar, and sake in a shallow glass dish; put ribs in and flip to coat. Place in the refrigerator, covered, for 2 hours to overnight.
- Preheat oven to 165°C or 325°F. Pour in enough water to cover the bottom of a broiler tray; place rack or grate on top. Put ribs on the rack.
- Set the rack in the middle of oven. Broil 40 minutes, flip the ribs and spread marinade on them every 10 mins. To glaze, allow the marinade to cook on during the last 10 minutes. If desired, finish cooking the ribs under the broiler. Get rid of the remaining marinade.

Nutrition Information

- Calories: 503 calories;
- Total Fat: 30.9
- Sodium: 1015
- Total Carbohydrate: 23
- Cholesterol: 121
- Protein: 30.4

663. Chinese Steamed Buns With Meat Filling

Serving: 24 | Prep: 50mins | Cook: 30mins | Ready in:

Ingredients

- 8 ounces chopped pork
- 1 (4 ounce) can shrimp, drained and chopped
- 1 teaspoon salt
- 2 green onions
- 1 tablespoon chopped fresh ginger root
- 1 tablespoon light soy sauce
- 1 tablespoon rice wine
- 1 tablespoon vegetable oil
- 1 tablespoon white sugar
- ground black pepper to taste
- 2 1/2 tablespoons water
- 1 recipe Chinese Steamed Buns

Direction

- Put the wok over medium heat and cook the chopped pork in it. You can add chopped shrimp if you prefer, add this after 3 minutes of cooking the pork. Continue to cook until the pork is no longer pink then drain and add salt to season. Set it aside to let it cool.
- Combine green onions, soy sauce, ginger, rice wine, sugar, oil, and pepper and mix them together. Add minced meat while stirring then as you continue to stir, add the water and blend completely. Put this in the freezer to chill for 2 hours or in a refrigerator to chill overnight so that the flavors would blend flavors and the filling firm up.
- Prepare the dough for the Chinese Steamed Buns.
- Form the dough into balls and roll each one out into a circle, wonton wrapper-like. Get 1 tablespoon of the prepared meat mixture and place it in the center of each circle then wrap the dough around it. Place each bun seam down onto wax paper squares. Leave it to stand for about 30 minutes until it has doubled.
- Put water in the wok and bring it to a boil then lower the heat to medium but the water should still be boiling. Place a small wire rack in the middle of the wok and put the steam-plate on it. Put as many buns on the wax paper as will comfortably fit on the steam-plate. There should be 1-2 inches of space between the buns, and at least 2 inches space between the steam-plate and the wok. Cover the wok and leave the buns to steam for 15-20 minutes over the boiling water.
- Remove the lid first before turning off the heat. This will avoid the water from dripping back onto the bun surface, as it will leave yellowish marks on the surfaces of the buns. Do the process of steaming with the rest of the buns until all of them are cooked.

Nutrition Information

- Calories: 33 calories;
- Cholesterol: 14
- Protein: 3
- Total Fat: 1.8
- Sodium: 132
- Total Carbohydrate: 0.8

664. Chinese Steamed Cake

Serving: 12 | Prep: | Cook: | Ready in:

Ingredients

- 6 eggs

- 1 1/4 cups white sugar
- 2 1/2 tablespoons water
- 1 1/2 cups cake flour
- 1/2 teaspoon baking powder
- 1 1/2 teaspoons almond extract
- 1/4 cup confectioners' sugar for dusting

Direction

- Place a big bamboo steamer or veggie steamer in pot above simmering water. It should be spacious enough to hold a baking pan. Prepare a square nine-inch baking pan, lined with waxed paper.
- Separate eggs into bowls. Put yolks in with water and sugar. Use an electric mixer on medium speed. Whip until the mixture has increased thrice in size. Whisk baking powder and flour in. Sift them on the egg mix and gently fold in. Add extract and mix.
- In another bowl, whip egg whites until stiff peaks, but they should not be dry. Fold this into the yolk mix. Transfer the batter to the baking pan. Make sure all edges are smooth. Tap pan on a solid surface to remove all the air bubbles.
- Put the pan in the steamer. Place a kitchen towel on top of the steamer to cover. Put the lid on. This lets the towel absorb steam collecting from the lid and prevents it from dripping down on the cake. Steam until an inserted toothpick comes out clean, for 20 minutes. Let it cool on a rack.
- Top with confectioners' sugar.

Nutrition Information

- Calories: 193 calories;
- Total Fat: 2.7
- Sodium: 56
- Total Carbohydrate: 37.6
- Cholesterol: 93
- Protein: 4.6

665. Chinese Steamed White Fish Fillet With Tofu (Cantonese Style)

Serving: 4 | Prep: 25mins | Cook: 5mins | Ready in:

Ingredients

- 1 Thai chile, chopped
- 2 cloves garlic, chopped
- 1 (1/2 inch) piece fresh ginger, minced
- 1 tablespoon black bean sauce
- 2 tablespoons dark soy sauce
- 2 tablespoons white soy sauce
- 1 tablespoon vegetable oil
- 1 tablespoon white sugar
- 1 pinch white pepper
- 1 tablespoon cornstarch
- 1 tablespoon cold water
- 3/4 pound white fish fillets
- 1 (16 ounce) package tofu, drained and cubed
- 1 cup green onion, finely chopped

Direction

- Boil 1 1/2-inches of water in a pot that is fitted with a steamer basket.
- Whisk black bean sauce, garlic, chili, and ginger in a big bowl. Add white pepper, sugar, dark and white soy sauce, and vegetable oil. Mix water and cornstarch in a small cup and add it to the sauce. Slice the fish fillets to thin strips, and then add the strips in the bowl. Coat each strip thoroughly.
- Place the tofu cubes in one layer in the prepared basket once the water in the steamer boils. Cover and steam for 2 minutes. Slowly place the fish strips on the tofu. Cover and steam again for 3 more minutes.
- Before serving, garnish it with chopped green onion on top. Serve together with steamed Asian veggies or steamed jasmine rice and stir-fried.

Nutrition Information

- Calories: 280 calories;
- Protein: 27.3
- Total Fat: 14.1
- Sodium: 801
- Total Carbohydrate: 12.6
- Cholesterol: 51

666. Chinese Style Sesame Sauce

Serving: 4 | Prep: 10mins | Cook: 10mins | Ready in:

Ingredients

- 1 cup white sugar
- 1/4 cup cornstarch
- 1 cup chicken broth
- 1/2 cup water
- 1/8 cup white vinegar
- 2 tablespoons dark soy sauce
- 2 tablespoons sesame oil
- 1 teaspoon chile paste
- 1 clove garlic, minced

Direction

- Combine cornstarch and sugar in a saucepan. Mix in water, sesame oil, garlic, chili paste, soy sauce, chicken broth, and vinegar. Let it boil on medium heat while constantly stirring. Reduce the heat and bring to simmer for 5 minutes.

Nutrition Information

- Calories: 293 calories;
- Total Fat: 7
- Sodium: 463
- Total Carbohydrate: 58.9
- Cholesterol: 0
- Protein: 0.6

667. Chinese Sweet And Sour Spare Ribs

Serving: 4 | Prep: 10mins | Cook: 21mins | Ready in:

Ingredients

- 1 pound pork spare ribs, cut into 1 1/2-inch pieces
- 2 tablespoons soy sauce
- 2 teaspoons rice wine, divided
- 1/4 teaspoon salt
- 2 cups vegetable oil for frying
- 1/3 cup white sugar
- 1/4 cup water
- 2 teaspoons Chinese black vinegar

Direction

- Mix 1 tsp. of rice wine, salt, pork ribs, and soy sauce together in a large bowl. Store it inside the refrigerator to marinate for 20 minutes.
- Put oil in a deep saucepan or wok that is placed over medium-high heat. Fry the ribs in hot oil for 10 minutes until the ribs are no longer pink in the middle and they're golden brown in color.
- In a separate saucepan, mix and boil sugar, 1 tsp. of rice wine, and water. Add ribs and adjust the heat to low. Let it simmer for 5 minutes, just enough for the flavors to combine. Stir in black vinegar and adjust the heat to high. Cook and stir the mixture for 1-2 minutes until the sauce is thick and it completely coats the ribs.

Nutrition Information

- Calories: 367 calories;
- Protein: 14.9
- Total Fat: 26
- Sodium: 643
- Total Carbohydrate: 17.8
- Cholesterol: 60

668. Chinese Take Out Shrimp With Garlic

Serving: 4 | Prep: 15mins | Cook: 10mins | Ready in:

Ingredients

- 2 tablespoons canola oil
- 10 cloves garlic, chopped
- 1 teaspoon minced fresh ginger root
- 1 (8 ounce) can sliced water chestnuts, drained
- 1 cup snow peas
- 1 cup small white button mushrooms
- 1 teaspoon crushed red pepper flakes
- 1/2 teaspoon salt
- 1 teaspoon ground black pepper
- 1 pound peeled and deveined jumbo shrimp
- 1/2 cup chicken broth
- 1 tablespoon rice vinegar
- 2 tablespoons fish sauce
- 2 tablespoons dry sherry
- 1 tablespoon cornstarch
- 1 tablespoon water

Direction

- Heat a big skillet or wok with oil until the oil is very hot. Put in the ginger and garlic and sauté in hot oil for 30 seconds or until fragrant. Mix in the mushrooms, shrimps, red pepper flakes, water chestnuts, snow peas, pepper and salt. Cook and stir the mixture for 2-3 minutes until the shrimps are pink in color.
- In a small bowl, mix rice vinegar, dry sherry, chicken broth and fish sauce together. Put in the sauce mixture into the shrimp mixture then cook and stir for several seconds to mix well. Mix the water and cornstarch together and pour it into the wok. Cook and stir the mixture for 2 minutes or until the sauce is thick in consistency.

Nutrition Information

- Calories: 226 calories;
- Total Fat: 8.3
- Sodium: 1090
- Total Carbohydrate: 16.1
- Cholesterol: 173
- Protein: 21.4

669. Chinese Tea Leaf Eggs

Serving: 8 | Prep: 20mins | Cook: 3hours | Ready in:

Ingredients

- 8 eggs
- 1 teaspoon salt
- 3 cups water
- 1 tablespoon soy sauce
- 1 tablespoon black soy sauce
- 1/4 teaspoon salt
- 2 tablespoons black tea leaves
- 2 pods star anise
- 1 (2 inch) piece cinnamon stick
- 1 tablespoon tangerine zest

Direction

- Mix a teaspoon of salt and eggs in a big saucepan then pour in cold water to cover; boil. Lower heat and let it simmer 20 minutes; take off heat. Drain eggs and let them cool down. Once cool enough to handle, crack the shells of the egg by tapping it with the back of a spoon. Do not detach the shells.
- Mix together tangerine zest, three cups water, cinnamon stick, soy sauce, star anise, black soy sauce, tea leaves, and salt in a big saucepan; boil. Lower heat and let it simmer, covered, 3 hours; take off heat. Put in eggs and let it steep for a minimum of 8 hours.

Nutrition Information

- Calories: 76 calories;
- Sodium: 659
- Total Carbohydrate: 1.2
- Cholesterol: 186
- Protein: 6.6

- Total Fat: 5

670. Chinese Yam Pudding

Serving: 4 | Prep: 10mins | Cook: 1hours | Ready in:

Ingredients

- 1 pound yams, peeled and cubed
- 2 cups white sugar
- 2 tablespoons vegetable oil

Direction

- Put metal steamer insert into a saucepan; fill using water to right under the bottom of steamer. Cover; boil. Add yam cubes and cover; steam for 30 minutes till very tender.
- Put steamed yam cubes in a bowl; mash with vegetable oil and sugar till very smooth.
- Clean the steamer insert; line with parchment paper. Put mashed yam pudding in a steamer above a saucepan with water like before; boil. Cover; steam for 30 minutes then serve hot.

Nutrition Information

- Calories: 581 calories;
- Cholesterol: 0
- Protein: 1.7
- Total Fat: 7
- Sodium: 10
- Total Carbohydrate: 131.6

671. Crab Rangoon I

Serving: 10 | Prep: 20mins | Cook: 10mins | Ready in:

Ingredients

- 1 (14 ounce) package small won ton wrappers
- 2 (8 ounce) packages cream cheese, softened
- 1 teaspoon minced fresh ginger root
- 1/2 teaspoon chopped fresh cilantro
- 1/2 teaspoon dried parsley
- 3 tablespoons dark soy sauce
- 1 pound crabmeat, shredded
- 1 quart oil for frying

Direction

- Set the heat to 180 degrees C or 360 degrees F. Use a large heavy skillet to heat the oil. You can also use a deep fryer for this.
- Combine soy sauce, cream cheese, ginger, garlic, cilantro, parsley, and crabmeat.
- Add 1/2 to 1 teaspoon of cream cheese mixture onto individual wonton wrappers at the middle.
- Fold the wrapper into a half moon or triangle depending on the shape of the wrapper, making sure to cover the stuffing. Use a bit of water to moisten the edges and seal. Transfer the wrapped wontons below a slightly damp paper towel until you are ready to fry.
- Cook three or for wontons in the hot oil to a golden brown color, flipping them once. Let it rest on paper towels, then drain. Do this with all the wontons until they are fried. Serve hot.

Nutrition Information

- Calories: 393 calories;
- Protein: 16.5
- Total Fat: 25.6
- Sodium: 778
- Total Carbohydrate: 23.9
- Cholesterol: 93

672. Crab Rangoon II

Serving: 10 | Prep: 15mins | Cook: 10mins | Ready in:

Ingredients

- 1 quart oil for frying

- 1 tablespoon vegetable oil
- 1 clove garlic, minced
- 2 tablespoons minced onion
- 1 medium head bok choy, chopped
- 2 tablespoons chopped snow peas
- 1 (6 ounce) can crab meat, drained
- 1 (8 ounce) package cream cheese, softened
- 1 tablespoon soy sauce
- 1 (14 ounce) package small won ton wrappers

Direction

- In a deep-fryer or a big cooking pan, heat the oil to 190°C or 375°F.
- In a big cooking pan, heat 1 tablespoon vegetable oil then sauté onion and garlic in the oil for 2 minutes. Add the pea pods and bok choy then stir fry them until the pea pods and bok choy are tender yet crisp.
- Combine the crab, soy sauce cream cheese and sautéed vegetables in a big mixing bowl. Scoop a 3/4 teaspoon of the mixture and place it into the middle of a wonton wrapper. Make a triangle by folding the wrapper in half. Dip your finger in cold water and press the ends of the wrapper together to seal it around the filling.
- Fry the dumplings in the deep-fryer with oil, in batches, until they are golden brown. Move to paper towels to drain.

Nutrition Information

- Calories: 312 calories;
- Protein: 10.4
- Total Fat: 19
- Sodium: 491
- Total Carbohydrate: 25.6
- Cholesterol: 43

673. Crispy Baked Gau

Serving: 48 | Prep: 15mins | Cook: 50mins | Ready in:

Ingredients

- 1 (16 ounce) box sweet rice flour (mochiko)
- 2 cups brown sugar
- 3/4 cup white sugar
- 1 teaspoon baking soda
- 1 (13.5 ounce) can coconut milk
- 2 cups milk
- 2 teaspoons vanilla extract
- 2 tablespoons sesame seeds

Direction

- Preheat the oven to 350°F (175°C). Use an aluminum foil to line the bottom and up the sides of an 8x12-inch pan.
- Sift the white sugar, rice flour, baking soda and brown sugar directly into a big bowl. Create a well in the middle of the flour mixture then put in the milk, vanilla extract and coconut milk. Mix everything together until the consistency of the mixture is smooth. Transfer the batter mixture in the prepared pan and scatter top with sesame seeds.
- Put it in the preheated oven and let it bake for 50-55 minutes until a poked toothpick in the middle comes out clean. Allow it to cool down in the pan for 30 minutes then peel off the foil and put it onto a cutting board with top side facing up. Slice the baked batter mixture into squares that are 1 inch in size.

Nutrition Information

- Calories: 104 calories;
- Cholesterol: < 1
- Protein: 1.2
- Total Fat: 2.2
- Sodium: 34
- Total Carbohydrate: 20.5

674. Crispy Chinese Noodles With Eggplant And Peanuts

Serving: 4 | Prep: 30mins | Cook: 25mins | Ready in:

Ingredients

- 1 medium eggplant, cubed
- 1 teaspoon salt
- 16 ounces fresh Chinese wheat noodles
- 2 tablespoons sherry
- 1 tablespoon cornstarch
- 1/4 cup red wine vinegar
- 1/3 cup water
- 1 tablespoon minced fresh ginger root
- 1 tablespoon white sugar
- 2 tablespoons vegetarian fish sauce
- 2 cups sliced onion
- 3 tablespoons canola oil
- 4 cloves garlic, minced
- 1 red bell pepper, julienned
- 4 tablespoons chopped, unsalted dry-roasted peanuts
- 1 tablespoon chopped fresh mint (optional)

Direction

- Put cubed eggplants in a colander. Drizzle with salt then toss adequately. Drain the eggplant for 15 minutes then wash off lightly with water. Drain the eggplants again in the colander.
- Boil water in a large pot then add the noodles and boil them in the water until they're tender, about 5 minutes. Drain the noodles and wash off properly with cold water. Let the noodles drain in the colander for at least 10 minutes.
- Mix together the sherry and the cornstarch in a small bowl. Blend adequately then set it aside.
- Mix together the red wine vinegar, water, ginger, imitation fish sauce, sugar, and onions in a cooking pan. Bring to a boil then lower the heat to low and allow the mixture to simmer for 5 minutes.
- Heat 1 1/2 tablespoon of oil over medium-high heat in a large cooking pan that is preferably non-stick. Cook the eggplant in the oil for 5 minutes with frequent stirring. Mix in the red pepper and garlic and cook for 5 minutes while stirring occasionally, until the eggplant has softened. Pour in the onion-vinegar mixture as well as the cornstarch-sherry mixture then let cook for 2-3 minutes more with occasional stirring. Make sure to keep this mixture warm.
- Heat the remaining 1 1/2 tablespoons oil in a large non-stick pan over medium-high heat just until the oil starts to smoke. Add the noodles then put 2-3 plates on top of the noodles so to brown more of the surface. Allow the noodles to sit for 5 minutes over medium-high heat. Take off the plates when the noodles have already formed a golden brown crust on its underside. Turn them over using a spatula then cook for 5 minutes on the other side. Turn the heat off.
- Mix the peanuts into the eggplant mixture then spoon them onto individual plates. Separate noodles into 4 parts. Place the noodles on top of the sauce and vegetables. If you prefer, drizzle with mint then serve.

Nutrition Information

- Calories: 558 calories;
- Total Carbohydrate: 88.2
- Cholesterol: 0
- Protein: 12.3
- Total Fat: 16.9
- Sodium: 1310

675. Crispy Ginger Beef

Serving: 5 | Prep: 25mins | Cook: 20mins | Ready in:

Ingredients

- 3/4 cup cornstarch
- 1/2 cup water
- 2 eggs
- 1 pound flank steak, cut into thin strips

- 1/2 cup canola oil, or as needed
- 1 large carrot, cut into matchstick-size pieces
- 1 green bell pepper, cut into matchstick-size pieces
- 1 red bell pepper, cut into matchstick-size pieces
- 3 green onions, chopped
- 1/4 cup minced fresh ginger root
- 5 garlic cloves, minced
- 1/2 cup white sugar
- 1/4 cup rice vinegar
- 3 tablespoons soy sauce
- 1 tablespoon sesame oil
- 1 tablespoon red pepper flakes, or to taste

Direction

- In a big bowl, put in the cornstarch and slowly mix in the water until it is smooth. Mix in the eggs into the cornstarch mixture and toss in the steak strips to evenly coat with the cornstarch mixture.
- Heat a 1-inch deep wok with canola oil over high heat until the wok is hot but not smoking. Put in 1/4 of the coated beef strips into the hot wok and use fork to separate each beef strip. Cook and stir the coated beef strips from time to time for about 3 minutes or until the coating is golden and crispy. Put the cooked beef strips on paper towels to drain excess oil and do the same cooking process with the remaining beef strips.
- Remove all but 1 tablespoon of oil from the wok and set over high heat then cook and stir in the green onions, garlic, carrots, ginger, green bell pepper and red bell pepper for about 3 minutes or until slightly brown but crispy.
- In a small bowl, combine soy sauce, sesame oil, rice vinegar, red pepper and sugar. Put in the sauce mixture over the vegetables in the wok and let it boil. Add in the cooked beef strips into the wok with vegetable mixture then cook and stir for 3 minutes or until heated through.

Nutrition Information

- Calories: 364 calories;
- Sodium: 614
- Total Carbohydrate: 45.4
- Cholesterol: 103
- Protein: 15
- Total Fat: 13.8

676. Deb's General Tso's Chicken

Serving: 6 | Prep: 25mins | Cook: 30mins | Ready in:

Ingredients

- 4 cups vegetable oil for frying
- 3 eggs
- 1/2 cup cornstarch
- 2 teaspoons cornstarch
- 2 pounds skinless, boneless chicken thighs, cut into bite-sized pieces
- 1 1/2 cups white sugar
- 1/4 cup distilled white vinegar
- 1/4 cup rice vinegar
- 1/4 cup dry sherry
- 2 1/2 tablespoons soy sauce
- 2 teaspoons minced garlic
- 2 tablespoons vegetable oil
- 12 dried whole red chilies, or to taste
- 2 tablespoons minced fresh ginger, or to taste

Direction

- In a large pot or deep fryer, heat oil until it reaches 375°F or 190°C.
- In a bowl, beat eggs until smooth. Add in half a cup and 2 teaspoons of cornstarch; stir until no lumps remain. Mix in the chicken until evenly coated in the batter. Drop the cubed chicken in the oil one by one and fry for 3 minutes until the chicken pieces turn golden brown and begin to float. Place the cooked chicken on paper towels and pat off oil.

- In a small skillet, mix white vinegar, sugar, garlic, sherry, rice vinegar, and soy sauce. Set on medium-high heat and leave the mixture to boil. Mix constantly for about 3 minutes or until the sugar is completely dissolved and the sauce becomes thick, similar to the consistency of pancake syrup. Take off from heat; keep warm.
- In a large pot or wok set over medium-high heat, heat two tablespoons of oil. Cook ginger and dried chiles for about 30 seconds or until the ginger begins to turn brown. Remove the ginger and chilies and add them to the sauce. Transfer the chicken cubes into the pot. Cook until they turn to dark golden brown and very crispy. Serve chicken with the sauce.

Nutrition Information

- Calories: 829 calories;
- Cholesterol: 189
- Protein: 36.4
- Total Fat: 37.3
- Sodium: 689
- Total Carbohydrate: 91.9

677. Duck Sauce

Serving: 8 | Prep: 20mins | Cook: 40mins | Ready in:

Ingredients

- 5 cups coarsely chopped mixed fruit (apples, plums, and pears)
- 1 cup water
- 3/4 cup apple juice
- 1 teaspoon soy sauce
- 1 tablespoon apricot preserves
- 1/2 cup packed light brown sugar
- 1/2 teaspoon garlic powder
- 1/2 teaspoon dry mustard

Direction

- In stock pot, put the fruit over medium-high heat. Put dry mustard, garlic powder, brown sugar, apricot preserves, soy sauce, apple juice and water. Simmer, mixing often to dissolve brown sugar. Lower heat, and keep simmering for 40 minutes, or till fruit is fully tender. Take off heat and let cool.
- In blender or food processor, process the sauce till fully smooth, putting more water to adjust consistency, if wished. Place cover, and chill till set to use.

Nutrition Information

- Calories: 224 calories;
- Sodium: 48
- Total Carbohydrate: 55.9
- Cholesterol: 0
- Protein: 2.4
- Total Fat: 0.4

678. Easy Chinese Broccoli

Serving: 2 | Prep: 5mins | Cook: 10mins | Ready in:

Ingredients

- 1 pound Chinese broccoli
- 3 tablespoons oyster sauce
- 1 teaspoon brown sugar
- 1/2 teaspoon sesame oil (optional)

Direction

- In a saucepan, pour in about 1 inch of water and bring water to a boil. Put into the saucepan the Chinese broccoli and place a lid to cover. Cook for 2-5 minutes until stems are soft, then transfer to a plate with tongs.
- In a bowl, combine together sesame oil, brown sugar and oyster sauce. Drizzle cooked Chinese broccoli with sauce.

Nutrition Information

- Calories: 116 calories;
- Total Fat: 2.5
- Sodium: 325
- Total Carbohydrate: 21.6
- Cholesterol: 0
- Protein: 5.4

679. Easy Fried Chinese Chicken Balls

Serving: 4 | Prep: 15mins | Cook: 10mins | Ready in:

Ingredients

- Batter:
- 1 cup all-purpose flour
- 2 teaspoons baking powder
- 1 pinch salt
- 1 teaspoon sesame oil
- 1/2 cup water, or more if needed
- vegetable oil for frying
- Chicken:
- 5 tablespoons cornstarch
- 1 pinch ground white pepper
- 4 boneless skinless chicken breasts, cubed

Direction

- Combine baking powder, salt, and flour in a bowl. Stir in sesame oil and add water gradually while whisking the mixture until smooth. The batter should have a consistency like cream. Set aside for a minimum of 30 minutes.
- Pour oil to fill a deep pan or wok and gradually heat to 375°F (190°C).
- In a large shallow dish, combine cornstarch and white pepper. Coat the chicken evenly with cornstarch mixture, dunk into batter and coat each piece evenly. Cook the chicken in the hot oil for 4-5 minutes until golden and no longer pink in the center. Use a slotted spoon to transfer the chicken onto a clean kitchen towel and allow it to drain. Cook the chicken in batches following the same steps mentioned above.

Nutrition Information

- Calories: 338 calories;
- Protein: 26.9
- Total Fat: 9.7
- Sodium: 341
- Total Carbohydrate: 33.8
- Cholesterol: 65

680. Easy Moo Shu Pork

Serving: 6 | Prep: 15mins | Cook: 5mins | Ready in:

Ingredients

- 2 tablespoons soy sauce
- 1 tablespoon sesame oil
- 1 tablespoon grated fresh ginger
- 1 teaspoon minced garlic
- 3/4 pound pork tenderloin, fat trimmed and pork cut into 1/4-inch strips
- 2 tablespoons vegetable oil
- 2 cups shredded napa cabbage
- 1 carrot, grated
- salt and ground black pepper to taste

Direction

- Combine sesame oil, soy sauce, garlic, and ginger in a bowl and mix them together until the marinade becomes smooth. Pour the marinade in a plastic resealable bag and add the pork in the bag. Coat the pork with marinade and squeeze out air from the bag and seal it. Leave it to marinate for 1 hour or overnight in the refrigerator.
- Pour vegetable oil in a big cooking pan or wok and heat it on medium heat. Cook the carrot and cabbage in the oil for 1-2 minutes while stirring. Push the cabbage and carrot mixture on the side of the wok or pan then place the

pork with the marinade in the center of the pan. Cook the pork for 3-4 minutes while stirring until it's cooked through. Draw the cabbage mixture back to the middle of the pan and continue to cook for 1-2 minutes while stirring. Add pepper and salt to season to taste.

Nutrition Information

- Calories: 118 calories;
- Sodium: 351
- Total Carbohydrate: 2
- Cholesterol: 24
- Protein: 9.5
- Total Fat: 8.1

681. Easy Shrimp Lo Mein

Serving: 2 | Prep: 10mins | Cook: 25mins | Ready in:

Ingredients

- 1 (8 ounce) package spaghetti
- 2 tablespoons soy sauce
- 2 tablespoons oyster sauce
- 2 tablespoons brown sugar
- 2 teaspoons fish sauce
- 1/2 teaspoon garlic powder
- 1/2 teaspoon ground ginger
- 2 teaspoons vegetable oil
- 1 pound uncooked medium shrimp, peeled and deveined
- 1 cup chopped broccoli
- 1/4 yellow onion, thinly sliced
- 3 crimini mushrooms, sliced
- 2 cloves garlic, minced
- 2 large eggs

Direction

- Boil a large pot of water with a bit of salt. Let the spaghetti cook for 12 minutes until cooked through yet firm to the bite, and then remove the water.
- In a bowl, combine the oyster sauce, soy sauce, brown sugar, garlic powder, fish sauce, and ground ginger until the sugar is completely dissolved.
- Set the heat to medium and use a large wok or skillet to heat the oil. Let the shrimp cook in the hot oil while stirring for 1 to 2 minutes until its color changes. Mix in the onion, mushrooms, and broccoli then cook for 3 to 5 minutes or until it starts softening. Add the garlic to the vegetable mixture. Position the vegetables onto a side of the pan. Then, cook eggs in the available space and lightly scramble them for 3 to 5 minutes, or until no longer moist. Mix the egg with the vegetables and shrimp. Combine the cooked noodles with the sauce, then stir them all together to cook for another 2 minutes until hot mixed well. Serve right away.

Nutrition Information

- Calories: 834 calories;
- Total Fat: 14.3
- Sodium: 2240
- Total Carbohydrate: 109.5
- Cholesterol: 531
- Protein: 63.9

682. Egg Drop Soup II

Serving: 4 | Prep: | Cook: | Ready in:

Ingredients

- 2 (14.5 ounce) cans chicken broth
- 1 tablespoon cornstarch
- 1 egg, lightly beaten
- 2 tablespoons chopped green onion

Direction

- Combine cold chicken broth with cornstarch in a medium stockpot. Heat it slowly over medium heat with frequent stirring.
- Add the beaten egg into the soup and break up the egg by very gently stirring around the stock pot once. Turn the heat off immediately and divide the soup into 4 separate bowls or dish. Add green onions for garnishing.

Nutrition Information

- Calories: 26 calories;
- Sodium: 18
- Total Carbohydrate: 2.1
- Cholesterol: 46
- Protein: 1.6
- Total Fat: 1.2

683. Eight Treasure Porridge Dessert

Serving: 10 | Prep: 10mins | Cook: 2hours5mins | Ready in:

Ingredients

- 1/4 cup dried small red beans (adzuki beans)
- water to cover
- 1/4 cup barley
- 1/2 cup glutinous sweet rice
- 1/4 cup dried mung bean
- 1/4 cup oats
- 1/4 cup millet
- 1/4 cup dried small pearl tapioca
- 1/2 cup brown sugar, or more to taste
- 1/4 cup raisins

Direction

- In a large container, place the red beans and add several inches of cool water to cover the beans. Allow this to stand for 3 hours to overnight. Drain the beans and wash off.
- Mix together the barley and red beans in a pot then pour enough water to fill half of the pot. Bring this to a boil then lower the heat to low, cover the pot and allow it to simmer for an hour until the barley and beans are tender.
- Combine the rice and the mixture of bean and barley, add more water if all has been absorbed. Cook rice mixture, about 20 minutes. Mix in mung beans and allow it to cook for 20 minutes.
- Add the millet, oats, and tapioca into the rice mixture, mix together and allow to cook for about 20 minutes, stirring every 5 minutes until all the grains have softened. Pour in more water until the porridge has reached your desired thickness. Add the raisins and brown sugar into the porridge while stirring and cook for another 5 minutes. Turn off the heat, occasionally stir to avoid the porridge from sticking. You can serve this chilled or hot.

Nutrition Information

- Calories: 164 calories;
- Total Carbohydrate: 35.8
- Cholesterol: 0
- Protein: 4.4
- Total Fat: 0.6
- Sodium: 7

684. Ginger Chicken With Cashews

Serving: 6 | Prep: 25mins | Cook: 15mins | Ready in:

Ingredients

- 1 1/2 cups chicken broth
- 1/2 cup soy sauce
- 1 tablespoon cornstarch
- 3/4 teaspoon ground ginger
- 3/4 teaspoon brown sugar
- 1/4 cup cornstarch
- 1 1/2 teaspoons ground ginger

- 1/4 teaspoon curry powder
- 2 pounds skinless, boneless chicken breast meat - cut into cubes
- 3 tablespoons extra-virgin olive oil
- 1 tablespoon sesame oil
- 3 green onions, chopped
- 1 bell pepper, chopped
- 1 teaspoon sesame seeds
- 1/2 cup cashews

Direction

- In a small bowl, combine 3/4 teaspoon of ground ginger, chicken broth, brown sugar, 1 tablespoon of cornstarch, and soy sauce.
- In a large, resealable bag, add curry powder, a quarter cup of cornstarch, and 1 1/2 teaspoon of ground ginger. Shake to mix then add chicken. Shake again until chicken pieces are well coated.
- In a large pan or wok set over high heat, heat up sesame oil and olive oil. Cook the chicken for 3 to 5 minutes until golden brown. Mix in bell peppers and green onions, then cook for another 2 to 3 minutes. Add the sauce into the veggie and chicken mixture. Adjust heat to medium. Add in sesame seeds, then allow the mixture to boil for 3 to 5 minutes or until the sauce thickens. Take off from heat. Garnish with cashews then toss before serving.

Nutrition Information

- Calories: 387 calories;
- Sodium: 1359
- Total Carbohydrate: 14.6
- Cholesterol: 92
- Protein: 37.5
- Total Fat: 19.4

685. Hainanese Chicken Rice

Serving: 8 | Prep: 30mins | Cook: 45mins | Ready in:

Ingredients

- 1 (3 pound) whole chicken
- salt to taste
- water to cover
- 1 onion, halved (skin on)
- 8 cloves garlic, peeled
- 1 (1 inch) piece fresh ginger, sliced
- salt and ground white pepper to taste
- Rice:
- 3 cups long-grain white rice
- 5 cloves garlic, sliced
- 1 (1/2 inch) piece fresh ginger, sliced
- 2 teaspoons oil
- 5 pandan leaves, knotted
- Dipping Sauces:
- 3 fresh red chile peppers, halved and seeded
- 1 lime, juiced, or as needed
- 4 cloves garlic, peeled
- 1 slice fresh ginger
- Garnish:
- 10 leaves lettuce, or as desired
- 1 cucumber, peeled and sliced
- 1 tomato, sliced
- 1 tablespoon light soy sauce
- 1 teaspoon sesame oil

Direction

- Take the fat out of the chicken and set it aside. Season chicken with salt all over.
- Boil water in a big pot then add the onion, chicken, 8 garlic cloves, salt, sliced 1-inch piece of ginger, and white pepper. Boil again, lower the heat and allow to simmer for 20-25 minutes until the chicken is completely cooked. Use an instant-read thermometer to insert into the biggest part of the thigh near the bones, and it should register 165° F (74° C).
- Take the chicken out carefully and immerse it in a big bowl of ice water until it has cooled. Take the chicken out and dry it then cut into bite-size chunks. Strain the chicken broth then set the liquid aside.
- Rinse the rice then drain it.
- In a cooking pan, heat the chicken fat on medium heat. Cook the 5 sliced garlic cloves

and the sliced 1/2-inch piece ginger in the fat for a minute while stirring until it's aromatic. Add in the oil and rice and continue to cook while stirring until the rice is covered in oil. Add 6 cups of chicken broth or enough to cook the rice. Add the pandan leaves, cover the pan and cook the rice for 20-30 minutes until the broth has absorbed and the rice becomes tender.
- Crush the red chili peppers with a bit of salt using a mortar and pestle until a fine paste is formed. Pour in enough lime juice to make the paste smooth then move it to a serving dish.
- Crush 1 slice of ginger and 4 garlic cloves using the mortar and pestle until it forms a paste then move it to another serving plate.
- Lay the lettuce leaves on a serving dish and place the tomatoes and cucumber slices around the dish, arranging them neatly. Put the pieces of chicken in the middle. Combine sesame oil and soy sauce in a bowl and mix them together then pour it on the chicken. Serve with a bowl of rice, a bowl of the reserved chicken broth and the 2 dipping sauces.

Nutrition Information

- Calories: 521 calories;
- Sodium: 231
- Total Carbohydrate: 64.5
- Cholesterol: 73
- Protein: 29.4
- Total Fat: 15.2

686. Hakka Style Squid And Pork Belly Stir Fry

Serving: 4 | Prep: 20mins | Cook: 20mins | Ready in:

Ingredients

- 1 teaspoon vegetable oil
- 1/2 pound pork belly, or more to taste
- 1 (6 ounce) package dried bean curd
- 1 squid
- 1 green bell pepper, chopped
- 1 clove garlic, chopped
- 1/4 cup water
- 2 1/2 tablespoons soy sauce
- 4 teaspoons cooking wine
- 1 tablespoon white sugar
- 1 teaspoon ground white pepper
- 3/4 cup chopped celery
- 1 cup garlic sprouts, chopped

Direction

- Spread oil in a large skillet and warm it over moderate heat. Cook the pork belly for 5-7 minutes until the oil is released. Stir in bean curd and cook for 3-5 minutes more until it turns yellow. Add the squid, garlic and bell pepper and cook for another 3-5 minutes.
- Add cooking wine, soy sauce, and water into the pork belly mixture. Sprinkle white pepper and sugar into the mixture, and then cook for 3 more minutes. Lastly, stir in garlic sprouts and celery and cook for another 3 minutes until the mixture is fragrant.

Nutrition Information

- Calories: 367 calories;
- Protein: 30.9
- Total Fat: 16.2
- Sodium: 1053
- Total Carbohydrate: 27.6
- Cholesterol: 44

687. Hoisin Pork Stir Fry

Serving: 4 | Prep: 30mins | Cook: 20mins | Ready in:

Ingredients

- 1 pound boneless pork chops, cut into stir-fry strips

- 1 tablespoon hoisin sauce
- 1 tablespoon cornstarch
- 2 tablespoons hoisin sauce
- 1/4 cup chicken broth
- 1 tablespoon cornstarch
- 1 tablespoon rice vinegar
- 1 tablespoon white sugar
- 1 teaspoon red pepper flakes, or to taste
- 1 tablespoon sesame oil
- 2 cloves garlic, minced
- 2 teaspoons minced fresh ginger root
- 1 carrot, peeled and sliced
- 1 green bell pepper, sliced
- 1 (4 ounce) can sliced water chestnuts, drained
- 2 green onions, sliced

Direction

- In a bowl, combine together a tablespoon of hoisin sauce, a tablespoon of cornstarch, and some sliced pork. Let rest. In a small bowl, mix the chicken broth, a tablespoon of cornstarch, and 2 tablespoons of hoisin sauce with sugar, cayenne pepper, and rice vinegar. Let stand.
- Use a skillet on medium high heat to heat sesame oil. Cook the pork by stirring for 5 minutes, or until it starts to brown. Add in the ginger and garlic, stirring until aromatic. Add in the bell pepper, water chestnuts, and carrot to soften. Pour the hoisin sauce mixture you saved while continuing to cook and stir for 3 minutes until all the flavors are blended well.

Nutrition Information

- Calories: 235 calories;
- Total Fat: 11.4
- Sodium: 295
- Total Carbohydrate: 17.5
- Cholesterol: 39
- Protein: 15.6

688. Homemade Hainanese Chicken Rice

Serving: 8 | Prep: 15mins | Cook: 1hours | Ready in:

Ingredients

- 2 teaspoons salt, divided
- 1 whole chicken
- 5 cloves garlic, crushed
- 20 slices fresh ginger, divided
- 2 spring onions, cut into 2-inch pieces
- 3 tablespoons sesame oil, divided
- 2 3/4 cups white rice
- 2 pandan leaves

Direction

- Get about 1 teaspoon of salt and rub it all over the chicken.
- Boil water, garlic, spring onions, 15 ginger slices, and 1 tablespoon of sesame oil in a big pot. Carefully add the chicken into the pot then bring the liquid back to a boil. Lower the heat and let it simmer over low heat for about 30 minutes until the chicken is cooked completely. Use an instant-read thermometer and insert it into the thickest part of the chicken thigh, near the bone. The thermometer should read 165° F (74° C). Take the chicken out of the pot and submerge it in a bowl of ice water, setting aside the chicken broth.
- Mix together rice, 3 cups of chicken broth, pandan leaves, 2 tablespoons sesame oil, and 1 teaspoon salt in a rice cooker. Follow the manufacturer's instruction for cooking and let it cook until the rice is tender.
- Serve this together with the chicken.

Nutrition Information

- Calories: 509 calories;
- Total Fat: 18.3
- Sodium: 662
- Total Carbohydrate: 52.7
- Cholesterol: 102
- Protein: 30.5

689. Honey Walnut Shrimp

Serving: 4 | Prep: 15mins | Cook: 15mins | Ready in:

Ingredients

- 1 cup water
- 2/3 cup white sugar
- 1/2 cup walnuts
- 4 egg whites
- 2/3 cup mochiko (glutinous rice flour)
- 1/4 cup mayonnaise
- 1 pound large shrimp, peeled and deveined
- 2 tablespoons honey
- 1 tablespoon canned sweetened condensed milk
- 1 cup vegetable oil for frying

Direction

- In a small saucepan, mix the sugar and water. Let it boil first before stirring in walnuts. Boil for 2 more minutes. Drain the mixture and transfer the walnuts to dry on a cookie sheet.
- In a medium bowl, beat egg whites until it is foamy. Add the mochiko and whisk until it reaches the desired pasty consistency. Place the deep heavy skillet on medium-high heat and heat enough oil. Coat the shrimp with mochiko batter before placing it into the hot oil. Cook the shrimp for 5 minutes until it is golden brown. Using a slotted spoon, transfer the cooked shrimp on the paper towels and allow it to drain.
- Whisk sweetened condensed milk, honey, and mayonnaise in a medium bowl. Toss in shrimp until well-coated. Top it with candied walnuts, and then serve.

Nutrition Information

- Calories: 605 calories;
- Cholesterol: 179
- Protein: 26.1
- Total Fat: 26.3
- Sodium: 340
- Total Carbohydrate: 68

690. Hong Kong Style Egg Tarts

Serving: 12 | Prep: 25mins | Cook: 20mins | Ready in:

Ingredients

- 1 cup confectioners' sugar
- 3 cups all-purpose flour
- 1 cup butter
- 1 egg, beaten
- 1 dash vanilla extract
- 2/3 cup white sugar
- 1 1/2 cups water
- 9 eggs, beaten
- 1 dash vanilla extract
- 1 cup evaporated milk

Direction

- In a medium bowl, combine flour and the confectioners' sugar together. Stir in butter using a fork till it is in small crumbs. Mix in vanilla and egg till forming a dough. The dough texture should be slightly moist. Put in additional butter if it is too dry, or more flour, if it is greasy. Form the dough into balls of 1 1/2 inch, then press into tart molds to cover the bottom and go up higher than the sides. Shape the edge into an A shape with two fingers.
- Set the oven to 450°F (230°C), and start preheating. In a medium saucepan, mix water and white sugar together, and let it come to a boil. Cook till the sugar is dissolved, discard from the heat and allow to cool to room temperature. Strain the eggs with a sieve, then whisk with the sugar mixture. Stir in vanilla and evaporated milk. Strain the filling through a sieve; then fill in the tart shells.

- Bake in the prepped oven for 15 - 20 minutes, until golden brown, and the filling is slightly puffed up.

Nutrition Information

- Calories: 421 calories;
- Total Carbohydrate: 47.8
- Cholesterol: 202
- Protein: 10.1
- Total Fat: 21.4
- Sodium: 190

691. Hong Kong Walnut Sweet Soup

Serving: 5 | Prep: 5mins | Cook: 10mins | Ready in:

Ingredients

- 1/2 cup uncooked white rice
- 1 cup chopped walnuts
- 4 1/4 cups milk, divided
- 1/4 cup sweetened condensed milk

Direction

- Let the rice soak in water for 1 hour then drain it. Blend the walnuts and rice with 1 1/4 cup of milk in a blender until smooth. Pour this mixture into a cooking pan and bring it to a boil over medium heat. Pour in gradually the remaining 3 cups of milk while stirring slowly. If the soup gets too thick, just add more milk. Add the sweetened condensed milk while stirring.

Nutrition Information

- Calories: 373 calories;
- Sodium: 106
- Total Carbohydrate: 36
- Cholesterol: 22
- Protein: 12.9
- Total Fat: 20.8

692. Hot And Sour Soup With Tofu

Serving: 4 | Prep: 20mins | Cook: 30mins | Ready in:

Ingredients

- 1 tablespoon vegetable oil
- 1 red bell pepper, chopped
- 3 green onions, chopped
- 2 cups water
- 2 cups chicken broth
- 1 tablespoon soy sauce
- 1 tablespoon red wine vinegar
- 1/4 teaspoon crushed red pepper flakes
- 1/8 teaspoon ground black pepper
- 1 tablespoon cornstarch
- 3 tablespoons water
- 1 tablespoon sesame oil
- 6 ounces frozen snow peas
- 1 (8 ounce) package firm tofu, cubed
- 1 (8 ounce) can sliced water chestnuts, drained

Direction

- In a large saucepan, heat the oil over medium heat. Sauté the green onions and red bell pepper in the oil for 5 minutes then pour in broth, 2 cups of water, and soy sauce. Lower the heat to medium-low and let the soup simmer for 5 minutes.
- Mix together the vinegar, ground black pepper, red pepper flakes, 3 tablespoons water, cornstarch, and sesame oil in a separate medium bowl. Pour this into the soup and let it simmer for another 5 minutes until the soup has become bubbly and thick.
- Lastly, combine the snow peas, tofu, and water chestnuts in the mixture then continue to cook until heated through, about 10 minutes.

Nutrition Information

- Calories: 211 calories;
- Cholesterol: 0
- Protein: 11.3
- Total Fat: 12
- Sodium: 243
- Total Carbohydrate: 17.3

693. Hot And Spicy Sichuan Chicken

Serving: 4 | Prep: 20mins | Cook: 47mins | Ready in:

Ingredients

- 1/2 (2 pound) whole chicken
- 1 (3/4 inch thick) slice fresh ginger, crushed
- 1 teaspoon Sichuan peppercorns
- 1/4 cup soy sauce
- 1/4 cup chile oil
- 2 tablespoons white sugar
- 1/4 teaspoon monosodium glutamate (MSG)
- 1/4 teaspoon Sichuan peppercorn oil
- 6 spring onions (white parts only), cut into 3/4-inch pieces
- 1 teaspoon toasted sesame seeds, or to taste

Direction

- Boil water in a big pot. Put the chicken into the boiling water and cook for 2-3 minutes. Drain the chicken, discarding the water.
- Boil fresh water in a large pot and add the chicken, peppercorns, and ginger. Make sure that the chicken is covered with water. Cover the pot and cook it on high heat for 35-45 minutes until the chicken is not pink and the juices are running clear. Drain and throw away the water.
- Chop the chicken horizontally, cutting the chicken through its skin and bone and create it into 3/4-inch pieces. Cut it vertically into 3/4-inch squares and transfer them in a bowl.
- In a bowl, mix sugar, Sichuan peppercorn oil, MSG, chili oil, and soy sauce and pour the mixture on the chicken. Toss the mixture well and garnish it with sesame seeds and spring onions.

Nutrition Information

- Calories: 376 calories;
- Sodium: 973
- Total Carbohydrate: 9.5
- Cholesterol: 40
- Protein: 11.3
- Total Fat: 32.7

694. Kerri's Szechuan Sauce

Serving: 6 | Prep: 5mins | Cook: 10mins | Ready in:

Ingredients

- 1/4 cup soy sauce
- 2 tablespoons oyster sauce
- 2 tablespoons rice wine
- 1 tablespoon white sugar
- 2 teaspoons ground white pepper
- 1/4 cup water
- 2 tablespoons cornstarch

Direction

- On medium-low heat, cook white pepper, soy sauce, sugar, oyster sauce, and rice wine together for 5mins in a small pot until completely heated.
- In a small bowl, stir cornstarch and water together; pour into the pot. Let it simmer for 5mins until the sauce is thick.

Nutrition Information

- Calories: 34 calories;
- Sodium: 638
- Total Carbohydrate: 6.3
- Cholesterol: 0
- Protein: 0.8
- Total Fat: 0

695. Lee's Incredible Momos

Serving: 4 | Prep: 30mins | Cook: 30mins | Ready in:

Ingredients

- 1 pound extra-lean ground beef
- 1 small onion, chopped
- 8 ounces spinach, rinsed and chopped
- 1 clove garlic, minced
- 1 teaspoon grated fresh ginger root
- 2 green onions, chopped
- 2 tablespoons chopped fresh cilantro
- salt to taste
- 12 wonton wrappers
- 1 tablespoon soy sauce
- 1 tablespoon rice vinegar
- 1 tablespoon chili oil
- 1 (1/2 inch) piece fresh ginger root, grated

Direction

- Boil 3 inches of water in a big cooking pot. This may also be done with steamer baskets and a wok.
- Combine the ground beef, spinach, onion, 1 teaspoon ginger, garlic, cilantro, salt, and green onion in a big bowl and mix them together. Scoop a spoonful of filling then place it on a wonton wrapper. Fold and press scrunch together to seal the wrapper. Wet the edges with water if needed. Do the same with the rest of the wrappers and filling.
- Place a steamer tray in the cooking pot then put the momos in the steamer. Steam them for 30 minutes on top of rapidly boiling water then eat with dipping sauce.
- For the dipping sauce, combine the rice vinegar, soy sauce, grated ginger, and chili oil in a small bowl and mix them together.

Nutrition Information

- Calories: 315 calories;
- Total Fat: 15.2
- Sodium: 469
- Total Carbohydrate: 18.8
- Cholesterol: 71
- Protein: 25.3

696. Lunar New Year Peanut Cookies

Serving: 54 | Prep: 30mins | Cook: 20mins | Ready in:

Ingredients

- 2 1/8 cups roasted unsalted peanuts
- 1 1/4 cups confectioners' sugar
- 2 cups all-purpose flour
- 2 tablespoons all-purpose flour
- 1 teaspoon salt
- 3/4 teaspoon baking powder
- 2/3 cup peanut oil
- 3 tablespoons unsalted butter, melted
- 1 egg
- 1 tablespoon water
- 54 peanuts

Direction

- Prepare the oven by placing a rack in the center and preheating it to 325° F. Get 2 baking sheets and line them using parchment paper.
- Put peanuts in a food processor and pulse until they form coarse crumbs. Mix in confectioner's sugar and process with the peanuts until the mixture is powder-like. Stop occasionally to scrape the bottom of the processor, if necessary. Do not process the mixture too much.
- Combine salt, baking powder, and 2 cups and 2 tablespoons flour in a big bowl and stir them together. Add the peanut mixture and stir it in until properly blended. Dribble it with melted butter and oil. Mix all of them together using your hands and knead for 5 minutes until it forms a coarse dough (Play-Doh® like). The

dough will soften the more you knead it but if it feels too soft or turns oily, allow it to chill for 15 minutes. On the other hand, if it feels dry, add 1 tablespoon of oil at a time until the dough is workable.
- Form 1-inch balls by rolling the dough and put them on the baking sheets keeping 1 1/2 inch of space in between them. In a small bowl, combine egg with water and lightly beat them together. Brush the cookie tops with egg mixture and bake the first sheet while covering the other sheet until it's ready to bake. Put a whole peanut on top of each dough ball, pressing it down gently.
- Bake the cookies for 20-22 minutes until they're light golden in color then move them to wire racks and let them completely cool.

Nutrition Information

- Calories: 99 calories;
- Total Carbohydrate: 8.1
- Cholesterol: 5
- Protein: 2.2
- Total Fat: 6.8
- Sodium: 52

697. Mapo Doufu

Serving: 4 | Prep: 15mins | Cook: 12mins | Ready in:

Ingredients

- 1 tablespoon red chile flakes
- 1 tablespoon hot water
- 1/4 cup soybean oil
- 1 1/2 teaspoons Sichuan peppercorns
- 1 large clove garlic, sliced thin
- 1/4 pound ground pork
- 2 1/2 tablespoons doubanjiang (spicy broad bean paste)
- 1 (15 ounce) container soft tofu, drained and cubed
- 1/4 cup water
- 3 green onions, sliced

Direction

- In a small bowl with hot water, put the red pepper flakes in and let them soak until they have softened.
- Place a wok over medium-high heat and heat it until it's very hot then pour in the oil. Briefly toss in the peppercorns in the oil until they're aromatic. Add the garlic and stir for 10-15 seconds until it's aromatic. Add the ground pork and sauté for about 2 minutes, until it's brown and crumbly.
- Add the red chile flakes and the doubanjiang into the pork mixture then let it simmer for another minute. Pour in the water and tofu and coat by stirring gently then bring it to a boil. Lower the heat to medium-low and simmer for 3-4 minutes until the flavors meld. Turn the heat off and add the green onions, tossing them in.

Nutrition Information

- Calories: 260 calories;
- Total Fat: 21
- Sodium: 604
- Total Carbohydrate: 7.9
- Cholesterol: 18
- Protein: 12.6

698. Mongolian Beef And Spring Onions

Serving: 4 | Prep: 12mins | Cook: 8mins | Ready in:

Ingredients

- 2 teaspoons vegetable oil
- 1 tablespoon finely chopped garlic
- 1/2 teaspoon grated fresh ginger root
- 1/2 cup soy sauce
- 1/2 cup water

- 2/3 cup dark brown sugar
- 1 pound beef flank steak, sliced 1/4 inch thick on the diagonal
- 1/4 cup cornstarch
- 1 cup vegetable oil for frying
- 2 bunches green onions, cut in 2-inch lengths

Direction

- Use medium heat in a saucepan to heat 2 teaspoons of vegetable oil, then stir in the ginger and garlic to cook for 30 seconds until aromatic. Add in the water, soy sauce, and brown sugar. Set the heat to medium-high, then stir for 4 minutes to dissolve the sugar and let the sauce boil to a thick consistency. Transfer the sauce away from the heat and let rest.
- Add the beef slices into a bowl, then mix with the cornstarch by stirring to coat well.
- Let the beef and cornstarch sit until most of the juices from the meat have been absorbed by the cornstarch, about 10 minutes.
- Use a deep-sided skillet or a wok to heat vegetable oil to 190 degrees C or 375 degrees F.
- Take the beef slices and shake away the excess cornstarch. Cook in the hot oil, making sure to portion a few at a time in the wok.
- Stir briefly, and let it cook for 2 minutes until the edges are crispy and it has a nice brown color. Use a large slotted spoon to strain the beef from the oil, then use paper towels to drain excess oil.
- Discard the oil from the wok or skillet, then set the pan over medium heat. Add the beef slices back onto the pan, then pour leftover sauce while briefly stirring. Mix well by stirring once or twice, then put in some green onions. Let it boil for 2 minutes until the onions turn a bright green color and are soft.

Nutrition Information

- Calories: 391 calories;
- Protein: 18
- Total Fat: 12.1
- Sodium: 1862
- Total Carbohydrate: 54.7
- Cholesterol: 27

699. One Egg Egg Drop Soup

Serving: 4 | Prep: 10mins | Cook: 10mins | Ready in:

Ingredients

- 1 egg
- 1/4 teaspoon salt
- 2 tablespoons tapioca flour
- 1/4 cup cold water
- 4 cups chicken broth
- 1/8 teaspoon ground ginger
- 1/8 teaspoon minced fresh garlic
- 2 tablespoons chopped green onion
- 1/4 teaspoon Asian (toasted) sesame oil (optional)
- 1 pinch white pepper (optional)

Direction

- Whisk salt and egg in a bowl until it is well-mixed. In a different bowl, mix cold water and tapioca flour until it dissolves completely.
- Boil ginger, garlic, and chicken broth. Remove the mixture from the heat and pour in dissolved tapioca flour. Boil again for 1 minute until the soup is thick and not cloudy anymore. Remove from heat and add in egg in a thin line. Mix the egg in a figure 8 shape (do not overmix). Sprinkle chopped onions, white pepper, and sesame oil on top. Serve.

Nutrition Information

- Calories: 51 calories;
- Total Carbohydrate: 5
- Cholesterol: 52
- Protein: 2.7
- Total Fat: 2.1
- Sodium: 1124

700. Oriental Tea Leaf Eggs

Serving: 10 | Prep: 10mins | Cook: 2hours45mins | Ready in:

Ingredients

- 1 tablespoon black tea leaves
- 2 (3 inch) cinnamon sticks
- 4 whole star anise pods
- 1 tablespoon five-spice powder
- 6 whole cloves
- 1 slice fresh ginger root
- 1/2 teaspoon Szechuan peppercorns
- 1 teaspoon licorice root
- 1 piece dried mandarin orange peel
- 1 ounce Chinese rock sugar
- 1/2 cup dark soy sauce
- 1/3 cup light-colored soy sauce
- 10 hard-cooked eggs

Direction

- Use a large saucepan to combine the cinnamon, star anise, tea, cloves, five-spice, ginger, peppercorns, licorice, rock sugar, orange peel, light soy sauce, and dark soy sauce. Let it boil, then set the heat to a medium-low and simmer for 15 minutes.
- Crack the shells of the hard-boiled eggs by tapping them lightly so the soy sauce can color the egg white through the cracks.
- Cook the eggs for 30 minutes while the mixture simmers. Transfer from the heat, then leave the eggs in it for two hours. Remove the eggs after 2 hours, and peel after letting it chill.

Nutrition Information

- Calories: 98 calories;
- Cholesterol: 212
- Protein: 6.6
- Total Fat: 5.5
- Sodium: 1261
- Total Carbohydrate: 5.6

701. Owen's Chicken Rice

Serving: 10 | Prep: | Cook: | Ready in:

Ingredients

- 1/2 (3 pound) whole chicken, cut into pieces
- 8 ounces Chinese-style sausages
- 1 teaspoon salt
- 1 tablespoon dark soy sauce
- 2 tablespoons sesame oil
- 1/2 slice fresh ginger root, chopped
- 12 dried shiitake mushrooms, soaked until soft
- 3 cups long-grain white rice
- 2 1/2 cups boiling water
- 3 tablespoons chopped fresh cilantro
- 3 tablespoons thinly sliced green onion

Direction

- Mix soy sauce and 1 teaspoon salt then marinate the sausages and chicken in it and put it aside.
- In a big nonstick wok, heat the sesame oil in it and stir fry the ginger in the oil until it's fragrant. Mix in the chicken and sausages and stir fry them until they are brown. Mix in the mushrooms then fry for 3 more minutes. Add the rice while stirring then add salt and pepper to season.
- Move the mixture to a rice cooker then pour in water. Once the rice has cooked, add spring onions and chopped coriander as toppings then serve.

Nutrition Information

- Calories: 469 calories;
- Sodium: 576
- Total Carbohydrate: 49.4
- Cholesterol: 51
- Protein: 22.1
- Total Fat: 20.1

702. Pineapple Fried Rice II

Serving: 4 | Prep: 15mins | Cook: 30mins | Ready in:

Ingredients

- 1 cup uncooked white rice
- 2 cups water
- 2 tablespoons sesame oil
- 3 green onions, thinly sliced including tops
- 1 cup diced ham
- 1/2 cup peas
- 1 (8 ounce) can pineapple chunks, drained
- 1 egg, beaten
- 1 tablespoon white sugar
- 1 teaspoon salt
- 1/2 teaspoon white pepper
- 1/2 teaspoon garlic powder
- 1/4 cup soy sauce

Direction

- Let a saucepan with water and rice boil over high heat. Lower the heat to medium-low then cover the pan and let it simmer for 20-25 minutes until the rice is soft and the water has been absorbed by the rice. Put the cooked rice evenly on a rimmed baking sheet and keep in the fridge for about 20 minutes until cold.
- Heat a big skillet or wok with sesame oil over medium-high heat. Put in the ham, peas and green onions and stir-fry in hot oil for roughly 2 minutes or until the onions are soft. Add in the pineapple chunks and cook for about 2 minutes or until the pineapple starts to darken. Gather the mixture on the side of the wok then put the beaten egg in the middle. Cook the eggs for about 30 seconds until the egg is starting to set. Mix everything until well combined.
- Add in the garlic powder, salt, white pepper, sugar and cooled rice into the wok then stir continuously to prevent the rice from sticking. Cook the mixture for about 3 minutes until heated through. Drizzle the soy sauce into the mixture and mix until well combined.

Nutrition Information

- Calories: 374 calories;
- Protein: 12.8
- Total Fat: 11.3
- Sodium: 2001
- Total Carbohydrate: 55.4
- Cholesterol: 60

703. Popcorn Chicken (Taiwanese)

Serving: 4 | Prep: 15mins | Cook: 20mins | Ready in:

Ingredients

- 1 1/2 pounds boneless chicken thighs, cut into bite-size pieces
- 1 tablespoon soy sauce
- 1/2 teaspoon rice vinegar
- 2 cloves garlic, finely chopped
- 2 teaspoons grated ginger
- 1 teaspoon Chinese five-spice powder
- 1 teaspoon ground white pepper
- 1 teaspoon salt
- 1/2 teaspoon cayenne pepper
- 1 egg
- 1 cup tempura batter mix, or as needed
- peanut oil for frying
- Garnish:
- 1 bunch Thai basil, chopped
- 2 green onions, chopped
- 1 pinch ground white pepper
- 1 pinch salt

Direction

- In a big bowl, mix together the chicken pieces, rice vinegar, soy sauce, garlic, 5-spice powder, ginger, salt, white pepper, and cayenne pepper. Leave it for 10 minutes to marinate.

- Pour oil in a big cooking pan or a deep-fryer and heat it to 200° C or 400° F.
- Put the egg in a small bowl and beat until it's smooth. In a separate small bowl, pour the tempura batter mix in. Dip the chicken pieces one by one in the egg and then into the tempura batter mix and make sure to shake off the excess. Carefully place the chicken pieces in the hot oil and do it in batches. Fry the chicken for 5-8 minutes until it's golden brown. Move them to a paper towel-lined plate to drain. Do this to the rest of the chicken pieces.
- Sprinkle the chicken pieces with green onions, white pepper, basil leaves, and salt, then serve.

Nutrition Information

- Calories: 524 calories;
- Sodium: 1057
- Total Carbohydrate: 14.3
- Cholesterol: 163
- Protein: 35.8
- Total Fat: 35.5

704. Pork Chop Suey

Serving: 6 | Prep: 45mins | Cook: 6mins | Ready in:

Ingredients

- 1 pound pork tenderloin
- 1/4 cup all-purpose flour
- 2 tablespoons vegetable oil, divided
- 2 cups thinly sliced bok choy
- 1 cup chopped celery
- 1 cup red bell pepper, cut into 1/4 inch strips
- 1 cup sliced mushrooms
- 1 (8 ounce) can water chestnuts, sliced
- 2 cloves garlic, minced
- 1/4 cup chicken broth
- 1/4 cup soy sauce
- 1 tablespoon cornstarch
- 1 tablespoon dry sherry
- 1/2 teaspoon ground ginger

Direction

- Cut fat from the pork and slice it into 1-inch pieces. In a ziplock bag, place the sliced pork together with flour, and shake it forcefully.
- Place a large pan over medium-high heat and heat about 1 tbsp. of oil. Cook the pork for 3 minutes until all sides are browned. Take out of the pan and keep warm.
- In the same pan, heat another tablespoon of oil and stir in the bok choy, mushrooms, garlic, red pepper, water chestnuts, and celery. Fry for 3 minutes. Combine thoroughly soy sauce, sherry, chicken broth, ginger, and cornstarch and whisk thoroughly in a bowl. Pour the mixture into the pan and add in the pork. Cook for 1 more minute until thick.

Nutrition Information

- Calories: 194 calories;
- Total Fat: 8.4
- Sodium: 712
- Total Carbohydrate: 13.6
- Cholesterol: 42
- Protein: 15.9

705. Pork Dumplings

Serving: 6 | Prep: | Cook: | Ready in:

Ingredients

- 100 (3.5 inch square) wonton wrappers
- 1 3/4 pounds ground pork
- 1 tablespoon minced fresh ginger root
- 4 cloves garlic, minced
- 2 tablespoons thinly sliced green onion
- 4 tablespoons soy sauce
- 3 tablespoons sesame oil
- 1 egg, beaten
- 5 cups finely shredded Chinese cabbage

Direction

- Mix together egg, sesame oil, green onion, ginger, pork, garlic, soy sauce, and cabbage in a large bowl. Stir until well-combined.
- Put a teaspoon-full of pork filling on each wonton skin. Wet the edges with water and seal to form a triangle by folding edges over. Slightly roll the edges to seal in the filling. Leave the dumplings on a lightly-floured surface or container until they are ready to be cooked.
- Cook the dumplings for about 15 to 20 minutes in a covered metal steamer or bamboo steamer. Serve right away.

Nutrition Information

- Calories: 752 calories;
- Total Fat: 28.8
- Sodium: 1449
- Total Carbohydrate: 81.1
- Cholesterol: 129
- Protein: 39.2

706. Pork Lo Mein

Serving: 4 | Prep: 15mins | Cook: 15mins | Ready in:

Ingredients

- 1 (8 ounce) package linguine
- 1/3 cup low-sodium soy sauce
- 2 tablespoons rice vinegar
- 2 teaspoons cornstarch
- 1 teaspoon white sugar
- 1/2 teaspoon sesame oil
- 2 tablespoons canola oil
- 2 cups snap peas
- 1 small sweet onion, chopped
- 1 (12 ounce) pork tenderloin, cut into thin strips
- 1 (8 ounce) package sliced white mushrooms
- 1 red bell pepper, chopped
- 1 clove garlic, chopped
- 1/2 teaspoon chopped fresh ginger, or to taste
- 2 cloves garlic, chopped
- 3 green onions, sliced

Direction

- Boil lightly salted water in a pot and cook the linguine in the boiling water for 8-9 minutes until it's tender yet firm to chew then drain it.
- Combine soy sauce, cornstarch, vinegar, sesame oil, and sugar in a small bowl and whisk them together.
- Pour canola oil in a big cooking pan and heat it on medium-high heat. Cook the onion and snap peas in the hot oil while stirring for 2 minutes until it's softened. Add in the mushrooms, pork, 1 clove garlic, red bell pepper, and ginger and cook for 2 minutes until the pork is not pink. Add 2 cloves of garlic in the pork mixture and mix it and cook for a minute. Add the soy sauce mixture by pouring it on the pork mixture and continue to cook for a minute more until the sauce thickens. Turn the heat off then add the linguine and toss it to coat. Drizzle with green onions.

Nutrition Information

- Calories: 419 calories;
- Sodium: 793
- Total Carbohydrate: 55.5
- Cholesterol: 37
- Protein: 25.6
- Total Fat: 11.3

707. Potstickers (Chinese Dumplings)

Serving: 12 | Prep: 50mins | Cook: 12mins | Ready in:

Ingredients

- 1 pound raw shrimp, peeled and deveined
- 4 pounds ground beef
- 1 tablespoon minced fresh ginger root
- 1 shallot, minced
- 1 bunch green onions, chopped
- 3 leaves napa cabbage, chopped
- 2 tablespoons soy sauce
- 1 teaspoon Asian (toasted) sesame oil
- salt and white pepper to taste
- 1 pinch white sugar
- 1 (10 ounce) package round gyoza/potsticker wrappers
- vegetable oil
- 1/4 cup water

Direction

- Process the shrimp in the work bowl in a food processor until it's very finely ground. Move it to a large bowl then set it aside. Process the ground beef in the food processor as well until it becomes a fine grind, doing it in batches, then set it aside as well. Mix together the ground beef and shrimp, shallot, ginger, green onions, soy sauce, napa cabbage, sesame oil, white sugar, and salt and pepper until all ingredients are well blended.
- Put a wrapper on a work surface and get a scant teaspoon of the filling then put it in the center of the wrapper to fill the pot stickers. Dip your finger in water to wet it then dampen the wrapper's edges. Enclose the filling by folding the dough into the shape of a half-moon then press and seal the sticker for removing extra air and tightly sealing the edges together. Create a traditional look by folding several small pleats in the wrapper's top half before sealing the filling in. Put the filled wrappers on a baking sheet lined with parchment paper, then refrigerate as you fill and seal the rest of the pot stickers.
- In a big nonstick cooking pan with a lid, heat the oil over medium heat. Fry the pot stickers in the hot oil for 1-2 minutes until the bottoms are golden, the flat sides down and with a few spaces apart so they don't crowd. Turn over the pot stickers then pour water over them. Cover the pan and leave the dumplings to steam for 5-7 minutes until they begin to fry in oil again and the water has nearly evaporated. Uncover the pan and leave the dumplings to cook for another 2-3 minutes, until the wrapper has shrunk tightly onto the filling and all the water has evaporated.

Nutrition Information

- Calories: 411 calories;
- Protein: 34.5
- Total Fat: 22.3
- Sodium: 454
- Total Carbohydrate: 16.1
- Cholesterol: 152

708. Prawn And Mussel Soup With Rice Noodles

Serving: 2 | Prep: 15mins | Cook: 24mins | Ready in:

Ingredients

- 4 ounces mussels, cleaned and debearded
- 1/2 (8 ounce) package dried rice noodles
- 1 quart water
- 1 tomato, diced
- 1/3 cup diced onion
- 2 tablespoons tomato puree
- 1 tablespoon sauerkraut
- 2 teaspoons chile oil
- 1 teaspoon sliced garlic
- 1/2 teaspoon salt
- 4 ounces prawns, peeled and deveined
- 1 tablespoon chopped fresh parsley

Direction

- Prepare a bowl of cold salted water, then soak mussels for 20 minutes then drain.
- Boil water in a small pot and add noodles. Bring it to simmer for 2-3 minutes until tender. Drain and wash with cold running water.

- In the same pot, boil 1 quart of water and then stir in onion, sauerkraut, tomato, tomato puree, chili oil, salt, and garlic. Let it simmer for 10 minutes until the onion softens. Add the drained mussels and simmer for 1 more minute. Stir in prawns and simmer for another 1 or 2 minutes until the mixture is non-transparent. Stir in rice noodles and garnish the dish with parsley.

Nutrition Information

- Calories: 386 calories;
- Total Fat: 6.6
- Sodium: 1054
- Total Carbohydrate: 56.9
- Cholesterol: 110
- Protein: 22.8

709. Razor Clam In Sha Cha Sauce

Serving: 2 | Prep: 15mins | Cook: 5mins | Ready in:

Ingredients

- 2 tablespoons vegetable oil
- 2 teaspoons finely shredded fresh ginger
- 1 pound live razor clams
- 1 1/2 tablespoons sa cha sauce
- 1/2 cup water
- 1 tablespoon thinly sliced red bell pepper
- 2 green onions, cut into thin strips

Direction

- Set a large pan set over high heat, and heat vegetable oil. Cook the ginger for about 30 seconds until fragrant. Add in the razor clams (with shells) for about 2 minutes until all the clams have opened. Pour in the sa cha sauce and water. Bring the mixture to a boil. Stir in green onions and bell pepper before serving.

Nutrition Information

- Calories: 235 calories;
- Total Fat: 19.4
- Sodium: 274
- Total Carbohydrate: 6.1
- Cholesterol: 18
- Protein: 8.6

710. Restaurant Style Beef And Broccoli

Serving: 4 | Prep: 15mins | Cook: 15mins | Ready in:

Ingredients

- 1/3 cup oyster sauce
- 2 teaspoons Asian (toasted) sesame oil
- 1/3 cup sherry
- 1 teaspoon soy sauce
- 1 teaspoon white sugar
- 1 teaspoon cornstarch
- 3/4 pound beef round steak, cut into 1/8-inch thick strips
- 3 tablespoons vegetable oil, plus more if needed
- 1 thin slice of fresh ginger root
- 1 clove garlic, peeled and smashed
- 1 pound broccoli, cut into florets

Direction

- In a bowl, combine the sesame oil, oyster sauce, sherry, sugar, soy sauce, and cornstarch and whisk them together and stir until sugar has completely dissolved. In a shallow dish or bowl, put the steak pieces in and pour the oyster mixture on them. Coat the meat well by stirring, put in the refrigerator and wait 30 minutes for it to marinate.
- In a big cooking pan or wok, heat the vegetable oil on medium-high heat. Cook the ginger and garlic in the oil while stirring. Allow them to sizzle for a minute in the oil to add flavor to it then take them out and

discard. Add the broccoli while stirring and continue to toss and stir in the hot oil for 5-7 minutes until it's bright green and starting to get tender. Take the broccoli out of the wok then put it aside.
- If needed, add a bit more oil in the wok and toss and stir the beef with the marinade for 5 minutes, until the meat is not pink and the sauce has formed a glaze on the beef. Put the cooked broccoli back to the wok and stir for 3 minutes, until the broccoli and the meat are heated through.

Nutrition Information

- Calories: 331 calories;
- Total Fat: 21.1
- Sodium: 419
- Total Carbohydrate: 13.3
- Cholesterol: 52
- Protein: 21.7

711. Roasted Szechuan Broccoli

Serving: 4 | Prep: 10mins | Cook: 20mins | Ready in:

Ingredients

- 1 pound broccoli florets, cut into bite-size pieces
- 1 tablespoon olive oil
- salt and ground black pepper to taste
- 1 tablespoon chile oil
- 1 tablespoon light soy sauce
- 1 tablespoon Chinese black vinegar
- 1 teaspoon white sugar (optional)

Direction

- Set the oven at 425°F (220°C) and start preheating. Use aluminum foil to line a baking dish.
- In a large bowl, toss broccoli with pepper, salt and olive oil. Arrange on the prepared dish.
- Bake for around 20 minutes in the preheated oven till browned.
- In a bowl, mix together sugar, black vinegar, soy sauce and chile oil. Toss with the roasted broccoli.

Nutrition Information

- Calories: 101 calories;
- Total Carbohydrate: 9.5
- Cholesterol: 0
- Protein: 3.4
- Total Fat: 6.6
- Sodium: 210

712. Scallops A La Peking House

Serving: 4 | Prep: 15mins | Cook: 20mins | Ready in:

Ingredients

- 1 tablespoon cornstarch
- 1/4 cup dry white wine
- 4 tablespoons peanut oil
- 2 green onions, minced
- 1 1/2 pounds scallops
- 1 cup clam juice
- 1/2 teaspoon salt
- 1/4 teaspoon ground cayenne pepper
- 1/2 teaspoon ground ginger
- 1/3 (8 ounce) can sliced water chestnuts

Direction

- Mix cornstarch and 1/4 cup dry white wine in a small bowl until the cornstarch is dissolved then set it aside.
- Pour the peanut oil in a big cooking pan and heat it on medium-high heat until it's almost smoking. Turn the heat off and add in the green onions. Turn the heat on again and cook

while constantly stirring until the scallions soften.
- Add the scallops to the pan and cook for a minute while constantly stirring.
- Pour in the clam juice or broth in the pan then continue stirring. Season with salt, red pepper, or hot sauce. Add the water chestnuts and ginger while stirring.
- Add the cornstarch and white wine mixture while stirring then turn the heat to high. Cook the mixture until it's boiling and has thickened.

Nutrition Information

- Calories: 304 calories;
- Sodium: 698
- Total Carbohydrate: 9.4
- Cholesterol: 58
- Protein: 29.2
- Total Fat: 14.9

713. Sesame Chicken

Serving: 4 | Prep: | Cook: | Ready in:

Ingredients

- 2 teaspoons cornstarch
- 2 tablespoons rice wine
- 1 tablespoon lemon juice
- 1 tablespoon soy sauce
- 1 dash hot pepper sauce
- 1 tablespoon grated fresh ginger
- 1 clove crushed garlic
- 1 pound skinless, boneless chicken breast halves, cut into bite size pieces
- 2 tablespoons sesame seeds
- 1 tablespoon sesame oil
- 2 tablespoons vegetable oil
- 4 ounces fresh mushrooms, quartered
- 1 green bell pepper, sliced
- 4 green onions, sliced diagonally into 1/2 inch pieces

Direction

- Prepare the marinade: Combine wine or sherry with some cornstarch using a bowl or nonporous dish. Add in soy sauce, lemon juice, ginger, garlic, and hot pepper sauce. Mix with the chicken strips by stirring. Put on the dish, cover then place in the fridge for 3 to 4 hours to let it marinate.
- Set the heat to medium, then use a large skillet or wok to dry-fry sesame seeds. Shake the wok until the seeds turn golden brown. Transfer the seeds and let rest.
- Using the same skillet or wok, pour some sesame oil and vegetable oil, then let it slowly heat. Remove the chicken while saving the marinade for later. Add pieces of chicken to the wok at a time and stir-fry until it turns a brown color. Use a slotted spoon to remove the chicken and let rest.
- Stir in the green bell pepper and mushrooms into the same skillet or wok and cook for 2 to 3 minutes. Stir-fry another minute when adding the scallions. Transfer the chicken back to the wok along with the leftover marinade. Set the heat to medium, then stir them for two to three minutes more to coat them with the glaze evenly. Top with some toasted sesame seeds, and serve right away.

Nutrition Information

- Calories: 279 calories;
- Protein: 28.8
- Total Fat: 14.1
- Sodium: 312
- Total Carbohydrate: 7.2
- Cholesterol: 66

714. Shrimp Egg Foo Young

Serving: 4 | Prep: 5mins | Cook: 15mins | Ready in:

Ingredients

- 4 eggs
- 8 ounces fresh bean sprouts
- 1/3 cup thinly sliced green onions
- 1 cup cooked small shrimp
- 1/4 teaspoon garlic powder
- 2 tablespoons vegetable oil
- 3 cups chicken broth
- 2 tablespoons cornstarch
- 2 tablespoons sugar
- 2 tablespoons distilled white vinegar
- 2 tablespoons soy sauce

Direction

- In a bowl, mix bean sprouts, shrimp, garlic powder, eggs, and green onions thoroughly until well-combined. Place the skillet over moderate heat, and heat oil. Spoon about half a cup of the egg mixture and drop it onto the skillet to make a patty. Cook each side for 4 minutes until the patty is golden brown. Do the same with the remaining egg mixture and then set patties aside after cooking.
- Combine chicken broth, soy sauce, cornstarch, vinegar, and sugar in a saucepan, and simmer the mixture over medium-low heat for 5 minutes until the sauce thickens. Drizzle sauce over the cooked patties.

Nutrition Information

- Calories: 239 calories;
- Protein: 16.1
- Total Fat: 12.6
- Sodium: 1318
- Total Carbohydrate: 15.7
- Cholesterol: 252

715. Shrimp Stirfry

Serving: 4 | Prep: 20mins | Cook: 10mins | Ready in:

Ingredients

- 1 tablespoon sesame oil
- 1 tablespoon olive oil
- 1 pound tiger shrimp, peeled and deveined
- 1 cup chopped onion
- 1 1/2 cups sliced king mushrooms
- 1/2 cup chopped green bell pepper
- 3 cloves garlic, finely chopped
- 1 teaspoon minced fresh ginger
- 1/2 cup water
- 1 teaspoon oyster sauce, or to taste
- 1 pound fresh Chinese wheat noodles
- 2 cups bean sprouts

Direction

- In a large pan or wok set over medium heat, heat up olive oil and sesame oil. Cook the onions and shrimps until well coated. Add in garlic, mushrooms, and green bell pepper and mix well. Mix in the ginger.
- Add oyster sauce and water to the shrimp mixture. Allow to simmer for about 5 minutes or until the meat is no longer transparent and outside of the shrimps is bright pink. Mix well
- Add bean sprouts and noodles, toss to combine. Cook for about 2 minutes or until the noodles are well heated. Toss again.

Nutrition Information

- Calories: 507 calories;
- Total Fat: 9.5
- Sodium: 896
- Total Carbohydrate: 73.3
- Cholesterol: 173
- Protein: 29.1

716. Shrimp With Broccoli In Garlic Sauce

Serving: 4 | Prep: 15mins | Cook: 15mins | Ready in:

Ingredients

- 2 cups fresh broccoli florets
- 1 tablespoon water
- 2 tablespoons peanut oil
- 4 large cloves garlic, minced
- 1 cup low-sodium chicken broth
- 1 tablespoon soy sauce
- 1 tablespoon oyster sauce
- 2 teaspoons grated fresh ginger root
- 1 pound uncooked medium shrimp, peeled and deveined
- 1/4 cup canned water chestnuts, drained
- 2 tablespoons cornstarch

Direction

- In a glass bowl, combine water and broccoli and place inside the microwave oven to steam for 2-3 minutes until slightly tender.
- Place the large skillet or wok over medium-high heat, and heat peanut oil. Cook the garlic in hot oil for 60 seconds until fragrant. Adjust the heat to low before stirring in chicken broth, oyster sauce, ginger root, and soy sauce. Allow the mixture to boil then stir in shrimp. Cook the mixture for 3-4 minutes until the shrimp turn pink. Add water chestnuts and the steamed broccoli into the mixture and toss them well to coat. Add cornstarch into the mixture, 1 tbsp. at a time, and simmer for 5 more minutes until the sauce thickens.

Nutrition Information

- Calories: 198 calories;
- Total Carbohydrate: 10.1
- Cholesterol: 174
- Protein: 21.2
- Total Fat: 8
- Sodium: 496

717. Sichuan (Szechuan) Cold Noodle

Serving: 1 | Prep: 15mins | Cook: 15mins | Ready in:

Ingredients

- 3 cloves garlic, minced
- 1 pinch kosher salt
- 1 tablespoon dark soy sauce
- 2 teaspoons red chile oil
- 1 teaspoon Szechuan peppercorn oil
- 1 teaspoon rice vinegar
- 1/2 teaspoon sesame oil
- 1 cup soybean sprouts
- 1 cup Chinese noodles (La mian)
- 1 teaspoon vegetable oil

Direction

- Put together the kosher salt and garlic in a mortar or in a small bowl. Using a wide spoon or pestle, crush the garlic mixture until it forms a paste.
- Mix together in a small bowl the soy sauce, garlic paste, red chile oil, rice vinegar, peppercorn oil, and sesame oil. Stir them all together until the sauce is properly blended.
- Pour cold water in a bowl, filling it. Boil water in a pot then put the bean sprouts in as you stir. Cook the beans for about 2 minutes until they're slightly softened, then drain. Transfer the beans to the cold water, immersing them until they're cool then move the beans to a serving bowl.
- Boil water in a pot then put the noodles in it while stirring. Cook the noodles while stirring for about 3 minutes until they are softened, then drain. Put the noodles in the cold water, submerging them, until they are cool. Place the noodles in a bowl then drizzle with vegetable oil, mixing it in. Put the noodles on top of the bean sprouts then dribble with sauce. Mix them together until they are well blended.

Nutrition Information

- Calories: 716 calories;
- Sodium: 1331
- Total Carbohydrate: 90.1
- Cholesterol: 0
- Protein: 36.8

- Total Fat: 33.4

718. Sichuan Cucumber Salad

Serving: 4 | Prep: 20mins | Cook: 5mins | Ready in:

Ingredients

- 5 dried red chile peppers
- 5 teaspoons soy sauce
- 1 spring onion, finely chopped
- 1 tablespoon sesame oil
- 2 teaspoons hot chile oil
- 1 teaspoon soft dark brown sugar
- 1 clove garlic, minced
- 1/2 teaspoon Chinese black vinegar
- 1/2 teaspoon toasted white sesame seeds
- 2 cucumbers - peeled, seeded, and cut into 2-inch strips

Direction

- Prepare a dry skillet and heat over medium heat. Add red chile peppers; cook and stir for about 5 minutes till fragrant. Allow to cool down and remove to a spice grinder; pulse till ground coarsely.
- For making a dressing, mix together in a bowl sesame seeds, black vinegar, garlic, brown sugar, hot chile oil, sesame oil, spring onion, soy sauce, and ground chile peppers.
- On a serving plate, lay the cucumbers. Pour dressing over the top and toss well. Before serving, let sit for about 3 minutes.

Nutrition Information

- Calories: 160 calories;
- Cholesterol: 0
- Protein: 4.6
- Total Fat: 8.3
- Sodium: 491
- Total Carbohydrate: 21

719. Singapore Noodles

Serving: 8 | Prep: 15mins | Cook: 15mins | Ready in:

Ingredients

- 1 pound dry vermicelli pasta
- 2 skinless, boneless chicken breast halves - cut into strips
- 2 butterfly pork chops, thinly sliced
- 2 cloves garlic, crushed
- 3 tablespoons vegetable oil
- 1/2 onion, thinly sliced
- 2 carrots, thinly sliced
- 2 stalks celery, thinly sliced
- 1/2 (12 ounce) package frozen shrimp, thawed
- 1 cup bean sprouts
- 2 tablespoons soy sauce
- 3 tablespoons yellow curry powder
- 1/4 cup water

Direction

- Boil lightly salted water in a large pot, add pasta and then cook for 8 to 10 minutes or until al dente. Drain the pasta.
- Use medium-high heat to brown garlic, chicken, and pork in the oil on a fry pan or deep skillet.
- Decrease the heat to medium-low and pour in water, onion and carrots. Cover and then steam for five minutes. Mix in shrimp and celery. Cover and then steam for two minutes.
- Stir in soy sauce, bean sprouts, and curry powder. Mix together for 4 to 5 minutes until hot and blended. Mix with noodles and then serve with the option of soy sauce and hot pepper sauce as condiments.

Nutrition Information

- Calories: 351 calories;
- Sodium: 310
- Total Carbohydrate: 46.2
- Cholesterol: 64

- Protein: 24.2
- Total Fat: 8.2

- Total Fat: 13
- Sodium: 2391

720. Slow Cooker Mongolian Beef

Serving: 4 | Prep: 10mins | Cook: 4hours10mins | Ready in:

Ingredients

- 1 pound flank steak, cut into bite-size pieces
- 1/4 cup cornstarch
- 2 teaspoons olive oil
- 1 onion, thinly sliced
- 1 tablespoon minced garlic
- 3 large green onions, sliced diagonally into 1/2 inch pieces
- 1/2 cup soy sauce
- 1/2 cup water
- 1/2 cup brown sugar
- 1/2 teaspoon minced fresh ginger root
- 1/2 cup hoisin sauce

Direction

- Combine the cornstarch and flank steak in a resealable plastic bag then shake the bag to coat the flank steak evenly with cornstarch. Leave the steak for 10 minutes to rest.
- In a big cooking pan, heat the olive oil on medium-high heat. Cook the steak in the oil for 2-4 minutes and stir until it's browned evenly. Combine the garlic, onion, flank steak, soy sauce, green onions, water, ginger, brown sugar, and hoisin sauce in a slow cooker. Allow this to cook on low for 4 hours.

Nutrition Information

- Calories: 450 calories;
- Total Carbohydrate: 55.4
- Cholesterol: 47
- Protein: 28

721. Spicy Beef Filet In Oyster Sauce

Serving: 4 | Prep: 15mins | Cook: 10mins | Ready in:

Ingredients

- 1 teaspoon vegetable oil
- 1 teaspoon oyster sauce
- 1/2 teaspoon cornstarch
- 3/4 pound beef tenderloin, cut into 1/4 inch strips
- 1 teaspoon water
- 1 teaspoon cornstarch
- 2 tablespoons oyster sauce
- 1 teaspoon sugar
- 1 teaspoon black pepper
- 1 tablespoon vegetable oil
- 1/2 onion, thinly sliced

Direction

- In a bowl, mix 1 teaspoon of oyster sauce, 1/2 teaspoon of cornstarch and 1 teaspoon of vegetable oil. Put in the beef and mix until the beef is well coated. Keep the marinated beef in the fridge for 30-45 minutes. Take the marinated beef out of the fridge 10 minutes before cooking.
- In a small bowl, mix 2 tablespoons of oyster sauce, pepper, water and 1 teaspoon of cornstarch and set aside. Heat a big skillet with 1 tablespoon of vegetable oil over high heat. Put in the onions and sauté for about 1 minute until the edges of the onion starts to turn brown. Put in the marinated beef and continue to cook and stir for approximately 5 minutes or until the beef meat is just a little bit pink. Put in the sauce and stir-fry the mixture for 1 more minute or until the sauce turns clear and has a thick consistency.

Nutrition Information

- Calories: 202 calories;
- Total Fat: 14.8
- Sodium: 94
- Total Carbohydrate: 3.8
- Cholesterol: 43
- Protein: 12.9

722.   Spicy Crispy Beef

Serving: 4 | Prep: 20mins | Cook: 20mins | Ready in:

Ingredients

- 1/4 cup cornstarch
- 1/4 tablespoon salt
- black pepper
- 12 ounces flank steak, thinly sliced
- 1 quart oil for frying
- 4 tablespoons soy sauce
- 1 tablespoon rice vinegar
- 1/2 tablespoon rice wine
- 1 1/2 tablespoons honey
- 7 tablespoons granulated sugar
- 1/2 tablespoon chile paste
- 1/4 cup water
- 3 tablespoons chopped fresh ginger root
- 1 tablespoon vegetable oil
- 2 cloves garlic, chopped
- 1/4 cup sliced onion
- 1/4 cup diced red bell pepper

Direction

- Pour oil in deep-fryer and heat it to 190° C or 375° F.
- While heating the oil, mix together the cornstarch, pepper, and salt in a mixing bowl. Coat the steak slices by tossing them in the cornstarch mixture. Make sure they are coated well.
- Deep fry them in the heated oil until they're golden brown. Make sure that the steaks are cooked through by checking them. Take them out of the oil once cooked and put them aside.
- Mix together the rice vinegar, soy sauce, honey and rice wine in a separate mixing bowl. Add in the ginger, chili paste, sugar, and water then mix thoroughly and put aside.
- Place a deep-frying pan or wok on medium heat then pour in 1 tablespoon of oil. Sauté the onion, red pepper, and garlic in the oil for 30 seconds. Pour in the sauce mixture and continue cooking for 30 seconds more. Add in the fried steak strips and toss to coat with sauce and heat through.

Nutrition Information

- Calories: 489 calories;
- Total Fat: 31.8
- Sodium: 1383
- Total Carbohydrate: 40.9
- Cholesterol: 27
- Protein: 11.4

723.   Spicy Orange Zest Beef

Serving: 4 | Prep: 20mins | Cook: 5mins | Ready in:

Ingredients

- 1 pound beef tenderloin, cut into 1/2 inch strips
- 1/4 cup orange juice
- 1/4 cup seasoned rice vinegar
- 2 tablespoons soy sauce
- 1 tablespoon hot chile paste (such as sambal oelek)
- 1 tablespoon brown sugar, or to taste
- 2 cloves garlic, minced
- 1/4 cup water
- 1 teaspoon cornstarch
- cooking spray
- 2 tablespoons grated orange zest
- 1 bunch green onions, sliced - white parts and tops separated

- salt and freshly ground black pepper to taste

Direction

- In a large bowl, mix together the beef, rice vinegar, orange juice, soy sauce, brown sugar, hot chili paste, and garlic then cover and leave it refrigerated for 1-2 hours.
- Set a colander over a big bowl and strain the beef in it allowing it to thoroughly drain for about 5 minutes. Set the marinade aside.
- Pour into the bowl of marinade the water and the cornstarch then whisk until the cornstarch is dissolved. Set it aside.
- Coat the skillet with oil using cooking spray and place over high heat. Cook the beef for a minute while undisturbed, then cook and stir for another minute.
- Add the orange zest and light parts of green onion, stirring it in then cook for 30 seconds.
- Add the green onion tops and the marinade, stirring it in. Cook while stirring for about 2-3 minutes, until the sauce is reduced and thick and the beef is no longer pink inside.
- Add salt and black pepper to taste.

Nutrition Information

- Calories: 267 calories;
- Total Fat: 14.3
- Sodium: 888
- Total Carbohydrate: 16.8
- Cholesterol: 58
- Protein: 18.7

724. Spicy Szechuan Green Beans

Serving: 2 | Prep: 15mins | Cook: 8mins | Ready in:

Ingredients

- 1/2 pound green beans, trimmed and cut into 1-inch pieces
- 1/4 cup water
- 1 tablespoon minced ginger
- 2 cloves garlic, minced
- 1 teaspoon sesame oil
- 2 tablespoons soy sauce
- 1 tablespoon rice vinegar
- 1/2 teaspoon white sugar
- 1/4 teaspoon red pepper flakes

Direction

- On medium-high heat, mix water and green beans in a pan; cover. Cook and stir time to time for 4-5mins until the beans are crisp-tender; put in sesame oil, garlic, and ginger. Cook and stir often for 1-2mins until the garlic is pale brown.
- In a small bowl, combine red pepper flakes, soy sauce, sugar, and rice vinegar; pour in the pan with beans. Cook for 3-5mins until the sauce is thick enough to cover the beans.

Nutrition Information

- Calories: 77 calories;
- Sodium: 911
- Total Carbohydrate: 12.1
- Cholesterol: 0
- Protein: 3.4
- Total Fat: 2.6

725. Spicy Tan Tan Soup (Tantanmen Or Dan Dan Noodles)

Serving: 2 | Prep: 10mins | Cook: 15mins | Ready in:

Ingredients

- 1 teaspoon sesame oil
- 2 teaspoons doubanjiang (soy bean paste)
- 1 tablespoon minced shallots
- 1 clove garlic, pressed
- 1 1/2 teaspoons grated fresh ginger

- 6 ounces ground pork
- 1/4 cup soy sauce
- 2 tablespoons tahini (sesame seed paste)
- 1 tablespoon sake
- 1 tablespoon miso paste
- 1 teaspoon tianmianjiang (sweet bean paste)
- 4 cups chicken stock
- 2 teaspoons rice vinegar
- 1 teaspoon rayu (chile oil)
- 1/2 cup fresh spinach, or to taste (optional)
- 2 cups ramen noodles, or to taste
- 3 green onions, thinly sliced
- 1 red Thai chile pepper, sliced

Direction

- Place the skillet over moderate heat, and heat sesame oil. Add the doubanjiang and cook it together with garlic, shallots and ginger until fragrant, about 30 seconds. Stir in ground pork and cook for 3 more minutes until browned.
- Add soy sauce, sake, tianmianjiang, tahini, and miso paste into the pork mixture and mix until evenly combined. Stir in chicken stock and bring it to boil. Add rayu, rice vinegar, and spinach into the pork mixture and let it simmer over low heat for 10 minutes.
- Separate the noodles by soaking them in a bowl of hot water. Drain the noodles and add them into the soup. Garnish the soup with Thai chili peppers and green onions before serving.

Nutrition Information

- Calories: 561 calories;
- Total Fat: 33
- Sodium: 5122
- Total Carbohydrate: 36.4
- Cholesterol: 65
- Protein: 27.9

726. Steamed Fish With Ginger

Serving: 2 | Prep: 15mins | Cook: 10mins | Ready in:

Ingredients

- 1 pound halibut fillet
- 1 teaspoon coarse sea salt or kosher salt
- 1 tablespoon minced fresh ginger
- 3 tablespoons thinly sliced green onion
- 1 tablespoon dark soy sauce
- 1 tablespoon light soy sauce
- 1 tablespoon peanut oil
- 2 teaspoons toasted sesame oil
- 1/4 cup lightly packed fresh cilantro sprigs

Direction

- Dry halibut with paper towels. Rub salt to both sides of the fillet. Sprinkle the ginger on top then place the fish on a heat proof ceramic dish.
- Put into a bamboo steamer and place over a few inches of gently boiling water. Cover the steamer and gently steam for 10-12 minutes.
- Pour out of the dish the accumulated water, then sprinkle the fish fillet with green onion. Pour both soy sauce on top of the fillets.
- In a small frying pan, heat peanut and sesame oils over medium high heat until they start to smoke. When the oil is already hot, slowly pour on top of the fillets. The very hot oil will make the water on top of the fish and green onions to spatter and pop so be very careful. Top with cilantro sprigs before serving right away.

Nutrition Information

- Calories: 361 calories;
- Total Fat: 16.8
- Sodium: 1908
- Total Carbohydrate: 2
- Cholesterol: 73
- Protein: 48.1

727. Steamed Garlic Prawns Chinese Style

Serving: 4 | Prep: 5mins | Cook: 15mins | Ready in:

Ingredients

- 20 large tiger prawns with shell
- 2 tablespoons light soy sauce
- 5 cloves garlic, minced
- 1 teaspoon brandy

Direction

- Thoroughly wash the prawns while leaving the heads and shell on. Combine the soy sauce, brandy, and garlic in a bowl. Using a dish, arrange the prawns and use the soy sauce mixture to pour over it.
- Use water to fill half of a wok or pot. Set the steamer basket on top of the water and let it boil. Top the steamer basket with the shrimp on its dish. Put the cover on top of the wok and let the prawns steam for 10 minutes. Serve hot.

Nutrition Information

- Calories: 67 calories;
- Cholesterol: 106
- Protein: 12.1
- Total Fat: 0.6
- Sodium: 574
- Total Carbohydrate: 1.8

728. Steamed Pork Spare Ribs

Serving: 4 | Prep: 10mins | Cook: 15mins | Ready in:

Ingredients

- 3 tablespoons shrimp paste
- 2 tablespoons fish sauce
- 2 tablespoons black soy sauce
- 1 tablespoon white sugar
- 1 1/2 pounds pork spareribs, cut into 1-inch pieces
- 1 tablespoon cornstarch
- 1 tablespoon peanut oil (groundnut oil)
- 1 tablespoon water

Direction

- In a bowl, combine the fish sauce, shrimp paste, sugar, and black soy sauce and mix them together. Add the spareribs in and coat it by stirring then let it marinate for 20 minutes.
- In a different bowl, combine the peanut oil, water, and cornstarch and mix them together then pour it on the spareribs and marinate for another 5-7 minutes. Take the spareribs out of the marinade and discard.
- Position a steamer insert in a cooking pan and fill the pan with water right below the bottom of the steamer. Boil the water, put the spareribs in, cover the pan and steam for 15 minutes until the meat is cooked.

Nutrition Information

- Calories: 541 calories;
- Total Fat: 43.3
- Sodium: 1145
- Total Carbohydrate: 7.1
- Cholesterol: 143
- Protein: 28.7

729. Stir Fried Chicken With Pineapple And Peppers

Serving: 6 | Prep: | Cook: | Ready in:

Ingredients

- 1/4 cup reduced-salt soy sauce
- 2 tablespoons white wine vinegar
- 2 tablespoons mirin (sweetened Asian wine)

410

- 1 teaspoon grated ginger root
- 2 crushed garlic cloves
- 1 tablespoon cornstarch
- 2 tablespoons oil, preferably sesame oil
- 1 pound boneless, skinless chicken breast, cut in 1-inch pieces
- 6 large green onions, cut in 1-inch pieces
- 2 cups fresh or frozen pepper strips
- 1 (20 ounce) can chunk pineapple in juice
- 1/4 cup sliced almonds (optional)

Direction

- Put the first 6 ingredients together and stir thoroughly.
- Pour oil in a big cooking pan and heat it. Add the chicken and stir-fry it for 5 minutes until it's brown and done.
- Take the chicken out then add peppers, green onions, and pineapple in the pan and allow them to heat through. Add the sauce in and stir until it has thickened. Put the chicken back in the pan and allow to heat through as well. Top with almonds if you want and eat with brown rice.

Nutrition Information

- Calories: 238 calories;
- Total Fat: 7.7
- Sodium: 412
- Total Carbohydrate: 21
- Cholesterol: 44
- Protein: 20.2

730. Stir Fried Chicken With Tofu And Mixed Vegetables

Serving: 6 | Prep: 15mins | Cook: 15mins | Ready in:

Ingredients

- 3 tablespoons light soy sauce
- 1 teaspoon white sugar
- 1 tablespoon cornstarch
- 3 tablespoons Chinese rice wine
- 1 medium green onion, diced
- 2 skinless, boneless chicken breast halves - cut into bite-size pieces
- 3 cloves garlic, chopped
- 1 yellow onion, thinly sliced
- 2 green bell peppers, thinly sliced
- 1 (12 ounce) package firm tofu, drained and cubed
- 1/2 cup water
- 2 tablespoons oyster sauce
- 1 1/2 tablespoons chili paste with garlic

Direction

- Combine the sugar, soy sauce, rice wine, and cornstarch in a medium bowl and mix them together. Add the chicken and green onion in the mixture then allow 15 minutes to marinate.
- Place a wok over medium-high heat, put the chicken with the marinade mixture in and cook while stirring until almost done, about 5 minutes. Add the onion, peppers, and garlic, tossing them in. Cook for 5 more minutes while stirring until the chicken is no longer pink, its juices run clear and the vegetables are tender-crisp.
- Mix in the water, tofu, chili paste, and oyster sauce into the wok then continue cooking while stirring until it has heated through.

Nutrition Information

- Calories: 172 calories;
- Sodium: 548
- Total Carbohydrate: 11.8
- Cholesterol: 20
- Protein: 17.8
- Total Fat: 6.4

731. Stir Fried Mushrooms With Baby Corn

Serving: 4 | Prep: 10mins | Cook: 15mins | Ready in:

Ingredients

- 2 tablespoons cooking oil
- 3 cloves garlic, minced
- 1 onion, diced
- 8 baby corn ears, sliced
- 2/3 pound fresh mushrooms, sliced
- 1 tablespoon fish sauce
- 1 tablespoon light soy sauce
- 1 tablespoon oyster sauce
- 2 teaspoons cornstarch
- 3 tablespoons water
- 1 red chile pepper, sliced
- 1/4 cup chopped fresh cilantro

Direction

- Heat a big skillet or wok with oil on medium heat then put in the garlic in hot oil and sauté for 5-7 minutes or until brown in color. Put in the baby corn and onion and cook and stir for 5-7 minutes until the onion is translucent. Mix in the mushrooms and cook for 2 minutes or until the mushrooms are a little bit soft. Put in the soy sauce, oyster sauce and fish sauce into the mixture and mix well until fully blended.
- In a small bowl, mix water and cornstarch together until the cornstarch has fully dissolved in water then pour it into the mushroom mixture. Stir-fry the mixture until it is glistening and the sauce is thick in consistency. Put the cooked mixture into a serving dish and top with cilantro and chile pepper then serve.

Nutrition Information

- Calories: 49 calories;
- Sodium: 448
- Total Carbohydrate: 8.3
- Cholesterol: 0
- Protein: 3.4
- Total Fat: 0.9

732. Stir Fried Pork With Sweet Bean Paste

Serving: 2 | Prep: 15mins | Cook: 8mins | Ready in:

Ingredients

- 2 tablespoons water
- 1 teaspoon cornstarch
- 9 ounces pork, cut into thin strips
- 2 teaspoons salt, divided
- 3 tablespoons water
- 1 teaspoon white sugar
- 1 teaspoon soy sauce
- 1/8 teaspoon monosodium glutamate (MSG)
- 3 1/2 tablespoons vegetable oil
- 2 tablespoons sweet bean paste
- 2 spring onions (white parts only), cut into matchstick-size pieces

Direction

- Combine cornstarch and 2 tablespoons of water in a bowl and stir them together.
- In a shallow dish or bowl, place the pork in then add in 1 teaspoon salt and the cornstarch mixture. Coat the pork by stirring then allow to sit for several minutes.
- In a bowl, combine 3 tablespoons water, soy sauce, sugar, 1 teaspoon salt, and MSG and mix them together until the sauce is smooth.
- Pour oil in a big cooking pan or wok and heat it on medium-high heat. Add the pork and sauté it in the oil for 5 minutes until it's thoroughly cooked. Push the pork to the side of the wok or pan then add the sweet bean paste. Cook the bean paste while stirring for a minute until it's fragrant. Add the sauce in and stir for 2-3 minutes until it has thickened.
- Move the pork mixture to a platter or dish and add spring onions as toppings.

Nutrition Information

- Calories: 510 calories;
- Sodium: 2573
- Total Carbohydrate: 11.3
- Cholesterol: 79
- Protein: 26.1
- Total Fat: 39.8

733. Stir Fry Pork With Ginger

Serving: 2 | Prep: 15mins | Cook: 15mins | Ready in:

Ingredients

- 2 tablespoons vegetable oil
- 1/2 inch piece fresh ginger root, thinly sliced
- 1/4 pound thinly sliced lean pork
- 1 teaspoon soy sauce
- 1/2 teaspoon dark soy sauce
- 1/2 teaspoon salt
- 1/3 teaspoon sugar
- 1 teaspoon sesame oil
- 1 green onion, chopped
- 1 tablespoon Chinese rice wine

Direction

- Pour oil in a wok or big cooking pan then heat it on medium-high heat. Add the ginger in the hot oil and fry it until it's fragrant. Add the soy sauce, pork, salt, dark soy sauce, and sugar and cook for 10 minutes while occasionally stirring.
- Add the green onion, rice wine, and sesame oil while stirring then allow it to simmer until the pork becomes tender.

Nutrition Information

- Calories: 322 calories;
- Total Fat: 29.7
- Sodium: 838
- Total Carbohydrate: 2.2
- Cholesterol: 41

- Protein: 9.4

734. Sweet And Sour Pasta

Serving: 5 | Prep: | Cook: | Ready in:

Ingredients

- 1 onion, chopped
- 1 leek, chopped
- 1 small carrot, grated
- 1 (5 ounce) can tuna
- 1 (16 ounce) can crushed tomatoes
- 2 tablespoons olive oil
- 2 tablespoons honey
- 2 tablespoons light soy sauce
- 1 tablespoon Worcestershire sauce
- 1 1/2 teaspoons Chinese five-spice powder
- 2 tablespoons creme fraiche
- 1 (16 ounce) package penne pasta

Direction

- Boil salted water and cook the penne pasta until al dente.
- Heat olive oil in a saucepan and then cook the carrot, leek, and onion for a few minutes until the onions are transparent.
- Stir in honey, Worcestershire sauce, Chinese five spice, soy sauce, and tomatoes and cook for 5 minutes over moderate heat.
- Drain tuna fish and add it into the saucepan; cook for 5-10 more minutes.
- Season it with salt before serving. Stir in spoonfuls of crème fraiche and then pour the sauce all over the penne.

Nutrition Information

- Calories: 505 calories;
- Total Fat: 10.4
- Sodium: 395
- Total Carbohydrate: 86.2
- Cholesterol: 16

- Protein: 21

735. Szechuan Beef

Serving: 6 | Prep: 10mins | Cook: 10mins | Ready in:

Ingredients

- 1 pound sirloin steak, cut into bite size strips
- 1 tablespoon soy sauce
- 2 teaspoons cornstarch
- 1/4 teaspoon crushed red pepper
- 1 clove garlic, minced
- 2 tablespoons vegetable oil
- 3 cups fresh broccoli florets
- 2 small onions, cut into wedges
- 1 (8 ounce) can water chestnuts, drained
- 1/4 cup chicken broth
- 1/2 cup peanuts

Direction

- Combine the beef with cornstarch, soy sauce, garlic, and crushed pepper in a non-metal bowl and toss them together. Cover then leave refrigerated for 20 minutes.
- Pour oil in a big cooking pan or wok then heat it on high heat. Add the beef and stir-fry it for 5 minutes until it's not pink. Add the onions, water chestnuts, and broccoli while stirring and cook for 2 more minutes. Add the broth then boil. Add the peanuts while stirring and cook for another minute then serve.

Nutrition Information

- Calories: 306 calories;
- Total Fat: 21.1
- Sodium: 243
- Total Carbohydrate: 13.3
- Cholesterol: 44
- Protein: 17.9

736. Szechuan Spicy Eggplant

Serving: 4 | Prep: 25mins | Cook: 20mins | Ready in:

Ingredients

- 1 (1 1/2 pound) eggplant
- 4 tablespoons soy sauce
- 1/4 cup chicken stock
- 1 teaspoon chili sauce
- 1 teaspoon white sugar
- 1/2 teaspoon ground black pepper
- 2 tablespoons oyster sauce (optional)
- 1 tablespoon cornstarch
- 4 tablespoons water
- 2 cloves garlic, minced
- 4 large green onions, finely chopped
- 1 tablespoon chopped fresh ginger root
- 1/4 pound fresh shrimp - peeled, deveined, and diced
- 1/3 pound lean ground beef
- 1 tablespoon sesame oil
- 4 cups hot cooked rice

Direction

- Cut the eggplant into 1-inch cubes, and discard the stem. Whisk oyster sauce, sugar, chili sauce, ground black pepper, soy sauce, and chicken stock together in a medium bowl. Mix well and set aside. Combine water and cornstarch on a separate small bowl then put aside.
- Spread a large and deep pan over high heat with cooking spray; wait a few minutes until it becomes very hot. Cook dried shrimp (if choosing), garlic, half of the green onions, and ginger for 3 to 5 minutes or until they begin to turn brown. Make sure to stir continuously. Add in the ground pork or beef and stir constantly for another 3 minutes or until browned.
- Place the eggplant in the pan and mix all the ingredients. Add the reserved soy sauce mixture, then cover the pan. Lower the heat to medium-low; leave to simmer for about 15

minutes while stirring sometimes. If using fresh shrimp, put it in during the last few minutes of cooking process. Mix in the remaining cornstarch mixture and allow to heat until the mixture thickens. Lastly, mix in sesame oil and the remaining green onions.
- Pour over hot rice for serving.

Nutrition Information

- Calories: 441 calories;
- Total Fat: 12.6
- Sodium: 1079
- Total Carbohydrate: 61.6
- Cholesterol: 71
- Protein: 20

737. Taiwanese Dumplings

Serving: 20 | Prep: 1hours15mins | Cook: | Ready in:

Ingredients

- 2 heads napa cabbage, finely chopped
- 1 bunch cilantro, chopped
- 2 pounds ground pork
- 2 egg whites
- 3 jalapeno peppers, minced
- 1 (2 inch) piece ginger root, peeled and minced
- 1 tablespoon sesame oil
- salt and ground black pepper to taste
- 3 (16 ounce) packages potsticker wrappers, or more as needed

Direction

- Lay the cilantro and cabbage on top of a clean dish towel. Gather the towel up then squeeze hard to release moisture from cabbage.
- Move the cilantro and cabbage to a bowl then add the pork, jalapeno peppers, egg whites, sesame oil, and ginger. Mix them together thoroughly using your hands then add pepper and salt to season to taste.
- Line 2 baking sheets using waxed paper. Pour water in a small bowl.
- Place a pot sticker on your palm, scoop a tablespoonful of pork filling and place it in the middle of the wrapper. Dip your finger in water and brush it on the edges of the wrapper. Seal the dumpling by folding the edges and pinching it together. Place the dumpling on the baking sheet. Do the same with the rest of the pork filling and wrappers.
- Freeze the pot stickers for 2 hours until they are firm then move them to big resealable plastic bags.

Nutrition Information

- Calories: 304 calories;
- Total Fat: 8.3
- Sodium: 426
- Total Carbohydrate: 40.6
- Cholesterol: 35
- Protein: 15.6

738. Taiwanese Spicy Beef Noodle Soup

Serving: 8 | Prep: 25mins | Cook: 8hours15mins | Ready in:

Ingredients

- 2 pounds beef stew meat, cut into 1-inch cubes
- water to cover
- 3 tablespoons vegetable oil, or more as needed
- 8 cups water, or more as needed
- 1 (14 ounce) can beef broth
- 1 cup soy sauce
- 1/2 cup rice wine
- 1 bunch green onions, cut into 2-inch pieces
- 1/4 cup brown sugar
- 10 cloves garlic, peeled, or more to taste
- 4 small chile peppers, halved and seeded, or more to taste
- 2 tablespoons chile paste

- 1 (1 1/2 inch) piece fresh ginger, peeled and cut into 5 pieces
- 3 star anise pods, or more to taste
- 1 teaspoon Chinese five-spice powder
- 4 small heads baby bok choy
- 1 (10 ounce) package udon noodles
- 1 tablespoon chopped pickled Chinese mustard greens, or to taste (optional)

Direction

- Use a stockpot to place the beef inside. Pour water into the pot enough to cover the beef. Let it boil, then transfer and drain.
- Using a slow cooker, pour vegetable into it then add in 8 cups of water, beef, beef broth, soy sauce, rice wine, brown sugar, green onions, chili paste, chili peppers, ginger, garlic, star anise, and Chinese five-spice powder.
- Let it cook for 8 to 9 hours while set to Low.
- Use a slotted spoon to remove the beef. Strain broth into a bowl, then remove the solids.
- Boil a pot of water, then cook the bok choy in for 30 seconds. After removing, use cold water to run it.
- In boiling water, add bok choy for 30 seconds. Remove and run under cold water. Cook the udon noodles for 4 minutes, just until it becomes tender yet firm to bite. Remove the water.
- Prepare the serving bowls by portioning the noodles. Serve with broth, baby bok choy, and beef. Use Chinese pickled mustard greens to garnish.

Nutrition Information

- Calories: 482 calories;
- Sodium: 2366
- Total Carbohydrate: 41.5
- Cholesterol: 63
- Protein: 27
- Total Fat: 22

739. Taiwanese Style Three Cup Chicken

Serving: 4 | Prep: 20mins | Cook: 40mins | Ready in:

Ingredients

- 1 tablespoon vegetable oil
- 1 1/2 pounds skinless, boneless chicken thighs, cut into chunks
- 1/2 cup sesame oil
- 10 slices fresh ginger
- 2 cloves garlic, sliced
- 1/2 cup dry sherry
- 1/3 cup soy sauce
- 1/4 cup water
- 3 tablespoons white sugar
- 1/2 cup fresh Thai basil leaves
- 3 dried whole red chilies

Direction

- Place a large skillet over medium-high heat, and heat vegetable oil. Stir in chicken pieces and cook for 5 minutes until lightly browned on all sides. Remove the chicken pieces from the skillet; set aside.
- Heat sesame oil and stir in garlic and ginger. Cook for 30 seconds until the ginger begins to brown. Add the reserved chicken, sugar, soy sauce, sherry, and water. Let it boil before reducing the heat to medium-low. Simmer for 20 minutes until the liquid is reduced to about 1/4 cup. Stir in chilis and basil, and adjust the heat to medium. Cook until the liquid is almost gone.

Nutrition Information

- Calories: 653 calories;
- Sodium: 1554
- Total Carbohydrate: 28.4
- Cholesterol: 108
- Protein: 33.7
- Total Fat: 44.9

740. Ten Minute Szechuan Chicken

Serving: 4 | Prep: 20mins | Cook: 10mins | Ready in:

Ingredients

- 4 boneless skinless chicken breasts, cut into cubes
- 3 tablespoons cornstarch
- 1 tablespoon vegetable oil
- 4 cloves garlic, minced
- 5 tablespoons low-sodium soy sauce
- 1 1/2 tablespoons white wine vinegar
- 1/4 cup water
- 1 teaspoon white sugar
- 3 green onions, sliced diagonally into 1/2 inch pieces
- 1/8 teaspoon cayenne pepper, or to taste

Direction

- Place the chicken in a bowl or bag and coat it with cornstarch. Put oil in a large skillet or wok and heat it over medium-high heat. Cook and stir chicken pieces and garlic until lightly browned. Add water, vinegar, sugar, and soy sauce and cover the skillet or wok. Fry for 3-5 minutes until the chicken pieces are no longer pink inside.
- Add cayenne pepper and green onion, and cook for 2 more minutes uncovered. You can serve this dish over white rice.

Nutrition Information

- Calories: 206 calories;
- Protein: 28.7
- Total Fat: 4.9
- Sodium: 745
- Total Carbohydrate: 10.1
- Cholesterol: 68

Chapter 7: Vietnamese Cuisine Recipes

***

741. Amanda's Quick Pho

Serving: 10 | Prep: 10mins | Cook: 10mins | Ready in:

Ingredients

- 3 quarts fat-free chicken broth
- 1 onion, sliced into rings
- 2 tablespoons hoisin sauce
- 1 tablespoon oyster sauce
- 1 tablespoon minced garlic
- 1/2 teaspoon ginger powder
- 1/2 teaspoon curry powder
- 1 pinch ground cinnamon
- 1 (16 ounce) package dried rice noodles
- 1 roasted chicken

Direction

- In a saucepan, combine curry, broth, ginger, onion, oyster sauce, garlic and cinnamon and hoisin sauce. Bring to a boil then lower the heat. Simmer the mixture for 5 minutes until onions have softened.
- Fill a large bowl with hot water and soak the noodles. Put aside for about 15 minutes until softened. Drain the noodles and rinse well.
- Shred the meat from roasted chicken thickly. Stir in to broth. Ladle chicken and broth over noodles.

Nutrition Information

- Calories: 283 calories;
- Cholesterol: 34

- Protein: 20.4
- Total Fat: 3.4
- Sodium: 647
- Total Carbohydrate: 40.2

742. Asian Garlic Beef Cubes (Vietnamese Bo Luc Lac Or Shaking Beef)

Serving: 6 | Prep: 30mins | Cook: 5mins | Ready in:

Ingredients

- 1 1/2 pounds beef tenderloin, cut into cubes
- Marinade:
- 2 tablespoons olive oil
- 2 tablespoons oyster sauce (such as Maekrua®)
- 4 large cloves garlic, minced, or more to taste
- 1 tablespoon Cabernet Sauvignon wine
- 1 teaspoon fish sauce
- 1 teaspoon ground black pepper, or more to taste
- 1 teaspoon soy sauce (optional)
- 1 teaspoon dark soy sauce (optional)
- 2 drops sesame oil, or more to taste
- Dipping Sauce:
- 1 tablespoon fish sauce (optional)
- 1 tablespoon lemon juice (optional)
- 1 tablespoon ground black pepper (optional)
- 2 tablespoons olive oil
- 2 tablespoons oyster sauce (such as Maekrua®)
- 4 cloves garlic, minced, or more to taste

Direction

- Place the beef cubes in a container with cover. Whisk 2 tablespoons oyster sauce, wine, 2 tablespoons olive oil, 4 minced garlic cloves, 1 teaspoon black pepper, dark soy sauce, soy sauce, sesame oil and 1 teaspoon fish sauce together in a bowl until is well blended; pour the marinade over beef. Let the beef cubes marinate for about 10 to half an hour.
- Whisk lemon juice, a tablespoon of black pepper and 1 tablespoon fish sauce in a bowl until the sauce for dipping is well combined.
- Place a wok or a large skillet over high heat. Heat 2 tablespoons of olive oil; add the beef together with the marinade. Cook beef mixture, 4 cloves minced garlic and 2 tablespoons oyster sauce together in hot oil while stirring for about 5 to 10 minutes until the sauce starts to get thick and the beef is completely cooked. Adding in garlic into the mixture over numerous times while cooking produces a better combination of flavors.
- Serve the beef with dipping sauce on side.

Nutrition Information

- Calories: 329 calories;
- Cholesterol: 60
- Protein: 17.7
- Total Fat: 26.8
- Sodium: 458
- Total Carbohydrate: 3.4

743. Authentic Oxtail Pho

Serving: 8 | Prep: 20mins | Cook: 6hours5mins | Ready in:

Ingredients

- water to cover
- 1 1/2 pounds beef oxtail, or to taste
- 2 Spanish onions, peeled, divided
- 1 tablespoon fish sauce, or to taste
- 1 tablespoon whole star anise pods
- 1 cinnamon stick
- salt to taste
- 3 tablespoons beef pho flavor paste
- 2 bunches scallions, chopped
- 1 bunch fresh cilantro, chopped

- 1 (16 ounce) package dried rice noodles, or to taste
- 1 (12 ounce) package beef pho meatballs, halved, or to taste
- 1/2 pound sirloin steak, thinly sliced, or to taste
- 1 lime, cut into 8 wedges
- 4 teaspoons white sugar, or to taste
- 1 (8 ounce) package bean sprouts
- 1 bunch Thai basil leaves, torn into bite-size pieces
- 1 (2.8 ounce) can crispy fried shallots, or to taste

Direction

- Boil a pot with water and the oxtail. Remove the oil and froth and oil off the surface. Stir in star anise, fish sauce, 1 onion, salt and cinnamon. Mix in pho flavor paste and put lid loosely to cover. Lower the heat and simmer the broth for 6 hours.
- Slice the rest of the onion in half and cut into extremely thin. Put in a bowl together with cilantro and scallions.
- Place noodles and rinse in a large bowl. Fill with warm water enough to cover the noodles and let it soak for an hour.
- Add the meatballs into the soup on the last 20 minutes of cooking.
- Place water in a small saucepan and bring to a boil. Drain the noodles and submerge for half minute into the boiling water. Divide the noodles between 8 large bowls.
- Place sliced sirloin on top of each bowl. Ladle in meatballs, broth and oxtail. Taste and spice if necessary. Squeeze 1 or 2 lime wedges into each bowl and mix in half teaspoon of sugar. Top it off with cilantro-onion mixture, shallot, basil and bean sprouts.

Nutrition Information

- Calories: 566 calories;
- Cholesterol: 92
- Protein: 30.4
- Total Fat: 18.3
- Sodium: 744
- Total Carbohydrate: 69.7

744. Authentic Pho

Serving: 4 | Prep: 20mins | Cook: 8hours | Ready in:

Ingredients

- 4 pounds beef soup bones
- 1 onion, unpeeled and cut in half
- 5 slices fresh ginger
- 1 tablespoon salt
- 2 pods star anise
- 2 1/2 tablespoons fish sauce
- 4 quarts water
- 1 (8 ounce) package dried rice noodles
- 1 1/2 pounds beef top sirloin, thinly sliced
- 1/2 cup chopped cilantro
- 1 tablespoon chopped green onion
- 1 1/2 cups bean sprouts
- 1 bunch Thai basil
- 1 lime, cut into 4 wedges
- 1/4 cup hoisin sauce (optional)
- 1/4 cup chile-garlic sauce (such as Sriracha®) (optional)

Direction

- Heat oven to 425 deg F or 220 deg C.
- Put beef bones on a cookie sheet. Roast for 1 hour in heated oven until they turn brown.
- Place onion on a cookie sheet and roast for 45 minutes in heated oven until black and soft.
- In a large stockpot, put onion, ginger, bones, fish sauce, star anise, and salt and add 4 quarts of water to cover. Heat to a boil and lower heat to low. On low, simmer 6-10 hours. Strain broth into a pot and let rest.
- In large bowl filled with water at room temperature, place rice noodles and soak 1 hour. Boil a large pot of water, and when noodles are done soaking, add them the boiling water a minute. Heat stock to simmering.

- Separate noodles between 4 serving bowls. Add cilantro, sirloin, and green onion on top. Pour the hot broth over. Stir and set aside for 1 to 2 minutes until the beef is not pink and is partly cooked. On the side, serve Thai basil, hoisin sauce, lime wedges, bean sprouts, and chile-garlic sauce.

Nutrition Information

- Calories: 509 calories;
- Sodium: 3519
- Total Carbohydrate: 65.6
- Cholesterol: 74
- Protein: 34.9
- Total Fat: 11

745. Banh Mi Burgers

Serving: 6 | Prep: 30mins | Cook: 10mins | Ready in:

Ingredients

- 1/2 cup chopped cucumber, seeded if large
- 1/4 cup thinly sliced green onion
- 1/4 cup chopped carrot
- 1/2 cup rice vinegar
- 2 tablespoons mirin (Japanese rice wine)
- 1 teaspoon white sugar
- 2 pounds ground pork
- 2 tablespoons tamari sauce
- 1 tablespoon toasted sesame oil
- 1 teaspoon mirin (Japanese rice wine)
- 1 tablespoon grated fresh ginger
- 1 tablespoon chili garlic sauce
- 1 teaspoon fish sauce
- 6 sesame seed hamburger buns
- 1 teaspoon chopped fresh basil (optional)
- 1 teaspoon chopped fresh mint (optional)

Direction

- Mix together the carrot, cucumber, 2 tablespoons of mirin, green onion, sugar and rice vinegar in a bowl until the mixture is well combined. Place in the fridge for 3 hours up to overnight.
- Put the pork in a mixing bowl, and gently combine with sesame oil, chili garlic sauce, fish sauce, tamari sauce, ginger and 1 teaspoon of mirin. Split the meat into 6 even portions, and shape each portion to a patty. Chill in the fridge for an hour.
- Set an outdoor grill for preheating to medium-high heat, and oil the grate lightly.
- Place the burgers on the grill and grill for 5 minutes each side until the outside is brown and crisp and the meat have no visible pink inside. Assemble the burger. Arrange the patty on a sesame seed bun, and pile about a quarter cup of the pickle mixture on top of the burger. Top with mint and a bit of fresh basil if preferred.

Nutrition Information

- Calories: 487 calories;
- Total Fat: 27
- Sodium: 803
- Total Carbohydrate: 26.6
- Cholesterol: 98
- Protein: 32.7

746. Banh Mi Style Vietnamese Baguette

Serving: 2 | Prep: 20mins | Cook: 25mins | Ready in:

Ingredients

- 2 portobello mushroom caps, sliced
- 2 teaspoons olive oil
- salt and pepper to taste
- 1 carrot, sliced into sticks
- 1 daikon (white) radish, sliced into sticks
- 1 cup rice vinegar
- 1/2 cup fresh lime juice
- 1/2 cup cold water

- 1/2 cup chilled lime juice
- 2 teaspoons soy sauce
- 1 teaspoon nuoc mam (Vietnamese fish sauce)
- 1/2 teaspoon toasted sesame oil
- 2 tablespoons canola oil
- 2 teaspoons minced garlic
- 1/3 cup white sugar
- 1/3 cup cold water
- 1 jalapeno pepper, thinly sliced
- 8 sprigs fresh cilantro with stems
- 1 medium cucumber, sliced into thin strips
- 2 sprigs fresh Thai basil
- 2 (7 inch) French bread baguettes, split lengthwise

Direction

- Set the oven to 450°F (230°C) for preheating. Arrange the mushrooms on a baking sheet. Drizzle with a bit of olive oil and spice up with pepper and salt. Roast the mushroom for about 25 minutes inside the prepped oven. Let it cool slightly, and cut into strips.
- Meanwhile, put a water in a saucepan and let it boil. Drop the radish sticks and carrot into the boiling water and remove after a few seconds, and submerge them in an ice water placed in a bowl to prevent the vegetables from cooking. In another bowl, stir a half cup of lime juice, rice vinegar and half cup cold water together. Place the radish and carrot to the vinegar and lime marinade and allow soaking for 15 minutes, much longer if it's convenient.
- Make the sandwich sauce: Combine together 1/3 cup water, the remaining lime juice, fish sauce, 1/3 cup sugar, sesame oil, soy sauce and canola oil, mix in a small bowl,.
- To arrange the sandwiches, drizzle a bit of a sandwich sauce on each half of the French loaves. Put the roasted mushrooms on the bottom half of each roll and drizzle with a little more sauce. Top it off with a couple sticks of carrot and radish (without the marinade), a few slices of jalapeno, basil, cilantro and cucumber. Place the other half of the bread on top to close. Serve.

Nutrition Information

- Calories: 760 calories;
- Total Fat: 22.8
- Sodium: 1282
- Total Carbohydrate: 128.4
- Cholesterol: 0
- Protein: 19.5

747. Beef Pho

Serving: 6 | Prep: 30mins | Cook: 6hours | Ready in:

Ingredients

- 5 pounds beef knuckle, with meat
- 2 pounds beef oxtail
- 1 white (daikon) radish, sliced
- 2 onions, chopped
- 2 ounces whole star anise pods
- 1/2 cinnamon stick
- 2 whole cloves
- 1 teaspoon black peppercorns
- 1 slice fresh ginger root
- 1 tablespoon white sugar
- 1 tablespoon salt
- 1 tablespoon fish sauce
- 1 1/2 pounds dried flat rice noodles
- 1/2 pound frozen beef sirloin
- TOPPINGS:
- Sriracha hot pepper sauce
- hoisin sauce
- thinly sliced onion
- chopped fresh cilantro
- bean sprouts (mung beans)
- sweet Thai basil
- thinly sliced green onion
- limes, quartered

Direction

- In a very big (9-quart of more) pot, put in beef knuckle. Season using salt then put in 2

gallons of water. Boil then cook for about 2 hours.
- Skim fat off the soup's surface. Add onions, radish, and oxtail. Tie ginger, peppercorns, cloves, cinnamon stick, and anise pods in a spice bag or cheesecloth. Add to soup. Mix in fish sauce, salt, and sugar. Simmer for at least 4 hours or more (the longer it simmer, the better) on medium-low heat. Taste when done cooking, adding salt to your preference. Strain the broth and put back in the pot to simmer. Get rid of bones and spices. Keep beef knuckle meat for another use if you want.
- Boil lightly salted water in a big pot. Soak rice noodles for about 20 minutes in water then cook for about 5 minutes in boiling water until its soft yet not mushy. Cut frozen beef to paper thin slices. It should be able to instantly cook. Put some noodles in every bowl and put several raw beef slices on top. Place boiling broth on beef and noodles into the bowl. Serve with Sriracha sauce and hoisin sauce on the side. Put lime, green onions, basil, bean sprouts, cilantro, and onion on the table to add as toppings.

748. Braised Green Beans With Fried Tofu

Serving: 4 | Prep: 20mins | Cook: 20mins | Ready in:

Ingredients

- 2 tablespoons white sugar
- 3 tablespoons soy sauce
- 1 cup dry white wine
- 1/2 cup chicken broth
- 1 (14 ounce) package tofu, drained
- salt and pepper to taste
- 1 tablespoon cornstarch
- 3 cups oil for frying, or as needed
- 1 onion, chopped
- 4 plum tomatoes, sliced into thin wedges
- 12 ounces fresh green beans, trimmed and cut into 3 inch pieces
- 1 cup bamboo shoots, drained and sliced
- 1 cup chicken broth, or as needed
- 2 tablespoons cornstarch
- 3 tablespoons water

Direction

- Stir together the soy sauce, a half cup of chicken broth, white wine and white sugar in a small bowl. Set aside the sauce.
- Pat the tofu dry using paper towels, and slice into cubes. Spice up the cubes with pepper and salt. Sprinkle a tablespoon of cornstarch all over the sides.
- Pour a little more than 1 inch of oil in a big deep skillet and heat over medium-high heat. If you are using a deep-fryer, fill to the advisable level, and heat the oil to 375°F (190°C). Once the oil is hot, add the tofu; fry until it turns golden brown on all over. Flip occasionally. Transfer to a paper towels using a slotted spoon to drain excess oil.
- Pour one tablespoon of oil in another skillet and heat over medium-high heat. Drop the onions and add the green beans; sauté for 3 to 5 minutes. Spice it off with pepper and salt. Add in the tomatoes, stir and cook for about 4 minutes until they start to break apart. Stir in the bamboo shoots to blend.
- Combine the sauce into the skillet with the beans, stir and allow boiling. Cook the mixture for 5 minutes while stirring from time to time. If the liquid begins to disperse too much, add up to a cup of chicken broth and give it a stir.
- Combine together the water and remaining 2 tablespoons of cornstarch and mix until cornstarch has dissolved. Pour the slurry into the sauce while stirring in the skillet. Simmer while gently stirring, until the sauce turns thick and clears. Add the fried tofu, and toss to coat with the sauce.

Nutrition Information

- Calories: 380 calories;

- Total Fat: 21.6
- Sodium: 699
- Total Carbohydrate: 28.2
- Cholesterol: 0
- Protein: 11.7

749. Cao Lau (Vietnamese Noodle Bowl)

Serving: 6 | Prep: 20mins | Cook: 10mins | Ready in:

Ingredients

- 2 tablespoons soy sauce
- 4 cloves garlic, minced, or more to taste
- 2 teaspoons Chinese five-spice powder
- 2 teaspoons white sugar
- 1 teaspoon paprika
- 1/4 teaspoon chicken bouillon granules
- 1 1/2 pounds pork tenderloin, cut into cubes
- 2 tablespoons vegetable oil
- 2 tablespoons water
- 2 pounds fresh thick Vietnamese-style rice noodles
- 2 cups bean sprouts
- 1 cup torn lettuce leaves
- 1 bunch green onions, chopped
- 1/4 cup fresh basil leaves
- 1/4 cup fresh cilantro leaves
- 1/4 cup crispy chow mein noodles, or more to taste

Direction

- Mix chicken bouillon, paprika, sugar, Chinese 5-spice, garlic, and soy sauce in a ceramic bowl or a big glass. Add the pork cubes then evenly coat by tossing. Use plastic wrap to cover the bowl then marinate for at least an hour in the fridge.
- Take pork out of marinade then shake off the excess. Throw out leftover marinade.
- In a big skillet or wok, heat oil on medium heat. Sauté pork for 4-7 minutes in the hot oil until its brown. Add water then sauté for another 2 minutes until pork is cooked through and water evaporates.
- Boil a big pot of water. Rinse the rice noodles in cold water and break noodles apart gently. Submerge noodles in the boiling water for about 30 seconds until half tender. Put bean sprouts in the noodles and water. Keep cooking for another 30 seconds until tender yet firm to chew. Drain.
- Mix pork mixture and noodles together in a big serving dish. Top with crispy chow mein, cilantro, basil, green onion, and lettuce on the noodles.

Nutrition Information

- Calories: 488 calories;
- Sodium: 373
- Total Carbohydrate: 78.1
- Cholesterol: 49
- Protein: 23.7
- Total Fat: 8.1

750. Caramel Coated Catfish

Serving: 4 | Prep: 15mins | Cook: 30mins | Ready in:

Ingredients

- 1/3 cup water
- 2 tablespoons fish sauce
- 2 shallots, chopped
- 4 cloves garlic, minced
- 1 1/2 teaspoons ground black pepper
- 1/4 teaspoon red pepper flakes
- 1/3 cup water
- 1/3 cup white sugar
- 2 pounds catfish fillets
- 1/2 teaspoon white sugar
- 1 tablespoon fresh lime juice
- 1 green onion, thinly sliced
- 1/2 cup chopped cilantro

Direction

- Combine fish sauce and 1/3 cup of water in a small bowl; mix and put aside. Combine together shallots, red pepper flakes, black pepper and garlic in another bowl and put aside.
- Heat 1/3 cup of sugar and 1/3 cup of water in a big skillet placed over medium heat, stirring from time to time until sugar becomes deep golden brown. Stir in the fish sauce mixture gently and let the mixture boil. Mix and cook the shallot mixture. Once the shallots have softened, add the catfish to the mixture. Cook the catfish with cover for about 5 minutes each side until the fish can be easily flake using a fork. Transfer the catfish to a large plate, place a cover, and put aside. Adjust the heat to high and mix in a half teaspoon of sugar. Stir in any sauce that left on the plate and the lime juice. Let it boil and simmer until the sauce has cooked down. Drizzle the sauce on top of the catfish and sprinkle with cilantro and green onions.

Nutrition Information

- Calories: 404 calories;
- Total Carbohydrate: 24.1
- Cholesterol: 107
- Protein: 36.8
- Total Fat: 17.4
- Sodium: 676

751. Caramelized Pork Belly (Thit Kho)

Serving: 6 | Prep: 20mins | Cook: 1hours13mins | Ready in:

Ingredients

- 2 pounds pork belly, trimmed
- 2 tablespoons white sugar
- 5 shallots, sliced
- 3 cloves garlic, chopped
- 3 tablespoons fish sauce
- ground black pepper to taste
- 13 fluid ounces coconut water
- 6 hard-boiled eggs, peeled

Direction

- Cut the pork belly into 1-inch pieces with layers of meat, fat and skin in each cut.
- Heat a pot or big wok with sugar over medium heat for about 5 minutes or until the sugar has caramelized into a light brown syrup. Put in the pork and increase the heat setting to high. Stir-fry for 3-5 minutes to render some of the pork fat.
- Add in the garlic and shallots into the wok. Put in the black pepper and fish sauce and mix well to evenly coat the pork. Mix in the coconut water and let it boil. Put in the eggs then lower the heat to low and let the pork mixture simmer for about an hour until the pork is tender.
- Remove the wok from heat and keep it warm for about 10 minutes. Remove the fat from the surface of the dish then serve.

Nutrition Information

- Calories: 410 calories;
- Cholesterol: 267
- Protein: 26.7
- Total Fat: 26.3
- Sodium: 1832
- Total Carbohydrate: 15.6

752. Cha Gio Vietnamese Egg Rolls

Serving: 12 | Prep: 45mins | Cook: 5mins | Ready in:

Ingredients

- 1 cup uncooked bean threads (cellophane noodles)
- 1 large dried shiitake mushroom
- 1 pound ground pork
- 1/2 pound shrimp, chopped
- 1 large carrot, peeled and grated
- 1 small shallot, minced
- 2 1/4 teaspoons Vietnamese fish sauce
- 1 1/4 teaspoons white sugar
- 1 1/4 teaspoons salt
- 1 1/4 teaspoons ground black pepper
- 24 egg roll wrappers
- 1 egg, beaten
- oil for deep frying

Direction

- Soak the shiitake mushroom and vermicelli in warm water for about 15 minutes until pliable; drain thoroughly and mince the mushrooms.
- Combine shiitake, carrot, shrimp, shallot, sugar, fish sauce, pepper, salt, pork and vermicelli in a big bowl. Toss them well to pull apart the pork and equally distribute the ingredients for the filling.
- Diagonally lay 1 piece of egg roll wrapper on a flat surface. Spread a little 2 tablespoons of filling across the middle of the wrapper. Fold the bottom corner over the filling, then fold in the corners to secure the filling. Brush the top corner of wrapper with egg and continue to roll to secure. Make more egg rolls using the same method.
- In a deep-fryer, large saucepan or wok, heat the oil to 350°F (175°C), or test a drop of water if it sizzle on the surface.
- Fry the egg rolls for 5 to 8 minutes until it turns golden brown. Place the rolls on paper towels to drain, or you may also use paper bags.

Nutrition Information

- Calories: 227 calories;
- Total Fat: 13.5
- Sodium: 464
- Total Carbohydrate: 13.8
- Cholesterol: 68
- Protein: 12

753. Chicken Pho

Serving: 24 | Prep: 30mins | Cook: 1hours30mins | Ready in:

Ingredients

- 10 quarts water
- 3 pounds chicken bones
- 1 whole chicken
- 1 medium onion
- 1 (1 inch) piece ginger
- 1 (32 fluid ounce) container chicken broth
- 1/4 cup rock sugar
- 3 teaspoons fish sauce
- 2 cubes pho ga soup seasoning
- 1 1/2 teaspoons salt
- 2 (16 ounce) packages rice stick noodles (banh pho)
- 1/2 pound bean sprouts
- 1 bunch green onion, chopped
- 1 bunch cilantro, chopped
- 6 sprigs Thai basil, or as needed
- 1 lime, cut in wedges

Direction

- Fill a stockpot with water and let it boil. Meanwhile, put the chicken bones under hot water and rinse to remove impurities.
- Put the bones in the pot of boiling water. Lessen the heat and simmer for about an hour until it is beginning to soften, removing any fat off the surface of the broth. Remove parboiled bones.
- Put the whole chicken into the pot and make it simmer for about 30 to 40 minutes until no visible pink color in the middle. Take the chicken out from broth and set aside, allowing it to cool. An instant-read thermometer poked near the bone should register 165°F (74°C).

- Mix together the ginger and onion in a skillet over medium-high heat. Sauté for about 7 minutes until both turns nicely browned and aromatic. Smash the ginger using the backside of a knife placed into a chopping board. Place the ginger and onion into the broth. Mix with rock sugar, pho ga seasoning, salt, fish sauce and chicken broth.
- Fill a big pot with water and let it boil. Stir in the rice noodles and boil for about 2 to 3 minutes until soft yet firm to the bite. Drain the noodles.
- Peel off the skin of the cooled chicken; get rid of the bones and skin, and set aside the meat.
- Serve the noodles in bowls and put the chicken meat and broth on top. Garnish with Thai basil, bean sprouts, cilantro and green onion. Squeeze a wedge of lime in each bowl.

Nutrition Information

- Calories: 324 calories;
- Sodium: 520
- Total Carbohydrate: 34.1
- Cholesterol: 73
- Protein: 19.9
- Total Fat: 11.1

754. Crabmeat And Asparagus Soup

Serving: 6 | Prep: 10mins | Cook: 45mins | Ready in:

Ingredients

- 1 (10 ounce) can asparagus tips, drained
- 2 (6 ounce) cans crabmeat, drained and flaked
- 2 tablespoons fish sauce
- 1 tablespoon oyster sauce
- 1 cup chopped fresh spinach
- 1 cup diced firm tofu
- 2 teaspoons dried oregano
- 1 clove garlic, crushed

Direction

- Combine the fish sauce, garlic, asparagus, tofu, crabmeat, spinach and oregano in a slow cooker. Add water enough to cover the mixture, about 2 inches. Cook on High setting with cover for 45 minutes, or until the spinach has cooked down dramatically and aromatic.

Nutrition Information

- Calories: 100 calories;
- Cholesterol: 50
- Protein: 16.2
- Total Fat: 3
- Sodium: 695
- Total Carbohydrate: 2.7

755. Day After Thanksgiving Turkey Pho

Serving: 4 | Prep: 15mins | Cook: 2hours15mins | Ready in:

Ingredients

- 1 whole cardamom pod
- 2 whole cloves
- 1 star anise pod
- 1 teaspoon fennel seeds
- 2 teaspoons coriander seed
- 1 (2 inch) piece fresh ginger, peeled and smashed
- 1/2 onion, peeled
- 1 turkey carcass
- 8 cups water, or more as needed
- 1 (16 ounce) package dried flat rice noodles
- 1/4 cup fish sauce
- salt to taste
- 1 cup shredded leftover cooked turkey
- 1 tablespoon shredded fresh basil leaves (optional)
- 1 tablespoon chopped fresh cilantro (optional)
- 1/4 onion, thinly sliced (optional)

- 1 lime, cut into wedges (optional)
- 1 tablespoon chile-garlic sauce (such as Sriracha®), or to taste (optional)

Direction

- Toast coriander, fennel, star anise, cloves, and cardamom pod in a small skillet on medium-low heat for 5-7 minutes until fragrant. Put spices onto the middle of an 8-inch square cheesecloth. Bring edges of cheesecloth together then tie using kitchen twine to make it secure. Sear ginger on both sides and half the onion for about 3 minutes per side in the same skillet until charred slightly.
- Put onion, ginger, sachet, water, and turkey carcass in a big pot on medium-high heat. Boil then bring down to simmer. Simmer it for 2 hours.
- Put a big pot full of lightly salted water to a rolling boil on high heat. When water is boiling, mix in rice noodles then boil again. Cook noodles, occasionally stirring and uncovered, for 4-5 minutes until noodles are cooked through yet firm to chew. Drain it well inside a colander in the sink.
- Take out onion, ginger, sachet, and carcass from soup. Strain soup to get rid of meat that fell of the bones if needed. Season with salt and fish sauce. Distribute turkey meat and rice noodles into 4 big bowls evenly. Scatter sliced onion, cilantro, and basil on the top. Pour soup on top. Eat with hot sauce and a lime wedge.

Nutrition Information

- Calories: 755 calories;
- Protein: 24
- Total Fat: 27.3
- Sodium: 1524
- Total Carbohydrate: 99.7
- Cholesterol: 87

756. Dragon Fruit Shake

Serving: 2 | Prep: 10mins | Cook: | Ready in:

Ingredients

- 1 dragon fruit (pitaya)
- 2 tangerines, peeled and segmented
- 1 lime, juiced
- 4 leaves fresh basil
- 2 tablespoons brown sugar
- 1 cup sparkling mineral water, chilled
- 1 cup crushed ice

Direction

- Cut two quarter inch slices thickly from peeled dragon fruit for garnishing; put aside. Combine the remaining dragon fruit, with the lime juice, brown sugar, sparkling water, tangerine segments and basil into a blender. Puree until the consistency turns smooth. Add in the crushed ice and put in each glasses. Use the reserved dragon fruit slices to garnish and serve.

Nutrition Information

- Calories: 149 calories;
- Sodium: 9
- Total Carbohydrate: 40
- Cholesterol: 0
- Protein: 1.4
- Total Fat: 0.8

757. Fried Squid With Pineapple (Muc Xao Thom)

Serving: 4 | Prep: 10mins | Cook: 10mins | Ready in:

Ingredients

- 2 tablespoons vegetable oil
- 3 cloves garlic, minced
- 1 onion, cut into wedges

- 2 pounds squid, cleaned and cut into 1/2 inch rings
- 1/2 fresh pineapple - peeled, cored and chopped
- 4 stalks celery, cut into 2 inch pieces
- 4 tablespoons fish sauce
- 1 teaspoon white sugar
- 1 teaspoon ground black pepper

Direction

- Heat oil and garlic in a big skillet on medium-high heat. Fry until garlic becomes golden brown.
- Add onion then stir fry for 1 minute. Add squid then cook until they become white, don't overcook. Add pepper, sugar, fish sauce, celery, and pineapple. Stir fry it for 2 minutes.

Nutrition Information

- Calories: 330 calories;
- Sodium: 1228
- Total Carbohydrate: 21.1
- Cholesterol: 529
- Protein: 37.2
- Total Fat: 10.1

758. Goi Cuon (Vietnamese Spring Roll With Pork And Prawns)

Serving: 6 | Prep: 45mins | Cook: 10mins | Ready in:

Ingredients

- 1/2 pound pork tenderloin, cut into thin strips
- 1/2 pound prawns, peeled and deveined
- 1/4 pound rice vermicelli noodles
- 1 (12 ounce) package rice wrappers (such as Blue Dragon®)
- 1 bunch fresh cilantro, leaves picked from stems
- 5 spring onions, cut in half
- 1/4 cup fresh mint leaves, or more to taste
- 1/4 head romaine lettuce, cut into bite-size pieces

Direction

- Place a skillet and heat over medium heat; once hot, add the pork, cook and stir for about 5 to 7 minutes until cooked well.
- Fill a pot with water and bring to a boil; stir in prawns and cook until the meat turns pink. Drain water and cut the prawns in half lengthwise.
- In big pot, add water with light salt and bring to a rolling boil. Mix in vermicelli and return to a boil. Cook the vermicelli for 2 to 4 minutes until soft yet firm to the bite. Drain.
- Put warm water in a big shallow bowl.
- Submerge the rice wrapper into the bowl of warm water for about 3 to 5 seconds until softened. Put the rice wrapper on your work surface. Allow the rice paper to soften for about half minute. Assemble the roll and place the pork, followed by a prawn half, then the vermicelli noodles, mint leaves, spring onions, cilantro and finish the layer with romaine lettuce, placing on the bottom third of the wrapper; roll it up halfway. Fold in each side and finish rolling the rest of the wrapper. Repeat with the rest of the ingredients.

Nutrition Information

- Calories: 328 calories;
- Total Carbohydrate: 56.6
- Cholesterol: 74
- Protein: 19.6
- Total Fat: 2
- Sodium: 88

759. Grilled Shrimp Rice Noodle Bowl

Serving: 2 | Prep: 25mins | Cook: 10mins | Ready in:

Ingredients

- 8 large fresh shrimp, peeled and deveined
- 3 tablespoons olive oil
- 3 cloves garlic
- 1/2 cup fresh mint
- 1/4 cup chopped fresh cilantro
- 3 tablespoons fish sauce
- 2 tablespoons honey
- 1 lime, juiced
- 1/4 teaspoon ground white pepper
- 2 tablespoons fresh ginger root, minced
- 3/4 cup shredded cabbage
- 1 (6.75 ounce) package dried rice noodles

Direction

- Heat grill for high heat. Mix white pepper, lime juice, honey, fish sauce, cilantro, 1/4 cup of mint, and garlic in a blender or food processor. Puree it until smooth.
- Boil a big pot of water. Cook cabbage and noodles until done for 2 minutes.
- As it cooks, use olive oil to coat shrimp then grill on high heat, flipping once, until golden.
- Mince leftover 1/4 cup of mint. Serve cabbage and noodles inside a bowl. Top with shrimp and sauce. Sprinkle with mint.

Nutrition Information

- Calories: 565 calories;
- Total Fat: 21.3
- Sodium: 1757
- Total Carbohydrate: 85
- Cholesterol: 44
- Protein: 10

760. Instant Pot® Beef Pho

Serving: 6 | Prep: 20mins | Cook: 53mins | Ready in:

Ingredients

- 3 pounds beef soup bones
- 3 whole cloves
- 3 whole star anise pods
- 1 (1/2 inch) piece cinnamon stick
- 1 teaspoon olive oil
- 1 large onion, chopped
- 1 (2 inch) piece ginger, peeled
- 1/2 pound chuck roast
- 2 tablespoons fish sauce
- 1 tablespoon raw sugar
- 2 teaspoons kosher salt
- 9 cups water
- 1/2 pound top round beef
- 12 ounces dry rice stick noodles
- 1/4 cup chopped cilantro
- 2 green onions, chopped

Direction

- Program a multi-functional pressure cooker like Instant Pot® to Sauté. Put in water and beef bones; cover and vigorously boil for 3 minutes. Drain and place the bones on a plate. Dry the pot and put it back in the pressure cooker.
- Set on the Sauté function, combine the cinnamon stick, star anise, and cloves at the bottom of the pressure cooker. Toast for 5 minutes until fragrant, stir once to prevent the ingredients from burning. Place the ingredients in a bowl.
- In a hot pot, heat olive oil and add the sliced ginger and onion. Cook for 10 minutes until it begins to brown, stir occasionally.
- Add sugar, beef bones, salt, fish sauce, chuck roast, and the toasted spices to the pot. Fill the pot with 9 cups of water until 3/4 full. Secure the lid and set the pressure to high as specified in the maker's instructions; cook for half an hour. Let pressure release naturally for 20 minutes.
- Take the chuck roast out of the cooker and sieve the stock in a separate pot. Get rid of the spices and bones. Place the pot on the stove and heat on low heat and cover.
- Freeze the top round for 15 minutes. In a bowl, pour warm water over the rice noodles until

sufficiently covered. Soak for 15 minutes until soft; drain.
- Take the top round out of the freezer and cut thinly against the grain. Cut the chuck roast.
- In a soup bowl, place in a little pile of rice noodles; top with green onions and cilantro. Put the chuck roast and pieces of sliced, raw top round all over the noodles. Fill the bowl with hot stock. Repeat the process for the next servings.

Nutrition Information

- Calories: 367 calories;
- Total Fat: 8.7
- Sodium: 1050
- Total Carbohydrate: 52.1
- Cholesterol: 40
- Protein: 17.5

761. Lemon Grass And Chicken Summer Rolls

Serving: 16 | Prep: 1hours | Cook: 20mins | Ready in:

Ingredients

- 2 pounds skinless, boneless chicken breast
- 2 tablespoons minced fresh ginger root
- 2 tablespoons minced fresh jalapeno chile
- 1/2 cup peeled and thinly-julienned seedless cucumber
- 1/4 cup minced fresh Thai basil leaves
- 1/4 cup minced fresh mint leaves
- 1/4 cup minced fresh cilantro
- 1 1/2 tablespoons minced lemon grass
- 1/2 cup ground peanuts
- 1/4 cup fish sauce
- 3 tablespoons lime juice
- 2 teaspoons white sugar
- 1 tablespoon sesame oil
- 1 tablespoon peanut oil
- 16 rice paper wrappers
- 16 leaves red leaf lettuce

Direction

- Put a lightly salted water in a large pot and bring to a boil. Sprinkle the chicken with salt to season and cook in the boiling water for about 7 to 10 minutes until the pink color is no longer visible in the middle. Place the chicken in a big platter and let it cool completely inside the fridge. Shred the chicken into small pieces once it can be easily handled.
- Mix together the cucumber, ginger, basil, jalapeno pepper, cilantro, lemon grass, mint, peanuts and the shredded chicken in a big mixing bowl; give it a toss until equally distributed. In a small bowl, whisk together the fish sauce, lime juice, sesame oil, peanut oil and sugar; pour it off to the chicken mixture and give it a mix with your hands until coated equally.
- Place a hot water in a shallow pan. Dip the wrappers in a hot water until it turns soft. Make sure to do this one at a time. Lay the wrapper on a clean and flat surface. Arrange a leaf of lettuce into the middle of a sheet of the rice paper; scatter about a third cup of the chicken mixture on the lettuce. Fold the bottom end part of the wrapper on top of the mixture and then roll it forming a cylinder. Repeat until the rest of the ingredients are consumed. Cut into halves and serve.

Nutrition Information

- Calories: 137 calories;
- Total Fat: 6.9
- Sodium: 301
- Total Carbohydrate: 6.5
- Cholesterol: 28
- Protein: 12.4

762. Maho, Vietnamese Chicken Recipe

Serving: 4 | Prep: 15mins | Cook: 30mins | Ready in:

Ingredients

- 2 cups uncooked white rice
- 4 cups water
- 3 tablespoons vegetable oil
- 2 cloves garlic, minced
- 3 skinless, boneless chicken breast halves - cut into bite-size pieces
- 2 tablespoons soy sauce, or to taste
- 1/2 cup dry-roasted, unsalted peanuts
- 4 large leaves of iceberg lettuce
- 1 (11 ounce) can mandarin oranges, drained

Direction

- Combine the water and rice a saucepan and bring to a boil over high heat. Adjust the heat to medium-low and cover. Simmer for 20 to 25 minutes until liquid has been absorbed and the rice has softened. Allow the rice to sit with cover while you working on the dish.
- Put the oil in the skillet and heat over medium heat until shiny. Add the garlic and sauté for a minute until it smells nice. Add in the chicken and cook about 5 minutes while stirring until it starts to brown and seared. Mix in the peanuts and soy sauce; cook for additional 5 minutes while stirring until the chicken and peanuts has coated by the soy sauce and the chicken is no longer pinkish in the inside. Take off the chicken mixture from heat.
- Arrange 4 plates with lettuce, and spoon a cup of cooked rice over each leaf. Place the chicken-peanut mixture on top, and scatter with mandarin orange slices.

Nutrition Information

- Calories: 693 calories;
- Sodium: 511
- Total Carbohydrate: 91
- Cholesterol: 50
- Protein: 31.4
- Total Fat: 22.2

763. Minh Ai's Bitter Melon Soup

Serving: 3 | Prep: 15mins | Cook: 30mins | Ready in:

Ingredients

- 1/2 pound ground pork
- 2 tablespoons soy sauce
- 1/8 teaspoon garlic powder
- 1/8 teaspoon ground black pepper
- 1 bitter melon
- 4 cups water
- 1 teaspoon soy sauce, or to taste
- 1 teaspoon fish sauce, or to taste
- 1 green onions, sliced

Direction

- Combine garlic powder, 2 tablespoons of soy sauce, pepper and pork in a bowl. Cover the bowl using a plastic wrap and place in the fridge for 30 minutes up to an hour. Slice the bitter melon thickly to 1 to 1 1/2 inches rounds. Get rid of the spongy, seeded interior with the tip of a small knife. Put the pork mixture to fill each bitter melon ring and ensure that each ring is entirely stuffed. Shape similar sized meatballs with the rest of the pork.
- Put a water in a saucepan and bring to a boil. Add in the stuffed bitter melon rings and meatballs. Simmer over medium heat for 30 to 45 minutes until the bitter melon is softened and can cut easily using a spoon. Take off from heat. Add a teaspoon of soy sauce and fish sauce for added taste and stir in green onions.

Nutrition Information

- Calories: 171 calories;
- Total Fat: 10.9
- Sodium: 873
- Total Carbohydrate: 3
- Cholesterol: 49
- Protein: 14.8

764. My Chicken Pho Recipe

Serving: 2 | Prep: 10mins | Cook: 30mins | Ready in:

Ingredients

- 4 ounces dry Chinese egg noodles
- 6 cups chicken stock
- 2 tablespoons fish sauce
- 4 cloves garlic, minced
- 2 teaspoons minced fresh ginger root
- 1 tablespoon minced lemon grass
- 5 green onions, chopped
- 2 cups cubed cooked chicken
- 1 cup bean sprouts
- 1 cup chopped bok choy

Direction

- Put a water in a big saucepan and boil over high heat. Stir in the noodles and let it boil for about 8 minutes until tender. Drain the water and set aside the noodles.
- Combine garlic, green onions, fish sauce, chicken stock, lemon grass and ginger in a large pot; bring to a boil. Lessen the heat to a simmer and cook for about 10 minutes. Mix in the chicken, bok choy and bean sprouts. Cook pho for about 5 minutes until heated through.
- Distribute the noodles among 2 big bowls. Ladle the pho over noodles and serve quickly.

Nutrition Information

- Calories: 521 calories;
- Protein: 49.8
- Total Fat: 13.7

- Sodium: 3270
- Total Carbohydrate: 54.4
- Cholesterol: 107

765. Nuoc Cham (Vietnamese Dipping Sauce)

Serving: 20 | Prep: 15mins | Cook: | Ready in:

Ingredients

- 1/4 cup white sugar
- 1/2 cup warm water
- 1/4 cup fish sauce
- 1/3 cup distilled white vinegar
- 1/2 lemon, juiced
- 3 cloves garlic, minced
- 3 Thai chile peppers, chopped
- 1 green onion, thinly sliced

Direction

- Combine the sugar and warm water together in a bowl and stir until the sugar dissolves completely; add the vinegar, fish sauce, garlic, lemon juice, green onion and Thai chile peppers to the mixture.

Nutrition Information

- Calories: 15 calories;
- Total Fat: 0
- Sodium: 220
- Total Carbohydrate: 3.7
- Cholesterol: 0
- Protein: 0.4

766. Nuoc Cham (Vietnamese Sauce)

Serving: 4 | Prep: 5mins | Cook: | Ready in:

Ingredients

- 3 tablespoons lime juice
- 2 tablespoons fish sauce, or more to taste
- 2 tablespoons white sugar, or more to taste
- 1 tablespoon water
- 1 red chile pepper, thinly sliced, or more to taste (optional)
- 1 clove garlic, thinly sliced (optional)

Direction

- Combine garlic, lime juice, water, sugar, red chile pepper and fish sauce together in a bowl. Mix to combine until well blended.

Nutrition Information

- Calories: 35 calories;
- Sodium: 549
- Total Carbohydrate: 8.7
- Cholesterol: 0
- Protein: 0.7
- Total Fat: 0.1

767. Nuoc Cham (Vietnamese Spicy Dipping Sauce)

Serving: 10 | Prep: 5mins | Cook: 5mins | Ready in:

Ingredients

- 3 1/2 fluid ounces water
- 6 spicy red chile peppers, seeded and minced
- 6 cloves garlic, minced
- 1/4 cup fish sauce
- 1/4 cup rice vinegar
- 1/4 cup white sugar
- 1/4 cup lemon juice

Direction

- Combine together the garlic, rice vinegar, water, sugar, chile peppers and fish sauce in a saucepan. Heat the mixture on medium-low heat until the sugar has dissolved; take off from heat and put aside for about an hour to cool completely.
- Mix in lemon juice into the sauce.

Nutrition Information

- Calories: 36 calories;
- Protein: 0.9
- Total Fat: 0.1
- Sodium: 441
- Total Carbohydrate: 8.7
- Cholesterol: 0

768. Nuoc Cham Sauce

Serving: 6 | Prep: 5mins | Cook: | Ready in:

Ingredients

- 2 cloves garlic, minced
- 1 teaspoon crushed red pepper flakes
- 3 tablespoons white sugar
- 2 tablespoons lime juice
- 4 tablespoons fish sauce
- 1 cup water

Direction

- Mix the fish sauce, lime juice, sugar, red pepper flakes, water and garlic in a medium bowl. Combine all the ingredients together, adjusting according to your taste. Serve the sauce with grilled lemon grass beef.

Nutrition Information

- Calories: 32 calories;
- Cholesterol: 0
- Protein: 0.6
- Total Fat: 0.1
- Sodium: 730
- Total Carbohydrate: 7.6

769. Pasta With Vietnamese Pesto

Serving: 4 | Prep: 30mins | Cook: 5mins | Ready in:

Ingredients

- 1 pound dried rice noodles
- 1 1/2 cups chopped fresh cilantro
- 1/2 cup sweet Thai basil
- 2 cloves garlic, halved
- 1/2 teaspoon minced lemon grass bulb
- 1 jalapeno pepper, seeded and minced
- 1 tablespoon vegetarian fish sauce
- 4 tablespoons chopped, unsalted dry-roasted peanuts
- 7 tablespoons canola oil
- 1/2 lime, cut into wedges
- salt and pepper to taste

Direction

- In a big bowl, soak rice noodles for half an hour in cold water. Drain noodles then put aside.
- Pesto: Combine 2 tablespoons peanuts, salt or imitation fish sauce, jalapeno peppers, lemon grass, garlic cloves, basil, and chopped cilantro in a food processor or blender. Whirl until peanuts and herbs are chopped coarsely. As machine runs, run a thin stream of oil into it. Add leftover peanuts then run machine in short spurts to coarsely chop peanuts.
- In a big skillet, put soaked rice noodles and half a cup of water on medium-high heat. Mix until majority of water absorbs and noodles become tender.
- Add nearly all the pesto and mix it well. Add several tablespoons of water if pesto begins clumping.
- Taste pasta and add more pepper, salt, imitation fish sauce, lime juice, or pesto if you want. Top pasta with leftover 2 tablespoons of peanuts then immediately serve.

Nutrition Information

- Calories: 694 calories;
- Total Fat: 29.8
- Sodium: 217
- Total Carbohydrate: 98.8
- Cholesterol: 0
- Protein: 6.8

770. Pho

Serving: 3 | Prep: 30mins | Cook: 4hours30mins | Ready in:

Ingredients

- 4 pounds bone-in beef shank
- 1 onion
- 5 slices fresh ginger root
- 1 pod star anise, whole
- 1 teaspoon salt
- 2 1/2 tablespoons fish sauce
- 1 (8 ounce) package dried rice noodles
- 1/2 pound cooked beef sirloin, thinly sliced
- 3 green onions, chopped
- 1 1/2 cups fresh bean sprouts
- 6 sprigs cilantro

Direction

- Place 3 quarts water and the beef shank in a big pot over medium heat; boil. Skim the foam and discard. Lessen the heat and simmer for about 4 hours with cover.
- Prepare the oven broiler by preheating. Put the unpeeled whole onion under broiler until tender. Remove and peel.
- Stir fish sauce, onion, salt, anise and ginger into beef mixture.
- Put a lightly salted water in a large pot and bring to a boil. Stir in the rice noodles and cook until al dente, for 8 to 10 minutes; drain the water.
- Distribute the noodles between three serving bowls. Arrange the cooked sirloin over the

pasta. Top it off with cilantro, bean sprouts and green onions equally in each bowls. Drain beef broth and distribute evenly among serving bowls, pouring over the prepped ingredients. Serve all together.

Nutrition Information

- Calories: 1100 calories;
- Total Carbohydrate: 54.7
- Cholesterol: 267
- Protein: 107.7
- Total Fat: 46.8
- Sodium: 1938

771. Pho Ga Soup

Serving: 6 | Prep: 15mins | Cook: 15mins | Ready in:

Ingredients

- 1 tablespoon vegetable oil
- 1 small yellow onion, chopped
- 1 (8 ounce) package baby bella mushrooms, chopped
- 4 cloves garlic, minced
- 8 cups water
- 1 (6.75 ounce) package rice stick noodles (such as Maifun®)
- 8 teaspoons chicken bouillon
- 2 cooked chicken breasts, shredded
- 4 green onions, chopped
- 1/3 cup chopped fresh cilantro
- 2 cups bean sprouts
- 1 lime, sliced into wedges
- 1 dash Sriracha hot sauce, or more to taste

Direction

- In a big saucepan, heat vegetable oil on medium-high heat. Sauté garlic, mushrooms, and onion for 5-10 minutes until tender. Add chicken bouillon, rice noodles, and water to the onion mixture. Boil. Bring heat down to low.
- Mix cilantro, green onions, and shredded chicken in soup. Simmer for another 5 minutes. Place soup in serving bowls then top with Sriracha hot sauce, a bit of lime juice, and bean sprouts.

Nutrition Information

- Calories: 231 calories;
- Total Fat: 5.4
- Sodium: 149
- Total Carbohydrate: 32
- Cholesterol: 28
- Protein: 13.5

772. Pickled Daikon Radish And Carrot

Serving: 4 | Prep: 20mins | Cook: | Ready in:

Ingredients

- 1/2 cup distilled white vinegar
- 1/4 cup white sugar
- 1 small carrot, peeled and cut into matchsticks
- 1 daikon radish, peeled and cut into matchsticks
- 2 tablespoons chopped fresh cilantro
- 1 Thai chile pepper, seeded and chopped

Direction

- On low heat, heat sugar and vinegar until the sugar dissolves. Take off heat then place in the refrigerator for cool. Put carrot, daikon, chile peppers, and cilantro in a glass jar. Add the cooled vinegar mixture until the vegetables are submerged; cover. Place in the refrigerator for at least 4hrs to overnight.

Nutrition Information

- Calories: 70 calories;
- Total Fat: 0.1
- Sodium: 27
- Total Carbohydrate: 17.2
- Cholesterol: 0
- Protein: 0.7

773. Roasted Pork Banh Mi (Vietnamese Sandwich)

Serving: 1 | Prep: 25mins | Cook: 7mins | Ready in:

Ingredients

- 1/4 cup julienned (2-inch matchsticks) daikon radish
- 1/4 cup julienned (2-inch matchsticks) carrots
- 1 tablespoon seasoned rice vinegar
- 1/4 cup mayonnaise
- 1 teaspoon hoisin sauce, or to taste
- 1 teaspoon sriracha hot sauce, or more to taste
- 1 crusty French sandwich roll
- 4 ounces cooked pork roast, thinly sliced
- 2 ounces smooth pate, thinly sliced
- 6 thin spears English cucumber, diced
- 6 thin slices jalapeno pepper, or more to taste
- 1/4 cup cilantro leaves

Direction

- Set the oven for preheating to 400°F. Prepare a baking sheet lined with aluminum foil.
- Mix together the carrot and julienned daikon with seasoned rice vinegar and toss to coat well. Let the mixture stand for 15 to 20 minutes until the vegetables are a bit wilted. Drain. Place inside the fridge or just set aside.
- Combine together the sriracha, hoisin sauce and mayonnaise in a small bowl.
- Slice the French roll on the side just enough to open it like a book. To accommodate the filling better, scoop out some of the bread from the top half if preferred.
- Scoop a mayo mixture and spread the interior surfaces of the roll generously. Arrange the roll placing cut side up in the prepared baking sheet. Bake inside the preheated oven for about 7 minutes until edges begins to get brown, crisp, and heated through.
- Assemble sliced pork, jalapeno, cucumber, picked daikon and carrots, pate and cilantro leaves in the roll. Cut evenly into 2 portions and serve.

Nutrition Information

- Calories: 1263 calories;
- Sodium: 1994
- Total Carbohydrate: 91.3
- Cholesterol: 188
- Protein: 54.2
- Total Fat: 75.9

774. Spicy Vietnamese Quick Pickled Vegetables

Serving: 10 | Prep: 20mins | Cook: 10mins | Ready in:

Ingredients

- 1/2 pound carrots, peeled and cut into matchsticks
- 1/2 pound purple daikon radish, peeled and cut into matchsticks
- 1/2 pound English cucumber, sliced into thin rounds
- 2 jalapeno peppers, sliced into rings
- 2 cups water
- 1 1/2 cups rice vinegar
- 2 tablespoons white sugar
- 2 teaspoons salt
-

Direction

- Examine 2 mason jars for cracks and rings for rust, get rid of any damaged ones. Submerge in simmering water till vegetables are ready.

- Use warm soapy water to rinse new, unused rings and lids.
- Distribute jalapeno peppers, cucumbers, radishes and carrots equally between 2 clean jars.
- In a medium saucepan, mix salt, sugar, vinegar and water together. Boil and cook for 3 minutes till sugar has dissolved. Switch heat off and allow to cool for 2 minutes. Put mixture on top of vegetables in jars and allow to come to room temperature, about half an hour.
- Screw on lids and chill for a minimum of 1 hour prior to serving.

Nutrition Information

- Calories: 27 calories;
- Total Carbohydrate: 6.3
- Cholesterol: 0
- Total Fat: 0.1
- Protein: 0.7
- Sodium: 487

775. Steamed Vegan Rice Cakes (Banh Bo Hap)

Serving: 12 | Prep: 10mins | Cook: 15mins | Ready in:

Ingredients

- 4 cups rice flour
- 2 cups lukewarm water
- 1 (14 ounce) can coconut milk
- 1 cup white sugar
- 4 teaspoons tapioca starch
- 1 1/2 teaspoons active dry yeast
- 1/2 teaspoon vanilla extract
- 1/4 teaspoon salt
- 2 teaspoons oil, or as needed

Direction

- Combine salt, rice flour, yeast, coconut milk, tapioca starch, vanilla extract, water and sugar together in a bowl and whisk until it turns smooth. Cover with a lid and allow the batter to rest for about 2 hours until the bubbles rise on top. Stir the mixture well.
- Grease cake molds using an oil. Put a steamer insert in a saucepan and put water just below the bottom of a steamer. Position the cake molds on top of the steamer and spoon the batter into each molds, leaving 1 3/4-inch space at the top to give a space once the batter risen. Bring water to a boil. Cover and steam for about 10 minutes. It should be done once a toothpick inserted into a cake comes out clean.

Nutrition Information

- Calories: 334 calories;
- Sodium: 54
- Total Carbohydrate: 60.8
- Cholesterol: 0
- Protein: 4
- Total Fat: 8.5

776. Stir Fry Spicy Green Beans

Serving: 4 | Prep: 15mins | Cook: 15mins | Ready in:

Ingredients

- 1/2 teaspoon vegetable oil
- 1/2 yellow onion, chopped
- 1 teaspoon minced garlic
- 1 pound fresh green beans, trimmed and halved
- 1/4 cup soy sauce
- 3 tablespoons nuoc mam (Vietnamese fish sauce)
- 1/4 cup water
- 1 medium tomato, diced
- salt and pepper to taste

Direction

- Place a skillet over medium heat and heat the oil. Stir in the garlic and onion; cook for a few minutes while mixing and add the green beans. Mix to coat with the flavors in the pan. Spice it up with fish sauce and soy sauce and let the mixture simmer for about 2 minutes while stirring from time to time. Add in the water and let it simmer until green beans have softened, for about 10 minutes. Mix in tomato and sprinkle with salt and pepper to season before serving.

Nutrition Information

- Calories: 64 calories;
- Total Fat: 0.8
- Sodium: 1732
- Total Carbohydrate: 12.4
- Cholesterol: 0
- Protein: 4.1

777. Thai Chicken Spring Rolls

Serving: 4 | Prep: 40mins | Cook: 5mins | Ready in:

Ingredients

- 1 cup peanut sauce
- 1 (1 1/2 inch) piece fresh ginger root, minced
- 2 cloves garlic, minced
- 1 teaspoon soy sauce
- 1 pound skinless, boneless chicken breast halves - cut into 1 inch pieces
- 1 teaspoon peanut oil
- 6 ounces fresh snow pea pods
- 12 ounces bean sprouts
- 4 green onion, chopped
- 1 pound watercress, chopped
- 1/4 cup chopped fresh cilantro
- 2 large carrots, peeled
- 1 teaspoon peanut oil
- 1 teaspoon soy sauce
- 12 spring roll wrappers
- 1/2 cup peanut sauce

Direction

- Combine ginger, 1 teaspoon soy sauce, garlic and a cup peanut sauce in a bowl. Add the chicken and toss the chicken to coat. Place in the fridge to marinate for half an hour.
- Set a wok or skillet over medium heat. Heat a teaspoon of peanut oil, add the bean sprouts, green onion and snow peas; cook for 3 to 4 minutes till heated yet remain crisp. Transfer to a big bowl. Stir in the cilantro and watercress. Get long slices of carrot using a vegetable peeler into the watercress mixture. Sprinkle a teaspoon of soy sauce in the watercress mixture; mix to coat.
- Heat a teaspoon of oil to the skillet or wok. Cook the marinated chicken for about 10 minutes until a color pink is no longer visible inside.
- Put a hot water on a large bowl. Submerge the wrappers one at a time for about 2 seconds each. As soon as the wrappers were taken off water, filling each wrapper with a small handful of the watercress mixture and 2 large spoonful of the chicken. Fold in two opposite ends of the wrapper to meet the filling. And fold the bottom of the wrapper on top of the filling and roll. Serve with half cup of peanut sauce for dipping.

Nutrition Information

- Calories: 595 calories;
- Sodium: 647
- Total Carbohydrate: 40.5
- Cholesterol: 71
- Protein: 46.9
- Total Fat: 30.5

778. Thit Bo Xao Dau

Serving: 4 | Prep: 10mins | Cook: 20mins | Ready in:

Ingredients

- 1 clove garlic, minced
- 1/4 teaspoon ground black pepper
- 1 teaspoon cornstarch
- 1 teaspoon vegetable oil
- 1 pound sirloin tips, thinly sliced
- 3 tablespoons vegetable oil
- 1/2 onion, thinly sliced
- 2 cups fresh green beans, washed and trimmed
- 1/4 cup chicken broth
- 1 teaspoon soy sauce

Direction

- Combine a teaspoon vegetable oil, garlic, cornstarch and black pepper in a large mixing bowl. Add the beef, and mix thoroughly.
- Heat 2 tablespoons of oil in a big wok over high heat for a minute. Add the meat; cook while stirring for about 2 minutes, or until it starts to brown. Place the beef in a large bowl, and put aside.
- Heat the remaining tablespoon oil in wok. Stir in onion and cook until softened. Add in green beans and mix; add the broth. Adjust the heat to medium. Simmer with cover for about 4 to 5 minutes, or until beans are tender crisp. Mix in soy sauce and beef. Cook while stirring from time to time, for a minute or 2, or until heated completely.

Nutrition Information

- Calories: 376 calories;
- Protein: 23.1
- Total Fat: 28.6
- Sodium: 199
- Total Carbohydrate: 6.3
- Cholesterol: 76

779. Vegetarian Pho (Vietnamese Noodle Soup)

Serving: 6 | Prep: 30mins | Cook: 1hours4mins | Ready in:

Ingredients

- Broth:
- 10 cups vegetable stock
- 1 onion, peeled and halved
- 1/4 cup soy sauce
- 8 cloves garlic, coarsely chopped
- 2 (3 inch) cinnamon sticks
- 2 teaspoons ground ginger
- 2 pods star anise
- 2 bay leaves
- Soup:
- 1 (16 ounce) package thin rice noodles (such as Thai Kitchen®)
- 2 tablespoons vegetable oil, or as needed
- 2 (14 ounce) packages firm tofu, drained and cut into 1/4-inch slices
- 8 ounces enoki mushrooms
- 4 scallions, thinly sliced
- 1/2 cup coarsely chopped cilantro
- 1 lime, cut into wedges
- 2 jalapeno peppers, sliced into rings
- 1/4 cup mung bean sprouts
- 1/4 cup Thai basil leaves, torn into bite-size pieces

Direction

- Combine star anise, onion, garlic, ground ginger, cinnamon sticks, soy sauce, bay leaves and vegetable stock in a large pot and bring to a boil. Lessen the heat and cover. Make it simmer for half an hour to 45 minutes until flavors blend together. Take away the solids using a slotted spoon and keep the broth warm.
- Place the noodles in a large bowl and pour the boiling water to cover the noodles. Set aside for about 8 to 10 minutes until noodles are

tender. Drain the noodles and rinse well. Distribute the noodles between 6 serving bowls.
- In a large skillet, pour the oil and heat over medium-high heat until shimmering. Fry tofu in a single layer, cooking in batches for about 6 minutes per side until turns golden brown.
- Simmer mushrooms and fried tofu for about 5 minutes in broth until heated completely. Place to serving bowls. Top it off with cilantro and scallions and spoon in hot broth.
- Serve alongside the basil, jalapeno peppers, lime wedges and bean sprouts for garnishing each bowl.

Nutrition Information

- Calories: 483 calories;
- Sodium: 1209
- Total Carbohydrate: 77.7
- Cholesterol: 0
- Protein: 16.6
- Total Fat: 12.6

780. Vermicelli Noodle Bowl

Serving: 2 | Prep: 35mins | Cook: 25mins | Ready in:

Ingredients

- 1/4 cup white vinegar
- 1/4 cup fish sauce
- 2 tablespoons white sugar
- 2 tablespoons lime juice
- 1 clove garlic, minced
- 1/4 teaspoon red pepper flakes
- 1/2 teaspoon canola oil
- 2 tablespoons chopped shallots
- 2 skewers
- 8 medium shrimp, with shells
- 1 (8 ounce) package rice vermicelli noodles
- 1 cup finely chopped lettuce
- 1 cup bean sprouts
- 1 English cucumber, cut into 2-inch matchsticks
- 1/4 cup finely chopped pickled carrots
- 1/4 cup finely chopped diakon radish
- 3 tablespoons chopped cilantro
- 3 tablespoons finely chopped Thai basil
- 3 tablespoons chopped fresh mint
- 1/4 cup crushed peanuts

Direction

- In a small bowl, combine red pepper flakes, vinegar, garlic, fish sauce, lime juice, and sugar; set aside.
- On medium heat, heat vegetable oil in a small pan. Cook and stir in shallots for 8 mins until soft and a bit caramelized.
- Set the outdoor grill on medium heat; grease the grate lightly. On each skewer, spike four shrimps; grill for 1-2 mins on each side until pink and the outsides are charred. Set aside.
- Boil a big pot of water. Cook vermicelli noodles for 12 mins until soft; drain and rinse the vermicelli with cold water. Stir to detach the noodles.
- To make the vermicelli bowl, put the noodles in one side of every serving bowl. Place bean sprouts and lettuce on the other side. Add caramelized shallots, cucumbers, peanuts, carrots, mint, daikon, Thai basil, and cilantro on top. Serve vermicelli bowls with sauce on the side; top with shrimp skewers. Drizzle sauce on top and toss to coat.

Nutrition Information

- Calories: 659 calories;
- Total Fat: 12.8
- Sodium: 2565
- Total Carbohydrate: 112.3
- Cholesterol: 36
- Protein: 26.2

781. Vietnamese Aromatic Lamb Chops

Serving: 5 | Prep: 10mins | Cook: 20mins | Ready in:

Ingredients

- 15 (3 ounce) lamb loin chops (1-inch thick)
- 2 cloves garlic, sliced
- 1 teaspoon garlic powder, or to taste
- 1 pinch chili powder
- 2 tablespoons white sugar
- freshly ground black pepper to taste
- 1 tablespoon fresh lime juice
- 1 tablespoon soy sauce
- 2 tablespoons olive oil
- 1/4 cup chopped fresh cilantro
- 2 lime wedges
- 2 lemon wedges

Direction

- Arrange the lamb chops in a roasting pan and spice it up evenly with the chili powder, garlic, pepper, garlic powder, salt and sugar. Sprinkle with a tablespoon of lime juice, olive oil and soy sauce. Chill in the fridge with cover overnight.
- Set the oven for preheating to 400°F (200°C). While preheating, let the lamb sit at room temperature.
- Remove the cover and allow to roast in the preheated oven to your preferred degree of doneness, about 20 minutes for medium, or half an hour for well done. Squeeze a lemon and lime juice over and top with cilantro before serving.

Nutrition Information

- Calories: 555 calories;
- Total Fat: 40.4
- Sodium: 301
- Total Carbohydrate: 7.4
- Cholesterol: 151
- Protein: 38.6

782. Vietnamese Beef And Lettuce Curry

Serving: 4 | Prep: 15mins | Cook: 45mins | Ready in:

Ingredients

- 1 cup uncooked long grain white rice
- 2 cups water
- 5 teaspoons white sugar
- 1 clove garlic, minced
- 1/4 cup fish sauce
- 5 tablespoons water
- 1 1/2 tablespoons chile sauce
- 1 lemon, juiced
- 2 tablespoons vegetable oil
- 3 cloves garlic, minced
- 1 pound ground beef
- 1 tablespoon ground cumin
- 1 (28 ounce) can canned diced tomatoes
- 2 cups lettuce leaves, torn into 1/2 inch wide strips

Direction

- Put the water and rice on a pot and bring to a boil. Adjust the heat to low and simmer with cover for about 25 minutes.
- Combine 1 clove garlic and sugar and mash with a pestle. Stir in the water, fish sauce, lemon juice and chile sauce.
- Place a wok over high heat and heat the oil and immediately sauté the 3 cloves of garlic. Add the beef and sprinkle with cumin to taste; continue to cook until browned evenly. Pour about half of the fish sauce mixture and tomatoes. Adjust the heat to low, and simmer for about 20 minutes until it gets thick.
- Stir the lettuce in the beef mixture. Serve once on top of the cooked rice alongside the rest of the fish sauce mixture.

Nutrition Information

- Calories: 529 calories;

- Total Fat: 21
- Sodium: 1481
- Total Carbohydrate: 56.9
- Cholesterol: 69
- Protein: 26.3

783. Vietnamese Beef Noodle Soup

Serving: 4 | Prep: 30mins | Cook: 15mins | Ready in:

Ingredients

- 4 ounces dried rice noodles
- 6 cups cold water
- 3 (10.5 ounce) cans condensed beef broth
- 1 teaspoon chopped fresh ginger root
- 1/2 teaspoon kosher salt
- 1 Thai chile, chopped
- 1/2 pound boneless top round steak, sliced very thin
- 1/4 pound fresh basil
- 4 tablespoons snipped fresh cilantro
- 1/4 pound mung bean sprouts
- 4 green onions, thinly sliced
- 4 wedges lime
- hot pepper sauce (optional)
- oyster sauce (optional)

Direction

- In cold water, soak noodles for 30 minutes then drain. Boil water in a big pot. Add the noodles then boil for 3-5 minutes without overcooking. Drain and rinse under cold water. Put aside.
- As that happens, mix ginger, Thai pepper, salt, and beef broth in a saucepan. Boil then simmer for 15 minutes.
- Put even portions of noodles in 4 big soup bowls. Put raw beef over it. Place hot broth over beef and noodles. Garnish with green onions, mung beans, cilantro, basil leaves, and lime wedges. Eat with oyster sauce and hot pepper sauce.

Nutrition Information

- Calories: 258 calories;
- Total Fat: 5.8
- Sodium: 2160
- Total Carbohydrate: 30.9
- Cholesterol: 43
- Protein: 20.9

784. Vietnamese Beef Pho

Serving: 6 | Prep: 10mins | Cook: 1hours20mins | Ready in:

Ingredients

- 4 quarts beef broth
- 1 large onion, sliced into rings
- 6 slices fresh ginger root
- 1 lemon grass
- 1 cinnamon stick
- 1 teaspoon whole black peppercorns
- 1 pound sirloin tip, cut into thin slices
- 1/2 pound bean sprouts
- 1 cup fresh basil leaves
- 1 cup fresh mint leaves
- 1 cup loosely packed cilantro leaves
- 3 fresh jalapeno peppers, sliced into rings
- 2 limes, cut into wedges
- 2 (8 ounce) packages dried rice noodles
- 1/2 tablespoon hoisin sauce
- 1 dash hot pepper sauce
- 3 tablespoons fish sauce

Direction

- Mix peppercorns, cinnamon, lemon grass, ginger, onion, and broth in a big soup pot. Boil, reduce the heat, then cover. Simmer for an hour.
- Place cilantro, basil, mint, and bean sprouts onto a platter with lime and chilies.

- Soak noodles for 15 minutes in hot water, covering the noodles, until soft. Drain. Put even noodle portions in 6 big soup bowls then put raw beef on the top. Place hot broth on beef and noodles. Pass along the platter with sauces and garnishes.

Nutrition Information

- Calories: 528 calories;
- Total Fat: 13.6
- Sodium: 2844
- Total Carbohydrate: 73.1
- Cholesterol: 51
- Protein: 27.1

785. Vietnamese Beef And Red Cabbage Bowl

Serving: 4 | Prep: 25mins | Cook: 5mins | Ready in:

Ingredients

- 1 head red cabbage
- 1 red onion, halved
- 3 tablespoons canola oil, divided
- 1 pound lean ground beef
- 1 red Fresno chile pepper, sliced very thinly
- 2 teaspoons paprika
- 1 teaspoon kosher salt
- 2 tablespoons lime juice
- 1 tablespoon fish sauce
- 1 teaspoon packed brown sugar
- 1/2 teaspoon grated lime zest
- 1/2 cup chopped fresh cilantro
- 1/4 cup chopped fresh mint
- 1 lime, cut into wedges

Direction

- Halve the cabbage on a flat surface. Empty one half of the core and most of the leaves inside to act as a bowl. Thinly slice the other half.

- Chop half of the red onion finely and the other half thinly.
- Place a large skillet over medium heat then heat a tablespoon of canola oil. Stir in the chopped onion, ground beef, paprika, salt and Fresno chile. Cook the beef for 5 to 7 minutes and break it up while stirring from time to time, until the beef is crumbly and had turned brown.
- Whisk the fish sauce, lime zest, remaining oil, lime juice and brown sugar together in a small bowl. Pour into the beef mixture and stir to combine well. Spoon the heated mixture in the cabbage bowl. Top it off with the sliced onion, sliced cabbage, mint and cilantro. Serve alongside lime wedges.

Nutrition Information

- Calories: 410 calories;
- Protein: 23.8
- Total Fat: 26.6
- Sodium: 878
- Total Carbohydrate: 22.5
- Cholesterol: 68

786. Vietnamese Caramelized Pork

Serving: 4 | Prep: 15mins | Cook: 20mins | Ready in:

Ingredients

- 1 tablespoon vegetable oil
- 1 cup white sugar
- 2 pounds pork spareribs, cut into 1-inch pieces
- 2 green onions, cut in 2-inch lengths
- 1 green chile pepper, chopped
- 1 teaspoon ground black pepper
- 2 shallots, finely chopped
- 2 cloves garlic, minced
- salt to taste
- 1 teaspoon Asian (toasted) sesame oil

- 1 tablespoon green onion, thinly sliced and separated into rings

Direction

- Set a large heavy skillet or wok over high heat, add the oil into the pan and the sugar over the oil. Cook while stirring continuously until the sugar has dissolved and light brown in color. Take note that the melted sugar is very hot, so be careful. Add in 2 green onions, pork, shallots, chile pepper, black pepper, salt and garlic. Stir to toss them in the caramelized sugar until the pork is golden brown. Pour the sesame oil on top of the vegetables and pork, adjust the heat to low, and allow to simmer to lessen the juices.
- Once the most of the juices were absorbed, adjust the heat to high. Cook and stir the vegetables and pork for about 5 minutes until the sauce thickens and coated the pork. Garnish with a tablespoon of green onion rings over.

Nutrition Information

- Calories: 657 calories;
- Protein: 29.9
- Total Fat: 34.7
- Sodium: 98
- Total Carbohydrate: 56.8
- Cholesterol: 120

787. Vietnamese Chicken Cabbage Salad

Serving: 6 | Prep: 15mins | Cook: | Ready in:

Ingredients

- 1 head cabbage, cored and shredded
- 2 onions, halved and thinly sliced
- 2 cups shredded, cooked chicken breast
- 1/4 cup olive oil
- salt and pepper to taste
- 3 tablespoons lemon juice, or to taste

Direction

- In a big bowl, stir together the chicken, cabbage and onions. Drizzle with olive oil and toss to coat everything lightly. Sprinkle with salt and pepper to taste. Keep on tossing while pouring lemon juice. Add enough lemon juice so you can taste it in every bite. Refrigerate, covered, for at least 4 hours then serve. Keep it chilled for a longer time so the flavors have more time to blend, giving an even better taste.

Nutrition Information

- Calories: 231 calories;
- Total Fat: 12.7
- Sodium: 66
- Total Carbohydrate: 15.5
- Cholesterol: 35
- Protein: 15.7

788. Vietnamese Chicken Salad

Serving: 4 | Prep: 30mins | Cook: | Ready in:

Ingredients

- 1 tablespoon finely chopped green chile peppers
- 1 tablespoon rice vinegar
- 2 tablespoons fresh lime juice
- 3 tablespoons Asian fish sauce
- 3 cloves garlic, minced
- 1 tablespoon white sugar
- 1 tablespoon Asian (toasted) sesame oil
- 2 tablespoons vegetable oil
- 1 teaspoon black pepper
- 2 cooked skinless boneless chicken breast halves, shredded

- 1/2 head cabbage, cored and thinly sliced
- 1 carrot, cut into matchsticks
- 1/3 onion, finely chopped
- 1/3 cup finely chopped dry roasted peanuts
- 1/3 cup chopped fresh cilantro

Direction

- Combine the sugar, lime juice, chopped green chiles, sesame oil, fish sauce, garlic, vegetable oil, rice vinegar and black pepper together. Stir until the sugar has dissolved and the mixture is thoroughly blended.
- Put the carrot, peanuts, cabbage, onion, cilantro and chicken in a salad bowl, and toss well together using the tongs. Drizzle the dressing over the salad and toss to coat again. Serve quickly.

Nutrition Information

- Calories: 303 calories;
- Sodium: 991
- Total Carbohydrate: 19.3
- Cholesterol: 37
- Protein: 19.2
- Total Fat: 17.9

789. Vietnamese Chicken And Long Grain Rice Congee

Serving: 4 | Prep: 10mins | Cook: 2hours | Ready in:

Ingredients

- 1/8 cup uncooked jasmine rice
- 1 (2.5 pound) whole chicken
- 3 (2 inch) pieces fresh ginger root
- 1 stalk lemon grass, chopped
- 1 tablespoon salt, or to taste
- 1/4 cup chopped cilantro
- 1/8 cup chopped fresh chives
- ground black pepper to taste
- 1 lime, cut into 8 wedges

Direction

- Put the chicken in a stock pot and place enough water to cover the chicken. Drop the lemon grass, salt and ginger; bring to a boil. Lessen the heat and gently simmer with cover for an hour to 1 1/2 hours.
- Strain the broth, and place back the broth to stock pot. Allow the chicken cool, debone and remove the skin, and pull apart into bite-size pieces; put aside.
- Stir in rice in the broth, and bring to a boil. Adjust the heat to medium, and cook for about half an hour while stirring from time to time. If needed, adjust with additional salt or water. The congee is done, but you can leave it to cook 45 minutes more for better consistency.
- Pour congee using the ladle into each bowls, and place with chicken, chives, pepper and cilantro on top. Squeeze lime juice to season.

Nutrition Information

- Calories: 642 calories;
- Total Fat: 42.3
- Sodium: 1943
- Total Carbohydrate: 9.8
- Cholesterol: 210
- Protein: 53

790. Vietnamese Coffee

Serving: 1 | Prep: 10mins | Cook: | Ready in:

Ingredients

- 2 tablespoons sweetened condensed milk, or more to taste
- 2/3 cup strong brewed coffee
- 1 teaspoon non-dairy creamer (such as Coffee-Mate®), or more to taste
- 1 teaspoon hot cocoa mix (such as Godiva®), or more to taste (optional)

Direction

- Add in a glass some boiling water. Leave to sit for 1 minute to warm the glass. Remove water. Into the warmed class, add condensed milk and coffee on top. Stir in hot cocoa mix and creamer.

Nutrition Information

- Calories: 158 calories;
- Total Fat: 5.1
- Sodium: 65
- Total Carbohydrate: 26.1
- Cholesterol: 13
- Protein: 3.4

791. Vietnamese Crispy Fish

Serving: 4 | Prep: 15mins | Cook: 16mins | Ready in:

Ingredients

- 2 (1 pound) whole red snapper
- sea salt to taste
- 1/4 cup vegetable oil, divided
- 6 tomatoes, seeded and coarsely chopped
- 2 bird's eye chiles, seeded and finely sliced
- 3 cloves garlic, chopped
- 6 tablespoons water
- 2 tablespoons Asian fish sauce (nam pla)
- 1 tablespoon palm sugar
- 2 green onions, chopped
- 2 tablespoons coarsely chopped cilantro
- 1 teaspoon cornstarch

Direction

- Chop off the heads of each of the snappers and slice incisions through the skin on both sides of the snapper; season it with sea salt.
- In a big skillet, put in 2 tablespoons of vegetable oil and heat over medium heat setting. Put in the scored snapper and cook for 6-8 minutes on every side until you could flake the fish meat apart with ease using a fork and the skin turns crispy and brown in color. Put the cooked snapper onto a serving platter and put the skillet back onto the stove.
- Put the chiles, remaining oil, garlic and tomatoes into the same skillet and cook for 2-3 minutes over high heat setting until the tomatoes have softened. Put in the fish sauce, palm sugar and water and allow the mixture to simmer for 1-2 minutes until the mixture has reduced a little bit in volume. Add in the cilantro, cornstarch and green onions and mix everything together; let the mixture simmer for about 1 more minute until it has reduced in volume and has a sticky texture. Serve the cooked snapper with the prepared sauce drizzled on top.

Nutrition Information

- Calories: 401 calories;
- Sodium: 740
- Total Carbohydrate: 12.8
- Cholesterol: 82
- Protein: 48.3
- Total Fat: 17

792. Vietnamese Dipping Sauce

Serving: 16 | Prep: 5mins | Cook: | Ready in:

Ingredients

- 1 cup fish sauce
- 3/4 cup rice vinegar
- 3 tablespoons water
- 1/2 cup white sugar
- 1/2 teaspoon garlic powder
- 1 dried red chile pepper, seeded and thinly sliced

Direction

- Combine the water, fish sauce, garlic powder, sugar, chile pepper and rice vinegar in a medium bowl. Stir until the sugar has dissolved. Check for taste to ensure the spicy, sweet, salty and sour flavors are balanced and adjust the spice if needed. Place into bottles; cover and seal the lids.

Nutrition Information

- Calories: 30 calories;
- Cholesterol: 0
- Protein: 0.7
- Total Fat: 0
- Sodium: 1094
- Total Carbohydrate: 6.9

793. Vietnamese Eggplant With Spicy Sauce

Serving: 2 | Prep: 25mins | Cook: 11mins | Ready in:

Ingredients

- 3 tablespoons vegetable oil, divided
- 1 white eggplant, sliced
- 3 tablespoons minced lemongrass
- 1 tablespoon crushed garlic
- 1 tablespoon chopped green onion
- 1 tablespoon chopped fresh basil
- 1 teaspoon minced red chile pepper
- 1 teaspoon minced fresh ginger
- 1 tablespoon oyster sauce
- 1 teaspoon white sugar

Direction

- Put a tablespoon of oil in a skillet placed over medium heat. Drop the eggplant and let it cook for 3 to 5 minutes per side until it turns golden brown and soft, but not mushy.
- Combine remaining 2 tablespoons oil, red chile, garlic, basil, green onion, ginger and lemongrass and stir together in a bowl. Pour the mixture over eggplant in the skillet. Cook for about 3 minutes until green onion wilts. Mix in sugar and oyster sauce; cook for 2 to 3 minutes until flavors blend. Remove the skillet off the heat.

Nutrition Information

- Calories: 273 calories;
- Total Fat: 21.2
- Sodium: 62
- Total Carbohydrate: 21.6
- Cholesterol: 0
- Protein: 3.3

794. Vietnamese Fresh Spring Rolls

Serving: 8 | Prep: 45mins | Cook: 5mins | Ready in:

Ingredients

- 2 ounces rice vermicelli
- 8 rice wrappers (8.5 inch diameter)
- 8 large cooked shrimp - peeled, deveined and cut in half
- 1 1/3 tablespoons chopped fresh Thai basil
- 3 tablespoons chopped fresh mint leaves
- 3 tablespoons chopped fresh cilantro
- 2 leaves lettuce, chopped
- 4 teaspoons fish sauce
- 1/4 cup water
- 2 tablespoons fresh lime juice
- 1 clove garlic, minced
- 2 tablespoons white sugar
- 1/2 teaspoon garlic chili sauce
- 3 tablespoons hoisin sauce
- 1 teaspoon finely chopped peanuts

Direction

- Boil water in a medium saucepan. Boil the rice vermicelli for 3-5 minutes or until al dente. Drain.

- In a big bowl, fill with warm water. Dip a wrapper in hot water to soften for a second. Lay the wrapper flat. Put lettuce, cilantro, mint, basil, a handful of vermicelli, and 2 shrimp halves into a row across the middle. Leave about 2 inches on each side uncovered. Fold the uncovered sides going in, then roll wrapper tightly, starting at the end with lettuce. Repeat process with the rest of the ingredients.
- Mix chili sauce, sugar, garlic, lime juice, water, and fish sauce in a small bowl.
- Mix peanuts and hoisin sauce in a separate small bowl.
- Serve the spring rolls with hoisin sauce mixtures and fish sauce mixtures.

Nutrition Information

- Calories: 82 calories;
- Total Fat: 0.7
- Sodium: 305
- Total Carbohydrate: 15.8
- Cholesterol: 11
- Protein: 3.3

795. Vietnamese Golden Chicken Wings

Serving: 4 | Prep: 15mins | Cook: 30mins | Ready in:

Ingredients

- 12 chicken wings, tips removed and wings cut in half at joint
- 2 cloves cloves garlic, peeled and coarsely chopped
- 1/2 onion, cut into chunks
- 1/4 cup soy sauce
- 1/4 cup Asian fish sauce
- 2 tablespoons fresh lemon juice
- 2 tablespoons sesame oil
- 1 teaspoon salt
- 1 teaspoon freshly ground black pepper
- 1 tablespoon garlic powder
- 1 tablespoon white sugar

Direction

- Put the onion, garlic and chicken wings in a large bowl. Mix in fish sauce, lemon juice, sesame oil and soy sauce. Spice it up with garlic powder, salt, sugar and pepper; mix together and toss until well coated. Cover the bowl and put in the fridge for about 2 hours up to overnight.
- Set the oven for preheating to 200°C (400°F.) Prepare a 9x13 inches baking dish and line with aluminum foil.
- Take away the wings from the marinade, keeping the extra. Assemble wings in a single layer on the bottom of baking pan. Place inside the preheated oven and bake for roughly 30 minutes, flipping once and brushing with the reserved marinade. Bake until deep golden brown and until meat juices run clear.

Nutrition Information

- Calories: 716 calories;
- Protein: 53
- Total Fat: 50.9
- Sodium: 2781
- Total Carbohydrate: 9.1
- Cholesterol: 213

796. Vietnamese Grilled Lemongrass Chicken

Serving: 4 | Prep: 10mins | Cook: 10mins | Ready in:

Ingredients

- 2 tablespoons canola oil
- 2 tablespoons finely chopped lemongrass
- 1 tablespoon lemon juice
- 2 teaspoons soy sauce
- 2 teaspoons light brown sugar

- 2 teaspoons minced garlic
- 1 teaspoon fish sauce
- 1 1/2 pounds chicken thighs, or more to taste, pounded to an even thickness

Direction

- Mix canola oil, fish sauce, lemon juice, brown sugar, garlic, lemongrass and soy sauce in a mixing bowl until the sugar has dissolve; add chicken in the marinade and flip to coat.
- Let the chicken marinate in the fridge for 20 minutes up to an hour.
- Set grill to medium heat for preheating and grease the grate lightly.
- Take off the chicken thighs from the marinade and shake to get rid of excess marinade. Dispose the remaining marinade.
- Grill the chicken for about 3 to 5 minutes each side until it's' juices run clear and the pinkish color in the middle is no longer visible. An instant-read thermometer poked in the middle should reach 165°F (74°C).

Nutrition Information

- Calories: 308 calories;
- Cholesterol: 105
- Protein: 29
- Total Fat: 19
- Sodium: 339
- Total Carbohydrate: 3.9

797. Vietnamese Grilled Pork Skewers

Serving: 6 | Prep: 30mins | Cook: 8mins | Ready in:

Ingredients

- 1 pound pork belly, cubed
- 1 fresh red chile pepper, minced
- 3 stalks lemongrass, minced
- 3 tablespoons fish sauce
- 3 cloves garlic, minced, or more to taste
- 1 teaspoon monosodium glutamate (MSG)
- 1 teaspoon white sugar
- 1 teaspoon Chinese five-spice powder
- bamboo skewers
- Dipping Sauce:
- 1/4 cup fish sauce
- 1/4 cup white sugar
- 1 fresh red chile pepper, minced, or more to taste
- 1 lime, juiced
- 5 cloves garlic, minced, or more to taste
- 1 teaspoon monosodium glutamate (MSG), or to taste
- 1 cup water

Direction

- In a bowl, mix together pork belly, lemongrass, 1 red chile pepper, 3 cloves garlic, 3 tablespoons fish sauce, 1 teaspoon each of white sugar and MSG, and five-spice powder. Cling wrap and marinate in the refrigerator for 1 to 3 hours.
- Take another bowl and mix together lime juice, 1/4 cup fish sauce, 1/4 cup sugar, 5 cloves garlic, 1 teaspoon MSG, and 1 red chile pepper. Let the flavors come together for half to a full hour, then pour in water.
- Take the pork belly and thread them onto skewers.
- Set grill on high to pre-heat and grease the grates lightly. Grill, turning occasionally, for 8-10 minutes or until crisp. Serve with sauce on the side.

Nutrition Information

- Calories: 204 calories;
- Protein: 10.8
- Total Fat: 10.6
- Sodium: 2020
- Total Carbohydrate: 16
- Cholesterol: 27

798. Vietnamese Iced Coffee

Serving: 4 | Prep: 5mins | Cook: 5mins | Ready in:

Ingredients

- 4 cups water
- 1/2 cup dark roast ground coffee beans
- 1/2 cup sweetened condensed milk
- 16 ice cubes

Direction

- Brew the coffee added with water using your desired method to make a brewed coffee. Scoop 2 tablespoons of condensed milk (sweetened) in every of the 4 coffee cups. Pour a cup of freshly brewed coffee on each cup, and stir to blend the milk.
- Give your guests cups of coffee, and serve each one a tall glass filled with 4 ice cubes, and a spoon with a long handle. Guests can pour out the hot coffee on top of the ice cubes and stir quickly with the spoon, making the drink a pleasant clash with the ice cubes to get the coffee chill.

Nutrition Information

- Calories: 129 calories;
- Total Carbohydrate: 22
- Cholesterol: 13
- Protein: 3.3
- Total Fat: 3.3
- Sodium: 64

799. Vietnamese Lemon Grass Chicken Curry

Serving: 4 | Prep: 15mins | Cook: 25mins | Ready in:

Ingredients

- 2 tablespoons vegetable oil
- 1 lemon grass, minced
- 1 (3 pound) whole chicken, cut into pieces
- 2/3 cup water
- 1 tablespoon fish sauce
- 1 1/2 tablespoons curry powder
- 1 tablespoon cornstarch
- 1 tablespoon chopped cilantro (optional)

Direction

- Prepare a skillet over medium heat. Heat the vegetable oil and stir in the lemon grass for 3 to 5 minutes until aromatic. Add the chicken and cook for about 10 minutes while stirring the chicken until no longer pink in the middle and the skin turns brown. Mix in the water, curry powder and fish sauce. Adjust heat to high; bring to a boil. Lessen the heat and simmer for about 10 to 15 minutes.
- Combine 2 tablespoons of the curry sauce and cornstarch in a small bowl and stir until smooth. Mix cornstarch mixture into the skillet and make it simmer for about 5 minutes until sauce turns thick. Top it off with cilantro before serving.

Nutrition Information

- Calories: 813 calories;
- Total Carbohydrate: 4.6
- Cholesterol: 255
- Protein: 63.8
- Total Fat: 58.4
- Sodium: 515

800. Vietnamese Meatballs

Serving: 6 | Prep: 20mins | Cook: 35mins | Ready in:

Ingredients

- 1 1/2 pounds ground chicken
- 1 clove garlic, minced

- 1 egg white
- 1 tablespoon rice wine
- 2 tablespoons soy sauce
- 1/2 teaspoon Worcestershire sauce
- 2 teaspoons fish sauce
- 1/2 teaspoon white sugar
- salt and white pepper to taste
- 2 tablespoons cornstarch
- 1 tablespoon sesame oil

Direction

- Set the oven's broiler for preheating.
- Combine the Worcestershire sauce, fish sauce, garlic, rice wine, pepper, sugar, cornstarch, sesame oil, salt, soy sauce, egg white and ground chicken and mix together in a large bowl,.
- Shape the mixture into small round balls, and thread on a skewer 3 or 4 at a time. Arrange on a broiling rack or baking sheet.
- Cook and broil for about 15 to 20 minutes, flipping it from time to time, until completely cooked.

Nutrition Information

- Calories: 184 calories;
- Cholesterol: 69
- Protein: 26.5
- Total Fat: 5.9
- Sodium: 497
- Total Carbohydrate: 4.1

801. Vietnamese Pho Ga (Chicken)

Serving: 8 | Prep: 15mins | Cook: 46mins | Ready in:

Ingredients

- 1 (16 ounce) package 1/4-inch thick dried rice noodles
- 1 whole chicken
- 1 (2 inch) piece peeled ginger
- 2 whole star anise
- 1/2 teaspoon monosodium glutamate (MSG) (optional)
- 2 teaspoons salt
- water to cover

Direction

- Soak the noodles in a cold water; cover and set aside for 30 minutes.
- Put the star anise, chicken, monosodium glutamate and ginger together in a big pot. Add the salt and fill with water enough to cover the chicken. Cook on medium heat for 40 minutes until juices run clear. An inserted instant-read thermometer to the thickest portion of the thigh, near the bone should register 165°F (74°C).
- Take out the chicken from pot and let it cool for about 15 to 20 minutes until easily handled. Remove the chicken skin and shred its' meat.
- Drain the noodles. Put water on a large pot and bring to a boil. Cook for 1 to 2 minutes while stirring occasionally in boiling water until noodles are soft yet firm to the bite. Drain the noodles and distribute among serving bowls.
- Place the shredded meat on top and ladle in broth.

Nutrition Information

- Calories: 373 calories;
- Protein: 17.7
- Total Fat: 11.4
- Sodium: 761
- Total Carbohydrate: 47
- Cholesterol: 46

802. Vietnamese Pickled Daikon Radish And Carrots

Serving: 10 | Prep: 15mins | Cook: | Ready in:

Ingredients

- 4 cups warm water
- 3/4 cup rice vinegar
- 3 tablespoons sugar
- 2 tablespoons salt
- 1/2 pound carrots, julienned
- 1/2 pound daikon radish, julienned

Direction

- Combine salt, water, sugar and vinegar in a bowl. Mix until sugar and salt dissolves.
- Put the daikon and carrots and in a sterilized jar. Fill vinegar mixture over, enough to completely cover the vegetables. Seal the jar tightly and put in the fridge for at least a day, preferably up to 3 days.

Nutrition Information

- Calories: 28 calories;
- Total Carbohydrate: 6.9
- Cholesterol: 0
- Total Fat: 0.1
- Protein: 0.3
- Sodium: 1416

803. Vietnamese Pork And Five Spice

Serving: 8 | Prep: 10mins | Cook: 2hours10mins | Ready in:

Ingredients

- 4 pounds pork shoulder, cut into cubes
- 1 teaspoon salt
- 1 teaspoon ground black pepper
- 1/4 cup olive oil
- 2 cloves garlic, minced
- 2 tablespoons brown sugar
- 2 tablespoons soy sauce
- 1 tablespoon fish sauce
- 1 teaspoon Chinese five-spice powder

Direction

- Spice up the pork with pepper and salt.
- Pour the olive oil in a large pot and heat over medium heat; cook pork and garlic in hot oil for 7 to 10 minutes until the pork turns fully brown.
- Combine fish sauce, soy sauce, five-spice powder and brown sugar and stir together with the pork. Adjust the heat to medium-low and cook mixture at a simmer for about 2 hours while stirring from time to time, until the pork is softened enough that it can easily pull apart using a fork.

Nutrition Information

- Calories: 288 calories;
- Total Carbohydrate: 4.4
- Cholesterol: 85
- Protein: 29.5
- Total Fat: 16.4
- Sodium: 713

804. Vietnamese Rice Noodle Salad

Serving: 4 | Prep: 15mins | Cook: | Ready in:

Ingredients

- 5 cloves garlic
- 1 cup loosely packed chopped cilantro
- 1/2 jalapeno pepper, seeded and minced
- 3 tablespoons white sugar
- 1/4 cup fresh lime juice
- 3 tablespoons vegetarian fish sauce

- 1 (12 ounce) package dried rice noodles
- 2 carrots, julienned
- 1 cucumber, halved lengthwise and chopped
- 1/4 cup chopped fresh mint
- 4 leaves napa cabbage
- 1/4 cup unsalted peanuts
- 4 sprigs fresh mint

Direction

- Mince garlic with hot pepper and cilantro. Place mixture in a bowl. Add sugar, lime juice, and salt or fish sauce. Mix well. Let sit for 5 minutes.
- Boil a big pot of salted water. Add rice noodles and boil for 2 minutes. Drain it well. Rinse noodles under cold water until cool. Let drain again.
- Combine Napa cabbage, mint, cucumber, carrots, noodles and sauce in a big serving bowl. Toss it well then serve salad topped with mint sprigs and peanuts.

Nutrition Information

- Calories: 432 calories;
- Sodium: 188
- Total Carbohydrate: 89.5
- Cholesterol: 0
- Protein: 6.6
- Total Fat: 5.3

805. Vietnamese Salad Rolls

Serving: 8 | Prep: 20mins | Cook: 5mins | Ready in:

Ingredients

- 1 (8 ounce) package rice vermicelli
- 8 ounces cooked, peeled shrimp, cut in half lengthwise
- 8 rice wrappers (6.5 inch diameter)
- 1 carrot, julienned
- 1 cup shredded lettuce
- 1/4 cup chopped fresh basil
- 1/2 cup hoisin sauce
- water as needed

Direction

- Boil a medium saucepan full of water. Take off heat. Put rice vermicelli in the boiling water, take off heat, and soak for 3-5 minutes until they're soft. Drain then rinse using cold water.
- Fill hot water into a big bowl. Dip a rice wrapper in hot water for a second to make it soft. Lay the wrapper down flat and put in your preferred amount of basil, lettuce, carrot, shrimp, and noodles in the middle. Roll wrapper edges inward slightly. Starts at the bottom edge of the wrapper, wrap the ingredients tightly. Repeat process with the rest of the ingredients.
- Mix water and hoisin sauce in a small bowl until you get your preferred consistency. Heat in the microwave for a few seconds.
- Serve spring rolls with warm dipping sauce.

Nutrition Information

- Calories: 187 calories;
- Total Fat: 1.5
- Sodium: 344
- Total Carbohydrate: 31.2
- Cholesterol: 57
- Protein: 11.6

806. Vietnamese Sandwich

Serving: 4 | Prep: 10mins | Cook: 5mins | Ready in:

Ingredients

- 4 boneless pork loin chops, cut 1/4 inch thick
- 4 (7 inch) French bread baguettes, split lengthwise
- 4 teaspoons mayonnaise, or to taste
- 1 ounce chile sauce with garlic

- 1/4 cup fresh lime juice
- 1 small red onion, sliced into rings
- 1 medium cucumber, peeled and sliced lengthwise
- 2 tablespoons chopped fresh cilantro
- salt and pepper to taste

Direction

- Set the oven's broiler for preheating. Put the pork chops on a broiling pan and place under the broiler. Cook for about 5 minutes, flipping once, or until it turns brown per side.
- Open the French rolls and spread mayonnaise inside. Arrange a piece of a cooked pork chop into each roll. Scatter the chile sauce straight on the meat. Sprinkle with a bit of lime juice and top it off with slices of onion, cilantro, cucumber, pepper and salt. Finish with one more quick drizzle of lime juice.

Nutrition Information

- Calories: 627 calories;
- Total Carbohydrate: 72.1
- Cholesterol: 124
- Protein: 55.3
- Total Fat: 12.1
- Sodium: 908

807. Vietnamese Spring Rolls

Serving: 4 | Prep: 10mins | Cook: 15mins | Ready in:

Ingredients

- 1/2 (6.75 ounce) package dried rice noodles
- 8 rice wrappers (8.5 inch diameter)
- 8 fresh mint leaves
- 8 cooked medium shrimp, sliced in half lengthwise
- 1 1/2 cups bean sprouts
- 3 tablespoons fish sauce, or to taste
- 1/2 cup cilantro leaves

Direction

- In a big bowl with hot water, put rice noodles in and soak for about 15 minutes until cooked. Drain then rinse using cold water. Fill hot water in a big bowl then soak rice wrapper sheets, one by one, for about 20 seconds until soft yet rather firm. Put sheets on a big dish cloth, then separate from each other. Put a mint leaf in the middle of every wrapper. Put two halves of shrimp on mint leaf, then top with a small handful of noodles, then add 5-6 bean sprouts. Season with fish sauce to taste then top with cilantro leaves.
- Roll, burrito style, by folding the wrapper's bottom on the filling in the middle. Fold in right and left sides, then roll the whole thing tightly away from you.

Nutrition Information

- Calories: 145 calories;
- Cholesterol: 20
- Protein: 5.2
- Total Fat: 0.4
- Sodium: 890
- Total Carbohydrate: 29.7

808. Vietnamese Spring Rolls With Dipping Sauce

Serving: 4 | Prep: 20mins | Cook: 5mins | Ready in:

Ingredients

- 1/4 cup white vinegar
- 1/4 cup fish sauce
- 2 tablespoons white sugar
- 2 tablespoons lime juice
- 1 clove garlic, minced
- 1/4 teaspoon red pepper flakes
- 2 ounces rice vermicelli
- 8 large shrimp, peeled and deveined
- 4 rice wrappers (8.5 inch diameter)

- 2 leaves lettuce, chopped
- 3 tablespoons finely chopped fresh mint leaves
- 3 tablespoons finely chopped cilantro
- 4 teaspoons finely chopped Thai basil

Direction

- Mix red pepper flakes, garlic, lime juice, sugar, fish sauce, and vinegar in a small bowl. Put dipping sauce aside.
- In a big bowl, fill with room temperature water. Put in rice vermicelli and soak for an hour.
- Boil a big pot of water. Place in shrimp then cook for about a minute until pink in color and curled. Take out shrimp then drain. Cut every shrimp lengthwise in half. Place rice vermicelli noodles in a pot with boiling water. Cook for a minute. Take out then strain in a colander. Rinse vermicelli immediately with cold water. Mix to separate noodles.
- To make rolls, dip a rice wrapper in a big bowl full of room temperature water for several seconds to make it soft. Put wrapper on a work surface. Top with 1/4 each of Thai basil, cilantro, and mint then 1/2-ounce vermicelli, 1/4 chopped lettuce, and 4 shrimp halves. Fold left and right edges of the wrapper on the ends of the filling then roll up the spring roll. Repeat process with leftover ingredients and wrappers. Cut every roll to half then serve with the dipping sauce.

Nutrition Information

- Calories: 137 calories;
- Sodium: 1170
- Total Carbohydrate: 22.5
- Cholesterol: 64
- Protein: 10.1
- Total Fat: 0.7

809. Vietnamese Steamed Buns (Banh Bao)

Serving: 20 | Prep: 15mins | Cook: 15mins | Ready in:

Ingredients

- 5 cups self-rising flour
- 2 cups milk
- 1 cup white sugar

Direction

- Combine the flour, sugar and milk, and mix together in a bowl. Cover the bowl and allow the dough to rise for half an hour up to 1 hour.
- Punch the dough down and split into 20 evenly sized shapes of a bun.
- Position a steamer insert into a saucepan and put water just below the bottom of the steamer. Allow water to boil, arrange the buns and cover; steam for about 15 minutes until softened.

Nutrition Information

- Calories: 162 calories;
- Sodium: 407
- Total Carbohydrate: 34.3
- Cholesterol: 2
- Protein: 3.9
- Total Fat: 0.8

810. Vietnamese Stir Fry

Serving: 6 | Prep: 30mins | Cook: 25mins | Ready in:

Ingredients

- 1/4 cup olive oil
- 4 cloves garlic, minced
- 1 (1 inch) piece fresh ginger root, minced
- 1/4 cup fish sauce
- 1/4 cup reduced-sodium soy sauce
- 1 dash sesame oil

- 2 pounds sirloin tip, thinly sliced
- 1 tablespoon vegetable oil
- 2 cloves garlic, minced
- 3 green onions, cut into 2 inch pieces
- 1 large onion, thinly sliced
- 2 cups frozen whole green beans, partially thawed
- 1/2 cup reduced-sodium beef broth
- 2 tablespoons lime juice
- 1 tablespoon chopped fresh Thai basil
- 1 tablespoon chopped fresh mint
- 1 pinch red pepper flakes, or to taste
- 1/2 teaspoon ground black pepper
- 1/4 cup chopped fresh cilantro

Direction

- Combine the olive oil, soy sauce, ginger, sesame oil, fish sauce and 4 cloves of garlic and whisk in a bowl; pour them out in a resealable plastic bag. Add the beef sirloin tip to the marinade and coat, release out the air and seal the bag. Keep inside the refrigerator for 2 hours to marinade. Take the beef sirloin tip off from the marinade, and shake off to remove excess. Dispose the remaining marinade.
- In a big skillet set over medium-high heat, heat the vegetable oil. Stir in the beef and cook until it turns brown evenly and no longer pink. Transfer the beef to a plate and put aside. Adjust the heat to medium; pour additional vegetable oil in the skillet if necessary. Stir in 2 cloves of garlic, onion and green onion; cook and stir for about 5 minutes until the onion turned translucent and has softened. Stir in beef broth, green beans, basil, lime juice, mint, pepper and red pepper flakes. Put back the beef sirloin to skillet and stir it to combine. Take it off from heat and toss in cilantro.

Nutrition Information

- Calories: 475 calories;
- Sodium: 1174
- Total Carbohydrate: 8.8
- Cholesterol: 101
- Protein: 31.7
- Total Fat: 34.4

811. Vietnamese Style Vegetarian Curry Soup

Serving: 8 | Prep: 30mins | Cook: 1hours30mins | Ready in:

Ingredients

- 2 tablespoons vegetable oil
- 1 onion, coarsely chopped
- 2 shallots, thinly sliced
- 2 cloves garlic, chopped
- 2 inch piece fresh ginger root, thinly sliced
- 1 stalk lemon grass, cut into 2 inch pieces
- 4 tablespoons curry powder
- 1 green bell pepper, coarsely chopped
- 2 carrots, peeled and diagonally sliced
- 8 mushrooms, sliced
- 1 pound fried tofu, cut into bite-size pieces
- 4 cups vegetable broth
- 4 cups water
- 2 tablespoons vegetarian fish sauce (optional)
- 2 teaspoons red pepper flakes
- 1 bay leaf
- 2 kaffir lime leaves
- 8 small potatoes, quartered
- 1 (14 ounce) can coconut milk
- 2 cups fresh bean sprouts, for garnish
- 8 sprigs fresh chopped cilantro, for garnish

Direction

- In a large stock pot placed over medium heat, pour the oil. Sauté shallots and onion until they get translucent and soft. Add ginger, curry powder, garlic and lemon grass, stir properly. Cook for 5 minutes, to release the flavors of the curry. Pour in water, vegetable stock, carrots, green pepper, mushrooms, tofu and stir. Use red pepper flakes and fish sauce to season. Boil; then stir in coconut milk and potatoes. When soup begins to boil again, reduce heat and simmer for 40 to 60 minutes, or until potatoes are soft. Use a pile of cilantro and bean sprouts to garnish each bowl.

Nutrition Information

- Calories: 479 calories;
- Total Carbohydrate: 51.4
- Cholesterol: 0
- Protein: 16.4
- Total Fat: 26.5
- Sodium: 271

812. Vietnamese Table Sauce

Serving: 12 | Prep: 10mins | Cook: | Ready in:

Ingredients

- 1/4 cup lime juice
- 1/4 cup Thai fish sauce
- 2 tablespoons rice vinegar
- 1 tablespoon white sugar
- 1 bird's eye chile, minced
- 1 clove garlic, minced

Direction

- Combine fish sauce, bird's eye chile, vinegar, sugar, garlic and lime juice together in a bowl and mix until the sugar has dissolve. Serve it in a small bowl.

Nutrition Information

- Calories: 7 calories;
- Total Fat: 0
- Sodium: 365
- Total Carbohydrate: 1.7
- Cholesterol: 0
- Protein: 0.3

813. Vietnamese Style Shrimp Soup

Serving: 6 | Prep: 15mins | Cook: 20mins | Ready in:

Ingredients

- 1 tablespoon vegetable oil
- 2 teaspoons minced fresh garlic
- 2 teaspoons minced fresh ginger root
- 1 (10 ounce) package frozen chopped spinach, thawed and drained
- salt and black pepper to taste
- 2 quarts chicken stock
- 1 cup shrimp stock
- 1 teaspoon hot pepper sauce (optional)
- 1 teaspoon hoisin sauce (optional)
- 20 peeled and deveined medium shrimp
- 1 (6.75 ounce) package long rice noodles (rice vermicelli)
- 2 green onions, chopped (optional)

Direction

- In a big pot, heat vegetable oil on medium heat. Mix in ginger and garlic then sauté for a minute. Add spinach then season with pepper and salt. Cover then cook for about 3 minutes until spinach becomes hot. Pour chicken stock in, hoisin sauce, hot pepper sauce, and shrimp stock. Cover again then simmer on medium-high heat.
- When soup simmers, mix in noodles and shrimp. Cover then cook for 4 minutes. Mix in green onions then cook for another 5 minutes. Season with pepper and salt to taste then serve.

Nutrition Information

- Calories: 212 calories;
- Cholesterol: 52
- Protein: 14.4
- Total Fat: 4.7
- Sodium: 1156

- Total Carbohydrate: 28.6

Chapter 8: Asian Dinner Cuisine Recipes

***

814. Apricot Chicken Stir Fry

Serving: 4 servings. | Prep: 10mins | Cook: 20mins | Ready in:

Ingredients

- 1/2 cup dried apricot halves, cut in half
- 1/4 cup hot water
- 1 tablespoon all-purpose flour
- 1 tablespoon chopped cilantro, optional
- 1/2 teaspoon salt
- 1/8 teaspoon pepper
- 3/4 pound boneless skinless chicken breasts, cut into 1/2-inch pieces
- 3 tablespoons canola oil, divided
- 1 medium onion, halved and sliced
- 1 cup chopped celery
- 1/2 cup halved snow peas
- 1/2 teaspoon ground ginger
- 1 garlic clove, minced
- 1 to 2 tablespoons lemon juice
- Hot cooked rice

Direction

- Steep apricots in a small bowl of water; put to one side (do not drain). Combine pepper, salt, flour, and cilantro (if desired); scatter over the chicken and put to one side.
- In a wok or large skillet, heat 1 tablespoon oil over medium heat; sauté celery and onion in heated oil until tender, about 2 to 3 minutes. Add apricots, garlic, ginger, and peas; sauté for 2 minutes. Take everything out and keep warm.
- Add the rest of oil to the skillet; cook and stir chicken until no longer pink, about 6 to 7 minutes. Add lemon juice to the skillet. Pour apricot mixture back into the skillet and cook until heated through. Serve warm with rice.

Nutrition Information

- Calories: 268 calories
- Sodium: 364mg sodium
- Fiber: 4g fiber)
- Total Carbohydrate: 20g carbohydrate (12g sugars
- Cholesterol: 47mg cholesterol
- Protein: 19g protein.
- Total Fat: 12g fat (2g saturated fat)

815. Apricot Filled Pork Tenderloin

Serving: 6 servings. | Prep: 10mins | Cook: 30mins | Ready in:

Ingredients

- 2 pork tenderloins (1 pound each)
- 1 package (6 ounces) dried apricots
- MARINADE:
- 1/3 cup sweet-and-sour salad dressing
- 1/4 cup packed brown sugar
- 3 tablespoons teriyaki sauce
- 2 tablespoons ketchup
- 1 teaspoon Dijon mustard
- 1 onion slice, separated into rings
- 1 garlic clove, minced
- 2 teaspoons minced fresh gingerroot
- 1/4 teaspoon pepper
- 1/8 teaspoon pumpkin pie spice

Direction

- Cut three-quarters of the way through each tenderloin; pound to flatten evenly. Put 3 apricots aside for marinade. Within 1/2-in. from ends, stuff leftover apricots into pork; use kitchen string or toothpicks to secure.
- Mix reserved apricots and remaining ingredients till smooth in a blender, covered; put 1/3 cup aside. Put leftover marinade into a big resealable bag; add tenderloins and seal bag. Turn to coat; refrigerate, turning meat often, for at least 2 hours.
- Drain then discard marinade. Put pork into a greased 13x9-in. baking dish; drizzle with reserved marinade. Bake for 30-35 minutes at 400° till thermometer reads 160°, uncovered.

Nutrition Information

- Calories:
- Cholesterol:
- Protein:
- Total Fat:
- Sodium:
- Fiber:
- Total Carbohydrate:

816. Asian Beef Noodle Toss

Serving: 4-6 servings. | Prep: 30mins | Cook: 0mins | Ready in:

Ingredients

- 1 pound ground beef
- 2 packages (3 ounces each) Oriental ramen noodles
- 1 package (16 ounces) frozen stir-fry vegetable blend
- 2 cups water
- 4 to 5 tablespoons soy sauce
- 1/4 teaspoon ground ginger
- 3 tablespoons thinly sliced green onions

Direction

- Cook the beef in a large skillet that is set over medium heat until it is no longer pink; drain. Pour in all the contents of a packet of noodle seasoning. Put the mixture aside and keep it warm.
- Break the noodles and pour it into the large saucepan. Add all the contents of another seasoning pack, soy sauce, ginger, water, and vegetables. Let the mixture boil. Lower the heat and cover the pan. Simmer the mixture for 6-10 minutes until the noodles and vegetables are tender. Mix in onions and beef.

Nutrition Information

- Calories: 208 calories
- Total Fat: 9g fat (4g saturated fat)
- Sodium: 978mg sodium
- Fiber: 2g fiber)
- Total Carbohydrate: 13g carbohydrate (3g sugars
- Cholesterol: 37mg cholesterol
- Protein: 17g protein.

817. Asian Beef Ribbons

Serving: 2 servings. | Prep: 10mins | Cook: 10mins | Ready in:

Ingredients

- 1 beef flank steak (3/4 pound)
- 2 tablespoons teriyaki sauce
- 1-1/2 teaspoons vegetable oil
- 1 garlic clove, minced
- 1 teaspoon minced fresh gingerroot
- 1/8 teaspoon crushed red pepper flakes
- 1/2 teaspoon sesame seeds, toasted

Direction

- Cut quarter-inch strips of beef across the grain. Mix together red pepper flakes, teriyaki sauce, ginger, oil, and garlic in a big ziplock bag; put in meat strips then seal. Flip the bag to coat meat with marinade. Let it chill in the refrigerator for 8 hrs or overnight; turn the bag regularly.

- Drain beef and get rid of the marinade. Lace meat strips on metal or soaked wooden skewers. On medium heat, grill beef while covered or broil four inches from the heat for 2-4mins per side until it reaches the preferred doneness. Take it off the grill or broiler. Add sesame seeds on top.

Nutrition Information

- Calories:
- Sodium:
- Fiber:
- Total Carbohydrate:
- Cholesterol:
- Protein:
- Total Fat:

818. Asian Beef And Cauliflower Stew

Serving: 6 servings. | Prep: 20mins | Cook: 01hours05mins | Ready in:

Ingredients

- 2 tablespoons vegetable oil
- 1-1/2 pounds lean round steak, cut into 1-inch cubes
- 3 cups beef broth
- 1 small head cauliflower, separated into florets
- 1 green pepper, cut into chunks
- 1/4 cup reduced-sodium or regular soy sauce
- 1 garlic clove, minced
- 1-1/2 teaspoons grated fresh gingerroot, optional
- 2 to 3 tablespoons cornstarch
- 1/2 teaspoon sugar
- 1/4 cup water
- 1 cup sliced green onions
- Cooked rice

Direction

- Heat oil in a frying pan over medium-high heat. Brown all sides of the meat. Pour in broth, simmer with a cover for 1 hour or until the beef is soft. Add ginger root (if wanted), garlic, soy sauce, green pepper, and cauliflower. Simmer with a cover for 5-7 minutes or until the vegetables are soft. Mix together water, sugar, and cornstarch. Mix into the meat mixture. Boil it while stirring continuously, cook until thickened, about 2 minutes. Mix in green onions. Enjoy with rice.

Nutrition Information

- Calories: 165 calories
- Cholesterol: 82mg cholesterol
- Protein: 23g protein. Diabetic Exchanges: 2-1/2 lean meat
- Total Fat: 4g fat (0 saturated fat)
- Sodium: 771mg sodium
- Fiber: 0 fiber)
- Total Carbohydrate: 8g carbohydrate (0 sugars

819. Asian Pork Chops

Serving: 4 servings. | Prep: 5mins | Cook: 10mins | Ready in:

Ingredients

- 3 tablespoons soy sauce
- 3 tablespoons honey
- 1 tablespoon lemon juice
- 1 tablespoon olive oil
- 3 garlic cloves, minced
- 1/2 teaspoon ground ginger
- 4 boneless pork loin chops (1/2 to 3/4 inch thick)

Direction

- Mix the first six ingredients in a shallow glass container or a large resealable plastic bag. Add pork, turning to coat. Cover the container or seal the bag; keep cool in refrigerator for 4-8 hours.
- Drain and dispose of marinade. Grill, uncovered, over medium heat until a thermometer reads 145deg, 4-5 minutes on each side. Let stand for 5 minutes before serving.

Nutrition Information

- Calories: 225 calories
- Cholesterol: 55mg cholesterol
- Protein: 21g protein. Diabetic Exchanges: 3 lean meat
- Total Fat: 9g fat (0 saturated fat)
- Sodium: 420mg sodium
- Fiber: 0 fiber)
- Total Carbohydrate: 16g carbohydrate (0 sugars

820. Asian Pork Stir Fry

Serving: 4 servings. | Prep: 20mins | Cook: 10mins | Ready in:

Ingredients

- 2 tablespoons cornstarch
- 1/2 cup water
- 1/2 cup reduced-sodium chicken broth
- 2 garlic cloves, minced
- 2 teaspoons minced fresh gingerroot
- 1 pound pork tenderloin, cut into 1/2-inch pieces
- 2 tablespoons sesame or canola oil, divided
- 1-1/2 cups sliced fresh mushrooms
- 1 cup bean sprouts
- 1 cup sliced bok choy
- 1 cup fresh snow peas
- 1 small sweet red pepper, cut into 3/4-inch pieces
- 2 tablespoons reduced-sodium soy sauce
- 2 cups hot cooked brown rice

Direction

- Mix water and cornstarch together in a small bowl until tender. Mix in ginger, garlic, and broth. Put aside.
- Stir-fry pork with 1 tablespoon of oil in a big wok or skillet until not pink anymore. Take out and keep warm.
- Stir-fry soy sauce, pepper, peas, bok choy, bean sprouts, and mushrooms in the leftover oil until the vegetables are soft and crunchy, about 4-5 minutes.
- Whisk the cornstarch mixture and pour in the pan. Boil; stir and cook until thickened, about 1 minute. Add pork and thoroughly heat. Enjoy with rice.

Nutrition Information

- Calories: 386 calories
- Fiber: 6g fiber)
- Total Carbohydrate: 38g carbohydrate (7g sugars
- Cholesterol: 63mg cholesterol
- Protein: 32g protein. Diabetic Exchanges: 3 lean meat
- Total Fat: 12g fat (3g saturated fat)
- Sodium: 565mg sodium

821. Asian Salmon Fillets

Serving: 4 servings. | Prep: 10mins | Cook: 15mins | Ready in:

Ingredients

- 4 green onions, thinly sliced
- 1 garlic clove, minced
- 1 teaspoon olive oil
- 1 teaspoon minced fresh gingerroot
- 4 salmon fillets (5 ounces each)

- 1/4 cup white wine or reduced-sodium chicken broth
- 2 tablespoons reduced-sodium soy sauce
- 2 tablespoons oyster sauce

Direction

- Cook garlic with onions in a big nonstick skillet with oil on medium heat about one minute. Put in ginger and cook for another minute. Turn out to a small bowl and put aside.
- Use cooking spray to spritz the fillets, then put into skillet. Cook until browned slightly, or about 4 to 6 minutes per side.
- Mix together the reserved onion mixture, oyster sauce, soy sauce and wine or broth, then transfer over salmon. Cook until it is easy to make fish flake using a fork, or about 2 to 3 minutes. Cook the sauce until thickened, or about 1 to 2 more minutes. Serve on top of salmon.

Nutrition Information

- Calories: 300 calories
- Fiber: 0 fiber)
- Total Carbohydrate: 3g carbohydrate (0 sugars
- Cholesterol: 84mg cholesterol
- Protein: 30g protein. Diabetic Exchanges: 4 lean meat
- Total Fat: 17g fat (3g saturated fat)
- Sodium: 725mg sodium

822. Asian Slow Cooker Pork

Serving: 12 servings. | Prep: 25mins | Cook: 04hours30mins | Ready in:

Ingredients

- 2 large onions, thinly sliced
- 3 garlic cloves, minced
- 1/2 teaspoon salt
- 1/2 teaspoon pepper
- 1 boneless pork loin roast (3 pounds)
- 1 tablespoon canola oil
- 3 bay leaves
- 1/4 cup hot water
- 1/4 cup honey
- 1/4 cup reduced-sodium soy sauce
- 2 tablespoons rice vinegar
- 1 teaspoon ground ginger
- 1/2 teaspoon ground cloves
- 3 tablespoons cornstarch
- 1/4 cup cold water
- Hot cooked rice
- 2 tablespoons sesame seeds, toasted
- Sliced green onions, optional

Direction

- Add onions to a 5-quart slow cooker. Combine pepper, salt, and garlic. Slice the roast in half; rub the garlic mixture over the roast. Coat a big nonstick skillet with cooking spray; put in oil and cook the pork until browned on all sides. Move the pork to the prepared slow cooker and put in bay leaves.
- Combine the honey and hot water in a small bowl, whisk in the spices, vinegar, and soy sauce. Spread the mixture all over the pork. Cook while covered for 4-5 hours on low until the meat becomes soft.
- Take the pork out of the slow cooker and keep warm. Remove the bay leaves. Combine the cold water with the cornstarch until smooth and gradually whisk into the slow cooker. Cook while covered for half an hour on high until thickened, only stir two times.
- Shred the pork coarsely into bite-sized pieces and serve with sauce over rice. Top the dish with sesame seeds and green onions (optional).

Nutrition Information

- Calories: 203 calories
- Cholesterol: 56mg cholesterol
- Protein: 23g protein. Diabetic Exchanges: 3 lean meat

- Total Fat: 7g fat (2g saturated fat)
- Sodium: 342mg sodium
- Fiber: 1g fiber)
- Total Carbohydrate: 11g carbohydrate (7g sugars

823. Asian Steak

Serving: 4 servings. | Prep: 10mins | Cook: 10mins | Ready in:

Ingredients

- 1/2 cup soy sauce
- 2 tablespoons brown sugar
- 2 tablespoons vegetable oil
- 2 teaspoons onion powder
- 2 teaspoons lemon juice
- 1/4 teaspoon ground ginger
- 4 T-bone steaks (about 3/4 inch thick)

Direction

- Put the initial six ingredients into a big resealable plastic bag before adding the steak and sealing the bag. Turn to coat the meat and cover it up. Refrigerate for a minimum of 4 hours. Drain the meat and throw the marinade away. Over medium heat, grill the steaks without cover until meat is at desired doneness, about 3 to 4 minutes per side. To get medium-rare meat, an inserted thermometer should register at 145°F.

Nutrition Information

- Calories:
- Sodium:
- Fiber:
- Total Carbohydrate:
- Cholesterol:
- Protein:
- Total Fat:

824. Asian Sweet And Sour Pork

Serving: 4 servings. | Prep: 15mins | Cook: 15mins | Ready in:

Ingredients

- 4 teaspoons cornstarch
- 1/2 teaspoon salt
- 1/2 teaspoon ground ginger
- 1/8 teaspoon pepper
- 1 can (8 ounces) unsweetened pineapple chunks
- 1/4 cup cider vinegar
- 1 pork tenderloin (1 pound), cut into 1-inch cubes
- 5 teaspoons canola oil, divided
- 1 medium green pepper, cut into 1-inch pieces
- 1 medium sweet red pepper, cut into 1-inch pieces
- 1 small onion, cut into 1-inch pieces
- 1/3 cup red currant jelly
- Hot cooked rice, optional

Direction

- Mix the pepper, salt, ginger, and cornstarch in a small bowl. Drain the pineapple and reserve its juice; put the pineapple aside. Mix the vinegar and juice into the cornstarch mixture until smooth; put aside.
- Stir-fry the pork in a wok or large nonstick skillet with 3 tsp. of oil until it is no longer pink. Remove from the heat and keep it warm. Stir-fry the onion and peppers in the same pan with its remaining oil until crisp-tender. Mix in jelly, pork, and pineapple.
- Whisk the cornstarch mixture first before adding it into the pan. Let it boil. Cook and stir the mixture for 2 minutes until its thick. Serve the mixture with rice, if desired.

Nutrition Information

- Calories: 311 calories
- Total Carbohydrate: 33g carbohydrate (26g sugars
- Cholesterol: 63mg cholesterol
- Protein: 23g protein. Diabetic Exchanges: 3 lean meat
- Total Fat: 10g fat (2g saturated fat)
- Sodium: 347mg sodium
- Fiber: 2g fiber)

825. Asparagus Mushroom Beef Stir Fry

Serving: 4 servings. | Prep: 15mins | Cook: 15mins | Ready in:

Ingredients

- 1 pound lean ground beef (90% lean)
- 2 cups cut fresh asparagus (1-inch pieces)
- 1 can (8 ounces) sliced water chestnuts, drained
- 1/3 pound sliced fresh shiitake mushrooms
- 1 teaspoon minced garlic
- 2 teaspoons sesame oil
- 2 tablespoons cornstarch
- 1-1/2 cups beef broth
- 1/3 cup hoisin sauce
- 2 tablespoons reduced-sodium soy sauce
- 1 teaspoon minced fresh gingerroot
- 1 large tomato, chopped
- Hot cooked rice, optional

Direction

- Cook the beef in a large skillet or wok that is set over medium heat until it is not anymore pinkish. Drain the beef and put it aside. Stir-fry the water chestnuts, garlic, mushrooms, and asparagus in the same pan with oil for 5 minutes until crisp-tender.
- Mix the broth and cornstarch in a small bowl until smooth. Mix in soy sauce, ginger, and hoisin sauce. Pour the mixture all over the vegetables. Add the beef back into the pan; boil. Cook and stir the mixture for 2 minutes until thick. Remove it from the heat and mix in tomato. Serve the mixture with rice if desired.

Nutrition Information

- Calories: 338 calories
- Cholesterol: 56mg cholesterol
- Protein: 27g protein.
- Total Fat: 12g fat (4g saturated fat)
- Sodium: 1040mg sodium
- Fiber: 5g fiber)
- Total Carbohydrate: 31g carbohydrate (4g sugars

826. Beef Asparagus Stir Fry

Serving: 3 servings. | Prep: 15mins | Cook: 15mins | Ready in:

Ingredients

- 2 tablespoons reduced-sodium soy sauce, divided
- 2 tablespoons dry red wine or beef broth, divided
- 1/2 pound beef top sirloin steak, cut into thin strips
- 1 tablespoon cornstarch
- 1/2 cup water
- 4 teaspoons canola oil, divided
- 1 small onion, thinly sliced
- 1 pound fresh asparagus, trimmed and cut into 1-inch pieces
- 2 celery ribs, thinly sliced
- 1 garlic clove, minced
- 1/8 to 1/4 teaspoon crushed red pepper flakes
- Hot cooked rice, optional

Direction

- Mix 1 tbsp. of broth or wine and 1 tbsp. of soy sauce in a large resealable plastic bag. Add the beef inside the bag. Seal the bag and flip it until the beef is well coated. Refrigerate the bag for 30 minutes. Mix the remaining soy sauce, wine or broth, water, and cornstarch in a small bowl until smooth; put aside.

- Stir-fry the beef in a wok or large nonstick skillet with 2 tsp. of oil for 3-4 minutes until it is not anymore pinkish. Use a slotted spoon to remove the beef from the pan; keep warm. In the remaining oil, stir-fry the onion for 1 minute. Add the asparagus and stir-fry for 2 minutes. Add the red pepper flakes, garlic, and celery. Stir-fry the mixture for 4-6 minutes until crisp-tender.
- Whisk the cornstarch mixture and pour it into the pan. Let the mixture boil. Cook and stir the mixture for 2 minutes until thick. Add the beef and heat the mixture through. If desired, serve this stir-fry with rice.

Nutrition Information

- Calories: 211 calories
- Fiber: 3g fiber)
- Total Carbohydrate: 11g carbohydrate (0 sugars
- Cholesterol: 42mg cholesterol
- Protein: 18g protein. Diabetic Exchanges: 2 lean meat
- Total Fat: 10g fat (2g saturated fat)
- Sodium: 461mg sodium

827. Beef Pineapple Stir Fry

Serving: 4 servings. | Prep: 20mins | Cook: 15mins | Ready in:

Ingredients

- 1 cup unsweetened pineapple juice
- 1/4 cup white wine or reduced-sodium chicken broth
- 2 tablespoons brown sugar
- 2 tablespoons reduced-sodium soy sauce
- 1/4 teaspoon cayenne pepper
- 1 beef top sirloin steak (1 pound), cut into thin strips
- 2 tablespoons cornstarch
- 1-1/2 teaspoons olive oil, divided
- 2 large carrots, sliced
- 1 small onion, halved and sliced
- 1 medium green pepper, julienned
- 1/2 cup fresh snow peas
- 3/4 cup unsweetened pineapple tidbits
- 2 cups cooked brown rice

Direction

- Mix the first 5 ingredients in a small bowl. Transfer 2/3 cup of the marinade into the large resealable plastic bag. Add the beef inside the bag. Seal the bag and flip it until coated. Place the bag inside the fridge for 30 minutes. Also, cover and place the remaining marinade inside the fridge.
- Mix the reserved marinade and cornstarch in a small bowl until smooth; put aside.
- Drain the beef, discarding the marinade. Stir-fry the beef in a large and nonstick skillet or wok with 1 tsp. of oil for 2-3 minutes until the beef is no longer pink. Use a slotted spoon to remove the beef; keep warm.
- Stir-fry the onion and carrots in the remaining oil for 4 minutes. Add the snow peas and green pepper. Stir-fry for 2-3 more minutes until the vegetables turn crisp-tender.
- Whisk the cornstarch mixture before adding it into the pan. Let the mixture boil. Cook for 2 minutes, stirring until thick. Add the pineapple and beef and heat through. Serve the hot mixture with rice.

Nutrition Information

- Calories: 388 calories
- Cholesterol: 46mg cholesterol
- Protein: 29g protein.
- Total Fat: 7g fat (2g saturated fat)
- Sodium: 324mg sodium
- Fiber: 5g fiber)

- Total Carbohydrate: 51g carbohydrate (19g sugars
- Protein:
- Total Fat:

828. Beef Stir Fry On A Stick

Serving: 4 servings. | Prep: 20mins | Cook: 15mins | Ready in:

Ingredients

- 1/2 cup hoisin sauce
- 3 tablespoons water
- 2 tablespoons canola oil
- 1 tablespoon reduced-sodium soy sauce
- 1 garlic clove, minced
- 1/4 to 1/2 teaspoon crushed red pepper flakes
- 3 cups large fresh broccoli florets
- 2 medium yellow summer squash, cut into 3/4-inch slices
- 1 large sweet red pepper, cut into 1-inch pieces
- 1 pound beef tenderloin, cut into 1-inch cubes
- Hot cooked rice

Direction

- For glaze, in a small bowl, combine the water, hoisin sauce, soy sauce, oil, pepper flakes and garlic.
- On four soaked wooden or metal skewers, alternately thread the squash, broccoli, beef and red pepper. Grill with cover over medium heat or broil 4 inches away from the heat for approximately 6-7 minutes of each side or until vegetables are tender and meat reaches desired doneness, basting with glaze from time to time. Serve with rice.

Nutrition Information

- Calories:
- Sodium:
- Fiber:
- Total Carbohydrate:
- Cholesterol:

829. Calypso Pork Chops

Serving: 6 servings (3 cups salsa). | Prep: 30mins | Cook: 10mins | Ready in:

Ingredients

- 2/3 cup reduced-sodium soy sauce
- 1/3 cup packed brown sugar
- 1/3 cup water
- 1/4 cup rice vinegar
- 2 tablespoons minced fresh gingerroot
- 2 garlic cloves, minced
- 6 boneless pork loin chops (4 ounces each)
- SALSA:
- 2 cups cubed fresh pineapple
- 1 cup chopped peeled papaya
- 1 small sweet red pepper, chopped
- 1 small onion, chopped
- 1 serrano pepper, seeded and minced
- 1 garlic clove, minced

Direction

- Mix the initial 6 ingredients in a little pot. Let it boil while stirring constantly until sugar crystals disappear. Take from heat to let it cool at room temperature.
- Put one cup marinade into a big closable plastic bag; mix in pork chops. Close the bag and mix to cover pork well; store overnight in the refrigerator. Transfer remaining marinade into a little glass bowl for basting; put plastic wrap and chill.
- Blend salsa ingredients in a big glass bowl. Let it sit at room temperature for an hour.
- Drain the pork and throw out marinade. Use tongs with long handles to dampen paper towel with cooking oil and slightly rub all over grill rack. Grill pork chops 4 to 5 minutes per side, covered with lid over medium heat or broil 4 to 5 inches away from the heat until an

instant-read thermometer shows 145°. Baste constantly with reserved marinade. Let it sit 5 minutes before serving it with salsa.

Nutrition Information

- Calories: 214 calories
- Total Carbohydrate: 15g carbohydrate (11g sugars
- Cholesterol: 55mg cholesterol
- Protein: 23g protein. Diabetic Exchanges: 3 lean meat
- Total Fat: 7g fat (2g saturated fat)
- Sodium: 297mg sodium
- Fiber: 2g fiber)

830. Catfish In Ginger Sauce

Serving: 4 servings. | Prep: 5mins | Cook: 10mins | Ready in:

Ingredients

- 1/2 cup chopped green onions
- 1 tablespoon vegetable oil
- 1/4 teaspoon ground ginger
- 1 teaspoon cornstarch
- 2 tablespoons water
- 1 cup chicken broth
- 1 tablespoon soy sauce
- 1 tablespoon white wine vinegar
- 1/8 teaspoon cayenne pepper
- 4 catfish fillets (6 ounces each)

Direction

- Mix oil, onions and ginger in a 2 cup microwave-safe bowl. Place in the microwave and heat it uncovered on high temperature. Cook for 1 and a half minutes until onions are softer.
- In a small bowl, mix water and cornstarch until smooth. Add in the broth, vinegar, soy sauce, and cayenne. Add the onion mixture.
- Put inside the microwave, without cover, for 2-3 minutes at 70 % power. Stir after each minute until sauce is boiling.
- Put catfish in a microwave-safe 3 qt. bowl. Put sauce over fish. Place cover and heat on high in the microwave for 5-6 minutes until fish flakes easily with a fork.

Nutrition Information

- Calories: 274 calories
- Total Carbohydrate: 2g carbohydrate (1g sugars
- Cholesterol: 80mg cholesterol
- Protein: 28g protein.
- Total Fat: 16g fat (3g saturated fat)
- Sodium: 555mg sodium
- Fiber: 0 fiber)

831. Chicken Long Rice

Serving: Serves 8 | Prep: 25mins | Cook: 2hours | Ready in:

Ingredients

- 2 1/2 lb chicken thighs (8)
- 2 teaspoons salt
- 1 1/2 tablespoons minced fresh ginger
- 2 1/2 qt water
- 1 large onion, finely chopped
- 1 1/2 extra-large (Knorr) chicken-bouillon cubes
- 4 small dried shiitake mushrooms
- 1/2 lb Chinese bean-thread (cellophane) noodles, cut into 3-inch lengths with kitchen scissors
- 1/2 cup chopped scallion
- 1 teaspoon black pepper

Direction

- In 2-quart water, let chicken simmer with ginger and salt in one 5-quarts pot for 40 minutes, cover slightly, scooping off foam from time to time, till extremely tender. Using tongs, turn the chicken to bowl, setting broth aside. Once chicken is cool, throw the bones and skin and pull meat apart.

- Into a bowl, pass broth through a fine sieve and clean the pot. Put broth back to pot along with mushrooms, bouillon cubes, onion and leftover 2 cups of water and boil with cover. Put in noodles and cook with cover for 5 minutes, on medium heat, mixing from time to time. Switch off heat and rest for 30 minutes with cover. Mix in chicken and heat till hot. Mix in salt to taste, pepper and scallion.

Nutrition Information

- Calories: 439
- Saturated Fat: 7 g(34%)
- Sodium: 932 mg(39%)
- Fiber: 2 g(7%)
- Total Carbohydrate: 24 g(8%)
- Cholesterol: 163 mg(54%)
- Protein: 28 g(56%)
- Total Fat: 25 g(38%)

832. Chicken Spareribs

Serving: 4 servings. | Prep: 5mins | Cook: 30mins | Ready in:

Ingredients

- 8 bone-in chicken thighs (about 3 pounds)
- 2 tablespoons canola oil
- 1 cup water
- 2/3 cup packed brown sugar
- 2/3 cup reduced-sodium soy sauce
- 1/2 cup apple juice
- 1/4 cup ketchup
- 2 tablespoons cider vinegar
- 2 garlic cloves, minced
- 1 teaspoon crushed red pepper flakes
- 1/2 teaspoon ground ginger
- 2 tablespoons cornstarch
- 2 tablespoons cold water

Direction

- In a Dutch oven over medium heat, heat the oil and cook the chicken in batches until browned on both sides then drain the pan. Move all of the chicken back into the pan.
- Combine the ginger, pepper flakes, garlic, vinegar, ketchup, apple juice, soy sauce, brown sugar and water together in a big bowl. Pour the mixture over chicken and bring it to a boil. Lower the heat and cover it up. Let it simmer until a thermometer reads 180°F, about 20-25 minutes. Transfer the chicken to a platter and keep warm.
- Mix water and corn starch together until smooth then stir it into the cooking juices and bring it to a boil. Cook and stir until it thickens, about 2 minutes. Serve with chicken.

Nutrition Information

- Calories: 583 calories
- Total Carbohydrate: 48g carbohydrate (41g sugars
- Cholesterol: 116mg cholesterol
- Protein: 37g protein.
- Total Fat: 26g fat (6g saturated fat)
- Sodium: 2753mg sodium
- Fiber: 0 fiber)

833. Chicken Stir Fry With Noodles

Serving: 4 servings. | Prep: 10mins | Cook: 20mins | Ready in:

Ingredients

- 8 ounces uncooked whole wheat spaghetti
- 1/2 head bok choy (about 1 pound)
- 2 tablespoons canola oil, divided

- 1 pound boneless skinless chicken breasts, cubed
- 1 celery rib, sliced
- 1/2 cup coarsely chopped green pepper
- 1/2 cup coarsely chopped sweet red pepper
- 1/3 cup coarsely chopped onion
- 6 tablespoons reduced-sodium teriyaki sauce

Direction

- Following package directions to cook spaghetti, then drain. In the meantime, cut the root end of bok choy and throw away. Cut stalks into pieces with 1 inch size. Chop the leaves of bok choy coarsely.
- Heat 1 tbsp. of oil in a big skillet on moderately high heat. Put in chicken and stir-fry until it is not pink anymore, 5-7 minutes. Take away from pan.
- Stir-fry onion, peppers, celery and bok choy stalks in the leftover oil for 4 minutes. Put in leaves of bok choy and stir-fry until leaves are soft, about 3 to 5 more minutes. Stir in teriyaki sauce, then put in chicken and spaghetti. Heat through and toss together to mix well.

Nutrition Information

- Calories: 434 calories
- Cholesterol: 63mg cholesterol
- Protein: 35g protein.
- Total Fat: 11g fat (1g saturated fat)
- Sodium: 623mg sodium
- Fiber: 9g fiber
- Total Carbohydrate: 53g carbohydrate (10g sugars

834. Chicken And Rice Chow Mein

Serving: 3-4 servings. | Prep: 15mins | Cook: 25mins | Ready in:

Ingredients

- 1 cup cubed cooked chicken
- 1/4 cup chopped celery
- 1/4 cup chopped onion
- 2 teaspoons canola oil
- 1 can (10-3/4 ounces) condensed cream of chicken soup, undiluted
- 2 tablespoons reduced-sodium soy sauce
- 1 to 1-1/4 teaspoons ground ginger
- 2 cups cooked rice
- 1/2 cup chow mein noodles

Direction

- Sauté onion, celery, and chicken with oil in a big frying pan until the chicken is not pink anymore. Add ginger, soy sauce, and soup; cook while stirring until bubbling. Mix in rice.
- Remove into a 1-quart baking dish coated with cooking spray. Put a cover on and bake at 350° until fully heated, about 25 minutes. Remove the cover, sprinkle the noodles over. Bake until the noodles are crunchy, about 5-10 minutes more.

Nutrition Information

- Calories: 0
- Sodium: 1,100 mg sodium
- Fiber: 2 g fiber
- Total Carbohydrate: 32 g carbohydrate
- Cholesterol: 37 mg cholesterol
- Protein: 16 g protein.
- Total Fat: 11 g fat (3 g saturated fat)

835. Chicken And Shrimp Satay

Serving: 6 servings. | Prep: 20mins | Cook: 10mins | Ready in:

Ingredients

- 3/4 pound uncooked medium shrimp, peeled and deveined

- 3/4 pound chicken tenderloins, cut into 1-inch cubes
- 4 green onions, chopped
- 1 tablespoon butter
- 2 garlic cloves, minced
- 1 tablespoon minced fresh parsley
- 1/2 cup white wine or chicken broth
- 1 tablespoon lemon juice
- 1 tablespoon lime juice
- SAUCE:
- 1/4 cup chopped onion
- 1 tablespoon butter
- 2/3 cup reduced-sodium chicken broth
- 1/4 cup reduced-fat chunky peanut butter
- 2-1/4 teaspoons brown sugar
- 3/4 teaspoon lemon juice
- 3/4 teaspoon lime juice
- 1/4 teaspoon salt
- 1/4 teaspoon each dried basil, thyme and rosemary, crushed
- 1/8 teaspoon cayenne pepper

Direction

- Alternately thread chicken and shrimp on 12 metal or water-soaked wooden skewers. Arrange skewers in a large, shallow container. Heat butter up in a small skillet and sauté green onions until crisp-tender. Add the garlic and cook for one more minute before stirring in the parsley, wine, and lemon and lime juices. Remove from heat, let it cool a little, then pour it over the chicken-and-shrimp skewers in the shallow container. Put the lid on the container and let the meats soak in the marinade for 4 hours in the fridge, turning the skewers over occasionally. Put butter in a small saucepan and heat enough to sauté the onions in it. Stir in the remaining ingredients for the sauce until they are well-blended. Remove the saucepan from the heat and set aside. Take the skewers out, discarding the marinade. Take a paper towel with long-handled tongs, dip it in cooking oil, then dab on grill rack to lightly coat it. Set grill for medium indirect heat. Place the skewers on the rack, cover the grill, and cook for 7-8 minutes, or broil 4 in. from the heat for the same cooking time. Flip the skewers frequently. Baste with 1/4 cup of the sauce at the last minute of grilling, then serve warm with remaining sauce.

Nutrition Information

- Calories: 190 calories
- Total Fat: 7g fat (3g saturated fat)
- Sodium: 339mg sodium
- Fiber: 1g fiber)
- Total Carbohydrate: 7g carbohydrate (3g sugars
- Cholesterol: 126mg cholesterol
- Protein: 25g protein. Diabetic Exchanges: 3 lean meat

836. Chow Mein Chicken

Serving: 4 servings. | Prep: 15mins | Cook: 15mins | Ready in:

Ingredients

- 2 celery ribs, chopped
- 1 medium onion, chopped
- 1/4 cup butter
- 1 can (10-3/4 ounces) condensed cream of mushroom soup, undiluted
- 1/2 cup chicken broth
- 1 tablespoon soy sauce
- 3 cups cubed cooked chicken
- 1/2 cup sliced fresh mushrooms
- 1 can (3 ounces) chow mein noodles
- 1/3 cup salted cashew halves

Direction

- Sauté celery and onion with butter in a saucepan till soft. Mix in soy sauce, broth and soup. Put in the mushrooms and chicken; heat through.

- Move to a 2-qt. greased baking dish. Scatter cashews and chow mein noodles. Without cover, bake at 350° till heated through, about 15 to 20 minutes.

Nutrition Information

- Calories: 578 calories
- Cholesterol: 127mg cholesterol
- Protein: 37g protein.
- Total Fat: 36g fat (13g saturated fat)
- Sodium: 1283mg sodium
- Fiber: 3g fiber)
- Total Carbohydrate: 26g carbohydrate (5g sugars

837. Cranberry Turkey Stir Fry

Serving: 4 servings. | Prep: 10mins | Cook: 15mins | Ready in:

Ingredients

- 2 garlic cloves, minced
- 1 tablespoon canola oil
- 2 cups julienned carrots
- 2 cups uncooked turkey breast strips
- 2 cups julienned zucchini
- 1 cup canned bean sprouts
- 1 can (8 ounces) jellied cranberry sauce
- 1/3 cup apple juice
- 1/4 cup reduced-sodium soy sauce
- 1/4 cup cider vinegar
- 1 tablespoon cornstarch
- 1/4 cup cold water
- 4 cups hot cooked rice

Direction

- Stir-fry the garlic in a wok or nonstick skillet with oil for 30 seconds. Add the carrots and stir-fry for 2 minutes. Add the bean sprouts, turkey, and zucchini and stir-fry for 3 minutes. Mix the apple juice, cranberry sauce, vinegar, and soy sauce and pour the mixture into the skillet. Bring the mixture to a boil.
- Mix cold water and cornstarch until smooth. Pour the mixture into the skillet gradually. Let the mixture boil. Cook and stir for 1-2 minutes until the turkey juices run clear and the mixture is bubbly and thick. Serve this stir-fry over the rice.

Nutrition Information

- Calories: 530 calories
- Fiber: 5g fiber)
- Total Carbohydrate: 83g carbohydrate (0 sugars
- Cholesterol: 55mg cholesterol
- Protein: 26g protein. Diabetic Exchanges: 3 starch
- Total Fat: 10g fat (2g saturated fat)
- Sodium: 696mg sodium

838. Crunchy Curried Chicken

Serving: 6-8 servings. | Prep: 15mins | Cook: 35mins | Ready in:

Ingredients

- 4-1/2 cups cooked long grain rice
- 1 cup cubed cooked chicken
- 1 cup cubed fully cooked ham
- 1 can (8 ounces) water chestnuts, drained and chopped
- 1 can (10-3/4 ounces) condensed cream of chicken soup, undiluted
- 1-1/4 cup milk
- 1/2 cup mayonnaise
- 1/4 cup minced fresh parsley
- 3/4 teaspoon salt
- 1/8 to 1/4 teaspoon curry powder
- 1/3 cup sliced almonds

Direction

- In a greased 13-in. x 9-in. baking dish, place the rice. Sprinkle with water chestnuts, ham, and chicken. Mix the next 6 ingredients, then pour over the chicken mixture.
- Bake at 350°, uncovered, until bubbly for 30-35 minutes. Sprinkle with almonds and continue to bake for 5 minutes more.

Nutrition Information

- Calories: 372 calories
- Sodium: 847mg sodium
- Fiber: 2g fiber)
- Total Carbohydrate: 34g carbohydrate (3g sugars
- Cholesterol: 38mg cholesterol
- Protein: 14g protein.
- Total Fat: 19g fat (4g saturated fat)

839.   Curried Shrimp Stir Fry

Serving: 4 servings. | Prep: 10mins | Cook: 20mins | Ready in:

Ingredients

- 1 cup chopped peeled tart apple
- 1/2 to 3/4 cup chopped onion
- 1/2 cup sliced celery
- 1/4 cup butter, cubed
- 3 tablespoons all-purpose flour
- 1 teaspoon curry powder
- 1/2 teaspoon salt
- 1/4 teaspoon ground ginger
- 1/8 teaspoon pepper
- 1-1/2 cups chicken broth
- 1/2 cup milk
- 1 teaspoon Worcestershire sauce
- 3/4 pound cooked shrimp, peeled and deveined
- Hot cooked rice

Direction

- Stir-fry celery, onion and apple with butter in a wok or big skillet until softened, about 10 minutes. Mix together pepper, ginger, salt, curry powder and flour, then put into the apple mixture and combine well. Stir in Worcestershire sauce, milk and broth gradually, then bring the mixture to a boil. Boil about 2 minutes while stirring continuously. Put in shrimp and heat through, then serve together with rice.

Nutrition Information

- Calories: 265 calories
- Sodium: 928mg sodium
- Fiber: 1g fiber)
- Total Carbohydrate: 14g carbohydrate (7g sugars
- Cholesterol: 164mg cholesterol
- Protein: 20g protein.
- Total Fat: 14g fat (8g saturated fat)

840.   Curried Tofu Stir Fry

Serving: 6 servings. | Prep: 25mins | Cook: 15mins | Ready in:

Ingredients

- 1 can (13.66 ounces) light coconut milk
- 1/4 cup reduced-sodium soy sauce
- 2 tablespoons cornstarch
- 1-1/2 teaspoons curry powder
- 1 teaspoon minced fresh gingerroot
- 1 teaspoon hoisin sauce
- 1/2 teaspoon salt
- 1/2 teaspoon brown sugar
- 1/2 teaspoon chili powder
- 1/2 teaspoon crushed red pepper flakes
- 1 package (16 ounces) firm tofu, drained and cubed
- 2 teaspoons canola oil
- 1 medium sweet yellow pepper, julienned
- 1/2 pound sliced fresh mushrooms

- 8 green onions, cut into 1-inch pieces
- 4 cups shredded cabbage
- 4 plum tomatoes, chopped
- 3 cups hot cooked brown rice

Direction

- Mix the first 10 ingredients in a small bowl; put aside. Coat the wok or large nonstick skillet with cooking spray. Stir-fry the tofu in oil until heated through, about 2-3 minutes. Remove from the heat and keep it warm.
- Stir-fry the yellow pepper in the same pan for 1 minute. Add the onions and mushrooms. Stir-fry for 2 more minutes. Add the tomatoes and cabbage. Stir-fry the mixture for 2 minutes.
- Whisk the coconut milk mixture and pour it into the skillet. Let the mixture boil. Bring the tofu back into the skillet. Cook and stir the mixture for 1-2 minutes until the vegetables are crisp-tender and the mixture are thick. Serve the mixture together with rice.

Nutrition Information

- Calories:
- Total Fat:
- Sodium:
- Fiber:
- Total Carbohydrate:
- Cholesterol:
- Protein:

841. Easy Marinated Sirloin Steak

Serving: 4 servings. | Prep: 10mins | Cook: 20mins | Ready in:

Ingredients

- 3/4 cup apple juice
- 3/4 cup soy sauce
- 1/4 cup olive oil
- 1 tablespoon each minced fresh oregano, rosemary and thyme
- 3 garlic cloves, minced
- 1 teaspoon ground ginger
- 1 beef top sirloin steak (1-1/2 pounds)

Direction

- Mix the soy sauce, apple juice, seasonings and oil together in a big ziplock plastic bag. Put in the beef then seal the ziplock bag and turn to coat the beef with the marinade. Keep in the fridge for at least 1 hour.
- Drain the marinated beef and throw away the marinade mixture. Put the marinated beef on a grill over medium heat then cover and let it grill for 8-10 minutes on both sides until the preferred meat doneness is achieved (a thermometer inserted in the meat should indicate 160°F for medium, 170°F for well-done and 145°F for medium-rare). Cut the beef into thin slices across the grain then serve.

Nutrition Information

- Calories: 277 calories
- Fiber: 0 fiber)
- Total Carbohydrate: 2g carbohydrate (2g sugars
- Cholesterol: 69mg cholesterol
- Protein: 38g protein.
- Total Fat: 11g fat (3g saturated fat)
- Sodium: 997mg sodium

842. Easy Shrimp Stir Fry

Serving: 4 servings. | Prep: 10mins | Cook: 20mins | Ready in:

Ingredients

- 2 tablespoons cornstarch
- 3/4 cup cold water
- 2 tablespoons reduced-sodium soy sauce

- 1 teaspoon garlic powder
- 1/2 teaspoon ground ginger
- 2 cups fresh broccoli florets
- 2 tablespoons olive oil
- 1 medium sweet red pepper, julienned
- 3 green onions, chopped
- 1 pound uncooked medium shrimp, peeled and deveined
- 1 cup frozen stir-fry vegetable blend, thawed
- 3 garlic cloves, minced
- 1/4 cup chopped peanuts

Direction

- Mix together water and cornstarch in a small bowl until smooth. Stir in ginger, garlic powder and soy sauce, then put aside.
- Stir-fry broccoli in a big nonstick skillet or wok with oil about 2 minutes. Put in onions and red pepper, then stir-fry until vegetables are tender but still crispy, or about 2 to 3 minutes. Put in garlic, Oriental vegetables and shrimp, then cook about 3 more minutes.
- Stir cornstarch mixture and stir into the shrimp mixture. Put in peanuts, then bring to a boil. Cook and stir until thickened, or about 2 minutes.

Nutrition Information

- Calories: 273 calories
- Sodium: 593mg sodium
- Fiber: 4g fiber)
- Total Carbohydrate: 18g carbohydrate (4g sugars
- Cholesterol: 129mg cholesterol
- Protein: 23g protein. Diabetic Exchanges: 3 lean meat
- Total Fat: 13g fat (2g saturated fat)

843. Eckrich® Sweet And Sour Sausage

Serving: 5 servings. | Prep: 10mins | Cook: 15mins | Ready in:

Ingredients

- 1 can (20 ounces) unsweetened pineapple chunks, undrained
- 1/3 cup packed brown sugar
- 2 tablespoons cornstarch
- 1/4 cup white wine vinegar
- 2 tablespoons soy sauce
- 1 package Eckrich® Smoked Sausage, cut into 1/2-inch slices
- 2 medium carrots, diagonally sliced
- 1 medium green pepper, cut into 1-inch pieces
- Hot cooked rice

Direction

- Drain pineapple, saving juices. Pour in enough water to the juice to measure 1 1/2 cups. Mix together cornstarch and brown sugar in a bowl. Slowly beat in juice mixture until thoroughly blended. Mix in soy sauce and vinegar; put aside.
- Stir-fry pepper, carrots, and sausage in a big skillet for 6 minutes, till carrots are crisp-tender. Mix juice mixture and blend into skillet.
- Heat to a boil; stir and cook until thickened, or about 1 minute. Mix in pineapple and cook, mixing occasionally, until heated through. Serve along with rice.

Nutrition Information

- Calories:
- Protein:
- Total Fat:
- Sodium:
- Fiber:
- Total Carbohydrate:
- Cholesterol:

844. Egg Foo Yong With Sauce

Serving: 4 servings. | Prep: 15mins | Cook: 15mins | Ready in:

Ingredients

- 4 teaspoons cornstarch
- 1 tablespoon sugar
- 2 teaspoons grated fresh gingerroot
- 1 cup reduced-sodium chicken broth
- 2 tablespoons reduced-sodium soy sauce
- 2 tablespoons sherry or apple juice
- EGG FOO YONG:
- 1-1/2 cups egg substitute
- 1/4 cup chopped green onions
- 2 cups canned bean sprouts, rinsed and drained
- 1 can (8 ounces) water chestnuts, drained and chopped
- 1 can (4 ounces) mushroom stems and pieces, drained
- 1/4 teaspoon salt
- 1/8 teaspoon Chinese five spice
- 2 tablespoons canola oil

Direction

- Mix ginger, cornstarch and sugar in a small pot. Add broth and stir until smooth. Pour in the soy sauce and apple juice or sherry. Heat to a boil and stir constantly until thick, 2-3 minutes. Take the pot off the heat. In a separate bowl, mix together onions and egg substitute. Let the mixture stand for 10 minutes. Mix in water chestnuts, Chinese five spice, bean sprouts, salt, and mushrooms. Make sure it is well combined. Heat oil in a nonstick frying pan and dump in batter 1/4 of a cup at a time. Cook for 2-2 1/2 minutes per side until color is golden brown. Enjoy with sauce.

Nutrition Information

- Calories: 209 calories
- Total Carbohydrate: 14g carbohydrate (0 sugars
- Cholesterol: 1mg cholesterol
- Protein: 14g protein. Diabetic Exchanges: 2 lean meat
- Total Fat: 10g fat (1g saturated fat)
- Sodium: 955mg sodium
- Fiber: 3g fiber)

845. Epiphany Ham

Serving: 12 servings. | Prep: 10mins | Cook: 03hours00mins | Ready in:

Ingredients

- 1 fully cooked bone-in ham (8 to 10 pounds; not spiral cut)
- 1 can (12 ounces) black cherry soda
- 2 teaspoons Chinese five-spice powder
- 2/3 cup duck sauce

Direction

- Preheat an oven to 350°. Put ham onto a rack in a baking dish/pan; pour soda over ham. Sprinkle five-spice powder over. Cover using aluminum foil; bake for 30 minutes.
- Remove foil; discard. Baste using duck sauce; put back in oven. Bake for 2 1/2 hours till thermometer reads 140°, uncovered, basting again halfway through baking.

Nutrition Information

- Calories: 303 calories
- Sodium: 1659mg sodium
- Fiber: 0 fiber)
- Total Carbohydrate: 13g carbohydrate (9g sugars
- Cholesterol: 133mg cholesterol
- Protein: 45g protein.
- Total Fat: 8g fat (3g saturated fat)

846. Firecracker Grilled Salmon

Serving: 4 servings. | Prep: 20mins | Cook: 5mins | Ready in:

Ingredients

- 2 tablespoons balsamic vinegar
- 2 tablespoons reduced-sodium soy sauce
- 1 green onion, thinly sliced
- 1 tablespoon olive oil
- 1 tablespoon maple syrup
- 2 garlic cloves, minced
- 1 teaspoon ground ginger
- 1 teaspoon crushed red pepper flakes
- 1/2 teaspoon sesame oil
- 1/4 teaspoon salt
- 4 salmon fillets (6 ounces each)

Direction

- Mix the first 10 ingredients together in a small bowl. Transfer a quarter (1/4) cup of marinade in a big resealable bag and place the salmon inside. Seal and turn to coat. Chill in the refrigerator for half an hour. Cover the remaining marinade and refrigerate.
- Remove the salmon from the bag and discard the marinade. Arrange the fish on a greased grill rack with its skin side down. On maximum heat, grill the salmon for 5-10 minutes, covered, or broil 3-4 inches from the heat until the flesh is flaky. Often baste using the remaining marinade.

Nutrition Information

- Calories: 306 calories
- Fiber: 0 fiber)
- Total Carbohydrate: 4g carbohydrate (3g sugars
- Cholesterol: 85mg cholesterol
- Protein: 29g protein. Diabetic exchanges: 5 lean meat
- Total Fat: 18g fat (4g saturated fat)
- Sodium: 367mg sodium

847. Garlic Chicken Kabobs

Serving: 8 servings. | Prep: 10mins | Cook: 10mins | Ready in:

Ingredients

- 8 garlic cloves, minced
- 1/2 teaspoon salt
- 1/4 cup minced fresh cilantro
- 1 teaspoon ground coriander
- 1/2 cup reduced-fat plain yogurt
- 2 tablespoons lemon juice
- 1-1/2 teaspoons olive oil
- 2 pounds boneless skinless chicken breasts, cut into 1-inch cubes
- GARLIC DIPPING SAUCE:
- 4 garlic cloves, minced
- 1/4 teaspoon salt
- 2 tablespoons olive oil
- 1 cup (8 ounces) reduced-fat plain yogurt

Direction

- Crush garlic and salt with the back of a sturdy spoon. Place them in a small bowl. Add coriander and cilantro, crush again with back of a spoon. Stir in lemon juice, oil, and yogurt. Pour the mixture over the chicken in a large re-sealable plastic bag. Seal the bag, turn to coat, and refrigerate for 2 hours. Make the dipping sauce: Crush garlic and salt with the back of a sturdy spoon. Add in oil then yogurt, mixing well. Cover and store in the fridge until ready for serving. Drain chicken and discard its marinade. Thread chicken onto eight metal or pre-soaked wooden skewers. Lightly oil the rack with an oil-moistened paper towel using long-handled tongs. Cook kabobs in a covered grill over medium heat, or broil 4 in. from heat, for 6-8 minutes or until juices come out clear. Flip kabobs from time to time.

Nutrition Information

- Calories: 186 calories
- Total Carbohydrate: 4g carbohydrate (0 sugars
- Cholesterol: 68mg cholesterol
- Protein: 28g protein. Diabetic Exchanges: 3 lean meat
- Total Fat: 6g fat (1g saturated fat)
- Sodium: 246mg sodium
- Fiber: 0 fiber)

848. Glazed Shrimp & Asparagus For 2

Serving: 2 servings. | Prep: 15mins | Cook: 15mins | Ready in:

Ingredients

- 4 ounces uncooked whole wheat angel hair pasta
- 1-1/2 teaspoons cornstarch
- 1/3 cup cold water
- 1-1/2 teaspoons soy sauce
- 1-1/2 teaspoons honey
- 1-1/2 teaspoons peanut or canola oil, divided
- 1/2 teaspoon sesame oil
- 1/2 pound uncooked large shrimp, peeled and deveined
- 1/2 pound fresh asparagus, trimmed and cut into 2- to 3-in. lengths
- 1-1/2 teaspoons minced fresh gingerroot
- 1 garlic clove, minced
- 1/8 teaspoon crushed red pepper flakes
- 1-1/2 teaspoons sesame seeds

Direction

- Follow the package instructions on how to cook the pasta. Mix the soy sauce, water, honey, and cornstarch in a small bowl until smooth; put aside.
- Stir-fry the shrimp in a wok or large skillet with sesame oil and 1/2 tsp. of peanut oil until the shrimp is already pink. Remove from the skillet and keep them warm.
- In the remaining peanut oil, stir-fry the asparagus for 2 minutes. Add the pepper flakes, sesame seeds, ginger, and garlic and stir-fry for 2 minutes until the asparagus is crisp-tender.
- Whisk the cornstarch mixture; pour to the pan. Let the mixture boil. Cook for 2 minutes, stirring until the mixture is thick. Add the shrimp and heat the mixture through. Drain the pasta before adding it into the shrimp mixture.

Nutrition Information

- Calories: 386 calories
- Cholesterol: 138mg cholesterol
- Protein: 29g protein.
- Total Fat: 8g fat (1g saturated fat)
- Sodium: 376mg sodium
- Fiber: 8g fiber)
- Total Carbohydrate: 53g carbohydrate (7g sugars

849. Grilled Curried Salmon

Serving: 2 servings. | Prep: 10mins | Cook: 10mins | Ready in:

Ingredients

- 2 salmon fillets (6 ounces each)
- 1 teaspoon lemon-pepper seasoning
- 1 teaspoon garlic powder
- 1 teaspoon curry powder
- 6 tablespoons reduced-sodium soy sauce
- 1/4 cup butter, melted
- 1/4 teaspoon Worcestershire sauce
- Dash Liquid Smoke, optional

Direction

- Season the fillets with curry powder, garlic powder, and lemon pepper. Seal with plastic wrap or cover with lid. Let it chill for half an hour (30 minutes).
- Mix the butter, Worcestershire sauce, soy sauce, in a large resealable bag. Adding Liquid Smoke is optional. Place the salmon in the bag, reseal and turn to coat the entire salmon; refrigerate for 30 minutes. Drain the fish and dispose the marinade.
- Set the salmon on a covered grill with its skin side down on the rack. Over a medium heat, cover and cook the salmon for about 8-12 minutes or until the flesh flakes easily with a fork.

Nutrition Information

- Calories: 381 calories
- Total Carbohydrate: 3g carbohydrate (0 sugars
- Cholesterol: 115mg cholesterol
- Protein: 36g protein.
- Total Fat: 25g fat (7g saturated fat)
- Sodium: 1222mg sodium
- Fiber: 0 fiber)

850. Grilled Lime Teriyaki Shrimp

Serving: 2 servings. | Prep: 10mins | Cook: 10mins | Ready in:

Ingredients

- 3 tablespoons lime juice
- 2 tablespoons olive oil
- 2 tablespoons reduced-sodium teriyaki sauce
- 1 tablespoon balsamic vinegar
- 1 tablespoon Dijon mustard
- 1 teaspoon garlic powder
- 6 drops hot pepper sauce
- 6 uncooked jumbo shrimp, peeled and deveined

Direction

- Mix the first 7 ingredients together in a big zip lock plastic bag then put in the shrimp. Seal the zip lock bag and turn to coat the shrimp. Keep in the fridge for an hour and occasionally turn.
- Drain the marinated shrimps and discard marinade. Insert the marinated shrimps onto 2 soaked wooden or metal skewers. Use tongs to lightly rub an oiled paper towel on the grill rack. Put the shrimp skewers on the grill over medium heat then cover or broil the shrimp 4 inches from heat for 3 to 4 minutes per side or until the shrimp turn pink in color.

Nutrition Information

- Calories: 98 calories
- Total Carbohydrate: 2g carbohydrate (1g sugars
- Cholesterol: 93mg cholesterol
- Protein: 13g protein. Diabetic Exchanges: 2 lean meat
- Total Fat: 4g fat (1g saturated fat)
- Sodium: 196mg sodium
- Fiber: 0 fiber)

851. Grilled Mahi Mahi

Serving: 12 | Prep: 20mins | Cook: 35mins | Ready in:

Ingredients

- 5 pounds skinned, deboned mahi mahi, cut into chunks
- 3/4 (4.5 ounce) jar bottled minced garlic
- 1/2 cup butter, diced
- 1 large onion, diced
- 1 1/2 lemons, juiced
- 1/2 cup dry white wine

- 1 1/2 (10 ounce) cans diced tomatoes with green chile peppers
- salt and pepper to taste
- 8 ounces shredded pepperjack cheese

Direction

- Preheat the grill for high heat. After inserting the mahi mahi into an aluminium foil pan, coat it tossing with garlic. Layer the butter evenly on the entire pan. Over the fish, scatter onions, followed by the green chilli peppers, diced tomatoes, wine and lemon juice. Add pepper and salt to season the fish. Use aluminium foil to cover the pan up firmly. Move the pan onto the grill grate and leave the fish cooking for 35 minutes. Use a fork to test if the fish flakes off easily. If it does, it's done. When ready to serve, scatter cheese over the top.

Nutrition Information

- Calories: 337 calories;
- Cholesterol: 179
- Protein: 40.1
- Total Fat: 15.3
- Sodium: 480
- Total Carbohydrate: 7.1

852. Grilled Marinated Pork Chops

Serving: Serves 6 to 8 | Prep: | Cook: | Ready in:

Ingredients

- 1 cup apple juice
- 3/4 cup soy sauce
- 1/2 cup honey
- 2 large garlic cloves, forced through a garlic press
- 2 tablespoons grated peeled fresh gingerroot
- 1 tablespoon dry mustard
- 2 dashes of Worcestershire sauce
- 1/2 cup golden or dark rum
- twelve 1-inch-thick pork chops
- a 12-ounce jar apple jelly
- 3 tablespoons lemon juice
- freshly grated nutmeg to taste

Direction

- Mix the honey, garlic, rum, apple juice, mustard, 1/2 cup of soy sauce, gingerroot and Worcestershire sauce in a bowl. Put a single layer of pork chops at the bottom of a shallow dish then pour the prepared marinade mixture evenly on top; cover the dish and let the pork marinate in the fridge overnight, turn it from time to time to let it marinate evenly.
- Drain off the marinade directly into a saucepan then put in the remaining 1/4 cup of soy sauce and jelly. Let the mixture boil until the mixture is about 1 1/2 cups; add in the nutmeg and lemon juice and give it a mix.
- Put the marinated pork chops on a greased grill rack placed about 6 inches above smoldering coals and let them grill for 20 minutes until they are cooked thoroughly. Turn and baste the pork chops with the prepared sauce mixture in 5-minute intervals to let them cook evenly. Serve the grilled pork chops along with the prepared sauce mixture.

Nutrition Information

- Calories: 991
- Saturated Fat: 12 g(60%)
- Sodium: 1992 mg(83%)
- Fiber: 1 g(5%)
- Total Carbohydrate: 65 g(22%)
- Cholesterol: 275 mg(92%)
- Protein: 86 g(171%)
- Total Fat: 37 g(56%)

853. Grilled Marinated Pork Tenderloin

Serving: 6 servings (2/3 cup sauce). | Prep: 15mins | Cook: 25mins |Ready in:

Ingredients

- 3/4 cup canola oil
- 1/3 cup soy sauce
- 1/4 cup white vinegar
- 2 tablespoons lemon juice
- 2 tablespoons Worcestershire sauce
- 1 tablespoon minced fresh parsley
- 1 garlic clove, minced
- 1/4 teaspoon salt
- 1/4 teaspoon pepper
- 2 pork tenderloins (1 pound each)
- MUSTARD SAUCE:
- 1/2 cup mayonnaise
- 2 tablespoons Dijon mustard
- 2 teaspoons prepared horseradish
- 1 teaspoon Worcestershire sauce
- 1/8 teaspoon crushed red pepper flakes, optional

Direction

- Mix the first 9 ingredients together in a big ziplock bag; put pork in. seal and flip the bag to coat the pork. Place in the refrigerator overnight.
- Set grill on indirect heat. Drain the pork and get rid of the marinade. Grease the grill rack lightly with a paper towel moistened with cooking oil and long-handled tongs.
- On indirect medium heat, grill tenderloins for 25 to 40 mins, covered, until an inserted thermometer registers 160 degrees F. Set aside for 5 mins then slice.
- Mix the sauce ingredients together in a small bowl. Serve tenderloins with the sauce.

Nutrition Information

- Calories: 442 calories
- Sodium: 781mg sodium
- Fiber: 0 fiber)
- Total Carbohydrate: 2g carbohydrate (1g sugars
- Cholesterol: 91mg cholesterol
- Protein: 31g protein.
- Total Fat: 33g fat (6g saturated fat)

854. Grilled Teriyaki Pork Tenderloin

Serving: 4 servings. | Prep: 10mins | Cook: 20mins |Ready in:

Ingredients

- 3/4 cup honey mustard
- 3/4 cup teriyaki marinade
- 1 pork tenderloin (1 pound)
- 2 garlic cloves, minced
- 1 green onion, chopped

Direction

- Mix teriyaki marinade and mustard in a small bowl, add 1 cup into a large resealable plastic bag. Put in garlic and pork, sealing bag and turning to coat. Keep in refrigerator for 6 hours or overnight. Refrigerate the remaining marinade covered.
- Set grill for indirect heat with a drip pan. Use cooking oil to moisten a paper towel; rub on to coat grill rack lightly with long-handled tongs. Drain and dispose of marinade from pork.
- In a drip pan, place pork, cover and grill for 25-40 minutes over indirect medium-hot heat (or desired doneness) for medium-rare, a thermometer should read 145deg; medium, 160deg. Baste with reserved marinade turning several times. Before slicing, let stand 5 minutes. Top with onion.

Nutrition Information

- Calories: 222 calories

- Cholesterol: 64mg cholesterol
- Protein: 25g protein.
- Total Fat: 6g fat (2g saturated fat)
- Sodium: 957mg sodium
- Fiber: 1g fiber)
- Total Carbohydrate: 19g carbohydrate (15g sugars

855. Grilled Turkey Tenderloin

Serving: 4 servings. | Prep: 5mins | Cook: 20mins | Ready in:

Ingredients

- 1/4 cup apple juice
- 1/4 cup reduced-sodium soy sauce
- 1/4 cup canola oil
- 2 tablespoons lemon juice
- 2 tablespoons dried minced onion
- 1 teaspoon vanilla extract
- 1/4 teaspoon ground ginger
- Dash each garlic powder and pepper
- 2 turkey breast tenderloins (1/2 pound each)

Direction

- In a large resealable plastic bag, blend pepper, garlic powder, ginger, vanilla, onion, lemon juice, oil, soy sauce, and apple juice; put in the turkey. Close the bag and shake to coat. Let cool in the refrigerator for a minimum of 2 hours.
- Drain turkey, discard marinade. Cover and grill turkey on medium heat, about 8 to 10 minutes per side, until a thermometer shows 170°.

Nutrition Information

- Calories: 157 calories
- Total Carbohydrate: 1g carbohydrate (1g sugars

- Cholesterol: 56mg cholesterol
- Protein: 27g protein. Diabetic Exchanges: 3 lean meat
- Total Fat: 5g fat (1g saturated fat)
- Sodium: 211mg sodium
- Fiber: 0 fiber)

856. Ground Beef Lo Mein

Serving: 6 servings. | Prep: 5mins | Cook: 20mins | Ready in:

Ingredients

- 8 ounces uncooked spaghetti
- 1/2 pound cooked lean ground beef (90% lean)
- 1 package (16 ounces) frozen stir-fry vegetable blend, thawed
- 1 jar (12 ounces) home-style beef gravy
- 1/4 teaspoon reduced-sodium soy sauce
- 1/4 teaspoon garlic powder
- 1/8 teaspoon pepper

Direction

- Following package directions to cook spaghetti. In the meantime, cook beef in a big skillet on medium heat until heated through, or about 2 to 3 minutes. Put in pepper, garlic powder, soy sauce, gravy and vegetables, then bring all to a boil. Lower the heat, then cover and simmer until vegetables are tender but still crispy, or about 8 to 10 minutes. Drain spaghetti and put into the beef mixture, stir well.

Nutrition Information

- Calories: 267 calories
- Total Carbohydrate: 42g carbohydrate (2g sugars
- Cholesterol: 21mg cholesterol
- Protein: 16g protein.
- Total Fat: 4g fat (1g saturated fat)

- Sodium: 425mg sodium
- Fiber: 4g fiber)

857. Hawaiian Stir Fry

Serving: 4 servings. | Prep: 20mins | Cook: 15mins | Ready in:

Ingredients

- 1 can (8 ounces) unsweetened pineapple chunks
- 2 tablespoons brown sugar
- 1 tablespoon cornstarch
- 1/3 cup water
- 2 tablespoons reduced-sodium soy sauce
- 1 carrot, cut into 2-inch julienne strips
- 2 tablespoons canola oil, divided
- 2 celery ribs, thinly sliced
- 1 medium sweet red pepper, julienned
- 1 medium sweet yellow pepper, julienned
- 1 medium onion, cut into thin wedges
- 2 cups frozen sugar snap peas, thawed
- 1 pound boneless skinless chicken breasts, cut into 2-1/2-inch strips
- Hot cooked rice, optional

Direction

- Drain pineapple and reserve the juice. In a small bowl, mix cornstarch and brown sugar. Blend in saved pineapple juice, soy sauce, and water, until smooth; put aside. In a large non-stick skillet (or wok), stir-fry carrot in 1 tablespoon of heated oil, about 1 minute. Combine in onion, sweet peppers, and celery; stir-fry for 3 minutes. Put in sugar snap peas; stir-fry about an extra 1 minute, or until crispy-tender. Take vegetables out and keep warm.
- Stir-fry chicken in the oil left in the same skillet, about 3 to 4 minutes, or until not pink anymore. Whisk soy sauce mixture; slowly blend into skillet. Bring to a boil; keep cooking and stirring for 1 to 2 minutes, or until thickened. Combine in pineapple chunks and vegetable mixture; heat through. Serve over rice if wanted.

Nutrition Information

- Calories: 314 calories
- Protein: 29g protein. Diabetic Exchanges: 3 lean meat
- Total Fat: 9g fat (1g saturated fat)
- Sodium: 413mg sodium
- Fiber: 5g fiber)
- Total Carbohydrate: 29g carbohydrate (0 sugars
- Cholesterol: 66mg cholesterol

858. Hoisin Shrimp & Broccoli

Serving: 4 servings. | Prep: 15mins | Cook: 15mins | Ready in:

Ingredients

- 1 tablespoon cornstarch
- 1/3 cup reduced-sodium chicken broth
- 4-1/2 teaspoons reduced-sodium soy sauce
- 4-1/2 teaspoons hoisin sauce
- 1 teaspoon sesame oil
- 3 cups fresh broccoli florets
- 1 tablespoon canola oil
- 4 green onions, chopped
- 3 garlic cloves, minced
- 1 teaspoon minced fresh gingerroot
- 1 pound uncooked medium shrimp, peeled and deveined
- 2 cups hot cooked rice

Direction

- Mix broth and cornstarch till smooth in a small bowl. Mix in sesame oil, hoisin sauce and soy sauce; put aside.

- Stir-fry broccoli till crisp-tender in canola oil in a big nonstick skillet/wok. Add ginger, garlic and onions; stir-fry till veggies are tender for 3-4 minutes. Add shrimp; stir-fry till shrimp are pink for 4-5 minutes.
- Mix cornstarch mixture; put in pan. Boil; mix and cook till thick for 2 minutes. Serve with rice.

Nutrition Information

- Calories: 289 calories
- Total Fat: 7g fat (1g saturated fat)
- Sodium: 524mg sodium
- Fiber: 2g fiber)
- Total Carbohydrate: 33g carbohydrate (3g sugars
- Cholesterol: 138mg cholesterol
- Protein: 23g protein. Diabetic Exchanges: 3 lean meat

859. Hoisin Glazed Pork

Serving: 2 servings. | Prep: 10mins | Cook: 15mins | Ready in:

Ingredients

- 3 green onions, cut into 2-inch pieces
- 1 tablespoon Dijon mustard
- 1 tablespoon hoisin sauce
- 1 tablespoon oyster sauce
- 1 tablespoon honey
- 1 teaspoon reduced-sodium soy sauce
- 1/2 teaspoon minced fresh gingerroot
- 2 boneless pork loin chops (1/2 inch thick and 5 ounces each)

Direction

- Combine the first 7 ingredients in a small bowl. Arrange the pork in a shallow 1-qt. baking dish coated with cooking spray; then pour sauce over the pork.
- Bake while uncovered for 15-20 minutes at 400°, or until a thermometer states 160°.

Nutrition Information

- Calories: 265 calories
- Total Carbohydrate: 17g carbohydrate (11g sugars
- Cholesterol: 69mg cholesterol
- Protein: 29g protein. Diabetic Exchanges: 4 lean meat
- Total Fat: 8g fat (3g saturated fat)
- Sodium: 789mg sodium
- Fiber: 1g fiber)

860. Honey Citrus Chops

Serving: 6 servings. | Prep: 5mins | Cook: 10mins | Ready in:

Ingredients

- 2/3 cup lemon-lime soda
- 1/2 cup soy sauce
- 1/4 cup honey
- 6 boneless pork loin chops (6 ounces each)

Direction

- Mix the honey, soy sauce, and soda in a large resealable plastic bag. Add the pork into the bag. Seal the bag and flip it until coated. Refrigerate the bag overnight while occasionally flipping it.
- Drain the pork and discard its marinade. Cover and grill the pork onto the oiled rack that is set over medium heat, or you can broil the pork 4-inches away from the heat source until the thermometer registers 160°, about 4-5 minutes per side.

Nutrition Information

- Calories: 260 calories

- Sodium: 662mg sodium
- Fiber: 0 fiber)
- Total Carbohydrate: 7g carbohydrate (7g sugars
- Cholesterol: 82mg cholesterol
- Protein: 34g protein. Diabetic Exchanges: 5 lean meat.
- Total Fat: 10g fat (4g saturated fat)

861. Honey Glazed Chicken Kabobs

Serving: 6 servings. | Prep: 20mins | Cook: 10mins | Ready in:

Ingredients

- 2/3 cup reduced-sodium soy sauce
- 2/3 cup honey
- 1/2 cup canola oil
- 1 tablespoon prepared horseradish
- 2 teaspoons steak seasoning
- 2 garlic cloves, minced
- 2 pounds boneless skinless chicken breasts, cut into 1-1/2-inch cubes
- 1 large sweet red pepper, cut into 1-1/2-inch chunks
- 1 large green pepper, cut into 1-1/2-inch chunks
- 1 large onion, cut into 1-1/2-inch wedges

Direction

- Combine the first six ingredients in a small bowl. Take a cup of the mixture and pour in a large re-sealable plastic bag with the chicken. Zip the bag, turn several times to coat, and let marinate in the refrigerator for 5-6 hours. Transfer the remaining marinade in a covered container and store in the refrigerator until time for grilling. Take the bag with the chicken out of the refrigerator, drain and discard marinade, and thread the chicken alternately with the vegetables on six metal or pre-soaked wooden skewers. Cook on a covered medium-hot grill, brushing often with reserved marinade, for 5-7 minutes per side or until chicken juices come out clear.

Nutrition Information

- Calories: 363 calories
- Sodium: 395mg sodium
- Fiber: 1g fiber)
- Total Carbohydrate: 14g carbohydrate (11g sugars
- Cholesterol: 73mg cholesterol
- Protein: 28g protein.
- Total Fat: 22g fat (2g saturated fat)

862. Honey Grilled Pork Tenderloin

Serving: 2 servings. | Prep: 10mins | Cook: 20mins | Ready in:

Ingredients

- 3 tablespoons reduced-sodium soy sauce
- 2 garlic cloves, minced
- 1/4 teaspoon ground ginger
- 1 pork tenderloin (3/4 pound)
- 4-1/2 teaspoons honey
- 1 tablespoon brown sugar
- 1 teaspoon sesame oil

Direction

- Mix ginger, garlic, and soy sauce together in a big ziplock bag; put pork in. Seal and flip the bag to coat the pork. Place in the refrigerator for 8 hours to overnight.
- Mix oil, brown sugar, and honey together in a small pot. On low heat, cook and stir the mixture until the sugar dissolves. Take off heat then put aside.
- Drain pork and get rid of the marinade. Grease the grill rack lightly. With a drip pan, set grill on indirect heat.

- Arrange pork on top of the drip pan. On indirect medium heat, grill pork for 20 to 25 mins, covered, until an inserted thermometer registers 160 degrees F. Use the honey mixture to baste the pork regularly. Set aside for 5 mins then slice.

Nutrition Information

- Calories: 298 calories
- Fiber: 0 fiber)
- Total Carbohydrate: 21g carbohydrate (20g sugars
- Cholesterol: 95mg cholesterol
- Protein: 34g protein. Diabetic Exchanges: 5 lean meat
- Total Fat: 8g fat (2g saturated fat)
- Sodium: 373mg sodium

863. Indonesian Peanut Chicken

Serving: 6 servings. | Prep: 15mins | Cook: 04hours00mins | Ready in:

Ingredients

- 1-1/2 pounds boneless skinless chicken breasts, cut into 1-inch cubes
- 1/3 cup chopped onion
- 1/3 cup water
- 1/4 cup reduced-fat creamy peanut butter
- 3 tablespoons chili sauce
- 1/4 teaspoon salt
- 1/4 teaspoon cayenne pepper
- 1/4 teaspoon pepper
- 3 cups hot cooked brown rice
- 6 tablespoons chopped salted peanuts
- 6 tablespoons chopped sweet red pepper

Direction

- Put the chicken into a 4-quart slow cooker. Mix pepper, cayenne, salt, chili sauce, peanut butter, water and onion in a small bowl; pour onto the chicken. Cook, with cover, for 4 to 6 hours on low until on top is not pink anymore.
- Using 2 forks, shred meat and put back into the slow cooker and heat fully. Serve along with rice. Scatter red pepper and peanuts over.

Nutrition Information

- Calories: 353 calories
- Sodium: 370mg sodium
- Fiber: 3g fiber)
- Total Carbohydrate: 31g carbohydrate (4g sugars
- Cholesterol: 63mg cholesterol
- Protein: 31g protein. Diabetic Exchanges: 3 lean meat
- Total Fat: 12g fat (2g saturated fat)

864. Lemon Plum Pork Roast

Serving: 6 servings. | Prep: 40mins | Cook: 60mins | Ready in:

Ingredients

- 1 boneless pork loin roast (2 pounds)
- 1/4 teaspoon garlic salt
- 1/4 teaspoon pepper
- 1/4 cup chopped onion
- 2 teaspoons butter
- 1/4 cup plum jam
- 3 tablespoons lemonade
- 2 tablespoons chili sauce
- 3/4 teaspoon soy sauce
- 1/2 teaspoon prepared mustard
- 1/4 teaspoon ground ginger
- GRAVY:
- 1 tablespoon all-purpose flour
- 1/4 cup water

Direction

- Season the roast with pepper, and garlic salt. Put roast in a shallow roasting pan with fat side up. Sauté onion with butter until tender in a skillet; stir in the reserved ingredients. Keep stirring until heated through. Pour over the roast.
- Bake without a cover for 1 hour at 350°, until a thermometer reaches 160°. Transfer roast to a platter and keep warm. Allow to sit for 10 minutes.
- Pour loosened brown bits and drippings into a bowl. Remove the fat. Mix flour into water in a small saucepan until smooth. Stir in drippings gradually. Bring to the boil; cook while stirring for 2 minutes until thickened. Cut roast into slices and serve along with gravy.

Nutrition Information

- Calories: 269 calories
- Total Fat: 9g fat (4g saturated fat)
- Sodium: 368mg sodium
- Fiber: 0 fiber)
- Total Carbohydrate: 16g carbohydrate (0 sugars
- Cholesterol: 87mg cholesterol
- Protein: 33g protein. Diabetic Exchanges: 4 lean meat

865. Marinated Beef Stir Fry

Serving: 3 servings. | Prep: 15mins | Cook: 15mins | Ready in:

Ingredients

- 1/2 cup dry red wine or beef broth
- 6 tablespoons olive oil, divided
- 1 teaspoon chili powder
- 1 teaspoon minced garlic
- 1/2 teaspoon ground cumin
- 1/4 teaspoon salt
- 1/4 teaspoon ground ginger
- 1/4 teaspoon pepper
- 1/2 pound beef flank steak, cut into 1/8-inch strips
- 1 medium onion, cut into thin strips
- 1/2 cup julienned zucchini
- 1/2 cup julienned carrot
- 1/2 cup each julienned green and sweet red peppers

Direction

- Mix the wine, chili powder, salt, pepper, ginger, 4 tbsp. of oil, garlic, and cumin in a large and resealable plastic bag. Add the beef inside before sealing the bag. Flip it until coated. Refrigerate the bag for at least 12 hours.
- Stir-fry the carrot, peppers, onion, and zucchini in a wok or large skillet with remaining oil for 4-5 minutes until they are crisp-tender. Remove from the heat and keep it warm.
- Drain the beef and discard the marinade. Stir-fry the beef for 5-6 minutes until it is no longer pink; drain. Add the vegetables to the pan, and then stir-fry for 2-3 minutes until the mixture is heated through.

Nutrition Information

- Calories: 268 calories
- Total Fat: 20g fat (4g saturated fat)
- Sodium: 112mg sodium
- Fiber: 3g fiber)
- Total Carbohydrate: 10g carbohydrate (6g sugars
- Cholesterol: 32mg cholesterol
- Protein: 14g protein. Diabetic Exchanges: 2 lean meat

866. Orange Turkey Stir Fry

Serving: 4 servings. | Prep: 30mins | Cook: 0mins | Ready in:

Ingredients

- 3/4 cup orange juice
- 1/4 cup orange marmalade
- 2 tablespoons soy sauce
- 2 tablespoons cornstarch
- 1/8 teaspoon ground ginger
- 1/8 teaspoon hot pepper sauce
- 1/4 cup all-purpose flour
- 1 pound turkey cutlets, cut into 1-inch strips
- 2 tablespoons vegetable oil, divided
- 4 green onions, cut into 1-inch pieces
- 1/2 cup coarsely chopped green pepper
- 1 seedless orange, peeled, sliced and halved
- Cooked rice

Direction

- Mix initial 6 ingredients in a small bowl; put aside. Put flour on waxed paper sheet. Coat turkey strips; shake excess off. Heat 1 tbsp. oil in 10-in. skillet on medium high heat. In 3 batches, cook turkey till all sides are lightly browned and strips are tender. Remove turkey; keep warm. Put leftover oil in skillet; mix and cook green pepper and green onions for 1 minute. Mix in orange juice mixture; boil. Lower heat; simmer for 3 minutes. Add orange slices and turkey; heat through. Serve on rice.

Nutrition Information

- Calories: 324 calories
- Protein: 29g protein.
- Total Fat: 9g fat (1g saturated fat)
- Sodium: 536mg sodium
- Fiber: 2g fiber)
- Total Carbohydrate: 34g carbohydrate (21g sugars
- Cholesterol: 56mg cholesterol

867. Orange Spiced Chicken

Serving: 4 servings. | Prep: 10mins | Cook: 10mins | Ready in:

Ingredients

- 1/2 cup thawed orange juice concentrate
- 1/4 cup honey
- 1/4 cup soy sauce
- 1 teaspoon Chinese five-spice powder
- 1/2 teaspoon garlic powder
- 4 boneless skinless chicken breast halves (5 ounces each)

Direction

- In a small bowl, blend the first 5 ingredients. Transfer 1/2 cup of marinade to a large resealable plastic bag; put in chicken. Close the bag and shake to coat; marinate in the refrigerator for 2 hours. Cover the marinate and put it in the refrigerator.
- Drain chicken, discard marinade. Use cooking oil to moisten a paper towel; with long-handled tongs, lightly rub on the grill rack. Cover and grill chicken over medium heat or broil 4-inch stayed from the grill for 5 to 7 minutes per side, until a thermometer shows 170°, basting regularly with saved marinade.

Nutrition Information

- Calories: 234 calories
- Total Carbohydrate: 19g carbohydrate (19g sugars
- Cholesterol: 78mg cholesterol
- Protein: 30g protein. Diabetic Exchanges: 4 lean meat
- Total Fat: 3g fat (1g saturated fat)
- Sodium: 643mg sodium
- Fiber: 0 fiber)

868. Pacific Rim Salmon

Serving: 8 servings. | Prep: 15mins | Cook: 15mins | Ready in:

Ingredients

- 1/2 cup unsweetened pineapple juice
- 1/4 cup reduced-sodium soy sauce
- 2 tablespoons prepared horseradish
- 2 tablespoons minced fresh parsley
- 5 teaspoons sesame oil, divided
- 2 teaspoons honey
- 1/2 teaspoon coarsely ground pepper
- 8 salmon fillets (6 ounces each)
- 5 green onions, coarsely chopped

Direction

- Mix the honey, pepper, pineapple juice, 3 teaspoons sesame oil, soy sauce, parsley, and horseradish in a small bowl. Transfer 2/3 cup of the marinade into a large plastic bag that is sealable. Place in green onions and salmon. Seal the bag and flip to coat. Chill for about 1 to 1-1/2 hours while flipping often. Pour the remaining sesame oil into the remaining marinade. Cover and chill for basting.
- Drain and get rid of the marinade. Use cooking oil to moisten a paper towel with the help of long-handled tongs and then coat the grill rack lightly. Grill the salmon with the skin side down while covered on medium heat or broil 4 inches away from the heat source for about 8 to 12 minutes or until the fish easily flakes with a fork. Baste often with the reserved marinade as you cook the fish.

Nutrition Information

- Calories: 333 calories
- Total Carbohydrate: 2g carbohydrate (2g sugars
- Cholesterol: 100mg cholesterol
- Protein: 34g protein.
- Total Fat: 20g fat (4g saturated fat)
- Sodium: 337mg sodium
- Fiber: 0 fiber)

869. Peanut Chicken Satay

Serving: 6-8 servings. | Prep: 10mins | Cook: 15mins | Ready in:

Ingredients

- 1/2 cup chunky peanut butter
- 1/2 cup vegetable oil
- 1/4 cup white wine vinegar
- 1/4 cup soy sauce
- 1/4 cup lemon juice
- 1 tablespoon brown sugar
- 2 teaspoons chili powder or crushed red pepper flakes
- 2 teaspoons ground ginger
- 2 garlic cloves
- 2 pounds boneless skinless chicken breasts
- 12 green onions

Direction

- Blend together the first nine ingredients until smooth, add a little water to move it along if it's too thick. Pour the mixture into a large re-sealable plastic bag and add in chicken that's been sliced into 1-in.-wide strips. Seal the bag, turn to coat, and refrigerate for at least 2 hours. Drain the chicken, discarding its marinade. Cut 3 in. off the green tops of the onions and then halve the onion. Thread a piece of onion per metal or water-soaked wooden skewer. Follow with two to three chicken strips then another onion. Repeat for all of the skewers. Cook on an open grill over medium-low heat, flipping every 3-5 minutes, for 15-20 minutes or until juices come out clear.

Nutrition Information

- Calories:
- Total Carbohydrate:

- Cholesterol:
- Protein:
- Total Fat:
- Sodium:
- Fiber:

- Protein: 14g protein.
- Total Fat: 13g fat (2g saturated fat)
- Sodium: 567mg sodium
- Fiber: 10g fiber)
- Total Carbohydrate: 57g carbohydrate (6g sugars
- Cholesterol: 0 cholesterol

870. Peanut Ginger Pasta

Serving: 4 servings. | Prep: 15mins | Cook: 15mins | Ready in:

Ingredients

- 2-1/2 teaspoons grated lime zest
- 1/4 cup lime juice
- 2 tablespoons reduced-sodium soy sauce
- 2 teaspoons water
- 1 teaspoon sesame oil
- 1/3 cup creamy peanut butter
- 2-1/2 teaspoons minced fresh gingerroot
- 2 garlic cloves, minced
- 1/4 teaspoon salt
- 1/4 teaspoon pepper
- 8 ounces uncooked whole wheat linguine
- 2 cups small fresh broccoli florets
- 2 medium carrots, grated
- 1 medium sweet red pepper, julienned
- 2 green onions, chopped
- 2 tablespoons minced fresh basil

Direction

- In a blender, add the first ten ingredients, then cover and process until blended. Following package directions to cook linguine while adding broccoli during the final 5 minutes of cooking process, then drain.
- Turn the broccoli as well as linguine to a big bowl. Put in leftover ingredients, then put in peanut butter mixture and toss well to mix.

Nutrition Information

- Calories: 365 calories

871. Pineapple Chicken Stir Fry

Serving: 4 servings | Prep: 30mins | Cook: | Ready in:

Ingredients

- 1/3 cup KRAFT Asian Toasted Sesame Dressing
- 1 Tbsp. lite soy sauce
- 2 tsp. oil
- 1 lb. boneless skinless chicken breasts, cut into thin strips
- 1 Tbsp. minced garlic
- 1 Tbsp. minced gingerroot
- 1 cup chopped fresh pineapple
- 1 red chile, cut into thin slices
- 2 cups cooked long-grain white rice
- 2 tsp. chopped fresh cilantro

Direction

- Combine the soy sauce and dressing until well-blended.
- Put oil onto the large nonstick skillet or wok and heat it over medium-high heat. Add the chicken and stir-fry it for 5 minutes until browned all over. Add the ginger and garlic. Stir-fry the mixture for 1 minute.
- Pour in dressing mixture, chilies, and pineapple. Stir-fry for 3 minutes until heated through.
- Serve the mixture over rice with cilantro sprinkled over it.

Nutrition Information

- Calories: 350
- Fiber: 1 g
- Cholesterol: 55 mg
- Total Carbohydrate: 42 g
- Sugar: 9 g
- Total Fat: 10 g
- Saturated Fat: 1 g
- Sodium: 370 mg
- Protein: 22 g

872. Pineapple Pork Stir Fry

Serving: 6 servings. | Prep: 20mins | Cook: 10mins | Ready in:

Ingredients

- 1 can (8 ounces) unsweetened pineapple chunks, undrained
- 3 tablespoons cornstarch, divided
- 1 tablespoon plus 1/2 cup cold water, divided
- 3/4 teaspoon garlic powder
- 1 pork tenderloin (1 pound), cut into thin strips
- 1/2 cup soy sauce
- 3 tablespoons brown sugar
- 1/2 teaspoon ground ginger
- 1/4 teaspoon cayenne pepper
- 2 tablespoons canola oil, divided
- 4 cups fresh broccoli florets
- 1 cup fresh baby carrots, cut in half lengthwise
- 1 small onion, cut into wedges
- Hot cooked rice

Direction

- Drain pineapple, keeping 1/4 cup juice; put aside. Mix 1 tbsp. reserved pineapple juice, garlic powder, 1 tbsp. water and 2 tbsp. cornstarch in a small bowl. Put in a big resealable bag then add pork; seal bag. Flip to coat.
- Mix reserved pineapple juice, cornstarch, leftover water, cayenne, ginger, brown sugar and soy sauce till smooth in a small bowl; put aside.
- Stir-fry pork till not pink in 1 tbsp. oil in a big skillet/wok on medium high heat. Remove; keep warm.
- Stir-fry onion, carrots and broccoli in leftover oil till tender. Mix cornstarch mixture; put in pan. Boil; mix and cook till thick for 2 minutes. Add pineapple and pork; heat through. Serve it with rice.

Nutrition Information

- Calories: 230 calories
- Sodium: 1295mg sodium
- Fiber: 2g fiber)
- Total Carbohydrate: 21g carbohydrate (13g sugars
- Cholesterol: 42mg cholesterol
- Protein: 19g protein.
- Total Fat: 7g fat (1g saturated fat)

873. Pineapple Red Pepper Beef Stir Fry

Serving: 4 servings. | Prep: 10mins | Cook: 20mins | Ready in:

Ingredients

- 1/2 cup soy sauce
- 2 garlic cloves, minced
- 1 teaspoon ground ginger
- 1 pound beef top sirloin steak, cut into 1/4-inch thin strips
- 1 tablespoon canola oil
- 2 celery ribs, thinly sliced
- 1 cup cubed sweet red pepper
- 1 cup sliced green onions
- 1 cup sliced fresh mushrooms
- 1 can (20 ounces) pineapple chunks
- 1 can (8 ounces) sliced water chestnuts, drained
- 2 to 3 tablespoons cornstarch

- 1/2 cup water
- Hot cooked rice

Direction

- Mix ginger, garlic and soy sauce in a big resealable plastic bag. Add beef; flip to coat. Stand for 15 minutes.
- Stir-fry beef mixture for 2 minutes in oil in a big skillet. Add red pepper and celery; stir-fry it for 2 minutes. Add mushrooms and onions; cook for 2 minutes.
- Drain pineapple; keep juice. Mix water chestnuts and pineapple into skillet. Mix reserved pineapple juice, water and cornstarch till smooth in a small bowl; mix into veggies and beef slowly. Boil; mix and cook till thick for 1-2 minutes. Serve with rice.

Nutrition Information

- Calories: 351 calories
- Total Fat: 9g fat (3g saturated fat)
- Sodium: 1916mg sodium
- Fiber: 5g fiber)
- Total Carbohydrate: 39g carbohydrate (21g sugars
- Cholesterol: 63mg cholesterol
- Protein: 28g protein.

874. Pineapple Shrimp Fried Rice

Serving: 4 servings. | Prep: 20mins | Cook: 10mins | Ready in:

Ingredients

- 2 tablespoons reduced-sodium soy sauce
- 1 teaspoon curry powder
- 1/2 teaspoon sugar
- 2 tablespoons peanut or canola oil, divided
- 1 pound uncooked shrimp (31-40 per pound), peeled and deveined
- 2 teaspoons minced fresh gingerroot
- 1 garlic clove, minced
- 1 medium sweet red pepper, chopped
- 1 medium carrot, finely chopped
- 1/2 cup chopped onion
- 1 can (20 ounces) unsweetened pineapple tidbits, drained
- 2 cups cooked rice, at room temperature
- 6 green onions, chopped
- 1/2 cup finely chopped salted peanuts
- Lime wedges

Direction

- Combine sugar, curry powder and soy sauce. In a large skillet over medium-high heat, heat 1 tablespoon oil; stir-fry shrimp for 2-3 minutes until it looks pink. Take out of pan.
- In same pan over medium-high heat, heat leftover oil. Put in garlic and ginger; cook for 10 seconds just until aromatic. Put in onion, carrot and pepper; stir-fry 2 minutes. Mix in shrimp and pineapple. Pour in soy sauce mixture and rice; heat through over medium heat, tossing to mix and crumble any clumps of rice. Mix in green onions. Top with peanuts; serve with lime wedges.

Nutrition Information

- Calories: 491 calories
- Sodium: 513mg sodium
- Fiber: 5g fiber)
- Total Carbohydrate: 54g carbohydrate (22g sugars
- Cholesterol: 138mg cholesterol
- Protein: 28g protein.
- Total Fat: 18g fat (3g saturated fat)

875. Pineapple Shrimp Kabobs

Serving: 4 servings. | Prep: 10mins | Cook: 10mins | Ready in:

Ingredients

- 1/4 cup each reduced-sodium soy sauce, balsamic vinegar and honey
- 1 garlic clove, minced
- 1 pound uncooked medium shrimp, peeled and deveined
- 1 large green pepper, cut into 1-inch pieces
- 1 can (8 ounces) pineapple, chunks, drained

Direction

- Mix garlic, soy sauce, vinegar and honey together in a small bowl. Put 1/3 cup of the marinade aside. Insert the shrimps, pineapple and green pepper alternately onto 8 skewers. Put in the kebabs and the leftover marinade into the big Ziplock plastic bag. Keep it in the fridge for 1 hour. Cover the leftover marinade and keep in the fridge as well.
- Drain the marinated kebabs and throw marinade. Use tongs to lightly rub an oiled paper towel on the grill rack. Put the kebabs on an open grill on medium heat or broil the kebabs in the oven 4 inches away from the heat for 5 to 8 minutes or until the shrimp turns pink in color, turn the kebabs from time to time to cook both sides and baste with leftover marinade each turn.

Nutrition Information

- Calories: 168 calories
- Total Fat: 2g fat (0 saturated fat)
- Sodium: 443mg sodium
- Fiber: 1g fiber)
- Total Carbohydrate: 19g carbohydrate (16g sugars
- Cholesterol: 138mg cholesterol
- Protein: 19g protein. Diabetic Exchanges: 2 lean meat

876. Pineapple Teriyaki Chicken

Serving: 4 servings. | Prep: 10mins | Cook: 15mins | Ready in:

Ingredients

- 1 can (20 ounces) sliced pineapple
- 1/2 cup teriyaki sauce
- 4 boneless skinless chicken breast halves (4 ounces each)
- 4 slices provolone cheese (1 ounce each)

Direction

- Drain pineapple. Set juice aside. Chill the pineapple. Mix the juice and teriyaki sauce in a bowl. Place 3/4 cup of marinade in a resealable bag. Put chicken in, seal, and turn to coat. Chill for 8 hours or overnight. Put a cover on the rest of the marinade for basting, and chill.
- Drain. Throw out marinade in bag. Cook chicken on grill, with cover on, over medium heat. You can also broil it 4 inches from the heat source until a thermometer reaches 170°F, or 4-6 minutes per side. Baste often with the saved marinade.
- Grill 8 pineapple slices until lightly browned, 2 minutes per side. Baste with the saved marinade. Save the rest of the pineapple for later use.
- Top each chicken with 2 pineapple slices and cheese. Grill for 1-2 minutes, covered, until cheese has melted.

Nutrition Information

- Calories: 305 calories
- Total Fat: 10g fat (6g saturated fat)
- Sodium: 1289mg sodium
- Fiber: 1g fiber)
- Total Carbohydrate: 19g carbohydrate (16g sugars
- Cholesterol: 82mg cholesterol
- Protein: 32g protein.

877. Polynesian Sausage Supper

Serving: 6 servings. | Prep: 10mins | Cook: 20mins | Ready in:

Ingredients

- 1 pound Johnsonville® Fully Cooked Smoked Sausage Rope, cut into 1/2-inch slices
- 1 medium onion, chopped
- 1 medium green pepper, cut into 1-inch chunks
- 1 can (14-1/2 ounces) diced tomatoes, undrained
- 1/2 cup beef broth
- 1 tablespoon brown sugar
- 1/4 teaspoon garlic powder
- 1/4 teaspoon pepper
- 1 can (20 ounces) unsweetened pineapple chunks
- 2 tablespoons cornstarch
- Hot cooked rice

Direction

- In a big skillet, cook green pepper, onion and sausage till vegetables are tender.
- Put in pepper, garlic powder, brown sugar, broth, and tomatoes. Drain pineapple, saving juice. Mix pineapple into the sausage mixture. Heat to a boil; cook for 5 minutes without a cover.
- Blend together reserved pineapple juice and cornstarch until smooth; slowly pour into sausage mixture. Heat to a boil then stir and cook 2 minutes or until thickened. Serve along with rice.

Nutrition Information

- Calories: 332 calories
- Protein: 12g protein.
- Total Fat: 20g fat (9g saturated fat)
- Sodium: 1021mg sodium
- Fiber: 3g fiber)
- Total Carbohydrate: 25g carbohydrate (18g sugars
- Cholesterol: 51mg cholesterol

878. Pork 'n' Pea Pod Stir Fry

Serving: 3 servings. | Prep: 10mins | Cook: 15mins | Ready in:

Ingredients

- 2 tablespoons reduced-sodium soy sauce
- 2 tablespoons honey
- 1-1/2 teaspoons minced fresh gingerroot
- 1/2 to 1 teaspoon crushed red pepper flakes
- 3/4 pound pork tenderloin, cut into 2-inch strips
- 2 teaspoons canola oil
- 1 tablespoon cornstarch
- 1/3 cup orange juice
- 2 tablespoons cider vinegar
- 1 pound fresh snow peas
- 2 teaspoons minced garlic
- 1 teaspoon grated orange zest

Direction

- Mix pepper flakes, ginger, honey, and soy sauce together in a small bowl. In a big bowl, put 3 tablespoons; add the pork and flip to blend. Put a cover on and chill for 1 hour. Put a cover on and chill the leftover marinade.
- Mix together the leftover marinade, vinegar, orange juice, and cornstarch; whisk until blended and put aside. Strain and dispose the marinade from the pork. Stir-fry the pork in oil in a big, nonstick wok or skillet until not pink anymore, about 4-5 minutes. Take the pork out and keep warm.
- Stir-fry snow peas in the same pan until crunchy and soft, about 2-3 minutes. Mix in orange zest and garlic. Whisk the cornstarch

mixture and mix into the pan. Boil; stir and cook until thickened, about 1-2 minutes. Put the pork back to the pan, thoroughly heat.

Nutrition Information

- Calories: 286 calories
- Sodium: 354mg sodium
- Fiber: 4g fiber)
- Total Carbohydrate: 26g carbohydrate (16g sugars
- Cholesterol: 63mg cholesterol
- Protein: 28g protein. Diabetic Exchanges: 3 lean meat
- Total Fat: 7g fat (2g saturated fat)

879. Pork Lo Mein With Spaghetti

Serving: 4 servings. | Prep: 10mins | Cook: 10mins | Ready in:

Ingredients

- 1 pork tenderloin (1 pound)
- 1/4 cup reduced-sodium soy sauce
- 3 garlic cloves, minced
- 1 teaspoon minced fresh gingerroot
- 1/4 teaspoon crushed red pepper flakes
- 2 cups fresh snow peas
- 1 medium sweet red pepper, julienned
- 3 cups cooked thin spaghetti
- 1/3 cup reduced-sodium chicken broth
- 2 teaspoons sesame oil

Direction

- Slice tenderloin lengthwise into two lengthwise. Slice each half widthwise into slices, about 1/4-inch each slice. Put aside. Mix pepper flakes, ginger, garlic, and soy sauce together in a big resealable plastic bag. Add pork. Close the bag and flip to cover. Chill for 20 minutes.
- In an oil-coated big, nonstick wok or skillet, stir-fry marinade and pork until the meat is not pink anymore, or about 4-5 minutes. Add red pepper and peas, stir-fry for 1 minute. Mix in broth and spaghetti, cook for another 1 minute. Take away from heat, mix in sesame oil.

Nutrition Information

- Calories: 343 calories
- Total Carbohydrate: 37g carbohydrate (0 sugars
- Cholesterol: 74mg cholesterol
- Protein: 31g protein. Diabetic Exchanges: 3 lean meat
- Total Fat: 7g fat (2g saturated fat)
- Sodium: 716mg sodium
- Fiber: 3g fiber)

880. Pork Tenderloin With Plum Sauce

Serving: 8 servings. | Prep: 15mins | Cook: 40mins | Ready in:

Ingredients

- 1/2 cup apple cider or juice
- 1/2 cup soy sauce
- 2 garlic cloves, minced
- 1 tablespoon ground mustard
- 1 teaspoon dried thyme
- 1 teaspoon ground ginger
- 2 pork tenderloins (about 1 pound each)
- PLUM SAUCE:
- 1/2 cup plum preserves
- 1/4 cup finely chopped onion
- 1/4 cup apricot preserves
- 2 tablespoons brown sugar
- 2 tablespoons apple cider or juice
- 2 tablespoons soy sauce
- 2 tablespoons ketchup
- 1 garlic clove, minced

Direction

- Mix the first six ingredients in a small bowl. Pour 3/4 cup of the mixture into a big resealable plastic bag; put in the pork. Seal the bag and turn over to coat; put in the fridge for minimum of 2 hours. Put the remaining marinade with a cover into the fridge for basting.
- Drain and remove the marinade from pork. Transfer the tenderloins to a rack in a shallow roasting pan. Bake at 425° without a cover for 40-45 minutes or until a thermometer indicates 160°, basting with reserved marinade twice.
- Mix sauce ingredients in a small saucepan. Boil. Reduce heat; simmer without a cover for 10 minutes or until the flavors blend together. Allow the pork to sit for 5 minutes before slicing. Serve the pork with plum sauce.

Nutrition Information

- Calories:
- Protein:
- Total Fat:
- Sodium:
- Fiber:
- Total Carbohydrate:
- Cholesterol:

881. Pork With Sugar Snap Peas

Serving: 4 servings. | Prep: 5mins | Cook: 15mins | Ready in:

Ingredients

- 1 pound pork tenderloin, cut into 1/4-inch slices
- 2 teaspoons olive oil
- 2 garlic cloves, minced
- 10 ounces fresh or frozen sugar snap peas
- 3 tablespoons reduced-sodium soy sauce
- 2 tablespoons white wine vinegar
- 1 tablespoon molasses
- 1 tablespoon minced fresh gingerroot
- 1/4 teaspoon crushed red pepper flakes
- Hot cooked rice

Direction

- Stir-fry pork in oil in a non-stick skillet about 6 minutes, or until no pink meat remains. Put in garlic; cook for an extra 1 minute. Take away from the skillet and keep warm.
- Cook red pepper flakes, ginger, molasses, vinegar, soy sauce, and peas for 4 minutes in the same pan, or until peas are crispy and tender. Transfer the pork back to pan; cook for 3 minutes, or until glazed. Better when served with rice.

Nutrition Information

- Calories: 226 calories
- Fiber: 2g fiber)
- Total Carbohydrate: 10g carbohydrate (0 sugars
- Cholesterol: 67mg cholesterol
- Protein: 27g protein. Diabetic Exchanges: 3 lean meat
- Total Fat: 6g fat (2g saturated fat)
- Sodium: 513mg sodium

882. Quick Almond Chicken Stir Fry

Serving: 4 servings. | Prep: 20mins | Cook: 0mins | Ready in:

Ingredients

- 1 cup whole unblanched almonds
- 1/4 cup canola oil
- 1 pound boneless skinless chicken breasts, cut into cubes
- 1 tablespoon cornstarch

- 1/2 cup chicken broth
- 3 tablespoons soy sauce
- 2 teaspoons honey
- 1 teaspoon ground ginger
- 1 package (14 ounces) frozen sugar snap peas
- Hot cooked pasta or rice

Direction

- Cook almonds with oil over medium heat for 3 minutes in a large skillet. Add in the chicken; cook till meat is not pink anymore.
- Mix ginger, honey, soy sauce, broth, and cornstarch together in a small bowl till it becomes smooth; pour into the chicken mixture. Bring to a boil; keep cooking and stirring till thickened or for 2 minutes. Lower heat. Mix in peas; cook until heated through. Pair with pasta and serve.

Nutrition Information

- Calories: 526 calories
- Protein: 35g protein.
- Total Fat: 35g fat (4g saturated fat)
- Sodium: 871mg sodium
- Fiber: 8g fiber)
- Total Carbohydrate: 21g carbohydrate (8g sugars
- Cholesterol: 63mg cholesterol

883. Quick Glazed Salmon

Serving: 4 servings. | Prep: 10mins | Cook: 10mins | Ready in:

Ingredients

- 4 salmon fillets (6 ounces each)
- 1/4 teaspoon salt
- 1/8 teaspoon pepper
- 2 tablespoons brown sugar
- 2 tablespoons lemon juice
- 2 tablespoons Dijon mustard
- 1 teaspoon ground cumin

Direction

- In a greased 7"x11" baking dish, arrange salmon, then sprinkle pepper and salt over. Mix the remaining ingredients together and scoop over fillets.
- Bake at 400 degrees without a cover until it is easy to use a fork to flake salmon, or for 10 to 15 minutes.

Nutrition Information

- Calories: 349 calories
- Protein: 34g protein.
- Total Fat: 19g fat (4g saturated fat)
- Sodium: 432mg sodium
- Fiber: 0 fiber)
- Total Carbohydrate: 9g carbohydrate (7g sugars
- Cholesterol: 100mg cholesterol

884. Quick Orange Chicken Stir Fry

Serving: 2 servings. | Prep: 15mins | Cook: 15mins | Ready in:

Ingredients

- 2 teaspoons cornstarch
- 1/2 cup reduced-sodium chicken broth
- 1/3 cup orange juice
- 2 tablespoons reduced-sodium soy sauce
- 2 teaspoons sugar
- 2 teaspoons white wine vinegar
- 1 teaspoon sesame oil
- 1/2 pound boneless skinless chicken breasts, cut into strips
- 2 teaspoons canola oil, divided
- 1 small sweet red pepper, julienned
- 1 cup fresh snow peas
- 1 small onion, halved and sliced

- 1 teaspoon grated orange zest
- 1 garlic clove, minced
- Hot cooked rice, optional

Direction

- Mix broth and cornstarch together in a small bowl until tender. Mix in sesame oil, vinegar, sugar, soy sauce, and orange juice. Put aside.
- Stir-fry chicken in 1 teaspoon canola oil in a big nonstick wok or skillet over medium-high heat until the juices run clear, or about 5-7 minutes. Take out and keep warm. Stir-fry garlic, orange zest, onion, peas, and red pepper in the leftover oil until crunchy and soft, about 3-5 minutes. Put the chicken back to the pan.
- Whisk the orange juice mixture, put on top of the chicken mixture. Boil; stir and cook until thickened, or about 1 minute. Enjoy with rice if wanted.

Nutrition Information

- Calories: 303 calories
- Total Carbohydrate: 24g carbohydrate (14g sugars
- Cholesterol: 63mg cholesterol
- Protein: 28g protein. Diabetic Exchanges: 3 lean meat
- Total Fat: 10g fat (1g saturated fat)
- Sodium: 820mg sodium
- Fiber: 4g fiber)

885. Quick Pork Chow Mein

Serving: 3 servings. | Prep: 15mins | Cook: 15mins | Ready in:

Ingredients

- 2/3 cup uncooked instant rice
- 2 tablespoons butter
- 1/2 teaspoon salt
- 1 large onion, chopped
- 2 celery ribs, sliced
- 1 medium green or sweet red pepper, chopped
- 1 teaspoon chicken bouillon granules
- 1-1/2 cups boiling water
- 1 cup cubed cooked pork roast
- 1 tablespoon cornstarch
- 1 tablespoon cold water
- 1 tablespoon reduced-sodium soy sauce
- Chow mein noodles

Direction

- Sauté rice in salt and butter in a large skillet until golden. Add green pepper, celery, and onion; cook until tender-crisp. Dissolve the bouillon in the boiling water; pour into the rice mixture. Add pork; boil. Turn down the heat; put on a cover and cook until the rice becomes tender, 5 minutes.
- Blend soy sauce, cold water, and cornstarch until smooth; gradually put into the skillet. Boil; stir and cook until thickened, 2 minutes. Serve alongside chow Mein noodles.

Nutrition Information

- Calories: 291 calories
- Sodium: 1113mg sodium
- Fiber: 2g fiber)
- Total Carbohydrate: 28g carbohydrate (5g sugars
- Cholesterol: 63mg cholesterol
- Protein: 17g protein.
- Total Fat: 12g fat (6g saturated fat)

886. Ramen Chicken Stir Fry

Serving: 4 servings. | Prep: 5mins | Cook: 20mins | Ready in:

Ingredients

- 1 pound boneless skinless chicken breasts, cut into strips

- 2 tablespoons vegetable oil
- 1-1/2 cups water
- 2 garlic cloves, minced
- 2 packages (3 ounces each) chicken ramen noodles
- 1 package (16 ounces) frozen stir-fry vegetable blend
- 1 sweet red pepper, julienned
- 2 tablespoons soy sauce

Direction

- Stir-fry chicken in a wok or big skillet with oil. Put in garlic and water, then bring the mixture to a boil. Put in soy sauce, red pepper, vegetables and the contents of seasoning packets and noodles. Simmer, covered, until the vegetables and noodles are both softened, about 7 to 9 minutes.

Nutrition Information

- Calories:
- Protein:
- Total Fat:
- Sodium:
- Fiber:
- Total Carbohydrate:
- Cholesterol:

887. Saucy Beef With Broccoli

Serving: 2 servings. | Prep: 15mins | Cook: 15mins | Ready in:

Ingredients

- 1 tablespoon cornstarch
- 1/2 cup reduced-sodium beef broth
- 1/4 cup sherry or additional beef broth
- 2 tablespoons reduced-sodium soy sauce
- 1 tablespoon brown sugar
- 1 garlic clove, minced
- 1 teaspoon minced fresh gingerroot

- 2 teaspoons canola oil, divided
- 1/2 pound beef top sirloin steak, cut into 1/4-inch-thick strips
- 2 cups fresh small broccoli florets
- 8 green onions, cut into 1-inch pieces

Direction

- Combine the first 7 ingredients. Heat 1 tsp. of oil in a large nonstick skillet that is set over medium-high heat. Stir-fry for 1-3 minutes until the beef turns brown. Remove it from the pan.
- In the remaining oil, stir-fry the broccoli for 3-5 minutes until crisp-tender. Add the green onions and cook for 1-2 minutes until tender. Mix the cornstarch mixture then put into the pan. Boil the mixture. Cook for 2-3 minutes, stirring until the sauce is thick. Add the beef back into the pan and heat it through.

Nutrition Information

- Calories: 313 calories
- Total Carbohydrate: 20g carbohydrate (11g sugars
- Cholesterol: 68mg cholesterol
- Protein: 29g protein. Diabetic Exchanges: 3 lean meat
- Total Fat: 11g fat (3g saturated fat)
- Sodium: 816mg sodium
- Fiber: 4g fiber)

888. Sesame Beef Stir Fry

Serving: 2 servings. | Prep: 15mins | Cook: 15mins | Ready in:

Ingredients

- 2 teaspoons cornstarch
- 1/2 cup reduced-sodium beef broth
- 4 teaspoons reduced-sodium soy sauce
- 1 tablespoon minced fresh gingerroot
- 1 garlic clove, minced

- 1/2 pound beef top sirloin steak, thinly sliced
- 2 teaspoons sesame seeds, toasted, divided
- 2 teaspoons peanut or canola oil, divided
- 2 cups fresh broccoli florets
- 1 small sweet yellow pepper, julienned
- 1 cup hot cooked brown rice

Direction

- Mix the first 5 ingredients in a small bowl until blended; put aside.
- Stir-fry the beef and 1 tsp. of sesame seeds in a wok or large nonstick skillet with 1 tsp. of oil until the beef is not anymore pink. Remove from the heat and keep it warm.
- Add the broccoli into the remaining oil and stir-fry for 2 minutes. Add the pepper and stir-fry for 4-6 more minutes until the vegetables turn crisp-tender.
- Whisk the cornstarch mixture before pouring it into the pan. Let the mixture boil. Cook and stir the mixture for 2 minutes until thick. Add the beef and heat the mixture through. Serve this with rice and remaining sesame seeds sprinkled over it.

Nutrition Information

- Calories: 363 calories
- Cholesterol: 47mg cholesterol
- Protein: 31g protein. Diabetic Exchanges: 3 lean meat
- Total Fat: 12g fat (3g saturated fat)
- Sodium: 606mg sodium
- Fiber: 5g fiber)
- Total Carbohydrate: 33g carbohydrate (4g sugars

---

889. Sesame Flank Steak

Serving: 8 servings. | Prep: 5mins | Cook: 15mins | Ready in:

Ingredients

- 1-1/2 pounds beef flank steak
- 1/4 cup sesame seeds, toasted
- 1/4 cup thinly sliced green onions
- 3 tablespoons reduced-sodium soy sauce
- 2 tablespoons canola oil
- 1 tablespoon brown sugar
- 1 tablespoon ground ginger
- 3 garlic cloves, minced
- 1 teaspoon ground mustard
- 1 teaspoon Worcestershire sauce

Direction

- Etch steak and put in a big ziplock bag or big and shallow glass container. Mix remaining ingredients together and pour on the steak; seal or cover. Let it chill in the refrigerator for four hours to overnight. Drain steak and get rid of the marinade.
- On medium heat, grill steak while covered until it reaches the preferred doneness (an inserted thermometer in the steak should register 170° Fahrenheit for well-done, 160 degrees F for medium done, and 145° Fahrenheit for medium rare). Slice the steak thinly across the grain.

Nutrition Information

- Calories: 172 calories
- Protein: 19g protein. Diabetic Exchanges: 3 lean meat.
- Total Fat: 10g fat (0 saturated fat)
- Sodium: 169mg sodium
- Fiber: 0 fiber)
- Total Carbohydrate: 2g carbohydrate (0 sugars
- Cholesterol: 44mg cholesterol

---

890. Sesame Pork Kabobs

Serving: 6 servings. | Prep: 10mins | Cook: 10mins | Ready in:

Ingredients

- 3/4 cup finely chopped onion
- 1/2 cup soy sauce
- 1/4 cup sesame seeds, toasted
- 1/4 cup water
- 3 tablespoons sugar
- 4-1/2 teaspoons minced garlic
- 1-1/2 teaspoons ground ginger
- 1/8 teaspoon cayenne pepper
- 2 pork tenderloins (3/4 pound each), trimmed

Direction

- Mix all of the first 8 ingredients together in a big ziplock plastic bag. Cut the pork into slices that are 1/4 inch in thickness then put it into the marinade. Seal the ziplock bag and turn it to evenly coat the pork with the marinade then keep it in the fridge for not less than 1 hour. Drain and throw away the marinade mixture.
- Insert the marinated pork onto 6 pieces of soaked wooden or long metal skewers. Put the pork skewers on a greased grill rack placed over medium heat. Cover it and grill, or put the pork in a broiler and let it broil 4 inches away from the heat source for 9 to 12 minutes until the pork meat becomes tender, turn the pork skewers once to cook on both sides.

Nutrition Information

- Calories: 156 calories
- Protein: 25g protein. Diabetic Exchanges: 3 lean meat.
- Total Fat: 4g fat (0 saturated fat)
- Sodium: 385mg sodium
- Fiber: 0 fiber)
- Total Carbohydrate: 3g carbohydrate (0 sugars
- Cholesterol: 67mg cholesterol

891. Sesame Teriyaki Chicken

Serving: 24 servings. | Prep: 15mins | Cook: 20mins | Ready in:

Ingredients

- 3/4 cup vegetable oil
- 3/4 cup soy sauce
- 1/3 cup chili sauce
- 3 tablespoons sesame seeds
- 3 tablespoons white vinegar
- 6 garlic cloves, minced
- 1-1/2 teaspoons sugar
- 3/4 teaspoon ground ginger
- 3/4 teaspoon pepper
- 24 boneless skinless chicken breast halves (about 6 ounces each)
- Toasted sesame seeds

Direction

- Mix the first 9 ingredients together in a big bowl. Transfer 3/4 cup of the marinade to each of the 3 resealable plastic bags. Toss 8 breasts into each bag. Seal and shake to coat. Chill for 6 hours, or overnight while turning over once.
- Throw marinade out. Place contents on 2 greased 15x10x1-inch baking dishes. With no cover on, bake for 10-13 minutes per side at 350°F or until juices have run clear.
- Another option is to grill: Grill while uncovered for 5-7 minutes per side over medium heat until juices have run clear. Garnish with sesame seeds. Serve.

Nutrition Information

- Calories: 45 calories
- Cholesterol: 4mg cholesterol
- Protein: 2g protein.
- Total Fat: 4g fat (0 saturated fat)
- Sodium: 259mg sodium
- Fiber: 0 fiber)
- Total Carbohydrate: 1g carbohydrate (0 sugars

892. Sesame Crusted Pork Loin

Serving: 14-16 servings. | Prep: 15mins | Cook: 01hours45mins | Ready in:

Ingredients

- 1/2 cup soy sauce
- 3 tablespoons sugar
- 3 tablespoons finely chopped onion
- 2 tablespoons canola oil
- 2 teaspoons ground ginger
- 1 garlic clove, minced
- 3/4 cup sesame seeds
- 1 boneless rolled pork loin roast (about 5 pounds)
- 2 cups water

Direction

- Mix the first seven ingredients in a large resealable bag. Put in the roast; seal the bag then turn to cover the roast with the mixture. Let chill overnight in the fridge.
- Drain and remove the marinade. Put the roast onto a rack placed in a shallow roasting pan; then add water into the pan. Bake for 1-3/4 to 2 hours at 350°, or until a thermometer reaches 160°. Allow to sit for 10-15 minutes before carving.

Nutrition Information

- Calories:
- Cholesterol:
- Protein:
- Total Fat:
- Sodium:
- Fiber:
- Total Carbohydrate:

893. Shrimp Fried Rice

Serving: 4 | Prep: | Cook: 40mins | Ready in:

Ingredients

- 1½ cups water
- 1 cup instant brown rice
- 2 tablespoons hoisin sauce (see Tips)
- 4 teaspoons reduced-sodium soy sauce
- 2 teaspoons toasted sesame oil
- 4 teaspoons canola oil, divided
- 2 large eggs, lightly beaten
- 8 ounces peeled and deveined raw small shrimp (51-60 per pound; see Tips)
- 2 tablespoons minced fresh ginger
- 4 cups stringless snap peas (12 ounces)
- 1 medium red bell pepper, cut into ½-inch pieces
- 2 medium carrots, halved lengthwise and thinly sliced
- 4 scallions, chopped

Direction

- Fill a small saucepan with rice and water, place over high heat and bring to a boil. Cover with a lid and reduce to medium-low heat. Simmer for 10 to 12 minutes, or until the rice absorbs the water. Transfer rice to a large baking sheet, spread out and allow to cool.
- In a small bowl, combine sesame oil, soy sauce, and hoisin sauce and set aside.
- Place a large non-stick skillet over medium-high heat and heat 1 teaspoon of canola oil. Add eggs to the hot oil, cook and stir for 45 seconds, while breaking into smaller pieces, until eggs are just set. Transfer to a bowl.
- In the same skillet over medium-high heat, add 1 teaspoon of canola oil. Add shrimp; cook for 1 1/2 to 2 minutes, or until pink, stirring occasionally. Transfer to a bowl.
- In the same skillet over medium-high heat, heat the last 2 teaspoons of oil. Add ginger, cook and stir for 30 seconds, or until fragrant. Stir in scallions, carrots, bell peppers, and snap peas. Cook for 3 to 4 minutes, or until tender

and crisp, stirring occasionally. Stir in the reserved shrimp and eggs, and rice. Cook and stir for 1 more minute, or until heated through. Remove from the heat. Stir in the sauce mixture gently.

Nutrition Information

- Calories: 315 calories;
- Saturated Fat: 2
- Sodium: 446
- Fiber: 5
- Cholesterol: 185
- Total Fat: 11
- Total Carbohydrate: 34
- Sugar: 9
- Protein: 20

894. Shrimp Lettuce Wraps

Serving: 4 servings. | Prep: 20mins | Cook: 10mins | Ready in:

Ingredients

- 1/4 cup reduced-sodium soy sauce
- 3 tablespoons lime juice
- 2 tablespoons plus 1 teaspoon apricot preserves
- 2 tablespoons water
- 2 garlic cloves, minced
- 1/4 teaspoon ground ginger
- 1 large sweet red pepper, chopped
- 2 medium carrots
- 6 green onions
- 3 teaspoons olive oil, divided
- 1 pound uncooked medium shrimp, peeled and deveined
- 2 cups hot cooked rice
- 8 large lettuce leaves

Direction

- Combine the first 6 ingredients in a small bowl. Shave carrots lengthwise and very thinly into strips with a vegetable peeler. Cut white parts of green onions, then halve each green top lengthwise.
- Heat 2 tsp. of oil in a big skillet on medium high heat. Put in shrimp, then stir-fry until shrimp have pink in color. Take out of the pan.
- Stir-fry carrots and red pepper about 4 minutes with the leftover oil. Put in onions' white parts and stir-fry until vegetables are tender but still crispy, or about 1 to 2 more minutes.
- Put into the pan with 1/3 cup of the soy sauce mixture and bring to a boil. Put in shrimp and heat through. Put on each lettuce leaf with 1/4 cup of rice, then place 1/2 cup shrimp mixture on top. Use the leftover soy sauce to drizzle on top, then roll up. Use a green onion strip to tie each.

Nutrition Information

- Calories: 306 calories
- Sodium: 777mg sodium
- Fiber: 3g fiber)
- Total Carbohydrate: 41g carbohydrate (9g sugars
- Cholesterol: 138mg cholesterol
- Protein: 23g protein. Diabetic Exchanges: 3 lean meat
- Total Fat: 5g fat (1g saturated fat)

895. Shrimp Stir Fry

Serving: 4 | Prep: 25mins | Cook: 15mins | Ready in:

Ingredients

- 3 tablespoons cornstarch
- 1 3/4 cups Swanson® Chicken Stock
- 1 tablespoon soy sauce
- 1/2 teaspoon sesame oil (optional)
- 2 tablespoons vegetable oil

- 1 pound fresh or thawed frozen medium shrimp, peeled and deveined
- 4 cups cut-up fresh vegetables (see Note)
- 1/2 teaspoon ground ginger
- 1/8 teaspoon garlic powder
- 4 cups hot cooked regular long-grain white rice

Direction

- In a small bowl, add sesame oil, soy sauce, stock and cornstarch until the mixture is smooth.
- In a 12-in. skillet, heat 1 tbsp. of vegetable oil on moderately high heat. Put in shrimp and stir-fry until cooked through. Take the shrimp out of the skillet.
- In the skillet, heat leftover vegetable oil. Put in garlic powder, ginger and vegetables, then stir-fry until vegetables are crispy yet still tender.
- Stir into the skillet with cornstarch mixture. Cook and stir until boiled through and thickened. Turn the shrimp back to the skillet and cook until whole mixture is hot and bubbly. Serve together with rice.

Nutrition Information

- Calories: 428 calories;
- Cholesterol: 173
- Protein: 26.9
- Total Fat: 9.1
- Sodium: 653
- Total Carbohydrate: 58.4

896. Simple Marinated Chicken Breasts

Serving: 8 servings. | Prep: 10mins | Cook: 15mins | Ready in:

Ingredients

- 1 cup sugar
- 1 cup water
- 1 cup soy sauce
- 1/4 cup pineapple juice
- 1/4 cup vegetable oil
- 1 teaspoon garlic powder
- 1 teaspoon ground ginger
- 8 boneless skinless chicken breast halves (about 2-1/2 pounds)

Direction

- In a bowl, mix the first seven ingredients together; take out three quarters cup for the basting, then keep covered and refrigerated. In a big resealable plastic bag, add the rest of the marinade and chicken. Seal the bag and turn until coated, keep in the refrigerator 4 hours or overnight.
- Drain off and get rid of the marinade. Grill the chicken, covered, on medium heat for 3 minutes per side. Baste using the reserved marinade. Grill until the juices come out clear, 3 to 4 minutes more per side, basting a few times.

Nutrition Information

- Calories:
- Fiber:
- Total Carbohydrate:
- Cholesterol:
- Protein:
- Total Fat:
- Sodium:

897. Sizzling Chicken Lo Mein

Serving: 4 servings. | Prep: 20mins | Cook: 10mins | Ready in:

Ingredients

- 8 ounces uncooked linguine

- 3/4 pound boneless skinless chicken breasts, cubed
- 2 tablespoons olive oil
- 5 tablespoons stir-fry sauce, divided
- 4 tablespoons teriyaki sauce, divided
- 1 package (12 ounces) frozen stir-fry vegetable blend

Direction

- Follow the package cooking instructions to cook linguine. At the same time, stir-fry chicken in oil in a big wok or skillet until not pink anymore. Put in 2 tablespoons of each teriyaki sauce and stir-fry sauce. Take chicken out of pan.
- In the same skillet, stir-fry 1 tablespoon of each teriyaki sauce and stir-fry sauce and vegetables until vegetables are crisp-tender, 4 to 6 minutes. Drain the linguine. Put the remaining sauces, chicken, and linguine in the pan; stir-fry until heated through, 2 to 3 minutes.

Nutrition Information

- Calories:
- Protein:
- Total Fat:
- Sodium:
- Fiber:
- Total Carbohydrate:
- Cholesterol:

898. Slow Cooker Sweet And Sour Chicken

Serving: 5 servings. | Prep: 15mins | Cook: 03hours20mins | Ready in:

Ingredients

- 1-1/4 pounds boneless skinless chicken breasts, cut into 1-inch strips
- 1 tablespoon canola oil
- Salt and pepper to taste
- 1 can (8 ounces) pineapple chunks
- 1 can (8 ounces) sliced water chestnuts, drained
- 2 medium carrots, sliced
- 2 tablespoons soy sauce
- 4 teaspoons cornstarch
- 1 cup sweet-and-sour sauce
- 1/4 cup water
- 1-1/2 teaspoons ground ginger
- 3 green onions, cut into 1-inch pieces
- 1-1/2 cups fresh or frozen snow peas
- Hot cooked rice

Direction

- Sauté chicken in oil in a big skillet for 4-5 minutes; strain. Use pepper and salt to sprinkle. Strain pineapple, saving the juice; put pineapple aside. Mix pineapple juice, soy sauce, carrots, water chestnuts, and chicken together in a 5-quart slow cooker. Put a cover on and cook on low until the chicken juices run clear, about 3 hours.
- Mix ginger, water, sweet-and-sour sauce, and cornstarch together in a small bowl until tender. Mix into the slow cooker. Add the saved pineapple and onions, put a cover on and cook on high until thickened, about 15 minutes. Add peas, cook for another 5 minutes. Enjoy with rice.

Nutrition Information

- Calories: 293 calories
- Sodium: 753mg sodium
- Fiber: 3g fiber)
- Total Carbohydrate: 36g carbohydrate (23g sugars
- Cholesterol: 63mg cholesterol
- Protein: 25g protein.
- Total Fat: 6g fat (1g saturated fat)

899. Soy Ginger Grilled Swordfish

Serving: 4 servings. | Prep: 10mins | Cook: 10mins | Ready in:

Ingredients

- 2 tablespoons orange juice
- 2 tablespoons reduced-sodium soy sauce
- 1 tablespoon minced fresh parsley
- 1 tablespoon lemon juice
- 1 tablespoon ketchup
- 1 teaspoon minced fresh gingerroot
- 1/4 teaspoon dried oregano
- 1/4 teaspoon pepper
- 1 teaspoon olive oil
- 2 garlic cloves, minced
- 1-1/4 pounds swordfish steak

Direction

- Combine pepper, oregano, ginger, ketchup, lemon juice, parsley, soy sauce, and orange juice in a small bowl. Keep 2 tablespoons of mixture to use for basting.
- Combine remaining mixture with garlic and oil. In a large resealable plastic bag, add fish. Seal bag and turn to cover; let sit for 30 minutes in the refrigerator.
- Strain and discard marinade. Moisten a paper towel with cooking oil and cover the grill rack lightly using long-handled tongs. Cover and broil fish 4 inches from the heat or grill over high heat till fish is just turns opaque, or for 3-5 minutes every side; use reserved orange juice mixture to occasionally baste over fish.

Nutrition Information

- Calories: 178 calories
- Fiber: 0 fiber)
- Total Carbohydrate: 2g carbohydrate (1g sugars
- Cholesterol: 52mg cholesterol
- Protein: 27g protein. Diabetic Exchanges: 4 lean meat.
- Total Fat: 6g fat (2g saturated fat)
- Sodium: 328mg sodium

900. Spaghetti Hot Dish

Serving: 4 servings. | Prep: 20mins | Cook: 30mins | Ready in:

Ingredients

- 1 pound lean ground beef (90% lean)
- 2 medium onions, diced
- 3 celery ribs with leaves, diced
- 1/4 cup butter, cubed
- 5 tablespoons all-purpose flour
- Salt and pepper to taste
- 3-1/2 cups milk
- 2 tablespoons chopped pimientos
- 1 to 2 teaspoons soy sauce
- 1-1/4 cups broken spaghetti, cooked and drained
- 1 cup finely crushed butter-flavored crackers (about 25 crackers)

Direction

- Cook celery, onions and beef over medium heat in butter in a large skillet until no longer pink; drain. Stir in pepper, salt and flour until blended. Add pimientos, soy sauce and milk gradually. Bring to boiling; cook while stirring until thickened or for 2 minutes. Stir in spaghetti.
- Place into a greased 11x7-in. baking dish. Scatter with cracker crumbs. Bake without a cover at 350° until heated through or for 30-35 minutes.

Nutrition Information

- Calories: 653 calories
- Protein: 35g protein.
- Total Fat: 33g fat (16g saturated fat)
- Sodium: 587mg sodium

- Fiber: 4g fiber)
- Total Carbohydrate: 54g carbohydrate (17g sugars
- Cholesterol: 115mg cholesterol

901. Spareribs Cantonese

Serving: 4-6 servings. | Prep: 10mins | Cook: 01hours45mins | Ready in:

Ingredients

- 4 pounds pork spareribs
- 1 cup orange marmalade
- 3/4 cup water
- 1/2 cup soy sauce
- 1/2 teaspoon garlic powder
- 2 teaspoons grated fresh gingerroot
- 1/4 teaspoon salt, optional
- Dash pepper
- Lemon wedges, optional

Direction

- Cut ribs into serving-size pieces. Arrange in shallow roasting pan, meat side facing down. Cover using foil then bake for 45 minutes at 450°. Drain; flip the ribs.
- Combine seasonings, soy sauce, water and marmalade; spoon over the ribs. Bake, with no cover, basting with sauce occasionally, until tender, about 60 more minutes. If desired, decorate with the lemon wedges.

Nutrition Information

- Calories: 704 calories
- Protein: 44g protein.
- Total Fat: 43g fat (16g saturated fat)
- Sodium: 1387mg sodium
- Fiber: 0 fiber)
- Total Carbohydrate: 36g carbohydrate (35g sugars
- Cholesterol: 170mg cholesterol

902. Spicy Beef & Pepper Stir Fry

Serving: 4 servings. | Prep: 20mins | Cook: 10mins | Ready in:

Ingredients

- 1 pound beef top sirloin steak, cut into thin strips
- 1 tablespoon minced fresh gingerroot
- 3 garlic cloves, minced, divided
- 1/4 teaspoon pepper
- 3/4 teaspoon salt, divided
- 1 cup light coconut milk
- 2 tablespoons sugar
- 1 tablespoon Sriracha Asian hot chili sauce
- 1/2 teaspoon grated lime zest
- 2 tablespoons lime juice
- 2 tablespoons canola oil, divided
- 1 large sweet red pepper, cut into thin strips
- 1/2 medium red onion, thinly sliced
- 1 jalapeno pepper, seeded and thinly sliced
- 4 cups fresh baby spinach
- 2 green onions, thinly sliced
- 2 tablespoons chopped fresh cilantro

Direction

- Toss 1/2 tsp. salt, pepper, 2 garlic cloves, ginger and beef in a big bowl; stand for 15 minutes. Whisk leftover salt, lime juice, lime zest, chili sauce, sugar and coconut milk till blended in a small bowl.
- Heat 1 tbsp. oil on medium high heat in a big skillet. Add beef; stir-fry till not pink for 2-3 minutes. Take out of pan.
- Stir-fry leftover garlic, jalapeno, red onion and red pepper in leftover oil till veggies are crisp tender for 2-3 minutes. Mix in coconut milk mixture and heat through. Add beef and spinach; cook till beef heats through and spinach is wilted, occasionally mixing. Sprinkle cilantro and green onions.

Nutrition Information

- Calories: 312 calories
- Sodium: 641mg sodium
- Fiber: 2g fiber)
- Total Carbohydrate: 15g carbohydrate (10g sugars
- Cholesterol: 46mg cholesterol
- Protein: 26g protein. Diabetic Exchanges: 3 lean meat
- Total Fat: 16g fat (5g saturated fat)

903. Spicy Ginger Beef Stir Fry

Serving: 3 servings. | Prep: 10mins | Cook: 10mins | Ready in:

Ingredients

- 2 teaspoons sugar
- 1/2 teaspoon each cornstarch and ground ginger
- 1/4 teaspoon pepper
- 1/4 teaspoon crushed red pepper flakes
- 2 tablespoons sherry or beef broth
- 2 tablespoons reduced-sodium soy sauce
- 1 tablespoon barbecue sauce
- 1 teaspoon sesame oil
- 1-1/2 cups julienned carrots
- 1/2 cup sliced onion
- 2 teaspoons canola oil
- 12 ounces boneless beef top round steak, cut into thin strips
- 2 garlic cloves, minced
- 1/4 cup sliced green onion
- Hot cooked rice, optional

Direction

- Mix the cornstarch, red pepper flakes, sugar, pepper, and ginger in a bowl. Mix in soy sauce, sesame oil, barbecue sauce, and sherry or broth; put aside. Stir-fry the onion and carrots in a wok or large nonstick skillet with hot canola oil until they are crisp-tender. Remove from the heat and put aside. Stir-fry the garlic and beef in the same pan until the meat is not anymore pinkish. Whisk the sauce mixture and pour it into the pan, stir. Add the carrot mixture; boil. Cook and stir until thickened, for about 2 minutes. Garnish it with green onions before serving over rice, if desired.

Nutrition Information

- Calories: 254 calories
- Fiber: 3g fiber)
- Total Carbohydrate: 14g carbohydrate (0 sugars
- Cholesterol: 64mg cholesterol
- Protein: 27g protein. Diabetic Exchanges: 3 lean meat
- Total Fat: 8g fat (2g saturated fat)
- Sodium: 502mg sodium

904. Spicy Mongolian Beef Salad

Serving: 4 servings. | Prep: 20mins | Cook: 10mins | Ready in:

Ingredients

- 1/4 cup olive oil
- 2 tablespoons rice vinegar
- 1 tablespoon reduced-sodium soy sauce
- 1 tablespoon sesame oil
- 2 teaspoons minced fresh gingerroot
- 1 small garlic clove, minced
- 1 teaspoon sugar
- BEEF:
- 1 tablespoon reduced-sodium soy sauce
- 2 garlic cloves, minced
- 2 teaspoons sugar
- 1 to 2 teaspoons crushed red pepper flakes
- 1 teaspoon sesame oil

- 1 beef top sirloin steak (1 pound), cut into 1/4-inch strips
- 1 tablespoon olive oil
- SALAD:
- 8 cups torn mixed salad greens
- 1 cup shredded carrots
- 1/2 cup thinly sliced cucumber
- 4 radishes, thinly sliced

Direction

- To make dressing, mix together first 7 ingredients.
- Whisk first 5 beef ingredients; mix with beef strips. Heat olive oil on medium-high heat in a big skillet; stir-fry beef mixture for 2 to 3 minutes till browned. Take out of the pan.
- Mix salad ingredients; separate between four dishes. Add beef on top. Sprinkle with dressing.

Nutrition Information

- Calories: 396 calories
- Fiber: 3g fiber)
- Total Carbohydrate: 15g carbohydrate (7g sugars
- Cholesterol: 46mg cholesterol
- Protein: 27g protein.
- Total Fat: 26g fat (5g saturated fat)
- Sodium: 550mg sodium

905. Spicy Turkey Stir Fry

Serving: 4 servings. | Prep: 5mins | Cook: 10mins | Ready in:

Ingredients

- 1 tablespoon cornstarch
- 1 tablespoon sugar
- 1 cup reduced-sodium chicken broth
- 1/4 cup reduced-sodium soy sauce
- 2 tablespoons cider vinegar
- 1/8 to 1/4 teaspoon cayenne pepper
- 3 cups fresh broccoli florets
- 2 tablespoons water
- 1 pound boneless skinless turkey breast, cut into 3/4-inch pieces
- 2 teaspoons canola oil
- 1 medium sweet red pepper, cut into 3/4-inch pieces
- 1 garlic clove, minced
- 1 teaspoon minced fresh gingerroot
- 2 green onions, sliced
- 2 tablespoons dry roasted peanuts
- Hot cooked rice

Direction

- Mix first six ingredients in a bowl until smooth. Set aside for later. In a greased nonstick frying pan, stir-fry hot oil and turkey, 2-3 minutes. Add garlic, broccoli, sweet pepper, and ginger; continue stir-frying until veggies are crispy and tender, 3-4 minutes. Stir the broth mixture and put in pan. Heat to boiling, stir constantly, and cook until thick, 1-2 minutes. Spread peanuts and onions on top. Eat with rice.

Nutrition Information

- Calories: 233 calories
- Protein: 33g protein. Diabetic Exchanges: 3 lean meat
- Total Fat: 6g fat (1g saturated fat)
- Sodium: 866mg sodium
- Fiber: 3g fiber)
- Total Carbohydrate: 13g carbohydrate (0 sugars
- Cholesterol: 70mg cholesterol

906. Steak Lo Mein

Serving: 6 servings. | Prep: 20mins | Cook: 10mins | Ready in:

Ingredients

- 1 pound beef top round steak, trimmed
- 2 tablespoons cornstarch
- 1 teaspoon beef bouillon granules
- 3/4 cup water
- 1/4 cup soy sauce
- 2 tablespoons vegetable oil
- 1 garlic clove, minced
- 2 cups shredded cabbage
- 1 cup diagonally sliced carrots, partially cooked
- 1 medium onion, sliced into rings
- 1/2 cup sliced fresh mushrooms
- 1/2 cup diagonally sliced celery
- 1/3 cup sliced green onions
- 15 fresh snow pea pods, trimmed
- 1 can (8 ounces) sliced water chestnuts, drained
- 4 ounces thin spaghetti, cooked and drained

Direction

- Put steak into the freezer just until firm enough. Slice the steak diagonally across grain into 1/4-inch strips.
- Combine soy sauce, water, bouillon, and cornstarch until no lumps remain; put aside.
- Heat oil in a large skillet or wok over medium-high heat. Add garlic and meat; sauté for about 5 minutes until meat is no longer pink. Transfer meat to a platter.
- Add green onions, celery, mushrooms, onion, carrots, and cabbage to the skillet; sauté for about 3 minutes. Stir in water chestnuts and pea pods; cook for 2 more minutes. Add cooked meat.
- Stir bouillon mixture and add to the skillet; cook, stirring, until the sauce thickens. Add spaghetti and gently toss for 1 minutes until thoroughly heated.

Nutrition Information

- Calories: 329 calories
- Sodium: 834mg sodium
- Fiber: 0 fiber)
- Total Carbohydrate: 34g carbohydrate (0 sugars
- Cholesterol: 52mg cholesterol
- Protein: 29g protein. Diabetic Exchanges: 2 lean meat
- Total Fat: 8g fat (0 saturated fat)

907. Steaks With Cucumber Sauce

Serving: 4 servings. | Prep: 10mins | Cook: 10mins | Ready in:

Ingredients

- 4 boneless beef New York strip steaks (8 to 10 ounces each)
- 3/4 cup teriyaki sauce
- 1/2 cup chopped seeded peeled cucumber
- 1/2 cup sour cream
- 1/2 cup mayonnaise
- 1 tablespoon minced chives
- 1/2 to 1 teaspoon dill weed
- 1/4 teaspoon salt

Direction

- In a big resealable plastic bag, insert the steaks before adding teriyaki sauce. Close the bag up and turn to coat the meat. Keep the bag inside of a fridge through the night. Combine the salt, dill, chives, mayonnaise, sour cream and cucumber together in a bowl then cover it up and refrigerate. Drain the meat and discard the marinade. Over medium-hot heat, grill the steak on a covered grill until the meat reaches desired level of doneness. Grill for about 4 to 5 minutes per side. For medium-rare meat, a thermometer should register at 145°F and for medium, it should be 160°F. For well done, it should read 170°F. Serve the steak together with cucumber sauce.

Nutrition Information

- Calories:
- Sodium:
- Fiber:
- Total Carbohydrate:
- Cholesterol:
- Protein:
- Total Fat:

908. Stir Fried Beef 'n' Beans

Serving: 4 servings. | Prep: 10mins | Cook: 25mins | Ready in:

Ingredients

- 1/4 cup cornstarch
- 1/2 cup soy sauce
- 2 tablespoons water
- 4 teaspoons minced fresh gingerroot
- 4 garlic cloves, minced
- 4 tablespoons canola oil, divided
- 1 pound beef top sirloin steak, cut into 1/4-inch strips
- 1/2 pound fresh green beans, cut in half lengthwise
- 1 teaspoon sugar
- 1/2 teaspoon salt
- Hot cooked rice

Direction

- Mix 2 tbsp. oil, garlic, ginger, water, soy sauce and cornstarch till smooth in a small bowl; put 1/2 cup aside. Put leftover marinade into big resealable plastic bag. Add beef then seal bag; flip to coat then refrigerate it for 25-30 minutes.
- Drain marinade from beef; discard. Stir-fry beef in leftover oil in a wok/skillet till brown for 4-6 minutes. Remove; keep warm.
- Stir-fry salt, sugar and beans till crisp tender for 15 minutes in the same skillet; mix in reserved marinade and beef. Boil; mix and cook till thick for 1-2 minutes. Serve with rice.

Nutrition Information

- Calories:
- Sodium:
- Fiber:
- Total Carbohydrate:
- Cholesterol:
- Protein:
- Total Fat:

909. Stir Fried Beef On Lettuce

Serving: 4 servings. | Prep: 15mins | Cook: 10mins | Ready in:

Ingredients

- 1/3 cup reduced-sodium soy sauce
- 1/3 cup white wine or chicken broth
- 1 pound beef top sirloin steak, cut into 1/8-inch strips
- 1 teaspoon cornstarch
- 1/2 pound fresh mushrooms, sliced
- 2 cups fresh snow peas
- 4 teaspoons vegetable oil
- 4 cups shredded lettuce

Direction

- Mix broth or wine with soy sauce in a small bowl. Save 1/4 cup. In a big resealable plastic bag, add the leftover soy sauce mixture; add beef, close the bag and flip to cover. Chill for 15 minutes. Mix the saved soy sauce mixture and cornstarch together in a small bowl until tender, put aside.
- Stir-fry snow peas and mushrooms in 2 teaspoons oil in a nonstick skillet until the snow peas are crunchy and soft, about 3-4 minutes. Take out and keep warm.
- Strain and dispose the marinade from beef. Stir-fry the beef with the leftover oil in the same skillet, about 2 minutes. Whisk the cornstarch mixture, pour in the skillet. Boil;

stir and cook until slightly thickened, or about 1-2 minutes. On 4 serving dish, put lettuce. Put the snow pea mixture and beef mixture on top.

Nutrition Information

- Calories: 246 calories
- Cholesterol: 64mg cholesterol
- Protein: 26g protein. Diabetic Exchanges: 3 lean meat
- Total Fat: 10g fat (2g saturated fat)
- Sodium: 856mg sodium
- Fiber: 3g fiber)
- Total Carbohydrate: 8g carbohydrate (0 sugars

910. Sweet 'n' Tangy Shrimp

Serving: 4 servings. | Prep: 20mins | Cook: 10mins | Ready in:

Ingredients

- 1/2 cup ketchup
- 2 tablespoons sugar
- 2 tablespoons cider vinegar
- 2 tablespoons reduced-sodium soy sauce
- 1 teaspoon sesame oil
- 1/4 teaspoon crushed red pepper flakes
- 1-1/2 pounds uncooked medium shrimp, peeled and deveined
- 1 tablespoon minced fresh gingerroot
- 1 tablespoon canola oil
- 3 garlic cloves, minced
- 2 green onions, sliced
- 1 teaspoon sesame seeds, toasted
- Hot cooked rice, optional

Direction

- Mix the first 6 ingredients together in a small bowl, then set bowl aside. Stir-fry ginger and shrimp with oil in a wok or big nonstick skillet until shrimps are pink. Put in garlic and cook for 1 minute more.
- Put in ketchup mixture, then cook and stir until heated through, about 2 to 3 minutes. Sprinkle sesame seeds and onions over, then serve together with rice, if wanted.

Nutrition Information

- Calories: 241 calories
- Protein: 28g protein.
- Total Fat: 7g fat (1g saturated fat)
- Sodium: 954mg sodium
- Fiber: 1g fiber)
- Total Carbohydrate: 17g carbohydrate (10g sugars
- Cholesterol: 252mg cholesterol

911. Sweet Beef Stew

Serving: 4 servings. | Prep: 10mins | Cook: 35mins | Ready in:

Ingredients

- 1-1/2 pounds beef stew meat, cut into 1-inch cubes
- 2 medium onions, chopped
- 3 garlic cloves, minced
- 1 tablespoon canola oil
- 1/2 teaspoon salt
- 1/4 teaspoon ground ginger
- 1/4 teaspoon pepper
- 1/8 teaspoon ground nutmeg
- 3/4 cup apricot nectar
- 3 tablespoons soy sauce
- 2 tablespoons molasses
- 1 teaspoon brown sugar
- 1 teaspoon cornstarch
- 1 tablespoon water
- Hot cooked rice or noodles

Direction

- In a pressure cooker over medium heat, cook garlic, onions and beef in oil until browned.

Stir in salt, nutmeg, pepper and ginger. Combine the apricot nectar, brown sugar, molasses and soy sauce; spread over meat. Securely close cover; on vent pipe, place pressure regulator.
- Bring cooker to full pressure over high heat. Cook for 20 minutes over medium-high heat. (Pressure regulator should keep a slow steady rocking motion; adjust heat if needed.) Take away from the heat; allow pressure to omit.
- Use a slotted spoon to transfer meat. Combine cornstarch and water until smooth; slowly add to pan drippings. Boil and stir for 2 minutes or until thick. Add in meat and serve with rice.

Nutrition Information

- Calories: 377 calories
- Total Fat: 15g fat (5g saturated fat)
- Sodium: 1063mg sodium
- Fiber: 2g fiber)
- Total Carbohydrate: 23g carbohydrate (18g sugars
- Cholesterol: 106mg cholesterol
- Protein: 35g protein.

912. Sweet Salsa Chicken

Serving: 6 servings. | Prep: 20mins | Cook: 20mins | Ready in:

Ingredients

- 1-1/2 cups salsa
- 2/3 cup honey
- 1/2 cup orange juice
- 1/2 cup reduced-sodium soy sauce
- 1/4 cup Dijon mustard
- 4 teaspoons olive oil
- 1/2 teaspoon ground ginger
- 6 boneless skinless chicken breast halves (4 ounces each)
- 1-1/2 teaspoons cornstarch
- 2 tablespoons cold water

Direction

- Combine the first seven ingredients in a small bowl. In a large resealable plastic bag, pour 1 and a half cups of the mixture; add the chicken. Seal bag and turn to coat; put in the fridge for 2 hours. Cover remaining marinade and cool in the refrigerator.
- Drain and dispose marinade from chicken. In a greased 11x7-inch baking dish, place the chicken; place reserved marinade on top.
- Uncover and bake at 375° for around 20 to 25 minutes till a thermometer reads 179°. Take chicken out and keep warm.
- In a small saucepan, combine cold water and cornstarch till smooth; mix in pan juices. Allow to boil; cook and stir for 2 minutes till thickened. Serve with chicken.

Nutrition Information

- Calories: 251 calories
- Protein: 24g protein.
- Total Fat: 5g fat (1g saturated fat)
- Sodium: 1039mg sodium
- Fiber: 2g fiber)
- Total Carbohydrate: 25g carbohydrate (21g sugars
- Cholesterol: 63mg cholesterol

913. Sweet Spicy Asian Meatballs

Serving: 4 servings. | Prep: 35mins | Cook: 20mins | Ready in:

Ingredients

- 1/4 cup panko (Japanese) bread crumbs
- 1 large egg
- 2 garlic cloves, minced
- 1/4 teaspoon crushed red pepper flakes
- 1 pound Johnsonville® Ground Mild Italian sausage

- 2 tablespoons sesame oil
- 1 small onion, finely chopped
- 1/2 cup finely chopped sweet red pepper
- 1 tablespoon grated fresh gingerroot
- 1/2 teaspoon garam masala
- 3/4 cup vegetable broth, divided
- 1/2 cup coconut milk
- 1 teaspoon sweet chili sauce
- 1/2 teaspoon Sriracha Asian hot chili sauce or 1/4 teaspoon hot pepper sauce
- 1 tablespoon cornstarch
- 1/2 cup finely chopped fresh pineapple
- 1 teaspoon reduced-sodium soy sauce
- 4 cups hot cooked rice

Direction

- Preheat oven to 350°. In a big bowl, mix pepper flakes, garlic, egg, and bread crumbs. Put in sausage; stir gently but thoroughly. Form into 1-inch balls.
- On a greased rack in a shallow baking pan, position meatballs. Bake for 20-25 minutes until no pink remains.
- Meanwhile, in a big frying pan, heat oil over medium-high heat. Put in garam masala, ginger, pepper, and onion; cook and mix for 6-8 minutes or until vegetables become softened. Whisk in chili sauces, coconut milk and half a cup of broth; let it boil.
- In a small bowl, mix the leftover broth and cornstarch until smooth; mix into sauce mixture. Bring back to a boil, stirring often; keep cooking and stirring for about 1-2 minutes or until condensed. Combine in soy sauce, pineapple and meatballs; let heat through. Use with rice.

Nutrition Information

- Calories:
- Sodium:
- Fiber:
- Total Carbohydrate:
- Cholesterol:
- Protein:
- Total Fat:

914. Sweet And Sour Baked Chicken

Serving: 6-8 servings. | Prep: 10mins | Cook: 01hours15mins | Ready in:

Ingredients

- 1 cup soy sauce
- 1 cup water
- 3/4 cup sugar
- 1/2 cup vegetable oil
- 1/2 cup white wine vinegar
- 1 can (6 ounces) pineapple juice
- 1-1/2 teaspoons ground ginger
- 1 teaspoon salt
- 3/4 to 1 teaspoon garlic powder
- 12 broiler/fryer chicken pieces (3-1/2 to 4 pounds)

Direction

- In a glass 13x9-in. baking dish or a big resealable plastic bag, mix the first 9 ingredients together. Put in chicken pieces, turn to blend. Close the bag or put a cover on the dish and chill for 8 hours or overnight. Strain, saving 1 cup marinade and discard the rest. In a 15x10x1-inch baking pan, put the chicken; pour in the saved marinade. Bake without a cover at 350° until the juices run clear, about 1 1/4 hours.

Nutrition Information

- Calories:
- Sodium:
- Fiber:
- Total Carbohydrate:
- Cholesterol:
- Protein:
- Total Fat:

915. Sweet And Sour Skewered Shrimp

Serving: 6 servings. | Prep: 15mins | Cook: 10mins | Ready in:

Ingredients

- 1/2 cup barbecue sauce
- 1/4 cup lemon juice
- 1/4 cup pineapple preserves
- 4 teaspoons soy sauce
- 1/2 teaspoon ground ginger
- 30 uncooked large shrimp, peeled and deveined (about 2 pounds)
- 1 to 2 large green peppers, cut into 1-inch pieces
- 1/2 pound fresh mushrooms, halved

Direction

- Boil the first five ingredients in a small saucepan over medium heat, stirring frequently. Remove from heat and let cool; set aside half a cup for basting. In a large zip-top bag, pour the remaining marinade and add in the shrimps. Close the bag and refrigerate for a half hour. Drain the shrimps and dispose of its marinade. Alternately thread shrimps, mushrooms, and green peppers on six metal or pre-soaked wooden skewers. Cook on an open grill over medium heat for 2 minutes per side, turning and basting with reserved sauce. Grill for another 4-8 minutes, turning and basting often, until shrimps just turn pink.

Nutrition Information

- Calories:
- Protein:
- Total Fat:
- Sodium:
- Fiber:
- Total Carbohydrate:
- Cholesterol:

916. Tangerine Cashew Snapper

Serving: 4 servings. | Prep: 15mins | Cook: 15mins | Ready in:

Ingredients

- 4 tangerines
- 2 tablespoons lime juice
- 2 tablespoons reduced-sodium soy sauce
- 1 tablespoon brown sugar
- 2 teaspoons minced fresh gingerroot
- 1 teaspoon sesame oil
- 1/8 teaspoon crushed red pepper flakes
- 4 red snapper fillets (4 ounces each)
- 1/3 cup chopped unsalted cashews
- 2 green onions, thinly sliced

Direction

- Peel then cut and get rid of seeds from 2 tangerines. Chop their fruit and put in a small bowl. Squeeze the remaining tangerines to draw out juice, then put into a bowl. Stir in pepper flakes, sesame oil, ginger, brown sugar, soy sauce and lime juice.
- Into a 9"x13" baking dish sprayed with cooking spray, arrange fillets, then pour over fillets with tangerine mixture. Sprinkle with green onions as well as cashews. Bake at 425 degrees without a cover until it is easy to use a fork to flake fillets, or for 15 to 20 minutes.

Nutrition Information

- Calories: 260 calories
- Protein: 26g protein. Diabetic Exchanges: 3 lean meat
- Total Fat: 8g fat (2g saturated fat)
- Sodium: 358mg sodium

- Fiber: 2g fiber)
- Total Carbohydrate: 22g carbohydrate (15g sugars
- Cholesterol: 40mg cholesterol

917. Tangy Tropical Chicken

Serving: 4 servings. | Prep: 20mins | Cook: 04hours00mins | Ready in:

Ingredients

- 1 pound boneless skinless chicken breasts, cut into 1-inch strips
- 2 cups chopped peeled mangoes
- 1 medium onion, chopped
- 1 medium green pepper, sliced
- 1 garlic clove, minced
- 1 cup unsweetened pineapple juice
- 1 cup orange juice
- 1/4 cup reduced-sodium soy sauce
- 2 tablespoons Thai chili sauce
- 1/4 teaspoon pepper
- 2 tablespoons cornstarch
- 2 tablespoons cold water
- Hot cooked rice

Direction

- In a 3-quart slow cooker, put the chicken. Put garlic, green pepper, onion, and mangoes on top. Mix pepper, chili sauce, soy sauce, orange juice, and pineapple juice in a small bowl; pour over the chicken. Put a cover on and cook over low heat until the chicken becomes tender for 4-5 hours.
- Transfer the chicken into a serving platter; keep it warm. Put the cooking juices into a small saucepan. Boil the juices. Blend water and cornstarch until they are smooth; mix gradually into the pan. Boil; stir and cook until thickened for 2 minutes. Serve alongside rice and the chicken mixture.

Nutrition Information

- Calories: 299 calories
- Sodium: 760mg sodium
- Fiber: 3g fiber)
- Total Carbohydrate: 42g carbohydrate (29g sugars
- Cholesterol: 63mg cholesterol
- Protein: 26g protein.
- Total Fat: 3g fat (1g saturated fat)

918. Tasty Tuna Steaks

Serving: 4 servings. | Prep: 15mins | Cook: 15mins | Ready in:

Ingredients

- 1/3 cup dry red wine or reduced-sodium beef broth
- 1/3 cup reduced-sodium soy sauce
- 2 teaspoons minced fresh gingerroot
- 1 teaspoon minced garlic
- 4 tuna steaks (6 ounces each)
- 1 bay leaf
- 1 tablespoon olive oil

Direction

- Mix together garlic, ginger, soy sauce and wine in a small bowl. Add to a big resealable plastic bag, then put in bay leaf and tuna steaks. Seal bag and turn to coat well, allowing to stand for 15 minutes.
- Drain and get rid of the bay leaf as well as marinade. Cook tuna in a big skillet with oil on moderately high heat until the center is pink a little bit, or 4 to 6 minutes per side for medium-rare.

Nutrition Information

- Calories: 224 calories
- Total Fat: 5g fat (1g saturated fat)
- Sodium: 366mg sodium

- Fiber: 0 fiber)
- Total Carbohydrate: 1g carbohydrate (0 sugars
- Cholesterol: 77mg cholesterol
- Protein: 40g protein. Diabetic Exchanges: 5 lean meat

- Sodium: 528mg sodium
- Fiber: 2g fiber)
- Total Carbohydrate: 17g carbohydrate (9g sugars
- Cholesterol: 94mg cholesterol

919. Teriyaki Beef Stew

Serving: 8 servings. | Prep: 20mins | Cook: 06hours30mins | Ready in:

Ingredients

- 2 pounds beef stew meat
- 1 bottle (12 ounces) ginger beer or ginger ale
- 1/4 cup teriyaki sauce
- 2 garlic cloves, minced
- 2 tablespoons sesame seeds
- 2 tablespoons cornstarch
- 2 tablespoons cold water
- 2 cups frozen peas, thawed
- Hot cooked rice, optional

Direction

- Cook beef in batches in a large nonstick skillet until evenly browned. Place into a 3-quart slow cooker.
- Stir sesame seeds, garlic, teriyaki sauce and ginger beer together in a small bowl; transfer to the beef. Cook on Low with a cover until the meat is soft, or for 6-8 hours.
- Stir cold water and cornstarch together until smooth; gradually mix into the stew. Mix in peas. Cook on High with a cover until thickened, or for 30 minutes. Couple with rice to your favorite. Serve.

Nutrition Information

- Calories: 310 calories
- Protein: 33g protein. Diabetic Exchanges: 4 lean meat
- Total Fat: 12g fat (4g saturated fat)

920. Teriyaki Beef Stir Fry For 2

Serving: 2 servings. | Prep: 15mins | Cook: 5mins | Ready in:

Ingredients

- 2 tablespoons cornstarch
- 2/3 cup reduced-sodium teriyaki sauce
- 1/4 cup canola oil, divided
- 10 ounces boneless beef top round steak, cut into thin strips
- 1 medium green pepper, coarsely chopped
- 3 green onions, cut into 2-inch pieces
- Hot cooked rice, optional

Direction

- Mix together 2 tbsp. of oil, teriyaki sauce and cornstarch in a small bowl until smooth. Add into a big resealable plastic bag with half of the sauce mixture and put in beef. Seal bag and turn to coat well, then chill for a half hour. Cover and chill the leftover marinade.
- Stir-fry onions and green pepper with remaining oil in a big nonstick skillet or wok about 2 to 3 minutes. Take out and keep warm.
- Drain beef and put into pan. Put in the leftover reserved marinade and stir-fry until meat is not pink anymore, about 2 to 3 minutes. Turn vegetables back to pan, then cook and stir until thickened, about 1 to 2 minutes. Serve together with rice, if wanted.

Nutrition Information

- Calories: 378 calories

- Total Fat: 19g fat (3g saturated fat)
- Sodium: 897mg sodium
- Fiber: 2g fiber)
- Total Carbohydrate: 17g carbohydrate (10g sugars
- Cholesterol: 80mg cholesterol
- Protein: 36g protein. Diabetic Exchanges: 4 lean meat

921. Teriyaki Mushroom Chicken

Serving: 4 servings. | Prep: 10mins | Cook: 15mins | Ready in:

Ingredients

- 4 boneless skinless chicken breast halves (6 ounces each)
- 5 tablespoons butter, divided
- 4 cups sliced fresh mushrooms
- 1 cup sliced onion
- 1/4 cup water
- 1/4 cup honey teriyaki marinade

Direction

- Cook chicken in a tablespoon of butter in a large pan over medium heat, for 5-7 minutes per side. Temperature should reach 170°F. Turn heat off. Keep it warm.
- Sauté mushrooms and onion in the same pan, with the rest of the butter. Cook until softened. Add marinade and water during the last 2 minutes of cooking. Put chicken back, heat through.

Nutrition Information

- Calories:
- Sodium:
- Fiber:
- Total Carbohydrate:
- Cholesterol:
- Protein:
- Total Fat:

922. Teriyaki Pork Tenderloin

Serving: 8 servings. | Prep: 5mins | Cook: 25mins | Ready in:

Ingredients

- 1/2 cup soy sauce
- 1/4 cup olive oil
- 4 teaspoons brown sugar
- 2 teaspoons ground ginger
- 1 teaspoon pepper
- 2 garlic cloves, minced
- 4 pork tenderloin (3/4 to 1 pound each)
- Coarsely ground pepper, optional

Direction

- Mix the first six ingredients in a large resealable plastic bag; add pork. Seal the bag and coat by turning; keep cool for 4 hours, turning several times.
- Drain and dispose of marinade. Cover and grill the tenderloins over indirect medium-hot heat until a thermometer reads 160deg, 25-40 minutes. Dust with pepper if desired.

Nutrition Information

- Calories: 216 calories
- Sodium: 859mg sodium
- Fiber: 0 fiber)
- Total Carbohydrate: 3g carbohydrate (2g sugars
- Cholesterol: 95mg cholesterol
- Protein: 36g protein.
- Total Fat: 6g fat (2g saturated fat)

923. Teriyaki Tangerine Ribs

Serving: 8 servings. | Prep: 5mins | Cook: 01hours30mins | Ready in:

Ingredients

- 4 pounds country-style pork ribs
- 2/3 cup fresh tangerine or orange juice
- 1/3 cup light corn syrup
- 2 tablespoons soy sauce
- 1 teaspoon grated tangerine or orange zest
- 1/2 teaspoon ground ginger
- 1 garlic clove, minced

Direction

- Arrange ribs on a rack in a shallow roasting pan lined with foil, meat-side down. Bake for 30 minutes at 425°. Strain; flip the ribs. Turn the temperature down to 350°; bake for 30 more minutes.
- Meanwhile, in a saucepan, mix together the remaining ingredients; boil the mixture. Take away from the heat; set aside. Take the ribs out of the rack; discard foil and drippings. Transfer the ribs back to the pan; transfer the tangerine mixture over the ribs.
- Bake without a cover for 30-40 minutes, flipping the ribs often, or till tender.

Nutrition Information

- Calories: 286 calories
- Protein: 27g protein.
- Total Fat: 14g fat (5g saturated fat)
- Sodium: 310mg sodium
- Fiber: 0 fiber)
- Total Carbohydrate: 13g carbohydrate (9g sugars
- Cholesterol: 86mg cholesterol

924. Teriyaki Turkey Meatballs

Serving: 2 servings. | Prep: 20mins | Cook: 15mins | Ready in:

Ingredients

- 1 egg
- 1/4 cup dry bread crumbs
- 2 tablespoons chopped celery
- 2 teaspoons dried minced onion
- Dash ground ginger
- Salt and pepper to taste
- 1/2 pound ground turkey
- SAUCE:
- 1 tablespoon cornstarch
- 1 teaspoon ground ginger
- 1 cup chicken broth
- 2 tablespoons soy sauce
- 2 tablespoons sherry or additional chicken broth
- 2 tablespoons pineapple juice
- Hot cooked rice or noodles

Direction

- Combine pepper, salt, ginger, onion, celery, bread crumbs and egg together in a bowl. Crumble turkey over the mixture; mix properly. Form into 1-in. balls. Place on a rack coated with grease in a shallow baking pan. Bake without a cover at 400° till not pink anymore, or for 12-18 minutes; drain.
- Combine broth, ginger and cornstarch together in a saucepan till smooth. Mix in juice, more broth or sherry and soy sauce. Allow to boil; cook while stirring till lightly thickened, or for 2 minutes. Include in the meatballs; cook till heated through. Serve over noodles or rice.

Nutrition Information

- Calories: 379 calories
- Fiber: 1g fiber)

- Total Carbohydrate: 20g carbohydrate (4g sugars
- Cholesterol: 183mg cholesterol
- Protein: 26g protein.
- Total Fat: 20g fat (6g saturated fat)
- Sodium: 1658mg sodium

925. Thai Barbecued Salmon

Serving: 4 servings. | Prep: 10mins | Cook: 5mins | Ready in:

Ingredients

- 2/3 cup barbecue sauce
- 1/3 cup Thai chili sauce
- 1/4 cup minced fresh cilantro
- 4 salmon fillets (1 inch thick and 4 ounces each)

Direction

- Mix cilantro, chili sauce and barbecue sauce in a small bowl. Reserve 1/4 cup for serving.
- Cook the salmon for 4 to 5 minutes over an indoor grill that is greased with cooking spray, basting often with the sauce mixture or until the fish easily flakes with a fork. You can serve the salmon along with the reserved sauce.

Nutrition Information

- Calories: 283 calories
- Sodium: 701mg sodium
- Fiber: 1g fiber)
- Total Carbohydrate: 15g carbohydrate (12g sugars
- Cholesterol: 67mg cholesterol
- Protein: 24g protein.
- Total Fat: 13g fat (3g saturated fat)

926. Thai Salmon Brown Rice Bowls

Serving: 4 servings. | Prep: 5mins | Cook: 10mins | Ready in:

Ingredients

- 4 salmon fillets (4 ounces each)
- 1/2 cup sesame ginger salad dressing, divided
- 3 cups hot cooked brown rice
- 1/2 cup chopped fresh cilantro
- 1/4 teaspoon salt
- 1 cup julienned carrot
- Thinly sliced red cabbage, optional

Direction

- Preheat oven to 400°. In a foil-lined 15x10x1-inch pan, place salmon; brush with 1/4 cup dressing. Bake for around 8 to 10 minutes till fish just starts to easily flake with a fork. In the meantime, toss cilantro and salt with rice.
- To serve, divide rice mixture among four bowls. Place carrots, salmon and, if wished, cabbage on top. Drizzle with the rest of the dressing.

Nutrition Information

- Calories: 486 calories
- Protein: 24g protein.
- Total Fat: 21g fat (4g saturated fat)
- Sodium: 532mg sodium
- Fiber: 3g fiber)
- Total Carbohydrate: 49g carbohydrate (8g sugars
- Cholesterol: 57mg cholesterol

927. Thai Shrimp Linguine

Serving: 3 servings. | Prep: 5mins | Cook: 10mins | Ready in:

Ingredients

- 1 package (9 ounces) refrigerated linguine
- 1 cup fresh snow peas
- 2 cups shredded carrots
- 1/2 pound sliced fresh mushrooms
- 1 tablespoon olive oil
- 1/2 pound uncooked medium shrimp, peeled and deveined
- 1 cup Thai peanut sauce

Direction

- Cook linguine as directed on the package, cooking snow peas and pasta at the same time in the same pot.
- In the meantime, sauté mushrooms and carrots in oil over medium heat in a large skillet for 3 minutes. Stir in shrimp; cook until pink for 3 more minutes, stir. Mix in peanut sauce; cook until thoroughly heated.
- Drain snow peas and linguine, then remove to a serving bowl. Add cooked shrimp mixture on top and toss to combine.

Nutrition Information

- Calories: 599 calories
- Total Fat: 22g fat (4g saturated fat)
- Sodium: 1814mg sodium
- Fiber: 9g fiber)
- Total Carbohydrate: 69g carbohydrate (10g sugars
- Cholesterol: 92mg cholesterol
- Protein: 34g protein.

928. Thai Shrimp Stir Fry

Serving: 4 servings. | Prep: 15mins | Cook: 10mins | Ready in:

Ingredients

- 2 medium sweet red peppers, cut into thin slices
- 1 teaspoon canola oil
- 1 cup fresh snow peas
- 1/2 cup thinly sliced green onions
- 1 garlic clove, minced
- 1/2 cup reduced-sodium chicken broth
- 2 tablespoons reduced-fat peanut butter
- 4-1/2 teaspoons reduced-sodium soy sauce
- 1 tablespoon rice vinegar
- 1 teaspoon sesame oil
- 1 teaspoon minced fresh gingerroot
- 1/2 teaspoon crushed red pepper flakes
- 1 pound uncooked medium shrimp, peeled and deveined
- Hot cooked fettuccine

Direction

- Stir-fry red peppers in hot canola oil in a big nonstick wok or skillet, about 1 minute. Add garlic, green onions, and snow peas; stir-fry until the vegetables are crunchy and soft, about another 2-3 minutes. Take out and keep warm.
- Mix pepper flakes, ginger, sesame oil, vinegar, soy sauce, peanut butter, and broth together in the same skillet. Stir and cook until the mixture boils and peanut butter melts. Mix in shrimp. Stir and cook until the shrimp is pink, or about 2 minutes. Put the red pepper mixture back to the skillet, thoroughly heat. Enjoy with fettuccine.

Nutrition Information

- Calories: 206 calories
- Protein: 22g protein. Diabetic Exchanges: 3 lean meat
- Total Fat: 8g fat (1g saturated fat)
- Sodium: 565mg sodium
- Fiber: 3g fiber)
- Total Carbohydrate: 12g carbohydrate (0 sugars
- Cholesterol: 168mg cholesterol

929. Thai Shrimp And Noodles

Serving: | Prep: | Cook: 30mins | Ready in:

Ingredients

- 1/4 cup Soy Sauce
- 2 tablespoons Peanut Butter
- 2 tablespoons Vegetable Oil
- 2 tablespoons Sesame Oil
- 1 tablespoon Honey
- 1 tablespoon Light Brown Sugar
- 1 tablespoon Red Chili Paste
- 1 tablespoon Olive Oil
- 1 pound Medium Shrimp, Peeled and Deveined
- 1 teaspoon Salt
- 1 teaspoon Pepper
- 1 pound Pad Thai Style Rice Noodles or Linguine
- 2 pieces Carrots, Peeled and Shredded
- 1/2 cup Dry Roasted Peanuts, Chopped
- 2 pieces Green Onions, Thinly Sliced
- 4 tablespoons Cilantro, Chopped

Direction

- Whisk red chili paste, brown sugar, honey, sesame oil, vegetable oil, peanut butter and soy sauce together. Reserve.
- Preheat an oven to 400 degrees F.
- Heat the olive oil in the wok, add the shrimp and let cook for 6 to 8 minutes until opaque and pink. Season with pepper and salt. Then maintain low heat.
- Cook the noodles in a large pot containing boiling salted water, then drain thoroughly and transfer to the wok containing the shrimp.
- Mix in half of the cilantro, green onions, half of the peanuts, carrots, soy sauce mixture.
- Mix to combine and serve right away. Stud with the remaining cilantro and peanuts.

930. Tropical Turkey Meat Loaf

Serving: 8 servings (2/3 cup sauce). | Prep: 10mins | Cook: 60mins | Ready in:

Ingredients

- 1/2 cup egg substitute
- 1 can (8 ounces) unsweetened crushed pineapple, undrained, divided
- 3 tablespoons reduced-sodium soy sauce
- 1 teaspoon sugar
- 3/4 teaspoon ground ginger
- 1/2 teaspoon ground mustard
- 1/4 teaspoon garlic powder
- 1 cup dry bread crumbs
- 1-1/2 pounds lean ground turkey
- 1 tablespoon finely chopped onion
- 1 green onion, finely chopped
- 2 teaspoons finely chopped jalapeno pepper
- 1 teaspoon honey
- 1 teaspoon lime juice
- Pinch pepper

Direction

- Mix together the seasonings, 1/3 cup of pineapple and egg substitute in a bowl. Put in breadcrumbs, then mix well. Add crumbled meat to the mixture then stir well. Push into an 8x4-in. loaf pan greased with cooking spray. Put 1 tablespoon of pineapple on top. Bake for 1 to 1-1/4 hours at 350°, until a thermometer shows 165°.
- Allow to sit for 5 minutes before serving. In the meantime, combine the rest of pineapple, pepper, lime juice, honey, jalapeno and onions in a small bowl. Well-served with the meat loaf.

Nutrition Information

- Calories: 174 calories
- Protein: 24g protein. Diabetic Exchanges: 3 lean meat
- Total Fat: 2g fat (0 saturated fat)

- Sodium: 387mg sodium
- Fiber: 0 fiber)
- Total Carbohydrate: 15g carbohydrate (0 sugars
- Cholesterol: 25mg cholesterol

931. Turkey With Curried Cream Sauce

Serving: 3 servings. | Prep: 15mins | Cook: 15mins | Ready in:

Ingredients

- 2 tablespoons butter
- 2 tablespoons all-purpose flour
- 1/2 teaspoon curry powder
- 1 cup chicken broth
- 1/4 cup 2% milk
- 2 teaspoons canola oil
- 1 small yellow summer squash, sliced
- 1 small zucchini, sliced
- 1/2 small onion, thinly sliced
- 2 cups cubed cooked turkey breast
- 1/2 teaspoon grated lemon peel
- Hot cooked rice
- 3 tablespoons chopped cashews

Direction

- Melt butter in a small saucepan over medium heat. Add curry powder and flour until smooth. Slowly stir in milk and broth. Bring to a boil, stirring frequently; cook and stir for 1 to 2 minutes until mixture thickens. Put off from the heat and put to one side.
- Heat oil over medium-high heat in a large skillet. Sauté onion, zucchini, and squash; cook and stir until soft. Add reserved sauce, lemon peel, and turkey; cook until thoroughly heated. Serve with rice; garnish top with cashews.

Nutrition Information

- Calories: 331 calories
- Sodium: 504mg sodium
- Fiber: 2g fiber)
- Total Carbohydrate: 13g carbohydrate (4g sugars
- Cholesterol: 104mg cholesterol
- Protein: 33g protein.
- Total Fat: 17g fat (6g saturated fat)

932. Vegetable Beef Stir Fry

Serving: 4 servings. | Prep: 15mins | Cook: 15mins | Ready in:

Ingredients

- 1 teaspoon cornstarch
- 2 tablespoons reduced-sodium soy sauce
- 1 teaspoon minced fresh gingerroot
- 1/2 teaspoon sugar
- 1/4 teaspoon pepper
- 1 beef top sirloin steak (1 pound), cut into thin strips
- SAUCE:
- 1 teaspoon cornstarch
- 1/2 cup reduced-sodium chicken broth
- 2 tablespoons ketchup
- 1 tablespoon reduced-sodium soy sauce
- 2 teaspoons sesame oil
- 2 teaspoons canola oil, divided
- 1 medium sweet onion, cut into chunks
- 1 medium green pepper, cut into chunks
- 3 plum tomatoes, cut into chunks

Direction

- Mix the first five ingredients in a big bowl; throw in beef and mix to coat. Place in refrigerator for 15 minutes. For the sauce, mix soy sauce, broth, sesame oil, cornstarch, and ketchup in a little bowl until smooth. Set it aside. In a big greased nonstick wok or frying pan, place 1 teaspoon canola oil and stir-fry beef mixture until not pink. Remove beef mixture and keep warm. Add the remaining canola oil to pan and stir-fry onion, 2 minutes. Add in the green pepper and stir-fry, 2 minutes. Mix in tomatoes and stir-fry for 1 more minute. Put the beef back in. Mix the sauce and add to veggies and beef. Heat to a boil and cook until thick, 2 minutes.

Nutrition Information

- Calories: 240 calories
- Total Carbohydrate: 12g carbohydrate (6g sugars
- Cholesterol: 63mg cholesterol
- Protein: 24g protein. Diabetic Exchanges: 3 lean meat
- Total Fat: 11g fat (3g saturated fat)
- Sodium: 673mg sodium
- Fiber: 2g fiber)

933. Vegetarian Pad Thai

Serving: Makes 4 to 6 servings | Prep: 1hours | Cook: 1hours | Ready in:

Ingredients

- 12 ounces dried flat rice noodles (1/4 inch wide; sometimes called pad Thai or banh pho)
- 3 tablespoons tamarind (from a pliable block)
- 1 cup boiling-hot water
- 1/2 cup light soy sauce
- 1/4 cup packed light brown sugar
- 2 tablespoons Sriracha (Southeast Asian chile sauce)
- 1 bunch scallions
- 4 large shallots
- 1 (14- to 16-ounce) package firm tofu
- 1 1/2 cups peanut or vegetable oil
- 6 large eggs
- 4 garlic cloves, finely chopped
- 2 cups bean sprouts (1/4 pound)
- 1/2 cup roasted peanuts, coarsely chopped
- Equipment: an adjustable-blade slicer; a well-seasoned 14-inch flat-bottomed wok
- Accompaniments: lime wedges; cilantro sprigs; Sriracha

Direction

- In a big bowl of warm water, let the noodles soak for 25-30 minutes until soft. Drain the water from noodles completely using a colander and cover the drained noodles with a slightly wet paper towel.
- Meanwhile, start making the sauce by putting a boiling hot water in a small bowl and soaking the tamarind pulp in it for about 5 minutes until soft. Stir the tamarind pulp occasionally. Squeeze the soaked tamarind pulp through a sieve and into a bowl then throw away the fibers and seeds. Put in the Sriracha, soy sauce and brown sugar and mix well until the sugar has fully dissolved.
- Chop the scallions into 2-inch slices. Cut the white and pale green parts lengthwise in half.
- Use a slicer to cut the shallots crosswise into very thin slices.
- Wash the tofu and cut it into 1-inch cubes then pat dry completely.
- Heat a wok with oil over medium heat until the oil is hot. Lower the heat to medium-low setting and fry 1/2 of the shallots while stirring often for 8-12 minutes until the shallots are golden brown in color. Use a fine-mesh sieve to carefully drain the fried shallots, put a heatproof bowl below the sieve to catch the shallot oil. Spread the fried shallots on paper towels to drain excess oil and reserve the shallot oil. (Shallots will become crispy as they cool down.) Wipe the wok clean.
- Reheat shallot oil in the same wok over high heat until hot. Fry the cubed tofu in 1 layer for 5-8 minutes until golden brown, carefully turn the tofu occasionally to evenly fry all sides. Use a slotted spoon to put the fried tofu onto the paper towels to drain any excess oil. Remove the frying oil from the pan and reserve.
- Whisk the eggs lightly with 1/4 teaspoon of salt. Heat a wok with 2 tablespoons of shallot oil over high heat until the oil is shimmering.

Put in the beaten eggs and swirl to coat the sides of the wok then use a spatula to carefully stir the eggs until cooked through. Use the spatula to break the eggs into pieces then put it on a plate.
- Heat a wok over high heat until when a drop of water is dripped onto the wok's cooking surface the water evaporates right away. Put in 6 tablespoons of shallot oil into the wok then swirl to coat the sides of the wok. Stir-fry the garlic, remaining uncooked shallots and scallions for about 1 minute until soft.
- Put in the noodles then lower the heat setting to medium heat and stir-fry the mixture (use 2 spatulas to stir the mixture if need be) for 3 minutes. Put in the bean sprouts, 1 1/2 cups of sauce and tofu then let it simmer for about 2 minutes until the noodles are soft. Turn the noodles over while simmering to evenly absorb the sauce.
- Put in more sauce into the noodle mixture if you like then mix in the eggs and put the noodle mixture in a big shallow serving dish.
- Top off the Pad Thai with fried shallots and peanuts then serve with Sriracha, lime wedges and cilantro sprigs.

Nutrition Information

- Calories: 1581
- Fiber: 10 g(39%)
- Total Carbohydrate: 113 g(38%)
- Cholesterol: 279 mg(93%)
- Protein: 43 g(85%)
- Total Fat: 110 g(170%)
- Saturated Fat: 10 g(52%)
- Sodium: 1637 mg(68%)

Chapter 9: Southeast Asian Cuisine Recipes

***

934. Arroz Caldo (Chicken Rice Porridge)

Serving: 6 servings | Prep: | Cook: |Ready in:

Ingredients

- 200 g (7 oz / 1 cup) white glutinous rice
- 100 g (3 1/2 oz / 1/2 cup) jasmine or medium-grain rice
- 1.7 kg (3 lb 12 oz) whole chicken, jointed into 4 pieces, bone in
- 60 ml (2 fl oz / 1/4 cup) vegetable oil
- 9 garlic cloves, 6 thinly sliced, 3 finely chopped
- 1 large onion, finely chopped
- 4 cm (1 1/2-inch) piece ginger, peeled and cut into julienne
- 60 ml (2 fl oz / 1/4 cup) fish sauce
- 2 spring onions (scallions), very thinly sliced
- 6 hard-boiled eggs, peeled and halved
- Sesame oil (optional) and 8 kalamansi or lime wedges, to serve

Direction

- In a bowl, put the sticky rice together with the regular rice and soak covered in cold water. Set the bowl aside. Pour 10 cups/ 2.5 liters of water into a stockpot and place the chicken in it. Boil over medium heat and skim any scum from the surface while lowering the heat to low-medium and simmer until the juices appear clear when pierced at the thigh using a knife. This usually takes 40 minutes. Take the chicken out of the stock and let it rest to cool. Save the stock.

- Place a large saucepan over medium heat and pour in vegetable oil and chopped garlic, stir until the garlic turns golden, 5 minutes. Using a slotted spoon, remove the garlic and place on paper towel to drain. Heat the saucepan again, and stir in the onion until it softens, 5 minutes, then add ginger and the chopped garlic. Stir for 2 minutes, or until aromatic.
- Get the soaked rice and drain. Once drained, add it to the pan along with the onions and stir until thoroughly mixed, 2 minutes. Pour in 8 cups (2 liters/ 68 fl oz) of the stock with fish sauce and let it boil. Bing down the heat to medium and simmer until the mixture has thickened, and the rice is very soft, 20 minutes. Add a little extra stock to achieve a porridge-like texture, season with salt flakes.
- Discard the skin and bones when shredding the chicken. Ladle the rice mixture in serving bowls and take 3/4 of the chicken and divide it between them. Sprinkle on remaining chicken and top with spring onion, fried garlic, hardboiled eggs, kalamansi and sesame oil, if desired.

Nutrition Information

- Calories: 6089
- Total Fat: 87 g(133%)
- Saturated Fat: 19 g(96%)
- Sodium: 1217 mg(51%)
- Fiber: 1 g(5%)
- Total Carbohydrate: 1127 g(376%)
- Cholesterol: 362 mg(121%)
- Protein: 155 g(311%)

935. Beef Stew With Curry And Lemongrass

Serving: Serves 6 | Prep: | Cook: | Ready in:

Ingredients

- 4 cups water
- 2 extra-large beef bouillon cubes (each 1/2 ounce)
- 2 tablespoons olive oil
- 2 1/4 pounds trimmed boneless beef chuck, cut into 1 1/2-inch cubes
- 2 cups coarsely chopped onions
- 3 garlic cloves, minced
- 1 14 1/2-ounce can diced tomatoes in juice
- 1/3 cup finely chopped fresh lemongrass
- 1 tablespoon curry powder
- 2 bay leaves
- 2 large carrots, peeled, cut into 1/2-inch pieces
- 2 small potatoes, peeled, cut into 1/2-inch pieces
- 8 ounces button mushrooms, trimmed
- Chopped fresh parsley

Direction

- In a large saucepan, pour in 4 cups of water and boil. Stir in bouillon until it dissolves; set it aside. In a big pot, heat one tablespoon oil over high heat. Add beef in batches and sauté for 6 minutes per batch, or until brown. Place beef on to bowl using a slotted spoon. To the pot add onions, a tablespoon of oil, and garlic. Sauté onions fort 5 minutes, until tenderize. Add tomatoes with juices, bouillon mixture, curry powder, lemongrass and bay leaves. Add the beef back in along with any juices and boil. Lower the heat to medium-low, put the lid on and stir every now and then while simmering for about an hour.
- Put potatoes, mushrooms and carrots in the stew and simmer for 20 minutes to tenderize vegetables. Remove the lid and simmer for 10 minutes until stew thickens and potatoes are very soft (the potatoes will thicken the liquid). Season with pepper and salt according to preference and ladle into a serving bowl. Finish with sliced parsley on top.

Nutrition Information

- Calories: 370
- Saturated Fat: 4 g(21%)
- Sodium: 608 mg(25%)

- Fiber: 5 g(21%)
- Total Carbohydrate: 24 g(8%)
- Cholesterol: 107 mg(36%)
- Protein: 41 g(83%)
- Total Fat: 13 g(21%)

936. Betel Leaf Wraps With Curried Squid And Cucumber Relish

Serving: Makes 8 servings (as part of a multi-course meal) | Prep: | Cook: | Ready in:

Ingredients

- 2 tablespoons distilled white vinegar
- 2 tablespoons sugar
- 1/2 cup finely diced unpeeled Persian cucumber
- 1/2 cup finely diced celery
- 1 red jalapeño chile, seeded, finely diced
- 1 1-inch piece peeled fresh ginger, cut into matchstick-size strips
- 10 long fresh cilantro stems, chopped
- 2 garlic cloves, halved
- 1 1-inch piece peeled fresh ginger, chopped
- 2 tablespoons vegetable oil
- 1 tablespoon Homemade Curry Powder
- 8 ounces cleaned squid bodies, cut crosswise into 1/4-inch-thick rings
- 1 red jalapeño chile, seeded, cut into matchstick-size strips
- 1 tablespoon fish sauce (such as nam pla or nuoc nam)
- 1 tablespoon oyster sauce
- 1 teaspoon sugar
- 1/2 cup coconut cream
- 2 tablespoons low-salt chicken broth
- 16 betel leaves, small Boston lettuce leaves, or small romaine lettuce leaves

Direction

- For the relish, stir sugar and vinegar together in a little bowl until the sugar has dissolved then set it aside to be used as dressing. In a different small bowl, mix ginger, celery, chile and cucumber together then mix the dressing in by the spoonful, stopping when taste is as desired.
- To make the wraps, mix ginger, garlic and cilantro stems together in the mini processor and grind until it turns into a paste.
- In a big, sturdy skillet over medium-high heat, heat the oil and stir the cilantro paste in for 1 minute. Stir the curry powder in for 30 seconds. Mix chile strips and squid in and stir-fry for 1 minute or until squid is nearly tender. Stir in sugar, oyster sauce, coconut cream, fish sauce and chicken broth for 1 minute until the sauce thickens a little.
- Place the betel leaves on a platter and put the squid mixture on top of each leaf using a slotted spoon. Set the relish over it with a spoon.

Nutrition Information

- Calories: 136
- Sodium: 263 mg(11%)
- Fiber: 1 g(6%)
- Total Carbohydrate: 8 g(3%)
- Cholesterol: 66 mg(22%)
- Protein: 6 g(12%)
- Total Fat: 9 g(14%)
- Saturated Fat: 5 g(25%)

937. Candy Pork

Serving: 6 servings | Prep: | Cook: | Ready in:

Ingredients

- 8 ounces palm sugar, finely chopped (dark brown sugar can be substituted)
- 3/4 cup fish sauce
- 3 tablespoons canola oil

- 4 pounds boneless pork shoulder, cut into 2-inch-by-3-inch chunks
- Kosher salt and freshly ground black pepper
- 1 cup thinly sliced shallots
- 1 (2-inch-by-1-inch) piece fresh ginger, peeled and julienned
- 2 cloves garlic, peeled and crushed
- 2 to 3 Thai chilies (substitute 1 serrano chile), stemmed and crushed
- 3 cups coconut water

Direction

- In a mid-sized saucepan with a sturdy base, cook the palm sugar over medium-low heat until it melts, 8 to 10 minutes. Stir the sugar regularly to make sure it doesn't burn. When sugar is thoroughly melted and smooth, move the pan away from the heat and gently mix the fish sauce in. If the mixture does not mix well, stir it gently on low heat until it becomes smooth again.
- Start reheating the oven to 300 degrees F. Heat the canola oil in a big Dutch oven over high heat. Rub salt and pepper everywhere on the pork pieces to season. Once the oil is heated, sear some of the pork pieces for 8 minutes or until the meat is browned all over. Move pork to a rimmed baking tray then repeat the process with the remaining pork. Once all the pork is cooked, lower the heat to medium. Start cooking the shallots for 2 minutes or until they soften; then add the chilies, garlic and ginger and cook for 1 minute. Place coconut water, caramel sauce, and the pork as well as any accrued juices to the pot. The meat should be seen poking above the liquid level. If the meat is entirely beneath the liquid level, transfer the liquid and meat to another pot. Heat to a boil; then lower the heat and let the liquid simmer. Cover the pot up and transfer it to oven.
- Let it cook for 15 minutes then remove the cover of the pot; the liquid must be gently simmering. If there is intense bubbling, the temperature of the oven needs to be reduced to 275 degrees F. Let it continue cooking for 70 minutes until the meat is tender and juicy but not breaking apart. Remove the cover from the pot and cook for 30 more minutes until the parts of the pork that are exposed become caramelized and meat becomes tender. Move this away from the oven and place together with steamed rice. Serve.

Nutrition Information

- Calories: 982
- Protein: 56 g(111%)
- Total Fat: 62 g(95%)
- Saturated Fat: 20 g(98%)
- Sodium: 3164 mg(132%)
- Fiber: 3 g(11%)
- Total Carbohydrate: 49 g(16%)
- Cholesterol: 215 mg(72%)

938. Chicken Curry

Serving: 6 | Prep: 40mins | Cook: | Ready in:

Ingredients

- 2½ to 3 pounds meaty chicken pieces (breast halves, thighs, and/or drumsticks)
- 2 tablespoons cooking oil
- 1 medium onion, finely chopped
- 4 cloves garlic, minced
- 2 teaspoons finely chopped fresh ginger
- 1 teaspoon ground cumin
- 1 medium tomato, finely chopped
- 1 tablespoon ground coriander
- 1 teaspoon coarsely ground black pepper
- ½ teaspoon salt
- ½ teaspoon fennel seeds, coarsely ground or crushed
- ½ teaspoon ground turmeric
- ¼ to ½ teaspoon cayenne pepper (optional)
- ½ cup plain fat-free yogurt
- ½ cup water
- 2 tablespoons snipped fresh cilantro
- 1 tablespoon lemon juice

- 3 cups hot cooked brown or white basmati rice or 6 pieces flatbread
- Fresh cilantro sprigs (optional)
- Lemon wedges (optional)
- 2 cups red onion slivers, carrot sticks, sliced radishes, and/or quartered cherry tomatoes (optional)

Direction

- Remove the fat and the skin from the chicken and cut 2 or 3 slits per piece, with each slit measuring 1 inch long and half an inch deep.
- Heat oil on medium-high heat in a big skillet and cook chicken pieces until lightly browned, turning it from time to time to brown each side evenly, 5 to 8 minutes. Transfer the chicken from the skillet using a tongs, or a slotted spoon, seal with foil to keep warm and let it rest.
- In the same skillet, lower the heat to medium and add onion, ginger, garlic, and cumin. Stir regularly until onion is golden brown, 6 to 8 minutes.
- Stir in tomato, fennel seeds, black pepper, cayenne pepper if desired, salt, coriander, turmeric and cook for two minutes, occasionally stirring.
- Beat yogurt gently with a fork or whisk in a small bowl. One tablespoon at a time, add yogurt to tomato mixture, stirring thoroughly in between tablespoons. Stir occasionally while cooking for 2 minutes.
- Add and boil chicken pieces and the water in skillet. Reduce heat and add two tablespoons of cilantro. Ladle liquid over chicken. Seal top and simmer until chicken is white and tender, 20 to 25 minutes at 180°F for drumsticks and thighs and 170°F for breast.
- Place chicken on serving plate and ladle sauce over it. Drizzle with lemon juice. A cilantro garnish with an extra lemon squeeze on the chicken is optional. Serve with flatbread or rice and with desired vegetables.

Nutrition Information

- Calories: 312 calories;
- Sodium: 286
- Fiber: 3
- Total Carbohydrate: 28
- Cholesterol: 79
- Protein: 30
- Total Fat: 8
- Saturated Fat: 2

939. Chile Lime Sauce

Serving: Makes about 1/2 cup (120 ml) | Prep: | Cook: | Ready in:

Ingredients

- 1/4 cup (60 ml) fresh lime juice
- 2 tablespoons fish sauce
- 1 large garlic clove, minced
- 1/4 red or green jalapeño, unseeded and thinly sliced crosswise, or more to taste
- 1 packed tablespoon light brown sugar

Direction

- Mix together garlic, jalapenos, fish sauce, lime juice, and brown sugar in a small bowl. You can also do this in either a large jar with lid or in a 180mL/12-ounce jar, cover and shake to mix the ingredients. Taste the sauce by dipping in a piece of lettuce. You can place more jalapenos if you wish for a little more kick. Check for a balance of flavors of sweetness, saltiness, sourness, and a kick of heat. This melding of flavors shows the typical Thai cuisines we've come to know. You can store this sauce in the fridge for future use, just place it in a covered container, up to 2 weeks.

Nutrition Information

- Calories: 88
- Total Fat: 0 g(0%)
- Saturated Fat: 0 g(0%)
- Sodium: 2832 mg(118%)

- Fiber: 0 g(2%)
- Total Carbohydrate: 22 g(7%)
- Protein: 2 g(5%)

940. Chili Crab

Serving: Makes 4 servings | Prep: | Cook: | Ready in:

Ingredients

- 8 soft-shelled crabs, cleaned, or 2 whole Dungeness crabs
- 2 tablespoons vegetable oil
- 1 (3-inch) knob ginger, minced (about 3 tablespoons)
- 5 cloves garlic, minced (about 2 tablespoons)
- 3 to 4 fresh red bird's-eye chiles, seeded and minced
- 1 tablespoon Chinese fermented black beans or black bean sauce
- 1 tablespoon shaohsing rice wine or sherry
- 1/2 cup plain tomato sauce, purchased or homemade
- 1/4 cup mild chili sauce, such as Heinz
- 1 tablespoon sugar
- 2 teaspoons kosher salt
- 1/4 teaspoon ground white pepper
- 2 teaspoons cornstarch
- 2 large eggs, lightly beaten
- 2 tablespoons fresh cilantro, chopped
- 1 scallion, thinly sliced on bias
- Accompaniments: steamed Chinese buns or baguette slices

Direction

- Cut Dungeness crabs lengthwise in half and remove back shell and spongy green matter using a large chef's knife or a cleaver. Using the back of cleaver of chef's knife, crack the crab claws in different areas and to remove from body section. Slice body section into 2 or 3 pieces with the legs attached. Rinse and then pat to dry completely.
- Heat oil in a large skillet or a wok until it is hot but not yet smoking; add garlic, ginger and chiles. Stir-fry for 30 seconds, to make it aromatic. Stir in black beans and stir-fry for a few seconds; add the crab. Stir-fry or 1 minute until it turns opaque. Add rice wine, chili and tomato sauces, salt, pepper, sugar and a cup of water; stir. Boil and lower the heat to low; keep lid off. Simmer for 3 to 4 minutes until crab meat is cooked through.
- Whisk 2 tablespoons water and cornstarch together in a bowl. Pour into pan with crab mixture and stir. Simmer with lid off for 1 minute, or until the sauce is thick. Add eggs and simmer with the lid off for another minute until small pieces of egg are cooked fully; mix in scallion and cilantro. Serve. Best when paired with baguette slices or Chinese buns.

Nutrition Information

- Calories: 460
- Saturated Fat: 2 g(9%)
- Sodium: 1422 mg(59%)
- Fiber: 2 g(10%)
- Total Carbohydrate: 20 g(7%)
- Cholesterol: 285 mg(95%)
- Protein: 62 g(124%)
- Total Fat: 13 g(20%)

941. Coconut Chicken Soup

Serving: 4 | Prep: 15mins | Cook: 15mins | Ready in:

Ingredients

- 1 cup coconut milk
- 2 lemon grass, chopped
- 4 slices (1/2-inch) piece peeled fresh ginger
- 5 kaffir lime leaves, torn in half
- 3/4 pound skinless, boneless chicken breasts, cut into strips
- 5 tablespoons fish sauce
- 2 tablespoons white sugar

- 1 cup coconut milk
- 1/2 cup lime juice
- 1 teaspoon red curry paste
- 1/4 cup coarsely chopped cilantro
- 15 green Thai chiles, crushed

Direction

- In a big skillet over medium-high heat, bring the combination of kaffir lime leaves, ginger, lemon grass and 1 cup of coconut milk to a boil. Mix the fish sauce, chicken and sugar in; then reduce the heat to medium. Cook until the centre of the chicken is not pink anymore, about 5 minutes. Mix the remaining cup of coconut milk in and let it simmer, about 3 minutes.
- In 4 different bowls, distribute the curry paste and lime juice equally; then pour the soup in, topping each bowl with Thai chiles and cilantro.

Nutrition Information

- Calories: 436 calories;
- Total Fat: 25.6
- Sodium: 1477
- Total Carbohydrate: 32
- Cholesterol: 49
- Protein: 26.7

942. Coconut Tart

Serving: Makes 8 servings | Prep: 25mins | Cook: 4.5hours | Ready in:

Ingredients

- Pastry dough
- 2/3 cup whole milk
- 2 large whole eggs
- 1 large egg yolk
- 1 cup confectioners sugar
- 1/4 teaspoon salt
- 1 3/4 cups sweetened flaked coconut (5 ounces)
- Equipment: a pastry or bench scraper; pie weights or dried beans; a 9 1/2-inch fluted tart pan (1 inch deep) with removable bottom

Direction

- Dust a clean work surface with flour. Sprinkle a little flour on rolling pin and roll dough into a 13-inch round. Snug tightly into tart pan and trim excess dough. Refrigerate for 30 minutes to make it firm.
- Set the oven to 375°F and place rack in the center.
- Using a fork, gently prick all around bottom of shell and line with foil. Put pie weights over it and bake for 20 to 30 minutes, until edges appear light golden in color. Take off weights gently along with foil and bake for an additional 10 to 18 minutes until shell appears completely golden.
- In a large bowl, whisk together eggs, yolk, milk, salt and confectioner's sugar until smooth then add shredded coconut and stir.
- Transfer filling to hot tart shell, using a fork to even it out and bake for 35 minutes until top becomes golden. Place the pan on a rack for 5 minutes to cool it down and take off pan sides to cool tart for 2 hours at room temperature.
- Cooks' notes:• Tart shell may also be baked 24 hours earlier and set aside, as long as it is sealed in a plastic wrap at room temperature.
- Chilled tart from the refrigerator can be reheated with the lid off in a 350°F oven for 10 to 15 minutes, until pastry crisps. It can be baked a day early but it certainly tastes the best the day it is baked.

943. Coconut Marinated Short Rib Kebabs With Peanut Chile Oil

Serving: Serves 4 | Prep: | Cook: | Ready in:

Ingredients

- 1 lemongrass stalk
- 1 large shallot, chopped
- 2 garlic cloves, chopped
- 1 (1-inch) piece ginger, peeled, chopped
- 1/2 cup vegetable oil
- 1/2 teaspoon kosher salt
- 4 guajillo or New Mexico chiles or 2 ancho chiles, seeds removed, flesh torn
- 1 teaspoon crushed red pepper flakes
- 1/4 cup crushed salted, roasted peanuts
- 2 teaspoons fish sauce
- 1 1/4 pounds boneless beef short ribs
- 1 lemongrass stalk
- 2 garlic cloves, finely grated
- 1 (2-inch) piece ginger, peeled, finely grated
- 3/4 cup unsweetened coconut milk
- 2 tablespoons fish sauce
- 2 tablespoons light brown sugar
- 1 tablespoon fresh lime juice
- 1 teaspoon ground turmeric
- Vegetable oil (for grill)
- Kosher salt
- 8 (8–12-inch-long) metal skewers

Direction

- To make the peanut chili oil, get rid of the outer tough layers of the lemongrass and cut off top third of stalk; throw out. Beat the remaining stalk on the cutting board to bruise. Heat a small saucepan and add lemongrass, oil, shallot, garlic, ginger and salt and simmer on medium heat. Keep on a low boil for 15-20 minutes to soften the shallot and glaze it golden around the sides. Take it off the heat and add red pepper flakes and chili, mash with spoon until chili is tender. Blend in a processor just enough to break the chili down into small bits but do not over process. Stir into a small bowl together with fish sauce and peanuts.
- Freeze ribs for 20 to 30 minutes, just until they firm up along the sides to make them easier to cut.
- Peel off the outer tough layers of the lemongrass and grate bottom third of stalk finely; throw out remainder of keep in freezer for a different use. Using a large sealable plastic container, mix the lemongrass with garlic, coconut milk, ginger, brown sugar, fish sauce, turmeric and lime juice. Cut short ribs against the grain, lengthwise in 1/4 inch thick strips before putting them inside the bag. Remove any excess air from the bag before sealing it tight. Refrigerate as preferred, from 2 to 48 hours.
- Set the grill on medium-high heat and grease grates. Drain off excess marinade form chilled beef and impale on 6-8 skewers by folding it in an accordion style. Lightly season with some salt. Grill for 5 minutes until heated through and brown, turning once. Remove from grill and serve with peanut-chili oil.
- You can make the Peanut- chili oil a week early. Seal it tight and refrigerate. Best served at room temperature.

Nutrition Information

- Calories: 868
- Sodium: 1069 mg(45%)
- Fiber: 6 g(22%)
- Total Carbohydrate: 26 g(9%)
- Cholesterol: 103 mg(34%)
- Protein: 31 g(63%)
- Total Fat: 74 g(114%)
- Saturated Fat: 22 g(112%)

944. Crispy Fried Shallots

Serving: Makes 1 cup fried shallots | Prep: | Cook: | Ready in:

Ingredients

- 2 cups thinly sliced shallots (about 4 large shallots)
- 2 cups canola oil

Direction

- 1. Cook shallots on medium-high heat to 275°F in a small saucepan for eight minutes until they turn light golden brown. Remove shallots using slotted spoon and transfer to a plate lined with a paper towel to drain.
- 2. Place a fine-mesh strainer on top of a heatproof bowl; adjust heat to high for the saucepan. Add the fried shallots once the oil is at 350°F and cook for 1 to 2 seconds, just enough to make them brown and crispy. Make sure the shallots don't burn.
- 3. To quickly stop cooking, pour the shallots and the oil through the strainer and place the shallots on a plate lined with a paper towel to drain. The leftover oil can be kept to use for another dish. Keep the shallots for 24 hours in an airtight container and seal it tight. Although it is better to consume them on the day they were prepared.

Nutrition Information

- Calories: 164
- Sodium: 10 mg(0%)
- Fiber: 3 g(10%)
- Total Carbohydrate: 13 g(4%)
- Protein: 2 g(4%)
- Total Fat: 12 g(19%)
- Saturated Fat: 1 g(4%)

945. Cucumber Ajat

Serving: Makes 2 cups | Prep: | Cook: |Ready in:

Ingredients

- 4 ounces (112 grams) medium pickling cucumbers, quartered lengthwise, sliced 1/4-inch thick
- 1/4 cup (40 grams) thinly sliced shallots
- 2 fresh Thai chiles, thinly sliced (3 grams)
- 1/4 cup (56 grams) distilled white vinegar
- 1/4 cup (50 grams) granulated sugar
- 1 teaspoon (4 grams) kosher salt

Direction

- In a serving bowl, mix shallots, chiles and cucumbers. Whisk vinegar together with salt and sugar in another bowl until completely sugar dissolves completely. Pour the vinegar mixture into the bowl containing the cucumbers. Cover with lid and set aside for 15 minutes to pickle it before serving.

Nutrition Information

- Calories: 125
- Fiber: 1 g(4%)
- Total Carbohydrate: 31 g(10%)
- Protein: 1 g(2%)
- Total Fat: 0 g(0%)
- Saturated Fat: 0 g(0%)
- Sodium: 305 mg(13%)

946. Curried Shrimp

Serving: makes 4 servings | Prep: | Cook: |Ready in:

Ingredients

- 1 large baking potato, peeled and chopped into ½-inch pieces
- 1 tbsp canola oil
- 2 tbsp curry powder
- 1/2 cup thinly sliced onion
- 1 1/2 lb large shrimp, shelled and deveined
- 1 green bell pepper, cored, seeded and cut into thin strips
- 1 mango, cut into thin strips
- 1 cup light coconut milk
- 2 tbsp fish sauce
- 1/2 tsp sriracha
- 1 tsp sugar
- 1/3 cup chopped fresh basil

Direction

- Put 1 tbsp. of water on potato pieces; microwave potato pieces, covered up, until they are fork-tender, about 3 minutes. In a big skillet, heat curry powder and oil together over medium heat. Cook the onion for 3 to 4 minutes until it softens; then push it to one side of the skillet. Mix the shrimp in and cook for 2 minutes on each side. Add and cook potatoes and bell pepper until the pepper becomes soft, about 1-2 minutes. Combine sriracha sauce, mango, sugar, fish sauce and coconut milk in and let it simmer for 2 minutes. Move it away from the heat and top off with basil.

Nutrition Information

- Calories: 349
- Protein: 27 g(54%)
- Total Fat: 10 g(16%)
- Saturated Fat: 4 g(19%)
- Sodium: 1690 mg(70%)
- Fiber: 5 g(20%)
- Total Carbohydrate: 38 g(13%)
- Cholesterol: 214 mg(71%)

947. Filipino Style Beef Steak With Onion And Bay Leaves (Bistek)

Serving: 8 servings | Prep: | Cook: |Ready in:

Ingredients

- 2 (1-inch-thick) boneless rib-eye steaks, excess fat trimmed
- 2 tablespoons vegetable oil, divided
- 8 fresh bay leaves
- 1 large white onion, sliced into 1/2" thick rounds
- 1/4 cup fresh lemon juice
- 1/4 cup soy sauce
- Kosher salt

Direction

- Portion steaks into 2 lengthwise pieces and cut each half into 2-3 pieces following natural seams in meat. Set on the side.
- In a large skillet, warm a tablespoon of oil on medium heat. Cook bay leaves for 1 minute, just enough to start browning the edges. Pour in half a cup of water along with onion. Put lid on skillet and cook for 5 minutes until onion is slightly tender (you don't need to cover if using a cookie sheet). Using tongs or a spatula, remove bay leaves and onion and place on a plate.
- Adjust heat to medium-high to boil liquid. When only 2 tablespoons of liquid are left, remove from heat and pour into a small bowl. Add in soy sauce and lemon juice. Set on the side.
- Clean the skillet. Set temperature to medium-high and heat the remaining 1 tablespoon of oil in pan. Add salt to the rested meat. Cook meat in batches, for 2 minutes each batch or until dark brown. Flip and cook opposite side for 45 seconds, enough to brown it slightly. Remove and place on a platter.
- Lower the temperature to medium and let the skillet cool a bit. Cook the sauce for 1 minute, enough to blend the flavors together and if the sauce is too thick, add 1 to 2 tablespoons of water. Drizzle on meat and sprinkle onion and bay leaves on top.

Nutrition Information

- Calories: 268
- Saturated Fat: 8 g(40%)
- Sodium: 482 mg(20%)
- Fiber: 1 g(2%)
- Total Carbohydrate: 3 g(1%)
- Cholesterol: 60 mg(20%)
- Protein: 17 g(34%)
- Total Fat: 21 g(32%)

948. Filipino Style Roast Pork Belly With Chile Vinegar

Serving: 8-12 servings | Prep: | Cook: | Ready in:

Ingredients

- 1 (4-5-pound) skin-on, boneless pork belly
- Kosher salt
- 1 tablespoon vegetable oil
- 1 (12-ounce) bottle unseasoned rice vinegar
- 12 garlic cloves, chopped
- 6-12 green Thai chiles, lightly crushed but left whole
- 2 serrano chiles, torn into small pieces
- 4 (12-oz.) bottles hard apple cider
- 2 tablespoons honey

Direction

- Rub salt all over the pork generously. Set it on a wire rack placed inside a rimmed baking tray with the skin side facing up. Let it chill for a minimum of 12 hours up to a maximum of 2 days.
- Preheat the oven to 350 degrees F. Disperse 4 cups of water on baking tray with pork then rub oil and additional salt onto the pork skin. Begin roasting it for 1-1/2 to 1-3/4 hours, pouring more water into the pan when necessary. It is ready when the skin turns a nice golden brown or when an instant read thermometer reads 195 degrees F-200 degrees F when poked in the thickest portion of the pork.
- In the meantime, pour 1/2 cup of vinegar out of bottle to be saved for another use. Take the spout for pouring off bottle and mix chiles, garlic and a large pinch of salt into the bottle then cover it up and shake it well to distribute. Leave it to sit until serving time. Alternately, this can be done in a bowl or glass jar.
- In a big saucepan, bring honey and hard cider to a boil and cook until texture turns extremely syrupy and thick, about 30-45 minutes.
- Increase the temperature on the oven to 450°F. Leave the pork roasting until its skin is puffed and browned, about 15-20 minutes. Splash a little bit of water over baking sheet if juices begin to scorch. Move the rack together with pork onto a cutting board and let it sit for 20 minutes.
- Drain the fats off from the baking sheet, pour 1/2 cup of water in and scrape the browned parts up. If help is needed in loosening the browned parts up, place the baking sheet back in the oven for several minutes. Mix this into the reduced cider mixture.
- Use the tip of the knife to remove the pork skin, which with a little help should come off in one whole piece. Cut the lengthwise pork into pieces 2" wide and then 1/2"- thick crosswise. Move the cut up pieces onto a platter and sprinkle with the reduced cider mixture. Take the skin and break it up into big pieces and place on top of the dish. Decorate with a few chiles from the vinegar and serve with chile vinegar.
- The chile vinegar can be prepared one week in advance as long as it is stored at room temperature.

Nutrition Information

- Calories: 396
- Fiber: 1 g(3%)
- Total Carbohydrate: 13 g(4%)
- Cholesterol: 110 mg(37%)
- Protein: 38 g(76%)
- Total Fat: 16 g(24%)
- Saturated Fat: 3 g(14%)
- Sodium: 989 mg(41%)

949. Garlic Chile Ground Pork

Serving: 4 servings | Prep: | Cook: | Ready in:

Ingredients

- 1 tablespoon vegetable oil
- 1 shallot, chopped
- 4 garlic cloves, finely chopped
- 1 dried chile (such as chile de árbol)
- 1 pound ground pork
- 1 tablespoon fish sauce
- 1 tablespoon soy sauce
- Pinch of sugar
- 1 cup low-sodium chicken broth
- 2 teaspoons unseasoned rice vinegar
- Kosher salt

Direction

- In a mid-sized skillet, heat the oil over medium high. Cook the chile, garlic and shallot until the shallot turns translucent and soft for about 4 minutes, stirring regularly. Mix the pork in and stir every now and then until the meat is thoroughly cooked, 3 minutes. Pour in the soy sauce, fish sauce and sugar and cook for about 5 minutes or until all moisture in the skillet evaporates, stirring sporadically. Pour the broth in and lower the heat. Leave it uncovered and let it simmer for 12-18 minutes until the liquid evaporates, stirring every so often.
- Move the skillet away from the heat then pour vinegar into the pork mixture, taste then season it with salt if desired.

Nutrition Information

- Calories: 359
- Total Fat: 28 g(43%)
- Saturated Fat: 9 g(46%)
- Sodium: 657 mg(27%)
- Fiber: 1 g(2%)
- Total Carbohydrate: 5 g(2%)
- Cholesterol: 82 mg(27%)
- Protein: 21 g(43%)

950. Ginger Salad

Serving: 6 | Prep: 20mins | Cook: | Ready in:

Ingredients

- 2 tablespoons fried shallot oil (see Tips) or canola oil
- ¼ cup thinly sliced pickled ginger plus 1 tablespoon pickling liquid
- 2 tablespoons lime juice
- 1 tablespoon fish sauce (see Tips)
- 6 cups sliced romaine or Little Gem lettuce
- 2 cups shredded green cabbage
- ¼ jalapeño pepper, seeded and minced
- 3 tablespoons fried garlic (see Tips)
- 2 tablespoons chopped roasted peanuts
- 2 tablespoons toasted sunflower seeds
- 1 tablespoon toasted sesame seeds
- ½ cup fresh cilantro
- 1½ tablespoons toasted chickpea flour (see Tips)
- ¼ teaspoon crushed red pepper

Direction

- In a big bowl, combine the fish sauce, lime juice, pickling liquid and oil together then mix. Put in the lettuce, peanuts, cabbage, pickled ginger, sesame seeds, jalapeño, garlic and sunflower seeds then mix well until blended. Place it in a bowl or on a serving platter and garnish with crushed red pepper, cilantro and chickpea flour on top.

Nutrition Information

- Calories: 127 calories;
- Protein: 3
- Fiber: 3
- Cholesterol: 0
- Saturated Fat: 1
- Sodium: 276
- Total Carbohydrate: 10
- Sugar: 3
- Total Fat: 8

951. Ginger And Honey Baby Back Ribs

Serving: Makes 6 servings | Prep: | Cook: | Ready in:

Ingredients

- 2 2 1/4-to 2 1/2-pound baby back pork rib racks, cut into 6-to 7-rib sections
- 1/4 cup chopped peeled fresh ginger
- 6 garlic cloves, chopped
- 1 tablespoon sugar
- 1 tablespoon coarse kosher salt
- 1 tablespoon freshly ground black pepper
- 2 tablespoons honey
- 2 tablespoons soy sauce
- 2 tablespoons fish sauce (such as nam pla or nuoc nam)*
- 6 teaspoons coarse kosher salt, divided
- 6 teaspoons ground white pepper, divided
- 3 large limes, halved
- Nonstick vegetable oil spray

Direction

- On a clean working surface, position the rib racks and cautiously pry paper membrane off each rib section using a sharp knife (meat can be slippery). Once done, put ribs on a baking sheet with a large rim.
- In a processor, add 1 tablespoon coarse salt, sugar, black pepper, garlic and ginger and blend thoroughly. Pour in soy sauce, fish sauce, and honey and blend again. Rub marinade on each side of the rib, you will need about 2 tablespoons of marinade per side. Seal with plastic wrap and put inside refrigerator for 4 hours. Can be done 1 day before, occasionally rub the marinade on each side with the marinade that settles on baking sheet. Let it chill.
- Prepare 6 small bowls and position on 6 small plates. Put 1 teaspoon ground white pepper beside 1 teaspoon salt in neat mounds in each bowl together with half a lime on the plate next to each bowls. This will serve as the dipping sauce.
- Use a nonstick spray to grease the grill rack and set to medium heat. Lather the juices from the baking sheet on to the ribs just before starting to grill. Position rib racks on the rack with the meat side on the bottom. Grill 8 minutes each side without covering until ribs are heated through, cover the grill and another 8 minutes.
- Remove ribs from grill and place on cutting board. Slice in between bones to separate ribs individually. Place on a platter. To prepare the dipping sauce, squeeze lime juice into the bowl with white pepper and coarse salt, stir to mix. Dip ribs into sauce.
- The ingredients we used are commonly found throughout most Asian supermarkets, or in the Asian foods section of most supermarkets. You can request the butcher to take off the membrane on the underside of ribs, as it is often quite hard to do.

Nutrition Information

- Calories: 917
- Total Carbohydrate: 17 g(6%)
- Cholesterol: 246 mg(82%)
- Protein: 70 g(140%)
- Total Fat: 64 g(99%)
- Saturated Fat: 21 g(105%)
- Sodium: 1077 mg(45%)
- Fiber: 2 g(9%)

952. Green Papaya Salad With Shrimp

Serving: Serves 4 | Prep: | Cook: | Ready in:

Ingredients

- 1/4 pound small shrimp (about 9), shelled
- 1 large garlic clove, forced through a garlic press

- 3 tablespoons fresh lime juice
- 1 1/2 tablespoons Asian fish sauce (preferably nuoc mam)
- 1 tablespoon sugar
- 1 small thin fresh red or green Asian chili (1 to 2 inches long) or serrano chili, or to taste, seeded and chopped fine (wear rubber gloves)
- 3/4 pound green papaya, peeled, seeded, and coarsely shredded, preferably in a food processor (about 3 cups)
- 1 carrot, shredded fine
- 1/3 cup fresh coriander leaves, washed well and spun dry
- 2 tablespoons roasted peanuts, crushed

Direction

- Cook shrimps in a small pan with boiling salted water from 45 seconds to about 1 minute. Once shrimp is completely cooked, drain shrimp in a strainer and rinse with cold water to stop cooking. Slice shrimp horizontally and remove vein.
- Mix dressing ingredients together in a bowl until the sugar dissolves.
- Toss in shrimp, carrot, papaya, and coriander with the dressing. Salad may be prepared 2 hours early and refrigerated with a sealed top, but it is best served at room temperature.
- Sprinkle peanuts over the salad before serving.

Nutrition Information

- Calories: 108
- Protein: 6 g(12%)
- Total Fat: 3 g(4%)
- Saturated Fat: 0 g(2%)
- Sodium: 710 mg(30%)
- Fiber: 2 g(10%)
- Total Carbohydrate: 16 g(5%)
- Cholesterol: 36 mg(12%)

953. Grilled Pork Chops With Sweet Lemongrass Marinade

Serving: Serves 6 as a main course | Prep: | Cook: |Ready in:

Ingredients

- 3/4 cup sugar
- 1/4 cup plus 1 tablespoon fish sauce
- 1 lemongrass stalk, finely chopped
- 1 1/2 tablespoons minced garlic
- 2 tablespoons minced shallot
- 1 Thai chile, stemmed and finely chopped
- 1/4 teaspoon freshly ground black pepper
- 3 bone-in center cut pork chops, each about 12 ounces and 1 inch thick

Direction

- Whisk the chile, shallot, black pepper, fish sauce, garlic, lemongrass and sugar together in a bowl until the sugar has dissolved. In a rimmed dish, place the pork chops in one layer then dump the marinade over it. Cover the dish up with plastic wrap then leave it for 1 to 2 hours to marinate at room temperature. It can also be kept in the fridge overnight, just let the meat warm to room temperature before starting to grill.
- In a charcoal grill, prep a hot fire that a hand can only withstand from 1 to 2 inches above for about 2 to 3 seconds before having to move it away. Create a hot zone by putting two-thirds of the coals on half of the grill once the coals are ready. On the opposite side of the grill, create a less heated zone by spreading the remaining one-third of the coals there.
- Extract the pork chops from the marinade and throw the marinade away. On the warmest part of the grill, put the chops and let them cook for 1 minute before flipping to cook the other side for 1 minute as well.
- Transfer the pork chops to cook it on the less heated side of the grill for a total of 10 minutes, flipping it over once in between. It is ready when the thickest part of the chop

registers as 140 degrees F on an inserted instant-read thermometer. If needed, move the coals over from the hotter side of the grill in order to keep it at an even temperature. Have a spray bottle of water ready nearby to spritz out any flare-ups.
- On a big plate, place the pork chops cover loosely with aluminium foil and let sit for 10 minutes. Remove the meat from the bone and slice the meat diagonally across the grain. Serve the slices and bones on a separate serving platter.

Nutrition Information

- Calories: 241
- Sodium: 1221 mg(51%)
- Fiber: 0 g(1%)
- Total Carbohydrate: 28 g(9%)
- Cholesterol: 51 mg(17%)
- Protein: 17 g(33%)
- Total Fat: 7 g(10%)
- Saturated Fat: 2 g(11%)

954. Home Style Chicken Kebat

Serving: 3-4 servings or 6 servings as part of a larger meal | Prep: | Cook: | Ready in:

Ingredients

- 1 1/2 pounds boneless, skinless chicken thighs (5 to 6 thighs)
- 1 1/2 teaspoons Madras curry powder
- 1 teaspoon fish sauce
- 1/2 teaspoon salt
- 1 small-to-medium yellow onion
- 2 tablespoons canola oil
- 2 tablespoons minced garlic
- 2 tablespoons water
- 2 Roma tomatoes, each cut into 6 to 8 wedges
- Handful of cilantro sprigs, coarsely chopped, for garnish
- 1 lime or lemon, cut into wedges, for garnish

Direction

- Cut the chicken up into 1/2 inch strips. Place chicken strips in a bowl and layer the chicken with a combination of salt, fish sauce and curry powder mix with your hands. At room temperature, let the chicken sit and marinate while you prep the other things or keep it in the fridge overnight.
- Core, peel and halve the onion. Dice half the onion into fine little bits and chop up the other half into thin slices. Set the slices aside for later.
- Heat the oil in a wok or big skillet over moderately high heat. Mix in the diced onions and let them cook for 3 to 4 minutes or until they soften; then mix the garlic in and stir for 1 minute.
- Place the chicken in over medium heat and leave it cooking for about 5 minutes. Pour the water in and continue cooking until the water has evaporated and the chicken is thoroughly cooked, 5 minutes. Stir the tomatoes and sliced onions in and cook for another minute. When done, the onions should not be entirely wilted and the centre should still be crisp. Garnish with lime wedges on the side and cilantro on top. Serve.

Nutrition Information

- Calories: 547
- Saturated Fat: 5 g(23%)
- Sodium: 886 mg(37%)
- Fiber: 2 g(7%)
- Total Carbohydrate: 8 g(3%)
- Cholesterol: 333 mg(111%)
- Protein: 71 g(142%)
- Total Fat: 24 g(37%)

955. Indonesian Fried Noodles

Serving: Makes 4 to 6 servings | Prep: 1.25hours | Cook: 1.25hours | Ready in:

Ingredients

- 3 large shallots (6 ounces)
- 1/2 cup peanut or vegetable oil
- 1 pound fresh flat Chinese stir-fry egg noodles (not cooked)
- 1/2 cup reduced-sodium chicken broth or water
- 3 tablespoons ketjap manis (Indonesian sweet soy sauce)
- 1 1/2 tablespoons Asian fish sauce
- 1 tablespoon sambal oelek or Sriracha (Southeast Asian chile sauce), or to taste
- 1/2 teaspoon black pepper
- 3/4 teaspoon salt
- 1 (14- to 16-ounce) package firm tofu
- 4 large eggs
- 2 large onions, halved lengthwise, then cut crosswise into 1/2-inch slices (4 cups)
- 2 teaspoons finely chopped garlic
- 1/4 teaspoon minced fresh red or green Thai or serrano chile, including seeds
- 6 ounce snow peas, cut diagonally into 1-inch pieces (2 cups)
- 6 ounce Chinese long beans or haricots verts, cut crosswise into 2-inch pieces (1 1/2 cups)
- 2 scallions, cut diagonally into very thin slices
- Garnish: sliced cucumber; sliced tomatoes; lime wedges; sambal oelek or Sriracha (Southeast Asian chile sauce)
- an adjustable-blade slicer; a well-seasoned 14-inch flat-bottomed wok

Direction

- Cut crosswise the shallots into slim slices (less than 1/8 inch in thickness) with a slicer.
- In a wok, heat the oil up over medium temperature until it is hot but not smoking. Lower the heat to medium low then add shallots. Fry 8-12 minutes until they turn golden brown, stirring regularly. Over a heatproof bowl, pour shallot mixture carefully through a fine-mesh strainer. Move the shallots onto a paper towel to drain them off, keeping the shallot oil. The shallots will turn crispy once they have cooled off. Use new paper towels to clean the wok.
- In a 6- to 8-quart pot of unsalted boiling water, cook the noodles for 15 seconds to 1 minute or until they turn tender. Stir occasionally to separate the noodles. Using a colander, drain the water off and place noodles under cold water to stop the cooking. Remove excess water by shaking the colander gently; then coat the noodles with 2 teaspoons of reserved shallot oil.
- In a small sauce bowl, mix 1/2 teaspoon of salt, pepper, fish sauce, broth, ketjap manis and sambal oelek together.
- Pat the tofu dry and cut it into 1-inch cubes.
- Whisk a pinch of salt and eggs together. In a wok, heat 1 tablespoon of reserved shallot oil over medium high heat until it's hot but not yet smoking. Swirl eggs around in the wok and cook until they are scarcely set in the middle, 2 minutes. Slip the egg crepe slowly onto the cutting board and roll it up into a loose tube. Cut crosswise the egg cylinder into 1/2 inch strips without unrolling it. Keep it warm by loosely covering it up with foil.
- In a wok over high heat, pour 3 tablespoons of reserved shallot oil. Once it's hot but not yet smoking, add the remaining 1/4-teaspoon of salt and onions and stir-fry until onions turn a dark golden colour, about 8 to 10 minutes. Stir-fry the garlic and chile for 1 minute, then stir-fry the tofu for 3 minutes. Mix long beans and snow peas in and continue stir-frying until the vegetables are crispy and tender, 5 minutes. Pour the sauce in and let it boil; add the noodles and continue to stir-fry until the noodles are hot (if needed, use 2 spatulas). Put on a big platter and place the eggs over the top of the noodles. Garnish with half of shallots and scallions. Have the remaining shallots on the side and serve.

- The shallots can be fried one day in advance. Let them cool down then store at room temperature inside an airtight container.
- The uncooked, fresh lo mein noodles can be a substitute for the stir-fry noodles. Follow the package instructions or boil until they become tender, about 2-3 minutes before proceeding with the recipe.

Nutrition Information

- Calories: 1013
- Sodium: 1475 mg(61%)
- Fiber: 11 g(45%)
- Total Carbohydrate: 107 g(36%)
- Cholesterol: 281 mg(94%)
- Protein: 45 g(90%)
- Total Fat: 47 g(73%)
- Saturated Fat: 6 g(31%)

956. Indonesian Fried Rice

Serving: 4 | Prep: 25mins | Cook: 15mins | Ready in:

Ingredients

- 1/2 cup uncooked long grain white rice
- 1 cup water
- 2 teaspoons sesame oil
- 1 small onion, chopped
- 2 cloves garlic, minced
- 1 green chile pepper, chopped
- 1 small carrot, sliced
- 1 stalk celery, sliced
- 2 tablespoons kecap manis
- 2 tablespoons tomato sauce
- 2 tablespoons soy sauce
- 1/4 cucumber, sliced
- 4 eggs

Direction

- Boil the rice and water in a pot. Put the lid on, adjust the heat to low and simmer for 20 minutes.
- Cook the garlic, green chili and onion in a heated wok with oil. Once tender, add celery and carrot. Slowly mix in the rice together with kecap manis, soy sauce and tomato sauce. Cook until evenly heated for about a minute or so and ladle into bowls with sliced cucumber as garnish.
- Cook eggs in the wok until set and place on top of the rice and vegetables.

Nutrition Information

- Calories: 215 calories;
- Protein: 10
- Total Fat: 7.7
- Sodium: 1033
- Total Carbohydrate: 26.7
- Cholesterol: 186

957. Instant Pot Vietnamese Chicken Noodle Soup (Pho Ga)

Serving: 4 servings | Prep: 10mins | Cook: 45mins | Ready in:

Ingredients

- 2 tablespoons canola oil
- 2 medium yellow onions, halved
- 1 (2-inch) piece ginger, cut into 1/4-inch slices
- 1 tablespoon coriander seeds
- 3 star anise pods
- 5 cloves
- 1 cinnamon stick
- 3 cardamom pods, lightly smashed
- 6 bone-in, skin-on chicken thighs
- 3 tablespoons fish sauce
- 1 tablespoon sugar
- 8 cups water
- Kosher salt
- Freshly ground black pepper

- 4 servings rice noodles, prepared according to package directions
- 3 scallions, sliced
- 1 small handful fresh herbs, such as mint, cilantro, and Thai basil, chopped
- 1 lime, cut into wedges
- Handful of bean sprouts (optional)
- 1 jalapeño, thinly sliced (optional)

Direction

- On an Instant Pot preheat by setting it on Sauté over high heat.
- When preheated, add oil. Add onions with cut side facing down together with the ginger. Cook without stirring for 4 minutes until charred.
- Stir in the star anise, cloves, coriander, cinnamon stick and cardamom; stir and cook for another minute. Add in the chicken, sugar, and fish sauce and pour the water in immediately. Cover it with the lid securely.
- Select Manual setting high pressure and cook for 15 minutes.
- Release the steam by natural release for 10 minutes then release remaining steam. Take out the chicken from the pot and drain the broth into a bowl through a sieve carefully. Add salt and pepper to taste.
- Shred the chicken and discard the bones. Divide cooked noodles among 4 bowls and add chicken meat on top. Pour the broth over and finish with scallions, lime, herbs and bean sprouts. Add in jalapeño if desired.
- Ingredient tip: Try your local health food store or local Asian market if you cannot find whole dried spices. You may also try ordering them online.

958. Lamb Larb

Serving: Serves 4 | Prep: | Cook: | Ready in:

Ingredients

- 1 lemongrass stalk
- 4 garlic cloves
- 1/2 bunch cilantro, stems and leaves separated, stems coarsely chopped, plus sprigs for serving
- 1 large shallot, coarsely chopped
- 4 red Thai chiles, divided
- 1/2 cup salted, roasted peanuts
- 3 tablespoons fresh lime juice
- 1 tablespoon (or more) fish sauce
- 1 1/2 teaspoons demerara sugar or dark brown sugar
- 2 tablespoons vegetable oil
- 1 pound ground lamb (at least 10% fat)
- Cooked white rice, Bibb lettuce leaves, sliced cucumber, lime wedges, and mint sprigs (for serving)

Direction

- From the lemongrass, peel off the hard-outer layers then thinly slice a 4" piece from the bulb end and keep the remainder of it for a different use. Place garlic and lemongrass in food processor and pulse to chop finely. Add shallot, 1-2 Thai chillies depending on preferred spice level and cilantro stems (keeping leaves for another time) in a food processor and pulse to finely chop. Move the mixture into a big bowl and put it aside. Place peanuts into the food processor and pulse until they are coarsely ground before transferring them to a small bowl and setting aside. Slice the remaining chiles into thin pieces then put them aside for serving.
- In a small bowl, whisk Demerara sugar, fish sauce and lime juice together to be used as dressing. Set aside.
- In a big skillet, preferably cast iron, heat oil over high. Press lamb into the skillet in one flat layer with flexible spatula. Leave it cooking without disturbance until the base turns brown and the edges turn crispy, about 5-7 minutes. Break the patty down into smaller pieces with the spatula and turn them over. Leave the pieces cooking on second side until thoroughly cooked and edges become crispy,

around 5 minutes. Use a slotted spoon to move the lamb into a mid-sized bowl and then use the spoon to break the meat up further into smaller pieces.
- Keep 3 Tbsp. of fat from the skillet and pour the rest off. Over medium heat set the skillet and stir the lemongrass mixture in consistently until it is aromatic and starts to stick to the pan. It should take about 3 minutes. Put the reserved peanuts and lime dressing as well as the reserved lamb into the skillet. Toss thoroughly until meat is coated well then remove it from the heat. If desired, season the lamb with additional fish sauce.
- Serve Larb with cilantro sprigs, mint sprigs, lettuce, rice, cucumber, limes and reserved chiles to make lettuce cups.

Nutrition Information

- Calories: 536
- Sodium: 431 mg(18%)
- Fiber: 3 g(12%)
- Total Carbohydrate: 15 g(5%)
- Cholesterol: 83 mg(28%)
- Protein: 25 g(51%)
- Total Fat: 43 g(66%)
- Saturated Fat: 13 g(66%)

959. Linguine With Shrimp And Scallops In Thai Green Curry Sauce

Serving: Makes 4 servings | Prep: 40mins | Cook: 40mins | Ready in:

Ingredients

- 2 1/2 tablespoons vegetable oil
- 1 (4-inch-long) fresh hot red chile, thinly sliced crosswise
- 3 scallions, white and green parts thinly sliced separately
- 1 lb sea scallops, tough muscle removed from side of each if necessary
- 3/4 lb large shrimp, shelled and deveined
- 1 (14-oz) can unsweetened coconut milk
- 1 tablespoon Thai green curry paste
- 1/4 cup chicken broth or water
- 1 tablespoon packed light brown sugar
- 1 1/2 tablespoons Asian fish sauce
- 1 tablespoon fresh lime juice
- 12 oz dried thin linguine
- 1/2 cup chopped fresh cilantro

Direction

- In a 12-inch nonstick skillet, set the temperature to moderately high heat and add 1 tablespoon oil heat until hot but not yet smoking; add chili and white parts of scallions. Sauté until lightly browned. Drain on to paper towels using a slotted spoon to remove them from the pan.
- Dry the shrimp and scallops separately by patting and add salt for seasoning. In the same skillet, set the temperature to moderately high until add remaining 1 1/2 tablespoons oil and heat until hot but not yet smoking; cook the scallops 2 to 3 minutes on each side, or until browned. Using a slotted spoon, place scallops to a bowl. Sauté shrimp. Stir occasionally until almost cooked through; around 3 minutes and then add to the scallops.
- In the same skillet, pour in coconut milk, broth, fish sauce, brown sugar, curry paste, lime juice and then simmer, occasionally stirring for 5 minutes.
- Fill a 6- to 8- quart pot with salted water and heat to a boil, then cook linguine until al dente. Drain in a colander.
- In a bowl, mix shrimp and scallops with any liquid. Add into skillet and boil. Adjust the heat to down and simmer for two minutes, or until shrimp and scallops are cooked through. Using a slotted spoon, place the seafood in a clean bowl and add cilantro and linguine to sauce in skillet. Toss to mix.
- Separate sauce and pasta between 4 bowls and

sprinkle with chili and green scallion mixture along with the seafood.

Nutrition Information

- Calories: 762
- Cholesterol: 135 mg(45%)
- Protein: 40 g(80%)
- Total Fat: 33 g(51%)
- Saturated Fat: 20 g(100%)
- Sodium: 1520 mg(63%)
- Fiber: 3 g(14%)
- Total Carbohydrate: 78 g(26%)

960. Lumpia Rolls

Serving: 40 | Prep: 1hours | Cook: 20mins | Ready in:

Ingredients

- 2 pounds ground beef
- 2 pounds ground pork
- vegetable oil
- 1 1/2 cups carrots, finely chopped
- soy sauce to taste
- 3 cups bean sprouts
- 1 cup sugar snap peas, chopped
- 1 cup fresh mushrooms, finely chopped
- 1 cup green onions, finely chopped
- salt to taste
- garlic powder to taste
- black pepper to taste
- 1 (14 ounce) package Lumpia Wrappers
- 1 egg white, beaten
- canola oil for frying

Direction

- In a large frying pan, pour a small amount of oil on medium heat and cook beef and pork until brown. Remove from pan, drain, and set aside in a large mixing bowl. Pour soy sauce in pan and cook the carrots in it until tender. Stir in snap peas, mushrooms, green onions and bean sprouts with a drizzle of each soy sauce, garlic powder, black pepper, and salt; stir and cook for 5 minutes, or until vegetables soften. Add to pork and beef and toss to mix.
- Cover spring roll wrappers with damp cloth to avoid drying them out and work in batches of about 5 or so at a time. On a clean work surface, position the wrapper in a way that one corner is facing you; put small amount of filling mixture on the closest corner to you. Fold over and fold the two outside corners inward. Roll it with the top corner open like a burrito. Using a brush, apply a small amount of egg white on top corner, roll it up and then seal. Do the same with the rest of the wrappers and filling.
- Fry rolls until golden brown, about 5 minutes in a deep skillet or a deep-fryer with vegetable oil heated to 190 degrees C or 375 degrees F, and then rest on paper towels to drain.

Nutrition Information

- Calories: 313 calories;
- Sodium: 170
- Total Carbohydrate: 7.2
- Cholesterol: 37
- Protein: 9.1
- Total Fat: 27.6

961. Malaysian Beef Curry

Serving: Makes 6 servings | Prep: 30mins | Cook: 6hours15mins | Ready in:

Ingredients

- 8 large dried New Mexico chiles
- 4 lemongrass stalks
- 1/2 cup chopped shallots
- 6 garlic cloves, peeled
- 2 teaspoons ground coriander
- 1 1/2 teaspoons ground cumin
- 1/2 teaspoon ground ginger

- 3 tablespoons fish sauce (such as nam pla or nuoc nam)
- 1 tablespoon golden brown sugar
- 3 pounds boneless beef chuck roast, trimmed, cut into 1 1/2-inch cubes
- 1 13.5- to 14-ounce can unsweetened coconut milk
- 8 kaffir lime leaves
- 2 whole star anise
- 1 cinnamon stick
- 1 tablespoon tamarind paste or tamarind concentrate
- Chopped fresh cilantro
- Steamed rice
- Ingredient info: New Mexico chiles can be found at some supermarkets and at Latin markets. Fish sauce and coconut milk are sold at supermarkets and Asian markets. Look for star anise, star-shaped seedpods, in the spice section of the supermarket. Tamarind is available in Asian and Indian markets.

Direction

- To make the spice paste, soak the chiles in very hot water until they soften for 45 minutes. Drain the chiles then seed, stem and chop them up.
- Remove 4 inches off of the bottom of lemongrass stalks then chop them up. Put into the processor (reserve the top of the lemongrass stalks for the stew). Mix 1 teaspoon of ground black pepper, ginger, shallots, cumin, coriander and garlic in food processor until ground finely. Add and blend into a paste fish sauce, 1/2 cup water, sugar, and chile. Transfer it to a bowl, cover it up and let it chill. This can be prepared 1 week ahead of time.
- To prepare the stew, take the reserved tops of lemongrass from spice paste and crush them up with a rolling pin or mallet. Bend them in half and bundle it together with kitchen twine. In the slow cooker, combine spice paste, beef, cinnamon, star anise, tamarind, lime leaves, lemongrass bundles and coconut milk together then stir. Submerge the meat completely by pressing it down. On a low heat, cook the stew until meat becomes extremely tender, about 4 1/2 to 5 hours. Slant the pot and remove the cinnamon stick, lemongrass bundles, star anise, lime leaves and the excess fat from the top of the stew.
- Place the stew into a bowl and scatter cilantro over the top before serving with steamed rice.

962. Marinated Thai Style Pork Spareribs

Serving: Serves 4 as a main course; 8 as an appetizer | Prep: | Cook: | Ready in:

Ingredients

- 1 cup sliced shallots
- 10 scallions, coarsely chopped
- One 3-inch piece fresh ginger, sliced
- 8 large cloves garlic, peeled
- 1 cup coarsely chopped fresh cilantro including thin stems (and roots, if possible)
- 6 tablespoons soy sauce
- 2 tablespoons Thai or Vietnamese fish sauce (nam pla or nuoc mam)
- 1 teaspoon kosher salt
- 1 teaspoon fresh coarsely ground black pepper
- 2 tablespoons sugar
- 4 pounds pork spare ribs, cut by your butcher across the bone into 2- to 3-inch "racks," each rack cut between the bones into individual 2- to 3-inch-long riblets
- Thai Chile-Herb Dipping Sauce

Direction

- In the bowl of a food processor, process the combination of sugar, garlic, pepper, salt, ginger, scallions, shallots, fish sauce, cilantro and soy sauce until it turns into a finely chopped loose paste. Scrape the sides of the bowl one or two times.
- Prepare sturdy resealable plastic bags or a big bowl to place the pork ribs in. Layer the ribs

- with marinade thoroughly by massaging the paste in for about a minute. Cover the ribs up and let it stand at room temperature for a minimum of 2 hours or in the fridge for a maximum of 5 hours. In between this time, move the ribs around once or twice.
- Preheat the oven to 350 degrees F and place ribs bone down and spread out on two big, parchment-lined baking trays. Let ribs bake for about 1-1/2 hours, rotating the pans from time to time to cook it evenly. The ribs can be removed from the oven when the colour deepens and the meat is tender but not falling off from the bone. Best enjoyed with small bowls of Thai Chile-Herb dipping sauce.

Nutrition Information

- Calories: 1365
- Total Carbohydrate: 23 g(8%)
- Cholesterol: 363 mg(121%)
- Protein: 75 g(151%)
- Total Fat: 107 g(164%)
- Saturated Fat: 34 g(171%)
- Sodium: 2409 mg(100%)
- Fiber: 3 g(13%)

963. Massaman Chicken

Serving: Makes 8 servings | Prep: 45mins | Cook: 2hours45mins | Ready in:

Ingredients

- 1 tablespoon vegetable oil
- 1 4–4 1/2-pound chicken, cut into 10 pieces
- Kosher salt
- 4 medium Yukon Gold potatoes (about 1 1/2 pounds), quartered
- 2 medium red onions, cut into wedges
- 3/4 cup prepared massaman curry paste
- 12 ounces Belgian-style wheat beer
- 4 13.5-ounce cans unsweetened coconut milk
- 2 cups low-sodium chicken broth
- 1/2 cup fish sauce
- 1/4 cup fresh lime juice
- 1 tablespoon palm or light brown sugar
- 1 teaspoon red chile powder
- Freshly ground black pepper
- Cilantro sprigs, fried shallots, and cooked rice (for serving)

Direction

- In a big sturdy pot, heat the oil over medium-high. Cook the salted chicken in batches with the skin side down without turning for 8 to 10 minutes. It can be transferred to a plate once it has turned golden brown.
- In the same pot, cook potatoes for 8-10 minutes until they turn brown, flipping them occasionally. Move them to another plate. Cook onions in the same pot for 5-8 minutes with occasional stirring until they turn brown then place them onto the plate with the potatoes.
- Cook and stir the curry paste in the pot for 4 minutes or until fragrant. Pour the beer in and bring it to a boil. Reduce the heat and let it simmer for 5-7 minutes until it has been halved. Mix broth, coconut milk and chicken in then bring it to a boil. Reduce the heat and let it simmer for 1 to 1-1/2 hours until the chicken is extremely tender.
- Place the onions and potatoes into the pot and cook for 30 minutes until the potatoes soften. Move it away from the heat and mix in chile powder, fish sauce, palm sugar, lime juice, pepper and salt. Finish it off with shallots and cilantro. Best enjoyed together with rice.
- The chicken can be prepared 2 days in advance, just remember to cover it up and let it chill.

Nutrition Information

- Calories: 880
- Cholesterol: 125 mg(42%)
- Protein: 40 g(80%)
- Total Fat: 69 g(106%)
- Saturated Fat: 44 g(219%)

- Sodium: 1710 mg(71%)
- Fiber: 4 g(14%)
- Total Carbohydrate: 29 g(10%)

964. Minted Eggplant Rounds

Serving: Serves 6 | Prep: | Cook: |Ready in:

Ingredients

- 6 Asian (long, thin) eggplants (about 2 pounds)
- vegetable oil for brushing eggplant
- 1/3 cup fresh lime juice
- 1/3 cup Asian fish sauce (preferably naam pla)
- 2 tablespoons sugar
- 4 large garlic cloves, minced
- 1/4 cup finely chopped fresh mint leaves

Direction

- Turn the broiler on to heat.
- Chop eggplants into 3/4-inch crosswise portions. Place eggplant pieces on baking sheets and brush both sides with oil. In batches, broil 3 to 4 minutes per side approximately 4 inches away from heat. When they are golden brown, they are done.
- In a bowl, stir lime juice together with garlic, mint, sugar, fish sauce and garlic. Continue stirring until sugar dissolves
- Place eggplant on a serving plate and pour the sauce over it. Enjoy!

Nutrition Information

- Calories: 86
- Total Fat: 3 g(4%)
- Saturated Fat: 0 g(1%)
- Sodium: 1261 mg(53%)
- Fiber: 4 g(16%)
- Total Carbohydrate: 15 g(5%)
- Protein: 2 g(5%)

965. Ode To Halo Halo

Serving: Serves 2 | Prep: | Cook: |Ready in:

Ingredients

- 2 very ripe bananas, sliced 1/4-inch thick
- 2 tablespoons light brown sugar
- 1/4 teaspoon vanilla extract
- Kosher salt
- 6 ounces fresh blueberries (about 1 cup)
- 6 ounces fresh blackberries (about 1 1/2 cups), cut in half if large
- 2 tablespoons fresh lime juice
- 1 tablespoon granulated sugar
- 3/4 cup unsweetened coconut milk
- 2 tablespoons sweetened condensed milk
- 4 cups shaved ice
- 1/2 pint vanilla or coconut ice cream
- Toasted unsweetened coconut flakes, gummi bears, and/or popcorn (for serving)

Direction

- In a small bowl, mix a pinch of salt, bananas, 2 tbsp. of water, vanilla and brown sugar together. Leave it to sit for 20 to 30 minutes, stirring from time to time. It is ready when the liquid has thickened a little and the texture of the bananas is jammy.
- In a mid-sized bowl, place a pinch of salt, lime juice, berries and granulated sugar together then mash the berries gently to let the juices flow out. Leave it to sit for 15 to 20 minutes, stirring every now and then until the juice thickens a little.
- In another small bowl, whisk sweetened condensed milk and coconut milk together until combined. Using pint glasses or 2 small bowls, place halo-halo in them, layering alternatingly with berries, shaved ice, bananas, ice cream and coconut milk mixture. Finish off with toppings of your choice.

Nutrition Information

- Calories: 621
- Sodium: 2262 mg(94%)
- Fiber: 11 g(44%)
- Total Carbohydrate: 92 g(31%)
- Cholesterol: 36 mg(12%)
- Protein: 9 g(18%)
- Total Fat: 28 g(43%)
- Saturated Fat: 22 g(109%)

966. Panang Vegetable Curry

Serving: Makes 8 servings | Prep: | Cook: |Ready in:

Ingredients

- 2 tablespoons vegetable oil
- 2 large shallots, thinly sliced
- 2 tablespoons Panang Curry Paste
- 2 tablespoons chopped peeled ginger
- 2 1/3 cups canned unsweetened coconut milk, divided
- 1 1/2 cups (or more) vegetable stock
- 8 fresh or frozen kaffir lime leaves
- 2 dried chiles de árbol
- 1 4-pound kabocha squash, cut into 8 wedges, seeded, or 2 acorn squash, quartered, seeded
- 1 small head of cauliflower (about 1 1/2 pounds), cored, broken into 1"-2" florets
- 1 pound carrots, peeled, cut on a diagonal into 1/2" slices
- 2 red bell peppers, cut into 1/2" squares
- 1/4 cup liquid tamarind concentrate or 2 tablespoons tamarind paste mixed with 2 tablespoons water
- 1/2 cup thinly sliced fresh basil, divided
- 2 tablespoons fish sauce (such as nam pla or nuoc nam)
- 1 tablespoon fresh lime juice
- 1 12-ounce package firm tofu, drained, patted dry, cut into 1" cubes
- Kosher salt
- 1/4 cup chopped peanuts
- Steamed jasmine rice
- Ingredient info: Unsweetened coconut milk, chiles de árbol, and fish sauce are sold at better supermarkets. Kaffir lime leaves and tamarind concentrate can be found at Southeast Asian markets.

Direction

- Set a large pot on medium heat and add oil. Stir in shallots, ginger and Panang Curry Paste for 2-3 minutes until shallots are tender; add 1/3 cup of coconut milk. Stir for 4 minutes, until brown.
- Stir in the remaining 2 cups coconut milk along with 1 1/2 cups of vegetable stock, chiles, and lime leaves. Stir to mix and scrape the brown pieces up. Add the kabocha squash to the pot, to fit in one layer set on the sides. Heat to a boil; lower the heat to medium-low and secure with lid. Let the squash simmer for 15 to 20 minutes, until almost softened. Take out the squash from the pot and mix carrots, cauliflower and pepper into pot. Place squash back in the pot on top of the vegetables and cook for 10 to 15 minutes, or until all the vegetables soften. Serve squash on a plate.
- Add lime juice, fish sauce, half of basil, tamarind concentrate, and tofu into the pot and secure with lid. Simmer for 2 minutes, enough to heat it through. If too thick, add additional stock. Season with salt to taste.
- Divide the curry between bowls and place one chunk of squash on top. Sprinkle peanuts and remaining basil on then serve with steamed jasmine rice.

Nutrition Information

- Calories: 396
- Total Carbohydrate: 39 g(13%)
- Cholesterol: 0 mg(0%)
- Protein: 14 g(28%)
- Total Fat: 24 g(38%)
- Saturated Fat: 14 g(69%)
- Sodium: 1393 mg(58%)
- Fiber: 9 g(36%)

967. Penang Rice Salad

Serving: Makes 4 snack or side-dish servings | Prep: 45mins | Cook: 45mins | Ready in:

Ingredients

- 1 3/4 cups jasmine rice* (11 3/4 oz)
- 3 cups water
- 1/3 cup packaged unsweetened dried coconut
- 1/4 cup fine-quality dried shrimp** (1 oz)
- 1 large fresh lemongrass stalk, 1 or 2 outer leaves discarded and root end trimmed
- 3 (2 1/2-inch-long) fresh or thawed frozen Kaffir lime leaves
- 1 (1/2-inch) piece peeled fresh or thawed frozen turmeric** (optional), finely grated
- 1 large shallot, halved lengthwise and very thinly sliced crosswise (3/4 cup)
- 5 tablespoons very thinly sliced fresh Vietnamese basil or fresh cilantro (from 1 bunch)
- 3 tablespoons very thinly sliced fresh mint
- 2 tablespoons fresh lime juice, or to taste
- 1/2 teaspoon freshly ground white pepper
- 1/4 teaspoon salt
- an electric coffee/spice grinder

Direction

- Drain and rinse rice with cold water in a bowl several times changing the cold water each time until water becomes clear. Put in a strainer to drain. In a 2 1/2 - quart saucepan, put rice with 3 cups of fresh water and boil. Lower the temperature to low and cook for 15 minutes, or until rice is fluffy and soft and the water has been absorbed. Take off heat and set aside for 5 minutes with the lid on. Open lid and using a fork gently fluff rice, take 5 cups and place on a shallow big baking pan. Let it cool to room temperature. Use the remaining rice for another dish.
- Meanwhile, in a heavy cast iron skillet, stir coconut on moderately low heat for 4 to 6 minutes or until it toaststo a golden color. Remove and set aside to cool in a bowl. Grind by pulsing in a grinder a couple of times be careful to not overgrind otherwise it will be coconut butter. Place back into small bowl and grind shrimp in grinder until finely ground and very fluffy, 1 minute. Cut thinly the lower part of lemongrass stalk, about six inches from bottom. Mince finely. Using a sharp knife, remove the central stems and veins of lime leaves and cut leaves into lengthwise strips as thin as hair.
- Mix rice together with dried shrimp, coconut, lime leaves, turmeric (if desired), lemongrass, basil, mint, shallot, white pepper, salt and 2 tablespoons lime juice. Mix until evenly combined and no lumps are visible. Add lime and salt to season as needed. Serve as soon as possible.

968. Pork Tenderloin With Turmeric, Squash, And Collard Greens Salad

Serving: Serves 4 | Prep: 40mins | Cook: 45mins | Ready in:

Ingredients

- 1 1/2 teaspoons ground turmeric
- 1 1/2 teaspoons kosher salt
- 1 teaspoon freshly ground black pepper
- 1 teaspoon ground cumin
- 1 medium butternut squash (about 2 1/2 pounds), peeled
- 4 tablespoons coconut oil, warmed, divided
- 3 tablespoons fresh lime juice
- 1 tablespoon honey
- 3 1/2 teaspoons fish sauce
- 2 small pork tenderloins (about 1 1/2 pounds total)
- 1 large bunch collard greens (about 12 ounces)
- 2 tablespoons vegetable or canola oil
- 1/4 cup toasted coconut chips
- 1 cup plain Greek yogurt

Direction

- Organize the racks in the middle and upper thirds of the oven then preheat it to 450 degrees F. In a small bowl, combine cumin, salt, turmeric and pepper together and set aside.
- Cut ribbons off the long neck of squash with a peeler until there is enough to fill 2 cups then set it aside. With the remaining squash, cut it in half lengthwise, remove the seeds and discard. Cut the squash up further into half-moons 1/2".
- In a big bowl, toss 2 tbsp. of coconut oil and pieces of squash, then add 1-1/2 tsp. of turmeric mixture and mix to coat. Reserve the large bowl for later and distribute the squash mixture onto a rimmed baking tray. Roast it in the upper third level of the oven for 20 minutes or until it turns tender and a nice golden brown.
- In another big bowl, whisk fish sauce, honey, and lime juice together. Throw the squash ribbons in and toss it around to coat. Set it aside.
- Using the reserved big bowl, rub the remaining turmeric mixture onto the pork. In a big heatproof cast iron skillet over high heat, heat up the remaining 2 tbsp. of coconut oil and sear the pork for about 5 minutes. Turn it frequently and cook until it turns brown on all sides. Move the skillet to the rack in the centre of oven and roast for 10-12 minutes, turning the pork over mid-way through. Insert an instant read thermometer into the thickest part of the tenderloin and if it registers as 145°F, it is ready to be transferred to a cutting board. Let it sit for 5 minutes before cutting it up.
- When the pork and squash are roasting, get rid of the stems from the collards and put the halved leaves in a neatly stacked pile. From 1 long side, start rolling it into a cylinder before slicing it at 1/2" intervals across the cylinder, creating the ribbons.
- Move the squash ribbons to a plate. Whisk vegetable oil into the dressing to combine. Massage the dressing into the collards with your hands until they turn a dark green shade then toss the squash ribbons into the bowl to combine.
- Distribute the salad on a serving platter or divide among plates, topping it off with coconut chips. Put some yogurt alongside the roasted squash and pork. Serve.

Nutrition Information

- Calories: 651
- Saturated Fat: 19 g(93%)
- Sodium: 1280 mg(53%)
- Fiber: 9 g(37%)
- Total Carbohydrate: 43 g(14%)
- Cholesterol: 133 mg(44%)
- Protein: 50 g(100%)
- Total Fat: 34 g(52%)

969. Pork And Lemongrass Meatballs In Lettuce Cups

Serving: Makes 4 servings | Prep: 30mins | Cook: 1hours30mins | Ready in:

Ingredients

- 1 pound ground pork
- 1 lemongrass stalk, bottom 5 inches only, smashed with rolling pin, then minced
- 1/4 cup chopped shallots
- 2 tablespoons chopped fresh cilantro
- 2 tablespoons fish sauce (such as nam pla or nuoc nam)
- 2 garlic cloves, chopped
- 1 tablespoon vegetable oil
- 1 teaspoon sugar
- 1/2 teaspoon ground white pepper
- 1 lemongrass stalk
- 1/4 cup fresh lime juice
- 1/4 cup fish sauce
- 2 tablespoons chopped fresh cilantro
- 2 tablespoons coarsely grated carrot
- 4 teaspoons (packed) golden brown sugar

- 2 teaspoons minced green Thai chile or serrano chile with seeds
- 2 tablespoons vegetable oil
- 1 head of butter lettuce, leaves separated
- 1 small persian cucumber, thinly sliced
- Ingredient info: Fish sauce can be found in the Asian foods section of many supermarkets.

Direction

- In the process of making the meatballs, let the pork chill in the freezer during the entire duration it takes to create the lemongrass paste. Pulse the remaining ingredients, 1/2 teaspoon salt and lemongrass in the processor until it forms a paste. Pulse chilled pork in until well blended. Roll 1 tablespoonful of mixture into a ball. Make about 24 balls then put them on a rimmed baking tray. Cover it up and let them chill for a minimum of 1 hour or even overnight.
- To make the dipping sauce and assemble dish, cut 3 inches off the bottom of lemongrass then smash it with the rolling pin and mince. In a small bowl, place 1 tablespoon and keep the remainder for a different use. Whisk chili, sugar, lime juice, carrot, cilantro and fish sauce into the bowl and stop when the sugar has dissolved.
- In a big skillet, heat the oil over medium heat. Put meatballs in and cook thoroughly for 15 minutes until they begin to brown, flipping them over from time to time. Move meatballs onto 1 side of a big platter.
- Put cucumber and lettuce leaves on the platter. Let the guests fill the leaves up with meatballs, cucumber and a sprinkle of dipping sauce on top.

970. Pork Belly Buns

Serving: Makes 16 buns | Prep: 1.25hours | Cook: 24hours | Ready in:

Ingredients

- 1/2 cup kosher salt
- 1/2 cup sugar
- 4 1/2 cups water, divided
- 2 1/2 lb skinless boneless pork belly, cut into quarters
- 1/2 cup reduced-sodium chicken broth
- 1 cup warm water (105-115°F), divided
- 1/2 teaspoon active dry yeast
- 3 tablespoons sugar plus a pinch
- 2 tablespoons nonfat dried milk
- 3 1/2 cups cake flour (not self-rising)
- 1 1/2 teaspoons baking powder
- Canola oil for greasing and brushing
- Equipment: a deep 12-inch skillet with domed lid or a 14-inch flat-bottomed wok with lid
- Accompaniments: hoisin sauce; thinly sliced cucumber; chopped scallions
- 0cucumber
- scallions

Direction

- To prepare the brine pork, mix sugar and kosher salt together with 4 cups of water until it dissolves into a solution. Place the pork belly inside a large sealable bag, and pour the brine in it. Release excess air and seal the bag. Place in shallow dish and chill for at least 12 hours.
- While the pork continues to brine, make dough by stirring together a pinch of sugar and yeast in 1/4 cup of warm water. Let it settle for 5 to 10 minutes. When it is foamy, proceed to whisk in dried milk along with remaining 3/4 cup warm water (if the yeast mixture does not get foamy, start with some new yeast).
- In a bowl, stir together remaining 3 tablespoons sugar with flour, then mix in yeast mixture using a fork until dough is formed (do not put in the baking powder at this point). Knead using hands in bowl until flour is evenly mixed. Dust a clean working surface and hands with just enough flour to keep dough from sticking and knead dough for 5 minutes, until dough remains soft but is smooth and elastic like.

- Grease a large bowl with oil, put dough in and flip to coat. Seal with plastic wrap and leave in a closed area with warm room temperature for 2 hours to allow the dough rise and double its size.
- While the dough continues to rise, set the oven to 300°F place a rack in the center of oven.
- Drain brine. In an 8- to 9- inch square baking pan, place the pork fat side up. Add in remaining 1/2 cup water and broth. Seal tight using a foil and roast for 2 hours and 30 minutes, or until the pork is very tender. Take off foil and set the temperature to 450°F for about 20 minutes, just enough to make the fat appear golden. Let it cool for half an hour and chill for an additional hour to make it cold.
- When slicing the pork, cut across the grain into 1/4-inch slices. While making buns, cover chilled pork slices in pan together with its juice.
- To prepare the buns, flatten the dough on a clean working surface lightly dusted with flour. Pat and flatten gently into a disk. Add baking powder to the center part of dough, then seal in the baking powder by gathering and pinching edges together. Knead dough with a little flour to prevent it from sticking until it mixes thoroughly with the baking powder, 5 minutes. Place the dough inside a bowl and seal the top with plastic wrap. Leave for half an hour to let it rise.
- Prepare at least 16 pieces of wax paper, each measuring approximately 3 inches by 2 inches.
- Shape a 16-inch-long log from the dough and divide into 16 pieces. Sprinkle flour over it and seal loosely with plastic wrap. Dust your hands and a rolling pin with flour, then roll a 6- by 3- inch oval out of 1 piece of dough. To remove excess flour, tap oval piece of dough between your palms. Lightly brush half of oval with the oil and fold in half crosswise. On a large baking sheet, set the bun on a piece of wax paper and seal loosely with plastic wrap. Use the remaining dough to make more buns, seal loosely with plastic wrap while allowing them to slightly rise, 30 minutes.
- Place a sizable steamer rack inside wok or skillet, then pour sufficient amount of water to reach within half an inch of rack and then boil. With the wax paper still on, set 5 to 7 buns gently in steamer rack, with enough space to not let the buns touch. Seal tight and set the temperature to high. Steam for 3 minutes just until buns are cooked through and puffed. Using tongs, place the buns on a plate and dispose wax paper. Wrap buns with kitchen towels to warm. Finish the remaining buns in a couple of batches, pouring in hot water as needed.
- Still wrapped in towels, put the buns back on the steamer rack in wok and cover with lid to keep it warm but off the heat.
- Set oven to 350°F and place rack in the middle. In a liquid baking dish, heat chopped pork, sealed, for 15 to 20 minutes.
- Using hoisin sauce, lather bottom half of each bun and insert 2 or 3 pieces of chopped pork along with scallions and cucumber.
- Cooks recommend brining pork belly for up to 24 hours.
- It is also possible to roast and chop the pork at least 48 hours in advance, sealed and cooled in liquid.
- Steam and cool buns completely. Chill and seal tightly with a double layer of plastic wrap for 24 hours or freeze for a week. Set the oven to 350°F and place the buns wrapped in a dampened kitchen towel and wrap tightly with foil in the oven. Heat for about 15 minutes, or until buns are soft.

971. Red Curry Noodle Bowls With Steak And Cabbage

Serving: 4 servings | Prep: 30mins | Cook: 30mins | Ready in:

Ingredients

- 4 ounces dried flat linguine-width rice noodles
- 2 1/2 teaspoons kosher salt, plus more

- 1 pound flank steak
- 2 tablespoons refined coconut or vegetable oil, divided
- 1/4 cup red curry paste
- 2 teaspoons freshly grated ginger
- 1 small head savoy cabbage (about 12 ounces), thinly sliced into long ribbons
- 2 1/2 cups low-sodium beef broth
- 1 (15-ounce) can coconut milk
- 2 tablespoons fresh lime juice, plus wedges for serving
- 4 ounces pea sprouts or shoots
- 1/2 cup basil leaves, preferably purple Thai
- 1/2 cup mint leaves
- Sliced red chiles (for serving)

Direction

- Follow the package directions to cook noodles in salted boiling water in a big pot. Strain the noodles before cleansing with cold water then straining them once more. Set noodles to one side.
- In the meantime, sprinkle 1 teaspoon of salt onto steak to season it. In a big skillet over high heat, pour 1 tablespoon of oil in heat until hot. For medium rare, sear the steak for 4-5 minutes on each side. Let it cool down for 10 minutes before slicing the steak thinly against the grain.
- In the same pan, heat up the remaining 1 tablespoon of oil over medium heat. Mix in ginger and curry paste. Add cabbage and the remaining 1-1/2 teaspoons of salt and stir to coat. Cook for 1 minute until the cabbage starts to shrivel up, tossing it periodically. Mix the coconut milk and broth in then bring to a simmer. Move it away from the heat; mix the lime juice and noodles in.
- On separate bowls, distribute the noodles equally. Finish off by topping with pea sprouts, chiles, mint, steak and basil. Place lime wedges on the side and it is ready for serving.

Nutrition Information

- Calories: 636
- Total Fat: 41 g(63%)
- Saturated Fat: 25 g(124%)
- Sodium: 1279 mg(53%)
- Fiber: 5 g(21%)
- Total Carbohydrate: 37 g(12%)
- Cholesterol: 79 mg(26%)
- Protein: 35 g(70%)

972. Rice Noodles

Serving: Makes about 3 pounds (8 to 10 cups cooked noodles) | Prep: | Cook: | Ready in:

Ingredients

- 4 cups rice flour, plus more for dusting
- 3 1/2 cups water
- 3 tablespoons shallot oil or canola oil
- 1 cup tapioca starch

Direction

- Preparation 1. Whisk 3 1/2 cups water along with the rice flour in a bowl until smooth. Cap the bowl and let it ferment for 4 days at room temperature.
- 2. Pour out 1 1/2 cups water from the bowl of settled rice flour gently. Then, stir in 1/4 cup fresh water to the batter until smooth.
- 3. Fill a large pot with salted water and boil over high heat, keep water hot while preparing the dough.
- 4. Heat the oil in a 4- to 6- quart pot over high temperature. Pour in the batter when the oil is hot and adjust the heat to low. You will need two people for this, one to thoroughly stir the batter using a wooden spoon, and the other to hold the pot down in the process. Once the dough thickens, keep on stirring and cooking until the dough is firm and thick, this usually lasts 5 to 8 minutes. Do not remove any dough that sticks to sides of the pot.
- 5. Place the dough hook on a stand mixer and pour in the dough together with tapioca

starch. Set to medium speed and mix for 10 minutes, until it resembles a sticky ball.
- 6. Turn the heat back up to bring the water to a boil, and then let it simmer. Transfer the dough to a clean surface, dusted with flour and knead for another 5 minutes or until the dough is smooth. To avoid drying the dough out, seal the dough with plastic wrap.
- 7. Place a large ice-water bath beside the stove. Keep the remaining dough covered as you put 1 1/2 cups of the dough into a potato ricer. Place the ricer on top of the center of the pot of boiling water and press thoroughly to squeeze out the noodles. Bring the ricer closer to the water and shake it lightly to allow the noodles to drop onto the simmering water. Leave the noodles to simmer until they gather at a side of the pot, 1 1/2 to 2 minutes. Gently transfer the noodles to the ice-water bath using tongs or a spider. Transfer and drain in a colander once cool enough to touch. Finish with remaining dough and once everything has been cooked and cooled, transfer to a colander and drain. To remove excess starch, rinse the noodles under cold running water and drain. The noodles can be sealed and refrigerated for up to 24 hours, but it is best used the same day it is made.

Nutrition Information

- Calories: 307
- Fiber: 2 g(6%)
- Total Carbohydrate: 61 g(20%)
- Protein: 4 g(8%)
- Total Fat: 5 g(8%)
- Saturated Fat: 1 g(3%)
- Sodium: 3 mg(0%)

973. Rice Noodles With Garlic And Herbs

Serving: Serves 6 | Prep: | Cook: | Ready in:

Ingredients

- 1 cup plus 2 tablespoons vegetable oil
- 1/2 cup thinly sliced shallot
- 1/3 cup thinly sliced garlic
- 1/4 cup tamarind (from a pliable block)
- 1/2 cup warm water
- 3 tablespoons Asian fish sauce (preferably naam pla)
- 3 tablespoons rice vinegar
- 1 1/2 tablespoons firmly packed brown sugar
- 1/4 cup water
- 3/4 pound dried flat rice noodles (about 1/4 to 1/2 inch wide)
- 1 small onion, sliced thin
- 1 small red bell pepper, cut into thin strips
- 3/4 pint vine-ripened cherry tomatoes, quartered
- 1/4 cup thinly sliced fresh Thai basil leaves or Italian basil leaves
- 1/4 cup chopped fresh coriander

Direction

- Over moderate heat, heat up 1 cup of oil in an 8- or 9-inch pan until it is hot but not yet smoking then stir the shallot in. Fry until it turns golden, about 1-2 minutes. Using a slotted spoon, move the shallot to paper towels and drain. In the same skillet, fry the garlic and drain it the same way.
- Mix warm water and tamarind together in a small bowl, squashing the tamarind softly and straining the mixture through a sieve placed over a bowl, pushing hard on the solids. Mix the sugar, fish sauce, water and vinegar in.
- Place enough cold water into a big bowl to soak noodles completely for 15 minutes then drain the noodles. Cook the noodles in a kettle of boiling water that has been salted until they turn tender, about 1 to 2 minutes. Drain the noodles in a colander then run cold water over it before draining the noodles again entirely.
- In a big skillet over moderate heat, put the remaining 2 tablespoons of oil in to cook the bell pepper and onion until softened, stirring, before adding in the sauce, noodles and

tomatoes. Continue to stir the mixture and cook until it is cooked through. Put in shallot, garlic and herbs and finish off by tossing with the noodles.

Nutrition Information

- Calories: 642
- Saturated Fat: 3 g(14%)
- Sodium: 820 mg(34%)
- Fiber: 3 g(11%)
- Total Carbohydrate: 60 g(20%)
- Protein: 5 g(11%)
- Total Fat: 43 g(65%)

974. Roasted Brussels Sprouts

Serving: 6 | Prep: 15mins | Cook: 45mins | Ready in:

Ingredients

- 1 1/2 pounds Brussels sprouts, ends trimmed and yellow leaves removed
- 3 tablespoons olive oil
- 1 teaspoon kosher salt
- 1/2 teaspoon freshly ground black pepper

Direction

- Set the oven to 400 deg F.
- In a large air-tight plastic container, add olive oil, kosher salt, and pepper together with trimmed Brussels sprouts. Cover tight and shake to mix thoroughly. Place on a baking sheet and set on the center oven rack.
- Cook for 30 to 45 minutes inside the oven, In 5 to 7 minute intervals, shake the pan to brown the sides evenly and adjust the heat as needed to avoid burning. If the Brussels sprouts appear dark brown to almost black, they are done. Remove from oven and add salt to taste. Serve right away.

Nutrition Information

- Calories: 104 calories;
- Sodium: 344
- Total Carbohydrate: 10
- Cholesterol: 0
- Protein: 2.9
- Total Fat: 7.3

975. Roasted Cauliflower Larb

Serving: 6 servings | Prep: | Cook: |Ready in:

Ingredients

- 1 large head of cauliflower, cut into large florets with some stalk attached
- 3 tablespoons olive oil
- 3 green Thai chiles, finely chopped
- 1 (3-inch) piece lemongrass, tough outer layers removed, finely chopped
- 4 kaffir lime leaves, finely chopped
- 1/4 cup fish sauce
- 1/4 cup fresh lime juice
- 1/4 cup glutinous (sticky) rice
- 5 scallions, thinly sliced
- 2 cups chopped pea shoots (tendrils)
- 1 cup chopped cilantro
- 1 cup chopped mint
- Kosher salt
- Sliced Persian cucumber and Bibb lettuce leaves (for serving)
- A spice mill

Direction

- Preheat the oven to 450 degrees F. On a rimmed baking tray, toss the cauliflower with oil. Let it cook until the vegetable turns brown and tender, about 35-45 minutes. Stir from time to time. Let it sit to cool off before chopping them into pieces as small as peas. Move it into a big bowl and toss it well with lime juice, chiles, fish sauce, lime leaves and lemongrass.
- In a mid-sized skillet, toast rice over medium heat until it is browned evenly, about 10-15

minutes. Jiggle the pan continually to keep moving the rice around. Place the rice on a plate and let it cool; then grind it inside of a spice mill until it turns into semi-fine powder.
- Stir 2 tsp. of toasted rice powder, mint, scallions, cilantro and pea shoots into the cauliflower mixture, seasoning with a little salt. Use the remaining rice powder, lettuce and cucumber to make lettuce cups. Serve.

Nutrition Information

- Calories: 151
- Saturated Fat: 1 g(6%)
- Sodium: 999 mg(42%)
- Fiber: 4 g(17%)
- Total Carbohydrate: 19 g(6%)
- Protein: 5 g(10%)
- Total Fat: 7 g(11%)

976. Salt And Pepper Seasoning Mix

Serving: Makes 2 tablespoons | Prep: | Cook: |Ready in:

Ingredients

- 1 tablespoon salt
- 1 teaspoon sugar
- 1 teaspoon fine white pepper
- 1 teaspoon ground ginger
- 1/2 teaspoon five-spice powder

Direction

- In a bowl, stir all the ingredients and mix thoroughly.

Nutrition Information

- Calories: 16
- Total Fat: 0 g(0%)
- Saturated Fat: 0 g(0%)
- Sodium: 11 mg(0%)
- Fiber: 1 g(2%)
- Total Carbohydrate: 4 g(1%)
- Protein: 0 g(0%)

977. Salt And Pepper Tofu

Serving: Serves 2 | Prep: | Cook: |Ready in:

Ingredients

- 1/2 pound tofu pillows (Chinese-style pressed firm tofu)
- Oil, for deep-frying
- 2 scallions, sliced
- 1 bird's-eye chile, sliced
- 1 teaspoon ground garlic
- Salt and pepper seasoning mix

Direction

- Chop the tofu into 1 1/2 by 3/4- inch slices. Set aside on a piece of cloth to dry. Heat a wok to 350°F with enough oil to deep-fry the tofu or until in 15 seconds a cube of bread put in the oil turns brown. Add the tofu and deep-fry until it is crisp and golden, 5 minutes. Drain oil from wok and keep for another use.
- Place wok on high heat and add 2 teaspoons of oil. Stir-fry the scallions, garlic and chile for 20 seconds then add the tofu back in. Season with salt and pepper and toss to mix the flavors. Serve with vegetarian or lemon dipping sauce, salt and pepper.

Nutrition Information

- Calories: 200
- Total Fat: 12 g(19%)
- Saturated Fat: 2 g(8%)
- Sodium: 360 mg(15%)
- Fiber: 3 g(14%)
- Total Carbohydrate: 9 g(3%)
- Protein: 19 g(37%)

978. Salt, Pepper, And Lemon Dipping Sauce

Serving: Makes 2 tablespoons | Prep: | Cook: | Ready in:

Ingredients

- 2 tablespoons freshly squeezed lemon juice
- 1/2 teaspoon salt
- 1 teaspoon fine white pepper

Direction

- Mix all the ingredients well.

Nutrition Information

- Calories: 7
- Saturated Fat: 0 g(0%)
- Sodium: 35 mg(1%)
- Fiber: 0 g(1%)
- Total Carbohydrate: 2 g(1%)
- Protein: 0 g(0%)
- Total Fat: 0 g(0%)

979. Saté Chicken Salad

Serving: Makes 6 to 8 servings | Prep: 10mins | Cook: 10mins | Ready in:

Ingredients

- 1/4 cup dry-roasted peanuts
- 1 large garlic clove
- 1 (1-inch) piece peeled ginger
- 2/3 cup smooth peanut butter (not natural-style)
- 6 tablespoons warm water
- 3 tablespoons rice vinegar (not seasoned)
- 2 1/2 tablespoons soy sauce
- 1 1/2 tablespoons Asian sesame oil
- 1 teaspoon sugar
- 1 teaspoon hot red-pepper flakes
- 3 cups sliced or coarsely shredded rotisserie chicken
- 1 pound coleslaw mix
- 3 celery ribs, thinly sliced diagonally
- 1 red bell pepper, sliced
- 1 bunch scallions, chopped
- 1 cup coarsely chopped cilantro
- Accompaniment: lime wedges

Direction

- Place peanuts in a food processor and pulse until they become chopped into coarse bits; move them to a bowl.
- Put ginger and garlic through feed tube with the motor running then chop fine. Blend in red pepper flakes, sesame oil, peanut butter, sugar, soy sauce, water and vinegar until texture is smooth.
- Coat vegetables and chicken with sufficient dressing by tossing them together then scatter cilantro and peanuts over top.

Nutrition Information

- Calories: 473
- Saturated Fat: 7 g(36%)
- Sodium: 461 mg(19%)
- Fiber: 5 g(18%)
- Total Carbohydrate: 22 g(7%)
- Cholesterol: 59 mg(20%)
- Protein: 23 g(47%)
- Total Fat: 34 g(52%)

980. Shredded Sweet Potato And Carrot Fritters (Ukoy)

Serving: Serves 4 | Prep: | Cook: | Ready in:

Ingredients

- 3 Thai chiles, thinly sliced
- 1 garlic clove, finely chopped
- 2 tablespoons chopped red onion

- 1/4 cup sugarcane vinegar or distilled white vinegar
- Kosher salt
- 1 medium sweet potato, peeled
- 4 medium carrots, peeled
- Kosher salt
- 8 cups (or more) vegetable oil
- 3/4 cup (or more) club soda
- 1 teaspoon fish sauce
- 1 1/4 cups cornstarch
- 4 ounces small or medium shrimp, peeled, deveined
- 1 cup cilantro leaves with tender stems
- A deep-fry thermometer

Direction

- To make the Chile Vinegar, combine vinegar, chiles, onion and garlic together in a tiny bowl and flavor with salt.
- For the fritters, cut the sweet potatoes and the carrots into 3x1/4" sticks using a mandolin if available then cut them into matchsticks lengthwise. Toss them together with a few touches of salt in a mid-sized bowl then let it sit for 30 minutes until it becomes a little soft. Rinse the salt off and pat them dry.
- Make sure to use a big pot with a minimum of 4" headspace and a minimum of 2" deep because oil will aggressively bubble when fritters are added. Fit the thermometer to pot and leave the oil over medium-high heat until the thermometer registers between 330 deg F–340 deg F.
- In the meantime, mix the fish sauce and club soda in a big measuring cup. Then whisk cornstarch in until it is smooth. In a mid-sized bowl, toss cilantro, half the carrot and sweet potato mixture, and shrimp until well combined; then toss half the cornstarch slurry in to coat. The slurry should adhere on vegetables and shrimp lightly and evenly in a thin layer.
- Put the slurry-layered shrimp and vegetable mixture into the oil slowly with a slotted spoon. As soon as the bubbling lessens, the mixture will scatter itself along the surface of the oil. With a clean clotted spoon or spider skimmer, hold the shrimp and vegetables together on one side of the pot until they pile together in a mound and can be flipped as one unit. Fry the fritter for about 4 minutes or until it is golden brown, and its edges are crispy, flipping it around occasionally; turn the heat up when necessary to ensure the oil temperature stays in between 330 deg F and 340 deg F. Set a wire rack inside a rimmed baking tray, then transfer the fritters onto it. Repeat procedure for the rest of the slurry-coated shrimp and vegetable mixture, mix in a bit of club soda to loosen the batter if necessary (the coating should be glossy).
- Make 2 more fritters using the remaining shrimp, carrot and sweet potato mixture, cilantro, and cornstarch slurry using the same process as before.
- Sprinkle salt lightly onto the fritters to season. Place chile vinegar on the side of fritters as a dip when serving.
- The chile vinegar can be prepared 3 days in advance.
- The vegetables can be drained, patted dry and salted 1 day in advance. Both should be covered and chilled.

Nutrition Information

- Calories: 4207
- Total Fat: 449 g(690%)
- Saturated Fat: 29 g(146%)
- Sodium: 1661 mg(69%)
- Fiber: 4 g(15%)
- Total Carbohydrate: 53 g(18%)
- Cholesterol: 36 mg(12%)
- Protein: 6 g(12%)

981. Shrimp In Ginger Butter Sauce

Serving: Makes 1 serving | Prep: 15mins | Cook: 15mins | Ready in:

Ingredients

- 6 ounces large shrimp in shell, peeled
- 2 tablespoons unsalted butter
- 1 1/2 teaspoons grated peeled ginger
- 2 tablespoons medium-dry Sherry
- 2 tablespoons coarsely chopped cilantro
- a baguette
- green beans

Direction

- Make sure the shrimp is completely dried off before seasoning with salt.
- In a sturdy mid-sized skillet, heat the butter over medium high until foam is gone; then sauté the ginger for 30 seconds. Sauté the shrimp in skillet for 2 minutes then add sherry. Continue sautéing the shrimp until they are thoroughly cooked for 1 to 2 minutes. Mix cilantro in and add pepper and salt to season.

982. Singaporean Chili Crab

Serving: 2-4 servings | Prep: | Cook: | Ready in:

Ingredients

- 3 cups Super-Concentrated Cantonese Chicken Stock, hot
- 1 cup Hunt's brand ketchup
- 4 tablespoons Lee Kum Kee brand chili garlic sauce
- 4 tablespoons rice vinegar
- 4 tablespoons sugar
- 1 fresh Dungeness crab, or equally large and meaty crab
- 1 cup cornstarch
- 2 tablespoons minced garlic
- 2 tablespoons minced shallots
- 1 tablespoon minced ginger
- 5 Thai chile peppers, chopped
- 1 stalk scallion, cut diagonally
- 4 cups Chili Crab Sauce
- 2 large eggs
- Scallions, for garnish, cut diagonally
- Cilantro sprigs, for garnish
- 5 Buttermilk Beer Beignets

Direction

- To create the Chili Crab sauce, mix all the ingredients in a bowl (optional: use a 22-quart plastic Cambro container) until it combines into a consistent red chilli sauce and tastes savoury, sweet and spicy but not like ketchup.
- To prep the crabs, clean them and cut them up into pieces. Use the Asian method of killing the crab immediately instead of the boiling method to get a fresher taste. Before breaking the crabs down, put them in the fridge or freezer to make them sleepy, as this will slow them down drastically. Alternately, gently pet the crabs on the soft spot on their shell repeatedly until they fall asleep.
- Hold the crab from its tail end to flip it over with the eyes and claws pointing away from you until with its belly side up. On the centre of the crab's abdomen, there is a long triangular lip that can be lifted up. Lift it up quickly with the tip of knife and fold it over completely by hand. Be careful, as the crab might be angered due to the exposure of its weakest spot.
- Stab it directly through the spot that has been exposed until the knife reaches the shell and hold it there for 10 to 20 seconds. The crab should die immediately.
- Next, cut the crab in half by pressing your knife firmly down across its middle and cleaving it through abdomen. The crab will break in half as the knife goes all the way down. The crab can also be pulled apart by pulling both of the claws.

- Turn each half of the crab over then detach all white gills and discard.
- Remove the lip and all loose appendages from the front and back areas of crab. Throw all black matter and white film within the shell but do not disturb the rest. In an Asian household, the orange, coral, fatty tissue part is the most desirable part of the crab that is often reserved for the head of the household. It is very rich and resembles sea urchins. When it is cooked, it goes very well with rice.
- With the same cleaving action used to halve the crab, break the two halves of crab legs into 2 or 3 more sections depending on the size of the crab.
- To cook the chili crab, clean the crab legs entirely and pat them dry with paper towels. Place them into a large bowl with enough room to coat the crab with the starch.
- Cover all crab pieces with the starch including the head and coral with starch meticulously, inside out. Ensure all exposed parts are covered up in starch and shake off the excess. This helps to keep the crab's flavor in during the cooking process, particularly if preparation is being done in advance.
- Fill up the pot or wok with enough cooking oil – about 2-3 inches – to place all parts of the crabs in, including its head. On a high heat, heat the oil to 350 degrees F and fry in batches. Arrange the crab pieces in oil in one layer then turn them over with tongs to cook evenly.
- Once the crab pieces are entirely red and the battered parts turn golden, take out the crab pieces and remove extra oil over pot place onto a rack in a baking sheet to let them drip off more oil. Keep refrigerated for up to 24 hours.
- Heat up a wok or pan on high heat, add 1 tablespoon of cooking oil for each crab and sauté the chiles, shallots, garlic and ginger until fragrant. Stir the crab in for 10 to 15 seconds before adding the chili crab sauce. Cover it up and leave it cooking on high heat for about 7 minutes.
- Transfer the crab from the pan and reconstruct on a serving dish but leave the pan over the heat together with its sauces still inside. Mix eggs into the sauce quickly to merge and thicken sauce. Turn the heat up to high and stop mixing when the sauce is at desired thickness. Remove the pan and drain the sauce onto the crab. Decorate with cilantro and chopped scallions and serve the dish with Buttermilk Beer Beignets. Eat like a Singaporean king by breaking down the crab and swishing it up with all the thick sauce!

Nutrition Information

- Calories: 1391
- Saturated Fat: 3 g(17%)
- Sodium: 2556 mg(106%)
- Fiber: 4 g(15%)
- Total Carbohydrate: 182 g(61%)
- Cholesterol: 416 mg(139%)
- Protein: 76 g(151%)
- Total Fat: 13 g(20%)

983. Southeast Asian Rice Noodles With Calamari And Herbs

Serving: Makes 4 servings | Prep: 10mins | Cook: 20mins | Ready in:

Ingredients

- 1 pound cleaned squid, bodies cut into 1/3-inch-thick rings and tentacles halved
- 8 ounces 1/8-inch-wide dried rice-stick noodles (rice vermicelli)
- 6 tablespoons fresh lime juice
- 1 tablespoon Asian fish sauce
- 2 teaspoons sugar
- 3/4 teaspoon hot red pepper flakes
- 6 tablespoons vegetable oil
- 1 Kirby cucumber, sliced into thin half-moons
- 2 scallions, thinly sliced
- 1 cup mixed coarsely chopped herbs such as mint, basil, and cilantro

Direction

- In a 5-quart pot, boil the calamari for a minute in salted water until the meat turns opaque or translucent, stirring once. Place the calamari in an ice bath using a slotted spoon. This will help stop the meat from cooking. Keep boiling water in pot.
- Crop the noodles on the same pot used for the calamari, and cook for 3 minutes until it softens.
- Remove the calamari from the ice bath when cooled, pat dry and place on a clean plate.
- Then place the noodles on the same ice bath, dry, and slice twice or thrice using kitchen shears.
- Meanwhile, in a big bowl, stir together sugar, fish sauce, lime juice, a teaspoon of salt, and red pepper flakes until the sugar fully dissolves. Stir in oil and mix to fully incorporate. Toss together the squid, noodles, and dressing; along with herbs, cucumber, and scallions.

Nutrition Information

- Calories: 528
- Saturated Fat: 2 g(10%)
- Sodium: 512 mg(21%)
- Fiber: 2 g(7%)
- Total Carbohydrate: 57 g(19%)
- Cholesterol: 264 mg(88%)
- Protein: 22 g(44%)
- Total Fat: 23 g(36%)

984. Southeast Asian Style Turkey Burgers With Pickled Cucumbers

Serving: Serves 4 | Prep: | Cook: | Ready in:

Ingredients

- 1/3 cup seasoned rice vinegar
- 1 tablespoon sugar
- 1/4 cup pickled ginger (optional)
- 1 English cucumber
- 1 large garlic clove
- 2 slices firm white sandwich bread
- 1 pound lean ground turkey
- 1/4 cup chopped fresh cilantro sprigs
- 1/4 cup chopped fresh basil leaves
- 1/4 cup chopped fresh mint leaves
- 2 tablespoons fresh lime juice
- 2 teaspoons sugar
- 1/4 teaspoon Tabasco
- 4 light hamburger buns

Direction

- To prepare pickled cucumbers, mix vinegar and sugar together in a bowl and stir until the sugar dissolves. Chop the ginger if using. Cut crosswise the cucumber in 1/8-inch-thick slices until there are enough to fill up 1-1/2 cups then toss well together with ginger and vinegar. Keep the mixture marinating for a minimum of 30 minutes up to 4 hours.
- To make the burgers, prep the grill.
- Mince the garlic. Tear up bread slices and place in a blender and in fine crumbs grind bread. Use your hands to mix the breadcrumbs, garlic and remaining burger ingredients in a bowl until combined, don't over mix. Divide the mixture into four 1-in.-thick patties. Use salt and pepper to season the burgers before grilling them on a slightly oiled rack, placed over glowing coals about 5 to 6 inches. Keep the burgers on the grill for about 5 minutes per side or until thoroughly cooked. Move the burgers to the buns and put on drained cucumbers.

985. Spicy Noodles With Ginger And Fresh Vegetables

Serving: Serves 4 | Prep: | Cook: | Ready in:

Ingredients

- 2 carrots, peeled
- 1 large zucchini
- 3 green onions
- 1 tablespoon vegetable oil
- 4 tablespoons matchstick-size strips fresh ginger
- 3 teaspoons chopped garlic
- 1 teaspoon oriental sesame oil
- 1 1/4 cups water
- 1 cup canned unsweetened coconut milk
- 1 tablespoon reduced-sodium soy sauce
- 1 1/2 teaspoons Thai red curry paste
- somen
- 1/2 cup finely chopped toasted peanuts
- 1/2 cup finely chopped fresh mint leaves

Direction

- Slice the green onions, carrots, and zucchini into strips with the size of a matchstick.
- Sauté the vegetables for 30 seconds in a big pan over high flame along with one and 1/2 teaspoons of garlic and two tablespoons of ginger. Toss in the sliced zucchini, carrots and half of the green onions, and sesame oil. Continue cooking for another 2 minutes. Stir in the remaining garlic and ginger into the pan and sauté for an additional minute until all the vegetables become soft and crispy. Place the cooked vegetable in a bowl using a slotted spoon.
- On the same pan; pour in soy sauce, 1 and 1/4 cups of water, curry paste, and coconut milk after lowering down the heat to medium. Boil for 6 minutes until about 1 and 1/4 cups of the liquid has evaporated. Toss in the cooked vegetables along with the leftover onions.
- Meanwhile, boil the somen noodles for 2 minutes on salted water in a big pot till just tender. Remove excess liquid from the noodles and place in a big bowl. Toss together with vegetables, and garnish with mint and nuts on top.

Nutrition Information

- Calories: 303
- Saturated Fat: 12 g(62%)
- Sodium: 185 mg(8%)
- Fiber: 5 g(18%)
- Total Carbohydrate: 14 g(5%)
- Cholesterol: 0 mg(0%)
- Protein: 8 g(17%)
- Total Fat: 26 g(40%)

986. Squid Salad With Tamarind Sauce

Serving: Serves 4 | Prep: | Cook: |Ready in:

Ingredients

- 2 tablespoons tamarind (from a pliable block)
- 1/4 cup warm water
- 2 tablespoons fresh lime juice
- 1 1/2 tablespoons Asian fish sauce (preferably nuoc mam)
- 2 garlic cloves, minced
- 2 teaspoons sugar
- Tabasco to taste if not drizzling sriracha sauce on salad
- 1 pound cleaned large squid
- 1/3 cup fresh basil leaves (preferably Thai basil), washed well and spun dry
- 1/3 cup fresh mint leaves, washed well and spun dry
- 1 cup thinly sliced red onion
- sriracha sauce (Asian chili sauce) to taste if desired

Direction

- To make the sauce, in a bowl put warm water. Mix in tamarind, slowly mashing it for 4 minutes. Drain into a bowl using a fine sieve press hard on the solids. Mix in remaining ingredients for the sauce until sugar dissolves.
- Slice squid sacs in 1/2inch crosswise rings. Do the same to the flaps. If you want to be a little

fancy, flower-cut the squid (see procedure below). Slice large tentacles in half and cook squid in a large skillet of boiling salted water for 45 seconds, until squid is opaque. Drain in a strainer and rinse with cold water to prevent overcooking. Drain thoroughly and add the sauce. Mix together. This may be prepared a day in advance, sealed tight and refrigerated. But make sure it is at room temperature before continuing with the dish.
- Toss the salad with onion and herbs. Drizzle with sriracha sauce and serve.
- The first step in flower-cutting the squid, is to cut off the flaps and slice each body sac lengthwise to form a flat piece. Rinse the squid and spread its inner side up on work area. Score squid diagonally every eighth to a quarter of an inch in a crisscrossing pattern with a sharp knife angled at 45 degrees. Do the same on flaps and cut the squid into 1-in. portions.

987. Squid And Pork Noodle Salad

Serving: Makes 8 servings | Prep: | Cook: |Ready in:

Ingredients

- 1 pound buckwheat noodles
- 2 teaspoons canola oil
- 3 cloves garlic, finely chopped
- 1/2 pound ground pork
- 1 teaspoon salt
- 3/4 pound fresh squid, cut into bite-size pieces
- 3-6 red Thai bird chiles, finely chopped (found in grocery stores' Asian section)
- 3 cloves garlic, finely chopped
- 1 cup lime juice (from 4 to 5 limes)
- 1/4 cup plus 1 tablespoon fish sauce
- 1/4 cup plus 1 tablespoon sugar
- 1 cucumber, seeded and sliced
- 1 cup grape tomatoes, halved
- 1 cup mixed fresh mint and cilantro
- 1/2 cup finely chopped celery hearts
- 1/2 cup thinly sliced red onion
- 1/4 cup crushed peanuts

Direction

- Boil noodles according to instructions on packet. Using a strainer, drain noodles and rinse with cold water. Set noodles aside. Using a large nonstick pan on medium-high heat for 1 minute, heat oil. Add garlic and cook for 30 seconds but do not let it brown, then reduce heat to medium. Put the pork in and season with salt; cook for 2 minutes, until it browns and take off the heat. Add the squid and sauté for 1 minute. Put lid on. Cook for 2 minutes until the squid is opaque. Take off heat. To make the sauce, mix all the ingredients in a bowl. In another bowl, make a salad by mixing all ingredients. Put the noodles in with squid and pork and pour half of the sauce on top; mix or toss. Portion in 8 separate bowls and place salad on top of each. Place remaining sauce on the side when serving.

988. Steak With Watercress Salad And Chile Lime Dressing

Serving: 4 servings | Prep: | Cook: |Ready in:

Ingredients

- 2 teaspoons Chinese hot mustard powder or English mustard powder (such as Colman's)
- 2 teaspoons fish sauce
- 1 teaspoon demerara or light brown sugar, divided
- Kosher salt, freshly ground pepper
- 1–1 1/2 pounds boneless rib eye
- 1 red Thai chile, very thinly sliced
- 2 tablespoons fresh lime juice
- 2 tablespoons olive oil, plus more for drizzling
- 1 tablespoon vegetable oil
- 2 tablespoons unsalted butter

- 1 bunch watercress, tough stems trimmed (about 6 cups)
- 2 Persian cucumbers, thinly sliced
- 1/4 cup mint leaves
- 1/4 cup salted, dry-roasted peanuts, lightly crushed

Direction

- In a medium bowl, whisk fish sauce, mustard powder, half a teaspoon demerara sugar, and one tablespoon of very hot water until it dissolves the sugar. Add salt and a lot of pepper to season. Place steal in bowl and toss to coat. Let it rest.
- To make the vinaigrette, whisk in remaining 1/2 teaspoon demerara sugar together with two tablespoons of olive oil, lime juice and chili in a large bowl. Set aside.
- In a medium sized cast iron skillet, heat vegetable oil on medium-high. Put in the steak and cook until medium-rare, flipping occasionally to brown both sides evenly, 7 to 10 minutes. Drop in butter, tilt pan forward, and baste the steak with the butter using a large spoon for another minute. Remove steak from skillet and place on cutting board to rest for 5 minutes.
- In the bowl containing the vinaigrette, toss in cucumbers, mint leaves and watercress. Add salt and pepper to taste and drizzle with olive oil. Sprinkle peanuts on top.
- Portion steak and serve along with the salad.

Nutrition Information

- Calories: 582
- Protein: 31 g(62%)
- Total Fat: 49 g(76%)
- Saturated Fat: 18 g(89%)
- Sodium: 683 mg(28%)
- Fiber: 2 g(8%)
- Total Carbohydrate: 7 g(2%)
- Cholesterol: 112 mg(37%)

989. Thai Beef Salad

Serving: 6 | Prep: 30mins | Cook: 15mins | Ready in:

Ingredients

- 2 green onions, chopped
- 1 lemon grass, cut into 1 inch pieces
- 1 cup chopped fresh cilantro
- 1 cup chopped fresh mint leaves
- 1 cup lime juice
- 1/3 cup fish sauce
- 1 tablespoon sweet chili sauce
- 1/2 cup white sugar
- 1 1/2 pounds (1 inch thick) steak fillet
- 1 head leaf lettuce - rinsed, dried and torn into bite-size pieces
- 1/2 English cucumber, diced
- 1 pint cherry tomatoes

Direction

- Combine the fish sauce, sugar, green onions, mint leaves, lime juice, lemon grass, chilli sauce and cilantro together in a big bowl until the sugar is dissolved and the mixture is thoroughly mixed. If desired, tweak the flavor by mixing in more fish sauce and/or sugar then set it aside.
- On a heated grill over high heat, cook the steak for roughly 4-6 minutes per side until it is medium cooked. Be careful as to not overdo the cooking of meat. Move it away from the heat before slicing the steak up into slim strips. Place the sliced strips and its liquids into the sauce and cover it tightly. Keep refrigerated for a minimum of 3 hours.
- In a salad bowl, place the lettuce that has been shredded into bite-sized portions. Layer the cucumber over the top of the lettuce then pour meat and sauce on top. Finish off by placing cherry tomatoes on top and decorating with fresh cilantro leaves.

Nutrition Information

- Calories: 211 calories;

- Total Fat: 5
- Sodium: 1051
- Total Carbohydrate: 27.4
- Cholesterol: 25
- Protein: 16

990. Thai Chile Herb Dipping Sauce

Serving: Makes about 2/3 cup | Prep: | Cook: | Ready in:

Ingredients

- 1 tablespoon jasmine or other long-grain rice
- 6 to 8 dried whole Thai chiles (each about 2-inches long)
- 1 heaping tablespoon finely chopped scallion
- 2 tablespoons finely chopped fresh mint
- 2 tablespoons finely chopped fresh cilantro leaves
- 2 teaspoons sugar
- 3 tablespoons Thai or Vietnamese fish sauce (nam pla or nuoc mam)
- 1/3 cup fresh lime juice

Direction

- In a small skillet over medium heat, put rice and cook until it is slightly toasted and aromatic for under a minute. Shake the pan a little while it is cooking. Move the rice to a coffee or spice grinder to let it cool down then process it until the texture resembles powder. Place mixture into a small bowl and set aside.
- Using the same pan over medium heat, cook the chiles for 30 to 45 seconds until slightly toasted. Move the skillet by shaking to prevent burning. Move the chiles to a coffee or spice grinder let them cool down. Pulse the chiles in grinder until they are chopped up coarsely. Move the chiles into the bowl of rice (alternatively, both the chiles and the rice can be grounded separately with a mortar and pestle).
- Stir lime juice, mint, sugar, scallion, fish sauce and cilantro into the bowl, stopping when sugar has dissolved. Cover it up and set aside (this can be made a few hours in advance and stored at room temperature). It can be kept for up to 1 week if stored in a tightly sealed container and refrigerated though the bright colors may become dull.

Nutrition Information

- Calories: 184
- Fiber: 4 g(17%)
- Total Carbohydrate: 41 g(14%)
- Protein: 8 g(15%)
- Total Fat: 1 g(2%)
- Saturated Fat: 0 g(1%)
- Sodium: 3206 mg(134%)

991. Thai Rice Curry With Herbed Chicken (Khao Mok Gai)

Serving: Makes 4 servings | Prep: | Cook: | Ready in:

Ingredients

- 300 ml (10 fl oz/ 1 1/4 cup) rice vinegar
- 260 g (9 oz) honey
- 360 g (12 oz) cucumber, peeled, cored and finely chopped
- 4 tbsp finely chopped long red chiles
- 3 tbsp chopped coriander
- 60 ml (2 1/4 fl oz / 1/4 cup) coconut milk
- 1 shallot, finely chopped
- 2 garlic cloves, finely chopped
- 1 tbsp finely chopped fresh ginger
- 4 chicken breasts, skinned and boned
- 1 tbsp curry powder
- 1/4 tsp turmeric powder
- 300 g (10 1/2 oz) brown jasmine rice
- 3 tbsp soy sauce
- 1 tbsp miso paste

- 4 cardamom pods
- 1 bay leaf
- 1 cinnamon stick

Direction

- To make the Cucumber Relish, boil honey and vinegar together in a saucepan, stirring often to make sure the honey dissolves. Keep cooking for 10-15 minutes then remove it from the heat. Let it cool down then stir coriander, chiles and cucumber in. Set this mixture aside until serving time.
- To make the Thai Rice Curry Herbed Chicken, use a casserole dish with a lid or a big saucepan. In either one of these, heat up the coconut milk. Over a low to medium heat, cook ginger, garlic and shallot for 3-5 minutes then add the chicken in and turn the heat up. Cook until the chicken turns brown evenly. Coat the chicken consistently by stirring turmeric powder and curry powder in. Add miso paste, soy sauce, rice and mix well; add 1 cup (9 fl oz. / 250ml) water and stir well. Combine cinnamon stick, bay leaf and cardamom pods in then cover it up and bring it to a boil. Lower the heat and let it simmer mildly until the rice is cooked and soft, about 30-35 minutes. Move it away from the heat and leave it with the lid on for 10 minutes. Next, use a fork to fluff up the rice and remove the cinnamon stick, bay leaf and cardamom pods. Place cucumber relish on the side and serve the rice curry while it's warm.

992. Thai Seafood Hot Pot

Serving: Makes 4 servings | Prep: | Cook: | Ready in:

Ingredients

- 4 oz dried rice stick noodles
- 1 tbsp vegetable oil
- 2 shallots, thinly sliced
- 2 cloves garlic, smashed
- 1/2 cup chopped onion
- 2 1/2 cups chicken stock
- 1 can (14 oz) diced tomatoes, with juice
- 1 cup light coconut milk
- 3 tbsp rice vinegar
- 2 tbsp fish sauce
- Zest of 2 limes (about 1 tbsp)
- 1–2 Thai red chiles, thinly sliced
- 1 tbsp sugar
- 1 stalk lemongrass, minced
- 6 sprigs cilantro, plus more for garnish
- 2 sprigs basil, plus more for garnish
- 1/2 cup canned straw mushrooms
- 12 large shrimp, peeled and deveined
- 4 large sea scallops, cut in half
- 1 cup frozen calamari rings, thawed
- Juice of 1 lime

Direction

- In a mid-sized saucepan, bring water to a boil. Mix the noodles in then move it away from the heat. Leave the noodles in the saucepan for 7-10 minutes until they soften; then drain water. In a big pot, heat the oil over medium heat. Cook the onion, garlic and shallots until they turn soft, about 3-5 minutes. Mix the lemongrass, coconut milk, chiles, juice from tomatoes, stock, sugar, vinegar, lime zest and fish sauce in. Over medium-high heat, bring it to a boil. Mix basil and cilantro in; then reduce the heat to medium low and let it simmer, about 10 minutes. Take the basil, cilantro and garlic out of the pot and replace with mushrooms and tomatoes. Let it simmer. Mix scallops and shrimp in and leave it cooking for 2 minutes. Mix in lime juice and calamari; use pepper and salt to season. In 4 bowls, distribute the noodles equally and top it off with seafood and broth. Decorate the bowl with the remaining cilantro and basil.

993. Thai Spiced Watermelon Soup With Crabmeat

Serving: Makes 4 first-course servings | Prep: | Cook: | Ready in:

Ingredients

- 5 cups coarsely chopped seeded watermelon (from a 4-lb piece, rind discarded)
- 1 fresh lemongrass stalk*
- 3 tablespoons finely chopped shallot
- 1 1/2 tablespoons finely chopped peeled fresh ginger
- 1 tablespoon finely chopped garlic
- 1 1/2 tablespoons mild olive oil
- 1 small hot green chile such as Thai or serrano, finely chopped (including seeds), or to taste
- 2 tablespoons fresh lime juice, or to taste
- 3/4 teaspoon salt, or to taste
- 10 oz jumbo lump crabmeat (2 cups), picked over
- 1/4 cup finely chopped fresh cilantro
- 1 1/2 tablespoons mild olive oil
- 1/4 teaspoon salt, or to taste
- Accompaniment: lime wedges

Direction

- Blend watermelon into a smooth purée with a blender. Place inside a bowl and set blender unwashed aside.
- Remove one to two outer leaves of lemongrass, cut off root edge; chop lower 5 to 6 inches of stalk into thin slices. Mince and throw away the rest.
- Using a 2- quart heavy saucepan, cook shallot, ginger, lemongrass, and garlic in oil on moderately low heat for 5 minutes until fragrant and pale golden in color. Stir in 1/3 of puréed watermelon; for 5 minutes and let it simmer on moderate heat.
- Take watermelon purée mixture off the heat. Blend mixture with lime juice, chile, and salt until smooth (be careful because it contains hot liquids).
- Pour in the rest of watermelon purée and blend a little. Add lime juice, salt and chile to taste and blend as needed. Using a strainer, pour soup into a bowl and discard any solid pieces. Refrigerate for 2 hours if you want it cold, or heat in saucepan if you want it hot.
- Season crabmeat with salt, cilantro and oil.
- Portion crab into 4 soup plates and pour hot or chilled soup over and around it.
- Cooks' notes: Crabmeat can be prepared 24 hours earlier and crab mixture can be made an hour prior to serving. Cover and chill. Soup can also be prepared 24 hours earlier. Just refrigerate and seal after 2 hours. These ingredients can be found at any Asian supermarket and at Asian food sections in some supermarkets.

Nutrition Information

- Calories: 221
- Protein: 14 g(28%)
- Total Fat: 11 g(17%)
- Saturated Fat: 2 g(8%)
- Sodium: 691 mg(29%)
- Fiber: 1 g(5%)
- Total Carbohydrate: 19 g(6%)
- Cholesterol: 65 mg(22%)

994. Thai Style Chicken Soup With Basil

Serving: Makes 4 to 6 (main course) servings | Prep: 45mins | Cook: 1hours |Ready in:

Ingredients

- 2 fresh lemongrass stalks, root end trimmed and 1 or 2 outer layers discarded
- 2 large shallots, thinly sliced
- 2 large garlic cloves, thinly sliced
- 2 tablespoons vegetable oil
- 2 quart rich and flavorful chicken stock ; 1 or 2 outer layers discarded

- 1 (14-ounce) can diced tomatoes in juice, drained, reserving juice
- 2 ounces tamarind from a pliable block (a 2-inch cube), chopped
- 3 tablespoon Asian fish sauce
- 2 (2-inch-long) fresh Thai chiles, thinly sliced
- 2 fresh or frozen Kaffir lime leaves
- 1 (2-inch) piece peeled ginger, thinly sliced
- 1 pound skinless boneless chicken breast
- 1/4 pound snow peas, sliced 1/4 inch thick
- 1/3 cup packed basil leaves (preferably Thai)
- Accompaniment: cooked jasmine rice

Direction

- Cut 6-inch stalks from the lemongrass then finely chop them, discarding the top. In a big, sturdy pot, cook garlic, shallots and lemongrass in oil over medium-low heat for 12-15 minutes until it turns brown. Stir occasionally while cooking.
- Mix ginger, lime leaves, tamarind, chiles, fish sauce, reserved tomato juice and stock in do not cover and let simmer for 30 minutes.
- As the soup is simmering, place chicken breast into the freezer for 20 to 30 minutes until it turns slightly firm then cut it up crosswise into thin slices.
- Using a fine mesh sieve, strain the stock into a large saucepan and press the solids hard before discarding. Let it simmer before mixing in basil, diced tomatoes, chicken and snow peas. Simmer gently until chicken is thoroughly cooked, about 1-2 minutes. Add extra salt and fish sauce to season.
- You can make the soup, leaving out the basil, snow peas, diced tomatoes and chicken 3 days in advance. Let it chill and keep it covered up once it has cooled off.

Nutrition Information

- Calories: 493
- Sodium: 1821 mg(76%)
- Fiber: 5 g(21%)
- Total Carbohydrate: 45 g(15%)
- Cholesterol: 97 mg(32%)
- Protein: 42 g(84%)
- Total Fat: 16 g(25%)
- Saturated Fat: 3 g(14%)

995. Thai Style Squid And Cucumber Salad

Serving: 4 servings | Prep: 40mins | Cook: 40mins | Ready in:

Ingredients

- 1/4 cup fresh lime juice (from about 3 limes)
- 1 garlic clove, finely grated
- 1 Tbsp. fish sauce
- 1 1/2 tsp. dark brown sugar
- 1/4 cup plus 1 Tbsp. (or more) vegetable oil
- 2 tsp. kosher salt, divided
- 4 mini seedless or Persian cucumbers, halved lengthwise, sliced diagonally into 1/4"-thick slices
- 1–2 Fresno chiles, seeded, thinly sliced
- 1/2 cup salted, roasted peanuts
- 1 1/2 lb. cleaned squid, patted dry
- 1/4 cup cilantro sprigs
- Steamed white rice (for serving; optional)

Direction

- In a big bowl, whisk 1/2 tsp. of salt, brown sugar, 1/4 cup oil, lime juice, fish sauce and garlic together; then use it to coat peanuts, chiles and cucumber. Put it aside.
- Prep the squid to ensure it is as dry as it can be before coating it with the remaining 1-1/2 tsp. salt. Remove the squids' tentacles from the bodies.
- In a big cast iron skillet, heat 1 tbsp. oil until it smokes. Place only half the tentacles in, being careful not to overcrowd the pan with too much, and start searing for about 2-3 minutes. Flip them over about halfway through. It is ready when squid turns opaque and appears slightly charred. Place them on a plate.

- Add a bit more oil if necessary then repeat the entire process with the remainder of the tentacles. Pour in a little more oil then start searing half of the bodies for about 2-3 minutes, turning them once. Pick the bodies up with tongs to drain the accumulated water inside the bodies into the skillet. Let the excess water evaporate. The bodies are ready when they turn opaque and slightly charred. Place them together with the cooked tentacles. Repeat the process with the rest of the bodies. Slice the bodies up in thin pieces then toss them together with the cucumber mixture to coat.
- Garnish the platter with salad and sprinkle the remaining dressing over it. Finish off with cilantro sprigs on top. Serve as is or together with rice, if desired.

Nutrition Information

- Calories: 446
- Protein: 32 g(65%)
- Total Fat: 29 g(45%)
- Saturated Fat: 3 g(15%)
- Sodium: 780 mg(32%)
- Fiber: 2 g(9%)
- Total Carbohydrate: 16 g(5%)
- Cholesterol: 396 mg(132%)

996. Toasted Coconut Sundaes With Candied Peanuts

Serving: Makes 8 servings | Prep: 30mins | Cook: 30mins | Ready in:

Ingredients

- 1/2 cup unsweetened shredded coconut
- 1/2 cup granulated sugar
- 1 cup unsalted, dry-roasted peanuts
- 1/2 cup palm or light brown sugar
- 2 cups heavy cream, divided
- 2 pints coconut ice cream or sorbet
- 8 butter coconut cookies (for serving)
- Ingredient info: Butter coconut cookies are available at many Asian markets.

Direction

- Toss coconut on a rimmed baking tray in a preheated oven at 350 degrees F for 5 minutes until it becomes toasted and golden brown. Remove from the oven and allow to cool.
- Boil and dissolve sugar together with 2 tablespoons of water in a big pan over medium-high heat for 10 to 12 minutes. Stir or swirl the pan constantly and use a wet brush to brush down sides as needed until the mixture turns golden brown. Toss in the peanuts and spread out the mixture in a baking sheet lined with parchment. Allow this to cool and then chop to pieces once hardened.
- Stir together half a cup of cream and palm sugar over medium heat on a medium-sized skillet. Cook and stir until sugar has melted. Allow the mixture to cool in medium-sized bowl before adding 1 and 1/2 cups of the remaining cream. Whip it up until you form soft peaks. Scoop ice cream on separate bowls and plopped the whipped cream on top. Garnish with the peanut brittle and coconut. You can serve this dessert with cookies.

997. Two Pepper Shrimp

Serving: Serves 4 | Prep: | Cook: | Ready in:

Ingredients

- 1 pound uncooked large shrimp, peeled, deveined
- 4 tablespoons dry white wine
- 2 teaspoons grated peeled fresh ginger
- 1/2 teaspoon cracked black pepper
- 1/4 teaspoon dried crush red pepper
- 8 tablespoons rice vinegar
- 2 cups plus 2 tablespoons cold water
- 5 cups shredded romaine lettuce

- 8 radishes, trimmed, thinly sliced
- 1/2 cup bottled clam juice
- 2 teaspoons cornstarch
- 1/2 teaspoon salt
- 1/4 teaspoon sugar
- 4 teaspoons vegetable oil
- 1 pound onions, thinly sliced
- 1/2 cup drained canned diced tomatoes
- 1 garlic cloves, minced
- 2 tablespoons chopped fresh parsley

Direction

- In a big bowl, combine crushed red pepper, ginger, shrimp, 2 tablespoons of wine and black pepper together before covering it up and letting it chill for 30 minutes. Strain off the liquids but reserve the marinade.
- In a separate big bowl, put 7 tablespoons of rice vinegar, 2 cups of cold water, radishes and shredded lettuce. Leave it to sit for about 5 minutes before draining it.
- Beat the remaining tablespoon of vinegar, 2 tablespoons of wine and clam juice until blended in a medium bowl. Mix salt, sugar and cornstarch in until cornstarch is fully dissolved. Then stir the reserved shrimp marinade in. Set the mixture aside.
- In a big non-stick skillet, heat up 2 teaspoons of olive oil over medium high heat then put the shrimp in and sauté for 2 minutes just until shrimp is heated through. Move them onto a plate with a slotted spoon. Add in remaining 2 teaspoons of oil into the same skillet on medium high heat; mix the onions in and sauté for 4 minutes until they start to turn soft. Pour the remaining 2 tablespoons of water in and stir it for 1 minute. Mix the garlic and tomatoes in and whisk for 30 seconds. Beat the clam juice again to combine. Pour the mixture into the skillet and leave it boiling until the texture begins to thicken, about 1 minute. Put parsley and shrimp in, tossing it around to coat then season with salt and pepper to taste. Move it away from the heat.
- On 4 plates, distribute the radishes and lettuces equally then use a spoon to distribute the shrimp mixture. Pour the sauce over the top and serve.

998. Vegetable Summer Rolls

Serving: Makes 4 servings | Prep: 50mins | Cook: 1hours | Ready in:

Ingredients

- 3 tablespoons finely chopped onion
- 1 small garlic clove, minced
- 3/4 teaspoon dried hot red pepper flakes
- 1 teaspoon vegetable oil
- 3 tablespoons water
- 1 tablespoon creamy peanut butter
- 1 tablespoon hoisin sauce
- 1 teaspoon tomato paste
- 3/4 teaspoon sugar
- 1 ounce bean thread noodles (cellophane noodles)
- 1 tablespoon seasoned rice vinegar
- 4 (8-inch) rice-paper rounds, plus additional in case some tear
- 2 red-leaf lettuce leaves, ribs cut out and discarded and leaves halved
- 1/4 cup fresh mint leaves
- 1/4 cup fresh basil leaves (preferably Thai)
- 1/2 cup thinly sliced Napa cabbage
- 1/4 cup fresh cilantro leaves
- 1/3 cup coarsely shredded carrot (1 medium)

Direction

- In a small saucepan, heat oil on moderate heat and cook onion, red pepper and garlic. Stir and cook to a light golden color, 4 minutes. Mix in the remaining sauce ingredients. Whisk and simmer for 1 minute and then set aside to cool.
- To make summer rolls, immerse noodles in boiling water and let it rest for 15 minutes to soak. Using a strainer, drain the noodles and dry them by placing them between paper

towels and lightly patting them dry. Season with salt and vinegar as preferred.
- On a clean work surface, spread a double thickness of paper towels. Soak one hole less rice-paper round in a shallow baking pan filled with warm water for 30 to 60 seconds or until flexible. Remove and place on paper towels.
- Open soaked rice paper and put a piece of lettuce on the bottom half and fold or tear lettuce to fit with an inch of gap at the edge. Lather onto the lettuce a quarter of peanut sauce and cover with a quarter each of basil, cabbage, noodles and mint. Slowly roll rice paper tightly around filling, add a quarter of carrot and cilantro on the crease once rolled halfway. Finish by folding in the sides and continue rolling; place on a plate. Cover using damp paper towels.
- Repeat steps for 3 more rolls and cut diagonally at the center of each roll when serving.
- Cooks' note: It is also a good option to prepare the summer rolls at least 6 hours early. Just wrap with damp paper towels and put inside a sealed plastic container. Rolls should be at room temperature prior to cutting in half and serving.

Nutrition Information

- Calories: 121
- Protein: 2 g(4%)
- Total Fat: 4 g(5%)
- Saturated Fat: 1 g(3%)
- Sodium: 108 mg(4%)
- Fiber: 2 g(6%)
- Total Carbohydrate: 21 g(7%)
- Cholesterol: 0 mg(0%)

999. Vegetarian Dipping Sauce

Serving: Makes 1 1/2 cups | Prep: | Cook: | Ready in:

Ingredients

- 1/4 cup superfine sugar
- 3/4 cup boiling water
- 3 tablespoons freshly squeezed lemon juice
- 3 tablespoons light soy sauce

Direction

- Boil water and add in the sugar. Wait for the sugar to dissolve before turning off the heat and allowing the liquid to cool. Stir in the soy sauce and lemon juice in the mixture and incorporate together.

Nutrition Information

- Calories: 73
- Saturated Fat: 0 g(0%)
- Sodium: 514 mg(21%)
- Fiber: 0 g(1%)
- Total Carbohydrate: 18 g(6%)
- Protein: 1 g(3%)
- Total Fat: 0 g(0%)

1000. Vietnamese Chicken Soup With Rice

Serving: Serves 4 | Prep: | Cook: | Ready in:

Ingredients

- 2 skinless, boneless chicken thighs
- 1 (4x4-inch) piece dried kombu
- 1 (2-inch) piece ginger, peeled, crushed
- 3 star anise pods
- 1 (2-inch) cinnamon stick
- 2 whole cloves

- 4 cups chicken stock or low-sodium chicken broth
- 1 cup glutinous (sticky) rice or sushi rice, rinsed
- 1 tablespoon (or more) fish sauce
- 1 teaspoon palm or light brown sugar
- 1 scallion, thinly sliced
- 1 jalapeño, thinly sliced
- 1/2 cup cilantro leaves with tender stems
- 1/4 cup thinly sliced white onion

Direction

- In a large pot, add the chicken together with the kombu, ginger, cinnamon, cloves, star anise, stock and two cups water. Simmer on medium heat. Lower the heat to keep simmering the chicken until it is cooked and tender. Remove chicken and rest it on a plate.
- Using a fine-mesh strainer, drain broth into a large bowl and discard the solids. Pour strained broth back into the pot and add fish sauce, rice and palm sugar. Simmer for 18 to 20 minutes until the rice is very tender. Shred the chicken and put it back in the pot. Add fish sauce to soup as needed.
- Ladle soup equally between bowls and sprinkle with onion, cilantro, scallion and jalapeño.

Nutrition Information

- Calories: 448
- Total Fat: 16 g(24%)
- Saturated Fat: 4 g(21%)
- Sodium: 769 mg(32%)
- Fiber: 1 g(4%)
- Total Carbohydrate: 52 g(17%)
- Cholesterol: 80 mg(27%)
- Protein: 22 g(45%)

1001. Vietnamese Style Spring Rolls With Shrimp

Serving: Serves 4 as an appetizer | Prep: | Cook: | Ready in:

Ingredients

- 1/4 cup fish sauce (nam pla)
- 2 tablespoons thinly sliced green onion
- 1 1/2 tablespoons fresh lime juice
- Pinch of dried crushed red pepper
- 2 teaspoons olive oil
- 2 teaspoons minced fresh ginger
- 16 uncooked medium shrimp, peeled, deveined, halved lengthwise
- 1/4 cup chopped fresh cilantro
- 4 cups hot water
- 8 6-inch-diameter Vietnamese spring-roll sheets
- 4 small Bibb lettuce leaves, halved
- 1/2 cup thin strips green onions
- 1/2 cup thin strips seeded peeled cucumber
- 4 teaspoons minced fresh mint leaves

Direction

- In a small bowl, mix the first four ingredients and set aside.
- In a medium skillet with oil, sauté ginger for about 10 seconds on medium-high heat until aromatic. Stir in cilantro and shrimp sauté for 1 minute, just enough to cook the shrimp. Take off the heat and sprinkle with salt and pepper to taste.
- In a large bowl, pour in hot water and dip 1 spring-roll sheet in for 5 seconds using tongs. Dry on wet towel and rest for 30 seconds. Check for stiffness and sprinkle water as needed. The spring rolls should be soft and flexible.
- On the top third sheet of spring-roll sheet, put half of a lettuce leaf across and arrange 4 half pieces of shrimp on the lettuce. Put 1 tablespoon each of cucumber and green onions and sprinkle half a teaspoon of mint over the filling. With the spring-roll sheet, fold the

sides over the edges starting with the filled side and roll into a tube. Put on a plate and repeat method on remaining rolls with the remaining lettuce, shrimp, green onions, mint and cucumber. Place dipping sauce on the side and serve.

Nutrition Information

- Calories: 54
- Sodium: 1563 mg(65%)
- Fiber: 1 g(3%)
- Total Carbohydrate: 3 g(1%)
- Cholesterol: 30 mg(10%)
- Protein: 5 g(9%)
- Total Fat: 3 g(4%)
- Saturated Fat: 0 g(2%)

Index

A

Almond 14,496

Anise 10,352

Apple 6,144

Apricot 13,458,459

Arborio rice 234

Asafoetida 190

Asparagus 7,12,13,209,426,464,465,477

Aubergine 6,168

Avocado 4,87

B

Baguette 12,421

Banana 4,6,7,8,9,61,69,146,204,238,283

Basil 3,4,15,28,38,47,58,62,567

Basmati rice 200

Beans 3,5,6,7,8,11,12,14,36,107,180,203,254,371,408,422,438,510

Beef 3,4,5,6,7,8,9,10,11,12,13,14,15,36,70,81,82,98,102,120,129,138,142,180,224,226,227,235,238,239,286,287,289,298,299,302,306,309,316,317,321,333,340,353,354,381,394,401,406,407,408,414,416,418,422,429,442,443,459,460,464,465,466,482,486,491,498,499,507,508,510,511,512,516,517,523,525,533,544,564

Beer 559,560

Bread 4,5,7,8,92,124,201,202,233,264

Brie 393

Broccoli 3,7,10,11,13,14,25,212,355,357,362,383,401,404,483,498

Broth 8,9,138,248,277,440

Brussels sprouts 554,555

Buns 9,11,13,15,278,371,374,456,551

Burger 12,15,420,561

Butter 3,4,5,6,15,40,45,64,83,100,120,125,128,154,166,177,186,521,558,559,560,569

C

Cabbage 6,9,11,12,15,171,284,310,362,443,444,552

Cake 4,5,7,10,11,12,69,73,108,111,227,317,325,332,342,345,370,375,437

Caramel 9,12,283,424,444

Carrot 6,10,12,13,15,170,260,339,355,436,452,521,557

Cashew 3,4,7,11,14,18,50,55,59,200,386,515

Cassava 7,227,233

Catfish 12,13,424,467

Cauliflower 6,7,13,15,143,152,159,163,191,212,460,555

Celery 6,158

Champ 4,5,7,92,109,228

Cheddar 212,240,247,320,363

Cheese 4,5,93,128,132

Chicken 3,4,5,6,7,8,9,10,11,12,13,14,15,18,19,21,22,23,25,26,31,37,42,46,47,53,55,56,57,58,59,62,68,71,76,80,85,86,107,108,112,120,141,145,148,150,151,152,153,154,156,158,165,169,172,177,178,181,186,189,195,204,206,208,210,211,213,228,229,230,231,232,239,240,241,242,252,253,256,257,268,271,279,280,292,293,294,314,319,320,329,334,340,341,350,352,357,358,359,360,363,364,366,369,381,383,386,388,391,395,397,402,411,416,417,426,430,431,432,438,444,445,448,449,450,451,458,468,469,470,471,472,477,484,485,488,489,490,493,496,497,498,501,503,504,512,514,515,517,525,528,530,538,541,545,557,559,565,567,571

Chickpea 6,7,154,162,203,216,217

Chilli 55

Chinese cabbage 138,309,355,398

Chocolate 6,8,172,234

Chorizo 7,227

Chutney 6,7,144,153,155,168,186,196,207,210,214

Clams 5,128

Coconut 3,4,6,7,8,9,14,15,23,26,30,35,41,49,54,55,59,68,74,76,79,154,155,166,182,204,225,226,234,252,260,281,530,531,569

Cod 5,6,103,156

Coffee 4,12,13,60,86,87,446,450

Collar 15,549

Crab 3,4,5,8,10,11,12,14,15,49,60,81,127,235,317,378,379,426,529,558,559,566,567

Cranberry 7,13,196,471

Cream 4,6,7,14,79,100,101,111,149,159,212,522

Crumble 182,519

Cucumber 3,4,5,7,9,10,12,14,15,16,60,79,87,91,105,130,188,212,290,318,337,339,405,510,526,532,561,565,568

Cumin 6,160,275

Curd 7,9,220,316

Curry 3,4,5,6,7,10,12,13,14,15,24,25,28,29,30,41,42,63,66,67,74,96,124,143,146,153,155,156,162,163,165,166,168,181,187,195,204,206,212,213,216,217,324,350,442,450,457,525,526,528,542,544,547,548,552,565

Custard 3,26

D

Daikon 12,13,436,452

Dal 6,7,161,189,196,198

Dandelion 11,365

Date 7,210

Demerara sugar 542

Dijon mustard 459,478,480,483,496,512

Duck 3,8,11,24,236,382

Dumplings 9,10,11,12,278,354,356,365,367,398,399,415

E

Edam 5,139,272

Eel 4,90

Egg 3,5,6,7,8,9,10,11,12,13,14,26,33,40,99,105,106,120,146,168,173,215,259,268,306,318,335,353,357,367,377,380,385,389,394,395,403,414,425,447,475,546

English mustard 563

F

Fat 16,17,18,19,20,21,22,23,24,25,26,27,28,29,30,31,32,33,34,35,36,37,38,39,40,41,42,43,44,45,46,47,48,49,50,51,52,53,54,55,56,57,58,59,60,61,62,63,64,65,66,67,68,69,70,71,72,73,74,75,76,78,79,80,81,82,83,84,85,86,87,88,89,90,91,92,93,94,95,96,97,98,99,100,101,102,103,104,105,106,107,108,109,110,111,112,113,114,115,116,117,118,119,120,121,122,123,124,125,126,127,128,129,130,131,132,133,134,135,136,137,138,139,140,141,142,143,144,145,146,147,148,149,150,151,152,153,154,155,156,157,158,159,160,161,162,163,164,165,166,167,168,169,170,171,172,173,174,175,176,177,178,179,180,181,182,183,184,185,186,187,188,189,190,191,192,193,194,195,196,197,198,199,200,201,202,203,204,205,206,207,208,209,210,211,212,213,214,215,216,217,218,219,220,221,222,223,224,225,226,227,228,229,230,231,232,233,234,235,236,237,238,239,240,241,242,243,244,245,246,247,248,249,250,251,252,253,254,255,256,257,258,259,260,261,262,263,264,265,266,267,268,269,270,271,272,273,274,275,276,277,278,279,280,281,282,283,284,285,286,287,288,289,290,291,292,293,294,295,296,297,298,299,300,301,302,303,304,305,306,307,308,309,310,311,312,313,314,315,316,317,318,319,320,321,322,323,324,325,326,327,328,329,330,331,332,333,334,335,336,337,338,339,340,341,342,343,344,345,346,347,348,349,350,351,352,353,35

4,355,356,357,358,359,360,361,362,363,364,365,366,367,368,369,370,371,372,373,374,375,376,377,378,379,380,381,382,383,384,385,386,387,388,389,390,391,392,393,394,395,396,397,398,399,400,401,402,403,404,405,406,407,408,409,410,411,412,413,414,415,416,417,418,419,420,421,423,424,425,426,427,428,429,430,431,432,433,434,435,436,437,438,439,440,441,442,443,444,445,446,447,448,449,450,451,452,453,454,455,456,457,458,459,460,461,462,463,464,465,466,467,468,469,470,471,472,473,474,475,476,477,478,479,480,481,482,483,484,485,486,487,488,489,490,491,492,493,494,495,496,497,498,499,500,501,502,503,504,505,506,507,508,509,510,511,512,513,514,515,516,517,518,519,520,521,522,523,524,525,526,527,528,529,530,532,533,534,535,536,537,538,539,540,541,542,543,544,545,546,547,548,550,553,554,555,556,557,558,560,561,562,564,565,567,568,571,572

Fish 4,8,9,10,11,12,75,241,248,277,281,354,369,375,409,446,544,550

Flank 3,10,14,19,323,499

Flour 110

French bread 124,139,317,421,454

Fruit 5,12,100,427

G

Garlic 3,8,11,12,13,14,15,29,251,359,377,404,410,418,477,535,554

Gin 3,4,5,8,10,11,12,13,14,15,40,91,97,101,120,125,238,251,252,340,381,386,409,413,467,489,505,507,536,558,561

Grain 12,445

Grapefruit 4,68

Gravy 6,7,145,195

H

Ham 7,8,11,13,220,254,368,476

Herbs 15,554,560

Honey 5,11,13,14,108,389,484,485,521,536

J

Jelly 4,87

Jus 567,570

K

Ketchup 22,44

Kidney 6,180

L

Lamb 3,6,7,12,14,29,169,179,183,184,185,189,441,541

Leek 3,10,26,347

Lemon 3,5,6,11,12,13,14,15,32,49,111,186,369,430,449,450,486,506,525,528,538,550,556

Lentils 6,7,10,161,198,325

Lettuce 9,12,14,15,287,442,502,511,550

Lime 13,14,15,478,492,529,563

Ling 14,520,521,542

Little Gem lettuce 536

M

Mackerel 8,9,250,301

Mango 3,4,6,7,8,35,49,51,52,69,174,188,199,233

Marshmallow 5,111

Marzipan 101

Meat 6,11,13,14,15,184,320,374,451,513,519,522,550

Melon 4,8,12,92,261,432

Milk 3,7,8,9,49,55,213,237,252,277,281

Mince 5,102,116,429,453,549,561,567

Mint 7,14,188,546

Miso 4,5,9,81,103,109,113,114,121,123,126,132,277,316

Monkfish 3,4,26,63

Mozzarella 5,132

Muffins 4,93

Mushroom 5,12,13,14,114,132,412,464,517

Mussels 8,275

Mutton 7,187

N

Noodles 3,4,5,7,9,10,11,12,13,14,15,18,40,44,71,94,104,206,229,305,307,328,330,349,359,380,400,405,409,469,521,539,553,554,560,561

Nori 4,5,83,124,140

Nut 4,10,16,17,18,19,20,21,22,23,24,25,26,27,28,29,30,31,32,33,34,35,36,37,38,39,40,41,42,43,44,45,46,47,48,49,50,51,52,53,54,55,56,57,58,59,60,61,62,63,64,65,66,67,68,69,70,71,72,73,74,75,76,78,79,80,81,82,83,84,85,86,87,88,89,90,91,92,93,94,95,96,97,98,99,100,101,102,103,104,105,106,107,108,109,110,111,112,113,114,115,116,117,118,119,120,121,122,123,124,125,126,127,128,129,130,131,132,133,134,135,136,137,138,139,140,141,142,143,144,145,146,147,148,149,150,151,152,153,154,155,156,157,158,159,160,161,162,163,164,165,166,167,168,169,170,171,172,173,174,175,176,177,178,179,180,181,182,183,184,185,186,187,188,189,190,191,192,193,194,195,196,197,198,199,200,201,202,203,204,205,206,207,208,209,210,211,212,213,214,215,216,217,218,219,220,221,222,223,224,225,226,227,228,229,230,231,232,233,234,235,236,237,238,239,240,241,242,243,244,245,246,247,248,249,250,251,252,253,254,255,256,257,258,259,260,261,262,263,264,265,266,267,268,269,270,271,272,273,274,275,276,277,278,279,280,281,282,283,284,285,286,287,288,289,290,291,292,293,294,295,296,297,298,299,300,301,302,303,304,305,306,307,308,309,310,311,312,313,314,315,316,317,318,319,320,321,322,323,324,325,326,327,328,329,330,331,332,333,334,335,336,337,338,339,340,341,342,343,344,345,346,347,348,349,350,352,353,354,355,356,357,358,359,360,361,362,363,364,365,366,367,368,369,370,371,372,373,374,375,376,377,378,379,380,381,382,383,384,385,386,387,388,389,390,391,392,393,394,395,396,397,398,399,400,401,402,403,404,405,406,407,408,409,410,411,412,413,414,415,416,417,418,419,420,421,423,424,425,426,427,428,429,430,431,432,433,434,435,436,437,438,439,440,441,442,443,444,445,446,447,448,449,450,451,452,453,454,455,456,457,458,459,460,461,462,463,464,465,466,467,468,469,470,471,472,473,474,475,476,477,478,479,480,481,482,483,484,485,486,487,488,489,490,491,492,493,494,495,496,497,498,499,500,501,502,503,504,505,506,507,508,509,510,511,512,513,514,515,516,517,518,519,520,521,522,523,524,525,526,527,528,529,530,532,533,534,535,536,537,538,539,540,541,542,543,544,545,546,547,548,550,553,554,555,556,557,558,560,562,564,565,567,568,570,571,572

O

Oil 5,14,92,98,101,106,110,127,164,287,302,309,314,316,342,521,531,556

Okra 7,202,209

Olive 521

Onion 5,6,7,9,11,14,104,175,178,181,214,302,394,521,533

Orange 5,8,12,13,14,119,234,408,487,488,497

Oxtail 10,12,323,419

Oyster 5,12,111,407

P

Paneer 6,7,164,192

Papaya 7,14,222,537

Pasta 3,6,12,13,48,160,413,434,489

Pastry 351,530

Peach 6,186

Peanuts 7,11,15,199,380,521,569

Peas 6,7,8,10,14,178,197,232,353,495

Peel 61,82,138,292,426,515,521,532

Pepper 3,9,11,12,13,14,15,29,297,311,360,371,411,491,507,521,555,556,569

Perry 7,212

Pesto 12,434

Pickle 4,12,13,15,97,436,437,452,561

Pie 7,226,372

Pineapple 4,11,12,13,62,396,411,428,465,490,491,492,493

Pizza 3,10,42,324

Plantain 8,268

Plum 13,486,495

Popcorn 11,397

Pork 3,4,5,6,7,8,9,10,11,12,13,14,15,28,31,37,38,65,72,101,122,137,138,167,193,222,243,244,245,259,269,270,271,276,279,291,300,303,324,355,356,361,371,383,387,388,397,398,410,412,413,424,428,436,444,449,452,459,461,462,464,467,479,480,481,483,485,486,490,494,495,497,500,501,518,527,534,535,538,545,549,550,551,562

Port 534,563,567

Potato 4,6,7,9,10,15,86,143,147,160,165,168,180,194,199,206,216,297,329,557

Prawn 3,8,11,12,29,32,271,400,410,428

Pulse 75,175,550,565

Pumpkin 3,4,41,66,73

R

Radish 9,12,13,301,313,436,452

Raisins 7,200

Raita 7,188

Rice 3,4,5,6,7,8,9,10,11,12,13,14,15,23,35,37,49,51,52,62,69,82,86,91,95,118,120,121,130,156,158,163,182,186,200,220,230,234,246,250,251,255,291,311,325,330,332,338,342,345,346,363,386,388,395,396,400,429,437,445,453,468,469,491,502,520,521,525,540,548,553,554,560,565,571

Ricotta 198

Rum 8,273

S

Saffron 7,200

Salad 3,4,5,6,8,10,11,12,13,14,15,16,20,21,23,37,38,40,60,67,68,79,81,90,105,106,127,130,140,154,170,175,241,276,318,329,338,339,362,364,405,444,445,453,508,536,537,548,549,557,562,563,564,568

Salmon 4,5,6,7,8,13,14,67,113,126,166,219,273,274,462,476,478,488,496,519,520

Salsa 14,512

Salt 15,281,505,506,519,521,555,556

Sauces 386

Sausage 4,7,8,13,91,189,267,475,493

Savory 7,8,197,200,275

Scallop 6,11,14,160,402,542

Seafood 5,9,10,15,130,302,326,566

Seasoning 9,15,282,555

Seaweed 4,5,9,10,83,124,297,333

Seeds 5,105

Sesame oil 525

Shallot 14,524,532

Sherry 558

Shin 5,115

Sichuan pepper 352,391,393

Sirloin 13,473

Snapper 14,515

Soup 3,4,5,6,7,8,9,10,11,12,13,14,15,32,33,34,42,43,46,48,63,66,70,74,75,76,77,81,104,114,124,132,135,159,181,190,208,209,212,220,262,271,276,284,297,298,311,316,323,326,331,332,333,338,340,357,364,365,368,369,370,373,385,390,394,400,409,416,426,432,435,440,442,457,458,530,541,566,567,571

Spaghetti 3,5,6,8,13,14,45,118,157,246,494,506

Spinach 5,105,113,140

Squash 3,9,10,15,28,281,329,549

Squid 5,7,11,12,14,15,127,221,387,428,526,562,568

Steak 3,5,9,10,13,14,15,19,134,283,323,463,473,499,509,510,516,533,552,563

Stew 3,7,8,9,10,11,13,14,31,215,226,227,230,241,244,247,262,274,277,281,292,294,328,334,341,344,368,460,512,516,525

Stock 4,57,88,503,559

Strawberry 5,7,115,200

Sugar 14,196,324,490,495,502,521,536

Swordfish 14,505

Syrup 3,10,36,40,334

T

T-bone steak 463

Tabasco 226,274,561,562

Taco 10,340

Tamari 7,9,15,210,277,544,562

Tangerine 3,14,36,515,518

Tapioca 3,4,7,54,73,199

Taro 3,55

Tea 3,4,5,6,11,45,92,93,101,112,149,377,395,561

Tempura 5,133

Teriyaki 5,8,10,13,14,134,231,286,334,478,481,493,501,516,517,518,519

Thai basil 28,30,35,39,352,353,397,417,419,420,421,422,426,430,434,440,441,448,455,456,541,554

Tilapia 3,8,28,248

Tofu 3,4,5,6,9,10,11,12,13,15,17,30,50,70,77,80,97,106,117,135,136,174,296,326,328,331,338,341,347,373,375,390,411,422,473,556

Tomato 6,7,22,177,186,204,207,208,212,214

Tongue 4,98

Turkey 12,13,14,15,427,471,481,487,508,519,522,561

Turmeric 7,15,213,549

Turnip 5,6,11,132,180,370

V

Vegan 4,5,7,10,12,77,139,140,216,330,346,347,437

Vegetable oil 288,531

Vegetables 3,12,15,50,77,411,437,561

Vegetarian 4,5,7,9,10,12,13,14,15,78,140,217,305,347,348,440,457,523,571

Vinegar 5,14,134,534,557

W

Walnut 11,389,390

Watercress 11,15,369,563

Watermelon 15,566

Wine 10,352

Worcestershire sauce 80,96,110,134,299,300,323,331,414,451,472,473,478,480,500

Wraps 9,14,287,502,526

Y

Yam 4,11,79,378

Z

Zest 12,408,566

Conclusion

Thank you again for downloading this book!

I hope you enjoyed reading about my book!

If you enjoyed this book, please take the time to share your thoughts and post a review on Amazon. It'd be greatly appreciated!

Write me an honest review about the book – I truly value your opinion and thoughts and I will incorporate them into my next book, which is already underway.

Thank you!

If you have any questions, **feel free to contact at:** *author@ontariorecipes.com*

Wendy Ross

ontariorecipes.com

Made in the USA
Columbia, SC
20 March 2024